Inclusive Teaching
The Journey Towards Effective Schools for All Learners

SECOND EDITION

J. Michael Peterson
Wayne State University

Mishael Marie Hittie
Eisenhower Elementary School, Southfield Public Schools

Pearson

Boston   Columbus   Indianapolis   New York   San Francisco   Upper Saddle River
Amsterdam   Cape Town   Dubai   London   Madrid   Milan   Munich   Paris   Montreal   Toronto
Delhi   Mexico City   Sao Paulo   Sydney   Hong Kong   Seoul   Singapore   Taipei   Tokyo

Vice President and Editor in Chief: Jeffery W. Johnson
Executive Editor: Ann Castel Davis
Editorial Assistant: Penny Burleson
Vice President, Director of Sales and Marketing: Quinn Perkson
Marketing Manager: Erica DeLuca
Marketing Assistant: Brian Mounts
Senior Managing Editor: Pamela D. Bennett
Project Manager: Sheryl Glicker Langner
Senior Operations Supervisor: Matthew Ottenweller
Operations Specialist: Laura Messerly

Art Director: Candace Rowley
Cover Designer: Diane Lorenzo
Cover Image: Corbis
Photo Coordinator: Valerie Schultz
Full-Service Project Management: Carol Singer, GGS Higher Education Resources
Composition: GGS Higher Education Resources, A Division of PreMedia Global, Inc.
Printer/Binder: Edwards Brothers
Cover Printer: Lehigh/Phoenix
Text Font: Sabon

Credits and acknowledgments borrowed from other sources and reproduced, with permission, in this textbook appear on appropriate page within text.

Every effort has been made to provide accurate and current Internet information in this book. However, the Internet and information posted on it are constantly changing, so it is inevitable that some of the Internet addresses listed in this textbook will change.

Photo Credits: p. viii, Sue Huellmantel; pp. 2, 4, 36, 72, 108, 117 (top), 136, 216, 230, 237, 248, 276, 283, 295, 301, 310, 319, 326, 338, 348, 352 (right), 359, 372, 386, 390, 400, 413, 424, 428, 437, 451, Michael Peterson; pp. 16, 24, 68, 97, 129, 254, 263, Scott Cunningham/Merrill; pp. 54, 60, 88, 165, 205, Anthony Magnacca/Merrill; pp. 79, 182, Anne Vega/Merrill; p. 117 (bottom), courtesy of the Fialka-Feldman family; p. 146, T. Lindfors/Lindfors Photography; p. 155, Laura Bolesta/Merrill; pp. 171, 191, Lori Whitley/Merrill; p. 196, Krista Greco/Merrill; p. 224, Tom Watson/Merrill; p. 270, Katelyn Metzger/Merrill; p. 352 (left), Rod Moeller; p. 463, courtesy of the McKenzie family; p. 475, Jessica Quick.

All cartoons are reprinted with permission: Giangreco, M.F. (2007). *Absurdities and realities of special education: The complete digital set [CD]*. Thousand Oaks, CA: Corwin Press.

Library of Congress Cataloging-in-Publication Data

Peterson, Michael (J. Michael)
    Inclusive teaching: the journey towards effective schools for all learners/J. Michael Peterson, Mishael Marie Hittie. — 2nd ed.
        p. cm.
    ISBN 13: 978-0-13-715218-6
    ISBN 10: 0-13-715218-3
1. Inclusive education.   I. Hittie, Mishael Marie.   II. Title.
    LC1200.P48 2010
    371.9'046—dc22

                                2008055798

10 9 8 7 6 5 4 3 2 1

www.pearsonhighered.com

ISBN 13: 978-0-13-715218-6
ISBN 10:   0-13-715218-3

To Georgie Ellen Peterson and Todd A. Hittie, without whose love and support this book would not have been possible.

Preface

Throughout the world, educators and policy makers talk about their commitment to educating all children well. Yet, at the same time it's hardly a secret that children in schools are segregated from one another on the basis of many characteristics, particularly race, wealth, and disability. Our read of the evidence, the research, is that this arrangement is harmful to children and does not teach them how to function in a healthy society. The good news, however, is that committed, courageous, creative people throughout the world are working very hard to create different types of schools: schools where all children learn well together; where separate schools and classrooms for students with various special needs are relegated to a painful past; where children learn how to function as an inclusive, caring community; and where real learning and thinking rises to new heights.

In this book, we invite you to join this worldwide movement, to journey toward becoming an inclusive teacher who values and celebrates all children, not just some. We use the metaphor of a *journey* because it fits the experience of those who have sought to become inclusive teachers. Few of us had experiences of inclusive teaching growing up, so learning about inclusive teaching truly *is* a journey.

We will also challenge you to think in new ways about teaching children with differences. Rather than accepting the way schools are as a given and "including" a few students, we will explore strategies by which you will seek to design your teaching from the beginning so that truly diverse children learn well together, are challenged at their own levels of ability, and receive the support they need within a community of learners to which they know they belong. You will find that inclusive teaching improves learning and growth for *all* students, including students with special needs. By the end of our quest together, we think you will find that this perspective makes a great deal of sense—and we hope that you will never think about teaching in the same way again.

Much of the information we share in *Inclusive Teaching* derives from our own teaching and action research in schools. We have particularly drawn from an intensive qualitative study of 15 inclusive schools that was conducted through the Whole Schooling Research Project, a 3-year study funded by the U.S. Department of Education that explored inclusive teaching on a daily basis (Peterson, Tamor, Feen, & Silagy, 2002). Our understandings have been further deepened as we have worked to connect schools in urban, suburban, and rural areas to promote effective learning for all students as part of the Whole Schooling Consortium (see www.wholeschooling.net). Finally, your two coauthors have collaborated in this work and have also spent much time talking and learning together in Mishael Hittie's elementary classroom where she has set out, over the last decade, to be an effective inclusive teacher.

Beyond "Inclusion" to Inclusive Teaching

The unique purpose of this book is captured in the following question, which we hope you will carefully ponder: **How can we teach so that children with dramatically different abilities, personality styles, cultures, and languages learn well together?**

This is what being an *inclusive teacher* and creating an *inclusive school* is all about.

Organization of the Book

Each chapter includes a mix of (1) theory and research; (2) concrete stories that help you visualize and feel the emotional impacts of issues and approaches; and (3) practice—applied strategies that can be used in the classroom. Each chapter also seeks to paint a picture of the sometimes painful realities we see in schools, realities that often sharply contrast with best practices. Our hope is that the mix of vision, theory, research, story, and practice will help you learn at a deeper level, to understand the why and how, and ultimately to link emotional and cognitive intuition with systematic, practical action. Each chapter contains some or all of the following special features:

- *Journey into the Classroom:* Detailed peek into a classroom to explore key strategies being implemented for inclusive teaching.
- *Bumps in the Road:* Exploration of problems and challenges that occur that hinder effective inclusive teaching from becoming a reality, and discussion of strategies regarding how to deal with these issues.
- *Champions of Inclusion:* This five-segment piece offers practical insights regarding small but important ways that inclusive teaching can be promoted by everyone in the school community, from janitors and secretaries to teachers and speech therapists.
- *Traveling Notes:* A summary of the key ideas at the end of each chapter.
- *Stepping Stones:* Ideas for activities to extend your understanding and moving toward putting ideas into practice.
- *Backpack:* Key online and print resources related to each chapter.
- *Sights to See:* Links to online videos that illustrate information and strategies in each chapter.
- *Schools to Visit:* Brief profiles of real schools—with contact information provided—that are seeking to include all children in learning together.
- *Cartoons* by Michael Giangreco that bring humor and truth to our theme.

Supplements for Students and Teachers

Several supplements are available for use in university classes and professional development to accompany this text.

PowerPoint. PowerPoint transparencies are available for each chapter. Designed by the authors, these can be downloaded to use in presentations and dialogue in classes and training sessions.

Web Site. The authors maintain a comprehensive Web site based on this text that they use in their own teaching. (see http://www.wholeschooling.net/InclTchingWeb/index .html). This site is available for use by anyone. Based on information in the chapter, the site provides many forms that can be downloaded and used in learning exercises, links to valuable resources related to each chapter, syllabi for courses, learning assignments, and examples of student work over the last 10 years.

Instructor's Manual. The Instructor's Manual provides resources and suggestions for learning activities that may be used in university classes and professional development sessions based on each chapter in the text. Rubrics are provided for learning assignments used by Michael Peterson in his university classes. Text questions are provided for each chapter in various formats.

About the Authors

For us, writing this book has also been a journey. We are a father–daughter, university professor–teacher team.

Michael Peterson is a professor in the College of Education at Wayne State University in Detroit, where he has taught courses in inclusive education since 1994; before this he directed the Developmental Disabilities Institute. He has more than 30 years of experience working with children and adults with disabilities and teachers and service providers. In 1997 Michael and colleagues organized the Whole Schooling Consortium, a school renewal network based on a framework in which inclusive education is a central component. The consortium works with schools in urban, suburban, and rural settings (see www.wholeschooling.net).

Mishael Hittie began her teaching career in 1997 as a support teacher in an inclusive school. She has taught third, fourth and fifth grade, often looping with her children, and a Grades 3 to 5 multiage class. In her classes she's had children with a variety of disabilities (cognitive, emotional, learning, blindness), children of different ethnic groups, and children from low- and high-income backgrounds all learning together. She participated in the Whole Schooling Research Project, in which the researchers studied her school and classroom to understand and document effective inclusive teaching practices.

We've been excited about our own journey—about learning, writing, thinking, and exploring together. Our goal is to share our discoveries with you and to help prepare you for your own trek of development and growth. We hope you find the path enjoyable, rewarding, and valuable as you seek to be an effective teacher of highly diverse children learning *together*.

Acknowledgments

Michael: I would like to thank the first teachers who taught me about inclusive community, my parents, J. W. and Juanita Peterson. Together they have modeled inclusion, support, and care. My wife, Georgie, taught me about good teaching as she taught our children and about community as we built a family. My son, Shawn, has helped me understand the importance of critical reflection, perseverance, and caring relationships. Joyful has been the opportunity to learn with and from my colleague and daughter, Mishael, who has become a passionate leader toward inclusive teaching.

Mishael: I would like to thank my parents for their demonstration of how to live in and create inclusive communities wherever they go. My mother, Georgie, taught me how to love with my whole heart and soul and that learning is a joyous part of daily life, not confined to school. I get my love of learning and reading from her. My father, Michael, taught me to persevere and to always strive to improve. From him I get my passion for teaching. He has become a friend and confidant who has challenged me in my teaching.

My husband, Todd, has been supportive and loving throughout countless dinners discussing teaching and writing. I love him for his loving patience, willingness to give of his time, and ideas for making learning interesting. He knows more about teaching than he realizes. Shawn Peterson, my brother, is a wonderful example of courage and creativity. I love his laughter and his willingness to always try something new. My long-time friends Jim Ford and Sarah Melamed have always been there for me. My friend, Jessica, is a great example of a caring, loving heart. We have been through a lot together and she continues to amaze me with her strength. Vivienne Collinson and Jim Gallagher of Michigan State University have also helped me learn more about teaching.

From both of us: We both have many colleagues who have influenced and supported us in learning about inclusive teaching. These include:

Students: For both of us, students have been key to our learning. In some cases these have been children and students in school classrooms. Mishael has taught children and Michael has visited her class and the classes of many other teachers. They've helped us understand how to make learning fun, to leave our comfort zones, to encourage them to think and grow, to give of ourselves, and to always keep their best interests in mind. They have touched our hearts, and the lessons we have learned from them grace this book in many ways. We particularly note Kareem Allen, Katie Basford, Micah Fialka-Feldman, Sydney Jones, Katie Loviska, Cassy McKay, Erin McKenzie, Shawnacy Parham, Christina Robinson, and Kyle Smith.

Parents of children with disabilities: We've had the opportunity to know and learn from and with many parents of children with special needs. We've been amazed at their courage, insight, and caring. They particularly include Katie Basford, Bev Crider, Carolyn Das, Janice Fialka and Rich Feldman, Marta Hampel, Caryn Ivey, Barb McKenzie, Joanne Murphy, Sharon Murphy, Orah Raia, and Lynne Tamor.

Teachers: We've also learned much from many wonderful, amazing master teachers. They include: Jim Anderson, Deb Badrak, Nancy Barth, Sharon Berke, Karen, Chiapella, Jon Chisek, Tricia Coger, Nancy Creech, Sue Grady, Dodie Harris, Chris Horrocks, Holly Koscielniak, Halina Leary, Sasha Roberts-Levi, Tanya Sharon, Melissa Silagy, Brenda Vaughn, Sandy Widmer, Denise White, and Vitas Underys.

Administrators: We've been blessed to see administrators providing exemplary leadership moving toward inclusive teaching. They include Jan Colliton, former assistant superintendent of the Farmington Public Schools; Carla Harting, special education director of Wyandotte Public Schools; Norma Hernandez, principal, Detroit Public Schools; Jennifer McFarlane, principal, Warren Woods Public Schools; Barbara Mick, principal, Ausable Primary; Mark Morawski, principal, Farmington Public Schools; and Terry Patterson, former principal, Southfield Public Schools.

Michael Peterson and Mishael Hittie with her Grades 3 to 5 multiage inclusive class.

Educators from around the world: Many educators from around the world have including provided leadership toward inclusive teaching, Naadia Momberg, Egypt; Sigamoney Naicker, South Africa; Umesh Sharma, Australia; and Jen Snape, Australia.

Members of the Rouge Forum: These educators taught us much about democracy in the classroom: Rich Gibson, Amber Goslee, Katy Landless, Greg Queen, Wayne Ross, and many more.

Colleagues: Sharon Elliot, Karen Feathers, Mark Larson, Gerry Oglan, Kathi Tarrant-Parks, Dean Paula Wood, Marshall Zumberg, and Greg Zvric.

Change agents and leaders: Over the years we have learned from and been inspired and challenged by many people who've led the way in working to include all children in effective schools and communities: Kim Beloin, Doug Fisher, Bill Henderson, Cheryl Jorgensen, Norm Kunc, Barbara LeRoy, Diane Ryndak, Jacqueline Thousand, and Rich Villa. We particularly honor the memory of Marsha Forrest, an international heroine and model extraordinaire of inclusion, courage, and care, and her amazing circle of friends that included Shafik Asante, John McKnight, John O'Brien, Jack Pearpoint, and Judith Snow.

To our reviewers: We also owe a great deal to the thoughtful reviewers who helped us shape the first edition of this text. All provided feedback and insight that were valuable in our writing. We also thank the reviewers of this second edition: Jane Brower, The University of Tennessee–Chattanooga; Scot Danforth, The Ohio State University; Amanda Fenlon, State University of New York–Oswego; Pam Fernstrom, University of North Alabama; E. Frank Fitch, University of Cincinnati Clermont College; and Bruce Saddler, University at Albany.

Our editor and staff: Finally, we owe a great debt to our editors and staff in developing this book. We began this book in its first edition with Allyn and Bacon with the support and direction of Virginia Lanigan. We have further valued greatly working with Ann Davis and her assistant Penny Burleson in this second edition.

Brief Contents

Part V: Utilize Multilevel, Differentiated Instruction

# Contents

Special Features

Cartoons

Journey into the Classroom

Sights to See

Champions of Inclusion

Inclusive Teaching

1

Celebrate Difference

Promoting an Inclusive and Caring Society Through Education

CHAPTER GOAL

Understand how inclusive teaching relates to the ongoing social struggle to develop communities in which difference is valued and celebrated and how teachers can be part of leadership to move toward inclusive teaching.

CHAPTER OBJECTIVES

1. Understand how society and schools have responded to people who are different in terms of ethnicity, culture, socioeconomic status, sexual orientation, and (dis)ability.

2. Understand the movement from segregation to inclusive schools and communities.

3. Explore how teachers can be leaders in helping move toward inclusive teaching and schooling.

Welcome!

We welcome you on a quest to improve schooling and learning for *all* children through inclusive teaching. We begin this chapter with the question: How does society deal with people considered 'different'? We will explore shifts in treatment of children and adults who are different in terms of ability, race/ethnicity, gender, culture, language, sexual orientation, and socioeconomic status.

To start, we ask you to close your eyes and picture inclusive teaching. Can you imagine teaching in a school where students with dramatically different academic, social–emotional, and sensory–physical abilities learn well *together,* rather than being separated from one another? Can you imagine classrooms where children who are gifted learn with children who have cognitive disabilities; where no student leaves to get special help and support teachers come into the class; where students are not grouped by ability; where children work at their own levels of ability, no longer bound by a one-size-fits-all curriculum? Can you picture a school in which students of various races and cultures learn with and about one another, where students learn to value one another's differences. Can you picture a school where students who are gay are not afraid of ridicule, where gay teachers do not have to fear for their jobs but are appreciated for the role models they provide for caring, committed relationships? Can you picture a school where children with behavioral challenges are rarely medicated and the school community is so strong that no one would think of sending a child to a segregated program because of emotional problems? Can you imagine a school where children are evaluated by how much each one has progressed rather than meeting an arbitrary standard?

Such schools are not imaginary. In schools throughout the world, inclusive teachers are creating a quiet revolution, discovering new energy and excitement as they learn how to teach very different children well together. Teachers *can make a difference.* We have important choices. We *do* have the power to create classrooms where difference is celebrated, embraced, and valued. So let's begin. As we travel, we encourage you to think deeply, take notes, and seek colleagues from whom you can gain support and with whom you can talk. We are off.

Sights TO SEE

Inclusive O's

A good friend says it works this way related to inclusive teaching: "You must first believe, and then you can see." We think that's true. If you don't believe in the need for and potential of inclusive teaching, you literally could go into a great inclusive classroom and not perceive what you see before you. On the other hand, it's helpful to actually see practices in action. In each chapter, we'll provide a couple of online links to video segments to give you a brief glimpse and experience of inclusive teaching practices and ideas. Here's the one we selected for Chapter 1.

Inclusive O's: The Advertizement You'll enjoy this! Three young elementary children act out a simulated advertisement for Inclusive O's, a great, multicolored cereal. The point is a good one. Think about your own views on inclusive teaching as you watch this. www.youtube.com/watch?v=ho3ioTigoD8

Pictures in Time: Shifting Possibilities

Jeffrey Regan became the first person with Down syndrome to graduate with a regular high school diploma from Kempsville High School in Virginia in June 1999. At home Jeffrey relaxes playing pool.

It is late August of 1950 in a small Texas town populated largely by immigrant farm workers from Mexico. The heat is sweltering as Juanita Garcia walks to enroll her son Lorenzo in school. Young Juanita has worried about Lorenzo ever since his birth. Her doctor says he has cerebral palsy and mental retardation (now known as a cognitive disability).

Together they walk down the hall to the principal's office, Mr. Foster. "Come in, Mrs. Garcia," he says briskly. "What can I do for you today?" "I have come to enter Lorenzo in school," she says, looking down in respect, wishing her husband Juan were here. Mr. Foster shifts uncomfortably. Clearing his throat, he says cautiously but firmly, "I am sorry. I thought you knew that children like Lorenzo do not come to school. He should go to the institution in the city. I am surprised your doctor did not tell you." Juanita is stunned. Indeed, the doctor did tell her, but her family felt that her child belonged with them. She leaves dismayed.

Lorenzo grew up without a day of schooling. Each morning he watched children get on the school bus. As a young adult, he learned to read, write, and talk, although he still walked awkwardly and had speech difficulties. He liked reading about sports and enrolled in an adult education program. He wanted to get his G.E.D.

We fast-forward to Sunday, June 20, 1999. Jeffrey Regan is graduating from Kempsville High School. Jeffrey is the first person with Down syndrome to receive a regular diploma in his school, part of a national trend. Elizabeth Simpson of the *Virginian-Pilot* talks with Jeffrey.

"I had to work really, really hard," Jeffrey says, shoveling in bites of mashed potatoes. "All kinds of study, homework, tests, back to back." He shakes his head. . . . "Your teachers say you're very conscientious. That true?" He puts his fork down, pushes his hands in two directions, Egyptian-style, one at head level, one at his waist. "That's me!" (Simpson, 1999, p. E1)

Indeed, Jeffrey did work hard. He attended summer school and did homework every night for two hours. He was school basketball team manager, "drawing applause from the crowd by taking a jog around the court after collecting balls."

At the Virginia Beach Pavilion, he stands amid a sea of blue graduation robes and straightens his tassel as he waits to walk in.... The moment arrives—"Jeffrey Thomas Regan"—and he strides across the stage to applause ... that's as thunderous as any valedictorian or class president will receive. (Simpson, 1999, p. E1)

After finishing high school Jeffrey planned to attend classes in a technical program at Old Dominion University and to live in an apartment with his friend Ian (Simpson, 1999, p. E1).

Lorenzo and Jeffrey's stories illustrate a dramatic change in schools and a struggle to open education to truly diverse children. As we'll see in the following text, much and little has also occurred related to diversity in schools. For many, segregation is still a common practice. The stories also illustrate the substantial difference that socioeconomic status can make, for students who are members of minority groups or have parents of low socioeconomic status are still most likely to be educated in segregated classrooms. Yet the stories also show the potential for a new vision. How much has changed? How might we move toward a society in which more people have Jeffrey's experience?

Dealing with Difference
The Opportunity to Build Community

If we seek to be inclusive teachers, we must commit ourselves to working toward a society in which people with differences value, support, and care about one another. We seek to build a school community that focuses on the strengths and gifts of each person, valuing people with differences as human beings. Across the world we see a picture of this type of *inclusive community* emerging. Segregation and discrimination based on race, culture, gender, and disability are now illegal. We see increasing numbers of caring relationships across these various categories of difference. People with disabilities, who have been the most segregated of all groups, are increasingly being included in schools as well as being able to work, have their own homes, and participate in community activities as full members.

However, it remains true that societies have difficulty dealing with those seen as different—with what sociologists call "the other" (Grabb, 1997). Norm Kunc (2000), a person who has cerebral palsy and is an international spokesperson for disability civil rights and social justice, identified four "stages" of responses to people with differences, each a step from barbarism to humanity (Figure 1.1). This four-stage framework helps us think about how people with differences are treated.

Extermination

The most extreme approach, of course, is to simply kill those considered different, or to cause such people not to be born at all. In early Rome, children with disabilities were left exposed to die (Kroll & Bachrach, 1986; Piers, 1978); in Germany in the 1940s, people with disabilities were the first sent to extermination camps (Disability Rights Advocates, 1999). In the early 20th century in the United States, states passed laws to sterilize people with disabilities to reduce numbers of undesirable individuals (Brantlinger, 1995). The

FIGURE 1.1

Four Key Stages in Human Responses to Others Perceived as Different

RESPONSES TO PEOPLE CONSIDERED DIFFERENT	RATIONALE AND EXPLANATIONS FOR THESE RESPONSES
Stage 1: Extermination People who are different are killed—by banishment, exposure, direct slaughter.	*To protect society.* People who are different are considered a threat or menace, often not viewed as human.
Stage 2: Segregation People who are different are segregated into "special places"—ghettos, inner cities, segregated schools, homes for aged.	*To protect society.* People are isolated and segregated for the express and overt purpose of protecting the larger society from their harmful influence. *To protect special people and allow them to be with "their own kind."* People are isolated to protect them from harm in the larger society and to allow them the comfort of being with "their own kind." *To provide specially designed, professional services based on the unique needs of a group.* People are isolated so that they can be in specially designed places served by a professional trained in meeting the unique needs of this group of people.
Stage 3: Benevolence People who are different are accepted into the community to be helped by their "betters," to receive charity and assistance.	*To provide special help to people who can't function.* People are not considered to be capable of being real friends or to have skills or gifts to offer the community. Those providing the help have the opportunity to feel they are caring while at the same time having a position of power or superiority.
Stage 4: Community People who are different are accepted as members of the community with the capacity to contribute as well as to receive.	*To benefit everyone; everyone has a gift, and the community is less when such gifts are not recognized.* All in the community are recognized as having differences. Each difference contributes to the total, and all people are needed to make a strong community.

issue lives on through assisted suicide, "do not resuscitate" (DNR) orders for children with significant disabilities, and genetic engineering practices that augur a growing devaluation of lives deemed imperfect.

Segregation

As societies decide that extermination of people with differences is inhumane, they typically develop segregated places for such people. As in the townships of South Africa or on the numerous reservations for Native Americans, entire geographical regions have sometimes been set apart. In the Deep South, segregation of Black and White people was enforced through separate water fountains, schools, places to sit, stores, and churches. For people with disabilities a host of separate places still exist—segregated schools, classrooms, workplaces, and living places (Heal, Haney, & Amado, 1988).

What is the rationale for segregation? One goal has been to protect the larger community from unwanted influences. Thus the Jewish ghettos in Europe (Prager & Telushkin, 1983), racial segregation in the United States in the 1800s and 1900s (Hacker, 1993), and the growth of institutions for persons with disabilities in the early 20th century (Katz, 1985) were all created to protect communities for the presumed negative impact of these individuals.

More recently, advocates of segregation argue that it is in the best interest of those being segregated, who need to be with others like themselves (Hacker, 1993; National Law Center on Homelessness and Poverty, 2000; Orfield, 2001). Some groups themselves argue for separation, often as a result of forced segregation. Examples include certain groups among the deaf community (Cogswell, 1984; Sacks, 1989) and some African Americans, who state that racial integration is not realistic and call for business, culture, and community by and for Black people (Hacker, 1993; West, 1993).

Finally, some say people with differences need segregated environments specifically designed for them, environments in which they receive services from trained professionals (Katz, 1985). In the 1970s, many states built schools for students with moderate to severe disabilities that featured swimming pools, accessible classrooms, and other specially designed services (Taylor & Searl, 1987). Similarly, proponents argue that specialists are needed for second-language learners and for students who are gifted and talented. A growing movement has also occurred in some minority communities to pull back from working toward integration given the lack of progress and focus only on members of their racial or cultural group.

Clearly, segregating individuals with differences because they are seen as inferior or evil is very different from segregating them in order to meet their needs. Many well-meaning, concerned people have established separate places for such individuals to learn, work, and live, often because other options were not clear.

For many, however, the issue of segregation is about values. Segregation presents questions regarding civil and human rights and the type of community in which we wish to live—one that separates people by characteristics of color, ethnicity, socioeconomic status, gender, sexual orientation, and ability, or one in which difference and diversity are valued.

Have you experienced segregation in your own life? How were you affected? Do you see segregation in your community? What do you think is the impact of segregation on children?

Benevolence

Benevolence occurs when people are tolerated but not considered as equals; treated patronizingly; or seen as lower in ability, status, and prestige. When people act benevolently, they are not cruel or rejecting. Rather, they seek to help. In so doing, however, the recipients of benevolence become people to pity; the recipients are not considered as potential partners or friends, do not share power, and are often not considered as contributing members. Benevolence thus can become another method of exclusion, a way of preventing real human interaction (Adam, 1978). Benevolence occurs, for example, when a teacher assigns students to help a classmate with a disability but never allows that classmate to help others, or when a wealthy community donates goods to a low-income community but does not enter into relationships with its members. Adam (1978) and Grabb (1997) found that benevolence often allows helpers to maintain a sense of self-esteem by seeming to confirm that they are "at least better than this person."

 Donald uses a wheelchair and can neither talk nor use his hands effectively. It's not clear how smart Donald is, though he sometimes seems to understand much. His eyes are alive and his laughter and enjoyment make others want to be around him. Some students in

Donald's seventh-grade biology class have attended school with him since kindergarten. Visiting Clover Middle School, we assumed that Donald and other students spent time together outside school. "I like Donald a lot," said Jeremy as he put his hand on Donald's wheelchair. "I help him in class." "So what do you do together on the weekend?" we asked. Jeremy looked confused, and it became clear he had never asked Donald over. Later that year we talked with Donald and his class about their experience in building a community. They were enthusiastic, and we were happy to hear that Donald had begun to be involved socially with his fellow students.

Think about how benevolence can be hurtful, even with good intentions. How might this occur in a classroom? How do we teach children the difference between benevolence and friendship?

Community

Our goal, however, is to create a community in which all are valued, respected, and supported, an *inclusive community*. In our society building community is very difficult because, beginning in the late 19th century, powerful economic and social forces push people apart. Many people move from town to town as they obtain new jobs. Neighbors often do not know one another. Teachers typically do not live in the same area as the schools in which we teach.

Community, however, is very important for human well-being. We are made to be in social relationships with one another. When we are not we become lonely, isolated, and despairing. Such isolation affects all parts of our lives, our capacities to learn and be productive, our quality of life, even our physical health. Recognizing the importance of community, many are involved in growing efforts to intentionally rebuild and strengthen a sense of community.

As we attempt to strengthen community, we find that schools are a critical element in this process. Schools are major tools by which children are socialized and learn how to function as adults. In school, we have the opportunity and the responsibility to help children learn how to be caring, responsible members of communities in which they contribute to the common good. This is particularly important since belonging and emotional support are critical for academic learning. To build real communities, we must be committed to including all students in a learning community so that no one is left out and rejected. We will spend much time throughout this book seeking to understand strategies for creative inclusive learning communities in our classes.

Judith Snow's story powerfully illustrates how community can support people with substantive life challenges. Judith lives in Toronto. She travels throughout the world with colleagues, helping people struggle to overcome differences that separate human beings. She lives in a cooperative living apartment and has been particularly helpful in describing how circles of friends assist vulnerable people and how all grow stronger in the process. Judith also has a severe physical disability: She gets around in a wheelchair, which she directs with a "puff and sip" switch. She relies on paid assistants to bathe, dress, and move her; she has very limited capacity to move her arms and hands, and she cannot walk.

Judith's life shows what is possible when inclusion, community, care, and a willingness to challenge come together. Judith attended a typical school (unheard of at the time) and she had caring, nurturing parents. However, this did not stop Judith from almost dying. In her twenties she had to live in a nursing home to receive needed support services as she was going to college. The care was poor at the nursing home and Judith's health began to deteriorate. Her friends concluded that if something were not done, Judith would die. What could they do?

Visioning and Team Development to Promote Effective Inclusive Schooling

Rincon Middle School
925 Lehner Avenue
Escondido, CA 92026

In 1997 Rincon Middle School in Escondido, California, started a journey that led to the complete revamping of its pull-out and special class model of services to a team-teaching and consultative approach that allowed all students to be fully included in general education classes. How did this happen? Their experience followed the four-phase model for values-based change articulated by Villa and Thousand (1992): (1) *visioning*, (2) *introducing change*, (3) *expanding change*, and (4) *maintaining changes made*.

Ginny Sharp, then principal of Rincon, and Lisa Houghtelin, a parent of a child with disabilities and spokesperson for a growing number of families seeking inclusion, had the initial *vision*. Together they assembled a team that visited inclusive schools, articulated commitment to inclusive education, and drew in special education teachers to devise a model for getting services into, rather than students out of, general education classrooms.

Phase two, *introducing* the change, required the visionaries to create discomfort and a sense of urgency by helping staff understand that old solutions were no longer working. They had frequent personal dialogues with staff and used outside helpers to redesign options and address questions. For more than 6 months the core team met regularly and publicly to develop a collaborative approach. The principal secured time for teachers to plan together. The trust that teachers had developed over the years, together with support from "outside" helpers, enabled them to overcome initial fears and take the risk.

In phase three, *expanding* the change process, the goal was to obtain commitment from all staff to the new direction and support them in developing needed skills. The school was divided into village teams composed of four subject-area teachers (i.e., humanities, social studies, mathematics, and science) and at least one special education professional and paraprofessional. Ongoing in-service training and consultation were provided to these teams. Team members were recognized for their risk taking and innovation. Education leaders and other leaders visited the school. Teachers were given a public forum to voice concerns and to celebrate one another's positive stories.

The fourth phase, *maintaining* changes, occurred as the school institutionalized this new approach. Despite the fact that the school has had three different principals since the inclusive model was conceptualized, the model is as strong as ever. At Rincon inclusive beliefs are key hiring criteria. Students with disabilities are scheduled first, not last, when it is time to match them with classes, teachers, and supports they need.

Advancing change and maintaining the change process requires that people understand that change is a journey, an ongoing process that engages every member of the community. At Rincon this is well understood and taken seriously.

By Jacqueline Thousand, professor, California State University–San Marcos, with Richard Villa, president, Bayridge Consortium; Sherri Zehnder, assistant principal; Lisa Houghtelin, parent; Terri Termath, sixth-grade humanities educator; Carolyn Zeisler, special educator; and Larry Welsch, seventh-grade humanities educator; also Ginny Sharp, former Rincon principal and instructor; and Janet McDaniel, professor, California State University–San Marcos. Edited by Michael Peterson.

They quickly formed a support group Judith dubbed the Joshua Committee, after Joshua in the Bible who led the Israelites around Jericho to conquer it. They convened to address a complex question: "How can Judith have the life she wants?" Judith slept exhausted as they met. Ultimately, Judith's circle convinced authorities to provide individualized funding to hire people to provide support in her own apartment. Since then many people have received such supports. Judith was the first.

Judith's circle continues to meet to support her and to enjoy one another's company. The individuals have influenced many people, particularly the late Marsha Forest, a member of Judith's circle. It was Marsha who made famous the sayings that "together we are better," "inclusion means *with*, not just in," and "the only requirement for inclusion is breathing." (See www.inclusion.com/C-Marsha.Forest.Centre.html.) The lessons of Judith's story repeat themselves over and over: When people are supported in being part of the community, all benefit.

Toward Inclusive Schools for Inclusive Communities
How People with Differences Have Fared in Society and Schools

So how are we doing in our society at including valuing all people across differences that sometimes divide? Let's explore this question. As you read, think about your community and school. How inclusive is it? Who is excluded? How? Why? What should be done to change this?

Many countries throughout the world have sought to establish democratic political processes where all have rights for equitable treatment. However, there has always been great tension between democracy for all and exclusion of some. From the beginning in the formation of the United States, for example, women could not vote and many Black people were enslaved. In all countries, the interests of the wealthy and others have often been in conflict. The struggle toward inclusion and equity for different groups has taken substantial effort, sometimes achieving positive outcomes, sometimes experiencing setbacks. We stand in the midst of history and our actions will help move us toward greater inclusion and justice or toward segregation and oppression. Let's consider where we've been, where we are, and where we might go.

Students from Diverse Races and Cultures

The move toward inclusive communities began and has been influenced by efforts to establish just relationships for people with racial and cultural differences. People of color have struggled for equal opportunities and valued social roles throughout the world. In the 19th century many, particularly those from Africa, were enslaved. The worldwide antislavery movement could be considered as one of the first struggles toward inclusive communities.

Equity for people of color, however, has been slow in coming. As slaves were freed in the United States and other countries, social conditions for Black people did not improve much. They were still segregated racially. Eventually, segregation became codified into "Jim Crow" laws mandating separate schools, separate places of eating, separate places to live, even separate water fountains. In other parts of the United States, racial segregation was not legally mandated. However, segregation occurred de facto and housing discrimination prevented racial integration.

In the 1960s the civil rights movement sought to address discrimination and these inequities. Through direct political action, such as sit-ins, marches, and other forms of protest, the leaders of the civil rights movement sought to change local practices and to push for policy changes. The Civil Rights Act of 1964 made discrimination based on race, color, religion, sex, or national origin illegal and encouraged the desegregation of public schools. This law has inspired similar work on behalf of others.

In the Deep South, separate schools had been established for Black children. As part of the civil rights movement, these practices were directly challenged in many cities, most prominently Little Rock, Arkansas, and New Orleans as parents sought to enroll Black children in previously all-White schools. These actions provoked angry, hostile resistance on the part of many White citizens and federal troops were brought in to protect the children. Similar direct action occurred in universities including the University of Mississippi.

In the landmark 1954 Supreme Court decision *Brown v. Board of Education*, "separate but equal" education was declared illegal based on its findings that segregated schools could never provide equitable opportunities and resources. The Court ordered the district to desegregate its schools. This action set an important precedent.

The Civil Rights Act of 1964 codified these court decisions into law. To receive federal education funds, states had to create plans to desegregate schools. Additional lawsuits resulted in court orders in which judges mandated desegregation plans. Increasing numbers of students from minority groups entered White middle-class schools. Many problems were reported and funds were provided from 1972 to 1981 to provide assistance racial desegregation initiatives and to conduct research in the Emergency School Fund Act. However, President Reagan ended this funding in 1981. Since that time no federal funds or resources have been provided to support racially inclusive education.

Important events have also reversed the movement toward racially integrated schools and created an increase in racial segregation (Orfield & Lee, 2005). In 1974 the Supreme Court overturned an earlier decision in *Milliken v. Bradley,* a case from Detroit that sought to desegregate schools across the metropolitan area. This ruling and the subsequent desegregation of Detroit exacerbated White flight from the city to the suburbs throughout the United States (Kozol, 1991). In 1983 a report titled *A Nation at Risk* provided impetus for the standards-based education reform movement. In this initiative, inequality, poverty, and segregation were ignored in favor of calling for high achievement on defined standards. Initially incorporated into Goals 2000: Educate America Act in 1993, standards-based reform was made more stringent under the demands of the 2001 No Child Left Behind Act which required that 100% of students pass state examinations by the year 2014. The law's sanctions have penalized schools with high concentrations of students who are poor and are members of racial minority groups (Frankenberg & Orfield, 2007). Finally, in 2007, the Supreme Court struck down voluntary desegregation plans in Louisville, Kentucky, and Seattle, Washington, ruling that race could not be used as a criteria for assigning students to schools. Advocates perceived this to be a dramatic move away from a commitment to racial integration. U.S. schools are 41% non-White and the great majority of non-White students attend racially segregated schools in large cities (Orfield & Lee, 2007). In this context, recent efforts to improve schools have been based on the thesis that it is possible to have quality education in racially segregated schools, thus repudiating the argument of the Supreme Court in 1954.

Children of color are also identified as having disabilities and needing special education services at a much higher rate than other racial groups. In addition, a substantive gap in achievement and learning exists between children of color and other students. These two realities are clearly interactive. Numerous initiatives have been developed to provide more effective instruction to both reduce inappropriate placement in special education and enhance academic achievement. These initiatives use strategies consistent with inclusive teaching as described in this book.

Racial and cultural segregation, consequently, and the racism upon which they are based, are still very much with us. A critical part of our work as inclusive teachers will be to work toward creating conditions in which racially mixed students learn together and develop caring interpersonal relationships.

Students Who Are Poor

Every community has children who are poor. In recent years, childhood poverty is again growing. These children have unique needs that often are not addressed by schools. Beegle (2003) noted that though "there has been some progress made in diminishing the educational barriers of race, gender, geography, and religion, poverty is the one barrier that has not been even partially overcome" (p. 11). Despite this, poverty has declined among children in the United States from 23% in 1964 to 16.3% in 2007, though poverty has begun to increase. In 2004, more than 35.9 million, or 12% of Americans including 12.1 million children, were considered to be living in poverty with an average growth of almost 1 million per year.

Historically, communities have had problematic responses to people who are poor. Often people who are poor are seen as irresponsible, lazy, and unintelligent. The degree our society has provided support and assistance to people who are poor has always been controversial. Many argue that no support should be provided at all; otherwise people will rely on such assistance and not work to solve their own difficulties. Early on, some people who were poor were considered *deserving* of assistance while others were not. In the 19th century, people who were poor lived in *poorhouses*, a conglomeration of the rejects of local communities. Those staying there had to work for their keep.

The last notable time in which poverty was addressed in the United States was in the War on Poverty legislation that the Johnson administration put into place. Numerous programs were aimed at reducing poverty. These included job training programs, community organizing, Head Start, assistance to schools with high incidence of low-income children, and more. Despite some important successes, these programs were never funded at substantive levels and efforts have occurred to scale back those modest efforts.

People who are poor typically live in substandard housing clustered together. Low-income housing programs created large housing complexes that totally segregated poor people rather than assisting them to live in typical homes. In recent times, small programs have provided support for people with low incomes to live in typical apartments and houses. There have also been a small number of efforts to build intentional communities that include people of very different socioeconomic status living next to one another.

In schools no real effort has been made to create learning communities where students from different socioeconomic backgrounds learn together. Rather, school improvement has been based on the thesis that schools could be improved without addressing socioeconomic segregation. Such efforts have included creating smaller higher schools or schools within schools, charter schools, and movements to create magnet schools. As efforts to integrate schools racially have slowed, the segregation of children in schools by socioeconomic status is a major reality in most communities. Wealthier students and poor students are clustered together in geographical areas and typically do not cross the wealth line when they go to school.

However, some communities are moving toward what has been called *economic integration* involving intentional efforts to mix children of different socioeconomic status in schools (Century Foundation, 2000). These initiatives, implemented in communities such as Cambridge, Massachusetts, La Crosse, Wisconsin, and Rochester, New York, hold great promise for moving toward higher academic achievement for poor children and increased racial and cultural integration (Kahlenberg, 2007).

To date, however, most children who are raised in families that are poor continue to remain poor as adults. This is a major challenge for us as inclusive teachers—to create conditions that will break this cycle. Most critical is helping children have a vision of a possible better life and confidence in their abilities to create such a new life. As we'll see, the strategies of inclusive teaching, thoughtfully used, can help students who are poor break this cycle.

Dominant-Language Learners

As countries throughout the world become increasingly diverse, the importance of addressing language diversity has grown. The United States has long simply assumed that all learning would be in English. However, language diversity has grown dramatically in the United States as well. In many schools, it is not unusual to have 30 languages or more represented.

Two primary philosophies and operational strategies of dealing with language diversity are apparent: (1) primary emphasis is on learning the dominant language; and (2) bilingual education may occur in which students learn first in their native language and gradually are also taught the dominant language. Within each of these general approaches, important differences exist.

Some in the dominant culture believe that only the dominant language should be allowed in public schools. Not too many years ago, students were not allowed to speak their native language on school grounds and could be expelled if they did so in some communities. This was during a time in which respect for racial and cultural diversity was not emphasized. Students were not provided assistance in learning the dominant language but were expected to do it on their own. Some continue to feel that "total immersion" programs are most effective in which students are immersed in classrooms in which only the dominant language is spoken.

As educators realized that prohibiting students using their native language was problematic, programs were designed to assist students in learning the dominant language. In English-speaking countries, these are known as **English as a second language (ESL) programs**. ESL programs are typically pull-out, separate classes taught by a teacher who does not necessarily know the native language of the student. The emphasis is on learning the dominant language rather than academic content.

Others believe that students should first be nurtured in their native language and then learn the dominant language through *bilingual education* (Cloud, 2004). Five types of bilingual programs exist: (1) developmental bilingual education where emphasis is placed on using the student's native language to develop academic skills while slowly transitioning to all-English classes; (2) transitional bilingual education that provides academic instruction in the student's native language but with greater emphasis on transition to all-English classes, typically limiting students' participation to 2 or 3 years; (3) two-way bilingual education where language majority and minority students learn together and act as peer teachers for one another; (4) sheltered instruction in which teachers support students by modifying their teaching approaches that allow the student to engage in simultaneous learning of the second language and academic content—the curriculum is taught in both the majority language and the student's native language; and (5) integrated bilingual education in which second-language learners are integrated with native speakers of the dominant language for one or more academic subjects during which the dominant language is used for instruction, though students may also use their native language (de Jong, 2006).

The Civil Rights Act of 1964 implied special educational support for students whose native language was not English, or **limited-English proficient (LEP)** students. In 1968, the Bilingual Education Act was passed which provided funds to assist schools in helping students overcome language barriers. In 1974 California advocates, concerned about overrepresentation of Mexican and Chinese children in special education, pursued litigation resulting in a decision that required assistance to second-language learners. The

Supreme Court in *Lau v. Nichols* upheld this expectation. However, in recent years bilingual education has been attacked politically and efforts to revoke this law have occurred.

These different approaches vary in the degree to which they promote inclusive teaching. Traditional ESL and developmental and transitional bilingual education have students in separate classes where they are largely segregated from the rest of the student population. However, two-way bilingual education, sheltered instruction, and integrated bilingual education involve second-language learners and other students learning together. As inclusive teachers, we will draw strategies from these approaches. As we shall see, inclusive instruction for all learners has similar characteristics to sheltered instruction. These approaches are also useful to other students who have limitations in their language use, such as students with learning and cognitive disabilities.

Students Considered Gifted and Talented

Students who have high abilities and substantial talents have long provided a challenge for schools organized by age levels aiming to have students function on "grade level." As students with cognitive disabilities have challenged that narrow framework with their lesser abilities, so students who are considered gifted and talented challenge this approach when they function four and five grades above their typical peers.

The launch of *Sputnik* by the Soviet Union in 1957 stimulated concern with education of students considered very bright. Schools soon increased efforts to identify students seen as gifted and provide enriched educational programs. In 1972, the U.S. Department of Education provided a definition of *giftedness* for the first time and identified needs of these students. In 1988 Congress passed the Jacob K. Javits Gifted and Talented Students Education Act to provide federal support to improve the education of students considered gifted and talented.

Educators have used a range of approaches with this group of students. Strategies that separate students who are gifted from their peers include separate accelerated classes in which students may skip grades or access early entrance to colleges; pull-out to a separate gifted class part-time and participating in a mixed-ability class; home schooling; and ability grouping within classes where students who are gifted work together.

Other strategies aim to challenge students who are gifted in the context of general education classes. Some approaches seek to challenge these students in the context of heterogeneous learning groups using a range of multilevel, differentiated instructional strategies that include multilevel lessons that allow students to work on the same content at different levels of sophistication; individual learning contracts; mentors and community-based experiences; and tiered assignments in which teachers develop lessons with different assignments for students having different abilities.

The debate between those promoting inclusive educational programs and those who advocate separate programs for students who are gifted has been very spirited. However, in recent years much work has been implemented in developing models that seek to challenge and support these students in general education classes while simultaneously supporting talent development in all students. Key approaches include (1) differentiated instruction (Tomlinson, 2004a,b); (2) depth and complexity instruction; and (3) the schoolwide enrichment model.

Students Who Are Gay

Gay students in schools are an invisible minority, a direct result of the ridicule, prejudice, and abuse that such students both fear and experience. Given that research indicates that around 10% of the population is gay, this presents a major challenge. Some Western countries have established legal safeguards for people who are gay. However, in the United States there is no federal legal protection for individuals who are gay, though several states and cities have passed such laws.

Students who are gay often have much difficulty. Antigay remarks and negative attitudes are frequent from both students and educators. These students are sometimes ridiculed, threatened with weapons, and even beaten or raped. Educators too often look the other way and do not protect gay students, thus indirectly encouraging these actions. Eighty percent of prospective teachers report negative attitudes toward gay students and a strong majority would not encourage class discussion of homosexuality or integrate this theme into the curriculum (Smith, 2008). As a result, gay students frequently cut class because they do not feel safe. Many problems are prevalent that include suicide, substance abuse, emotional isolation, low self-esteem, dropping out of school, and physical and verbal abuse (Smith, 2008).

However, many school districts are making efforts to change this oppressive treatment through four strategies: (1) support services for gay and lesbian students including support groups, counseling, student organizations and policies prohibiting harassment and discrimination; (2) discussion of homosexuality and the damaging impacts of prejudice in sex education programs; (3) staff development training; (4) and inclusion of gay and lesbian issues and information in their curriculum. There is no evidence that any of these efforts encourage or promote homosexuality (People for the American Way, 2008).

Clearly, if we are to be teachers who support students in becoming caring people and creating a supportive, inclusive community, we must work to ensure that students who are gay have our support. This begins with our taking a close look at our own attitudes and gaining information and understanding. As we discuss how to build a sense of care and community for all in later chapters, these strategies will particularly be important for gay and lesbian students.

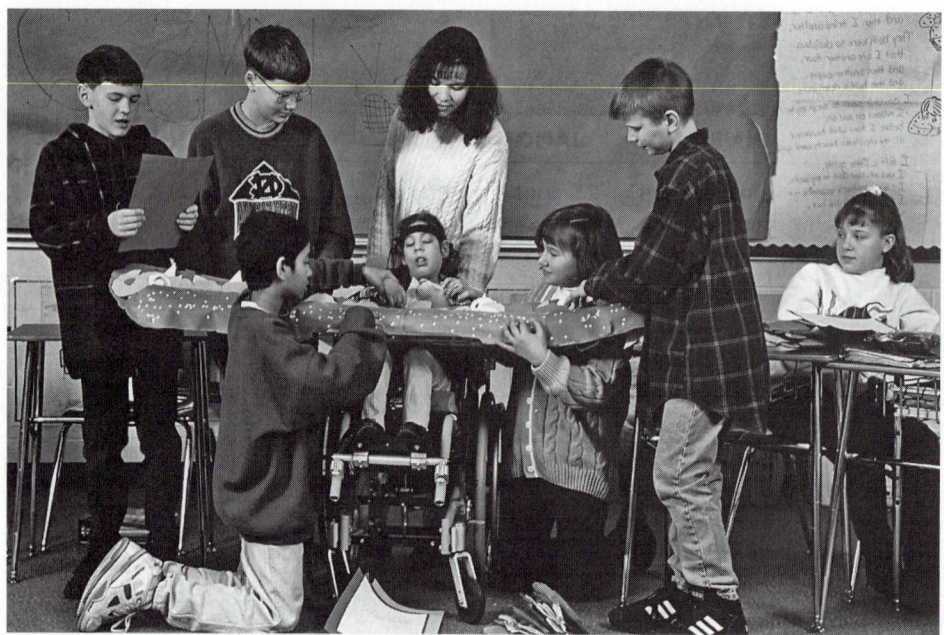

In this class all students pair at different times with the child with a severe disability. "We have learned so much by his being in our class," several students said one day in a class discussion about diversity.

Students with Disabilities

Including students with disabilities has grown as an initiative in schools throughout the world. The concept of disability itself, however, is not simple. Some writers emphasize that disability, like race and culture, is socially constructed. This means that human beings make judgments regarding characteristics that are considered to be a disability as well as the meaning of disability in the culture. Typically, disability has been considered a deficit, an imperfection often carrying many additional negative connotations. However, such viewpoints involve social judgment rather that being given truths. This is made clear with the different types of language used for specific disabilities. For example, individuals who are identified today as having a cognitive or intellectual disability have, in times past, been known as an idiot, cretin, feebleminded, and, more recently, mentally retarded. Additionally, countries throughout the world vary meaningfully in the types of disabilities identified. Most telling, some countries do not recognize the category of learning disabilities, a category that constitutes some 50% of students who have a labeled disability in the United States.

Disability as a social construct is also made apparent in the wide range of incidence in various school districts. In our own state of Michigan, we have known some schools that label only about 5% of their population as having a disability and other schools that labeled 25% of their students! These differences are not explained by objective differences in the children themselves but more in the perspective of the adults who provide the labels. The schools with lower incidence were using exemplary instructional strategies and support services in the general class, with the explicit goal of enhancing the success of students and reducing referrals to formal special education services.

Disability incorporates a wide range of conditions that affect cognitive, social–emotional, and sensory–physical functioning in complex ways. In the United States, the following categories are identified as eligible for special education services (note that the largest disability category, attention deficit/hyperactivity disorder [ADHD], is not eligible for special education as the primary diagnosis):

- Autism
- Deaf-blindness
- Deafness
- Emotional disturbance
- Hearing impairment
- Mental retardation
- Multiple disabilities
- Deaf and hearing impaired
- Orthopedic impairment
- Other health impairment
- Specific learning disability
- Speech or language impairment

Adults and children with disabilities have been the most segregated of all people. In many ways, parents and advocates of individuals with disabilities are driving the conceptualization of inclusive schools and communities as they seek to create new options for students with disabilities.

In many earlier societies, when children with significant disabilities were born they were simply killed so as not to be a burden on the community. However, communities also tended to have individuals in their midst who were considered different but accepted. In many rural settings, individuals with cognitive disabilities were able to fill meaningful roles on the farm and in the community.

Much of this changed with the scientific and industrial revolution. Scientists began to develop tests to predict effectiveness in industry and the military. These tests increasingly were used to identify "feebleminded" individuals. By the 17th century many forerunners of institutions were developed that housed people with cognitive or psychiatric disabilities. In the United States, however, these individuals were often placed in houses for poor people.

Early reformers, such as Dorothea Dix, believed that mixing people with disabilities with other social outcasts in poorhouses was problematic. They sought to develop special programs that would provide specialized training and care to help individuals develop skills and return to the community. Thus began the theory that segregation could benefit the person with a disability. The reality, however, has been that whenever segregated places are developed movement into the mainstream very seldom happens. Programs that began with beneficent goals ultimately became huge warehouses where individuals were kept in inhumane conditions.

By the early 20th century asylums had changed to huge edifices housing thousands of people. Their purposes shifted from training to custodial care and protection of the community from people viewed as menaces. This trend mushroomed as the **eugenics movement** in the early 20th century sought to promote a "pure" genetic strain. Beginning in Indiana in 1907, 17 states mandated involuntary sterilization of persons with disabilities (Katz, 1985; Rothman, 1990; Scotch, 1984; Shapiro, 1993a). Eugenics was discredited and died as a major movement after the Nazis killed millions of people in World War II in an effort to establish a pure master race. However, the thinking that underlies the eugenics movement has survived.

In the 1960s, reformers exposed shocking conditions in institutions. In 1966 Burton Blatt, accompanied by photographer Fred Kaplan with a hidden camera, toured back wards of institutions and published a pictorial exposé titled *Christmas in Purgatory.*

This book graphically documented naked men and women herded in groups, standing in their own excrement (Blatt, 1966; Shapiro, 1993a). Similar exposés occurred elsewhere.

As abuses in institutions were exposed, the public was outraged. In court cases in New York, Pennsylvania, Alabama, and Michigan, judges found that conditions violated constitutional protections of life, liberty, and the pursuit of happiness. Courts required improvements and established key legal principles:

1. *The right to treatment:* People's needs should be addressed through individual treatment plans.
2. *The right to services in the least restrictive environment:* People had a right to participate in the most typical setting possible.
3. *The right to due process:* Formal procedures designed to protect individual rights must be ensured.

Gradually, a controversial movement developed to move children and adults with disabilities out of institutions and into the community. Wolfensberger (1972) articulated an intellectual foundation for this movement through the concept of **normalization,** a highly influential philosophy that promoted the opportunity for people with disabilities to live normal lives. This view states that programs designed to benefit children and adults with disabilities should be as typical (or "normal") as possible.

The Community Mental Health Facilities and Construction Act was passed in 1963 to assist states in developing community-based programs. From 1977 to 1992 the number of people living in institutions in the United States dropped from 149,681 to 77,618, with proportionate increases in community-based programs. Most community support programs, however, were smaller versions of institutions. For example, the number of sheltered workshops expanded dramatically. These are workplaces for only persons with disabilities where they typically engage in repetitive work such as assembling or disassembling parts. They are typically paid only pennies an hour. Similarly, community-based institutions housing 50 to 100 individuals or, at best, group homes housing 6 to 10 people provided housing for individuals with disabilities (Katz, 1985; Taylor & Searl, 1987). While some strive to make such programs "homelike," they still remain segregated living places for people with disabilities where choice and engagement in the community typically are very limited.

Not surprisingly, little education was provided in large institutions. As more children with disabilities stayed in their homes and communities, parent groups began to advocate for education for their children and in 1975 were successful in mobilizing the passage of the Education for All Handicapped Children Act (PL 94-142). This groundbreaking law provided rights, protections, and entitlements for students with disabilities requiring that students be educated in the **least restrictive environment (LRE)**—that is, with typical students to the greatest degree possible—with needed supplementary services. PL 94-142 made it illegal, for the first time, for school to refuse to educate any student with a disability.

Many years would pass, however, before clear options for inclusive schooling were understood. Resource rooms were established for students with mild disabilities who were pulled out of general education classes to receive special assistance. Students with moderate disabilities typically were in separate special education classes. Students with severe disabilities were placed in segregated special education schools (Allington, 1991, 1994; Moody, Vaughn, & Hughes, 2000; Spear-Swerling & Sternberg, 1998).

In the 1970s, following the lead of the civil rights movement, adults with disabilities, parents, and other allies pushed ahead on many fronts to provide greater access for children and adults with disabilities. The *independent living* movement was particularly influential. Ed Roberts and other friends with disabilities began this movement at the

University of California at Berkeley in 1962. Roberts had barely survived polio in high school, had quadriplegia, used a wheelchair, and needed much assistance in daily living tasks. With struggle and support, he obtained housing on campus and an electric wheelchair and requested funding for attendants to assist him in daily tasks. In 1967 twelve other students with significant disabilities lived with Roberts in a dorm. This program was the first of a network of university support services and centers for independent living for people with disabilities that promoted a new philosophy of independent living. Key elements of this philosophy include:

- People with disabilities can live independently with appropriate supports.
- People with disabilities should direct the organization of independent living services.
- Integration and social inclusion is an issue of social justice.
- Political activism is necessary.

By 1980 people with developmental disabilities were creating a different type of disability rights movement. Composed of people who in many cases had been in institutions, group homes, and sheltered workshops, the *self-advocacy movement* encouraged people often considered unable to direct their own lives to speak out for their rights. At one organizational meeting, for example, the group passed resolutions calling for the closing down of all state institutions for people with retardation; sick leave, vacation time, and holidays at job sites and sheltered workshops; and recognition of the right to have sexual relationships.

Numerous other efforts soon developed to support individuals with disabilities participating in typical community settings. *Supported community living* allowed individuals to live in typical apartments and home where they received needed support and assistance rather than in group homes or small institutions. In the 1980s advocates and innovators developed *supported employment* in which individuals with significant disabilities received intensive training and support on the job from job coaches. Recreation specialists developed strategies to include individuals in typical recreation and sports events rather than in separate programs only for individuals with disabilities such as Special Olympics or "handicapped swimming."

In 1973, the first civil rights act for persons with disabilities was passed in Sections 503 and 504 of the Rehabilitation Act of 1973 (PL 93-112). **Section 504** prohibited discrimination against qualified persons with disabilities by any public organization receiving federal funds. In schools, Section 504 requires that all students with disabilities be educated in the least restrictive environment with reasonable accommodations. It covers students who have disabilities but are not eligible for special education, such as students diagnosed with ADHD and students in wheelchairs who need only assistance or adjustments in the physical environment.

The requirements of PL 93-112 were greatly expanded in 1990 with the passage of the **Americans with Disabilities Act (ADA)**. The ADA articulated rights in employment, public services, public accommodations, and telecommunications (Americans with Disabilities Act, 1990; Gostin & Beyer, 1993; Wehman, 1993). Employers cannot discriminate in the hiring process on the basis of disability. Disability could be considered in the hiring process only if it relates to a person's ability to perform essential functions of a job with reasonable accommodations. Employers are required to provide reasonable accommodations, but these cannot pose an "undue hardship" (Gostin & Beyer, 1993). ADA also requires access to all public services such as public schools, mental health services, and welfare programs as well as privately owned businesses and offices open to the public.

Through the world, individuals with disabilities are being included in all aspects of community life with needed supports and assistance. Numerous models of support and

BACK PACK

Inclusive Teaching

When we go somewhere and want to carry with us key but essential items, a backpack is often a great tool! But what shall we take? In each chapter, we'll provide a couple of relevant, online, rich resources to help you in your journey toward inclusive teaching. Here they are for Chapter 1.

Network for Inclusive Schooling The people who organized National Inclusive Schools week are forming an international network. You and your school can join. www.inclusiveschools.org/

Inclusion Solutions This site in the UK is packed with great resources for dealing with difficult situations in including students with differences. Photos illustrate practices. www.inclusive-solutions.com/research.asp

inclusion are in place. Despite this, however, many services and programs continue to be segregated in adult living services as well as in schools. In most locations, more funds are still provided for group homes rather than supported living, sheltered workshops still abound, and many students are educated in separate special education classes and schools. For sure, as we seek to be inclusive teachers we will have students with disabilities in our classes. We will be challenged to strengthen the movement toward inclusive education for these students.

The Growing Movement to Inclusive Schools
Welcoming the Children Home

Throughout the world, educators and community members are working toward creating and strengthening inclusive schools that welcome all children. A major effort has focused on racial, cultural, and linguistic differences. Others have focused on students who live in poverty and gay students. Yet others have focused primarily on inclusion of students with disabilities. On the one hand, the movement toward inclusive schools has been strengthened by this work. On the other hand, a focus on only one group, rather than on building schools and classrooms that address the needs of all groups, has often served to splinter the effort. For example, those concerned with students from racial minorities may or may not see common cause with those who advocate for students with significant disabilities. In the worst scenario, advocates actually work against one another and compete for resources. Yet, a growing number of leaders are increasingly recognizing the need to create schools and classrooms aimed at addressing the needs of all working together with representatives of all groups.

In dealing with multiple differences, similar dynamics have occurred in the movement from segregation to inclusive schooling. As we've already discussed, schools have often simply excluded students with differences. However, when they open their doors to educate students considered different, they have almost always initially created separate programs and places for these students. Thus, "separate but equal" schools were created for Black students in the southern United States. In the early days of immigration from other countries, separate classes were often established to "Americanize" children as well as adults. For students with disabilities, initial approaches separated special education schools and classrooms and resource rooms that provided services in separate

A Teacher Works to Provide Leadership

Malik started teaching at Stevens High School as an English teacher with a goal to be a good teacher. He was particularly committed to being an inclusive teacher, having become convinced in his student teaching placement that the segregation he observed in that school was harmful to the students. He was excited when the school principal told him that the school was "fully inclusive" and that he would be coteaching with a special education and bilingual support teacher. However, once he got to the school, he quickly discovered that only students with mild learning disabilities and emotional disturbance were included in general education classes. Students with cognitive disabilities were in "life skills" classes at the end of one wing in the school and students with severe disabilities went to a segregated school. He was also dismayed to find that his English classes were tracked (students were sorted into those with higher or lower abilities and clustered in classes based on their presumed ability). He had one section for students who had been identified as gifted who were in an honors program and another section for students at risk. However, Malik didn't give up.

He decided to talk with the principal, Shandra, about his ideas of inclusive teaching. He wanted to know if the principal would support changes. In fact, Shandra was pretty surprised at Malik's ideas. She was very committed to inclusive education and had worked to get coteaching and inclusion established in the building over the last 10 years. However, it had never occurred to her that students with cognitive disabilities could be included in general education classes. Malik explained some ways he thought this could work. When Malik asked, "Where do the other students who should come to this school go?" she was confused. Malik explained he meant students with more severe cognitive and physical disabilities. She had never even considered that some students who would typically attend Stevens were going elsewhere. Malik also suggested that they consider eliminating tracks in the school and develop a different approach to the honors program.

Malik and Shandra discussed ways they might involve the staff in considering these new ideas. Shandra agreed to read a book that Malik had used in an inclusive teaching class at the university. True to her word, at the next staff meeting Shandra discussed the commitment of the school to inclusive education and the journey they had been on over the last few years. "However, it's become clear to me that we still have a long way to go. I'd like to develop a working group of staff who could explore ways that our school can become truly inclusive" Shandra said. The staff had lots of questions. It was clear that a number of them were very uncomfortable with this new direction. However, 10 staff members representing various subject areas and support staff volunteered. Malik was both excited and a bit scared.

As it turned out, Jaclyn, a parent of Jady, a young man with a severe cognitive and physical disability, had been meeting with the director of special education for the district. She had advocated very hard to have her son fully included in general education classes. He was the only student with a severe disability to be included in the district. She was looking for a high school that would accept her son.

Over the next year Malik and others worked hard to develop a new, strengthened approach to inclusive teaching in the school. During that year the task force read materials, visited two other high schools that were trying to be inclusive, and attended two national conferences on inclusive education. By the end of the year, they developed a series of recommendations that included the following:

- Restructure the honors program. Eliminate the gifted-only class and develop a contract system where any student, not just those identified as gifted, could do extra, more in-depth work for honors credit.
- Eliminate all tracked classes. At the same time, make a commitment to learning new strategies for multilevel, differentiated instruction providing support for teachers to learn new skills.
- Obtain assistance from a consultant who could help the school move toward inclusive teaching and provide professional development and support. (The school contacted a professor at a local university who had written a book on inclusive education to work with the school.)

(continued)

- Obtain professional development in sheltered instruction for bilingual staff and all general education teachers to assists second-language learners. Pilot a two-way bilingual program.
- Begin including students with cognitive disabilities, phasing them into general education classes. Use the list of "functional life skills" that was the basis of the present segregated special education program and look at ways that these skills could be obtained in high school courses and extracurricular opportunities.
- Enroll students with severe disabilities in general education classes. (Jady attended general education classes held by Malik's interdisciplinary team.)

These were wonderful moves. The work had been hard. It was also clear to Malik and Shandra that they had much hard work ahead of them. However, a small group of teachers were angry at this direction and had begun talking with the union regarding whether this violated the union contract with the district. Yet, overall, the staff was supportive. Malik was proud that, as a new, young teacher, he had been part of helping create innovations.

Reflection: You might be thinking, "Well, Malik was lucky he had such a great administrator." For sure, he was. However, the point of the story is we never know what will happen when we reach out and take a risk. It's our challenge to find them and then figure how to make differences where we are.

locations. For students who speak a language different from the dominant language, educators have often created separate bilingual or ESL classes.

In all these cases, however, problems have been evident. Racial segregation has been shown to enhance racial discrimination and create poorer academic outcomes. Students of different races and cultures have often had limited opportunity to come to know one another and learn from and with each other. Separate programs for students with language differences isolate them from the rest of the student population, creating many social and academic problems. For students with disabilities, separate special education classes have prepared them for an entire lifetime of segregated living and working situations. As these problems have become more evident, educators concerned with different groups have pushed toward a similar outcome—creating inclusive schools and classrooms where students can learn together.

In recent years, advocates of individuals with disabilities have provided much leadership in articulating images of truly inclusive schools. Students with disabilities, of course, also possess other differences: race, culture, language, socioeconomic status, and sexual orientation. In the 1980s in the United States parents and professionals began to question the effectiveness of separate special education programs. Madeline Will (1986), assistant secretary of the Office of Special Education and Rehabilitative Services (OSERS), herself the parent of a child with a disability, developed the federal **Regular Education Initiative (REI)** calling for special and general educators to share responsibility for the education of children with disabilities. One organizational model during this time was *class merging*, in which a whole special education classroom of students with mild disabilities merged with a regular education class where teachers cotaught (Lipsky & Gartner, 1997). Others began to create approaches of **integrated education**, in which students in a special education classroom in a regular school had opportunities for integration at lunch, recess, or "specials" (art, music, etc.).

In the late 1980s in the United States, President George H. W. Bush called a governors' summit conference on education. This conference called for substantial restructuring (National Commission on Excellence in Education, 1983), for active learning approaches, and for the use of **push-in services** instead of **pull-out programs** for children at risk of educational failure. These ideas built on a growing base of research showing the negative effects of tracking children in homogeneous ability groups (Lipsky & Gartner, 1997; Oakes, 1985; Ogle, Pink, & Jones, 1990; Wheelock, 1992).

In this fertile climate, inclusive education was developed. Initially championed by advocates, parents, and educators of children with the most severe disabilities, **inclusive education** heralded a new and very different paradigm:

1. Inclusion of *all* students, including those with mild to severe disabilities, in general education classes.
2. Provision of supports and services within the general education class for both teachers and students (push-in services).

As schools began to implement inclusive education, researchers found that all students were learning more effectively (LeRoy, 1990a, 1990b, 1995; Stainback, Stainback, Moravec, & Jackson, 1992). The federal government in the United States funded a series of systems change grants to states to help local schools implement inclusive education. Many other nations have engaged in similar initiatives, often in collaboration with the United Nations. Beginning in small states such as New Hampshire and Vermont in the mid-1980s, by the end of the 20th century inclusive education was implemented in some schools throughout the United States (Lipsky & Gartner, 1997).

The movement toward inclusive schooling has had opponents. For example, Fuchs and Fuchs (1994) have argued that "**full inclusionists**" do not pay adequate attention to the individual needs of children with disabilities, that general education teachers will not accept students with disabilities, that students with disabilities will hinder learning of other students, and that schools may use inclusive education as an excuse to reduce funding and legal protection for students with disabilities.

The movement toward inclusive schooling, however, continues. In a nationally acclaimed report for *Newsweek* magazine, Joseph Shapiro (1993b) discussed the rising cost of special education and segregation of children with disabilities and stated that "we are spending billions on special education which is having little impact" (p. 10). In recent years a panel was convened to consider several problems with special education including the overrepresentation of children of color in special education and the continued segregation of students with disabilities. They concluded that efforts should be renewed to include students with disabilities, including those with the most severe disabilities, in general education classes.

In the United States, in 2001 the No Child Left Behind Act required schools to work toward providing high academic standards for all students in a common curriculum. While this law has remained controversial, it has also fueled the movement toward inclusive schools in the United States. Educators understand that if schools are judged based on the degree to which students acquire skills in a common curriculum, it only makes sense for all students to learn this curriculum together.

A new movement is growing naturally out of inclusive education for students with disabilities in K to 12 schools—the inclusion of students with cognitive and other related disabilities in colleges and universities. Increasing numbers of programs are supporting these students in various ways including taking classes for credit, participating in classes without credit, engaging in student activities throughout the campus, working in jobs on the campus, and more.

The movement toward inclusive schooling is occurring in countries throughout the world. In 1994 a United Nations conference developed the Salamanca Statement (United Nations Educational, Scientific and Cultural Organization [UNESCO], 1994), which outlined goals and strategies for inclusion of people with disabilities in school and society. With increased diversity of children in schools throughout the world, old models of separating students by various categories and labels have increasingly been seen as

Four high school students bring flowers from a local shop that they will use in creating pictures incorporating dried flowers in their art class.

unfeasible and oppressive (Booth & Ainscow, 1998; Vitello & Mithaug, 1998). International projects sponsored by the United Nations have promoted growth of inclusive schooling in countries all over the world, including Belgium, Great Britain (Ainscow, 1999), Germany (Hinz, 1996), Italy (Balboni, Giulia, & Pedrabissi, 2000; Berrigan, 1994); various African nations (Miles, 1999; Naicker, 1999), India, and China (Booth & Ainscow, 1998). Italy has become recognized as a leader in inclusive education, and as early as 1977 Italy passed National Law 517 requiring inclusion of students with disabilities, elimination of classes tracked by ability, and team teaching by general and special education teachers (Berrigan, 1994). More recently, South Africa, a country in which apartheid has existed for many years, has begun implementing a national inclusive education initiative as part of its efforts to transform its postapartheid educational system (Naicker, 1999).

Numerous educational organizations have also developed papers and position statements supporting inclusive schooling. In 1994 the National Association of School Boards of Education (NASBE) published *Winners All* and called on school boards to embrace inclusive education. Other organizations articulated similar statements of support, among them TASH, United Cerebral Palsy Association (1993), and the Council for Exceptional Children (CEC; 1993).

Individuals with Disabilities Education Act (IDEA)

In the movement toward inclusive schooling, law that governs educational services for students with disabilities is particularly important. In the United States, Congress passed the **Individuals with Disabilities Education Act (IDEA)** in 1997 as an update to PL 94-142 as passed in 1975. The most recent version of the law is PL 108-446, the Individuals with Disabilities Education Improvement Act of 2004. A summary follows of the key elements of the law as of 2008.

The law guarantees that all children with disabilities are entitled to a **free and appropriate public education (FAPE)**. All students with disabilities must be educated by public schools. All students with disabilities must have *access to the general education curriculum*. Education must be provided in the *least restrictive environment (LRE)*, which means that "to the maximum extent possible, children with disabilities must be educated with non-disabled children." A *continuum of placement options* requires that a range of services be available to meet the needs of the student.

An **Individualized Education Plan (IEP)** must be developed based on the needs of each student. Schools must involve parents in educational decisions and development of the IEP. This plan is a legal contract between the school and the parents. A general education teacher must be on the IEP team if the student is participating in general education classes. The IEP must contain annual goals and services aimed at helping the student be successful in general education. For students with behavioral challenges, a meeting

A TALE OF TWO SCHOOLS.

called a "manifest determination" must be held to determine if the problems are related to the student's disability. Functional assessment of behavior and behavior intervention plans must be developed based on need. Students also must be provided needed *supplementary and related services* to help students succeed in general education classes. Assistive technology must be considered in the IEP if needed by a student.

Early intervention services are provided to infants and toddlers with disabilities and those at risk through collaboration among human service agencies (this requirement was added in 1986 in PL 99-457). Services must be family centered and based on an **Individualized Family Services Plan (IFSP).** The law encourages serving children in natural environments and utilizes a noncategorical approach. All this has laid the groundwork for encouraging such children to move into inclusive education as they grow older.

An **Individual Transition Plan** must be developed for students with disabilities starting at age 16. (Schools may start earlier if they wish, but are required to do so only at age 16.)

The law also established processes to handle disagreements regarding the IEP. If conflicts cannot be resolved at the IEP meeting, the parents and/or the school may take the case to an impartial hearing officer, often a lawyer or a university professor. Such officers are charged with hearing arguments and making a decision. Dissatisfied parties may appeal this decision to federal court. *Mediation* programs have been developed in which trained individuals attempt to work out solutions as the number of hearings and court cases have risen.

Teacher Leadership for Inclusive Schooling

Let's now explore how, as teachers, we can be part of providing leadership for moving toward effective inclusive teaching.

One day we visited in a school that was working to be an inclusive school. The principal, Marleen, told us the story. It began with a lunch conversation one day. The teachers were talking about trying to get outside help. "Suddenly," Marleen said, "it hit us! No one is coming to save us. We are the ones we are waiting for! If we want to make a better school, it is up to us." For sure, if schools are going to become more effective in promoting caring, being places of belonging rather than segregation and isolation, the leadership of many people will be necessary. The leadership of teachers is particularly critical. We end this first chapter with a challenge for each of us to be the one for whom we are waiting, to be a leader in helping our school become an effective, inclusive school.

Many teachers are, in fact, leading. Here are a few examples we've seen:

- Teachers who collaborated with initiatives to develop partnerships between racially segregated inner-city schools and suburban schools to engage children in community learning together.
- A teacher who made sure that a student with mental retardation was placed in her room.
- A teacher working in a very segregated school who approached a special education teacher and invited her to include some of the special education students full-time in her class.
- A bilingual teacher who became a general education teacher and then worked to have both second-language learners and students with cognitive disabilities in his class.
- A teacher who challenged other educators to move away from negative statements, often overheard by students, regarding people who are gay.
- A teacher who taught a student with multiple, very severe disabilities and used this experience to question the existence of three separate special education classrooms in the school.

The Lessons of School Change: Not Easy but Worth the Trip

Schools are very difficult to change. The factory model of schooling has survived many efforts to reform it (Tyack & Cuban, 1995). However, when inclusive education becomes part of a school, it sometimes becomes the new reality and becomes equally resistant to change. So change is hard; but when good practices become part of the culture of a school, we have hope that they may last (Fisher, Sax, & Grove, 2000). In his book *Change Forces*, Michael Fullan (1997) describes eight key lessons for school renewal. Let's discuss these.

First, *change cannot be mandated* except in those concrete, specific areas that require little thought. Important change requires shifts in people's beliefs, skills, and behaviors. Moving toward inclusive teaching requires that educators explore beliefs about teaching, good instruction, and our hopes for the children we teach.

Second, *change is not linear*. Rather, we begin a journey, take the first steps, and reevaluate. We can't know how to teach inclusively before we start. We can't have an inclusive school *until* we start. We do the best we can and solve problems.

Third, *problems are our friends*. Inquiry, constant appraisal, analysis, and self-reflection on problems and solutions is critical. We expect that we will be confused and that conflict will occur but work toward creative solutions.

Fourth, *action and visioning must occur together*. Rather than the traditional "ready, aim, fire," the order must be "ready, fire, aim." In other words, only through action can we gain enough experience to create a vision and only through struggle can that vision be shared.

Fifth, we *balance individual and collaborative efforts*. These will remain in tension. On the one hand, we want shared vision and values. On the other hand, some of the worst atrocities in history occurred when groups decided to take oppressive courses of

CHAMPIONS OF INCLUSION
By Bill Henderson, Principal, O'Hearn Elementary School, Boston, MA

All across the country, individuals are being recognized for successfully promoting inclusive teaching in schools. These persons have helped make it more possible for students with a wide range of abilities, including students who have disabilities, to participate in meaningful ways with their peers in a wide range of activities. Although the quality of inclusion does indeed depend on many factors related to whole school change and improvement, it is important to acknowledge the people who really make it happen. In the Champions of Inclusion boxes featured in the text I will highlight some of the salient characteristics of these champions of inclusion. A few initial comments are in order, however.

First, most of the champions of inclusion I have highlighted do not depend upon advanced degrees and training. Although in many instances, special skills are certainly required, in most cases it is the accompanying positive beliefs, attitudes, and behaviors that are most significant. Indeed it is common for those who have been identified as champions of inclusion to state that what they are being recognized for is really quite ordinary.

Likewise it is important to note that many adults who have disabilities report that their impairments were not as challenging to them in school as were the ways others related to their impairments. For many persons with disabilities, stereotypic beliefs, negative attitudes, and inappropriate behaviors were common experiences that impeded opportunities for meaningful participation. In order for successful inclusion in schools to become more the norm than the exception, changes in how people relate to students who have disabilities must also occur.

Champions of inclusion are people who exemplify first and foremost that they can connect, communicate, challenge, and collaborate appropriately when dealing with students who have disabilities. They are certainly also people who have developed and/or creatively implemented specialized skills, but they recognize that this expertise must be accompanied by appropriate beliefs, attitudes, and behaviors in order for the skills being utilized to prove most beneficial. Indeed what makes champions of inclusion extraordinary is that they are demonstrating on a regular basis how ordinary it can be for students with disabilities to participate successfully in a wide range of activities with their peers. *These champions make inclusion extraordinarily ordinary.* I hope you enjoy and benefit from reading about these champions of inclusion!

action. Individual thought, risk taking, and initiative are always key in challenges to the status quo. Yet building a community is also critical.

Sixth, *top-down and bottom-up strategies must both work together.* Each of us can and must initiate change as well as respond to change efforts coming from above. Teachers can begin and challenge administration to remove segregating practices and to put resources in our schools and classrooms.

Seventh, school improvement must be *connected to issues in our community and society.* We are not islands unto ourselves. Schools support community and social needs.

Finally, *every person must be a change agent.* School dynamics are simply too complex for those "in charge." Fullan (1997) says that "every teacher has the responsibility to help create an organization capable of individual and collective inquiry and continuous renewal, or it will not happen" (p. 39).

Change Strategies for Moving Toward Inclusive Teaching

As the movement toward inclusive education has grown, several approaches to the change have emerged (Hoskins, 1996; Roach, Ascroft, & Kysilko, 1995; Villa & Thousand, 1996).

One Student at a Time: Parent Requests. This route is most typical in districts where segregated schooling for students with disabilities is the norm. Parents request their children be included in general education classes. For real change to begin, these requests must increase over time. This pattern puts the onus on parents, who are often very frustrated. For example, a parent insisted that a student with severe disabilities participate in general education. This student's success in these classes led staff to begin asking why separate classes existed.

Forced Change: Legislation and Class Action Suits. For all areas of difference, except sexual preference, laws prohibit segregation. However, this has not prohibited the ongoing segregation of many students. Court orders related to racial desegregation have increasingly been abandoned and racial segregation in schools has again grown. Related to disability, several lawsuits have been successful and courts have ordered action toward inclusive education. In some cases, parents will take court action regarding their child. However, the efficacy of these efforts has been questionable. Force from the outside is never as successful as work to change the minds and hearts of the educators involved.

Teacher-Initiated Inclusion. In many schools, teachers have taken the initiative to move toward inclusive teaching. In one school, for example, a teacher in a special education classroom made arrangements for some of her students to go to another teacher's class one period per day. Eventually the two teachers worked out an arrangement to team-teach together. Teacher-initiated efforts can help get things going. The danger is that change will stop there. However, we can reach out to other teachers, expand partnerships, and gradually expand inclusive strategies across the building and grade levels.

Building-Based Systemic Change. An entire school can work systemically toward inclusive schooling. Teachers may develop a proposal to the principal and leadership team. In other cases a principal may be the prime initiator. Typically a planning group is formed to collect information, obtain input, and develop a plan.

Districtwide Systemic Change. Some school districts develop districtwide initiatives to move toward inclusive schooling. Such an initiative sometimes grows out of the impact of a model effort in one school; in other cases it is the result of a court order; in yet other cases it emerges in response to combined pressures from parents and leadership from school administrators. In a districtwide effort a planning committee is often convened and includes teachers, parents, and administrators.

Teacher Leadership and Action: We Can Make a Difference

As teachers we owe our first allegiance, and the vast bulk of our energy, to what we do in our own classroom. However, we quickly learn that policies can either enhance or seriously undercut our ability to teach children effectively. We must also become effective agents of change to help create conditions for best practices. However, this work is not for the fainthearted. We must have courage and persevere.

Parker Palmer (1998) describes the process by which teachers move from lonely despair to activism for positive change. We begin isolated and disconnected, often feeling beaten down by problems and issues. However, as we look for opportunities to make change, we soon discover others who feel similarly. Gradually we get together as a group—as a study forum, an online chat, a discussion group and form what Palmer calls

<table>
<tr><td>**BUMpS IN THE ROAD**</td><td>*When Segregation, Expulsion, and Punishment Are Embedded in the Culture of the School*</td></tr>
</table>

In some schools, we may find a pervasive punitive culture where students are treated with disrespect. This particularly occurs in schools that serve low-income children, often also children of color. Tension is pervasive, students seem "out of control," and most educators don't seem to know any strategy other than to use authoritarian, punitive approaches. Segregation of many types of students is the norm.

One such middle school we visited was this way. It had separate classes for dominant language learners and special education classes where two teams of four special education teachers taught all subject to students with learning disabilities, mild cognitive disabilities, autism, and more. These students were totally separated from the rest of the student body. They didn't even get to go to assemblies (the principal said they would be disruptive), field trips, or eat lunch or take recess with the rest of the students. They also had tracked classes for "at-risk" youth who did not qualify for special education. June, one of the teachers in these classes, told us that the parents of these students did not know they were placed in this class.

We saw a class of six students with autism who were taking their recess together with three adults. They also were not allowed to be with other students at recess. The students were sitting on the ground on the basketball court as the adults talked with them.

We saw numerous instances where students were treated disrespectfully in our visits to the school. In each of the hallways we could hear a teacher literally screaming at the top of her lungs at some student. In one class, the teacher became frustrated at the small talk among students and told them they had to sit the last 10 minutes of class without moving. One girl rolled her eyes and the teacher put her livid face a quarter inch away from the student and screamed, "What are you saying?" At lunch a teacher was detaining a group of nine boys in the middle of the busy hallway. "They broke the rules and they have to sit here without moving during lunch this week," said Ramon. He explained that his strategy at the beginning of the year is to "take on any student who challenges me. I show them I am willing to take them out if they

mess with me. This really keeps them in line!" Later in the day we saw the principal in the hall with a student, small for his age. Suddenly, we heard the principal say, "You aren't going to talk to me that way young man," and he proceeded to grab the screaming and crying boy by his arm and drag him down the hallway to his office.

Reflection: This was an incredibly difficult school to be in. Many images play themselves over and over in our minds. Remembering the students with autism at recess amazed us. These students' main need is to learn how to interact with others. Yet, they were not allowed to do so. Even the educators related with them very little. When the principal dragged the student down the hall we were shocked. We were particularly struck that punishment, control, segregation, and tension formed a cohesive culture in this school.

What to do? Unfortunately, variations on this scene play out daily in schools. We don't have magic bullet answers, but here are a few ideas from experiences of some great teachers we've seen struggle in schools like this.

- First, don't lose your commitment to inclusive teaching. The tension between reality and your ideal is substantive. However, keep your goal clear and high. Otherwise, you will shortly become part of this dysfunctional school culture.
- Look for others who are concerned and willing to work toward inclusive teaching. In our experience, such people are always there. Look for teachers who seem to be particularly good at dealing with difficult children. As you go about the school look for evidence of activity-based learning and efforts to build community in the classroom. When you find someone, introduce yourself and get to know him or her. Go to lunch together.
- Work to make your own classroom a model of inclusive teaching. Get to know your students and help them learn to be a caring community. Design authentic multilevel lessons.

(continued)

- Look for ways to get students out of segregated settings and into general education classrooms. If you are a specialist (special education teacher, social worker) look for general education teachers who might be willing to take one or more of your students part- or full-time into their classes. If you are a general education teacher, ask the bilingual or special education teachers if they would like to have one of their students join your class full- or part-time. Make arrangements to work together with that student.
- Look for other opportunities to make a difference. If a new principal is hired, talk with the principal soon after he or she arrives. Maybe you will be as fortunate as Malik in this chapter's Journey into the Classroom feature.

a "community of congruence." Ultimately, our efforts lead us to create formal structures to support our community—structures that may range from a modest listserv to a collaborative center for teaching and research. At some point, we discover that our issues and the solutions we suggest have public importance. The group decides to go public—whether through conference presentations, demonstrations, articles in journals or letters to the local paper, creation of a newsletter, or other avenues. Finally, for a movement to prosper, alternative reward systems are critical. Institutions mete out their own rewards but activism for change can offer rewards of different kinds. We may experience connection, fellowship, and the support of others. As the effort grows and we have some impact, we feel rewarded and encouraged by seeing the fruits of our efforts. In the words of Palmer (1998).

> I am a teacher at heart, and I am not naturally drawn to the rough-and-tumble of social change. I would sooner teach than spend my energies helping a movement along and taking the hits that come with it. Yet if I care about teaching, I must care not only for my students and my subject, but also for the conditions . . . that bear on the work teachers do. (p. 182)

How does this play out in our own work? What can we do? Here are a few strategies.

Seek to Be an Inclusive Teacher. First, we can begin in our own class. We seek to construct our teaching inclusively. We can teach in ways that engage all students at their own levels of ability; and we can think ahead about what we might do if the ability range broadened, if we had a student who was "severely gifted" or "severely disabled" in our class. When the opportunity presents itself (and it will), we will be ready. As we teach inclusively we may have a rippling impact in our school as people become aware of what we are doing. At best, we'll form partnerships and develop a support network of teachers.

Know and Communicate a Philosophy of Inclusive Teaching. Most important is that we are able to articulate a philosophy of inclusive teaching to parents, other teachers, and our administrator. We should know that the inclusive classroom is based on research, law, and best practices. We'll get clearer over time; but even in the early stages, we'll be surprised at what impact we can have.

Welcome Students with Special Needs. Teachers can recruit students with special needs into our class. As we communicate to the special education teachers and parents that we'd like to have their children in our class, they will likely be surprised, grateful, and amazed. Here are some actions we might take.

1. Communicate to the principal, or other teachers, or the special education teacher that we're interested in having heterogeneous students in our class.

FIGURE 1.2

Sample Letter from an Inclusive Teacher

Note: Underlined items will change depending on the school, teacher, and class.

To Whom It May Concern:

My name is <u>Laura Johnson</u>. I am a <u>seventh-grade social studies</u> teacher at <u>Burbank Middle School</u>. I am writing this letter to anyone who may be interested to let you know about my desire to have students with "special needs" in my class.

I believe that all students ought to go to school together. That's where they develop friendships that will last them all their lives, where they learn how to deal with others and handle their frustrations and fears. I'd like to have a class with diverse students who have abilities ranging from gifted to severely cognitively impaired.

How will I teach such students? Well, please know that I am learning and that I expect to make mistakes. However, if we can work together, I know this can be a fun and valuable class for all my students. Students who can't yet talk will find a place, as will students who are exploring complex or advanced problems.

Building a community in which students can help and support one another is very important in my class. We have many ways to help that happen—peer buddies, cooperative work groups, and more. My classroom community gives students ways to lean on one another. If your child has some problem behaviors, we'll all be trying to understand what he or she feels and provide support.

I ask a few things. Here they are:

- That if you have a concern, you talk with me about it.
- That you be patient with me. I am learning.
- That students with special needs be the same age as my other students.
- That special education help will be delivered in my classroom and that I have some say in the type and extent of support I receive.
- That I not be sent *all* the students with special needs.

If you are a parent of a child with special needs, you may never have heard of a general education teacher who *wants* your child in her class. Trust me. I do.

If you are a student who they say has "special needs," I look forward to having you in my class.

Sincerely,

<u>Laura Johnson</u>

2. Put this in writing as part of the welcoming letter to parents and students at the start of the year, as an open letter to parents to be distributed at the PTA open house, or as a proposal to the principal (see Figure 1.2).
3. Find out if our school automatically sends some students to a special school or class based on their label. Consider sending a copy of the letter to those children's parents.

However, we'll also want to spell out some commonsense ground rules: some expectations based on best practices and on the reasonable supports available under the law. What might these expectations include?

1. That the student(s) will be the same age as all our other students (not the presumed same "mental ability level")
2. That special education services are provided in our class and negotiated with us

3. That we have time to plan collaboratively
4. That there is adherence to natural proportions—students with special needs will be the same approximate percentage in our class as they are in the district student population

Model for and Support Other Teachers. As we welcome students with special differences into our class, our class can become a model for the school. Some other teachers may be interested and seek advice. If we are a "new" teacher, we should not let our inexperience keep us from providing leadership. It may seem strange, at first, to find ourselves mentoring older teachers; but if we are being true to our journey toward inclusive teaching, we will be learning strategies that other teachers have never considered.

Question Problematic School Practices. Pretty quickly, we will notice practices that concern us. For example, we might find that the special education resource teacher is busy all the time doing pull-out services and can't help support a student in our class; there is no behavior support team; the school has a zero tolerance policy, so students are suspended for minor infractions; or students in special education attend a segregated class in the building. In each of these situations, we can question these practices. As we do so, we may become clearer about our own thinking and philosophy.

Form Alliances. On the one hand, we want to build a culture of community in the school. On the other hand, in any community differences exist—and we will want to identify who is likely to support authentic, inclusive teaching. As we build relationships, talking and engaging in dialogue will help us gain allies.

Support Change in Our School. A few of us will teach in schools where inclusive teaching is simply how work is done. In such a school, we will continue to learn and work with colleagues to improve practice. Many of us, however, will find ourselves in very segregated schools. Others will be in schools that have moved toward inclusive schooling but have stopped short of the goal. In all these situations, we have an important responsibility and an opportunity to seek ways to spur continued change. At best, we can get together with others. We might develop partnerships between general education teachers and teachers of special students—special education, ESL, and bilingual teachers; obtain videos or written materials to learn more about inclusive teaching; visit inclusive schools; develop plans for rearranging the roles of specialists and assigning students to classes; and find students who may be at a segregated school and work to invite them back to our school.

   The leadership of the principal is critical. If a school is violating both the letter and the spirit of the law, administrators are usually well aware of this—and of their potential liability in the case of a lawsuit. We may be able to help them avoid lawsuits that would be harmful to all involved. Figure 1.3 reviews a few core targets that must be addressed as a school moves toward inclusion. As we and other teachers in our school teach inclusively, other educators may visit our school. This recognition can help strengthen our school's commitment to inclusive teaching.

Be Involved in District Initiatives. As we work to make our school a better place for all children, we will inevitably run up against problems—and opportunities—that are tied to districtwide policies and practices. We can often find ways to confront these issues. For districtwide change we can mobilize strategies similar to those we employed

FIGURE 1.3

Key Areas of Focus for Schoolwide Movement Toward Inclusive Education

Welcoming all together: Commit to the idea that students of diverse abilities can learn well together. If opportunity presents itself, welcome a student with a severe disability into the school and class. Success with such students can provide a powerful model.

Instruction for all: Analyze methods of instruction. Does the curriculum require certain basal readers and texts that are at only one level? How can teachers teach at multiple levels, differentiating instruction? How might this teaching be improved?

Finding "lost" students: Many schools and districts send students with moderate to severe disabilities to special education programs without ever giving them the real chance to enter a regular school. We can identify these programs in our catchment area and find out

who is there. We can offer the parents the opportunity to have their children in our school.

Structuring in-class support: Develop strategies for shifting special services from a "pull-out" to a "push-in" model. Explore ways to assign the caseloads of special education teachers or related services personnel.

Building-based support team: Any school needs multiple support strategies for teachers and students. With a support team that meets regularly, we can ask for assistance and ideas when we are having difficulties with a student.

Community and positive behavioral supports: Both building a culture of community in the school and developing proactive ways of responding to behavioral challenges are particularly important.

in our own building. For example, we might develop relationships with other teachers and staff members. As we become effective in working with students of difference, we likely will find and be found by others who also are looking for allies. We can volunteer to serve on district committees; invite others to visit our class; offer to do presentations about how we teach, in collaboration with others; develop relationships with parents who would like to see inclusive education expanded, and offer to provide information about what we are doing; and work with others to present innovative proposals to the administration.

Traveling Notes

As we've discussed in this chapter, schools have made strides towards creating inclusive schools. However, many students are segregated or do not have a sense of belonging in schools. There is much work to be done. Here are key notes to remember from this chapter.

1. Historically, human beings have feared those considered different. The most typical responses have been extermination and segregation.
2. Initial movements toward including those considered different are often based on benevolence, still a pattern of inequality. Our goal is building an inclusive community where all are valued.
3. In our society schools provide the most important place for social development. Inclusive education is key to giving all students a valued role in our communities and society.

4. However, we have a long way to go. Strides have been made toward inclusive schooling for students from various races and cultures. However, in the last 20 years schools have grown more racially segregated.

5. Most prevalent is segregation based on socioeconomic status. Students who are poor are the most isolated of children.

6. Students who are gifted and talented also are often segregated from other students. Particularly for these future community leaders it is critical that they learn how to deal with diverse people.

7. Students who are gay are seldom overtly segregated. However, there is a pattern of ridicule and abuse that causes great harm.

8. Important movements have occurred to include students who are dominant language learners. However, many approaches and programs still exist that separate these students from others.

9. Students with mild to severe disabilities remain the most segregated of students. The movement toward inclusive education fits in a long history moving from segregation to inclusion in school and community. Parents, people with disabilities, and their allies have struggled to move from segregated institutions, schools, and group homes to being part of inclusive schools and communities. Their struggle parallels the struggle of other groups for civil rights, integration, and equality.

10. Despite these problems, a strong movement toward including all students in learning together is operating in countries throughout the world. In most communities, there is at least some movement toward inclusive teaching.

11. Laws passed over the last 30 years provide a legal basis for civil rights and inclusion.

12. PL 94-142—passed in 1975, updated over the years, and renamed in 1990 as the Individuals with Disabilities Education Act (IDEA)—guides the delivery of special education services in schools and mandates that students be educated in the least restrictive environment.

13. Teachers have both the opportunity and responsibility to provide leadership toward inclusive teaching in schools. Many teachers are doing so. Teachers can model for others, suggest educators in a school come together to plan for inclusive teaching, and be involved in district initiatives and policy discussions in their state.

Stepping Stones

Following are some activities that will help extend your understanding and actions you may take.

1. Consider what you really feel and believe about difference and inclusion in our society. What do you believe? How comfortable are you with students who have different disabilities and sexual orientation, who are from varied cultural and ethnic groups, who speak varied languages at home?

2. Visit an inclusive school. Talk with teachers about the roles that they played in helping the school become inclusive. What do they say? What patterns do you discern? Ask the general education teachers for their opinions about inclusive teaching. What do they see as their role in helping improve the school as a whole, and what do they think about having students with special needs in their classes? How do you interpret their responses?

3. Interview parents and students in your school in a small focus group discussion. What has been their experience? What do they feel about the school? What might make the school better? What role did they see teachers playing in making the school inclusive?

4. Write a letter setting forth your beliefs about teaching and about the inclusion of students with special needs. Share and discuss this letter with a small group of other teachers.

2 Introduction to Inclusive Teaching

Educating all Children Together Well

with contributions by **Douglas Fisher**

CHAPTER GOAL

Understand the research base for inclusive teaching and essential elements of inclusive teaching.

CHAPTER OBJECTIVES

1. Become knowledgeable concerning research about segregated and inclusive education.
2. Understand principles and practices of quality inclusive teaching and schooling.
3. Utilize response to intervention as a framework for developing individual differentiation and interventions for students with special needs.
4. Develop a mental picture of effective inclusive schools.

In this chapter we will begin to understand how teachers can teach, how schools can be, so that children with significant differences can learn together. We will leave behind the factory model of schooling moving beyond segregation and benevolence to community membership. We will visit classes, evaluate research on inclusive education, and visit effective inclusive schools. Let's pay careful attention to what we see.

What Is Wrong Here? The Frustrations of Coping with Diverse Children in a "Factory School"

We enter Lafayette Elementary School, where we'll be visiting several classrooms today. As we walk down the hall, we first observe Amanda, a child with a cognitive disability who attends a special education class in the morning and Head Start in the afternoon. Akira, the special education teacher, greets us; he introduces the paraprofessional, Jan, and the speech therapist, Anora, who is in the class once a week. These specialists have 14 children in three groups, each working on skills—learning colors, naming letters, cutting with scissors. Anora is working with Amanda one-on-one at a table. "She really needs individual attention," Akira explains.

In the afternoon Amanda goes to Head Start. The teacher there, Zola, has activity centers at which her 24 children are engaged. We are intrigued as we watch other children pull Amanda into the center activities, helping her select colors of paper and cut. Curiously, we see Amanda attending and performing in ways that Akira and Jan thought not possible. *not inclusion*

Next, we walk to the resource room at the end of the hall, a class for students with learning disabilities. We are warmly greeted by Gayle Horton. "Hi. Come in!" She is using reading and math worksheets with 10 students. After a while Gayle tells us about Robie, a student who "comes to me 2 hours each day for reading and math. I use a special curriculum so that he can have some success." We ask if she helps Robie with the reading and math in his regular class. "No," she says. "That is much too hard for him, and besides, there's no way I can keep up with all the different materials the different teachers are using." *so make changes* *How do they keep up?*

Gayle then expresses her frustrations and the pressures she feels. "They are on so many different levels!" she exclaims. "It's really hard to get to all the students. All are at different levels in every subject, and they are not able to help one another. So I do the best I can. It's really hard." She goes on to explain that it is virtually impossible to coordinate with the six teachers who send her students. "They are all at different places in the curriculum, using different materials. I am in this class all day with students and have no time to work with them." We ask Gayle what she thinks about having these students in the general education *have you kids?*

class full time. "Oh no!" she says. "They could never keep up. They would be lost and left behind! Also, the teachers would never want another teacher in their class."

Finally, we visit Jim Bridges's fifth-grade social studies class. The upper elementary grades are departmentalized, and Jim shares 75 students with two other teachers. He's been quite bothered with Lamar, a student classified as "educable mentally retarded." Lamar goes to Mrs. Horton's resource room for 1 hour daily but is in Jim's class the whole period. "Lamar can't function in my class at all," Jim says. "His academics are far too low, and he is always causing trouble. I have to spend so much of my time with this one child that I can't give other children what they deserve."

As we come in, Jim is passing out textbooks. "Turn to page 53 and begin reading about the Bill of Rights, then go to the questions on your worksheet." We look around at the class. The children are seated at tables in groups of four or five. A few commercial posters about social studies are on the wall; the only books in the room are the textbooks.

Indeed, Lamar is acting upset. He looks at the book, fidgets, and goes over to the trash can and throws something in it. "Lamar, sit down!" says Jim. Lamar returns and stares at the book.

Jim keeps a watchful eye on Lamar. "See, he won't do his work," says Jim. We ask if Lamar is able to read the textbook. "No, that's the problem. The textbook is at a fourth-grade reading level and Lamar is at a first-grade level." We ask Jim if he has books at a lower level and if he's paired Lamar with another student and let them read aloud together. Jim explains that he has no books Lamar can read and doesn't have the money to buy any. He further observes that students must do their own work and that pairing students for work is a bad idea. "We've got to do everything we can to get the test scores up," he points out. "So they need to do their worksheets on their own."

We leave for the car, deep in thought. In the two special education classrooms teachers are working hard, but the situation creates dynamics that appear to directly hamper the learning of the children. In Jim's class some obvious approaches that might help Lamar simply aren't being tried. Unfortunately, we are aware that Lafayette Elementary is too typical. Can it be different?

Toward Inclusive Schooling

A Glimpse of Teaching Practices That Honor All Children

We take our questions to another school, Thomas Jefferson Middle School. This school has children from many different ethnic groups and from both low and high socioeconomic backgrounds. The district has adopted a focus on both inclusion and improvement of instruction. As we walk in, students in the hall are noisy but not loud. There is an engaged, excited hum and periodic jovial outbursts. The phrase "learning noise" comes to mind.

Our first class is Bob Stephen's World Cultures class. At Lafayette Elementary the students were all seated at their desks, and the teachers put a lot of energy into keeping the students quiet and working. This class is different. Bob is discussing a project with a small group of students. The rest of the class is a buzz of activity—some students are standing, some sitting, some moving around the room, all engaged.

Bob points out a student to observe. Jonathan, he comments, has low reading and writing abilities and can be disruptive. However, he is very interested in learning and works very hard when he is engaged. He is also very good at singing and playing baseball.

The fourth-hour bell rings. Jonathan, restless, wanders to the back of the room, drumming his pencil on desks along the way. Bob watches Jonathan but says nothing. "Get in your work groups," he says, and Jonathan and the other students gather in circles. Jonathan's group is working on bartering; today he is the banker, tracking items his group receives in trade and money they have. He works very well and is totally engaged. Later we notice a paraprofessional working with Jonathan's group. Bob walks throughout the class, helping, encouraging, and coaching students. At the end of the activity, Jonathan reports the money and items to his group. He beams with pride.

Bob has been teaching the World Cultures class for 8 years. He uses teaching strategies such as cooperative learning, simulations, lectures, computer, video, reading supplements, and text reading. For assessment he uses rubrics for research projects, reports, papers, essay tests, oral presentations, and group projects (Peterson, 1999).

We ask him how including students with learning challenges has affected his class. Bob admits it was difficult at first but concludes that it has benefited everyone. "I have the support of a great special education department," he says. "The inclusion of students with special needs has really improved my teaching."

We next walk down the hall to Annette Smith's literacy class. Annette and her students are gathered in the rug area of the room. She is sitting in a chair reading a story to the students. The students listen intently. We wander around the room looking at learning projects: books read list; places we've been map; book recommendations (an envelope where students suggest books another student might like); personal "memoirs" projects (shoe boxes containing various personal archives and belongings that help explain students' lives); published books (three-ring binders filled with poems and writings of students—and of some parents as well).

As the next class comes in, Annette asks them to gather on the carpet. She asks for two or three volunteers. She reminds the other students how hard it is to go first and quietly encourages them to be supportive. Annette then exclaims, "Ladies and gentlemen! We now present Sharon." Sharon stands and faces the class, showing a picture drawn to illustrate a scene in the book she is reading. She explains what is happening in the scene. Two other students present scenes using characters made of paper or small dolls. Annette then passes out grading rubrics to all of the children. These have the key elements of the story scenes presentation: title, author, pages, presentation of setting, description of characters, the problem in the story, and how the problem was dealt with. She asks students to describe what they liked about the presentations and make suggestions for improvement. The presenting students call on those who raise their hands. We are amazed at their thoughtfulness.

Following a substantial amount of time on this activity and much clapping and appreciation, Annette directs the students to various projects—reading a "just right" book, working on memoirs, or doing group projects on the carpet. The children sort themselves with a bit of flurry but soon settle down to concentrate.

Annette talks with us and notes that among the students are children labeled ADHD, children diagnosed as learning disabled, and one child with severe brain damage. We are amazed that we simply did not notice these children in the classroom. The choices given, the requests for engagement that allowed for a range of ability levels, the respect for all children—all made the learning differences in this class invisible to us as outside observers.

We leave thoughtful and amazed. At Lafayette, even though teachers work hard, they don't know how to meet the multiple styles, abilities, and challenges of their students. Therefore, many students are referred to special education. At Thomas Jefferson Middle School, in contrast, each of the teachers we have seen is using engaging, interesting learning activities that allow students to work at their own level and encourage students to help one another. Although what we have seen at Jefferson is not perfect, it does represent what is both possible and needed.

What made the difference in these two schools? Engaging teaching techniques? A commitment to educating diverse children together? Supporting children in regular classrooms rather than in separate special education classrooms? Collaboration of teachers and specialists in the classroom? School administrative policies that support teachers? In these two schools we saw the difference between effective inclusive teaching and some of the problems associated with segregated special education, themes we will return to many times on our journey.

Research and Inclusive Schooling
The Effectiveness of Inclusive Versus Segregated Education

What does research show regarding inclusive education? Does it work to have students of such differing characteristics learning together? Can schools and teachers implement effective inclusive schooling? Let's look at a synthesis related to these questions with various types of students.

Students from Diverse Races and Cultures

Since the 1950s, schools have not been allowed to segregate students on the basis of race, culture, or gender. The Supreme Court stated that schools that are racially segregated can never be equal in the 1954 *Brown v. Board of Education* ruling. However, after some movement toward racial integration following this landmark case, racial segregation of schools has again increased in recent years. Some 73% of Black students and 77% of Latino students attend schools where students of color are the vast majority and more than one third attend schools that have more than 90% of students of color (Orfield & Lee, 2005). Conversely, some 90% of White students attend schools in which more than 50% of the students are White. The move toward racial resegregation has raised many issues.

Academic achievement of students is directly related to racial segregation (Borman, 2004; Orfield & Lee, 2007), impacts that are associated with greater poverty of children of color. Numerous negative indicators are associated with racially segregated schools. In the United States, 50% of Black and Latino students concentrated in racially segregated schools drop out of school (Orfield, 2004). In a Florida study, the authors concluded that "attempts to resolve the achievement gap by funding equity or classroom size changes" will fail if segregation is not addressed (Borman, 2004, p. 605).

Some have expressed concern that racial integration posits that for a child of color to learn well he or she must sit next to White children. However, race and culture are connected with many other issues. A much greater proportion of people of color have lower incomes so that issues related to poverty and quality schooling are evident. Further, even middle-income minority families end up in neighborhoods with high concentrations of poverty and in schools with high percentages of poor students (Harris & McArdle, 2004). Racial prejudice and discrimination continue. Students of color are identified as having disabilities and needing special education services at a much higher rate than their incidence in the population. Some argue that this is, in part, a result of racial discrimination and low expectations by educators of these students. This has been particularly the case as boys of color are identified as having behavioral problems and labeled as having emotional disturbance or social maladjustment.

Students Who Are Poor

Research is very clear that when schools have high concentrations of poor students academic achievement goes down. Poverty has many impacts on learning and human development and clustering of poor students in segregated schools expands the impacts of

SCHOOLS
to VISIT

Multilevel Teaching and Support for Inclusive Teaching

Dailey Elementary School
3135 N. Harrison
Fresno, CA 93710

Dailey Elementary is a K–6 school in Fresno Unified School District, an urban district in the agricultural heart of California. The city ranks sixth in the nation in childhood poverty, and students speak 101 languages. Seventy-nine percent of the approximately 630 students qualify for the free/reduced lunch program. The population is culturally diverse: 49% of students are Hispanic, 32% White, 9% Asian, and 8% African American. Just over 20% have been identified as learners of English as a second language.

The school district is now working to have all children with special needs included in general education classes. Beginning in the 2000–2001 school year, students with special needs in self-contained classes returned to Dailey fully included in general education classrooms. Since that time the school has included children with autism, Tourette syndrome, Down syndrome, cerebral palsy, developmental delays, hearing impairment, emotional/behavioral problems, and learning disabilities.

In 14 of 28 classrooms, in a mix of multiage and regular graded classes, a resource specialist and special day class teacher serve approximately 40 children identified with special needs. The school has one full-time and two part-time paraprofessionals as well as a half-day assistant for a student with autism. Specialists provide weekly support: an adaptive PE teacher, an occupational therapist, a speech therapist, and a school psychologist. One day a week an inclusion specialist observes children and helps teachers brainstorm solutions.

Although the teachers have concerns, they are working hard to differentiate instruction to accommodate all the children. Teachers use scaffolding, differentiated instruction, and multiple ways of knowing as a matter of course in many of the classrooms. Supported reading, choral reading, read alouds, interactive writing, reading and writing conferences, individualized spelling work, mini-lessons, and whole class discussions are all part of the picture. Some children use portable keyboards for writing. Others work on clipboards or use dry erase boards. Visual schedules, break cards, and individualized stories are used to help children who have difficulty staying on task or communicating with students or teachers.

Building community is important to the teachers at Dailey. Even before inclusion, several teachers insisted that I, a special education teacher, work with students with special needs in their classes. Because many teachers follow a workshop or inquiry model, I am able to work with individuals or small groups as needed. Instruction is more easily adapted to the needs of the students.

Our school's vision of inclusion continues to evolve as the general and special education teachers become comfortable with this new challenge, and as our student population ebbs and flows. There have been many positive experiences for the staff, parents, and students; and we continue to learn better ways to make everyone full members of the school community.

By Nancy Barth, inclusion teacher.

these difficulties. Children who are poor have much less exposure to language than middle school children. Families are often unstable, changing residence frequently and shifting their children from school to school. Neighborhoods are often considered unsafe and students frequently lack proper nutrition. Schools that have a high percentage of low-income students struggle to attract and retain good teachers and have higher rates of teacher turnover, often resulting in students having less able teachers. These schools also have a higher incidence of behavior problems, a high rate of dropouts, are most often racially segregated, and have large percentages of students whose first language is not

the predominant language. In addition, within schools peers are very important. Studies have shown that the absence of strong, positive influence of peers related to education has substantially lowered academic achievement (Orfield & Lee, 2005; Orfield, Losen, Wald, & Swanson, 2004).

What has been the impact of economic integration initiatives in which districts seek to heterogeneously mix students who are poor with middle-class students? Consistently, when implemented effectively, the achievement of low-income students has been higher and no negative impacts on other students have been reported. Students are exposed to higher expectations and have more educational and career options in these efforts. However, school districts must be careful to ensure that the percentage of low-income students does not grow too large. If this occurs, a tipping point may be reached where the impacts associated with poverty resurface. Finally, some studies have shown that when districts work effectively toward economic integration, racial integration follows as part of this process (Boger, 2005; Orfield & Lee, 2005). Research makes it very clear, then, if students of color and those who are poor are to narrow the achievement gap with their wealthier, White peers, economic and racial integration are critically important.

Dominant-Language Learners

Students who do not speak the dominant language often are segregated many times over, increasing their isolation. Such second-language learners are often from poor families and attend schools with high percentages of low-income students. As noted, these schools are often racially segregated as well. However, the pattern typically continues as second-language learners are put in separate classes to learn the dominant language or be taught in their first language. Most Latino students, for example, attend school where more than 60% of students are Latino (Orfield & Lee, 2005). Latino and Asian second-language learners are more than three times as isolated as their peers (Lee, 2004). The research regarding racial and economic segregation applies directly to many of these students.

What does research say about including students whose language is not the dominant one in general education classes using two-way bilingual education and sheltered instruction versus separate classes for either bilingual education or education in the dominant language (English as a second language in English-speaking countries)? This is a difficult question to answer. The debate among researchers regarding this and related questions has been substantial. Conclusions that can be drawn from research reflect tensions between the need to include students who are second-language learners with the peers in school and the need to provide the most effective means of learning a second language and learning academic content (de Jong, 2006; Ma, 2002; U.S. Department of Education, 1995).

First, immersion in dominant-language classrooms without meaningful and thoughtful language support is ineffective. The theory upon which this approach is built, that students will learn a second language more quickly if they are immersed in it full-time, simply hasn't worked. Quality instruction and time is more important. Languages take several years to learn fluently. Political efforts to eliminate bilingual education and institute full immersion programs have proven unsuccessful. *Because its Bull*

Second, researchers are clear that students need to learn using their native language where their culture is also honored. Programs that combine use of the native language with instruction in the dominant language are seen as effective.

Third, students also need to be integrated and educated with students who are fluent in the dominant language. Such inclusive educational approaches ensure that students develop relationships with others and feel a sense of belonging in the school that helps prevent social and emotional difficulties. Additionally, social integration with dominant-language speakers provides fluent role models in the use of language and does help students learn and apply language in ways that is not possible in a separate classroom.

Fourth, researchers have identified several characteristics of effective instruction of second-language learners that are applicable in both separate bilingual or ESL classrooms but particularly important in dominant-language classrooms. Particularly important is the need for teachers to "shelter" language demands using additional cues such as graphics, gestures, and pictures to enhance understanding and communication and reduce the demand on language alone. Instruction should also incorporate authentic learning that calls on higher cognitive abilities, engage student interest, offer student-directed activities, and make connections between school and home (Ma, 2002). Interestingly, these are exactly the type of supports that other students who have language difficulties (for example, children with cognitive disabilities) need.

While results are yet inconclusive, there is increasing evidence that inclusive, integrated approaches for students who are second-language learners can successfully incorporate all these findings. As noted in Chapter 1, two-way or dual-language bilingual education programs combined with sheltered instruction, an approach designed to incorporate key elements of effective instruction, and integrated bilingual education all provide options for inclusive strategies that have proven effective.

Students Considered Gifted and Talented

Much debate has occurred regarding whether students considered gifted and talented should be in separate programs or whether general education teachers should be trained to provide differentiated instruction to provide effective instruction for these students. In a comprehensive review of research, Oakes (1985) and Wheelock (1992) concluded that separate programs for high-ability students have only mild academic benefits but that they have negative impacts on average- to low-ability students. The removal of high-achieving classmates takes away role models whose work may strengthen learning for other students. Further, highly able students often feel isolated and cut off from their friends. Sapon-Shevin (1994b) found that such programs often promote elitism and break a sense of community. Most researchers agree that if teachers used multilevel, differentiated instruction segregated programs would be unnecessary (Clark, 1997; Cline, 1999; Kennedy, 1995; Sapon-Shevin, 1994a,b; Willis, 1995). Much work has occurred to develop programs and strategies for differentiated, multilevel instruction that provides a way to challenge all students at their ability level, including students considered gifted and talented using talent development of all students and consultation by gifted specialists with teachers (Kirschenbaum, Armstrong, Ciner, & Landrum, 1999; Stepanek, 1999; Tomlinson, 2004b; Tomlinson et al., 2002; Wilkes, 2000; Winebrenner, 2001).

Students Who Are Gay

Gay and lesbian students are included in general education classes. Despite much prejudice and poor treatment of these students, students who consider themselves gay have not been segregated in public schools. As reported in Chapter 1, we know that the typical negative, hostile treatment of students who are gay impacts them in many problematic ways. However, research has also found that proactive efforts can make a difference. When gay–straight alliance groups are formed in schools, this is a particularly effective strategy for making schools safe, more accepting places not only for students who are gay but for all students as well. When this occurs, gay and lesbian students have different feelings about themselves and achieve better academic and social outcomes. Additionally, there are no data that suggest that homosexuality increases among other young people when students are accepted and supported (GLSEN, 2007; MacGillivray, 2004; Smith, 2008).

Students with Disabilities

The move to including students with disabilities who have traditionally been served by special education is the newest, and, for some, most controversial part of the movement toward inclusive teaching. So we review the research in some detail regarding inclusion of these students. Figure 2.1 summarizes research on comparative academic and social outcomes of students in special and general education classes. You'll note that Figure 2.1 does not have a column headed "Segregated Classes Best." This is because no research to date has found better outcomes when comparing segregated and inclusive education. Figure 2.2 provides a summary of academic and social outcomes of students with varied levels of disability in inclusive education.

Educators have thought that segregated special education classes with smaller class sizes and additional adult resources would allow teachers to individualize instruction and focus on the learning styles and needs of each student, thus leading to improved learning. However, research overwhelmingly indicates that this has not occurred. For example, when Vaughn, Moody, and Schumm (1998) and Moody and colleagues (2000) studied instruction in resource rooms, they found that these programs constitute "broken promises" and are a "setup for failure" for students with disabilities. In both of these studies teachers taught mostly through whole class instruction; gave the same level of reading materials to students at obviously different levels of ability; used basals as the primary source of reading material; and used very little individualized, small group, or differentiated instruction. Others have reviewed instruction in special education classrooms with similar findings (Allington, 1991, 1993, 1994; McIntosh, Vaughn, Schumm, Haager, & Lee, 1993).

Advocates of inclusive education have hoped that greater academic expectations, a richer learning environment, more effective teaching strategies, and modeling by more able peers would enhance learning. With few exceptions, the research strongly supports these hopes. Again, note that no research findings in Figure 2.1 indicate segregated education is more effective. As early as 1968, Dunn questioned separate special education classes (Dunn, 1968). Waldron and McLeskey (1998), summarizing research related to segregated special education programs, indicated that "there is some controversy regarding whether separate class placement is *ever beneficial* for students with mild disabilities." Carlberg and Kavale (1980), Wang and Baker (1986), and Baker (1994) each conducted a **meta-analysis,** a statistical procedure by which findings from different studies are combined, of 74 studies; results showed that students with disabilities had more positive academic learning in integrated settings. Likewise, several studies found that achievement of

FIGURE 2.1

Impacts of Inclusive and Segregated Education for Students with Disabilities

INCLUSIVE EDUCATION BEST	MIXED RESULTS
Carlberg and Kavale (1980): Meta-analysis of 50 studies showed more positive academic learning in integrated settings.	
Brinker and Thorpe (1984) and Hunt, Goetz, and Anderson (1986): Greater integration associated with more IEP goals met.	
Wang and Baker (1986). Meta-analysis of 11 studies showed more positive academic learning in integrated settings.	Affleck, Madge, Adams, and Lowenbraun (1988): Study found no difference in academic performance; integrated education was more cost-effective.
Cole and Meyer (1991): Children in inclusive settings showed greater social competence, spent more time with peers and less time alone.	
Baker (1994): Meta-analysis of 13 studies showed more positive academic learning in integrated settings. Hunt, Farron-Davis, Beckstead, Curtis, and Goetz (1994): Students with severe disabilities had more engagement, higher quality IEPs, and higher levels of social interaction in inclusive education.	Baker and Zigmond (1995): 50% of students with LD made equal progress to classmates. Students with more severe LD made equal progress in both special education and general education classes.
Fryxell and Kennedy (1995) and Kennedy, Shulka, and Fryxell (1997): Studies showed larger social networks, substantial social benefits, interactions with general education students.	Marston (1996): 240 students with LD made better progress in partial pull-out than in full-time inclusion or pull-out only.
Waldron and McLeskey (1998): Mild LD students gained in reading in inclusive class, were equal in math; those with severe LD made equal progress in both inclusive and segregated settings.	Manset and Semmel (1997): Reviewed 11 studies but could not conclude that either segregation or inclusion was more effective. Recommended best practice teaching strategies in general education.
Buysse and Bailey (1993) and Hundert, Mahoney, and Mundy (1998): Children with severe disabilities in segregated preschools showed less developmental progress than comparable children in integrated settings.	
Freeman and Alkin (2000): Comprehensive review of studies for students with mental retardation concluded that the more students were integrated, the higher were their academic performance and social skills.	

LD = learning disability.

FIGURE 2.2

Outcomes of Inclusive Education for Students with Disabilities

	ACADEMIC	SOCIAL
Students with mild disabilities	Students with mild disabilities make better gains in inclusive programs than in pull-out programs (Banerji & Dailey, 1995; Deno, Maruyama, Espin, & Cohen, 1990; Fishbaugh & Gum, 1994; Jenkins et al., 1994; National Center for Educational Restructuring and Inclusion, 1995).	There is more active student engagement (Saint-Laurent & Lessard, 1991). Students develop enhanced social competence and improved behavior more than in segregated classes (Baker, Wang, & Walberg, 1994; Cole & Meyer, 1991; McLeskey, Waldon, & Pacchiano, 1993; Saint-Laurent & Lessard, 1991). Students with mild disabilities are less often accepted and are more likely to be rejected because of their behavior than students without disabilities (Roberts & Zubrick, 1992).
Students with moderate to severe disabilities	The quality of Individualized Education Plans is improved (Brinker & Thorpe, 1984; Hunt & Farron-Davis, 1992; Hunt, Farron-Davis, Beckstead, Curtis, & Goetz, 1994; Hunt, Goetz, & Anderson, 1986; Kaskinen-Chapman, 1992). For students with moderate to severe disabilities, achievement is enhanced or at least equivalent in inclusive versus segregated settings (Cole & Meyer, 1991; Giangreco, Dennis, Cloninger, Edelman, & Schattman, 1993; National Center for Educational Restructuring and Inclusion, 1995; Ryndak, Downing, Jacqueline, & Morrison, 1995; Saint-Laurent & Lessard, 1991).	Friendships and social interactions for students with disabilities expand in school and carry over to after-school contexts (Fryxell & Kennedy, 1995; Hall, 1994; Hunt, Farron-Davis et al., 1994; McDonnell, Hardman, Hightower, & Kiefer-O'Donnell, 1991; Ryndak et al., 1995; Salisbury, Palombaro, & Hollowood, 1993; Staub, Schwartz, Gallucci, & Peck, 1994). Students with severe disabilities have many social interactions, though these are often assistive. Over the course of the year, the numbers of interactions decrease but become more natural. Teachers can facilitate increased reciprocal interactions between students with and without disabilities (Hunt, Alwell, Farron-Davis, & Goetz, 1996).
Students without disabilities	There is no evidence that academic progress is impeded in inclusive classes, and in some cases it consistently increases (Fishbaugh & Gum, 1994; Hunt, Staub, Alwell, & Goetz, 1994; Kaskinen-Chapman, 1992; Odom, Deklyen, & Jenkins, 1984; Saint-Laurent, Glasson, Royer, Simard, & Pierard, 1998; Scruggs & Mastropieri, 1994; Sharpe, York, & Knight, 1994; Wang & Birch, 1984). Engaged time is not diminished (Hollowood, Salisbury, Rainforth, & Palombaro, 1995; McIntosh, Vaughn, Schumm, Haager, & Lee, 1993; Peck, Carlson, & Helmstetter, 1992; Pugach & Wesson, 1995). Problem-solving skills are acquired (Biklen, Corrigan, & Quick, 1989; Salisbury, Palombaro, & Hollowood, 1993).	Students view their involvement with peers with disabilities positively (Altman & Lewis, 1990; Helmstetter, Peck, & Giangreco, 1994; McLeskey et al., 1993; Pugach & Wesson, 1995; Stainback, Stainback, Moravec, & Jackson, 1992). There is an increased appreciation and understanding of diversity (Fisher, Pumpian, & Sax, 1998; Helmstetter et al., 1994; Peck et al., 1992; Scruggs & Mastropieri, 1994). Self-esteem and behaviors improve. (Staub, Spaulding, Peck, Gallucci, & Schwartz, 1996).

IEP goals was stronger in inclusive education (Brinker & Thorpe, 1984; Hunt, Farron-Davis, Beckstead, Curtis, & Goetz, 1994; Hunt, Goetz, & Anderson, 1986; Kaskinen-Chapman, 1992). Freeman and Alkin (2000) conducted a comprehensive review of research over the preceding 25 years concerning integration of children with mental retardation; they concluded that studies showed that the more time these children spent in general education, the more their academic growth improved.

A small number of studies (see Figure 2.1) have been less clear. Affleck, Madge, Adams, and Lowenbraun (1988) and Manset and Semmel (1997) found neither segregated nor inclusive education to be more effective. Baker, Zigmond, and colleagues (Baker & Zigmond, 1995; Zigmond, Jenkins, & Fuchs, 1995) showed that some 33 to 64% of students with mild learning disabilities in inclusive classes in three states made gains comparable to those of their general education peers. For those with more severe learning disabilities, however, progress was minimal and no differences in progress existed between general and special education. The researchers concluded that "general education settings produce achievement outcomes for students with learning disabilities that are neither desirable nor acceptable" (Zigmond et al., 1995, p. 539). Waldron and McLesky (1998) replicated the research and found similarly that 48% of students with learning disabilities made gains comparable to those of their general education peers. However, Waldron and McLesky saw the glass as half full: They were quite encouraged that approximately half of these students made progress equal to that of students without disabilities, and they suggested that the criterion for success cannot be "cure" but should be progress in learning. In fact, if achievement of students with learning disabilities is approximately equal, according to these two studies, in full-time general education and pull-out, separated services, ethically there is no reason that these students should be pulled out at all as evidence is clear that social and emotional problems occur when students are separated from their peers.

One final point is worth noting. Studies that compared inclusive and segregated education, for the most part, have made no attempt to evaluate the *quality of instruction* students are receiving. In other words, studies show that inclusive education is at least as effective as pull-out services whether or not the student is receiving quality instruction. If, as proposed in this book, teachers systematically used effective inclusive teaching approaches, we could reasonably expect that results would be much more positive.

Socially, the promise of segregated special education classes has been twofold. On the one hand, parents and educators have sought a place to protect students with cognitive and physical disabilities from feared ridicule or direct harm. On the other hand, segregated programs for students with behavioral difficulties have allowed greater control and promised more nurturing environments in which trained specialists can help students improve emotionally and socially.

Those calling for inclusive education, however, have been concerned about the isolation of children with disabilities from their neighborhood communities. Students in special education classes often go to a different school than neighborhood children, limiting opportunities for relationships. Parents of children in special schools typically come from a wide geographical area, making development of mutually supportive relationships difficult. Advocates of inclusive education hope that attending regular education classes, with needed support, will help children develop relationships, become a meaningful part of their community, and improve their self-esteem.

For students with behavioral problems, inclusive educators have been concerned that schools do not build a supportive learning community when students are removed—and that the self-esteem of such students is severely damaged. Kauffman, Lloyd, and Baker (1995) argue that general educators are not prepared to meet the behavioral challenges of students with emotional disturbances and that separate programs staffed by specially trained professionals are needed. However, problems in outcomes of segregated programs for students with emotional and behavioral problems are clear. Follow-up data indicate that once students are placed in a segregated program, the chances that they will drop out of school, be arrested, be imprisoned, and/or be unemployed all increase (Berg, 1989, p. 10B; Cheney & Harvey, 1994; Garbarino, Dubrow, Kostelny, & Pardo, 1992; Kay, 1999; Lantieri & Patti, 1996; Zionts, 1997). Researchers in this field hope that schools will work to develop nurturing communities that help prevent emotional problems and will use proactive strategies to help children learn social skills when problems do occur. Guidelines for practice resulting from research and demonstration efforts have been documented (Cheney & Muscott, 1996; Knoff & Batsche, 1995; March & Sprague, 1999; Meadows, 1996; Reavis & Andrews, 1999; University of Oregon, 1999; Zionts, 1997).

For students with academic and physical challenges, the social and emotional results of inclusion have been particularly positive. Inclusive education provides many more opportunities for interactions, development of relationships, and social skill enhancement (Fryxell & Kennedy, 1995; Hall, 1994; Hunt, Farron-Davis et al., 1994; McDonnell, Hardman, Hightower, & Kiefer-O'Donnell, 1991; Ryndak, Downing, Jacqueline, & Morrison, 1995; Staub, Schwartz, Gallucci, & Peck, 1994).

Research has also documented challenges and questions. With students who have more severe disabilities, typical students may provide help and assistance rather than playing or socializing (Salisbury, Palombaro, & Hollowood, 1993). Not surprisingly, students with disabilities, whether mild or severe, often have poorer social skills and are less often accepted and more often rejected (Freeman & Alkin, 2000; Salend & Duhaney, 1999), particularly because of behavioral problems, than students without disabilities. Studies have also shown, however, that teachers and other staff can facilitate relationships as part of community building, and that problem solving, conflict resolution, and social skills development can be effectively integrated into classes across the grade levels (Freeman & Alkin, 2000; Hunt, Alwell, Farron-Davis, & Goetz, 1996).

Research and Change

Many studies make it clear that proactive efforts to create an inclusive school can be effective, even invigorating for students and teachers. Some researchers, however, argue that educators are neither willing nor able to develop the innovative practices necessary to make inclusive teaching successful; these researchers have documented problems that include (1) poor planning and preparation, (2) inadequate supports for students and teachers, and (3) negative and adversarial attitudes of educators (Baines, Baines, & Masterson, 1994; McGregor & Vogelsberg, 1998; Salend & Duhaney, 1999; Zigmond & Baker, 1995).

Although change is always slow, increasing numbers of schools are successfully moving toward inclusive schooling. When change efforts involve faculty training, administrative leadership and support, in-class assistance, and other special services, the attitudes of teachers are positive (Phillips, Alfred, Brulli, & Shank, 1990; Villa, Thousand, Meyers, & Nevin, 1996; Werts, Wolery, Snyder, & Caldwell, 1996). Some teachers see inclusive schooling as building on positive teaching practices they already have in place (Fisher, Sax, Rodifer, & Pumpian, 1999; Rainforth, 1992). Teachers may fear having students with severe disabilities at first—but as teachers have come to know these students, they have engaged them and have been willing to have them again (Giangreco, Dennis, Cloninger, Edelman, & Schattman, 1993).

Despite the fact that much segregated education still exists, many schools are gradually moving toward inclusive education, as several comprehensive studies have documented. Among these are O'Hearn Elementary School in Boston (Henderson, 2000), Souhegan High School in New Hampshire (Jorgensen, 1998), and Purcell Marion High School in Cincinnati (Bauer & Myree-Brown, 2001). The National Center for Educational Restructuring and Inclusion (1995) conducted a national study of hundreds of schools throughout the United States that were implementing inclusive education.

Implications of Research. Research to date provides a solid foundation on which to expand inclusive schooling. Legally and ethically, students should not be segregated unless there is clear evidence of superiority for segregated classes and programs. The most important research questions for the future are not *whether* we should seek to build inclusive schools but *how* we may do so well. Clearly, as Zigmond and Baker (1995) state, for inclusive teaching to be successful, "business as usual" is not possible.

What Is School For?

To make sense of talking about whether schooling and teaching are being effective and how to create good schools and be a good teacher, we must ask a very fundamental question: "What are schools for?" Said a different way, "What do we hope that children will be as a result of schooling?" Peterson and Tamor (2009) discussed two clear options.

Two primary opposing views exist regarding the purpose of schools. Some, such as the Business Roundtable (Ryan, 2004) and Achieve (Achieve, 2004), an organization created by governors and business leaders, believe that the primary purpose of schools should be to *create workers* who have skills and personal styles to fill and perform available jobs. Others believe this outcome is too narrow (Freeman, 2005; Goodlad, 1984b; Hodgkinson, 2006; Postman, 1996). For them schools should seek to develop active *citizens,* helping children develop their own capacity for personal achievement and contributing to society as active citizens for democracy.

Relatedly we might consider these two goal statements for schools:

1. Children should learn to compete so they can be successful in business and work, become wealthy, and do better than others. They should focus on their own needs even to the detriment of others.
2. Children should learn to do their best and should take responsibility for themselves, their family, and others in their community. We would hope they would work to make their communities better, more caring places in which to live.

When we look at these two related options (training workers versus educating citizens; creating competitors or caring contributors), most people would opt for the second option. In fact, if you review mission statements of most public schools, you will often see clear statements that relate to option two. However, the way we evaluate the efficacy of schools and the way schools and classrooms are often organized promotes exactly the opposite.

In this context, three approaches to learning are apparent: (1) competition, (2) individualization, and (3) cooperation. When competition rules in schools and classrooms we are actively teaching children that what matters is not how good you are, how much you know, but whether you win. Winning, of course, is for the few; losing is for the many. When we use competition as the basis for learning we are also teaching children that their goal is to put others down so they can win. It is not surprising that in such environments children are often uncaring and create problems. We are actively teaching them to do so! We can also focus on individualistic learning approaches where students are expected to learn on their own based on their own goals. While this moves in a positive direction, when we use this approach we are teaching children that only they matter, that they have no responsibility to others. Finally, however, when we use cooperative, collaborative learning we actively teach children that all people are interdependent, that the success and quality of life of each individual is interactive with and related to the success of others and the existence of an effective community of people working together.

Unfortunately, too seldom do educators and community members clearly address this fundamental question and establish mechanisms for evaluating how well schools do. What schools, for example, assess students regarding their caring for others and their contributions to the community? What schools aggregate such information and report it to the community?

Despite these problems of evaluation, we believe that most people really do want schools that educate children to be caring citizens. If this is our goal, then it only makes sense that we create inclusive schools where all are valued. It's an inevitable part of meeting this mission and purpose of schooling.

Evaluating Success in Learning and Achievement
Toward Personal Best Learning

If we are to have schools that are effective in promoting learning and achievement for all students, we must have a clear picture of how we will determine if schools are successful. Three different approaches are evident: (1) traditional, (2) standards-based, and (3) personal excellence (see Figure 2.3). Let's briefly discuss these important concepts. (This information has been adapted from Peterson & Tamor, 2009.)

First, the **traditional model** posits that we teach all students the same content in the same way. We *expect* some to do well and some to fail and consider this the problem of the student, not of the educator. This approach has been problematic in that some students have poor learning outcomes and there have been no expectations that it will be otherwise. This has been particularly problematic related to students of color, students with low incomes, and students with disabilities.

More recently, throughout the world, **standards-based reform** (Koski, 2001; Silver, 2004) has established minimal standards of performance, typically as a score on a standardized test, which all students are expected to achieve. In this system, a student who is considered highly gifted and a student with a cognitive disability are expected to achieve at the same level. Schools, then, are evaluated based on their ability to achieve such *equal outcomes for all students, typically in a small subset of skills.*

The problems with this model, however, are substantial. Having one standard for all ensures that some students, the most capable, learn beneath their capacity and that other students, even though they work hard and learn a great deal, will be considered failures. It's hard to understand, for example, why we would expect the same learning outcomes of a student who is gifted and a student with a cognitive disability. Students who are gifted often can achieve expected outcomes without ever even attending school. They may skate through classes putting out minimal effort and learn little in school. For students with cognitive disabilities, expected outcomes may be far beyond their capacities, even when they put forth great effort and progress significantly. The standards-based movement, with its emphasis on standardized testing in selected curriculum areas, is being shown to deemphasize a focus on the whole child and the importance of building a social–emotional foundation in the culture of the school (Bull, 2006; Duttweiler & McEvoy, 2001).

FIGURE 2.3

TRADITIONAL EDUCATION	STANDARDS-BASED EDUCATION	PERSONAL EXCELLENCE
Differing Approaches to Learning Goals and Evaluation of Schools		
Same Teaching for All	**Same Standard for All**	**Different Standards**
Accept different outcomes	*Expect same outcomes for all*	*Based on personal excellence*
Develop curriculum strands across subjects guiding curriculum content.	Establish expectations of academic facts and knowledge for every age and grade level organized around traditional academic subjects—reading, writing, math, social studies, science.	Develop outcome goals for students that reflect the overall purpose of schools—citizenship, academic skills, social–emotional abilities, character. Develop strands for curriculum content linking subjects.
Provide the same instruction for all students.	Expect students to achieve these standards irregardless of ability, background, or prior knowledge.	Expect students to make ongoing growth and progress, starting with present understanding and deepening and widening.
Assessment is based on the ability of the school to provide equal educational experiences to all students.	All students take a standardized test as a measure of identified skills and content knowledge.	All students will be assessed to determine individual progress. Schoolwide reporting systems are developed to reflect this.

Source: From Peterson and Tamor (2009).

The next model we call **personal excellence.** In this model, we expect all students to achieve at their *personal best level* and for ongoing instruction to recognize where students are and engage them in learning using multiple modalities, approaches, and supports to move to the next level. In this scenario, a student would be considered successful if she were making progress and meeting learning goals. We would have very different expectations of students who are highly gifted and students with cognitive disabilities in, say, biology class though they may be working on similar content. In this scheme, we would evaluate schools based on (a) their ability to create instructional environments that support personal best and just right learning challenges without segregating students by ability, race, culture, language, or other variables; (b) the achievement of higher learning outcomes appropriate for each student; and (c) the evaluation of student learning on a holistic profile based on the stated purpose of the school district.

Key Elements of Effective Inclusive Teaching

Based on the research, what would an effective **inclusive school** look like, one designed to work toward personal excellence for all students? We'll sketch a picture of an inclusive school and inclusive teaching practice. Figure 2.4 shows how practices build on one another. (The following is adapted from Peterson & Tamor, 2009.)

FIGURE 2.4

Learning Pyramid in Effective Schools and Classrooms

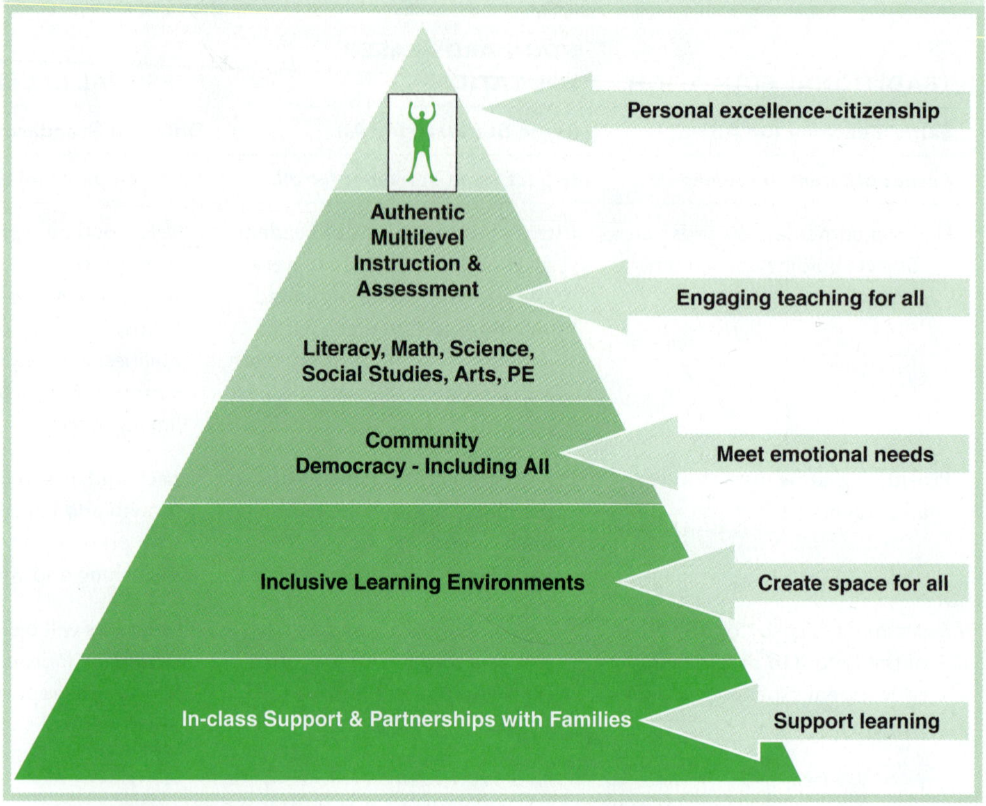

Personal excellence-citizenship

Authentic Multilevel Instruction & Assessment

Engaging teaching for all

Literacy, Math, Science, Social Studies, Arts, PE

Community Democracy - Including All

Meet emotional needs

Inclusive Learning Environments

Create space for all

In-class Support & Partnerships with Families

Support learning

Provide Support for Teachers, Students, and Parents (Chapters 4 and 5)

Supporting teachers in working with students at multiple ability levels, students who have emotional and social challenges in their lives, or students with sensory–physical differences is critical. Just as children need to feel safe and comfortable, so do adults. Teachers who are used to teaching at only one level sometimes have difficulty teaching to multiple levels and need help learning new ideas.

At most schools a range of specialists are available to deal with special needs and problems of children—social workers, special education teachers, bilingual teachers, psychologists, nurses, occupational therapists, speech therapists, and others. In a traditional school most of these people work on their own, with limited consultation from others, pulling children out of class for services. In an inclusive school, however, specialists work to support the general education classroom teacher as part of a *team*. Students are heterogeneously grouped in all classes and not ability grouped within classes. Support staff and the general education teacher work together with the whole class, and students with special needs are not taught at the side or at the back of the class.

Support teams often meet weekly to discuss the needs of children with special problems and brainstorm ideas for handling the issues, and planning meetings are scheduled at least every 2 weeks between the general education teacher and specialists who support

CLEARING A PATH
FOR PEOPLE WITH SPECIAL NEEDS
CLEARS THE PATH FOR EVERYONE!

the classroom. Special education teachers and other specialists—Title I teachers, speech therapists, occupational therapists—collaborate and support general education teachers in their classes. Teachers or **paraprofessionals** work with all the students in the class while ensuring that the students with special needs receive the help they need; such teachers often supervise small groups of children with mixed abilities who are engaged in different projects—centers, inquiry projects, and more. Teachers meet regularly in book study groups to learn new strategies.

Partner with Parents and the Local Community (Chapter 6)

Parents of children with special needs have typically gone through much. In traditional schools, such parents receive frequent negative feedback. However, we know that strong parent support is critical. Therefore, in an inclusive school we turn this pattern around through the following types of actions:

- Parents are *immediately* invited to have their children in inclusive classes.
- We meet with parents and listen carefully to their thoughts about their children, seeking to understand each child's gifts, strengths, needs, and interests from the parents' perspective, as well as to identify strategies that work with the child.
- We invite parents into the school and into class, making them feel welcome and a part of the school family and community.

In an inclusive school family members are often seen in the building. They read to classes, help during writing time, cut out materials, and demonstrate things they have learned in their career. Even parents whose work does not give them the flexibility to join the class during the day are often willing to do something at home for the class. They can read and record books on tape, put together books from a publishing center, or arrange for a field trip that involves touring their workplace. Family fun nights allow children and parents to engage in learning activities together in the evening. In an inclusive school parents are allies, discuss concerns freely and often, and see themselves as working as a team.

Create Space for All in Learning (Chapter 7)

In inclusive schools, whether newly constructed or older buildings, we do our best to take into account the multiple needs of children and staff in the way we use physical space and resources. We work to create places of beauty, peace, and fun; spaces where all have a place to belong and that respond to the different learning styles of children. Technology plays a key role in providing children expanded tools for learning and sources of information. In all this, we use **assistive technology,** whether simple devices such as nonskid desk pads that help a child with cerebral palsy place materials on his desk, software that reads words aloud or provides spelling and writing assistance, or more sophisticated electronic communication devices.

Empowerment, Leadership, and Democracy (Chapters 9–13)

Given the amount of segregation in our society based on race, class, culture, and ability, it is not surprising that building an inclusive school is a very challenging task and must be intentional, requiring a different way of thinking about teaching children. It takes a staff commitment that all students will be welcomed. For this commitment to become part of the culture of the school, the total staff must see inclusion as a value for children, must be able to articulate the reasons for their belief, must be willing to defend their work to those voicing concern, and must be willing to struggle when the inclusive approach doesn't seem to be working for a particular child. Effective inclusive schools, then, are also models of democratic practice. In them teachers and parents, supported by administrators, take responsibility both for leading and for listening, involving children in creating a school and classes where children learn together (Apple, 1995; Banks, 1990; Edelsky, 1999; Kozol, 1991).

Build Community and Meet the Needs of Children with Behavioral Challenges (Chapters 9 and 10)

If children are to learn, they must feel safe, secure, and cared for. When they don't, learning diminishes or ceases. Yet many children are at risk in our society. Teachers and schools are challenged to fill this void by providing comforting support structures. *Building community* in the school is critical, and intentional tools and strategies are needed. This is a complex process, however. Its many dimensions may include:

- Cultivating collaborative, supportive, respectful relationships among staff, parents, and the community—creating study groups, school teams that focus on different issues, team teaching, and so on.
- Building structures among children in the classroom so students can help one another—peer partners; circles of support; conflict resolution; and sharing of lives and feelings in conversation, writing, the arts, class meetings, and more.
- Giving children choices and teaching them responsibility—for example, letting children go to the bathroom on their own (rather than lining up a whole group); offering selection among several classroom activities; allowing students to sit, stand, move around, lie on the floor, and so on as they study or work together.

In an inclusive classroom, children are amazing in the way they know the strengths and problems of everyone in the classroom and are willing to share their own strengths and be guided in overcoming their challenges. They learn to share feelings with one another: "Please don't do that. It hurts me." Teachers help students learn how to brainstorm cooperative play activities so that some do not feel left out and how to include all in both play and academic work. Children are quick to point out positive attributes of their peers and have strategies for dealing with a classmate who is having a bad day. Students know if peers are upset and can request that the teacher call a class meeting to address their concerns. Students learn it is safe to take risks and to try more difficult work, knowing that others will not laugh at them and the teacher will not give them a bad grade for not getting it right. They know that all behavior involves choices and that they can make peaceful ones.

In such classes, behavior problems are much less frequent. Children know they belong; they have choices and do not feel constrained, yet are systematically taught responsibility. Of course students still cause problems. However, staff respect children and work to develop proactive solutions, involving the children in the process.

As inclusive teachers, we must consider carefully the way in which we approach problem behavior. Too often, in attempts to eliminate misbehavior without considering the underlying causes, schools actually *create* behavior problems. As inclusive teachers we work to foster a culture that meets students' needs. They understand that *all behavior communicates a message*. When a child acts out, this is his or her way of telling staff about a need. Teachers understand that motivation must come from inside the child—must be what psychologists call *intrinsic motivation*—rather than constantly being controlled by external forces through punishments or rewards (*extrinsic motivation*). Teachers in inclusive schools know that they must seek to understand the needs of the child and must identify and teach alternative strategies for helping the child meet his or her need in a positive way. Together with parents they ask questions: "What occurs before, during, and after the problematic behavior?" "What is going on in the child's life?" Together with the child and parents, staff then design strategies to meet the child's needs in positive ways. The aim is to help the child understand that the behavior is not good; that people care, but that there are other ways for a person to get what he or she needs.

Most centrally, inclusive teachers and their colleagues do their very best to avoid the use of rewards and punishments; and they do their very best to keep a child in their

school and classroom, resisting the frequent pressure and temptation to send children with behavior problems to separate classes or schools. They work hard to build a caring culture, help children support one another, learn about their own needs, and devise positive behavioral strategies for meeting them.

Include All in Learning Together (All chapters!)

For us, inclusive teaching is quite simple: We seek to educate *all children together well*. For us, "all" really does mean "all." As inclusive teachers, committed to the growth and development of all children, we see a quality school as a school that combines a focus on excellence and equity; that sees excellence and equity as mutually reinforcing, not as mutually exclusive. For us, teaching all children *together* is a cornerstone of good teaching and schooling.

In most schools a move to inclusive teaching will mean shifting students with special education needs, who are gifted, at-risk, and other students from separate classes into

---

JOURNEY into the CLASSROOM

Inclusive Teaching in a High School Government Class

As soon as the bell rings, Adalina Benini, the general education social studies teacher, asks all the students to get out their amendment reading packets. Ginger Kerby, the special education teacher, coteaches the fourth-hour Introduction to Government class with Adalina. The class is studying the major amendments of the constitution. Jonathan, a student with severe multiple impairments, has a bright smile on his face as Masa, one of his peers, gets out his reading packet for him. John, a student with a learning disability, has his packet out and is ready to go. Adalina divides the room in half. Students on the two sides of the room read the text aloud together. Bill stands in front of one group of students, and Ginger stands in front of the other group. Ginger explains the objectives of the class and then the students read chorally. She raises her hand to cue her group to read. When she puts her hand down, Adalina raises her hand to signal his group to read. The class alternates in this fashion until the reading packet is finished. Adalina follows along and reads aloud the words he knows. Jonathan's eyes follow the words on each page, and Devin, another peer, turns the pages for him.

After the class has completed the packet, Adalina goes to the board and uses graphic organizers to discuss prohibition and poll taxes. She invites students to come to the board as well to add to the ideas. After the graphic organizers are complete, he announces the variety of options available to complete the next assignment. John joins a group of four students to work on acting out the passage and removal of the prohibition amendment. Shelly and Devin invite Jonathan to join them in creating a song reflecting the meaning of the major amendments because they know how much he likes music. When they ask Jonathan if he would like to join their group, he responds by pushing "yes" on his communication board.

As the groups begin working, Ginger circulates the room and monitors Adalina's involvement in his group. He is participating actively by sharing his ideas and volunteering to act out certain parts. She also checks on Jonathan's progress with his group. Shelly and Devin are working well with him. As they test melodies to use for the song they wait for Jonathan to respond "yes" or "no" with his communication board to indicate if he likes the melodies or not. Soon the bell rings and Bill tells students to get into groups at the beginning of the next class so they can continue to work on their assignments.

Reflection: In this example, we see Adalina and Ginger working together effectively as coteachers supporting students with a wide range of abilities in a multilevel lesson that incorporates active learning.

Adapted from Brooks, Clarke, Green, Kerby, and Riley (2003).

general education; identifying students now in separate schools for special education or giftedness who would typically attend our school and inviting them back; and redesigning the roles of specialists to provide support for inclusive teaching.

Rather than separating children by abilities or other characteristics in special education classes, clustering them in general education classes, or grouping them according to ability within a class, inclusive teachers intentionally seek to have children of very different cultures, languages, and academic, social–emotional, and sensory–physical abilities learn *together.* Staff members are committed to **heterogeneous grouping** across and within classes. Fewer students are referred for special education services because teaching and individual support structures are in place and available to all students, based on their needs, consequently reducing the stress of referral and evaluation and freeing up more resources to provide direct assistance to children.

Inclusive schools spend much time putting in place practices in the classroom and schoolwide supports and instructional practices to make this possible. What are these practices? Here's a brief summary:

- Reaching out to parents of all children; paying particular attention to helping parents of children with special needs to know that their children are welcome and are part of the school community.
- Providing support for teachers and children in general education classes.
- Offering authentic, multilevel instruction specifically designed to engage children in meaningful activities in which they learn together at different ability levels; this may involve making adaptations and modifications in academic instruction.
- Building a community among children, staff, and parents: a community in which all feel welcome, all belong, emotional intelligence and social skills are taught, and relationships are nurtured. Part of building this community is responding proactively to the needs of children who have behavioral and emotional problems and challenges.
- Designing the physical environment of the classroom and school to promote learning and growth among children with diverse sensory and physical characteristics; adapting the environment and using assistive technology to help children learn more effectively.
- Demonstrating leadership and learning through dialogue and democratic decision making.

Does inclusive teaching mean that we *never* have students in separate classes or ability groups? We believe the evidence is clear that schools can and must work toward including all students in heterogeneous learning groups, in classes for all children. At the same time, we recognize that sometimes we just can't figure out how to make it work with a child. We recognize that when this happens, we've failed to create the type of school community to which we are committed, and we realize that our failure may have a negative impact on this child's life. Sometimes, however, that's the best we can do. In other situations, we may well find a school where the instruction in general education classes is ineffective for all students—and where the instruction in the segregated special education class is wonderful. In such a situation, we know we have a school that is not working for many of the children, a school that needs great improvement. For the time being, however, we may agree that a particular child would be better off, this semester, in the special education class. Yet, rather than negating the goal of inclusive teaching, these situations underscore the importance of working to improve it.

What about ability grouping or clustering students who are gifted in one class? Do we never do this? Our goal is that we meet the needs of all our students. We intentionally group children heterogeneously across classes; students labeled as gifted or having a disability are not grouped or clustered in a class. We use ability groups only for short-term, nonrecurring groupings for mini-lessons for specific skills or activities. We are very careful that such groupings are not stable ability groups but rather are flexible and have constantly shifting membership or methods of organization—by interest, topic, or type of project. No student in our class should be able to identify who is in the "low" group and who is in the "high" group.

In an inclusive school, literally every type of child attends and learns with other children. Inclusive schools follow both the spirit and the letter of IDEA: The general education classroom is the first choice for all students, and such classrooms are designed to meet the individualized educational needs of all students as they learn together. For example, activities in an inclusive classroom might include the following:

- A student of the highest ability works on a project involving a study of the polar ice caps in a small group that includes a student with severe mental retardation. Each of the students contributes to the total project at their own ability level; each is benefiting based on individual needs.
- A student who uses a wheelchair partners in science lab with a student who has immigrated recently from another country.
- A child who is blind intrigues his classmates with talking software on his laptop. A student who is deaf is aided by a signing interpreter; 90 students join the Sign Language Club, and the music teacher incorporates sign language into school musical productions.
- Students with social and emotional problems get help and support from a staff committed to helping them learn social skills, develop relationships, and know they are cared for and belong.

CHAMPIONS OF INCLUSION CONNECT
with students who have disabilities as individuals who are contributors first

There are still many who when dealing with a student with a disability focus on the limitations first. These folks start to think or talk about the impairment and the things that the individual cannot do. Sometimes these perceived inabilities are correct and sometimes they are incorrect or falsely magnified. What is significant though is that their first consideration is on deficits.

Champions of inclusion are:

- The classmates who describe Victoria as a good friend who has started skiing and who drives a cool wheelchair
- The English teacher who depicts Johnny (who has learning disabilities) as a kid who writes great stories using that special computer program
- The teacher aide who brags about how terrific a job Chuck (a boy with cognitive delays) has done combining geometric shapes

- The music specialist who relates how fantastically Ashley (who has autism) sings during performances
- The cafeteria worker who shares how helpful Diana (who has emotional disorders) has been cleaning up during the lunch period
- The special education teacher who points out to the physics teacher how Willy (who has ADHD) can fix all kinds of car problems
- The secretary who comments on how much more clearly Irma (who has speech and language delays) is communicating when she runs an errand to the office
- Maria (a girl with Down syndrome), who informs everyone that she is a fifth-grade super star because of all the books that she has read

By Bill Henderson, Principal, O'Hearn Elementary School, Boston, MA.

■ Circles of support meet for different types of students throughout the school—one for a little boy who does not understand English, another for a child who just lost both parents in a car accident, another for a child who was abused in the past and has many emotional and behavioral problems.

Utilize Authentic, Multilevel Instruction (Chapters 11–13)

A seventh-grade boy spends his time in English class struggling to read at a beginner's level. A girl at a nearby desk with her nose in a book could tackle a Harvard literature class. Seated in between is a youngster who's a whiz at math, but takes a whole period to write three English sentences because he is much more comfortable writing sentences in his native Spanish. (McAdamis, 2001, p. 48)

Schools are typically structured by grade levels and teach using standardized materials aimed at a middle ability level. However, we know that children of the same age do not necessarily learn at the same rate or level. In fact, any class, whether attempting to be inclusive or not, contains children functioning three to six grade levels apart. Therefore, inclusive teaching means designing for diversity from the beginning, rather than thinking of each type of special student as a separate challenge. Inclusive teachers use the growing understanding of differentiated instruction and universal design to:

■ Design lessons at multiple levels
■ Challenge students at their own level
■ Provide support to push children ahead to their next level of learning
■ Engage children in learning via activities that relate to the real world—to their lives at home and in the community
■ Engage the multiple intelligences and learning styles of children so that many pathways for learning and demonstrating achievement are available
■ Involve students in collaborative pair or group work in which children draw on each other's strengths

Many exciting methods of teaching may easily accommodate many levels of ability. These methods are part of what we call **multilevel teaching**: good teaching practices that actively engage children in real-world, problem-based projects. For example, a teacher may teach writing by having all students write about the same topic, but at different levels, expecting very different results from different children. The teacher helps students edit their work and provides specific instruction in needed skills via mini-lessons with individuals or with small groups that have similar needs cropping up in their writing. Instead of everyone's reading the same book, children choose books at their personal level, not too hard and not too easy. They read with a partner who is reading a similar book, or sit near a student who is at a higher level for ease of help with words. Teachers read with individual learners or sit in on a discussion group.

Teachers also help children draw from the knowledge and skill of their peers. The children know whom to ask for spelling advice, guidelines on quotation marks, or funny ideas for stories. They know who will allow them to practice reading out loud and always give positive feedback. Everyone, no matter what his or her ability level, has a needed role. Children who are gifted grow in their relationships with others through working with special education students, and lower functioning students may encourage a gifted but underachieving friend to improve his or her work. Students with mental retardation have models and a rich learning environment, picking up much by incidental learning yet benefiting from explicit, systematic instruction on needed skills. As children are expected to recognize each person's strengths and needs and to help one another achieve their goals, they rise to the occasion.

Four middle school students conduct a science experiment. A lowered table allows the student in a wheelchair to participate fully.

Use Authentic Assessment to Promote Learning (Chapter 11)

Effective inclusive schools resist the temptation to center the entire curriculum and student learning experiences around mandated standardized tests. Rather, teachers focus on effective instruction and curriculum-based assessment in which teachers maintain an ongoing assessment of important student skills and abilities. Teachers go far beyond typical ineffective classroom tests such as multiple choice and fill-in-the-blank, choosing instead assessment strategies that provide more authentic and engaging methods of assessing student skills while also providing multiple ways that students can use their multiple intelligences to demonstrate abilities. Teachers select products that students develop for learning assignments that demonstrate competencies. Options include creating physical models of content, writing in journals, creating fact and analysis papers, using art and drama, and student-developed posters, videos, or other graphics presentations of learning. **Assessment** is used to guide instruction and designed to meet the key goals of effective assessment: understanding what students know, identifying what students want to learn, and exploring how students best learn (Fairtest, 1995; Peterson, 2001a; Wormeli, 2006).

Designing Inclusive Instruction and Response to Intervention

These practices provide some very useful guidelines for us for structuring our teaching practice. Throughout the rest of this book, we will build on this introduction and explore many practical strategies for using these practices on a daily basis. Figure 2.5 illustrates how one teacher used these ideas to develop a sketch, an overview of how he wanted to teach his social studies this year. How will our class be laid out and organized? What learning resources do we have that accommodate different learning styles and abilities? When we ask such questions, constantly revising and seeking to do better, we will gradually develop good ideas and specific plans. Similarly, how will we deal with interactions of students? How can we build a sense of connection, community, or care in the class? Do we

FIGURE 2.5

Sketching Out Inclusive Teaching Strategies

WHAT ARE MY STRATEGIES FOR GRADE 9 SOCIAL STUDIES?

Academic Learning for All

Weekly journals to one another regarding personal life or news event.

Study project with seniors about issue in the community—identify, research, interview community people, prepare presentation and portfolio for class.

Weekly discussion and dialogue groups.

Assignments—optional. Reading, doing Internet research, listening to tapes of books, going to community meetings or conferences, interviewing community experts.

Social–Emotional–Behavioral Issues and Building Community

Cooperative work groups—teach how to work collaboratively.

Peer group "peacemakers" training for student leaders.

Circles of support—teach students how circles work and encourage participation; include in reflective journals.

Learning Environment

Room arranged in tables of 4.

Computers for Internet, graphics, and word processing next to wall.

Corner for small group and one-to-one conferencing and conflict resolution sessions.

Space to move around.

Music available—classical, jazz, rock, blues, folk. Use this to highlight periods.

Art examples from places and periods we are studying.

Collaboration with Parents and Specialists Working in My Classroom

Consult with gifted and bilingual specialist for multilevel teaching ideas.

Coteach with special education teacher and speech therapist including them in lesson design.

Develop positive relationships with parents by inviting them to the classroom and asking their opinions.

try to build community in the class, or do we see the students as "on their own"? What happens when students become angry or act out? What gets students in trouble? What strategies should we use to respond? Finally, what is our general approach to teaching? Will we use primarily lectures with some lab work? Community-based projects organized around themes?

When we use these strategies, we will find that we naturally help most of our students to be successful. However, we'll also find that some students continue to struggle. We'll want additional help. A multi-tiered approach is needed where we have ways of focusing more specifically on the needs of some students and providing strengthened interventions and services. The recent concept of **response to intervention (RTI)** provides a helpful way of organizing such a process. In 2004 federal legislation in the United States required a process of response to intervention as a new way of diagnosing students having learning disabilities. The law calls for provision of individualized interventions prior to formal referral for special education services. The framework, however, provides a useful tool that can be used for all students needing additional help.

Figure 2.6 illustrates graphically a response to intervention framework that is composed of three tiers. In *Tier I* we use effective practices we described previously to support learning of all students together. Of course, no matter how well we do, some students will have difficulties. For some, they will have difficulty learning math, reading,

FIGURE 2.6

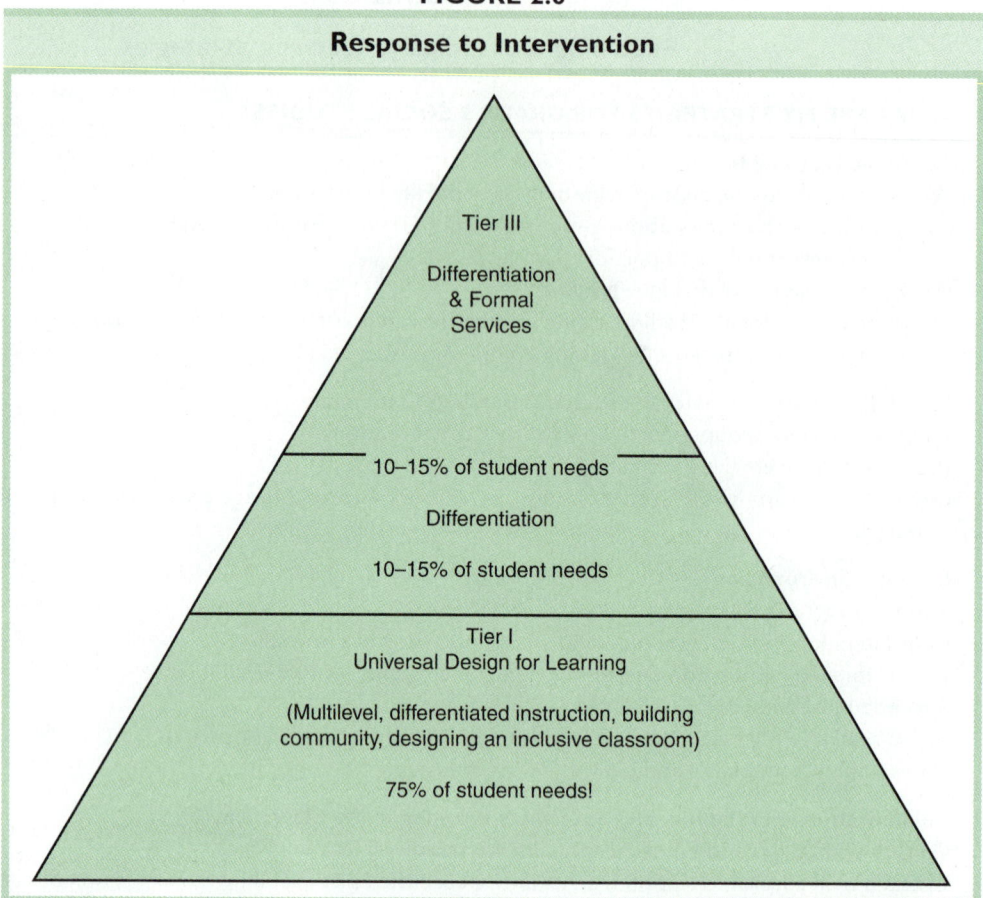

Response to Intervention

Tier III

Differentiation
& Formal
Services

10–15% of student needs

Differentiation

10–15% of student needs

Tier I
Universal Design for Learning

(Multilevel, differentiated instruction, building
community, designing an inclusive classroom)

75% of student needs!

social studies, or other academic content. Some will have difficulties managing their feelings and relating to others. Yet others may have difficulties with physical health and physical limitations and disabilities. We will work to identify ways to respond to individual student needs in *Tier II*. For example, when students learn much more than we anticipated, we develop learning activities that stretch them to go farther and deeper. When students have difficulty understanding, we give them simpler tasks, a reduced amount of work, and additional help. For students who bring emotional stress from home and act out or fight, we use positive approaches, seeking to understand them, listening, giving them alternative ways to express themselves, and helping build support systems for them. For a child who is blind or partially sighted, we obtain a computer with talking software. Note that these interventions may also be described using different terms in the educational literature. These include *curriculum adaptations or modifications* and *individualized differentiation of instruction*.

In inclusive schools where specialists provide push-in, rather than pull-out, services we can expect to have access to individuals who can help us think about the needs of students and strategies we might try with them. Note that such Tier II assistance can be expected to adequately address the needs of an additional 10 to 15% of our students.

Some students, however, will continue to have significant difficulties and we will want to provide additional assistance—*Tier III*. Here is where formal referral for services occurs for school programs. These include special education, bilingual education, gifted and talented, at-risk services, and services of community agencies. Federal law governs special education services and procedures for referral, eligibility, and individualized education programs must be followed. We'll discuss these in this Chapter 4. However, in an inclusive school such services will be implemented using a push-in approach so that specialists may already be working with a student in either Tier I or II. We've estimated that formal services may help meet the needs of some 10 to 15% of students. However, it is clear that the more effectively we implement Tier I and II strategies, the lower will be the number of students referred for formal services. We will suggest specific strategies for each of these tiers in subsequent chapters.

When we design individual interventions, we will always want to evaluate how effective they are and consider whether these strategies might be incorporated into instruction for all our students. For example, we read aloud to a student whose reading abilities are low—but then realize that reading to all our students would be beneficial; we come to see that a circle of friends used to provide assistance to a student with cerebral palsy is a powerful tool for other students; having purchased talking software for a blind student, it becomes clear we can use it with many students.

As we use this framework, we do so in three key areas: sensory-physical, social-emotional-behavioral, and academic. Figure 2.7 illustrates how each of these domains may interact in Tiers I to III. We will use these domains to organize sections III, IV, and V of this book. In Section III, we'll focus on how to use space and physical resources to create learning environments for all students. In Section IV, we focus on developing a sense of community and care in our classrooms where students' social and emotional needs are met, and where we respond proactively to behavioral challenges. Finally, in Section V we explore how to design lessons where students with very different levels of ability can learn well together. We think this is the way we most often think about our teaching—organizing and arranging our class, building community and responding proactively to behavior challenges, and using authentic, multilevel, differentiated instruction. As we proceed on our journey, we encourage you to revisit the concepts of designing teaching for all and response to intervention introduced in this chapter.

Visiting Two Inclusive Schools

Let's now visit an effective inclusive elementary school and high school. What is their experience related to the principles and practices of inclusive schooling we have outlined? How do they deal with the issues identified in research?

Gilman Elementary School

Gilman Elementary School is located in a small rural community. Many students ride buses a significant distance in order to attend school. Many people in Gilman have very limited incomes. There are few resources to assist families in the community. In recent years racial tensions have risen among White people, Native Americans who live on reservations, and a growing number of Asian American immigrants. Despite the idyllic and beautiful countryside, community life in this rural area can be both challenging and isolating for children and their families.

Despite these barriers, Gilman Elementary School is known as an effective inclusive school. Inclusive education began at Gilman Elementary in 1989 when the principal, Al Arnold, began a principal's math challenge class. The group needed space in the building, but the only space available was the special education resource room. On the first day of the challenge class, Al noticed that the children were very reticent. They did not want to sit and would not touch anything in the classroom. "What is going on?" Al asked. With a bit of questioning, he discovered that students were afraid because this was the special education room. Al was shocked. That evening he received phone calls from parents concerned that

FIGURE 2.7

Universal Design and Individual Interventions: Three Key Domains

	SENSORY–PHYSICAL	SOCIAL–EMOTIONAL	ACADEMIC
	Key elements (Chapter 2): *Designing space for all*	Key elements (Chapter 2): *Democracy, including all, building community*	Key elements (Chapter 2): *Multilevel, differentiated instruction; assessment for learning*
	Key elements: *Support for Learning* (Chapter 6) *Partnership with Families and the Community* (Chapter 5)		
	Chapter 7	*Chapter 9*	*Chapters 11–13*
Universal Design for Learning (Tier I)	Implement heterogeneous grouping Provide space for wheelchairs Use multiple learning modalities Design space for authentic teaching Obtain a talking computer for a blind student	Build community Promote caring Encourage friendships Teach social skills and "emotional intelligence" Identify interests	Promote authentic learning Use project learning Build a microsociety Recognize multiple intelligences Devise multilevel lessons
	Chapter 8	*Chapter 10*	*Chapters 11–13*
Individualized Differentiation (Tiers II & III)	Rearrange books so a student in a wheelchair can reach them Set aside areas to be alone or to get help	Understand needs and communication Provide positive alternatives Encourage peer support Create a circle of friends to assist student	Offer advanced projects Reduce difficulty Use drama to teach social studies Provide additional help and support Read stories to students with reading difficulties
Evaluate and Revise	Use talking computers for all students	Use circles of friends to build community	Read stories to all students Incorporate drama and art in all subjects

their children were being placed in special education. Al felt he had to take action: "If this is how general education students feel about a special education classroom, how do they feel about their classmates with disabilities?" He and a few teachers developed a school vision and plan in which all students could learn within the general education classroom.

As we walk into Gilman Elementary today, children with and without disabilities are learning together in the same classrooms. There are no special education rooms. The special education teacher, paraprofessionals, and other related service personnel teach in general education classrooms. As we walk around the school with Al, we notice that children are engaged in very exciting learning activities. There is a positive, busy atmosphere about each class and a comfortable, relaxed sense of respect between the principal and the teachers, children, and parents with whom we come in contact.

Al talks with us about how inclusive schooling is being implemented at Gilman Elementary. "Inclusion for us at Gilman," he says, "has several parts. First, we seek to deliver instruction to all students in a manner that meets individual needs and gives students the opportunity to develop to their full potential, academically and socially. Second, we do this by utilizing the team teaching of general and special teachers, who work together using diverse teaching strategies. We seek to respond to diverse learning styles, using individualized instruction and flexible grouping."

"To make these goals a reality," Al continues, "the school is using five key strategies to provide support to students and teachers." First, the staff designed a structure in which one specialist is assigned to each grade-level team as a support to all students with special needs. The specialists include a Title I teacher, gifted coordinator/reading specialist, guidance counselor, speech/language therapist, and one special education teacher (with cross-categorical experience). These specialists team-teach every day for a minimum of one-half day per week in each class.

Second, teams composed of two general educators and one specialist provide support to students. Each team member has equal responsibility for every student at their grade level. In essence, these three teachers are individually and collectively responsible for approximately 50 to 60 students. The grade-level teaching team is responsible for the success of their students with disabilities and all other students.

Third, the teaching staff redesigned the schoolwide schedule in order to create a daily block of *"sacred time"* during which there are absolutely no interruptions. During sacred time the grade-level classrooms have 100% of their students for 100% of the time. No music, art, physical education, or computer classes are scheduled. Sacred time is for grade-level teaching teams to go full speed ahead in teaching the core subject material without interruptions.

The fourth program feature involves *planning time* for grade-level teaching teams and the team of specialists. Thanks to the creation of the block schedule, each grade-level team now has 90 minutes of planning time each week, *in addition to* the designated amount of preparation time each teacher receives as specified in his or her teaching contract. Specialists also have a weekly 60-minute planning block in which they meet as a team to discuss specific students' needs, goals, and progress.

Fifth, to guarantee that students will never again identify a classroom as stigmatizing, Al explains, Gilman Elementary has implemented a system of flexible instructional grouping and utilization of instructional space. The staff change instructional groupings continually to eliminate the possibility of stigma becoming associated with a group. Similarly, all students work with each of the three teachers, so no stigma is associated with special teachers. The same is true of space usage. There is nothing unusual about a student's learning in any particular room or space, as all students work in those rooms at one time or another. The three teachers rotate and teach in each of the rooms (including the specialist's small room or office) so that the students will not associate a certain teacher with any specific room or space. (Figure 2.8 summarizes these five strategies.)

FIGURE 2.8

Inclusive Strategies in an Elementary School

- A specialist, drawn from several categorical programs, is assigned to each grade-level team to provide in-class support for teachers.
- Teachers and specialists work together as a team to assist all children at a grade level.
- "Sacred time" is established to create uninterrupted academic learning.
- A 90-minute planning block is set aside for grade-level teams and an additional 60-minute planning block with specialists each week.
- Flexible instructional groupings ensure heterogeneous grouping and prevent stigmatization of students.

As we finish our tour, Al leads us to a classroom at the end of the hall. There we see a general and special education teacher leading a rehearsal for a play students will present in an assembly for parents in the coming week. We see a child who typically experiences significant behavioral outbursts at the center of a small group of children singing a song. They are all holding hands, and the child smiles, making everyone in the room laugh. The teachers wave. We walk to our car wishing we could stay. (Account adapted from Arnold, 1998, and Beloin, 1998.)

BUMpS IN THE ROAD

Segregating Students Within the Classroom

Fields in education have been created to help respond to the needs of students with special needs. These include special education, bilingual education, second-language learning (English as a second language in English-speaking countries), and gifted education. Many professionals in these fields have been trained in approaches that separate students for instruction. We may well find that, for example, special education teachers and gifted education specialists are not interested in promoting inclusive teaching and only know how to work with students by pulling students into separate rooms or working with them individually or in small homogeneous groups at the back or side of the class.

For example, we visited a third-grade class where the teacher, Sheryl Harms, was working hard to include and educate a wide range of students—gifted, students representing six languages spoken in the home, students from eight different ethnic groups, a student with autism, and two students with cognitive disabilities. She was often frustrated, however, in dealing with the gifted specialist and special education teacher who worked with students in her class. She could certainly use their help. However, the special education teacher didn't seem to know how to work with her curriculum in the general education classroom. She constantly was pulling students off to the side keeping them there a long time. At other times she actually interrupted them in their work asking if they needed help. The gifted specialist, likewise, wanted constantly to pull out two gifted students. Sheryl tried to get both to help in her lessons but she also found that their philosophies about teaching were very different. Some days it seemed as if these well-meaning specialists caused more difficulty than providing help.

What do we do when we find ourselves in a situation like the one facing Sheryl? Here are some suggestions for both the general education teacher and specialist:

Strategies for general education teachers

- Be clear about your expectations and ask specialists to work with you in designing multilevel, differentiated instruction that will help all students. Explain that you would not like to see students pulled out since they will miss important experiences in class when they do.
- Initiate a conversation with specialists (as a group if, as with Sheryl, you are dealing with several people) regarding roles you'd like them to take in developing multilevel, differentiated instruction. Ask them about ideas for instruction that will help the students to whom they are assigned. As you work with specialists identify and use their strengths showing appreciation.

Strategies for specialists (special education teachers, gifted specialists, etc.)

- Examine your belief system carefully. Get help from the general education teacher to understand the curriculum and teaching strategies that are used.
- Think about the needs of your students and how these may be met in engaging, multilevel, differentiated lessons. Talk with the general education teacher about these ideas. Work to develop a collaborative working process where you can contribute your skills and knowledge.

Graham High School

"Urban high school"—in our mind's eye we picture security gates, metal detectors, graffiti, and gangs. However, we understand that Graham High School has developed an exemplary program for meeting the needs of all students, and we have been looking forward to visiting the school.

A junior named Thuy Nguyen greets us and tells us he will be our guide. Walking across the campus, we notice a group of students in the courtyard, one of whom is using a wheel-chair. Thuy says they are ninth graders working on a science project, creating their own measuring system. They are using Paulo's wheelchair as their measuring system, they explain: A full rotation of the wheel counts as one unit, and they are measuring the perimeter of the school.

We ask Thuy to introduce us to the special educators at the school. Again he looks puzzled; he says he doesn't know any special educators. We describe teachers who team-teach or who help students with disabilities in their classes. "Oh, you mean the resource teachers," he says. Then he asks, "for which department?" "English," we reply, feeling that this would be a safe bet in a high school. Thuy responds, "Do you mean humanities?"

Following more awkward interactions in which we discover that traditional stereotypes don't necessarily apply here, we meet Greg Allen, a member of the science team who coaches football and is the "advocate" for 27 students with disabilities. Graham High serves some 2,200 students and is organized into knowledge base groups, and all teachers in a knowledge base work together on curriculum and instruction. One member sits on the school curriculum council to negotiate schoolwide instructional themes and essential questions (see Jorgensen, 1998). All categorically funded teachers (special education, Title I, bilingual education, reading specialists, and migrant education), Greg explains, are called "resource teachers" and are members of knowledge base groups.

The school is organized into two divisions. Division I encompasses 9th and 10th grade and provides all students with a core curriculum. Classes are 90 minutes long on the block/quarter system. Division II is organized into curricular clusters: business, technology, engineering, communicative and fine arts, and human services. Within each cluster, students have classes that cover many disciplines.

We ask Greg about his role with students who have disabilities. He tells us that in addition to his role as a support teacher in science, he communicates regularly with each student and his or her family and chairs (or cochairs with the student) the IEP meeting. "I do not see all my students every day. If one is not in science this term, I may not see him or her very often. I rely on colleagues to provide support. I know the science curriculum quite well, and I support every student who has a disability in his or her science class. My colleagues support students in humanities, technology, communicative and fine arts, and other areas."

Greg says that every student with a disability who lives in the school catchment area attends Graham and that each student with a disability receives all special education supports and services within the general education classroom. Students with disabilities are not grouped by category, and no teacher has advocate responsibilities for a specific type of student disability (e.g., blindness, mental retardation).

We continue our tour and Thuy takes us to the technology cluster area where he attends class. We enter the humanities class for the Division II technology group and find two teachers and 35 students—a diverse group in terms of ethnicity, gender, age, and language background. Both adults look up from their tables and smile.

We talk with Felicia Conway, one of the two resource teachers in the humanities knowledge base. "I spend time 2 days a week with Ginger Ferrara working at learning centers, providing all students feedback and instruction on their writing." Four students in this section of humanities have IEPs, and every class in the school has a natural proportion of students with and without disabilities. Approximately 10% of the students in any class receive special education services. Felicia tells us that the school decided on this approach "many years ago, to avoid the idea that

These students are working as a group to investigate organisms in a local water sample. They are recording information and looking up tables they can use to make comparisons with other communities.

there were just a few 'inclusion classes' in which special education teachers and aides spent their time." We ask her what it took to ensure that all teachers were ready to teach all students. She shows us a list of interview questions used for all new teachers. Several of these questions make it clear that the ability to teach an inclusive, diverse group of students is a prerequisite for faculty. "I am a member of the professional development committee, and our staff development efforts focus on differentiating instruction," Felicia continues. Interestingly, she tells us that they have never done an "inclusion training." All staff development providers are selected based on their ability to share information about quality instruction for all students.

Our tour guide introduces us to his girlfriend, Jessica, who tells us about her fourth-block class. During that 90-minute period, Jessica is a peer tutor in a math class; she does not get math credit for the period but does receive an elective credit. "I provide assistance to any student in the class who needs it," she says. For example, Anthony "learns a bit different, moves his eyes to communicate, and uses a switch to talk. He has modified work that I help with, but mostly I make sure that he's involved with peers and stuff." Jessica tells us that she is in the technology cluster because she wants to be a teacher and knows that technology will be very important for teachers.

As we leave the technology cluster, we ask Thuy about how students get extra help if they need it. He tells us about the learning center. Thinking we've found the special education

Sights TO SEE

The Schools Our Children Deserve

The Schools Children Deserve: This is an enjoyable video that helps us think about what we want for children in schools that goes nicely with this chapter. www.youtube.com/watch?v=V1K_8jfXuTo

O'Hearn Elementary School: This school is a fully inclusive, high-achieving, multicultural school in Boston that implements the practices in this book. A nice video overview of work in the school. www.youtube.com/watch?v=Mnj7ZURXj20

FIGURE 2.9

Inclusive Practices in a High School

- Every student can access teachers—general and special education—for assistance, mentoring, or conflict resolution.
- Special education teachers provide in-class support and assistance for all students.
- Classes are structured to encourage peer support and a spirit of collaboration and collegiality among students.
- Special education and other categorical services are organized according to the overarching school governance structure (e.g., departments, knowledge base groups, academic families, academies).

- Class time is longer (90 minutes), allowing students to process information more deeply and ensuring that teachers get to know students well.
- Curriculum is planned and organized for all students, and accommodations and modifications are provided for those students who need them.
- Teachers are provided with the professional development resources they need to be successful.

room, we walk into the learning center—a room off the library/media center—and see students tutoring other students and teachers working with individuals and small groups of students. Students come in and out of the learning center.

Barbara Samimi coordinates the learning center. She is also the "coordinator of family and community involvement" for the school. Title I funds are used to support the learning center. Barbara is a bundle of energy, and every student seems to know her. We first ask her about attendance. She tells us that teachers "do all kinds of activities in their classes, and sometimes students just need a place to go and get caught up. The learning center is here for that." She adds that students come before or after school "to do homework without the pressure or to make sure that they're getting it done right."

We inquire about students with disabilities, asking her if, as happens in other schools, the learning center becomes a dumping ground for students the teachers don't want in their classrooms. Barbara looks troubled by our question. "A dumping ground? The learning center is not there for that! We are a place for students to get help; anyone can get help; not just students who have special needs. About your teachers not wanting kids... they shouldn't be teachers. Graham High School is a school for everyone—we figure it out and make sure that every student is provided the opportunity to be successful."

As we leave we consider the successes experienced by the students at this school. Figure 2.9 provides an overview of the inclusive practices at Graham High School, which typify exemplary approaches used in both middle and high schools. We realize that these practices are good for all students and serve to ensure that students feel welcomed and respected within the school walls.

Onward in Our Journey
The Sun Is High, the Road Is Wide

As we have begun our journey together, we have visited real schools and classrooms to see how an inclusive classroom and school looks; we have looked at the research and have introduced the principles and practices on which inclusive teaching is based. We hope that you are beginning to see how inclusive education can work and are excited about the possibility of being an inclusive teacher. Now, more than ever, in the midst of social change, children and families need good schools and effective education. Most of all they need caring teachers who reach out and welcome all children.

A former university student said this about a teacher who was working with students with special needs in her math class:

> The teacher sincerely believes that every student in her classroom has the ability to be successful and to learn. Her obligation is to discover how each student learns best and use that information to the student's advantage. . . . Her secret joy is defying visitors to correctly identify the "included" students. (Ceifetz, 1997, p. 5)

Before we continue, we invite you to reflect a few minutes. Think about your images of schools, families, and children with differences. Think about your own experiences as a young child and as a student. Think about your experiences with people who are different from you. Think about the possibilities of a school where all learn, all achieve, and all value one another. Think about the roles you might play in teaching in such a school and even in helping create one.

Traveling Notes

As we work to become effective inclusive teachers, we need key "big ideas" on which to hang the many details of our daily work. First, of course, we must be clear about our commitment to inclusive teaching. We now know that research validates the importance and positive impact of inclusive teaching. However, we also know from research that among the biggest hindrances to creating inclusive schools for all students are the attitudes and belief systems of many educators. Once we commit to being an effective inclusive teacher we can work toward practices introduced in this chapter. We can:

1. Intentionally design our classroom and our use of space to respond to a range of learning needs ensuring that students may work alone, in pairs, or in small groups with materials available at their own level of challenge.
2. Work to create a sense of care and community in our class, providing opportunities for democratic decision making and responsibility among our students.
3. Seek to understand the needs of students who have challenging behaviors, centering our approach on helping them know we care while expecting them to learn responsible behavior. We will be aware of students at the margins of our class and facilitate their developing positive relationships and a sense of self-worth.
4. We will welcome all students into our class and work to foster respect for all in the class. We will particularly seek out having students with heterogeneous characteristics and needs aiming to be known in our school as a teacher who works effectively with diverse, sometimes challenging students.
5. We will collaborate with specialists developing effective and positive coteaching relationships. We will work to use specialists in designing and implementing community and differentiated, multilevel instruction.
6. We will partner with parents, always seeking to understand their needs and gain their input into most effective ways to teach their children. We will work to make parents feel comfortable in our class, developing a trusting relationship.
7. We will work to design our lessons using principles and practices of authentic, multilevel instruction. We will avoid stable ability grouping and work to challenge all students at their own level of learning.
8. We will also use authentic assessment that allows us to document student learning at various levels of ability using a range of strategies and giving students options.

9. Response to intervention (RTI) provides a helpful framework to think about both universal design for learning and individualized interventions for students. In the foundation, Tier I, we seek to design our instruction and classroom culture to support diverse students. As students have special needs and require more assistance or support, we develop individualized interventions, adapting and modifying lessons as needed (Tier II). If students need more assistance we can refer them to a variety of formal services including bilingual education, gifted education, and special education. In inclusive schools, such services are provided in collaboration with teachers in the general education classroom.

The journey toward effective inclusive teaching is a lifelong quest. Most importantly, we'll plan for an enjoyable, challenging, thoughtful journey aiming to build a community of colearners in our school as partners on the way!

Stepping Stones

Following are some activities that will help extend your understanding and actions you may take in your journey toward becoming an inclusive teacher.

1. Visit a general education classroom that includes children from different races, cultures, and a range of disabilities. Observe the teaching and support provided in the regular classroom. Interview educators including the general education teacher and specialists such as special education teachers, paraprofessionals, and bilingual teachers. Ask them what their feelings are about what is happening in the classroom. Again, think about the reasons behind their responses. How do your two observations compare?

2. Interview a parent of a child with a special need who is being included and supported in a general education classroom. Ask about the parent's experiences with the child, the professionals, and the schools. Ask about his or her own experience in inclusive education—what is working and what is not. Again, explore the reasons for the answers the parent gives. What do these responses tell you?

3. Download a copy of the tool Quality Teaching for All: Self-assessment for Teachers at www .wholeschooling.net/WS/WSToolKit/Quality_ Tch for ALL.doc. Use this tool to assess yourself as a teacher. Share it with other teachers and use the tool to assess skills of your team. What did you learn? How might you work to improve your skills as an inclusive teacher based on your self-assessment?

4. Sketch ideas for how you might teach students with wide ranges of ability this year. Think about Tiers I, II, and III and how you may see implementing these.

5. It all starts with one teacher who cares enough about all children to say, "I want to have a student with special needs in my class. I think they belong here and I want to learn how." Is there one student in your school who is in a special education class that you could take into your class, perhaps part-time at first and building on this as you, the child, and the special education teacher feel comfortable?

3

Diverse Students in the Classroom

How Students Are Different and the Same

CHAPTER GOAL

Understand multiple dimensions of diversity and explore how using inclusive teaching instructional strategies can help meet very different needs.

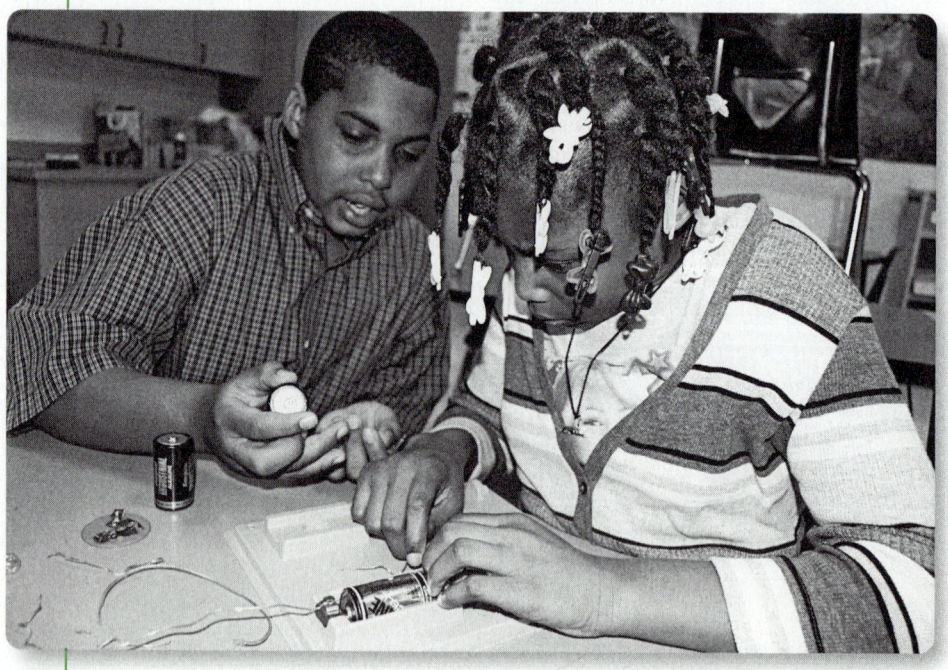

CHAPTER OBJECTIVES

1. Understand key needs of various groups of students with special needs and how these relate to exemplary inclusive teaching practices.

2. Understand the definitions and descriptions of various labels attributed to students.

3. Know how to consider strengths and needs of students in teaching that are related to multiple sources of diversity.

An Inclusive Middle School Language Arts Class: The Key Is—Teach Individuals, Not Groups

When we enter Aiyana Kitchi's Grade 7 Language Arts class, students are writing at desks, writing on the floor, or sitting at the back table working on editing with their peers. Kendrick has a moderate intellectual disability, Aiyana explains; he reads at a second-grade level, and the physical act of writing is difficult for him. However, he is writing many words. Although they are hard to read (many misspellings and letters run together), he is very busy. "What are you writing about?" Aiyana asks. Kendrick reads what he has written, and she quickly jots down his thoughts on the facing pages of the journal. "Kendrick, that's an interesting story. You have written a lot!"

Aiyana then walks over to Patrick, an extremely bright child who qualified for the gifted and talented program but wanted to stay with his friends. He is working on writing gripping beginnings and picturesque details. His language is amazingly sophisticated, with images and story lines that could have been created by a college student. As Patrick works, he periodically encourages Kendrick and spells words for him. Aiyana explains that they are good friends.

Shortly, Doria, a fifth-grade student who has autism, stands in the doorway as if she is paralyzed. The students say hello as she enters the room, but her face is frozen in a blank panicked stare, her hands twitching in response to the class noise. Aiyana watches as another student comes over and looks directly at Doria, not touching, and asks if she wants to sit down. She goes to her special place in the corner and sits on the cushions. She reads a book for the first 10 minutes of class. After a few minutes, some other kids come over and ask her to join them in working on a project. She does.

Aiyana explains that her classroom is filled with diversity of many forms—abilities, cultural and language diversity, socioeconomic status, the nature of families.

As you've seen already, students range in general abilities from pre-first grade to college in my class. I have students from a range of countries and cultures. These include three students from the Middle East (Iran and Afghanistan), one from Eastern Europe, two from Mexico, and one from Japan. The first language of six of my students is not English. We're working lots on helping them learn the language as well as the content of the class! In addition, some of our students are well off economically but 60% are from low-income families. My students come from all sorts of families as well. Four live with single parents while another four live in households with extended families. Two live with their grandmothers. It's a great class!

At break we ask Aiyana, "How do you manage with such diverse abilities, cultures, and characteristics?" She responds, "The key is learning how to teach to individuals, not groups." "I learn the strengths of each student and where they need to be pushed. The teaching activities I use allow students to work at different levels. I constantly ask myself, 'What is the best next step for this student?' instead of the traditional 'What should a seventh grader be able to do?' For example, look at Kendrick's writing," she says, pulling out his writing workshop folder. "He is writing simple ideas, spelling basic words, adding periods, and spacing letters. But these are huge steps for him."

She then shares how her students have learned to complement one another's strengths and needs. "They spell words for each other, listen for content, and edit each other's papers. When Amanda gets frustrated, her friend Christine listens and gets her past a tough spot. When Kendrick is staring at a blank page, Patrick asks what he is writing and gets him started. Patrick enjoys helping Kendrick. Sometimes Patrick even asks Kendrick for ideas to write about. These kids learn each other's goals, and they work to make sure that their friends are learning. I could not manage without them."

"Aren't there days you would rather teach children all on the same level?" we ask. She shakes her head "no," laughing. "Life would be too boring!" As we leave, we think about the concerns some people have that students with "special needs" and differences will hinder other students' learning. That doesn't happen in Aiyana's class. In fact, the different abilities in her classroom community seem to propel each student forward.

How are students different? What strategies can we use to teach students with a wide range of differences? We'll explore these questions in this chapter seeking to understand the needs of students with different types of characteristics. We encourage you to think how you might use this information to design instruction in ways that meets the needs of all students in the ways that we discussed in Chapter 2. Let's start by considering the notion of being both the same and different.

Special Needs and Good Teaching
Good Teaching Addresses Many Specific Needs

Often special needs of students are considered category by category. We might for example ask: "How can I best teach students of African descent?" Or "How can I best teach students who have a cognitive disability or students who are learning the primary language of my country?" Several tensions exist in these questions. First, the questions assume that students in a given category are enough alike that the question makes sense. However, this assumption and approach has the potential of stereotyping students and separating them from others in the school. For example, if teaching strategies for students of African descent are substantially different from other students, some might argue that separate classes for these students are needed. That same argument has been used often for students with various disabilities.

On the one hand, it makes sense to consider needs driven by characteristics such as disability, race, sexual orientation, and more. On the other hand, we have to understand that individual students may vary dramatically. Similarly, there is much overlap of recommended practices designed to meet needs of various groups with special needs. Said another way, if we use effective teaching techniques, we will go a long way toward meeting individual needs of students from various groups.

We'll explore these tensions in this chapter. We will introduce you to key needs of various categories of students and then provide strategies that have been found effective. In Chapter 2, we introduced you to strategies organized by the eight principles of whole schooling. You'll see those same strategies here. For example, promoting democracy and building community in a classroom are primary strategies in dealing with students from various cultural, ethnic, and lifestyle groups as well as students with social–emotional challenges. Similarly, multilevel differentiated instructional strategies are important for students who are second-language learners and students whose academic abilities are significantly above or below the average. We encourage you to seek to understand the needs of groups, think about needs of individual students, and recognize connections to exemplary teaching strategies.

Label Jars, Not People
Seeing Children as People First

In exploring issues related to student differences, we will encounter many labels given to children. Too often we forget that labels are attached to *people*. We hear students called "retards," "POHIs," LD students, or "the gifted." The starting point for labeling children is often the question, "What is wrong with this student?"—a *deficit-driven* approach—or its cousin, "Is this student smarter than others?"—a potentially *elitist* perspective. Both questions reflect the same underlying philosophy, the idea that inherent differences in children set them apart. This philosophy can lead to harmful attitudes. Students with presumed deficits may feel stupid and not worthy. Those with advanced skills can become isolated, compensating through attitudes of superiority. Students then *become* their labels. However, a student with a cognitive disability is mostly a child—happy, moody, fond of singing songs. A high school senior who is gifted is mostly an adolescent with dreams and fears like other teenagers. Using **people-first language**—speaking of a student *with* a cognitive disability, for example—helps us keep these truths in mind. We must be careful to see students with labels as children and students first.

With these cautions, let's now explore how students may differ and some ideas regarding how to address the needs of students.

Students from Diverse Cultural, Racial, and Ethnic Groups

Increasingly throughout the world, nations are becoming more racially and culturally diverse. How we respond to this diversity is very important. In the United States, a major focus of the civil rights movement in the 1960s was the elimination of enforced racial segregation. However, racial segregation has been again on the rise in the last 20 years. Despite this fact, schools and communities are increasingly diverse on many dimensions. As a key tool of socialization, schools provide a place where children can learn to accept, value, and interact with those who are different from them.

In our daily conversation we often speak of individuals being from different racial or ethnic groups having common cultures. However, a closer look reveals that these commonsense ideas are much more complex than it seems at first. **Race** largely has to do with genetics and certain physical characteristics that individuals hold in common. However, there has long been much interconnection between various racial groups so that, according to the American Association of Physical Anthropologists (AAPA), "pure races, in the sense of genetically homogenous populations, do not exist in the human species today, nor is there any evidence that they have ever existed in the past (AAPA, 1996). An **ethnic group** is a broader term referring to people who perceive a common bond based on a variety of factors including ancestry, geneology, common beliefs, language, religion, and culture. The famous sociologist Max Weber (1978) once said, however, that "the whole conception of ethnic groups is so complex and so vague that it might be good to abandon it altogether" (p. 389).

Cultural differences are closely connected with race and ethnicity as cultural variations are often associated with these two concepts. On the other hand, culture can vary dramatically within specific ethnic groups and a common culture may unite people across racial and ethnic differences. Culture involves many elements. One definition indicates that culture refers to "the beliefs, customs, practices, and social behavior of a particular nation or people" (Microsoft, 2008). Pang (2005) indicates that culture has three layers: (1) language, symbols, and artifacts; (2) customs, practices, and interaction patterns; and (3) shared values, norms, beliefs, and expectations. She further discusses the relationship between a particular cultural group and the dominant culture. Those considered *traditional* "follow the ways, beliefs, and patterns of the cultural group much of the time and continue to speak the native language" (p. 43). *Bicultural* members retain many of their cultural values but also have adopted practices and beliefs of the dominant culture, moving in and out of both cultures. Those who have *assimilated*, however, have largely rejected their original culture and adopted the beliefs and practices of the dominant culture. The concept of a **minority group** relates to individuals from various racial, ethnic, or cultural groups who may act in ways that are different from the predominant culture. Immigrants, for example, often bring the cultural values and practices from their home country that may be different or even in conflict with the culture of their new country.

Increasingly our classes will be filled with students who have a very wide range of racial and ethnic identities, backgrounds, and cultural perspectives. Most critical in working with students from differing racial, ethnic, and cultural groups is the building of a supportive and caring community within the classroom where students are taught explicitly how to value and support one another and to value and benefit from the differences that students bring.

Following are key strategies for responding to cultural, racial, and ethnic diversity in our classes (Burnette, 1999; Gross, 2008; National Council of Teachers of English, 2005). Note that these strategies, with minor modification, may be applied with all students in our class. In implementing these strategies, we will work with specialists and knowledgeable professionals who understand the culture of our students.

Promote respect for students' culture, race, and ethnic identity

- Recognize any biases or stereotypes you have.
- Positively acknowledge and validate individual, cultural, and lifestyle differences.
- Convey equal respect and confidence in all our students.
- Develop an understanding of diverse cultural practices and rituals.
- Choose texts and other learning materials that reflect cultural and ethnic diversity.
- Invite diverse parents into the classroom to share their expertise or tell about their family life and cultural traditions.
- Invite students to bring in materials that relate to various cultures and ethnic groups.
- Directly challenge racism.
- Be a role model to students for how to treat diverse individuals.

Promote respect for and understanding of each student as an individual

- Don't make assumptions based on stereotypes.
- Build relationships with your students and learn about their lives outside the school.
- Get a sense of how students feel about your classroom.

- Consider students' needs when assigning evening or weekend work.
- Avoid singling out a student as a spokesperson for his or her race, culture, or ethnic group.
- Observe and learn how students best learn. Seek to understand how their culture, race, language, or lifestyle affects learning.
- Use a variety of instructional strategies and learning activities.

Learn how to critique and challenge social injustice

- Develop sustained contact in the local community.
- Develop projects on different cultural practices.
- Encourage students to develop critical perspectives through community-based research and action projects.
- Use classroom approaches that empower students socially and academically.

Ensure that students are accepted and valued, have a sense of belonging, and develop friendships

- Suggest that students form study teams that meet outside of class.
- Assign group work and collaborative learning activities.
- Advise students to explore perspectives outside their own experiences.
- Provide opportunities for all students to get to know each other.
- Be a teacher in whom students can confide and in whom they can trust.

Students from Extreme Poverty

Perhaps one of the biggest challenges in building inclusive schools is teaching students who are extremely poor. By and large, parents and students who are very poor are judged and punished for their poverty and difficulties. The stereotype is that people who are poor are lazy, make bad choices, and are not motivated or intelligent. Yet studies find very different realities (Beegle, 2000; Danziger & Haveman, 2001). The fact also is, however, that most children who are raised in very poor families themselves will remain very poor. Many factors come together to make it difficult, though possible, for children who are poor to improve their lot in life. What's also clear, however, is that teachers have the potential to help break this cycle. The key is what we do and how we treat children who are poor.

We need to understand the life of people who are very poor. First, parents who are very poor are constantly in survival mode. On a daily, hour-by-hour basis, they are seeking food for the day, shelter, and other basic necessities. What is it like to be poor? People who are poor are humiliated, feeling that other people blame them for their poverty. They feel judged because of their appearance. One young woman stated that "no one wanted

BACK PACK

Urban and Cultural Diversity

National Center for Culturally Responsive Educational Systems NCCRESt works with schools to develop culturally responsive educational practices. Great information and resources. www.nccrest.org/

National Institute for Urban Inclusive Education This organization works with urban schools to encourage and facilitate inclusive schooling. Many excellent materials are at this site. urbanschools.org/index.html

us around" because "our hair was dirty and stringy, and most people made us feel like we didn't belong" (Beegle, 2003, p. 14). Their experience provides little understanding of professional jobs and ways to move toward higher incomes. Finding a place to live is always a problem due to poor housing conditions. Another person stated that "I could never bring anyone home to our dump" (Beegle, 2003, p. 14). Children may live in very messy conditions with many people in a small space, some even living in a car. Having enough food is often a problem and is often of poor quality. Many of these children come to school hungry. Families and children typically feel that there is literally nothing they can do to make their situation better. All is beyond their control.

As teachers we may feel these parents do not care about their children because they never come to school. However, they care very much but they have only so much energy. Beegle (2003) stated that "my mother . . . never went to a school conference. She'd say, 'I ain't going in there and make a fool of myself,' yet I have the most caring mother you could ever want" (p. 19). We also have to understand that education is not seen as important for many families who are poor. They are literally in a daily struggle for survival and often feel their children should be helping rather than doing schoolwork. Jobs most often pay minimum wage, not enough to live on. So the notion that children should study so that they can get a job doesn't make sense to them. They often have little understanding that education can help their children lead a more secure life.

Children who are poor often feel that teachers do not care about them and don't know how to respond to them. They and their parents often even feel that teachers are part of the "enemy," another group of people in power who humiliate and disrespect them. Too often teachers don't take the time to understand the lives of these children. Consequently, they often feel that they do not belong in school.

How does all this affect children and their behavior in school? First, because of low self-confidence and shame, students will often be silent and very quiet. This does not mean, however, that they understand the lesson. Also, children living with daily insecurity where basic needs are not met feel anger, have negative attitudes, and tend to be "smart alecks." Students may come to school with dirty bodies and clothes. They will often have great difficulty doing schoolwork at home and have difficulty keeping track of materials sent home.

What can we do to help children and youth who are very poor? Beegle (2003) has recommended the following:

- Show and tell students that they are special.
- Make extra efforts to ensure understanding of the material being covered.
- Ensure that the school and the classroom are safe, both emotionally and physically. Protect students from ridicule.
- Address social class as part of the curriculum and fight classism. Create learning opportunities for exploring structural causes of poverty.
- Examine our own attitudes related to people from generational poverty. Seek to understand and learn. Visit the children where they live, whether in the back of a truck or in a homeless shelter. Talk to the parents about their concerns.
- Work with others to ensure a school environment in which peers, teachers, and administrators try to understand and appreciate parents and children who are poor.
- Explore whether problematic behavior is related to conditions of poverty and find ways to respond to meet student needs.
- Connect students with mentors.
- Build a network of support with others who are working to address poverty issues and link students and families to them.
- Create incentives and motivators that are effective for all children who are poor. Ask students, "If you get knocked down, what are five things you would get back up for?" This will help us understand what really motivates a student.

Two students are involved in a service learning project where older students are paired with younger students. They have become best buddies in the process.

- Work to eliminate homework or create homework that could be reasonably done by children who have unstable home situations. Clearly understand the purpose for which we want to assign homework. Find ways to achieve this during the school day or in after-school tutoring programs.
- Bring in speakers, take field trips, and talk about career possibilities. Make sure there is time for the students to hear personal stories of how professionals came to be educated or obtained their jobs.
- Suspend judgment of parent/guardian behavior. Express appreciation of parenting efforts, even if the efforts are not what you might expect from a middle-class parent.

Students Who Are Gay

Students may also vary in their sexual orientation, heterosexual or gay. This will be particularly important in high school. However, actions toward gay and lesbian students are highly influenced by attitudes and information provided by teachers and other adults. Wood (1997) indicates that 10 to 30% of students are either gay or lesbian, or have an immediate family member who is. As with other differences, it is very important that we provide emotional support and acceptance of these students. Wood claims that "silence on these issues communicates values just as loudly as responding would. The values that should be taught are ones that encompass respect for one another and caring about one another's feelings, regardless of differences" (p. 2).

Students who are gay need particular understanding and support from us as teachers. These students need to know that ridicule and cruelty will not be tolerated in the class and that we will be working actively to create a caring classroom community. Most critically, they need to be able to trust and talk openly to us and know we will help them be accepted in the class. Wood (1997) suggested the following strategies:

- Make no assumption about sexual preference. Use neutral language such as, "Are you seeing anyone?" instead of "Do you have a boyfriend?" Additionally, do not assume that a female student who confides a crush on another girl is a lesbian.
- Have something gay-related visible in your office that will identify you as a safe person to talk to.

- Support, normalize, and validate students' feelings about their sexuality. Let them know that we are there for them.
- Work on our own biases by reading, learning, and talking to people.
- Do not advise youth to "come out." This is their decision to deal with in their own time. Many gay youth are forced to leave their home after they tell their parents. Help them figure out what makes sense for them.
- Guarantee confidentiality with students.
- Challenge homophobia immediately.
- Connect students with role models. Gay and straight students benefit from having openly gay teachers, coaches, and administrators.

Students with Differing Academic Abilities

All teachers know that their students vary dramatically in the level of skills and abilities in the classroom. Inclusive teachers intentionally plan for having students with a wide range of abilities ranging from students considered gifted and talented to those with significant cognitive disabilities. Here we will consider students who vary in their academic and cognitive abilities.

Peer Tutoring at an Inclusive High School

SCHOOLS to VISIT

Santana High School
9915 Magnolia Avenue
Santee, CA 92071

Santana High School is located in Santee, in Southern California. Students considered having moderate and severe disabilities are enrolled in general education classes. They attend classes according to their grade level, not according to their disability, and have done so since the early 1990s.

This high school provides a variety of supports to students with disabilities. The most essential is peer tutoring. Students from Grades 9 through 12 may enroll in a peer tutoring course that counts as an elective toward graduation credit. They tutor students who have moderate to severe disabilities and attend the general education classes with the student to provide academic and social support.

Special education teachers train them and provide support through five formal trainings throughout the 18-week term. These trainings focus on information

pertaining to inclusion, curriculum modification, support strategies, the use of people-first language (e.g., "a person with a disability," not "a disabled person"), and forms of communication. Major emphases of training are on respecting and empowering the student with a disability. Students learn to strive for social justice for people with disabilities and to celebrate human diversity.

Although the objective of the peer tutoring course is to provide support to students with disabilities who are included in general education courses, many other benefits also have evolved. Students and teachers have increased opportunities to interact with people at a variety of ability levels. Students discover the commonalities they share with people who have disabilities. Peer tutors also increase their own knowledge of the subject matter of classes as they provide tutoring. Friendships are developed; academics are effectively taught; and, most importantly, individual needs are being met in a supportive, inclusive environment.

By Rebecca Bond and Liz Castagnera. Edited by Michael Peterson.

Gifted and Talented

Parents of children with high abilities have been very concerned regarding the education of their children. In 1988 Congress passed the Jacob K. Javits Gifted and Talented Students Education Act to provide federal support to schools aimed at improving the education of gifted and talented students. In the 1994 reauthorization of PL 103-398, Title XIV:

> The term "gifted and talented" . . . means students . . . who give evidence of high performance capability in areas such as intellectual, creative, artistic, or leadership capacity, or in specific academic fields, and who require services or activities not normally provided by the school in order to fully develop such capabilities. (PL 103-398, Title XIV, p. 388)

Two points are noteworthy about this definition. First, a student can be "gifted" and also possess another label—such as "learning disabled" or "second-language learner." Second, this definition describes regular classrooms as being unable to challenge these students adequately. This description, however, is more an assumption and is based on traditional, one-level teaching practice.

How can students who are highly gifted and students with severe mental retardation or learning disabilities learn successfully together? The answer is that we can use techniques from gifted education to benefit all students. Strategies that use multiple intelligences and differentiated instruction can create classes aimed at the highest levels, in which the brightest students bring others along, yet structured so that students can begin where they are, however low or high their abilities. In addition, we must be concerned about the emotional well-being of students who are highly gifted. Do they feel set apart? When we build a strong community while providing opportunities for students to engage in learning at their own level, these students can be supported emotionally as well as academically.

A few examples may be helpful. We would expect students who are gifted to play leadership roles in class discussions, sharing their learning and extending issues to higher levels of complexity. As this happens, these students raise the level of understanding of all students. Teaching strategies that support students who are gifted and talented are expansions of multilevel teaching, introduced in Chapter 2 and discussed in detail in Chapters 11–13. Useful strategies include the following (Cline, 1999; Kronberg, 1999; Tomlinson, 2004a):

- *Curriculum compacting:* Pre-assess students to avoid teaching what they already know, and allow advanced students to pursue enrichment activities or explore units in additional breadth or depth.
- *Tiered lessons:* Structure lessons that allow students to move ahead as they are able and interested. Provide a range of activities students may select from at various levels of difficulty. Allow and teach students to choose their own activities at their own level.
- *Open-ended assignments:* Give assignments in which students can explore complexity, assignments that have open-ended rather than finite responses. Instead of saying, "Read this and answer the multiple-choice questions," we would say, "Read and write about how Columbus came to America."

Students who are gifted need scaffolds—technology, resources, and human help—to push and support them as they move to the next level. **Mixed-ability groups** can be structured as microcosms of the total class, mixing students of different ability levels, genders, and social, cultural, and ethnic backgrounds. We should aim to have at least two students with higher abilities in such groups. Some useful group learning approaches include:

- *Social action research projects:* Students investigate an area of concern in their community and take action (Cline, 1999; Sapon-Shevin, 1994a, 1999; Willis, 1995).
- *Literacy circles:* These are structured as cross-ability groups. A student with mental retardation listens to the book on tape while a student who is gifted reads the book and other resource information to enrich the discussion. The gifted student may help the student with mental retardation draw from his or her own perspective to interpret the story, a process that can increase interpersonal and leadership skills (Daniels, 1994).
- *Multiage grouping:* Multiage classes offer reciprocal benefits, as when an experienced 10-year-old with learning disabilities stimulates a bright 8-year-old. Also, mixing classes across age groups can be valuable, as in projects involving elementary and high school students or reading buddy programs mixing upper and lower elementary students (Banks, 1995; Hindley, 1996; Schiller, 1998).
- *Flexible grouping:* If we group kids flexibly and have students move in and out of groups, some short-term ability grouping can work in ways that do not undermine classroom community. However, we must be careful. Such groups should not last more than one day; also, different students should be in such groups around different subjects so that we don't have certain students clustered consistently in either high or low groups (Clark, 1997; Cline, 1999; Kennedy, 1995; Peterson, Tamor, Feen, & Silagy, 2002).
- *Collaborative pairing:* Students work together in pairs. We teach students to work together collaboratively, helping them understand how their differences can be interesting and powerful sources of learning (D. Cohen, 1990; Putnam, 1993; Tarrant, 1999a, 1999b).

Some fear that teachers will be tempted to say to gifted students, "Jennifer, tutor John"—and go off to grade their papers. Instead, we can, with the very same activity, say to our student who is gifted, "Jennifer, you know that John has difficulties learning to read. This is a very big issue in helping people learn and grow. I think John could benefit from your help. However, you may want to learn more about the controversies surrounding reading strategies as you work with him. Would you be interested?" Jennifer may spend extra time with John, reading to him, helping him develop webs, and working on collaborative projects that use language, all the time learning through other investigations about what researchers say about learning to read. Of course, collaborative cross-ability learning does not necessarily focus on the nature of difference. Almost any topic allows for expanding a knowledge base to help others.

Dominant-Language Learners

A growing number of students are attending our schools whose primary language is different from the predominant language and who are limited in their abilities to use oral or written in that language. Many schools have scores of languages represented (Peterson et al., 2002). Faltis (2000) suggests the term *second-language learners* refers to students who do not speak the language of the majority culture. In addition, some students may speak the language but use a dialect at home. Black English, or ebonics, has been much discussed, but numerous other nonstandard dialects exist—such as those spoken by Whites in the Appalachian region or other ethnic groups (Polish, Italian, German, etc.). We should not tell students that their home language is "incorrect." Rather, explain that we use language for different purposes in different places and that standard English is used in school, business, and many other settings. This helps us respect students' cultures while helping them learn the "language of power" (Delpit, 1995).

People disagree regarding whether students should be taught in pull-out bilingual classes or should learn in the general education class with a specialist providing collaborative support. Once again, we will see that good practices for second-language learners are based on good practices for all students, and that second-language learners enrich our class (Faltis, 2000; Miller-Lachmann & Taylor, 1995; Moore, 1999).

Faltis (2000) described four strategies for language learning:

1. *Recounts:* Students retell information known to both teacher and student: "What happened today when we visited the zoo, Juanita?"
2. *Accounts:* Student shares new information—a special event, weekend activities.
3. *Eventcasts:* Students talk about an event in process; for example, they might explain how to do an activity while it is being demonstrated.
4. *Stories:* Students read and write fictional accounts.

We must be aware of potential cultural mismatches of language use in the school and the home. In some families, for example, children are expected to listen and are not allowed to talk with adults. When such children are asked to talk with adults in school, they may have difficulty. Similarly, some cultures emphasize cooperation and group work over individual achievement. In classes in which children have frequent daily opportunities to use language, cultural mismatches become less problematic than in situations in which teachers do most of the talking (Faltis, 2000; Moore, 1999).

Faltis (2000) suggested the following strategies for second-language learners:

- High incidence of two-way communicative exchanges between teacher and students and among students;
- Social integration of second-language students with other students in all learning activities;
- Thoughtful integration of second-language acquisition principles with content instruction so that as students learn new subject matter knowledge, they develop language as well;
- Involvement and participation of second-language students' home community in classroom and school activities;
- Promotion of critical consciousness to oppose social stratification and promote equity; and
- Collaborative work with second-language learner specialists and paraprofessionals who can provide support and assistance within our class.

Learning Disabilities

Many students are intelligent yet have trouble with reading, writing, math, or related subjects—students with learning disabilities. The Individuals with Disabilities Education Act (IDEA) defines a **learning disability** as

> a disorder in one or more of the basic psychological processes involved in understanding or in using language, spoken or written, that may manifest itself in an imperfect ability to listen, think, speak, read, write, spell, or to do mathematical calculations. The term includes such conditions as perceptual disabilities, brain injury, minimal brain dysfunction, dyslexia, and developmental aphasia. The term does not apply to children who have learning problems which are primarily the result of visual, hearing, or motor

disabilities, of mental retardation, of emotional disturbance, or of environmental, cultural, or economic disadvantage. (Individuals with Disabilities Education Improvement Act [IDEA], 2004, p. 118)

When describing the characteristics of students with learning disabilities, professionals list many learning problems. These include hyperactivity or hypoactivity, distractibility, perceptual processing deficits, difficulty with social skills, confusing letters, comprehension difficulty, keeping work neat, writing their own thoughts, remembering math facts, and more. Often these statements are so general it is difficult to know what they mean. In addition, such characterizations treat student differences as deficits, often ignoring significant student strengths. Some researchers suggest that it is more effective to describe students in terms of their abilities to engage in learning tasks—such as their ability to frame questions while reading, trouble converting written print to words and sentences, difficulty understanding words that are "read," or difficulty in understanding mathematical calculations (Englert et al., 1995; Englert, Mariage, Garmon, & Tarrant, 1998; Spear-Swerling & Sternberg, 1998; Tarrant, 1999a).

From a multiple intelligences perspective, every individual possesses a profile of varied abilities. However, we focus only on selected areas as worthy of serious attention. For example, if a child is tone deaf and has difficulty succeeding in music, this is often noted but not treated as an issue of great concern. We certainly don't refer such a student for special education for learning disabilities in music. However, we could. If we think about it this way, almost everyone has some sort of "learning disability" (Armstrong, 1994; Gardner, 1993).

Until 2004, IDEA required that students have a severe discrepancy between achievement and intellectual abilities in at least one of seven areas: basic reading skill, reading comprehension, listening comprehension, oral expression, written expression, mathematics calculation, or mathematics reasoning. This approach was a "wait to fail" model since it required that students get more behind before they could be declared eligible for services. In 2004 the law *allowed* school districts to eliminate this requirement and Congress recommended that schools use a "response to intervention" model in which student responses to high-quality, research-based instruction are considered when diagnosing students with learning disabilities.

The response to the intervention model provides an approach to early intervening services. Response to intervention strategies involve tiers of assistance that begin with identifying student needs and then use a range of instructional strategies that may provide assistance to students. These strategies are consistent with those outlined in this book. Following are some key strategies that may be helpful for students with learning disabilities.

- Have positive expectations while affirming that students have different learning styles and rates of learning.
- Use authentic, activity-based learning that draws on multiple intelligences. (We'll find that students with learning disabilities often have strong abilities in art, physical movement, etc. These can be used as strengths and routes to typical academic abilities.)
- Seek to reduce stress and discouragement, providing experiences in which the students can be successful. We can do this by providing reading materials at their level of ability.
- Use assistive technology such as text to speech software, materials on tape or CD, software that provides writing assistance, speech to text software (see Chapter 8). When students with learning disabilities use these tools to gain meaning from text we help them have success, enjoy involvement in literacy, and function. It may be as important to help them learn to use these tools as to read in a conventional way!

- Provide scaffolding to help the student participate with support. Scaffolding support can come from the teacher (using read alouds, writing dictated stories), from other students (buddy reading, group reading), and from classroom volunteers.
- Help students learn to organize materials using calendars, organizers, story maps, and methods of filing.
- Provide student assignments ahead of time (perhaps on Friday) and send them home to parents so they and the student can prepare for the coming week.
- Give students social and emotional support. Value their contributions and help them deal with frustrations.

Cognitive Disabilities

Students with **cognitive disabilities** (previously referred to as mental retardation) have limitations in their intellectual and cognitive abilities as well as their abilities to engage in social and practical adaptive abilities of daily living. Students with intellectual disabilities will learn much slower than other students. There will be some skills they will never learn. For example, many students with cognitive disabilities may never develop reading skills higher than first- or second-grade level. Until recently, the term used for cognitive disabilities or intellectual disabilities was *mental retardation*. However, over the years that term has gained very negative connotations, as occurred with previous technical terms—*moron*, *idiot*, and *feebleminded*. In 2006, the American Association of Intellectual and Developmental Disabilities (AAIDD) changed its terminology from *mental retardation* to *intellectual disability*, which it defines as a "disability characterized by significant limitations both in intellectual functioning and in adaptive behavior as expressed in conceptual, social, and practical adaptive skills. This disability originates before age 18" (American Association of Intellectual and Developmental Disabilities, 2007).

IDEA still uses the term "mental retardation" but the definition uses similar language:

> "Mental retardation" means significantly sub-average general intellectual functioning existing concurrently with deficits in adaptive behavior and manifested during the developmental period that adversely affects a child's educational performance. (IDEA, 2004, section 300.7)

Intellectual abilities are measured by an individual intelligence test such as the Wechsler Intelligence Scales for Children (WAIS). Adaptive behavior is typically measured by a rating of functional and adaptive skills. Historically, IQ scores falling within certain ranges have defined the following levels of mental retardation: borderline (IQs of 70–85), mild or *educable* (55–70), moderate or *trainable* (40–55), *severe* (25–40), and *profound* (below 25).

Students with intellectual disabilities are among the most segregated and isolated of children. Despite the inclusive schooling movement, children with mental retardation often attend segregated schools or classes. Adults with intellectual disabilities are often segregated throughout their lifetimes, living either with their parents or, as explained in Chapter 1, in group homes (Braddock, Hemp, Bachelder, & Fujiura, 1995; Hill & Lakin, 1984). They often work in sheltered workshops (Murphy & Rogan, 1995; Weiner-Zivolich, 1995).

In recent years parents and people with mental retardation have rejected these limited options, demanding that children be included in general education and that adults be given support so they can live in their own homes, work in real jobs, marry, and participate in the community (Jupp, 1994; O'Brien, O'Brien, & Jacob, 1998; Schaefer, 1997; Schleien, Ray, & Green, 1997).

When we use good teaching strategies, students with intellectual disabilities learn much more than anyone thought possible (Beloin, 1997; Freeman & Alkin, 2000; Hunt, Staub, Alwell, & Goetz, 1994; Logan, Bakeman, & Keefe, 1997; McDonnell, Hardman, Hightower, & Kiefer-O'Donnell, 1997; Ryndak, Morrison, & Sommerstein, 1999). The strategies useful with students with learning disabilities are directly applicable to students with cognitive disabilities. Other useful strategies include the following:

- Facilitate supports for students to include circles of friends and peer buddies and helpers.
- Use paraprofessionals to work with students with cognitive disabilities. However, we often find they are not needed if we are using multilevel instruction (see Chapters 11–13). We want to ensure that a paraprofessional does not hover over students with cognitive disabilities and separate them from other students.
- Ensure that students are involved in age-appropriate activities. While we work with these students from their level of ability, we don't treat a 13-year-old, for example, as a 6-year-old even though the student may be functioning on the first-grade level.
- Use authentic, multilevel, and tiered instruction to involve students in the same topics and learning activities as other students but at their level of ability. Connect learning to real skills needed in life. We can use catalogs of life skills to connect these to academic instruction for all students such as "life-centered career education" (Brolin, 1993) and the "activities catalogue" (Wilcox & Bellamy, 1987).
- Provide students the opportunities to make choices and learn the skills of self-determination. Students with cognitive disabilities too often are given little opportunity to learn how to advocate for themselves. We can incorporate this into any class.
- Provide books at multiple levels of difficulty with good graphics and illustrations.
- Break complex activities into smaller, simpler parts (task analysis). However, take care not to overdo this.
- Promote connections of skills across home and school. For example, use similar labeling schemes for certain objects both at home and in school, or have books read at home that reinforce information at school.

Traumatic Brain Injury

In many ways, learning challenges faced by individuals who have a traumatic brain injury (TBI) are similar to those faced by individuals with learning disabilities and cognitive disabilities. A major difference is that these challenges are brought on suddenly. Thus, emotional reactions are of great concern. In terms of official definitions, IDEA states the following:

> "Traumatic brain injury" means an acquired injury to the brain caused by an external physical force, resulting in total or partial functional disability or psychosocial impairment, or both, that adversely affects a child's educational performance. Traumatic brain

Sights TO SEE

Peanut Butter and Micah in High School

Peanut Butter and Jelly Lesson The teacher "skillfully interweaves hands-on activities, rich language development dialogue, and writing practice to help her students learn." crede.berkeley.edu/research/crede/products/multimedia/pbj.html#

Micah: Senior Year in High School This site shares information about Micah Fialka Feldman's inclusion in high school. Includes video in classrooms, interviews of teachers, and Micah running a 200-meter race. www.wholeschooling.net/WS/Video/Micah.html

injury applies to open or closed head injuries resulting in mild, moderate, or severe impairments in one or more areas, such as cognition; language; memory; attention; reasoning; abstract thinking; judgment; problem solving; sensory, perceptual and motor abilities; psychosocial behavior; physical functions; information processing; and speech. Traumatic brain injury does not include brain injuries that are congenital or degenerative, or brain injuries induced by brain trauma. (IDEA, 2004, section 300.7)

Traumatic brain injuries are caused by injuries to the head. These include traffic injuries, sports accidents, and gunshot wounds. Auto accidents are frequently associated with alcohol consumption; gunshots with aggression, robberies, and gang wars; and blows to the head with child abuse (North et al., 1995). Students may have had serious problems in their lives prior to their injury that affect how they adjust.

Because the brain controls so many functions, the impacts of TBI can vary greatly. These may include (1) physical impairments such as speech loss, hearing loss, seizure disorders; (2) cognitive impacts such as reading and writing skills, concentration, memory, judgment, and communication; and (3) emotional responses that may include fatigue, depression, anger, mood swings, and low self-esteem. Some students will be able, with effort, to regain significant abilities. Others will not.

Students with TBI need support. They will likely be receiving ongoing medical attention, sometimes necessitating their missing school (Begali, 1992; Bell, 1994; North et al., 1995). At first, students' stamina may be limited and they may attend school a shorter day. We can help by having a place where the student can rest. Because impacts can be so variable, we pay close attention to academic performance and emotional responses. Given the devastation of loss, students need to capitalize on their strengths; similarly, we need to use these strengths as avenues to reach areas of weakness (Cohen, 1991; Gerring & Carney, 1992).

Strategies for Students with Differing Academic Abilities

Following are key strategies for students with different academic abilities. While it's helpful to think of strategies associated with each specific group, it's even more helpful to think about strategies to design instruction to accommodate students with various academic abilities. We will explore these in greater detail in later chapters.

- Have positive, high, but reasonable expectations coupled with emotional support.
- Expect all students, especially those with higher abilities, to play leadership roles in class discussions, sharing their learning and extending issues to higher levels of complexity.
- Have reading and instructional materials available that are high interest but are at wide-ranging levels of ability; picture books to highly technical materials on a particular subject, for example.
- Use multilevel, differentiated instruction to allow students to function at varying levels of ability in lessons. Expect performance that fits the ability level of each student. (See Chapters 11–13.)
- Use authentic and activity-based learning linking various subjects around key themes that are important and interesting to students.
- Identify and draw on the strengths of students (rather than emphasizing deficits). Use multiple intelligences to find areas of strength.
- Reduce stress and pressure concerning areas of student deficit by using authentic, multilevel teaching and celebrating their successes and growth.
- Provide scaffolds and supports to help students be able to participate in more complex activities than they could do alone and to challenge and support all students in learning at their own level.
- Help all students organize their materials and monitor their scheduling and completion of learning activities.

Three teachers are congratulating a student with special needs regarding his writing a poem related to the social studies unit on diversity. One teacher is a special education teacher who provides support in the general education classroom. The other two are English and social studies teachers who are collaborating on this unit.

- Mix groups heterogeneously giving all students opportunities to support other students in their learning, rather than just asking high-ability students to do this. Remember that teaching someone else deepens understanding.
- Help students connect with one another and develop relationships. Avoid stable ability grouping.
- Work collaboratively with other teachers and specialists, such as special education teachers, gifted specialists, speech therapists, psychologists, social workers, and others to design lessons that meet the needs of all students and to provide in-class support to students in learning.
- Resist the temptation to send students out to special education resources rooms, gifted classes, or other separate programs when it is difficult to figure out how to use multilevel, differentiated instruction.

Students with Behavioral and Emotional Challenges

Working with students who have emotional and behavioral issues will often challenge our commitment to being an inclusive teacher. When students cause disruptions, we may feel insecure in our own abilities. We may also be concerned for the safety of other students. It's also clear that schools don't do a very good job of dealing with the needs of students who exhibit challenging behaviors. The typical response is punishment or isolation—responses that make the problems worse, not better. Figure 3.1 identifies common emotional and behavioral difficulties, which are briefly described in the following text.

Attention Deficit/Hyperactivity Disorder

In recent decades a literal explosion has occurred in the number of students who are labeled as having **attention deficit/hyperactivity disorder** (ADHD) (G. Breggin, 2000; Diller, 1998). The term used in the most recent version of the *Diagnostic and Statistical Manual of Mental Disorders (DSM)*, the fourth edition, text revision (*DSM–IV–TR*;

FIGURE 3.1

Emotional and Behavioral Disorders

EXTERNALIZING DISORDERS

- Attention deficit/hyperactivity disorder (ADHD)
- Oppositional defiance disorder (ODD)
- Conduct disorder
- Pervasive developmental disorders (PDDs)

INTERNALIZING DISORDERS

- Substance abuse
- Feeding and eating disorders
- Anxiety and social withdrawal
- Depression
- Schizophrenia and psychosis

American Psychiatric Association, 2000), is ADHD. Several subtypes are identified: (1) *inattentive* (previously thought of as "ADD" without hyperactivity; (2) *impulsive and hyperactive*; and (3) *combined type*—exhibiting all three behaviors of concern.

The diagnostic criteria for ADHD are listed in Figure 3.2. For a child to be diagnosed as ADHD, he or she must exhibit at least six of the nine symptoms before age 7 in at least two situations (such as school or home). Behaviors must also cause significant problems in functioning and cannot be better explained by another diagnosis. Breggin and Ross-Breggin (1994) and Diller (1998) indicate that there is much overdiagnosis of students as ADHD with physicians often simply checking off criteria based on an interview with parents without adequately delving into the child's life. Stress, family dynamics, lack of time with teachers and parents, or simply boring instruction are seldom adequately considered. There is no evidence that ADHD has a biological cause (Coles, 1987, 1998).

Inattention. In ADHD, students shift between inattention and distractibility and bursts of "hyperfocusing" (Nelson, 1996, 1998).

Type 1: Hypofocus: Some students struggle to sustain concentration. They are kinesthetic learners who need movement and intense experiences.

Type 2: Hyperfocus: These students focus intensely blocking out other sources of input. Their minds race with ideas, and they are often physically overactive. They may need help to focus *less* so that they can switch to other activities. Such students may amaze teachers with their creativity.

Type 3: Mixed Focus: These children are inattentive one hour, overattentive the next, often mixing inattention with physical underactivity. The student may seem "spacey," prone to too much thinking and too little action.

Impulsivity. Students may jump from one idea to another and say what comes to mind. Such a student may hear something and run to the window (Bender, 1997). Yet impulsivity can be very valuable. Rather than hesitating, these students "act on instant decisions" with the "willingness to explore new and untested areas" (Hartmann, 1996, p. 24). They may be highly creative and stimulate lively discussion but need help in channeling this energy.

FIGURE 3.2

DSM–IV–TR Criteria for ADHD

INATTENTION

- Often fails to give close attention to details or makes careless mistakes in schoolwork, work, or other activities.
- Often has difficulty sustaining attention in tasks or play activities.
- Often does not seem to listen when spoken to directly.
- Often does not follow through on instructions and fails to finish schoolwork, chores, or duties in the workplace (not due to oppositional behavior or failure to understand instructions).
- Often has difficulty organizing tasks and activities.
- Often avoids, dislikes, or is reluctant to engage in tasks that require sustained mental effort (such as schoolwork or homework).
- Often loses things necessary for tasks or activities (e.g., toys, school assignments, pencils, books, or tools).
- Often is easily distracted by extraneous stimuli.
- Often is forgetful in daily activities.

HYPERACTIVITY

- Often fidgets with hands or feet or squirms in seat.
- Often leaves seat in classroom or in other situations in which it is inappropriate (in adolescents or adults, may be limited to subjective feelings of restlessness).
- Often runs about or climbs excessively in situations in which it is inappropriate.
- Often has difficulty playing or engaging in leisure activities quietly.
- Often is "on the go" or often acts as if "driven by a motor."
- Often talks excessively.

IMPULSIVITY

- Often blurts out answers before questions have been completed.
- Often has difficulty waiting turn.
- Often interrupts or intrudes on others (e.g., butts into conversations).

Source: Adapted from the American Psychiatric Association (2000), pp. 92–93.

Hyperactivity. Some students are full of energy and movement. According to the National Institute of Mental Health (2001), "people who are hyperactive always seem to be in motion. . . . They may roam around the room, squirm in their seats, wiggle their feet, touch everything, or noisily tap a pencil" (p. 1).

Ritalin and Related Drugs. Use of drugs to control ADHD behavior has grown dramatically. Drugs with three different names all use the same chemical, methylphenidate: Ritalin, Ritalin SR, and Concerta. Psychiatrists report that many parents come specifically to obtain prescriptions, and "Ritalin mills" have sprung up. A growing number of researchers and practitioners, however, are questioning drug use, analyzing both impact and side effects, and suggesting alternatives for both parents and teachers (Armstrong, 1997; Breeding, 1996; Breggin, 2001; Diller, 1998; Stein, 1999).

Ritalin does help students focus for a short time and helps moderate impulsivity. Ritalin has similar effects on those who are and are not considered to have ADHD (Diller, 1998). However, Ritalin has several potential side effects that can include increased blood pressure, convulsions, psychosis, depression, dizziness, headache, insomnia, nervousness, loss of appetite, nausea, vomiting, stomach pain, dry mouth, weight loss, growth suppression, blurred vision, and more. It tends to sap children of their spirit, creating a "zombie" demeanor. In addition, the **rebound effect,** typical withdrawal responses that can last up to 10 days after ingestion, may make a child's behavior worse than before. When this occurs, people often think that increased dosages are needed. Dependence on the drug shields children and adults from having to work through conflicts. Children on Ritalin tend to see their success as based on a drug rather than their own effort (Breggin, 2001).

Although ADHD is not a special education category, students with ADHD can qualify under the category of "other health impaired" if they need special education services (Office of Special Education and Rehabilitative Services, 1991). Many students labeled ADHD also are considered learning disabled. Even if they do not receive special education services, they are covered under Section 504 and schools must provide reasonable accommodations.

There is evidence that a combination of social supports, effective instruction, and reasonable drug use can be effective (Breggin, 2001; Monastra, 2004; Pierangelo & Giulani, 2007; Rief, 2005). With good teaching practice we should expect substantial reductions in the use of Ritalin and related drugs.

Labels of Serious Emotional Disturbance

The Individuals with Disabilities Education Act (IDEA) defines "serious emotional disturbance" as

a condition exhibiting one or more of the following characteristics over a long period of time and to a marked degree that adversely affects a child's educational performance:

A. An inability to learn that cannot be explained by intellectual, sensory, or health factors.
B. An inability to build or maintain satisfactory interpersonal relationships with peers and teachers.
C. Inappropriate types of behavior or feelings under normal circumstances.
D. A general pervasive mood of unhappiness or depression.
E. A tendency to develop physical symptoms or fears associated with personal or school problems.

The term includes schizophrenia. The term does not apply to children who are socially maladjusted, unless it is determined that they have an emotional disturbance. (IDEA, 2004)

This definition has caused much concern among professionals because the language is extremely vague. The number of students who are labeled as emotionally disturbed varies dramatically across districts and states. Some use the requirement that a student's difficulties "adversely affects a child's educational performance" to not qualify students who have emotional problems but who are making good grades (Kauffman, 2008). The term *socially maladjusted* is even more problematic. In the law it was not defined. Much effort has gone into efforts to distinguish between social maladjustment and emotional disturbance. Most often socially maladjusted students are considered not truly disabled. Rather, they "engage in deliberate acts of self-interest to gain attention or to intimidate others, while experiencing no distress . . . about their behavior" (RESA, 2004). Montgomery (2008) stated that conduct disorder, by definition, is social maladjustment. However, many professionals consider these ideas "incomprehensible. A youngster cannot be socially maladjusted . . . without exhibiting one or more of the five characteristics (especially B or C) to marked degree and over a long period of time. Neither logic nor research supports the discrimination between social maladjustment and emotional disturbance" (Kauffman, 2008, p. 30). If students truly have no conscience and engage willfully in bullying and hurting others, this should be considered a significant emotional disability. Clearly, schools using a punitive model have used this distinction to deny services and protection of the law to these difficult but troubled students (Kauffman, 2008; Merrell & Walker, 2004).

Five labels are used to describe students who "externalize" their difficulties via disruptive behaviors. ADHD and social maladjustment were discussed previously. Students with **oppositional defiance disorder (ODD)** exhibit negative, hostile behavior lasting at least 6 months in which they frequently do four of the following: lose temper; argue with adults; defy or refuse to comply with adults' requests; deliberately annoy people; blame others; and/or act touchy, angry, resentful, and spiteful. **Conduct disorder** involves persistent rule breaking and aggressive behavior such as defiance, fighting, and bullying. These students frequently are also diagnosed with other conditions such as ADHD, learning disabilities, anxiety disorders, and depression (American Academy of Child and Adolescent Psychiatry, 2008). In practice it is difficult to differentiate among these conditions (American Psychiatric Association, 2000; M. K. Cohen, 1994; Nelson, 1992; Skiba & Grizzle, 1992).

"Internalizing" disorders are those in which the impact of emotions is directed inward. These include the following (American Psychiatric Association, 2000):

- Substance abuse.
- Feeding and eating disorders—students with anorexia nervosa, bulimia, and related conditions.
- Anxiety and social withdrawal.
- Depression—signs typically include sad, lonely, or apathetic behavior; avoidance of social contacts; chronic problems with sleeping, eating, or elimination; fear of being with others in public places; and talk of suicide.
- Schizophrenia and psychosis—schizophrenia is diagnosed when two or more of the following symptoms are present: delusions, hallucinations, disorganized speech, disorganized or catatonic behavior, and problems in the ability to think logically or make decisions.

Unfortunately, we are failing to support these children whose lives are often very difficult. Research (Cullinan, Epstein, & Sabornie, 1992; Office of Special Education Programs, 1999; Wagner, 1995) indicates that students labeled emotionally disturbed are disproportionately likely to be:

- Male
- African American
- Economically disadvantaged
- In secondary school
- Living with one parent, in foster care, or in another alternative living arrangement

Boys are more likely to be aggressive and disruptive in the classroom (Boggiano & Barrett, 1992; Gresham, MacMillan, & Bocian, 1996). Young women are more likely to exhibit internalizing behaviors (Zahn-Waxler, 1993). Also, some teachers expect Black students to be problematic (Horowitz, Bility, Plichta, Leaf, & Haynes, 1998; Metz, 1994). No biological causes have been established for emotional disturbance. All of the following are significantly associated with emotional disturbance: poverty, malnutrition, homelessness, family conflict, divorce, inconsistent child-rearing practices, and child and sexual abuse (Eber, Nelson, & Miles, 1997; Kauffman, 2008). Fifty-five percent of students labeled emotionally disturbed drop out of school (Wagner, 1995). Black males from poor families are the most likely to be segregated and the least likely to receive counseling and graduate from high school (Osher & Osher, 1996). On leaving school, 73% of dropouts and 58% of graduates are arrested within 5 years (Wagner, 1995; Wagner, Blackorby, Cameto, Hebbeler, & Newman, 1993).

Treatment of students with emotional disturbances sometimes seems designed to exacerbate their problems. These students need "more security, more trust, more love" (Breggin & Ross-Breggin, 1994, p. 192). However, these students are most often (1) separated and isolated from other students, (2) punished, and (3) medicated (Lewis, Chard, & Scott, 1994). Schools often focus on controlling students instead of building on student strengths, and they frequently shift students from place to place (Kortering & Blackorby, 1992; Mayer, 1995; Osher & Hanley, 1996). Punishment may strengthen aggression when it causes pain, when there are no positive alternatives to the punished response, or when punishment provides a model of aggressive behavior. These dynamics play out in many schools where children, mostly low-income males, are not given support and modeling for new behaviors but are punished for aggression. Sometimes boys literally learn from family and teachers how to be aggressive and violent (Kauffman, 2008).

Clearly new directions are needed to help support students with emotional disturbance, including particularly those who are considered socially maladjusted. Students need opportunities to learn positive social behaviors from adults who care about them. For students considered the most difficult, it is particularly important that we help them develop prosocial behaviors. We must reach out to get through to these students helping them to know we care for them. One key element is central in every study that has documented strategies for moving students from violence to positive behaviors: a relationship with just *one* adult. We can be that one adult.

Autism (Autism Spectrum Disorder)

IDEA defines **autism** as

> a developmental disability significantly affecting verbal and nonverbal communication and social interaction, generally evident before age 3, that adversely affects a child's educational performance. Other characteristics often associated with autism are engagement in repetitive activities and stereotyped movements, resistance to environmental change or change in daily routines, and unusual responses to sensory experiences. Autism does not apply if a child's educational performance is adversely affected primarily because the child has a serious emotional disturbance. (IDEA, 2004, section 300.8)

Autism is a neurological disorder that interferes with the development of reasoning, social interaction, and communication. Five behaviors are common in many persons with autism, all related to these individuals' difficulty understanding and relating to social interactions (Koegel & Koegel, 1995; Wagner, 1999):

- *Deficits in language development:* At one point 50% of people with autism did not develop language; today, however, most learn to communicate via language or other tools such as communication boards. This process has led to a reduction in behavioral problems.
- *Self-stimulation:* Repetitive behaviors such as hand flapping, twirling of objects, body rocking, or staring at lights can be subtle or obvious.

The Class Community Deals with a Fight at Recess

One day in Sue's first-grade class two children, Ramone and Vista, got into a huge fight at recess. Students came in telling her, "They started hitting each other and calling each other names, Ms. Sue!"

Sue was very concerned. She had spent a lot of time working to build a sense of community in her classroom since the beginning of the year. Every day they sat in a circle and greeted one another, using a different language each week. Each morning one child was able to take the floor and share something important to him or her. She had students help one another in their work and used cooperative group projects often.

Sue knew that how she handled this problem was important. She could model positive responses; if she was harsh and uncaring, however, students would begin to understand that all her talk about care, respect, and community was just a cover to keep students under control.

"OK, class, let's get in our circle and talk!" says Sue. Her 26 students come to the area of the room that Sue had covered with soft rubber squares that fit together to form a comfortable base on which students could sit. They are quiet and subdued, uncomfortable with the anger and tension that had exploded on the playground.

"So, tell us what happened," Sue asks. "I wanted to play with Ramone and the others but he told me that I couldn't play. I felt left out," responds Vista. Sue replies, "I heard a feeling right there. You said, 'I felt left out.' What is the need that she is feeling?" Virginia, a cute little girl whose family had just moved from Appalacia to the city, says, "Love and belonging!" "Yes," says Sue. "She was not feeling that need being met. What could have happened?" Suzanne raises her hand and responds, "Ramone could have given Vista an 'I message.'" "Vista, did you walk up to Ramone and give him an 'I message'?" Sue asks. "No," says Vista. "What might have happened right then if you had done that?" Sue asks. "They might have told me that I could play with them," Vista responds.

Sue asks the children, "What can you do to make this better the next recess?" "We will be nice," says Ramone contritely. "But what will make it nice?" Sue queries. "Should we have a rule that you can't say to someone, 'You can't play with us'?" The rest of the students then begin to discuss this question. "Clearly both Vista and Ramone got their feelings hurt. But people respond in different ways to hurt feelings. Some people cry. Some get angry. But both have the same feeling. Ramone and Vista, do you think that the two of you can talk together and come up with some ways to prevent this happening again? Can you think of games where everyone can play, where everyone can belong?"

Ramone and Vista indicate that they can walk off together to the side of the class. For the next 20 minutes the two children work together on clipboards talking and writing down ideas. "Look here," says Ramone to Vista showing her his clipboard.

Shortly afterward, it is time for the daily reading of a book by the teacher to the children. "Look at what book I have here," Sue says laughing. The book's title is *You Aren't My Best Friend Anymore*. "How lucky is that," says Sue in amazement. "Molly and Ben were best friends . . . " she reads. Sue reads the book, stopping now and then to ask children questions and talk about what is happening in the story.

After the reading, Vista and Ramone get their list of games and stand in front of the class that is still sitting on the floor in the circle area. "Hide and go seek," says Vista. "Dances," says Ramone as they take turns reading their list of games.

After lunch the class meets on the carpet again. "OK, Ramone and Vista, how was lunch?" They sit next to each other, obviously friends again. "We played together and had fun," says Ramone. "I noticed that you were sitting together at lunch and talking," says Sue. "Class, do you have any questions for Vista and Ramone?" Courtney asks, "Can you tell us what games you played?" "Duck Duck Goose," says Vista. "I think that really improved your relationship," says Degas. "I think so too," Sue concludes. She then directs the class to the math center where she has manipulatives ready for them. "Now for math," thinks Sue contentedly.

Reflections: As Sue's story well illustrates, teaching children how to care for one another, improving their "social skills," is not a separate part of the curriculum but interwoven into every minute of the teaching day. It also requires flexibility. Sue had an important math lesson planned. Instead, she took the time to help her children solve a problem that was important to them. Had she not done so, she might have "gotten through" her math lesson but tension, anger, and hurt would have reigned. In these conditions, students would have learned little. Note also that these were two "labeled children," one as gifted, the other as having a cognitive disability. Sue paid attention to the needs and abilities of each child but in a way that was respectful to each person.

- *Self-injurious or aggressive behaviors:* These may include "skin cutting, skin burning, self-hitting, . . . and bone breaking" (Kauffman, p. 517).
- *Preoccupation with certain objects or a routine:* Individuals may become very upset if a routine is changed.
- *Poor social/communicative gestures and utterances:* Individuals with autism may be unable to make eye contact, acknowledge smiles, or return handshakes. They often use language only to obtain things, not for social interaction.

The incidence of autism has risen dramatically in recent years (Bertrand et al., 2001; Koegel & Koegel, 1995; Varin, 1998). Young children who have symptoms similar to those of autism are often classified as having pervasive developmental disorders (PDDs).

Two programs have been predominantly used with people with autism, each built on a very different philosophy. Lovaas (1987) developed an intense program involving intensive behavior modification techniques known as **applied behavior analysis (ABA)**. This controversial, expensive treatment takes place over 3 years and continues some 40 hours per week, 365 days per year. Some researchers have questioned the validity of claimed results; they have further expressed the concern that the program virtually demands a segregated setting (Gresham & MacMillan, 1997).

Other approaches rely on strategies for teaching positive behaviors using a range of tools in typical settings. **Treatment and Education of Autistic and Related Communication-Handicapped Children (TEACCH)** develops an individual program based on a child's skills, interests, and needs. Teachers organize the physical environment, create schedules, use visual materials, and make expectations very clear. This program seeks to foster independence by encouraging the development of skills to the point where the child can use them without adult prompting. This approach has been successful and is conducive to inclusive teaching (Varin, 1998).

Often people with autism do not understand their own feelings, as if their inner self is trapped behind fear and they are able to respond only by mimicking learned behaviors, such as motions or phrases they have been taught or seen on TV. Breaking out of this cage by communicating what they feel is a traumatic, intense experience. Basic things that are automatic processes for many people, such as knowing what food we like, holding someone's hand, or talking to new people, are extremely difficult for people with autism (Williams, 1994a,b).

Inclusive schooling is critical in helping students with autism develop social skills and become part of their communities. By sheer repetition of appropriate modeling, direction, and practice, children's social responses become more comfortable and their ability to think through a problem becomes more easily accessed (Wagner, 1999). Children with autism have strong visual skills, excellent ability to recognize details, and an amazing memory. These can become the basis for a successful life and can add to a classroom community.

Strategies for Students with Behavioral and Emotional Challenges

Following are key strategies for students who present behavioral, social, and emotional challenges. We will explore these in greater detail in later chapters.

- Commit ourselves to engaging, supporting, guiding, and teaching students with emotional and behavioral challenges and in working to develop relationships where we communicate that we care for them.

- Teach with creative and engaging activities to help provide a positive, meaningful school experience.
- Provide options and choices that respond to individual needs and learning styles. These include varied places to work (table, desk, floor, in the hall), places to be alone and comfortable (cushions, headphones, underneath the teacher's desk), varied lighting, and so on.
- Provide positive outlets for student energy—opportunities for movement and creative expression.
- Help all students organize their materials and monitor their scheduling and completion of learning activities.
- Develop class structures for emotional support through circles of support, peer partnerships, and class meetings.
- Develop predictable class routines and help students understand changes that may occur.
- Form a personal relationship with students.
- Build community and provide emotional support letting students know we are available to help.
- Help develop a place for supervised support where students can go to cool off, obtain academic assistance, or problem solve with an adult.
- Integrate social skills learning into all academic lessons on a moment-by-moment basis. Use a range of strategies to help students learn needed social skills including social stories that help a student rehearse behavior in a difficult situation and picture schedules.
- Use positive behavior supports strategies that affirm students' needs, explore the reasons for behaviors, and work to help students have their needs met in new ways and develop effective social skills.
- Help students understand their own needs and proactive ways to have those needs met.
- For students with seriously challenging behaviors, work with an interdisciplinary team to develop an intensive behavioral support plan.
- Use professional supports and services such as individual and group counseling, consultation with a psychologist of social worker, and support groups for students and families.
- Facilitate support for ourselves via informal and formal consultation with other teachers, behavior specialists, and other professionals.

Students with Differing Communication, Physical, and Sensory Abilities

Students also come to us with a wide range of disabilities that are based on physical functioning. These include communication, hearing, seeing, physical movement, and health and well-being. Here we'll introduce you to common disabilities we will see in the classroom.

Severe and Multiple Disabilities

Some children have severe disabilities that impact many areas—academic and physical abilities, adaptive skills, cognitive functioning (Meyer, Peck, & Brown, 1991, p. 19). The bodies—arms, legs, face, trunk—of many of these students are shaped very differently from those of other children, resulting in an appearance that seems disfigured to many people.

Traditionally these students were placed in separate schools or classes along with students with other severe disabilities. At first this makes sense, in light of their intense and specialized needs. However, observing such classes, even with the very best teachers and equipment, leads to other conclusions. Typically, a teacher might have 6 to 9 children in a class with two paraprofessionals. That's a ratio of 1:3. However, because these students need one-to-one attention, they sit waiting two thirds of the time. But when they are in a general education class, using learning activities based on the general curriculum yet adapted to their ability level, there is much ongoing interaction with other students that enhances communication, a key need of these students. Inclusive classrooms offer these students the equivalent of 24 teachers. Many studies have demonstrated the positive impact of inclusion for these students (Berrigan, 1994; Cole & Meyer, 1991; Hunt, Farron-Davis, et al., 1994; Janney & Snell, 1997; Meyer, Peck, & Brown, 1991; McGregor & Vogelsberg, 1998).

Communication Disorders

IDEA defines a **communication disorder** as "stuttering, impaired articulation, a language impairment, or a voice impairment, that adversely affects a child's educational performance" (IDEA, 2004, section 300.7). Children can become frustrated and humiliated when they have difficulty understanding others and expressing themselves. Some 7 to 10% of school-age children receive speech services. The vast majority of students with communication disorders also have another disability that is considered more significant (McCormick, Loeb, & Schiefelbusch, 1997).

Language disorders involve difficulty or delays in using oral and written symbols such as using words inappropriately and having difficulty learning grammatical patterns, distinguishing speech sounds, and comprehending. **Articulation disorders** occur when students have trouble articulating sounds, maintaining fluent speech rhythms, and controlling their voice (McCormick, et al., 1997).

Speech therapists (also called speech pathologists) work with students to improve their communication abilities. **Augmentative and alternative communication (AAC)** specialists are typically trained as speech therapists (McCormick et al., 1997). In the field of speech therapy, there is a growing movement toward "naturalistic" services (McCormick et al., 1997; Office of Special Education Programs, 2001) in observing language and providing services in natural environments, such as their classroom or homes. In inclusive schools speech therapists often come into the classroom to engage students in individual or group learning activities designed to improve both articulation and language development.

A teacher helps a student focus on strengthening the voice and interest in his lead sentence for a short story he is writing in a language arts class.

BUMpS IN THE ROAD   *Rejecting Students with Differences*

Sometimes teachers and other educators in your school will outright reject students with differences. While this has largely become unacceptable behavior related to students from various racial and cultural backgrounds, such rejection of students with disabilities and students who are gay is typically tolerated, sometimes overtly encouraged. Of course, racial discrimination often exists in more subtle ways.

One high school we visited was, for the first time, planning to fully include a student with severe, multiple disabilities. The student, Shawn, was in a motorized wheelchair. He did not have the strength or dexterity to propel himself and was unable to communicate verbally, but he did have a reliable sign with his hands for yes and no. He also had medical complications including a condition that made his bones very brittle. Shawn had been fully included in elementary school and middle school and many students knew him, some of whom had been in his circle of friends.

Shawn's parents had been anxious about his coming to the high school because the educational program there was rather rigid, rather than the flexible and student-centered experiences they had in elementary and middle school. The 9th-grade team that had agreed to work with Shawn had been very positive, however, so they felt more comfortable at the beginning of the year. But as classes started, two of the general education teachers suddenly became very resistant and angry. They approached the union representative complaining that teaching a student like Shawn was not in their contract. Jennifer, the special education coteacher, tried to talk with them but they remained hostile. She actually thought they might hit her! Phillip, one of these teachers, made the comment that really hurt: "Why is he in here? He can't do anything. He's just a vegetable!" It took some very hard work to get through this. Eventually Shawn was moved from this team to another 9th-grade team and his year progressed well after that.

This is but one example of many that we might encounter. Although this example related to a student with a severe disability, we've been aware of angry, hurtful comments about students who are gay, who have mild learning disabilities, or who are poor. Oftentimes we'll find that when educators reject children who belong to one category they do the same for other types of differences.

What do we do when we encounter such attitudes? As always, we don't have magic answers. Intolerance, discrimination, and hurtful comments are an unfortunate part of the human condition. However, here are a few suggestions:

- First, as you can't let your students harm others, neither can this action be tolerated by staff members. If we don't challenge such actions, we are actually encouraging this behavior. It's helpful to bring it back to questions like: "What do we want for our students? Do we want our students rejected? Do we want to commit to teaching all or just some students?"
- Second, don't draw away from a relationship with the person. Be there to talk through feelings. It may well be that if such people can be confronted while at the same time given opportunities to explore their feelings and emotions, they may change their perspective.
- On the other hand, it's clear that some people are so committed to intolerance that we may not be able, at this point at least, to help them. It's important that we not spend all our energy on these individuals. Rather, we seek to contain the harm they cause people and work around them, connecting with those who are more positive and with whom we can work. Over time, as we are successful and others sign on to the effort, those with negative attitudes will see they are in the minority and, at minimum, check their hurtful responses.

You might think about experiences you have had where educators rejected children. Why do you believe they did this? When you encounter such behavior again, what might you do?

Deafness and Hearing Impairment

IDEA defines these two conditions in the following way:

"Deafness" means a hearing impairment that is so severe that the child is impaired in processing linguistic information through hearing, with or without amplification, and that adversely affects a child's educational performance. "Hearing impairment" means an impairment in hearing, whether permanent or fluctuating, that adversely affects a child's educational performance but that is not included under the definition of deafness in this section. (IDEA, 2004, section 300.7)

Students who are **deaf** cannot use their hearing to understand speech, even with amplification. Students who are **hearing impaired** have a loss of hearing but they can often understand speech. Hearing loss can be slight (27–40 decibels) that causes difficulty in hearing faint or distant speech to profound (loss of 91 or more decibels) that results in ability to hear only occasional very loud sounds. Loss of the ability to hear speech profoundly influences social interactions (Gething, 1992; Hardman, Drew, & Egan, 1996; D. Smith, 1998; Vaughn, Bos, & Schumm, 1997).

We may come into contact with several types of professionals who specialize in dealing with individuals who are deaf or have a hearing impairment:

- *Audiologists* assess hearing loss and prescribe tools to improve hearing, such as hearing aids.
- *Sign language interpreters* translate spoken words into sign language. As the deaf person signs back, the interpreter speaks the signed words to other parties.
- *Augmentative hearing specialists* develop and prescribe devices such as hearing aids and speech augmentation tools.
- *Special education teachers* are certified to teach students who are deaf or hard of hearing.

Students who are deaf or hard of hearing will need assistance in being part of the class and in overcoming the isolation that can occur because of problems in receiving information. In addition, students who are deaf often struggle to develop academic language skills—both oral and written. Students who are deaf or hearing impaired have challenges both in *expressing* themselves and in *receiving* information. When communicating with students who are deaf or hearing impaired, the key is to be natural. What we *don't* want to do is yell or talk very loudly. This typically distorts our voice. Nor do we want to exaggerate our facial gestures. We will find many of the strategies for students with different academic abilities useful with students who are hearing impaired. Tools that are specific to hearing loss include the following:

- *Use alternative modes of communication.* **Sign language** involves signals using the hands and fingers. Signs are produced for each word using standard English syntax in **signed English,** a cumbersome process. **American Sign Language (ASL)** uses its own syntax. Signs may abbreviate or contain multiple words to allow more efficient communication. Many deaf adults prefer ASL. **Finger spelling** occurs when words are spelled using finger signs for each letter (Beukelman & Mirenda, 1992). When sign language is used in the classroom, an interpreter is often available. **Speechreading** occurs when a deaf person learns to understand by watching another person speak. Speechreading is an extremely difficult skill used by a small percentage of people who are deaf.
- *Use technology to enhance communication.* **Hearing aids** can help students with mild hearing losses. However, the hearing aid amplifies all sounds, not just speech, making sounds louder but not necessarily clearer. An **FM unit** is a device in which the teacher

SAM'S TEACHER IS DIAGNOSED WITH A
"TEACHING SPECTRUM DISORDER."

wears a wireless microphone and the student wears a wireless receiver. The unit amplifies the teacher's voice 12 to 15 decibels over the rest of the classroom noise.

- *Use sound field amplification.* The teacher wears a wireless microphone and the sound comes out of speakers placed around the room. A **cochlear implant** is surgically implanted inside the ear and picks up sounds from a microphone electrically stimulating the auditory nerve (Gething, 1992; Hardman, et al., 1996).
- *Use visual materials in instruction.* Use a range of tools and materials that do not rely on hearing for effectiveness. These can include written and pictorial directions, and written materials that use pictures and graphics along with the written word at various levels of ability. Also, using cooperative learning, experiments, learning projects, and other authentic learning strategies is very helpful. *Provide copies of notes* taken by another student (Banks, 1994; Vaughn, Bos, et al., 1997).

Visual Impairment and Blindness

The definition of **visual impairment** in IDEA is pretty simple and straightforward:

> Visual impairment including blindness means an impairment in vision that, even with correction, adversely affects a child's educational performance. The term includes both partial sight and blindness. (IDEA, 2004, section 300.7)

Visual problems are related to either (1) visual acuity or (2) field of vision. **Visual acuity**, or sharpness of vision, is measured based on the distance from which an object can be recognized. Perfect acuity is described as 20/20 vision. This means that an individual can see an object clearly at 20 feet. However, if an individual is able to read at 20 feet only what a person with 20/20 vision could read at 200 feet, we would describe that person's visual acuity as 20/200. **Visual field** refers to the angles from which the eye receives sensory input. Some individuals have narrow visual fields or *tunnel vision,* as low as 10 degrees. Others have limited vision in the center of the visual field but have *peripheral vision* (Gething, 1992).

The word *blindness* to most people means the inability to see at all in any functional way. However, many people considered blind still perceive some light or shapes. People who have low vision or who are partially sighted are considered *legally blind* when their visual acuity is better than 20/200 but not better than 20/70 in the best eye after correction or when their visual field is less than 20 degrees (Vaughn, Bos, et al., 1997). For clarification, simply ask the student how well she can see—in terms of light, shapes, acuity, and visual field.

Several professionals provide assistance to people who are blind or visually impaired, some of who—may assist us when blind or visually impaired students come to our class.

- *Ophthalmologists* are physicians who specialize in diseases, treatment, and functioning of the eye.
- *Optometrists* prescribe corrective lenses for visual difficulties.
- *Low-vision specialists* help individuals use tools to use their existing vision.
- *Rehabilitation teachers* help persons with blindness learn adaptive methods to function including Braille, taped books, and how to organize materials.
- *Assistive technology specialists* assist in identifying and helping students to use low and high tech assistive technology tools.
- *Orientation and mobility specialists* teach people how to use canes, sighted guides, and guide dogs. They orient a person to a new area—school grounds, a work site.
- *Special education teachers* provide instruction related to academic learning.

Following are specific strategies for assisting students who are blind or visually impaired:

- Provide learning activities that rely on senses other than sight, including groups working together, hands-on projects, and learning by doing. We give students with visual disabilities opportunities for obtaining input via touch, sound, even smell in ways that deepen and strengthen their learning (D. Smith, 1998).
- Learn how to be a good *sighted guide*. We should *not* take the student's hand and lead her around. Instead, have the student put a hand on the back of our elbow or arm. As we go through a narrow space, we walk first, putting our arm behind us so that the person can hang on. If there are overhanging obstacles, such as a low-hanging tree limb, warn the student. When we come to stairs, we stop and say, "Stairs," then proceed up or down at a smooth pace.
- Orient the child to the classroom by walking with him around the room explaining what is there, giving him an opportunity to feel with his hands—to touch the table, the globe, and so forth. For example, "Your pencil is right in front of you, about 1 foot" or, "The globe is at 45 degrees left." We might also use the numbering system on a clock face, as in "Your mashed potatoes are at twelve o'clock on your plate, and your steak is at nine." Also, if we change the layout of the room during the year, tell the student about these changes.
- Utilize an orientation and mobility specialist to help students learn to use these tools for getting around safely: (1) Use a *cane* by swinging it in front of the student from side to side to feel obstacles or dropoffs; barriers above waist level cannot be detected. If we see a student about to walk into an overhanging barrier, warn him or her. (2) Use a *guide dog*. The student and the dog learn to work as a team. However, the student is in charge and guides the general direction of the dog. The dog should not be petted when it is working.
- Use touch tools to access written materials. Touch-based strategies include *braille* and optacon. **Braille** uses six raised dots that represent different letters. Reading braille is much slower than visual reading and is difficult to learn. We can get books brailled through the Library of Congress and through local groups. In addition, braillers (braille typewriters) and braille printers for computers are available. We work with specialists to consider how a student will learn braille. This may occur on a pull-out basis or be incorporated into our class. Many students attend programs

outside of school where they learn braille. An **optacon** or similar tool scans text and converts the letters into vibrating tactile replicas.

- Use auditory tools to access written materials. These include software that speaks written words on a computer; a **Kurzweil scanner** that scans text and converts it to synthesized speech; tape-recorded words such as directions for activities; recorded books and other materials (many blind people use variable-speed tape recorders that allow them to listen to text at different paces to increase their "reading speed"); and sighted readers, which can include other students in the class or people who are paid to assist the student. Additionally, reading services could be provided by a teacher or a paraprofessional.

- Use large print for partially sighted students. Included are large-print books; low-vision aids: handheld magnifiers, desktop magnifiers, and devices designed to be used with computers: computer software and enlarged printouts: software is available that will increase the size of text and graphics on the monitor screen and will print enlarged text; and closed-circuit television (CCTV): a camera is pointed at printed text and magnifies it on a television screen.

- Use alternative methods to support students in writing using these tools: recording student work on a tape recorder or computer; type work on a typewriter or word processor; a sighted person takes dictation, then transcribes the material; and software that allows an individual to dictate responses, which are recorded in a word processer and printed.

- Help students organize and access materials. Use brailled tabs or other tactile tabs on materials so they can be identified via touch and organizing of materials where they are kept in routine locations.

- Help students participate in all class activities. Watch for visual information that other students are receiving. Sometimes we can give tactile (touch) alternatives. Often we will need to explain in words what is going on.

- Measurement devices. Many measuring devices are available that have either tactile markers or synthesized speech.

Orthopedic Impairment

Many states have grouped students with orthopedic and other health impairments under a category they label "physical and other health impairments (POHIs)" in their special education services. This section will discuss common orthopedic disabilities. IDEA defines orthopedic disabilities as follows:

> "Orthopedic impairment" means a severe orthopedic impairment that adversely affects a child's educational performance. The term includes impairments caused by congenital anomaly (e.g., clubfoot, absence of some member, etc.), impairments caused by disease (e.g., poliomyelitis, bone tuberculosis, etc.), and impairments from other causes (e.g., cerebral palsy, amputations, and fractures or burns that cause contractures). (IDEA, 2004, section 300.7)

One condition we will likely see is **cerebral palsy**, a neurological condition that affects the portions of the brain that control motor movements. Students with cerebral palsy often have other disabilities that may include intellectual disability, seizure disorder, and visual and/or hearing impairment (Gething, 1992). However, many people with cerebral palsy have normal intelligence and have distinguished themselves in their social contributions. An interdisciplinary team of specialists is often involved that may include physical therapists, occupational therapists, and assistive technology specialists (Bigge, 1991; Gething, 1992; Hardman et al., 1996; Orelove & Sobsey, 1987; Stolov & Clowers, 1981).

Spinal cord injuries occur when the spinal cord is damaged or severed. Essentially, the higher on the spinal cord the injury, the more disabling the effects. In addition, spinal cord injuries often occur together with damage to other body parts. Three general terms are used for individuals with different types and levels of injury:

- *Paraplegic:* The person's legs are immobilized but there is full use of the upper body and arms.
- *Quadriplegic:* Both legs and arms, as well as the upper body, are affected.
- *Hemiplegic:* The arm and leg on one side of the person's body are paralyzed.

Spinal cord injuries are traumatic events. Typically, young, active, athletic people must learn a new life. In the hospital physicians work to stabilize the spine, often with patients held in a special device that rotates them periodically. In the rehabilitation process individuals must learn new ways of managing their lives, using adaptive equipment and wheelchairs and moving from the wheelchair to a bed or couch.

In **spina bifida** an abnormal opening in the spinal column occurs at birth. Severe spina bifida often results in weakness or paralysis in the legs and lower body and an inability to control the bladder or bowel. The most serious form often involves other orthopedic difficulties, such as club feet or dislocated hips. About 90% of children with severe spina bidifa also develop **hydrocephalus**, an excessive accumulation of cerebral fluid in the brain. Untreated, hydrocephalus will result in an intellectual disability. However, physicians perform surgery to install a shunt, in which a tube is inserted between the ventricles of the brain and distributes fluids to an absorption site in the child's abdomen. Although students with spina bifida have little if any control over bowel or bladder, medical professionals assist them in learning to use a catheter to manage this process (Bigge, 1991). Spina bifida does not affect intellectual abilities, and most students have traditionally been in general education classes.

The muscles of students with **muscular dystrophy** will gradually degenerate, and they slowly lose their ability to walk and/or to use their arms and hands effectively. With this condition fatty tissue actually replaces muscle tissue over time. By age 20 individuals with muscular dystrophy use a wheelchair for mobility; they typically die in their twenties or thirties. Medicine has no cure, so the primary treatment consists of aiding the individual in maintaining functioning as long as possible, then providing supportive devices such as walkers, braces, and surgical corsets.

Other Health Impairments

Children have many health-related disabilities that IDEA calls *"other health impairments."* These involve limitations in

> strength, vitality or alertness, including a heightened alertness to environmental stimuli, that results in limited alertness with respect to the educational environment; that is due to chronic or acute health problems such as asthma, attention deficit disorder or attention deficit hyperactivity disorder, diabetes, epilepsy, a heart condition, hemophilia, lead poisoning, leukemia, nephritis, rheumatic fever, and sickle-cell anemia; and adversely affects a child's educational performance. (IDEA, 2004, section 300.7)

Not too many years ago, children died of serious diseases that physicians today can treat if not cure. If they lived, they would stay at home visited weekly by a special teacher for the "homebound" and later go to a separate school. However, many students with other health impairments are now returning to their school community. Common chronic health impairments include asthma, cystic fibrosis, diabetes, pediatric cancer, lead poisoning, and sickle-cell anemia.

Epilepsy and **seizure disorder** include a range of disorders in which abnormal neuro-chemical activity in the brain produces seizures. Although seizure disorders may occur alone, they also are frequently associated with other disabilities. About half of individuals with seizure disorders experience an "aura," a physical sensation that a seizure may soon occur—numbness, dizziness, or slight abdominal discomfort.

Tonic-clonic seizures (once known as *grand mal* seizures) cause a loss of conscious awareness, as the body goes rigid and convulsively jerks. If the person is standing, he or she will likely fall. Seizures typically do not last more than a few seconds. Once a seizure is over, the student will be tired and sometimes confused. **Absence seizures** (previously known as *petit mal* seizures) occur almost exclusively in young children and students often outgrow them. In these seizures students briefly lose consciousness where they appear to stare with slow rhythmic blinking of the eyes. Such seizures are difficult to notice at first. However, if students are "blanking out" many times an hour, they will have difficulty attending to the flow of learning. If we see these patterns occurring, talk with the school nurse and parents to facilitate a medical examination. **Psychomotor seizures** are so called because a part of the brain that controls physical activity is activated. However, psychomotor seizures are rare in children (Stolov & Clowers, 1981).

When a seizure occurs, or if the person has an aura, do the following (Gething, 1992; Hardman et al., 1996; Stolov & Clowers, 1981):

- Ease the student to the floor, preventing the student from falling and clearing an area to prevent banging against harmful objects. Put a pillow or jacket under the student's head and loosen tight-fitting clothes at the neck.
- Turn the student on the stomach with the head to the side to drain excess saliva.
- When the seizure has stopped, cover the student and let her rest.
- If the seizure lasts more than 10 minutes, contact a health professional. However, this is very rare.

We *should not* place anything in the student's mouth. This can result in the student's choking, cracking teeth, or even injuring us, as their biting movements are very powerful during the seizure. (Despite popular myths, it is not possible for people to swallow their tongue!) We will teach students in the class what to do as well so they can assist as needed. The pattern for seizures varies.

We will want to talk openly with the student and parents and get information about what happens and how best to respond.

- How often do your seizures typically occur?
- How long do they last?
- Are there stimuli that help set off the seizures? (Heat, stress, and light patterns can all have this effect.)
- How do you act when you have a seizure? What is best for us to do?
- Do you need or want to rest after seizures? For how long?
- What else should we know?

We engage our class in planning ahead for seizures and promote discussion in a calm manner. However, we want classmates to be able to share their feelings about the seizures in supportive ways. Sharing helps students with seizures feel accepted and helps other students obtain complete information.

Seizures are controlled through drug use in some 80% of people (Cornelius, 1980). However, medication can have some side effects—drowsiness, skin problems, or interactions with other drugs. Sometimes drugs are able to only partially control seizures.

Acquired Immune Deficiency Syndrome (AIDS)

In recent decades perhaps no health condition has caused so much concern as acquired **immune deficiency syndrome (AIDS). Human immunodeficiency virus (HIV)** and AIDS involve several stages over a number of years. For many years there may be no sign of the disease at all. At some point, however, the immune system will begin to break down and the person will be susceptible to infections and illnesses. Eventually the immune system collapses and the person dies of infections or tumors.

Most schools have established policies for inclusion of students with HIV. Information about a student's HIV status does not have to be disclosed. It is important that we maintain confidentiality regarding a student. Depending on their status and the stage of the disease, students with HIV/AIDS may be absent because of illness and medical problems. Their energy level may be low, and we may need to make adaptations by reducing their workload or finding other ways to reduce stress. These students may have difficulty with feelings of depression and be concerned about death. Our efforts to support them will be important.

Strategies for Students with Orthopedic and Other Health Impairments

Key considerations and strategies for students with orthopedic and other health impairments include:

- Organize the classroom so there is room for the student to traverse the room and arrange materials so that students can reach them easily.
- Use assistive technology to assist students. For example, use augmentative communication devices and adaptive equipment for computers such as keyboard guards, hardware, and software that will allow text to be scanned and read aloud via a computer and that will allow students to speak words into a microphone where they are translated into written text.
- For students in wheelchairs we will want to have tables at a slightly raised height so that the wheelchair can fit under the table.
- Some students will have difficulty grasping pencils or reaching for books, as well. Use low-tech strategies such as nonslip pads to help stabilize materials.
- Arrange assistance for going to the restroom or in eating, utilizing both the services of a paraprofessional as well as encouraging other students to assist if they are interested and willing. These could be same-age or older students. The paraprofessional or special education teacher may need to provide training for students. You may also want to inform and get approval of these students' parents.
- Ensure that these students are included in our class and the school, including field trips and extracurricular activities.
- Some students with serious conditions may die. We can help students who face death and the rest of our class process and deal with their fears and concerns through journal writing or having the student talk to the group, if he wants. We also can have students learn about the condition of the student with special needs with the student's and parents' permission.

Dealing with Real Diversity in the Classroom

In this chapter, we've viewed our classrooms from the eyes of students who have dramatic differences. We've thought about the needs and challenges of these students. We hope that you continue to see how the overall perspective of building a classroom designed for diversity applies to these students. Inclusive teaching is very different from teaching separately for each student, an impossible task even with a small number of students. Rather, we design classroom structures to incorporate ways of dealing with diverse abilities. Figure 3.3 illustrates a chart that may be a useful tool where you can make notes regarding special needs of each of your students and indicate possible helpful strategies. When you complete this, look down the right-hand column of strategies for the many common points that will occur. Here you will see connections of the needs of many of your students and how you can meet the needs of several students all at once!

If you find yourself feeling a bit overwhelmed, stop a minute. Take a deep breath. Try to capture for yourself a picture of a classroom that can incorporate diverse students. Don't feel that you need to have all the details worked out. If you have a philosophy, understand patterns, and have some beginning specifics, you can use this book and references to make it work. And it will!

FIGURE 3.3

Designing for Classroom Diversity Tool: Some Students in a Fifth-Grade Classroom

			DIVERSITY CATEGORY					
NAME	CULTURE	LANGUAGE	COGNITIVE ABILITY	EMOTIONAL NEEDS	SENSORY	PHYSICAL	SEXUAL ORIENTATION	STRATEGIES
Jawan	African American	English	2.5-grade level Learning disability	Gives up easily	Wears glasses— farsighted	Mild seizures		Daily encouragement Hourly report to mom
Paul	Multiracial	English	7th-grade level Gifted	Often acts bored				Independent study Lead math lessons in small groups
Sari	Middle Eastern	English/ Arabic	4th-grade level	Very strong social skills	Hearing loss in right ear			Invite to share about religion and language Use Arabic greeting at morning meeting
Shauna	African American	English	1.5-level grade level Cognitive disability	Easily upset with friends Hard time reading feelings	Visually impaired			Braille lite, 3-D maps, talking calculator Paired with partner to reexplain activities Partner read with Jawan
William	African American	English	5th-grade level	Loner, social outcast		Poor dexterity	Teased for being gay Has gay family member	Circle of support Counseling with social worker
Beth	Caucasian	English	4th-grade level	Cries easily Overreacts Retained in previous year				Pair with Colleen and Dane Suggest lunch club to hang out and work with them

Traveling Notes

As we seek to be inclusive teachers we will also become a real student watcher, learning daily about their individual strengths, needs, and unique characteristics. We'll continue to learn how best to teach them each as individuals and how to build a true learning community. Here are a few notes about our discussion in this chapter. Do well!

1. An inclusive class will, over time, have students with many different types of challenges. We should seek to understand the needs and characteristics of each individual student and connect these with best practices for inclusive teaching.
2. We should see students as individuals and people first, rather than a member of a group or having a particular label.
3. We will work with a range of specialists who can provide assistance in supporting diverse students in our class, rather than pulling them out of class to provide support and services.
4. We should seek to build a caring community in our classroom where diverse students are respected and supported—including students from various racial, cultural, and ethnic groups; students who are poor; students who are gay; students with a range of academic abilities, social and behavioral needs, and sensory and physical disabilities.
5. We will seek to teach using differentiated, multilevel instruction that allows students to learn together but at their own level of ability. We'll have learning materials on a subject at very different levels of ability and strategies for designing multilevel instruction.
6. When students have behavioral challenges, we will commit to having them in our class, learn how to respond to their needs, and teach them to understand themselves and learn to meet their needs in prosocial ways.
7. For students with sensory and physical disabilities, we will work to ensure that the school and classroom environment and materials are accessible to them. We will help them use assistive technology and other tools that can help them function in the class and learn. We will ensure that they are full members of the class.

Stepping Stones

Following are some activities that will help extend your understanding and actions you may take in understanding special needs of students you may teach.

1. Gather information about separation of students by race, language, and socioeconomic status in your area. What efforts have occurred to create more inclusive communities and schools? Journal the impact you think this has on learning and life success of students? How does your thinking fit with research?
2. Interview a student who attended a separate, special program and another individual who was integrated in a general education class. Ask them to describe their school experiences. What happened? How did they feel about the value of their learning and their experiences?
3. Investigate what happens with students who have significant disabilities in your community. Where do they go to school, work, live? What type of support is available to help them take part in community life?
4. Visit an inclusive school. Observe students with the differences discussed in this chapter in class. What type of instructional approaches are used, and how do these compare with best practices? What happens with these students? Talk with teachers. What do they do differently with these students, and how do they feel about having such students in their classes?
5. Interview parents of students with any of the labels in this chapter. What opinions do the parents have about what occurs in school? What is working and what is not for their child, and why?

4

Planning Individualized Differentiation

Interventions for Students with Special Needs

CHAPTER GOAL

Understand strategies, tools, and services for planning differentiation of instruction and interventions for students with special needs.

CHAPTER OBJECTIVES

1. Use tools for developing individualized differentiation and interventions for students with special needs.

2. Know how to access formal services for students with different types of special needs.

3. Know the procedures for referral and for developing Individualized Education Plans (IEPs) for students with disabilities in special education.

4. Develop an awareness of related planning processes for human service agencies that may collaborate with schools and teachers.

A Peek at Collaborative Consultation: Getting Help and Support

Today we are visiting Halloway Elementary School and will sit in on a collaborative consultation meeting that has been called to discuss the needs of a student who has medical issues. Sherie is a first-grade elementary teacher who works very hard to be a successful inclusive teacher. She has 25 students in her class. Her students include Kyle who has autism and Brent who has juvenile diabetes and a learning disability. Brent's blood sugar levels must be monitored and actions taken if they are problematic. Sherie feels she needs help and asked for a meeting with the building support team.

The support team typically meets every Wednesday at 2:00 p.m. for an hour and a half. Two teams meet simultaneously, and they meet with every teacher each month. The art and physical education teachers conduct special programs with students during this time so teachers can attend.

At this meeting, some additional professionals are present. They include Brandy, the special education teacher who will facilitate the meeting; Barbara, the principal; Rachel, a paraprofessional; Linda, the school secretary; Kris, the speech therapist; and Jo Ann Hardy, a nurse.

After welcome and introductions, Brandy asks Sherie, "How can we help you?" Sherie describes the situation saying, "I am just overwhelmed. He has to be monitored constantly. He knows how to do the measurements himself, but I need to check him. His sugar sometimes drops low and I don't know how much of that has impacted on his work. I have a lot of wonderful support from Jo Ann giving him insulin, but I know he is brittle. I need more help making decisions, monitoring him, and giving him assistance. Right now that is all up to me. Last week medical directions changed three times. I am trying to make a medical decision while attending to the rest of my class, particularly Kyle, my first grader with autism."

They discuss ideas. The nurse indicates that she could train Rachel, the paraprofessional who works with Kyle, in understanding what to do so that she could also provide help. "I would like to receive that training as well," Brandy says, "because I coteach with Sherie and am in her room often." "I would like that," Sherie responds. "I also think I could do two other things," Jo Ann, the nurse, adds. "I could come by your class every few days to check on how things are going so you have some regular medical help available. I could also give you my cell phone number so that if any question comes up you could call me immediately."

Brandy wonders out loud, "Does he need to be placed in the POHI class?" (This is a class for students with physical and other health impairments. While this school has been working toward inclusive teaching, it still has segregated classes for some students, a fact that has caused great concern among some of the teachers.) Sherie immediately says, "No. No. Brent is exactly where he needs to be. I am just feeling the need for some support to make sure that I don't make a mistake." Several others concur.

Sherie asks, "Could he be classified as a Section 504 student?" Barbara, the principal, says, "Well, that doesn't guarantee any help for him." Jo Ann disagrees, "Actually, if the 504 plan specifies what is needed, that is covered by law. I think this is a good idea. Brent is exactly the type of student for which 504 plans are intended."

"Well, thank you all very much," Sherie says. "This makes me feel much more comfortable. Jo Ann, could you come down and talk to Brent before you leave?" "Absolutely," Jo Ann replies.

As we walk out we talk about the meeting. We've been aware of meetings like this in other schools where the adults in the room simply complained a lot about students and their parents. In this meeting, however, everyone was intent on both helping the child and the teacher. They brought ideas together and were awesome in the way that they listened to and stimulated one another in coming up with good ideas. We understand that this process of collaboration is a centerpiece in this school. Not only are there formal meetings as this one but all teachers have been trained in collaborative consultation and often consult with one another on an informal basis. But even in these sessions the teachers document the plans they are going to try.

Individual Differentiation and Interventions for Students with Learning Challenges

As we identify challenges that students are experiencing, we will want to seek to understand their needs and identify strategies to assist them. Problems typically fall into the three key domains: (1) academic performance, (2) social and emotional needs, and (3) physical well-being and health. The **hypothesis testing** model is a helpful way to consider identifying strategies. In this model we work through several steps:

1. Develop a profile of the strengths and needs of the student.
2. Gather information that helps us understand the needs of the student through student-centered observations, student work, and input from parents and others.
3. Articulate a theory regarding the student's challenges and needs.
4. Identify strategies that have potential to assist the student.
5. Use these strategies while collecting information and data to see how well they are working.
6. Review the information and make needed changes.

Too often, as a student is having difficulty, we only attend to the problems we see inherent in the student. This approach, however, is very limiting and often leads to strategies that may deepen rather than help the student's problems. We need to understand the people and environments are mutually interactive. We also need to be clear that keeping a student in a typical environment is key to their growth in learning. Thus, we need a way of thinking that accounts for the interaction of student characteristics and the environment, particularly our

Sights TO SEE

Including Students with Autism and Multiple Disabilities

Student with Autism Included This story is about a child with autism being included in a general education class on YouTube. www.youtube.com/watch?v=qwBvfyVpWUc

Aaron Aaron, a 13-year-old boy who has multiple disabilities, is assisted by a range of assistive technology tools. From the *I Can Soar* video of the National Center for Technology Innovation. www.nationaltechcenter.org/index.php/2007/03/04/aaron/

FIGURE 4.1

Ecological Framework for Individualized Differentiation and Interventions

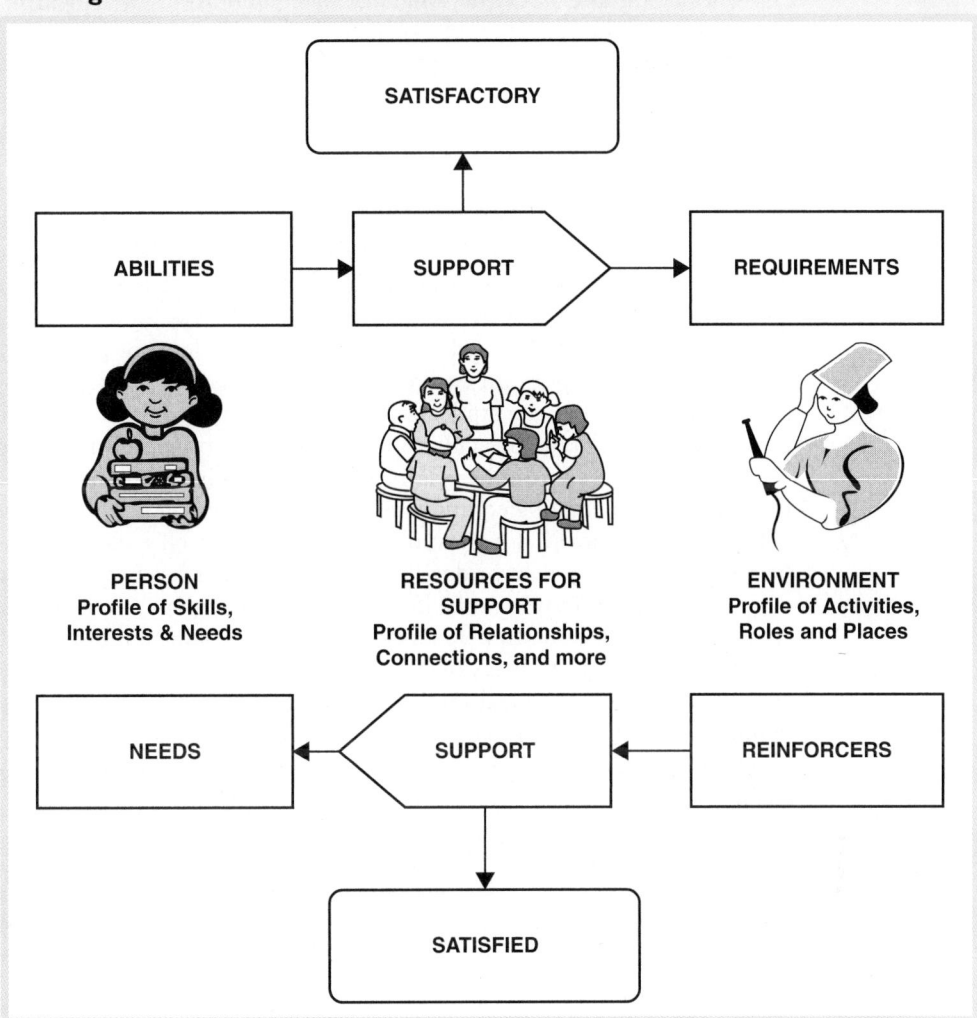

class. The **ecological model of differentiation and interventions** (Figure 4.1) helps us do this. (This model has been adapted from the work of Lofkuist and Dawes [1980] who used it to develop matches between individuals and jobs.)

Let's explore how this model can help us think about differentiation for individual students and how we can use it to think about helping students be more successful in our classes. First, if the needs of a person match the resources provided by an environment, we say the person is "satisfied" and will *prefer to stay* in that setting. Relatedly, if the abilities of the individual meet the minimum "requirements," the person is considered "satisfactory" and is *allowed to stay*. For a person to fit well into a setting, both conditions must be in place: Others must consider the individual to be satisfactory and the person must be reasonably satisfied.

Let's consider two examples:

1. The assignment is to read a book and write a play based on it. I am teaching in a seventh-grade language arts class. However, one student does not read or write well enough to complete this assignment. What do I do?

2. I am a band instructor in high school. A student with a severe physical disability comes to my class. She has very little motor control in her upper arms, is in a wheelchair, and has little language. She cannot play a typical instrument or read music. Yet she is excited about being in my class, the other students think it is neat that she is there, and I would like to involve her. What to do?

In each situation the student's abilities do not meet typical expectations. Traditionally, two strategies are used: (1) Try to change the skills of the person; (2) if this does not work, remove the person. In the first example, the teacher might try to improve the student's writing skills. Yet let us look again at the person (needs and abilities) and the classroom environment (requirements and resources). What could change to improve the student–lesson match? True, we can try to change the student—but we can also change the environment. We can differentiate expectations making adjustments in what is to be done, how a task is performed, or the level of performance expected. We can adjust the resources an environment provides. Perhaps our class is very competitive and this causes many students difficulty, creating feelings of anger and inadequacy. We can work to change our classroom to focus on cooperation and caring.

However, there is another major strategy. Looking again at Figure 4.1, you will see that we have a mediating component between the person and the environment: *support*. What does this mean? If a person's skills do not match expectations, various types of help or support may help bridge the gap. If a student needs to read aloud but has difficulty, a "reading buddy" can be helpful. If a child can't climb the stairs because she is in a wheelchair, someone can help navigate the wheelchair up the stairs. (Of course, an elevator or ramp ought to be available.)

We hope this ecological model establishes a fundamental concept in your mind: If people don't "fit" in our classes, we can differentiate and provide support. This is not about changing people to fit our classrooms. It is about how we design, differentiate, and provide supports to include everyone. Using this model, how might we deal with the situations we described previously?

The assignment is to read a book and write a play based on the book but the student cannot do this. We could change the requirement so that the student is asked to "read" a book on tape and then to "create" a play drawing pictures, recording on the tape recorder, and so on. We involve the student in developing these strategies.

Concerning the student who can't play an instrument but is in the band, we can involve the student and the class. Maybe one of the drummers and this student can work together; he could hold her hand and together they could carry the bass percussion with a simple rhythm. Maybe several students can trade off helping. If the student can use a head-directed signaling device, maybe she could direct a computerized music synthesizer.

Figure 4.2 provides us with an example of individualized differentiation. A high school history class is studying the U.S. Constitution. However, one student reads only at a third-grade level. The three-part form shown here can help us organize our thoughts as we consider individualized differentiation.

Building on the ecological model we already discussed, we can develop individualized differentiation using the four steps outlined in Figure 4.2. When we are learning, we may use these steps sequentially, overtly, and consciously. As with learning to ride a bicycle, however, these strategies will become much more intuitive as they become an integral part of our teaching practice. Note that we will use these steps to help us identify strategies for working with students that may be part of the three-step response to intervention process discussed in Chapter 2. We may discuss these ideas with other team members in collaborative consultation and/or the development of Individualized Education Plans.

FIGURE 4.2

Steps for Differentiating for an Individual Student and an Example

1. Understand student profile and needs—abilities, interests, fears, resources, supports.
2. Analyze our classroom and lesson(s).
3. Determine problems in the student participating and learning due to mismatches between the student and the environment and lesson requirements.
4. Develop solutions—manageable strategies to help the student participate meaningfully, learning at his or her own level.

Here's an example that illustrates steps 3 and 4.

LEARNING ACTIVITY	PROBLEM	SOLUTION
High school history class is to read about the U.S. Constitution and complete a worksheet of questions and answers for comprehension.	Student reads at third-grade level and can't read the text. She also has difficulty writing answers and understanding complex material.	■ Student is given simplified material about the Constitution at her reading level. ■ A peer buddy summarizes key points and explains them. ■ The student works with a group illustrating some key points.

Step 1: Understand Student Needs. As we work with students, we constantly ask the question, "Why does this student act and perform in these particular ways?" When we phrase the question this way, we move toward positive strategies as opposed to asking: "What is wrong with this child?" Notice how we frame the issue. We do not identify a problem as "not keeping up with Grade 3 or Grade 8 work." Rather, we ask, "How do we help the student participate and learn at his or her own level?" This moves us away from the one-size-fits-all curriculum.

We must focus on both student strengths and needs. All students have important strengths, even those with severe disabilities. The danger is that we literally can see only a student's problems. Teachers often send negative notes home. When parents receive only negative feedback, they begin to be defensive and wary. Increasingly, a teacher may see a student as a problem and the student may react by withdrawing or acting out. In turn, the teacher is frustrated and parents are angry and afraid. In effective inclusive classes we communicate about both student strengths and challenges and ask for input from students and their parents.

We cannot progress by focusing only on problems. We can try to make problems go away, but this doesn't necessarily promote growth which can happen only if we *build on strengths* (Falvey, Forest, Pearpoint, & Rosenberg, 1998). When we are concerned about a student, we step back and ask, "What are the strengths of this student?" Then we ask, "How can I use this student's strengths to deal with problems? How can we build on those strengths in a way the student likes?" For example, Julie sometimes acts out and disrupts class, but she also has a talent for making her classmates laugh, and she has shown leadership skills. Perhaps she could be given a responsible role in an oral reading lesson.

This leads us to "needs." *Need* is a powerful word. Asking the question "What do I need?" requires that we also ask the related question "For what?" The needs of students are tied to goals they want to accomplish. For example, a student may need to learn math because he wants to own a bicycle repair shop. Another student may need to improve her reactions to criticism because she wants to have friends. However, the word *need* is often used to express adults' wishes for a student to be a certain way. We hear statements like "Mark, you *need* to do your homework. You *need* to sit in your seat." These things are more *our needs* than those of the student. As we talk with students, we need to own our needs—"Mark, I need you to sit down right now! I am very frustrated." You may find it helpful to write down notes about the strengths and needs of the child related to school as well as home and community. Figure 4.3 provides an example of a student profile that can help us consider both the student strengths and needs.

FIGURE 4.3

Profile for Jonathan

WHAT ARE DREAMS (FOR THIS CHILD)?	NEEDS FOR SUPPORT AND ASSISTANCE
He is happy, gets a job that can support him. He lives near us. He has many friends and has many things he enjoys doing.	He needs encouragement when he is frustrated. Sometimes he gets angry and throws things. He needs help learning alternative ways to express frustration. He needs help in learning to read and write. He needs help in developing his abilities in art.

STRENGTHS OF THE STUDENT?	SUCCESSES?
Great sense of humor. Really likes to draw and is good at it for his age. Good in math.	He was recognized for his drawing ability in an art contest last year.

LIKES? DISLIKES?	GREATEST CHALLENGES?
Likes computers, snakes, doing hands-on activities. Doesn't like group activities often. Loves to draw and likes math and science.	He gets frustrated when he does not do well. He doesn't know how to deal with conflict with other kids and either runs off or gets in a fight.

READING	WRITING	MATH
Limited. Doesn't like to read. Feels like he can't so doesn't.	Very limited. Can write his name. Does like to tell stories with drawn pictures.	Excellent math skills. Best in the class.

WORK HABITS	COMMUNICATION	SOCIAL
Most of the time he attends to work and will turn in homework. When he is frustrated he may lose materials or just not do them.	Poor verbal skills and difficulties getting ideas in writing.	He has two friends. Has difficulty sometimes interacting with kids.

BEHAVIOR	MOTOR	OTHER
See comments about frustration.	Somewhat clumsy and poor at sports. Is self-conscious about this sometimes.	

Step 2: Analyze Our Classroom Environment. When students are having difficulty, we should step back and look closely at our class and school. What do we expect of students? What are the rules? What flexibility is there? How does our class function? How supportive is it? Figure 4.4 illustrates a class profile that we can use to analyze our

FIGURE 4.4

Class Profile

GENERAL APPROACH TO CURRICULUM

- ☐ Interdisciplinary
- ☐ Hands-on
- ☐ Community projects–oriented
- ☐ Project-based
- ☐ Student-directed
- ☐ Textbook-driven

CURRICULUM MATERIALS

For planning
- ☐ _____
- ☐ _____
- ☐ _____
- ☐ _____

For student use
- ☐ _____
- ☐ _____
- ☐ _____
- ☐ _____

ADVANCE PLANNING MEANS . . .

- ☐ Weeks ahead of time.
- ☐ One or two days in advance.
- ☐ As I enter the room.

CONTENT

- ☐ Tend to cover it all.
- ☐ Decide what's essential and add/subtract based on individual needs.
- ☐ Readily depart to follow students' interests.
- ☐ Tend to have single-concept lessons.
- ☐ Anchor it to a major project.

PHYSICAL ENVIRONMENT/SEATING

- ☐ Desks are clustered to promote peer-to-peer interaction.
- ☐ There are small group spaces.
- ☐ Computer stations are available.
- ☐ Bulletin boards are used for:

  _____

- ☐ Students have assigned seats.

STUDENT PARTICIPATION

Peer to peer
- ☐ Mutual helping by students
- ☐ Cooperative groups
- ☐ Peer partners
- ☐ Peer tutors

Self-management
- ☐ Schedule reminders
- ☐ Assignment booklets
- ☐ Study guides
- ☐ Contracts and self-checklists
- ☐ Organizers
- ☐ Frequent self-evaluation

TEACHER PRESENTATION/FACILITATION

- ☐ Moves around a lot
- ☐ Fairly structured
- ☐ Uses questioning techniques
- ☐ Involves all students
- ☐ Gives specific feedback and guidance
- ☐ Gives lots of praise
- ☐ Tolerates low levels of noise
- ☐ Lectures a lot
- ☐ Leads lots of large group discussions
- ☐ Demonstrates and models
- ☐ Uses video, film, audio

TESTS, ASSIGNMENTS, AND EVALUATION

- ☐ Portfolios are used.
- ☐ Grading tends to be based on: ___ curve ___ mastery criteria ___ IEP ___ individual student progress ___ contracts ___ multiple grading (effort and achievement)
- ☐ Maintenance of journal/class notebook
- ☐ Homework given: ___ daily ___ 2–3 times per week
- ☐ Usually takes: ___ 15 ___ 30 ___ 60 minutes
- ☐ Students demonstrate what they learn through: ___ projects ___ written/oral tests ___ written/oral reports.

(continued)

FIGURE 4.4

Continued

CLASSROOM CLIMATE AND MANAGEMENT	HOME–SCHOOL COMMUNICATION
☐ Students must raise hand to talk.	☐ Class newsletter
☐ Students move around a lot.	☐ Assignment notebook
☐ Students have assigned jobs.	☐ Special rules
☐ Students routinely conference with teacher.	☐ Regularly scheduled phone calls
☐ Students select their own work to display.	☐ Homework hotline
☐ Rewards include: ___ praise ___ special privileges such as _____	☐ Daily journals
☐ Corrective strategies include: ___ time out ___ loss of privilege ___ ignoring ___ staying after school ___ peer mediation	

teaching and classroom (Ford, Fitzgerald, Glodoski, & Waterbury, 1997). The profile also provides a menu of potential strategies. For example, under "General Approach to Curriculum" we note that our 10th-grade biology class is largely textbook driven, with some hands-on activities as part of the labs. We consider other options listed.

Step 3: Determine Discrepancy Between Student and Our Classroom Environment. What is the discrepancy between expectations and abilities of a student? Do we expect more than the student demonstrates? Does the student have needs that are unmet? These discrepancies will often be experienced as problems. Using the class profile, we can compare our class assessment with student characteristics and target discrepancies for individualized differentiation. Sometimes such detailed assessment and planning is useful. Many teachers find, however, that the forms are less important than the thinking on which they are based. Such tools can be useful in developing and documenting IEPs and Section 504 plans.

Step 4: Differentiate Instruction to Solve Problems. When there are discrepancies between student characteristics and our class, we can use several strategies.

First, if the student does not have skills we typically expect of students, we can:

- Work to help the student improve his or her skills. This is the most traditional response. However, there are other options.
- Use a different method of performing a task or activity. Perhaps vision is typically required to read. The student might use software that reads aloud messages.
- Modify the level of learning expectations and use adapted learning materials.
- Modify the tasks required so that different skills are required.
- Look for other roles in lessons that have different skills requirements.
- We can also provide support as a teacher or get help from peers.
- Partial participation allows students to participate in the parts of learning activities of which they are capable.

If, on the other hand, our class does not meet the needs of the student, a related set of strategies can be used:

- The class or assignments can be changed or adapted. We can change expectations of classroom assignments or work to have other students be more accepting.

Micah said, "I want to go in the same door as other students."

Micah Fialka-Feldman attends Oakland University in a suburb of Detroit, Michigan through the Options Program. Micah is one of the most popular and involved students on campus and is known by his friends as a very sensitive, caring person. Alex, one of his friends, said recently, "There are many kinds of intelligence. And Micah is one of the most socially, personally intelligent people that I know." Alex is Micah's friend and is also being paid by an adult service agency, the Macomb-Oakland Regional Center, to provide support to Micah as he attends classes and engages in college life.

Micah has a moderate cognitive disability. He is working hard now on learning to read but, until recently, he could only read by the many sight words he knows. He keeps up with current events and his e-mails on the Internet via a screen reading program. He is able to respond to his e-mails and write short paragraphs by using a text-to-speech software program called DragonSpeak®.

In recent years, Micah has spoken all over the United States telling his story. Listening to Micah, you'd be amazed how able he is, how well he communicates given his disability. He has received many standing ovations.

Micah running a 200 meter race.

In Grades K–2, Micah was in a separate special education class called the "opportunity room." It was at the end of the hall and students came in a side door. One day Micah said to his parents, "I want to go in the same door as other students." "What?" said Janice, his mother. He repeated his desire. It was clear. Micah didn't want to be in a separate special education class.

So began a long journey. For Micah's parents it was not always easy because the school administration had very limited experience with having students with disabilities in the general education classes. For Micah, he says, "It was fun! It was what I wanted." To help Micah, other students were invited to join a circle of friends in the third grade. Though some of the students changed throughout the years, this circle of friends was always active and supported Micah all through his high school years. They problem solved issues that came up, but most importantly they had fun together playing basketball, eating pizza, visiting senior citizens, hanging out, and going to dances together. In the tenth grade they noticed that Micah hung out only with the teachers at the school dances. At one of the circle meetings, they challenged Micah to dance with five girls at the next dance. They gave him practical tips on how to ask a girl to make that happen. Sure enough, at the next dance Micah danced with five girls and the teachers rarely saw him

Micah Fialka-Feldman.

(continued)

again. At the last meeting of the circle, they helped him get ready for the school prom. Micah was also elected to the homecoming court.

In high school, students supported Micah in another way, through the LINKS program. Oliver was one student who received credit for helping Micah in his science class. Oliver said, "I took the class to be a LINK because I though this would be an easy A. More than getting an easy A, I got a best friend. I taught Micah about science but he taught me how to teach." Oliver now lives outside of Chicago and he and Micah are still friends. He is a middle school math teacher and relishes teaching students with disabilities. Recently Oliver and Micah presented together at a teacher training workshop on inclusive education.

Since fifth grade, Micah attended and participated in his IEP meetings. He says now, "Nothing about me without me." He learned how to create PowerPoint® presentations to express what he wanted in his IEP. "Here's what I told my teachers so they could teach me," says Micah. "Talk to me. Show me pictures. Send me e-mails so I can hear it on my computer. Ask me questions and give me choices. Give me lots of new sight words. Let me use the Internet to learn."

Micah received support from a paraprofessional, and special education teachers helped general education teachers make adaptations to assignments. In history class, for example, students had to research an influential person in the Civil War and write a paper. Micah created a PowerPoint® presentation with some text and pictures. In a political science class students read materials on Vietnam, explored the politics regarding the war, and wrote a paper. Micah interviewed people who had protested against the war and then made a videotape. Mrs. Schultz, his current events teacher, said, "I was so amazed and pleased how well the other students accepted him. We do a lot of group work and they invited him to join their group. They asked his opinion even though it took him a bit of time to get it out. He gave great presentations using PowerPoint.® I would base his grade on these." Micah also joined the track team in high school. When he started he could run only one block! By his senior year in high school he was running 2 miles and received his varsity letter.

Micah has influenced hundreds of people, helping them see new possibilities for students with cognitive disabilities. You can read more about Micah's experience and watch the award-winning video of his experiences as a student on the college campus at www.throughthesamedoor.com/. Additional materials written by and about Micah can be obtained at www.danceofpartnership.com/.

Reflection: Some people have said, "Well, Micah is 'higher functioning' than students with cognitive disabilities I know. They could never do what Micah does. "Ah!" we think. "They don't understand. For Micah is who he is *because of his experiences*. He was given a chance to learn and grow and he did! How much more might other students grow and develop were they given the chance!" As Oliver, Micah's friend and now middle school teacher says, "Micah and our friendship shows what inclusive education is all about and what it can produce."

- The student might reevaluate his or her interests and needs. Care is needed here, however, so that the student's real needs are not ignored.
- We can also look at having a student play a different role in the class. Perhaps, for example, we devise ways a student can help other students as well as getting help.
- Numerous ways of providing students support may also help meet student needs.

As we are considering strategies, three guidelines are important. First, we seek to differentiate in ways that are the *least intrusive and most inclusive*, keeping students connected. For example, although we could adapt the curriculum by having a paraprofessional and student work on a different activity at the back of the class, this would separate the student. Second, we *provide challenges at her zone of proximal development*, starting where she is and going to the next level. Finally, we select strategies that will *impact on instruction for all students*. For example, a boy is having difficulty reading but shows signs of athletic abilities. We could incorporate more movement into reading lessons. Perhaps he and other students could create and act out a play. Perhaps the whole class could line up to spell words on the playground. Perhaps the student could stand while reading with the book on a podium. We decide to use these ideas for other students.

Tools for Individualized Differentiation and Interventions (Tiers II and III)

Let's discuss several tools useful in developing individualized differentiation and interventions in Tiers II and III of response to intervention (see Chapter 2).

Collaborative Consultation

In effective inclusive schools specialized support staff (special education teachers, gifted consultants, bilingual teachers, and aides) provide ongoing assistance in the general education classroom (see Chapter 5) and all staff learn to collaborate in developing strategies to assist students. Thus, teachers in inclusive settings have daily opportunities to talk with staff about a special student, brainstorm ideas, and develop collaborative strategies. Specialists are often assigned a caseload of students who are being served through formal services but also work with students who have not been referred. Sometimes individual teachers and support staff talk one-on-one. However, effective schools have a team of teachers and specialists that meets on a regular basis to discuss children's needs with us. We'll discuss such "child study" teams in more detail in Chapter 5.

While consultation and discussion can be informal, the more serious the student concerns are the more important it is to develop an intentional, systematic approach with a written plan. Figure 4.5 provides an example of such a plan for an individual student. First, we identify the resources and strengths of the student. Next, we focus on barriers and problems, listing these so we can be specific. We want to break down the problem so we can see it in detail rather than making global statements. Is the student having trouble reading? If so, what specifically do we mean—is the problem understanding text (orally or via print), reading at a certain level, knowing certain types of letter combinations, not wanting to read? At this point, we prioritize issues, asking the question: "What one or two things could we do to make the most difference?" These become a plan of action, describing who will do what, when, and how progress will be assessed. This process provides a valuable base for developing an IEP (see below) if further referral and intervention is needed. However, special education referral rates often decline in schools using collaborative consultation (Hiibner & Fracassi, 1999; Idol, Paolucci-Whitcomb, & Nevin, 1994).

MAPS—A Student-Centered Planning Process

In the early 1980s, allies of both adults and children with disabilities became concerned about the system-centered approaches used in planning for people with disabilities. These advocates recognized, however, that bringing people together could be an important source of support. They created a new form of gathering: the **circle of support**, a group that would engage in person-centered planning and harness the resources of the group to help an individual, a "focus person," achieve his or her dreams and goals. The approach used most often in schools is **Making Action Plans** (**MAPS**) (Falvey et al., 1998; O'Brien & O'Brien, 1998; Snow, 1998b). (Many books, videos, and articles on this process are listed at www.inclusion.com.)

The MAPS process is simultaneously simple, complex, and powerful. MAPS can be conducted as a way to develop the IEP. MAPS includes the planning requirements of an IEP but goes much further. Alternatively, a family or student may meet with a circle of support and develop a MAPS statement that identifies what is needed from the school and/or other human service organizations. A person or family might subsequently ask a member of the circle to attend the IEP meeting.

FIGURE 4.5

Collaborative Consultation Plan for a Student

Student Name: Sasha Levine   **Birthdate:**   **Date:**
School: Bernard Middle School   **Teacher:** Horton   **Grade:** 7
Team members: Horton, Juanita (school psychologist), Barry (special education teacher), Beth (social worker), Jameson (general education teacher), Mona (grandmother).
Initial concern: Reading and behavioral problems

STRENGTHS/RESOURCES	BARRIERS/PROBLEMS/NEEDS
When knows she's being listened to will work hard. Less impulsive lately. Likes hands-on activities. Enjoys reading and learning about astronauts and astronomy. Has a strong sense of family. Loves animals and small children.	Easily distracted. *Textbook in social studies is too hard for her and she gets angry. *Has difficulty making friends. Gets upset when someone talks about her. *Taking medications and seems to get worse when she does not take them.

TARGET GOAL(S)

(Select one or more barriers from above to identify a target goal and devise a plan of action that builds on strengths and resources of the student.)

Help Sasha get materials to read in areas of her interest on her own level that are still age appropriate.
Help her to connect with friends and deal with anger.
Evaluate her medication dosage.

PLAN OF ACTION

What	Who	When	Assessment
Circle of friends.	Social worker and parent help Sasha to get a meeting after school.	Within one month.	Sasha's self-report about her feelings and others' observations of relationships
Get trade books regarding social studies and areas of interest to be included in the curriculum.	General and special education teacher.	This week. More throughout the year. Begin having these types of books for all students.	Record of books read. Observations of Sasha's reading behavior and skills.
New physician visit. Consider effect of medications, whether they are making the problem worse.	Grandmother contact Dr. Diller. Support from social worker if needed.	Within two weeks.	Whether contact was made. Evaluate impact of any changes on behavior and initiative.

MAPS meetings include individuals invited by the student, such as family, friends, community members, educators, and other professionals. While MAPS sessions can be conducted anywhere, they are most effective in informal, welcoming, and comfortable settings. MAPS have been held in homes, community centers, churches, and restaurants,

FIGURE 4.6

Questions for a MAPS Meeting

1. *Story:* What is your history and experience?
2. *Dreams:* What are your dreams?
3. *Nightmares:* What are your nightmares?
4. *Who:* Who are you?
5. *Strengths:* What are your strengths?
6. *Needs:* What are your needs?
7. *Action:* What is the action plan?

as well as schools. At a MAPS gathering, as at an IEP meeting, one person acts as facilitator to help the group answer questions, ensure that all have a chance to talk, and keep the focus on the dreams of the individual. Another person acts as a graphics recorder and documents what individuals say through a combination of words and pictures on a flip chart or long piece of paper on the wall. This use of graphics and color in recording the session helps create a person-friendly dynamic and opens up the more creative, intuitive parts of people's brains. Recording all responses on the wall helps people vividly see ideas and words communicated all at once.

Figure 4.6 outlines the overall agenda for the MAPS meeting. The facilitator first introduces the group, saying something like "We are here to help Mary describe a dream for her life and develop an action plan to move toward that dream." She then leads the group through each of the questions shown in Figure 4.6, always allowing the focus person to speak first, followed by others who add to the question based on their own experience. "Mary, tell us your story. What has happened in your life?" the facilitator may begin. As Mary begins to talk, the facilitator summarizes. When Mary is finished, she asks others to add their perspectives.

The power of the MAPS process derives from the fact that as the group addresses each question, group members often bond over common understandings and deep feelings. Telling the story of the person from multiple perspectives brings the group together. We see the person, not just the disability.

The "nightmares" discussion allows the person and the group to name and identify what would happen if the worst scenario occurred. In this very important part of the process, the unspoken is confronted directly. Naming nightmares allows the person, family, and circle to face their fears and removes some of those fears' destructiveness.

In a typical MAPS meeting, members of the circle give one-word answers to the question "Who is Mary?" This is an amazing time, because the group almost always describes the positive essences of the person. It's encouraging and strengthening.

Then the group talks about strengths and needs. We ask, "What needs to happen for Mary to reach her goals?" The answer might involve Mary's improving skills or getting support and assistance from a peer or teacher. She might need to gain friends to feel comfortable in the classroom.

Finally, the circle articulates an action plan—steps toward the realization of Mary's dreams. This is the phase on which typical IEP meetings spend most of their time. What people discover in a MAPS process, however, is that often the action plan goes quickly, building on the previous discussion. During this phase, we prioritize needs. We can use additional tools such as the curriculum matrix (Figure 4.7) and individual class schedule (Figure 4.8) to develop an action plan regarding what happens in our classes.

The information from the MAPS can be translated into the formal documentation required by the IEP. Needs statements can easily be translated into more formal goals and objectives on a typical IEP form. Sometimes a separate short meeting is held to translate the MAPS ideas into more specific plans within the school and classroom (Knowlton, 1998).

MAPS are often used in schools to plan for students with great life challenges. However, MAPS can be used in many other ways as well. One fifth-grade teacher in Wisconsin divided her class into small groups as circles of support, and over the course of the year each circle did a MAPS on each student. This was done as part of a required curriculum on career guidance. Another teacher used circles and MAPS when students were having problems in her class and needed help and support (Knowlton, 1998; Peterson et al., 2002).

Curriculum Matrix: Connecting Individualized Plans to the Curriculum

The **curriculum matrix** provides a useful tool that answers the question, "How do goals and objectives designated on an IEP relate to the work of the class?" Figure 4.7 illustrates a sample curriculum matrix for a high school student. Key goals for the student are listed in the left-hand column. The curriculum units and school activities are listed

FIGURE 4.7

Curriculum Matrix

FRED BORDEN
First-Year Student, HILLSDALE HIGH SCHOOL

			SCHOOL DAY		
IEP GOALS	Math	Social Studies	Physical Education	Language Arts	Machine Shop
Read six books he enjoys over the semester.		X		X	X
Express himself in writing and through other tools, using his own life and other topics of interest.		X		X	
Learn to use math skills to make daily purchases, manage bank account, and pay bills.	X				
Increase ability to express himself orally.	X	X	X	X	X
Increase positive interactions with peers.	X	X	X	X	X
Improve stamina by walking two miles each week.			X		

across the top. For an elementary class a typical daily schedule might include beginning activities, math, centers time, and so forth. The curriculum matrix helps us plan how to maximize learning for the student in the existing curriculum and helps us identify gaps and appropriate adaptations. For example, if John is working on improving social interaction skills, we can target particular times when this area needs attention. In recording progress regarding each goal, the curriculum matrix again helps us focus: We can make notes on the matrix daily or weekly regarding specific progress. We may find a particular unit or class that has no goals or has a goal not adequately addressed. If this occurs we can revise our plans. The matrix can help identify such gaps (Ford et al., 1997).

Daily Schedule with Supports, Interventions, and Adaptations

One of the key questions we must address in this part of the IEP or any Tier III planning process is: "How much assistance and of what type does the student need to be successful in the general education classroom?" In poorly planned sessions, there is an automatic assumption that a particular disability means a particular type of service. For example, teacher aides may be routinely assigned to every student with mental retardation. What is more helpful, however, is to consider the school day from start to finish and develop specific plans for supports and adaptations. We should ask, "What is going on at this hour? What problems are apparent? How will we solve these?" When we do this, we anticipate problems, work out satisfactory solutions, and clearly identify the specific types of assistance needed. The individual class schedule can be a helpful tool for this purpose. Figure 4.8 shows an example; note that we've included the schedule for home activities to help the team see the connection between school and home.

When we work step by step as a problem-solving group, we often find multiple options to difficult challenges. Take the example of a student with multiple disabilities who uses a wheelchair. We want her to come to school like everyone else. However, neither the school bus nor the school is wheelchair accessible. What might we do? The team brainstorms solutions. In difficult situations like this, having the student and peers there can also make a huge difference. Often they are able to identify solutions not at first apparent (Ford et al., 1997; LeRoy, England, & Osbeck, 1994). Figure 4.9 illustrates a similar planning tool—an overall semester planning format, showing possible differentiation for each subject and responsibilities of support staff.

Putting it All Together: An Example of Individual Differentiation

Let's explore a plan for an actual student in the fifth grade whom we will call Shannell. Shannell has a moderate cognitive disability. She is a very quiet student most of the time. Periodically, however, she gets frustrated and strikes out at other students. Both her parents are supportive, though they are divorcing and there has been much stress in the home in the last 2 years. Shannell reads at about a first-grade level and began to write discernible sentences only last year. The plan for individualized differentiation adaptations for Shannell is summarized in Figure 4.10. Note how strategies related to academics, social-emotional needs, and physical- sensory needs are intermixed and interactive.

When we observe Shannell in the classroom, it's not at all obvious that she is a student classified as having special needs. As we watch her work, it's clear she is functioning at a lower level than many students in the class. However, she participates in the full curriculum—most of which is designed in the first place to allow students to work at different levels. In many ways, differentiation for Shannell simply fits within the teaching used in the class.

FIGURE 4.8

Individual Class Schedule with Accommodations and Supports

Linda Donatello's Schedule
7th grade, McConnell Middle School

Linda has mild cerebral palsy but can walk and speak understandably. She is very pleasant and well liked by her classmates. However, she also has learning disabilities. Her reading and math abilities are at a fifth-grade level, but she's had good instructors and she is enjoying learning.

TIME	ACTIVITY	SUPPORTS AND ADAPTATIONS
7:30	Come to school	Assistance from bus driver in getting safely off bus.
8:00	World cultures	John, a classmate, will make a copy of his notes for her. She will use a tape recorder as well.
9:00	Social studies—literacy team	She will use a computer with a typing guard to do her work. The special education support teacher, Janice, will be available for special assistance as needed.
10:30	Science—math team	Cooperative work groups on projects—take parts of the project she can do.
12:00	Lunch	None.
1:00	Physical education	Once a week the physical therapist will come and help the PE teacher include PT exercises for Linda in his class.
2:00	Technology studies	The class will explore various assistive technology devices, including talking software, as part of the curriculum. Meet with special education support teacher briefly before leaving school.
3:30	After school: Synchro swimming club	Randi will buddy with Linda.
4:30	Goes home	Randi and Linda's parents will carpool.
6:00	Dinner and family time	
8:00	School studies	John, Lisa, and Janeen will team study once per week. Self-monitoring checklist developed with special education support teacher Janice.
10:00	Bedtime	

Michelle, her teacher, laughs as she tells us what happened yesterday in class. It's obvious that she likes and enjoys Shannell. "It was wonderful. We were doing multiplication or column addition, depending on their working level, to find distance on a map. The students needed 640 times 4. I knew Shannell would have problems even adding 640 four times, so I gave her a different strategy to use. I asked her to add 640 plus 640. She was able to do this fine. Then I had her add the resulting sum together again. I pulled all

FIGURE 4.9

Differentiation for an Individual Student and Support in School Subject

STUDENT: *Shane French,* *Grade 9*	ADAPTATIONS	STAFF SUPPORT (if needed)	EVALUATION NOTES
Literacy: Reading and writing workshop. Guided reading. Read alouds. *Adele Smith, teacher*	Books on same topic at Grade 3 level. Focus on periods. Sit next to Christopher to model/ ask questions.	Visits Student Support Center during study hall to read orally and edit stories.	Keep daily log on progress toward goals.
Social studies: Group projects related to poverty in community. *Russell Lee, teacher*	Group asks him questions to draw into discussion. Shane draws picture to illustrate issue.	Supply Support Room with reading about topics so can support if needed.	Ask oral questions to test knowledge of issues. Make up rubric for group project.
Math: Manipulatives, interest groups based on curriculum goals. *Sydney Blanning, teacher*	Working on addition using real-life questions. Use calculator to subtract and multiply.	Works with whole class, checking in daily. Plans block with teacher.	Mark date on checklist when goals are achieved.
Music: Choral production of *Fiddler on the Roof.* *Connie Bueller, teacher*	Listens to songs on tape to memorize. Practices with partner.		Participation in class.
Art: Study impressionist paintings. Do own nature paintings. Self-portraits. *Marjorie Sanchez, teacher*	Shares work with buddies in other classes. Receives help on art he is doing for social studies.		Keep log of strengths seen. Positive aspects to boost morale. Self-evaluate progress.
Physical education: Daily calisthenics, volleyball, team running races. *Harvey Stott, teacher*	Gross motor development worked into curriculum. Cooperative, not individual, work stressed.	Therapist plans with teacher to incorporate goals. Works in class twice a week to assist.	Log of progress kept by teacher. Add notes from therapist in planning. Self-evaluate progress.

the students together and we talked about the different strategies they used to solve this problem. Her peer buddy for this activity, Pedro, explained what they had done as Shannell wrote it on the board. The other students loved this strategy. They decided to call it "Shannell's invention"!

In many ways, Michelle's thinking about adaptations for Shannell is not all that different from her thinking about any of her students. "They all are different," she says. "My job is to know where my students are and to design lessons and adjust as we go to help them grow and develop." She does have assistance and support from Sarah, a special education teacher, who comes in for 45 minutes a day. Sarah does not work only with Shannell, however, but provides support when the class does centers for math or reading and writing workshop. Sarah has been helpful in coming up with hands-on ways to teach subjects.

FIGURE 4.10

Individualized Differentiation for a Fifth Grader

Arrival
- Check in with Michelle and share backpack contents
- Buddy reminds her to sign up for lunch

Choice time
- Works with buddies: reading out loud, listening center, math activities

Reading / Writing workshop
- Scaffolds writing with lines for each word
- Reads books read first with teacher

Science
- Gathers group materials
- Draws / labels in journal
- Books on tape

Shannell

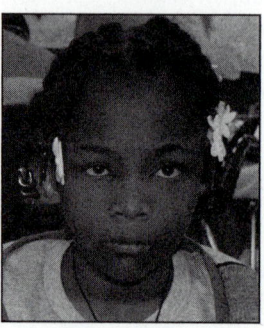

Math
1. Buddy explains directions
2. Manipulatives for concepts
3. Simple goals

Social studies
- Pair for research and write 3 facts
- Group act out historical events
- Draw pictures for notes

Art
- Buddy explains directions one step at time
- Sit with buddy who models what to do

Physical education
- Team games
- Buddy Pair: build friends and directions

Support Staff
- In room 40 minutes a day
- Work with his math group

Relationships
- Circle of support
- Peer buddies
- Discuss feelings and how to handle

Accessing Formal Services
Developing More Intense Individualized Classroom Interventions for Students (Tier III)

If we need more assistance in working with a student and the student could benefit from formal program services in the school, we may want to initiate a referral. Some programs in the school may also provide assistance to our students who do not have individual eligibility requirements, but are provided as teachers identify needs in their classrooms. These may include:

- Media center programs related to literacy and developing computer skills
- At-risk initiatives in which staff provide teachers support in dealing with social and emotional needs of students
- Tutoring and mentoring programs using peer supports and/or community volunteers— these may be implemented during the school day or after school

- Programs aimed at increasing skills of staff related to multicultural education, gay or lesbian issues, needs of students with disabilities, strategies for teaching gifted students, and more
- Supports by school staff including counselors and social workers

Some programs in schools have eligibility requirements and may also have procedures for developing individualized service plans. These most often include the following:

- Dominant-language learners
- Gifted and talented
- Individualized Family Services Plan (IFSP)
- Section 504
- Human service agencies including vocational rehabilitation and community mental health that provide collaborative services with educators
- Special education

Of these, the requirements for referral, eligibility determination, and service planning are very specific for special education.

Dominant-Language Learners

As we discussed in Chapter 1, schools may operate very different types of services for students who are considered having limited proficiency in the dominant language. This term refers to students with "sufficient difficulty speaking, reading, writing, or understanding the English language to deny such individuals the opportunity to learn successfully in classrooms where the language of instruction is English" (PL 95-561). If we are fortunate, these programs will provide push-in, inclusive services rather than pull-out or separate

classes. (We will discuss these in Chapter 5.) When we become aware that students may be having difficulty understanding or expressing themselves verbally or in writing due to language differences we will want to obtain assistance to help these learners. Parents must be informed, however, and agree to proceed.

There are no uniform guidelines or definitions for assessing students as needing second-language services, so specifics will vary among different school districts. A variety of assessments are used to determine students' eligibility for specialized instruction in English. These include home language surveys which parents complete regarding languages used at home; standardized achievement tests; and oral language proficiency tests which most often include the Language Assessment Scales, Oral (LAS-O) and Reading and Writing (LAS-R/W) and the Woodcock-Muñoz Language Survey. Sometimes several tools are used. Most often, however, only one is used as a screening tool. Some schools use criteria other than assessment tools that include parent recommendations, teacher referrals, and oral interviews. Once eligibility is determined, we can work with specialists to develop a plan for students and how they may collaborate with us in the classroom to provide interventions and support (Hull, 2006; U.S. Department of Education, 1995).

Gifted and Talented

Schools and school districts also vary widely in how they determine whether students are eligible to receive services as part of the gifted and talented program. Typical procedures include the following:

Nomination or referral can be initiated by anyone who knows a student, most often the parent or teacher. Often schools will ask a teacher to submit an assessment of the student's ability in "verbal skills, thinking skills, learning behaviors, motivation, and social/emotional development and their potential for meeting eligibility criteria and benefiting from program participation." (Seattle Public Schools, 2008, p. 12). For the referral to proceed parents must provide their consent.

Assessment and eligibility determination can involve formal testing or tools to be completed by teachers and parents. Often schools use the results on state standardized tests to measure academic achievement. Teachers and parents can provide input regarding other qualities not conducive to standardized tests. Some districts will provide additional tests for students who are dominant-language learners or who receive free and reduced lunches, a rough indicator of poverty. For students who are considered talented, information regarding their creative achievements may be obtained. An eligibility committee composed of gifted and talented specialists and other educators will review information and compare this to criteria established by the school or district. For example, the Seattle Public Schools expects a 98th percentile ranking in two of three domains on the tests that they use (Seattle Public Schools, 2008).

Enrollment then occurs in services that the district offers. As we will discuss more in Chapter 5, in an inclusive school, specialists will provide in-class support for students and teachers helping us develop lessons that will be multilevel and differentiated to support these students (Cline, 1999; Kirschenbaum, Armstrong, Ciner, & Landrum, 1999; Seattle Public Schools, 2008; Winebrenner, 2001).

Individualized Family Services Plan (IFSP): Parents of Young Children with Disabilities

With the passage of Part H of PL 94-142, special education began to provide early intervention services for young children with identified disabilities or children at risk of having such disabilities. Such services coordinate multiple service agencies—education, welfare, medical, and others—in providing assistance to children and their families to reduce the

In this middle school, students are practicing dance movements as part of a performance they will do related to the school-wide theme that has been selected this year—"making a better community".

impact of disabling conditions and to promote increased health and skills. Federal legislation requires an **Individualized Family Services Plan (IFSP)** that articulates how integrated services will assist families and their children with special needs. The IFSP seeks to provide family-centered assistance to children (McGonigel, Kaufmann, & Johnson, 1991). IFSPs include the following components:

1. A statement of the child's present level of functioning
2. A description of the status and needs of the family
3. Goals selected by the family and other professionals collaboratively
4. Services, including frequency and duration
5. Evaluation methods to determine whether goals were met

Section 504 Plans: Students with Disabilities Not Eligible for Special Education

Section 504 of the Rehabilitation Act of 1973 requires that all organizations receiving public funds provide equal access to persons with disabilities. Section 504 requires that students have access to the least restrictive environment and be provided with accommodations to enable them to participate in the general education class or to engage in formal assessment programs, such as standardized tests. Schools are required to develop 504 plans to document the accommodations that they provide. Unlike IDEA, however, Section 504 does not provide funding assistance or prescriptive guidelines for how these plans are developed or documented. Typically, schools develop 504 plans for students with ADHD, as well as for students with other disabilities that do not qualify them for special education services. The collaborative consultation plan we discussed previously provides one format for documenting an effective Section 504 plan for a student.

Human Service Agencies: Students with Disabilities

Many human service agencies provide specific services to adults and children with disabilities. Many students will receive services from these agencies. Each agency must, like schools, develop its own written plan of services. Agency and school services should be developed collaboratively and should work in concert. In each state a vocational rehabilitation agency employs counselors who coordinate services designed to help youth and adults with disabilities obtain employment or increase their ability to live independently. For each client vocational rehabilitation agencies are required to develop an Individualized Written Rehabilitation Plan (IWRP) that describes employment, independent living goals, services to be provided, and evaluation mechanisms. Mental health agencies also require individualized plans, most often governed by state law and/or accreditation standards rather than by federal law. Plans associated with these agencies go by many names—Individual Program Plan (IPP), Individual Plan of Services (IPOS),

---

BUMpS IN THE ROAD   *No Child Left Behind and Students with Special Needs*

In the United States, in 2001 Congress passed an educational law that has had great impact. Known as No Child Left Behind (NCLB), the law has required that all students be tested with a standardized test in Grades 3 to 8 and that by the year 2014 100% of students pass the test. The law also has sanctions against schools that do not make "adequate yearly progress" toward this goal. If a school continues not to meet targets, school improvement strategies are mandated; ultimately the school may be disbanded. Parents have the option of sending their children to another school that is seen as more successful. Further, the law mandates that all subgroups—including students from racial minorities, dominant-language learners, and students with disabilities—all make adequate progress. Less than successful performance by any subgroup can cause a school to be considered a "failing school."

This requirement has been very controversial. Educators have been particularly concerned with the requirement to test students with limited skills in the English language and students with disabilities. While up to 2% of students with disabilities may be assessed on an alternative test, many examples have been reported of schools being declared as failing when students with disabilities did not meet the target toward the goal of 100% pass rates.

How has this law impacted on inclusive teaching? Interestingly, it has worked both for and against movements toward inclusive teaching. On the one hand, educators may not want students with special needs in their school for fear that these students will bring down the school's score. In districts where teachers are, in part, evaluated on the basis of pass rates on the standardized test, they may also work to keep students with special needs out of their classes.

From one district perspective, some might argue that all students with special needs be put in one school. This would help strengthen the scores of other schools. The district would have to be content with having this as a failing school. Fortunately, this obviously cynical strategy has not been reported.

On the other hand, many educators have reasoned in ways that actually strengthen the move toward inclusive teaching. "If students with disabilities, second-language learners, and others with special needs are all going to be assessed based upon their performance in a test related to the core curriculum, then we'd better have all students included in those classes!" Numerous school districts have strengthened or initiated inclusive education for this reason. In addition, several districts including those in Boston and Arizona have reported significant differences in the test scores of schools that have been in the forefront of inclusive education.

We've also had many conversations with teachers who expressed concerns that using multilevel teaching will lower their test scores. However, it's also clear that if we teach students at their own level, rather than expecting levels of performance they simply can't do, they will learn more effectively and this learning will also be demonstrated in standardized test scores.

What to do? We suggest that you adopt the language of those who have realized that the best option for improving school district test scores is to include all students in core curriculum classes where multilevel, differentiated instruction is the norm. Be part of discussions in your school and you may help them see how inclusive teaching will help the school be viewed as more successful.

and Individual Habilitation Plan (IHP), among others. It is particularly important to collaborate with these agencies in assisting students in high school develop a plan for making the transition from school to adult life.

Special Education: Services for Students with Disabilities

We may decide to refer a student for special education services. In inclusive schools this is most often done to help the student qualify for specific assistance and resources not already provided. Given that in inclusive schools special education and other support resources work effectively with all students, referral rates are much lower in such schools, often ranging from 2 to 5% rather than the 11% that is now the national average (Office of Special Education Programs, 2000b; Peterson et al., 2002). Of all the formal services, special education has very clear and extensive requirements that are governed by federal law and regulations. Consequently, we will describe methods of accessing and planning formal special education services in some detail.

Referral for Special Education Services. Special education in a school can operate as a wonderful support for students, teachers, and families. Services that can be accessed through special education are numerous—essentially consisting of whatever a student needs to be successful in school. The specific procedures for referral vary across school districts and states. In some schools we complete a simple referral form and document strategies we have tried and the student's response. In other schools we may complete a comprehensive checklist of behaviors and other types of information (Parent Education Project, 1998a; Riester, 1998).

Interdisciplinary Evaluation. Once a student is referred for special education, an interdisciplinary team of professionals conducts a formal assessment to determine if the student has a disability and needs special services. Typically, an evaluation will, at minimum, include an individualized intelligence test and a standardized test of academic achievement, teacher reports, and information from parents. Specialized evaluations from various professionals also may be included—speech and language evaluation, occupational and physical therapy assessments, psychiatric evaluation, and more. For students aged 16 and above, assessment must also consider the transition needs of the student related to employment, independent living, and community participation (Procedures for Evaluation and Determination of Eligibility, 1999).

In most states professionals with special training in individualized assessment conduct and coordinate these evaluations. These individuals' professional titles vary by state—in Michigan, for example, school psychologists do evaluations; in Texas, educational diagnosticians test students. Evaluations must not discriminate against students from different cultural and ethnic backgrounds. Tests must be given in the primary language or other mode of communication, such as sign language, of the student.

The team develops a formal report describing the student's present levels of performance, the needs of the student for services and assistance, and the eligibility of the student for special education services. Eligibility is based on two factors: (1) whether the student has a disability in the categories identified in the federal law and (2) whether the student needs special education services. Parents have the right to receive a copy of this evaluation report and to have input into the decision regarding student eligibility for services and must agree with the decision to provide special education services. Whether the multidisciplinary team actually meets depends on local and state procedures. If the team does meet, however, the parent must be invited to participate

(Michigan Department of Education, 1999; Parent Education Project, 1998b; Riester, 1998).

Collaboration Between General and Special Education. Key in effective educational services to students with disabilities is collaboration between all parties involved, particularly between general education teachers, parents, and special educators. In inclusive schools, of course, such collaboration is built into the daily operation of the school as special education teachers, speech therapists, and other specialists coteach and collaborate with general education teachers. Specialists are an integral part of the building support team and collaborative consultation meetings we described. They will be involved in both Tier I design of classroom instruction and Tier II design of individual interventions for students even prior to their involvement in formal special education services. The current version of IDEA particularly emphasizes the involvement of special educators in such early intervention efforts to increase student success and reduce the number of referrals to special education.

Individualized Education Plan. Once the evaluation team declares the student eligible for special education services, a different team is convened to develop an Individualized Education Plan (IEP) for the child, a document intended to address the unique educational needs of the child. Figure 4.11 describes the legally required members of the team. Parent participation is particularly important; in addition, starting at age 14, when appropriate, students are required by law to attend. Many educators recommend that students participate at all ages, suggesting that their presence encourages those attending to focus more directly on the needs of the child. Parents also may invite other participants such as a parent advocate, a university professor, or staff of the state protection and advocacy agency (see Chapter 6) (Gibb & Dyches, 2000; Michigan Department of Education, 1999; Parent Education Project, 1998a; Riester, 1998; Seyler & Buswell, 2001).

FIGURE 4.11

Individualized Education Plan Team

The law requires that the following individuals participate in the development of the IEP. Other people *may* participate—family, friends, peers of the student, and others.

- The *parents* of a child with a disability
- At least one *regular education teacher* if the child is, or may be, participating in the regular education environment
- At least one *special education teacher*
- *Administrator:* A representative of the local educational agency who is qualified to provide, or supervise the provision of, specially designed instruction to meet the unique needs of children with disabilities
- *Evaluator:* An individual who can interpret the instructional implications of evaluation results
- *Other individuals* who have knowledge or special expertise regarding the child, including related services personnel
- The *child with a disability* (whenever appropriate)

Source: IDEA (2004).

FIGURE 4.12

What Is Required in an IEP? What the Law Says

The term *Individualized Education Plan* or *IEP* means a written statement for each child with a disability that . . . includes:

■ A statement of the child's *present levels of educational performance*, including—how the child's disability affects the child's involvement and progress in the general curriculum

■ A statement of measurable *annual goals*, including benchmarks or short-term objectives

■ A statement of the *special education and related services and supplementary aids and services*

■ An explanation of the *extent, if any, to which the child will not participate with nondisabled children in the regular class*

■ A statement of any individual modifications in the administration of state or districtwide *assessments of student achievement*

■ The *projected date* for the beginning of the services and modifications . . . and the anticipated frequency, location, and duration of those services and modifications

■ Beginning at age 14, and updated annually, a statement of the *transition service needs* of the child

■ A statement of *how the child's progress toward the annual goals . . . will be measured;* and *how the child's parents will be regularly informed*

Source: IDEA (2004).

Figure 4.12 describes the required components of an IEP from the Individuals with Disabilities Education Act (IDEA, 2004). In the IEP we:

1. Identify goals for children with special needs, select services to help them reach such goals, and decide how they will be involved in general education;
2. Specify the placement of the student, particularly related to participation in general education;
3. Describe the services to be provided in terms of amount, frequency, and duration; and
4. Develop a plan for evaluating the student's progress (Federal Register, 1999).

An IEP is a legal contract between the school and the parents. We have the responsibility of helping plan and carry out the services described in the IEP. The legal mandate for IEPs was created, as with all laws, to solve a problem. In this case the problem was that schools were simply putting children in special education without consultation with parents, oftentimes in programs that did not attend to the unique needs of the child.

IEPs can provide powerful opportunities for parents and educators to work collaboratively to develop strategies for supporting a student with special needs. In addition, IDEA provides parents a powerful tool for seeking inclusive education for their children. Parents can go to court to request placement in the least restrictive environment and services that will provide help for the teacher and student so that inclusion is successful. The number of such legal actions, on the one hand, demonstrates that many schools resist inclusive education. On the other hand, the courts are increasingly clear in supporting the move toward inclusive education. Yet parents often feel caught in a bind. Legal action is time-consuming and emotionally draining. Although IDEA requires that schools pay legal costs if the parents win, parents must foot the bill until such a decision is made, and sometimes they lose. Further, forcing a school to comply with a law or regulation often works against parents, as the goodwill and support of teachers and school staff are critical.

We talk with Cathy and Steve about their experience with their son Michael and his IEP meeting. Cathy explains that Michael, who is diagnosed as having mental retardation, had a hard time in first grade. He had attended an inclusive kindergarten program, so "we just assumed he would continue to receive his education in a general education class," Cathy says. Unfortunately, this assumption was incorrect. In Michael's first year in first grade, the teacher did not expect him to learn anything. "In a meeting before the end of the school year, a few members of the IEP team felt Michael should receive his education in a special education class and be 'included' only for music, PE, lunch, and recess. We couldn't believe it!" she exclaims, the tears welling up. "We finally had to tell them that it was not Michael who was failing. Rather, we had failed him. The expectation was that Michael should 'fit in' instead of being accepted for who he is."

Cathy and Steve educated themselves about their legal rights, "arming ourselves with every bit of information we could get our hands on about inclusion." In addition Cathy put together what she called "The Michael Book," a collection of pictures and stories illustrating her son's positive attributes. She hoped that the educators would look beyond Michael's Down syndrome. She presented the book to his new first-grade teacher along with other books and articles on inclusion and Down syndrome.

"At our first IEP meeting for the new year we decided to bring a parent advocate with us," she says. "Fortunately for us, staff had changed and the people who were pushing for a segregated classroom were gone."

Cathy and Steve were wary and cautious as they walked into a room full of unfamiliar people, only a few of whom even knew Michael. "We were totally prepared to battle," Cathy recalls, "but to my surprise and delight, they never even talked about having Michael in a separate class! Instead we all talked about our expectations for Michael, his strengths, and roles for each of us." The general and special education teacher used an "IEP matrix" to match Michael's learning goals to the curriculum. They looked at units of study—for example, America: community formation, community contributors, early settlements, animal habitats, and environment—and identified learning goals for Michael, using the matrix to plan lessons in which Michael could participate. Cathy says ecstatically, "I never in a million years thought I'd see that level of commitment to do whatever it takes. Michael is doing so well. He loves school, he adores his teacher, and his classmates think the world of him. In fact, Michael came home yesterday and told me 'Tiffany . . . wow!'" The delight on his face fills the room with warmth.

Michael's story richly illustrates both what can go wrong and what can go right as we work with students with special needs. The first IEP team had difficulty looking beyond Michael's disability and seeing a whole child. The second group worked collaboratively with the family and were able to see Michael's strengths and capabilities as well as his needs.

At best, all IEP meetings should be like this: meetings where educators and parents positively look at the needs and the strengths of a child. In Figure 4.13 we list a few practical steps to help you prepare for participating in an IEP. In fact, these are the same steps to consider for any child who is having difficulty in your class. First, develop a good picture of the student's strengths, challenges, and needs. Second, make notes on any other information that would be helpful. Finally, identify ideas for working with the student, including supports and assistance you need as a teacher. If you and others bring this kind of thinking to the meeting, you will be able to pool ideas and identify ways to work together. Focus on how this student can be successful in your class. Be open and honest about your concerns, and ask for help and input (Ford et al., 1997; Gibb & Dyches, 2000).

Parents often experience IEP meetings as extremely intimidating, which may cause them to become angry or withdrawn. In addition, often educators have focused only on the deficits of children, leaving their parents with a sense of hopelessness. In Figure 4.14

FIGURE 4.13

Steps in Preparing for an IEP

1. Identify the student's strengths and needs in your class.
2. Identify questions to understand the student's needs and potential strategies.
3. List ideas to meet student needs—teaching practices, support, adaptations, etc.

FIGURE 4.14

Advice for Professionals Who Must Conference Cases

Before the case conference,
I would look at my almost five-year-old son
And see a golden haired boy
Who giggled at his new baby sister's attempts
   to clap her hands.
Who charmed adults by his spontaneous hugs
   and hello's,
Who captured his parents with his rapture with
   music and
His care for white-haired people who walked
   a walk
A bit slower than younger folks,
Who often became a legend in places visited
   because of his
Exquisite ability to befriend a few special souls,
Who often wanted to play "peace marches,"
And who, at the age of four
Went to the Detroit Public Library
Requesting a book on Martin Luther King.

After the case conference
I looked at my almost five-year-old son.
He seemed to have lost his golden hair.
I saw only words plastered on his face.
Words that drowned us in fear and revolting
   nausea.
Words like:
Primary expressive speech and language disorder
Severe visual motor delay
Sensory integration dysfunction
Fine and gross motor delay
Developmental dyspraxia and RITALIN now.

I want my son back. That's all.
I want him back now. Then I'll get on with my life.
If you could see the depth of this wrenching pain.
If you could see the depth of our sadness
Then you would be moved to return
Our almost five-year-old son
Who sparkles in the sunlight despite his faulty
   neurons.

Please give me back my son
Undamaged and untouched by your labels, test
   results,
Descriptions and categories.
If you can't, if you truly cannot give us back our son
Then just be with us quietly,
Gently and compassionately as we feel.
Just sit patiently and attentively as we grieve and
   feel powerless.
Sit with us and create a stillness
Known only in small, empty chapels at sundown.
Be there with us
As our witness and as our friend.

Please do not give us advice, suggestions,
   comparisons or
Another appointment. (That's for later.)
We want only a quiet shoulder upon which to rest
   our too-heavy heads.
If you can't give us back our sweet dream
Then comfort us through this nightmare.
Hold us. Rock us until morning light creeps in.
Then we will rise and begin the work of a new day.

Source: Taken from *It Matters: Lessons from My Son,* Janice Fialka, 10474 LaSalle Boulevard, Huntington Woods, MI 48070. www.danceofpartnership.com copyright Fialka, 1997. Used with permission.

Janice Fialka, a parent of a child with a cognitive disability, gives advice to those of us who are involved in individualized planning in a poem that she wrote after such a meeting. If we come to a meeting frustrated, aiming to remove a child from our class or feeling the need to blame parents, we will make the process very difficult for all. One key strategy is to begin meetings by giving people the opportunity to state and own how they are feeling.

These meetings can either be family- and child-centered or system-centered. System-centered approaches are typically built around defending what the school has in place rather than responding to needs of the child and family. Complex reports, provided in the technical language of a professional discipline, can be overwhelming and confusing to parents, adding to their sense of powerlessness. On the other hand, IEP meetings can be used to develop partnerships between families and school personnel. In the poorest IEP meetings, educators come with everything typed out, expecting parents simply to listen and sign. In an effective meeting, in contrast, the components of the IEP serve as the agenda, and parents, the child, peers, and other educators bring their own ideas and make decisions collaboratively. As we discuss aspects of IEPs you may want to refer to Figure 4.15, which shows a partially completed IEP. However, the goal of the IEP meeting is not to complete a form but to develop a genuine plan to help the student.

Present Levels of Performance: Strengths and Needs. After introductions, the person facilitating the IEP meeting asks the team to review the present functioning of the student. In some meetings individual specialists report one at a time. In more effective meetings, however, team members address key areas of functioning together: academic, emotional–social, and physical across environments in which the student functions. For example, the facilitator might ask people to give brief summaries of Jenny's academic strengths and needs. In response, classroom teachers first share work samples of the student that show Jenny's skill level and needs for improvement. The parents share

Three students work together providing peer editing assistance in Mishael Hittie's fifth-grade class. One student, Clarissa, has a cognitive disability and both gives and gets assistance from her peers.

their observations regarding Jenny's use of academic skills at home. The facilitator may ask the child herself to add comments: "How do you use reading, writing, and math at home, Jenny? What are some things you would like to do better?" These discussions would be followed by specialists' testing reports and observations related to academic performance. Similar discussion would address other key areas in turn—social, emotional, sensory–physical, and more (Parent Education Project, 1998a; Williams, Fox, Monley, McDermott, & Fox, 1989).

Annual Goals and Measurable Objectives. The IEP must describe annual learning goals for most students and short-term objectives for each goal for students with severe disabilities who will take an alternative assessment to the state achievement test. These requirements are intended to help ensure accountability, and part of our responsibility will be to document the progress of a child related to these goals and objectives.

From time to time, educators have developed highly detailed and sometimes trivial goals in order to state objectives in measurable terms. For example, one might find statements in IEPs such as, "Lamar will learn to spell all words with 95% accuracy; Lamar will complete oral sentences correctly 90%, and respond to criticism appropriately 80%, of the time." However, there are several problems with these types of goal statements. On the one hand, their specificity and detail makes them difficult to document. In addition, while they lead to lists of skills and subskills that are immediately observable, they do not tend to evaluate complex cognitive, emotional, and physical learning goals. We see many examples of pseudobehavioral language in IEPs, and too few examples of goals that consist of complex skills.

However, we can develop more effective goal statements that fit best teaching practice and relate to critical skills. For example, in some cases we can use curriculum guidelines in our own lesson plans to target skills for which our lessons are designed, generating goals that focus on meaning, practical application, and the ability to use skills in authentic community settings. Here are some examples:

1. Improve reading abilities and enjoyment of reading.
2. Develop basic math skills and apply these in simple daily money management.
3. Increase oral expression abilities.

Typically, measurable objectives are subunits of the overall goal. For the first goal listed, for example, we might identify the following objectives:

1.1. Manuel will learn to monitor whether the text is making sense to him as he reads.
1.2. Manuel will discover meaning-based strategies for figuring out words.
1.3. Manuel will participate in oral storytelling based on stories he has read (Rhodes & Dudley-Marling, 1996).

In other cases, IEP goals will be directly related to the student's disability and to provision of specific special education services. If a student has difficulties in articulation of words, a speech therapist may target improvement of articulation as a goal. If a student needs to learn how to use a piece of assistive technology, such as a talking calculator, this can be identified as a goal with appropriate objectives.

Special Education and Related Services. Related services are services—such as occupational therapy, physical therapy, speech therapy, counseling, and so on—that provide needed assistance to a student. If a student is to receive in-class support from a special education coteacher or paraprofessional, this will be written in the IEP. As appropriate, the

IEP must also address issues of language acquisition, assistive technology, behavioral interventions, and other special needs.

One important issue is how special education service time is articulated on the IEP. As we will discuss in Chapter 5, special education supports can include both direct instruction or therapy as well as indirect supports—consultation with the teacher, accessing or developing instructional materials, and monitoring student progress. It's often helpful to write a range of services and specify that such services may involve both direct and indirect services. This maximizes the impact of special education service resources in the general education class, providing flexibility while ensuring accountability.

Students' Ownership of Their IEPs. We also should help students themselves understand and own their plans promoting student ownership and empowerment. When students participate in IEP meetings and provide input we help students' making choices for their lives and strengthen their own self-determination (Field, Martin, Miller, Ward, & Wehmeyer, 1998; Hughes & Agran, 1998). This also provides a wonderful opportunity to demonstrate to the child that people care, as well as to teach the child to take responsibility.

Several strategies for student involvement are helpful. At minimum, when the student attends the meeting, we should explain what is happening and ask for the student's input. We will ask for and rely on the student's input and choices more as the child grows older. We can help the student use the IEP to track his or her own learning by developing a booklet with the student that identifies goals and provides a way to record progress. This can easily become part of the class portfolio. In addition, as students enter middle and high school, we can provide them training and support to provide substantive input into their IEP. One young man, Micah, began in middle school using a PowerPoint® presentation to tell those at the IEP meeting what he saw as his needs and goals in which he was interested. This makes the IEP a living instrument, owned by the person it is intended to benefit, rather than a bureaucratic document.

Placement: The Degree of Involvement in General Education. Historically, the most controversial decision in IEP meetings has involved the educational placement of the student with a disability—the type of class or school where the student will be educated. Referral to special education has often meant a separate special education classroom. Since the passage of PL 94-142, however, the legal presumption has been that students would be educated in the general education class. When this does not occur, the IEP team must justify that decision. In almost all cases the needs of the child can be met in general education when, as the law requires, appropriate services and supports are provided. The questions then involve politics, how resources are used, and the willingness of schools to include students. For every student with a disability who is denied inclusion, there is most often a comparable student in another school who thrives academically and is a valued member of the classroom. In truly inclusive schools, placement is not often an issue. The child with a disability is part of the general education class like everyone else. What changes is not the location of the student but the degree of support and assistance provided in that class to aid both the student and the teacher (LeRoy, England, & Osbeck, 1994; Parent Education Project, 1998a; Saha, Enright, & Timberflake, 1996).

There are still a small number of students whose needs are so complex that educators have not yet come up with ways to include them successfully. Other programs, such as separate schools, may be seen as the best alternative. Our goal, however, should be to include all students. If we are committed to inclusive teaching, it is painful when we find

FIGURE 4.15

Individualized Education Plan (IEP)

Student Name Fred Borden	**Date of Meeting** April 23

Present Levels of Educational Performance

How does the child's disability affect the child's involvement and progress in the general curriculum; or, for preschool children, how does the disability affect the child's participation in appropriate activities?

> Fred is 14. Fred is able to read at a third-grade level but can understand at a higher level than he reads. He likes to read but is hesitant to write or express himself. He can do basic math functions and has begun to keep a checking account but would like to learn more daily math skills. He likes electric motors and machines and spends time with his dad at his car garage. Fred likes to be around people, but his oral communication skills are limited. He has a few friends but often seems awkward socially.

> Fred is not sure what he wants to do when he graduates from high school. He could use exploration of the community and job options, thinking about where he might like to live. A MAP might be useful with his friends and family to provide input into his transition plan and IEP.

Eligibility

Does the student have a disability and need special education and related services?

> Fred is diagnosed with mental retardation.

Measurable Annual Goals and Short-Term Objectives

How will these goals enable the child to be involved in and progress in the general curriculum or, for preschool children, to participate in appropriate activities? What other educational needs result from the child's disability? What services or interagency linkages are needed for transition, including instruction, related services, community experiences, employment, postschool adult living, daily living skills, and functional vocational evaluation?

Annual goal: Improve Fred's ability to read and express himself effectively in writing and with other tools.

Objective	Service/Person	Assessment
Over the semester Fred will read six books he enjoys and will develop interesting responses and share key ideas and issues in each of the books.	1. Fred will participate in a literature circle where he will be part of sharing group. 2. Special education teacher will coteach literacy class twice a week and monitor Fred's progress and provide support as needed. 3. Peer partner in the literacy group will work together with Fred in designing a project reporting on book via a play, computer graphic, or art. 4. General and special education teacher with librarian will help Fred pick out books at his level that he finds interesting. 5. Parent and Fred go to library together once a month.	General and special education teacher observation, Fred's self-report, summary record sheet for each book (location, main characters, plot, key message). Actual reporting project. Criteria: number of books read, Fred's evaluation of these books, rubric on report and reporting project.

(continued)

FIGURE 4.15

Continued

Objective	Service/Person	Assessment
Fred will learn to express himself in writing and through other tools, using his own life and other topics of interest.	1. General education teacher will use writing workshop approach in English class for development of written pieces. 2. Fred and small group will work together reviewing and editing one another's pieces, providing encouragement. 3. Special education teacher will work with Fred and the group to help them use tools for expression to focus and expand their writing, such as stick figures and graphics as a tool for storytelling, Inspiration software for graphic organizers, PowerPoint®, use of movies with I-Move to go with text.	General and special education teacher observation, Fred's self-report, rubric on written stories (teacher and student evaluation) and related expression products.

How Child's Parents Will Be Regularly Informed of Child's Progress

Regular report cards, parent conferences, and biweekly notes of learning activities and progress from the special education teacher.

Placement

What percentage of the time will the child be in general education or in a special education setting? What is the rationale for placement?

Location	% of time	Rationale
General education (specify) Fred will be involved in a schedule of classes that fit his interests and IEP goals. Special education (specify)	100%	Fred has been included in general education full time his entire school career. Teachers are working hard to teach at multiple levels and modify instruction to meet his needs.

Special Education and Related Services

What services, modifications, and supports are needed to help the child advance appropriately toward attaining the annual goals, be involved and progress in the general curriculum, participate in extracurricular and other nonacademic activities, and be educated and participate with other children with and without disabilities?

Service or Support	Start Date	Location	Frequency	Duration
MAPS facilitated by social worker.	9-3	Fred's home	Once per year	Time necessary
Coteaching support by special education teacher in language arts.	8-15	Language arts class	2 classes per week	Year

Supplementary Aids and Services/Interagency Linkages

Service or Support	Start Date	Location	Frequency	Duration
Refer to vocational rehabilitation for job exploration summer program.	November	Counselor's office	NA	NA

FIGURE 4.15

Continued

Program Modifications or Supports for School Personnel

Modifications or Supports	Start Date	Location	Frequency	Duration
Allowing Fred to read and write at his own level in language arts class.	8-15	Language arts class	Ongoing	Year
Modified grading in machine shop based on project rubric designed with special education teacher.	9-15	Machine shop class	Each card marking	Year

Extent, If Any, to Which Child Will Not Participate with Children without Disabilities

None.

State and Districtwide Assessments

In what state and district assessments will the student participate? What individual modifications are needed? What alternative assessment, if appropriate, will be used?

Fred does not want to participate in the statewide assessment, and his parents support this decision.

Source: Adapted from Office of Special Education and Rehabilitative Services (2000).

we do not, today, know how to include a student. Yet such instances offer us opportunities to reflect. "How can we do better? How might we have helped this student if things had been different in our school?" These are critical questions that will, we hope, lead to better answers in the future.

IDEA does require that school districts provide a "continuum of placement options" that range from inclusive to more restrictive. This requirement is based on the presumption that more restrictive settings may better meet the needs of some students. However, it is important to understand that *special education is a service, not a place.* As we will see in Chapter 5, we can develop an **inclusive continuum of services** where a range of supports and services are provided in general education based upon the needs of the student.

Evaluation of Progress. The law requires that educators report the progress students make on the goals and objectives identified in their IEPs. Evaluation criteria and tools need to be clear, so that we can track and report on a student's progress. If we incorporate goals for the student into the structure of our curriculum, and if we use assessment that is the same as or similar to what we use with all our students, this process is much easier to manage. We may need to make adaptations, but most often we should evaluate progress toward IEP goals in the same way that we evaluate progress made by other children. Most students with disabilities take the state standardized test that is required by the No Child Left Behind Act of 2001 while a small number who have more severe disabilities will take an alternative examination.

Mediation, Hearings, and Appeals. Sometimes school personnel and parents cannot agree on the IEP. Federal law has established procedures for the appeal of decisions. However, jurisdictions also encourage mediation, a process by which parents and school representatives come together with an individual who facilitates dialogue and discussion. Many states have established formal mediation services to achieve more amicable outcomes and reduce legal costs.

If parents and the school continue to disagree, however, the first level of appeal is an impartial hearing. This is a quasi-judicial meeting at which a court-appointed hearing officer, most often a university professor or a lawyer, hears the sides presented by the parents and the school system and makes a decision. If either side disagrees with this decision, the case can be appealed to federal court. Special education law is now a sub-specialty of law practice. In every state multiple hearings are conducted yearly. This is costly and emotionally stressful for parents.

Behavioral Intervention Plan. If students have behavioral challenges a Behavioral Intervention Plan (BIP) should be part of the IEP. In 1997, a multistep process was written into law. First, if a student with disabilities displays dangerous actions and the

---

SCHOOLS to VISIT

Committing to Including and Supporting All Children

Ausable Primary School
306 Plum Street
Grayling, MI 49738

Ausable Primary is a K–2 school located in the rural community of Grayling, Michigan. Grayling is a resort town known for canoeing and snowmobiling; however, the prevalence of poverty is high, and some 56% of Ausable's 430 students receive free or reduced-cost lunch. The incidence of significant disabilities is also high—in a county with the highest infant mortality rate in the state.

The design of Ausable Primary, a relatively new school, was shaped by the dreams of a principal, staff, and community members who wished for a school that would meet the developmental needs of young children. From the beginning the school has been fully inclusive, reaching out to children and their families and seeking to keep all children in general classes. In 2001 the school included in general education classes children with autism, mental retardation, cerebral palsy, learning disabilities, and emotional disturbance.

What's particularly amazing about Ausable is the degree to which all staff genuinely have adopted

inclusion as a value. They struggle with students, but the commitment they share is clear. The principal, Barbara Mick, has been a leader in developing this philosophy, carefully selecting new staff and gathering all staff in yearly retreats.

Ausable has developed a particularly strong support system for inclusive education. The special education teacher, speech therapist, counselor, and occupational therapist share an office in the center of the school and coordinate support services in collaboration with general education teachers. Once a month each teacher in the school has a Wednesday afternoon planning session with the specialist team. All specialists provide in-class collaborative teaching and support. In addition, almost every classroom has a full-time paraprofessional to assist with students with special needs. Support staff and general education teachers have learned to work as a family team. Every adult takes responsibility for all children in the school, and all constantly share information and ideas, particularly in informal lunchtime discussions when specialists and teachers eat together in the office. Finally, school staff are active in accessing community agencies to provide support to families and children.

school wants to expel the student, a multidisciplinary team must conduct a manifest determination review—a review to determine whether or not the behavioral issues were directly related to the disability of the student. If the actions were related, the school must develop a BIP as part of the IEP (Riester, 1998).

Individual Transition Plan (ITP) and Inclusive High Schools. The transition of students with disabilities from school to adult life has been a concern for many years. Students with disabilities often have much higher rates of unemployment and more difficulty accessing postsecondary educational opportunities than their peers. Students with mild to severe disabilities may spend years on waiting lists for adult service systems. The Individual Transition Plan (ITP), a required component of the IEP starting at age 16, is a central tool. According to IDEA, the purpose of the ITP to is promote

> movement from school to post-school activities, including postsecondary education, vocational training, integrated employment (including supported employment), continuing and adult education, adult services, independent living, or community participation [that is] based on the individual student's needs, taking into account the student's preferences and interests; and . . . includes—(i) Instruction; (ii) Related services; (iii) Community experiences; (iv) The development of employment and other post-school adult living objectives; and (v) If appropriate, acquisition of daily living skills and functional vocational evaluation. (IDEA, 2004, Section 300.42)

The law requires that students attend the transition planning meeting to develop the ITP and that schools work with adult service agencies to develop collaborative services to assist students with disabilities (Ludlow, Turnbull, & Luckasson, 1988). Inclusive high schools are very important in a successful transition from school to adult life as a member of the community. It is here that students with special needs develop relationships and are known by the future employers and leaders in local communities.

Getting Started and Going On

We've explored how to design our classes for all students and have surveyed ways to develop individualized support plans. Let's connect with DeMarcus, a beginning biology teacher and see how things are going.

Well, it's the end of the first week of school. It's been a good week. My strategy for teaching eighth-grade biology this year combines several practices that are new for me, exciting but scary at the same time. We still have the district's required text, and my principal insists that we target our instruction within the state's curriculum framework. However, I have decided I am not going to "cover" these objectives week by week in the textbook. No, I am going to involve my students in real, authentic experiences. First, I am involving my students in planning the class. This week we spent half our time discussing what they want to learn in biology this year. We brainstormed ideas on the board. There were a lot. Then we spent time organizing the ideas around learning themes and activities. That was a good beginning. Following this, the students and I together compared the state curriculum objectives to what we had done in our own planning. This helped us focus on certain activities we wanted to do. It was amazing how much we had addressed based on their own interests. I then taught them about multiple intelligences and the need to have students work at different levels. Together we came up with fun, thought-provoking lessons that will include working in

BACK PACK

Language, Culture, and Individualized Differentiation

Center for Research on Education, Diversity, and Excellence CREDE is a federally funded research and development program focused on improving the education of students whose ability to reach their potential is challenged by language or cultural barriers, race, geographic location, or poverty. crede.berkeley.edu

Teacher Vision This site has many resources for individualized differentiation and adaptations for a wide range of students. www.teachervision.fen.com/special-education/resource/5347.html

groups with different abilities (we talked about how to ensure each person was responsible and what would happen if they were not); developing our own experiments; using drama, art, and music to portray concepts; and conducting community projects both during and after school. The kids seem excited and so am I.

I was worried about the students with disabilities in my class. However, as we planned together, I asked the students to come up with ideas to ensure that everyone was learning and could participate. We will work out these plans in more detail as we go, but they had some terrific suggestions. In fact, I took their concepts into the IEP meeting for Joe, my student who has mental retardation and cerebral palsy. You should have seen Joe's parents. They actually looked shocked. They smiled and came up to me after the meeting. His dad shook my hand heartily and his mom hugged me! They both had tears in their eyes. Wow! Makes me glad I am a teacher. At least today. (Thomas, personal communication, September 2001)

Traveling Notes

In this chapter we explored the relationship between designing our teaching for diverse learners and developing individualized intervention and support plans. Here are some notes for you to review on your journey.

1. As we work to develop individualized differentiation and interventions for students with learning challenges, an ecological framework can help us think systematically regarding how students fit into our classroom. We can consider adaptations of our classroom to help the student be successful.
2. Useful tools include collaborative consultation, person-centered planning using the MAPS process, curriculum matrix, and daily schedule with supports.
3. Many formal services are available for students with special needs to which we may refer them. We want to work with specialists in these programs to support and strengthen effective inclusive teaching in our classroom.
4. If the student has a disability, we can refer him or her for special education services and will serve on a team to develop an Individualized Education Plan (IEP), which specifies goals, objectives, placement, services, and evaluation criteria. We take our ideas to the IEP meeting to contribute to a plan that works for our class.

Stepping Stones

Following are some activities that will help extend your understanding and actions you may take to plan for teaching diverse students.

1. Complete a class profile on your class. Do the same in the classroom of a colleague on your teaching team. What does this tell you? Is there a relationship between the problems students have in your class and the way that you teach? If so, what could you do?

2. Select one of your students who is having difficulty. Complete a student profile and identify some strategies you would like to try. Collect information. How well did this work? What did you learn?

3. Engage in collaborative consultation with another educator obtaining input and advice regarding a student who is having difficulty.

4. Obtain information about formal services in your school for students who are gifted, dominant-language learners, at-risk students, and students with disabilities. What collaborative programs are operated with community agencies?

5. Develop a plan for a student with a disability to be included in a general education class. Include the following components: (a) curriculum matrix; (b) daily schedule showing supports and adaptations as needed; and (c) summary narrative description regarding how the student will participate in the general education curriculum.

6. Participate in an IEP meeting. What occurred, and how did you feel about it?

7. Interview community agencies that work with people with disabilities about their individualized planning processes. What do they do that is similar to and different from the IEP process?

8. Talk with the principal and other teachers about the tools in this chapter and how they might be used in your school.

5

Provide Support and Collaborate

Getting Help and Building a School Community

CHAPTER GOAL

Understand how the concept and practice of support for teachers and students works in effective inclusive schools to strengthen learning and the school community.

CHAPTER OBJECTIVES

1. Understand effective methods of grouping students and ways in which students may provide assistance to one another with teacher guidance.

2. Develop skills in collaborating with other professionals in the classroom in teaching students with a wide range of abilities and needs.

3. Recognize the roles of various support staff in working in the general education classroom.

4. Comprehend practices and principles of effective support for inclusive teaching.

When we think about having students of truly different abilities and backgrounds in our classes, students who may not be able to talk, who may read far below or above grade level, who may not speak English, who are poor, who may have seizures or use a wheelchair, or who may be unable to see, we may feel overwhelmed. How can we manage? Our teaching methods make a great difference. However, we also need *support*. As we shall see in this chapter, support involves multiple forms of assistance from others—the emotional sustenance afforded by a listening ear, ideas to help us improve our teaching or deal with challenging students, solutions to problems with parents, and more. When we are asked to perform a task in which we are unsure of our abilities, we often ask, "How can I get help? Can someone help me learn how to do this? Can someone help me feel like I am not alone?" This is natural. Support is critical in successful inclusive teaching. Let us visit a classroom where teachers are getting help in teaching students with special needs.

Coteaching in a Middle and Elementary School: A Study in Contrasts

Mona has begun her 20th year as a middle school science teacher with excitement and trepidation. Last year she attended workshops on project-based learning and decided to take a risk and organize her teaching around problem-based projects, using textbooks only as a reference. She and the social studies teacher, Mark, are teaming to link science and social issues. It's been hard work but has gone pretty well so far.

Monclair Middle School is also including students with special needs, even bringing two students with severe mental retardation back from a segregated school. Teachers met at the end of last year and planned carefully to place students in heterogeneous groups; they made sure not to cluster students with academic or behavioral problems in any one class and to ensure a distribution of races and genders, even matching students to teachers based on their personalities. One student with severe mental retardation, Hasna, was in Mona's class. Terrified at first, Mona was relieved to have the full-time help of a paraprofessional, Jan, and part-time support from the special education teacher, Bob. However, she became increasingly concerned as Jan and Bob both worked with Hasna on separate activities at the back of the class, isolating her from the other students. What to do? One day she talked with Bob. "I am wondering," she said, "could you help Mark and me design our lessons so that Hasna can participate?" This idea was foreign to Bob and Jan. "We don't really know your curriculum," they said.

However, they decided to try, and the situation is slowly improving. For example, last week they studied the environmental impact of pollution, and the class divided into two groups. One group took water samples from the pond next to the school. Another interviewed local environmentalists. Hasna chose to go with classmate Amy in the interview group. The children and their teacher discussed how to include Hasna and decided to videotape the session. Hasna would turn the videotape on and off. The school technician helped them connect the camera to a switch. Hasna ran the camera with some help from Amy. She was so proud! "Since this first time, we daily figure out ways to include Hasna and meet her IEP goals. It's funny that before we had no clue."

Mona has avoided some problems we've sometimes seen. She proactively, respectfully brought the special education teacher and paraprofessional into the class curriculum, simultaneously ensuring that Hasna could participate at her own level. She took responsibility for Hasna, rather than leaving this to the special education staff, while also inviting collaboration. She has set up a situation where all can be part of the classroom community.

At Eubanks Elementary School, arriving for a visit in Hannah Abano's fourth-grade classroom, we find country music playing loudly and children milling about the room. "This is a transition time," Hannah says, "when the kids unwind a bit." Hannah's room is designated as the "inclusion classroom": All fourth graders with disabilities are in her class—4 children labeled as having learning disabilities, 2 with a cognitive disability, and 1 with emotional disturbance in a class of 25. Usually a paraprofessional works in the class in the morning and a special education teacher in the afternoon. Today, however, both are in the class together. Students sit at tables arranged in a U shape. However, Nathan, who has a cognitive disability, has a desk at the side of the room.

After Hannah shuts off the music, we are surprised to see the students divide into three obvious ability groups. One group is working with the special education teacher on forming letters in colored sand. Another group is reading a short book together as the paraprofessional follows a scripted lesson on phonics. The final group is in the hall with Hannah, reading an interesting book together and sharing stories written from the perspective of a character in the story. Nathan continues to work on a puzzle, totally separate from the other students.

We are concerned. We've seen other schools where teachers have students of different ability levels working together, learning skills such as letter recognition and phonics as they are reading and writing. Hannah clearly doesn't know how to do this, however. The special education teacher and paraprofessional are re-creating the equivalent of segregated special education within this classroom. Those with lower abilities don't have the benefit of interacting with higher ability students, and the more able children themselves are not learning leadership skills.

Support is important. Teachers need support from peers, principals, and families. As Joan, a high school teacher, said about her collaboration with a special education teacher, "The kids love having help when and where they need it. For me, it has been so wonderful because it gives me more comfort in knowing I have support. I don't feel so alone anymore" (Peterson, 1999). In this chapter we explore how we can obtain support as inclusive teachers. As you journey with us, think carefully about support you might need in order to teach children with different academic, social–emotional, and sensory–physical abilities, as well as children who come from different socioeconomic, cultural, or religious backgrounds.

In this chapter we will explore some details regarding how support is provided for inclusive teaching. Let's start by first looking at how traditional segregated models of education are organized. We'll then look at inclusive models for organizing supports. This will provide us a base to explore specific collaborative support that occurs in the general education classroom.

Traditional Service Models for Students with Special Needs

As we discussed in Chapter 1, the key underlying principle for traditional, segregated educational programs could be stated as follows: *special people belong in special places.* That one statement is also the most descriptive of what we see in schools.

Separate Classes

Separate, segregated classes have been developed for every type of difference in schools. These include separate classes for students with disabilities, students who are gifted and talented, dominant-language learners, and students who are pregnant or at risk. In many cases, a separate class for a category of students may be used for students throughout the school district. For example, a gifted class or class for students with moderate cognitive disabilities might be in one school and students bussed to that school. In such districts, each elementary school might have a class for a specific disability category such as hearing impaired, blind, emotionally disturbed, and so on.

The stated rationale for such classes is that they can better meet the needs of these students. However, as we discussed in Chapter 2, such efforts have not been successful. In fact, the evidence suggests that segregated programs have impacted very negatively on the lives of not only students with special needs but the general student body as well who do not have the opportunity to get to know these students.

Despite the stated rationale, often an underlying reason has also been to protect the general student body and teachers from what are perceived as deficits and negative influences of students with special needs. This even includes students considered gifted who are seen as causing challenges for general education teachers that are too stressful for a regular classroom.

The organizing models of separate classes are varied. In some cases, most often in elementary schools, students literally stay in one classroom all day long. It is common for such students to even go to lunch, gym, and art classes as a group. In middle and high school, sometimes students are in one class all day long. Other schools, however, create departments in which several special teachers teach different subjects. In a high school, for example, four special education teachers might respectively teach language arts, science, math, and social studies. Another model involves the tracking of the entire student body into perceived ability-based tracks with students who are gifted at the top and students with disabilities at the bottom.

In other cases, students many spend most of their time in a general education class but leave to obtain tutoring and remediation instruction in what is most often called a **resource room**. Remediation aims to improve student functioning in identified deficit areas. The assumption is that students possess within themselves either a deficit or a special ability that cannot be met in the regular classroom and that services must be provided elsewhere by a specialist. In most cases special instruction is provided in a separate classroom or therapy room. Such approaches may become self-reinforcing, perpetuating rather than diminishing a student's need for special services. As students are withdrawn from typical activities in the classroom, they often fall farther behind, creating the perception that they need even more remedial education (Spear-Swerling & Sternberg, 1998; Sternberg & Grigorenko, 1999).

From the perspective of the general education teacher other problems occur. When students are pulled out for services, the need for the teacher to seek strategies for effectively teaching the student in the subject for which he is receiving services is diminished.

The teacher may rely on the special services teacher. This limits the improvement of instruction, not only for this student but other students as well. Further, having several students coming in and out of the classroom is chaotic, making it difficult to having consistency and continuity in teaching students.

Separate Schools

Most school districts that use the principle of special places for special people also have segregated schools for some students where students have no opportunities for social interaction with other students. Students with moderate to severe disabilities are most often sent to separate schools. Such schools have also been used for students considered gifted and talented, at risk, and students with problematic behaviors. Such schools are typically called **alternative schools**. The best intent of all separate schools is, again, to better meet the needs of students who have not been considered successful in the general education school.

Separate schools often take students from multiple school districts. In many states, educational services are organized, often by county, to service school districts in their area. These go by different names such as regional districts, intermediate school districts, regional educational services, and so on. Students will be carried by bus to these schools, frequently riding as many as 2 to 3 hours a day on a bus.

Numerous problems with such schools are evident, however. By removing students with special needs, the general education school does not grapple with improving practices to support all students in their learning. This impacts negatively on all students. From the viewpoint of students with special needs, they are segregated from social interactions with other students and the opportunities to learn from peers with differing abilities and characteristics. Often this leads to a lifetime of segregated services and isolation in the community, dramatically reducing quality of life.

Inclusive Schoolwide Models of Support

As schools are becoming more inclusive, teachers and support staff are constantly experimenting with ways to provide support. As we've studied school implementation of support, important principles of effective inclusive support have become apparent. These are listed in Figure 5.1. First and foremost, effective support promotes and strengthens inclusion in our classes—it helps us group children heterogeneously, distribute both children with special needs and those who are gifted learners across classes, and teach children of differing abilities together rather than pulling children out to a resource room or to the back of the classroom. Inclusive support helps us build community to deal with behavioral

Sights TO SEE

Talking Coteaching

Coteaching Three teachers talk about their collaboration in coteaching. www.youtube.com/watch?v=_BKCur0DvRo

FIGURE 5.1

Principles of Support for Inclusive Teaching

1. *Inclusive classrooms:* Students are grouped heterogeneously, pull-out services are minimized, and segregation is not re-created in the general education classroom.
2. *Building community and meeting behavioral challenges:* Teachers are assisted in building a classroom community in which children help one another.
3. *Multilevel, authentic instruction:* Faculty and staff design and implement multilevel, authentic, challenging, and scaffolded instruction.
4. *Adaptations:* Teachers and support staff design and use needed instructional adaptations.

5. *Child services coordination:* Support staff coordinate services across multiple classes and professionals.
6. *Teacher support coordination:* Multiple services in a teacher's room are coordinated to ensure consistency of approach.
7. *Professional growth:* Teachers are given opportunities for collaborative growth and learning.
8. *Emotional support:* Teachers have forums through which they can get emotional support, opportunities to share with one another, and a time and place for all this to happen.
9. *Teacher empowerment:* Support staff seek to empower rather than to displace teachers in working with special students.

Source: Adapted from Peterson, Tamor, Feen, and Silagy (2002).

challenges rather than to focus only on a specific child. Support specialists help us design instruction at multiple levels, teach collaboratively with us, and help track each child's progress and needs, coordinating services so that we do not have specialists doing parallel activities. Such support implies the building of a culture of community and care for one another, as well as for children, within the school (Carpenter, King-Sears, & Keys, 1998; Giangreco, 1997; Peterson et al., 2002).

Support Personnel

In schools in most countries many specialists provide supports and services to students and teachers. Schools working to implement inclusive teaching will develop organizing strategies to use the services of these professionals to provide support and assistance. Figure 5.2 shows the types of personnel that are typically funded by special programs and those from general school funds.

Effective schools will develop a process by which all these professionals work together as a team. It is possible, of course, for each professional to "do their own thing" with little coordination with other services. However, this is often problematic. In such situations professionals often end up working at cross-purposes and frustrate teachers, students, and parents by sending mixed signals.

Interactions of Support, Teaching, and Student Success

A typical pattern is evident as schools begin and move along a journey toward inclusive teaching. We can see various models in the effectiveness and sophistication of organizing structures for inclusive teaching. Often, schools will start their journey by bringing much of the old thinking of separation and special places for special people into their practice. These schools typically believe the key to success is classroom support via direct instruction and therapy. Such schools tend to spend little if any time in rethinking how they

FIGURE 5.2

Support Personnel for Inclusive Teaching

SPECIALIZED SERVICES	SCHOOLWIDE SUPPORT PERSONNEL
Support teacher (special education, gifted, Title I, at risk)	Media specialist
Teacher consultant	Counselor
Related service specialists (speech therapist, occupational therapist, physical therapist, rehabilitation teacher, sign language interpreter)	Social worker
	School nurse
Paraprofessional	
Psychologist	

provide instruction so all students can be successful. They often use practices that are very traditional and use support personnel to provide individualized differentiation and adaptations. Schools that are more effective typically begin by looking at their teaching and schooling practices and work toward creating more effective classrooms based on the principles and practices introduced in Chapters 2 and 4. General education teachers and support personnel are expected to collaborate in using space effectively for all students, using specific strategies to build an inclusive community of learners in the classroom, and develop multilevel, differentiated instructional approaches. In a study by Peterson (2003) several hundred classroom observations identified a pattern in the interaction between the quality of support and quality of instruction on the outcomes for students (see Figure 5.3). At its simplest level, this chart illustrates the importance of multilevel teaching. However excellent the support, it cannot compensate for poor teaching practices. On the other hand, the more effective are instructional practices, the less impact that support has on the judged outcomes.

FIGURE 5.3

Interaction of Quality of Teaching, Support, and Student Outcomes

SUPPORTS/TEACHING	POOR TEACHING	FAIR TEACHING	GOOD TEACHING
Good in-class supports	Poor	Good	Excellent
Fair to poor in-class supports	Poor	Fair	Good
Pull-out supports: resource room; coordinated	Poor	Fair	Good
Pull-out resource room or special class; uncoordinated	Poor	Poor	Good

Poor, fair, and good are perceived outcomes for student academic achievement and social–emotional well-being as perceived by their teachers.

Source: Peterson (2001a).

Models of Student Placement and Support

Schools have developed a range of models to organize such support staff. Some are more effective than others in enhancing and strengthening inclusive teaching. Let's review some of these approaches. As we describe them, you might refer back to Figure 5.1 and see how well you think each approach implements these principles of support for inclusive teaching.

Include Some, Segregate Some. In this approach, some students are included in general education classes and coteachers support them in the class. These are typically students with mild disabilities such as learning disabilities and mild emotional impairment. Students with cognitive disabilities or other moderate to severe disabilities are placed in either separate special education classes in the school or go to another school in the district or a separate school that draws students from multiple districts.

Include All—Clustered Class Placement and Ability Grouping. Some schools who are seeking to be inclusive use a model in which students with special needs are clustered in some classes. Other classes would have no such students. Hamilton Elementary, for example, put all students who are in gifted one class, students with learning disabilities in another class, all dominant-language learners in one class, and students with cognitive disabilities in one class. Such schools often will also ability group students within. Typically, there will be little emphasis on developing multilevel, differentiated instruction. The support people will often develop individualized adaptations and work individually or in small groups with students with special needs to the side and back of the class.

With the emphasis on support as the key to success, these schools often provide at least one full-time educator to work in a classroom. A special education teacher may work in one third-grade class for the full day. Evergreen Elementary School had a special education teacher in two classes for a half day, morning in one, afternoon in another; a paraprofessional did the same thing and was in each class the half day the special education teacher was in another class.

Support staff—special education teachers, bilingual or gifted teachers, speech therapists—in such schools typically believe clustering helps them organize their efforts, minimizing the number of classes in which they work. Harmon Middle School, for example, assigns all students with learning disabilities to one class, second-language learners to another class, and students considered gifted to yet another class. Similarly, Oakdale Elementary School uses a common pattern in which students with special needs are in only one of the four classes at each grade level; a special education teacher works with only two of the four classes. In Eagle Mountain Elementary School, a special education teacher is in the general education class in the morning and is replaced by a paraprofessional in the afternoon. In a variation of clustering, an entire special education class (usually 10 to 15 students) may be merged with a general education class and two teachers may teach the class together.

Despite perceived administrative benefits of clustering for support staff, the practice violates the underlying educational theory of inclusive schooling, replicating the kinds of practices that led to segregated education in the first place. Even with professional support, overloading one classroom with a disproportionate number of students with special needs can mean fewer opportunities for students to model learning, thus creating over-taxed, highly stressed teachers (Blanksby, 1999). Some teachers do not have students with special needs; therefore, teachers who do may feel overburdened. Other teachers may receive no support even though many unidentified students in their room need assistance. We've seen teachers essentially bartering for who "gets" special students. Classes with special students may become labeled and stigmatized. Coteachers of these classes, too,

CHAMPIONS OF INCLUSION COMMUNICATE
enthusiasm and act comfortably around students with disabilities.

Many people still feel uncomfortable around students with disabilities. They have had less experience with persons with disabilities, and they are unfamiliar with much of the accompanying equipment and adaptations. They tend to interact awkwardly with the students who have disabilities and sometimes even avoid encounters altogether.

Champions of inclusion are:

- The classmates who nonchalantly pass a tissue to Keith (who has cerebral palsy) so that he can wipe off the drool that sometimes emerges while he is talking.
- The nurse who slips into a classroom, whispers to Nancy who is reading, and then changes the food cartridge in her backpack which is hooked up to her feeding tube.
- The special education administrator who warmly greets Scott (who has autism) as he brings up the attendance to the office in the morning.

- The parent leader who welcomes new parents and tells them how wonderful it has been for her daughter who does not have a disability to learn in an inclusive school.
- The vision teacher who works with her student Ryan to show off some of the gadgets that he will be using to take notes in braille.
- The history teacher who talks privately with John (who has significant dyslexia) and assures him that his test grade will not be affected by spelling.
- The custodian who asks Charlene (who is deaf) to teach him how to sign "have a good day."
- Judy, who extends an offer to her tired friend to hop on the back of her electric wheelchair and get a ride.

By Bill Henderson, Principal, O'Hearn Elementary School, Boston, MA.

---

may experience the type of stigma that has typically occurred in segregated classes in schools (Peterson et al., 2002).

Include All: Heterogeneous Class Placement and In-Class Grouping. Schools who have a clearer vision about inclusive teaching make a commitment to heterogeneous placement of students in classes. In elementary schools, grade-level teams often work together to create profiles of their students showing various characteristics and then make recommendations for the next grade-level placement. Two schools we have studied used the following categories:

1. Academic abilities
2. Behavioral and social challenges and needs
3. Socioeconomic status
4. Race
5. Gender

This allows staff to systematically heterogeneously group children while also thinking about the match of specific students and teachers. Once students have been distributed, support staff develop a plan with the general education teachers for how and when they will provide support. Figure 5.4 illustrates how such a distribution looks (Peterson et al., 2002; Walther-Thomas, Korinek, McLaughlin, & Toler Williams, 2000).

In middle schools or high schools, scheduling is more complex because students no longer remain in one classroom all day. An inclusive secondary school eliminates tracked classes—lower level and upper level English and biology, for example. Similarly, it does not have special classes for students with special needs: students with disabilities, students who are gifted, and so on. Students select classes based purely on graduation requirements

FIGURE 5.4

Heterogeneous Student Distribution: An Example

	CLASS 1	CLASS 2	CLASS 3
Academic Ability			
High	4	5	4
Medium	15	13	16
Low	6	7	5
Behavior			
Excellent	8	7	6
Average	12	14	13
Poor—high support needs	5	4	6
Socioeconomic Status			
High	5	2	5
Middle	14	15	13
Lower	6	8	7
Total in Class	**25**	**25**	**25**

and their interests. The elimination of tracked and separate special classes most often ensures a heterogeneous mix of students. When schools find clusters of students developing, they initiate efforts to recruit students from underrepresented categories or to deal with underlying issues. For example, if groups of students with disabilities were signing up for one class, the school staff would want to understand why. Similarly, if classes became racially segregated, this would be a sign of issues to be addressed. Some secondary schools have also found it helpful to schedule students with special needs *first* to ensure that they can access classes that are most helpful to them. This simplifies the scheduling process.

Melissa is upset. The special education teacher helps her understand the assignment and helps her with a problem she has with another student.

Inclusive Grouping of Students for Learning and Support

Since the beginning of compulsory education, schools have sorted children many ways—by age (thus the creation of grades), by ability, by language, and, for many years, by race. The theory for such sorting is seldom articulated and little researched, despite its prevalence as a fundamental organizing premise. When public schools were first developed in rural areas, children of all ages learned together in one-room schoolhouses. As schools grew, however, experts began using the factory as a model for educational design, and these heterogeneous classes disappeared. Children were organized by age-bound grades. Curriculum was developed based on narrow expectations at each grade, and special programs were created for those who did not fit. This is the basic model by which schools are still organized (Tyack & Cuban, 1995).

However, children don't all develop at the same rates (Bredekamp & Copple, 1997). As with adults, their abilities vary dramatically. In any typical school classroom, reading abilities, for example, will range across four to six theoretical grade levels (Allington, 1994; Peterson et al., 2002). Recognizing this problem, schools have begun to group children in ways that keep with children's natural development. The move toward inclusive schooling is consistent with this effort. Effective inclusive schools develop strategies for **inclusive grouping:** grouping across and within classes in heterogeneous groups of children with different abilities, styles, ethnicity, and other characteristics. Schools are seeking ways to allow students and teachers come to know one another well and to foster continuity across several years. Such connection and support is particularly important for students with special needs.

Students Helping Students: The Power of Peers

In inclusive schools we intentionally group children heterogeneously to build a sense of community and support. Students themselves can be the most valuable resource for student support. Teachers often take responsibility for helping students and don't create structures whereby students are taught to support one another in learning. Students can support one another, however, and several strategies help make this possible. We discuss these strategies in detail in Chapter 11.

Multiage Teaching

In multiage teaching, students from two to three typical grades learn together in one classroom, using the same curriculum and staying with that teacher for 2 to 3 years. Teachers engage students in projects that explore questions and facilitate mutual helping by older and younger students. In a multiage classroom, students work in pairs or small groups as the teacher moves from group to group or conferences with students.

Research has shown that multiage settings offer substantial academic and social advantages compared to single-age classrooms, not only for students with special needs but also for all other students (Feldman & Gray, 1999; McClellan, 1994; McClellan & Kinsey, 1999). Vygotsky (1978) based his influential work on the idea that children learn best from others who differ in ability and that "by playing and working with older and more competent partners, children are able to engage in and master more difficult tasks than they can handle alone" (Feldman & Gray, 1999, p. 508). Younger children learn from older children, and older children learn skills of teaching and nurturing. Students have opportunities to seek out a wider range of styles, interests, and expertises: Sometimes very able younger students are ready to be challenged by older students; at the same time, less able older students have the opportunity to deepen their own skills by leading and helping younger students. Such instruction also naturally enhances social and emotional learning and the development of a sense of community (Chase & Doan, 1994; Feldman & Gray, 1999; McClellan & Kinsey, 1999; Miller, 1995).

Looping

The term **looping** refers to a teacher's moving from one grade level to another along with his or her students. For example, Nancy is a third-grade teacher who is looping with her children and will continue to be their teacher in the fourth grade. The following year she will drop back to third grade and start the same process with another group of children. The effect of looping is that, as in multiage classes, a teacher spends 2 or more years with the same group of students. This allows the teacher to build a strong relationship with students and parents and to start off each new year more seamlessly. Students and teachers alike find this practice emotionally supportive as well as beneficial to learning (Gaustad, 1998; Grant, 1996).

School Within a School

A school within a school is another helpful strategy. Large schools can create a sense of anonymity in which students often feel literally lost in the crowd. To counter this, some schools, particularly middle and high schools, divide the school population into smaller groups in order to build a sense of community, collaboration, and support among teachers and students. A group of 100 to 200 students go through their school careers together, often assigned to teachers who work with students over several years. These groupings go by different names in different schools—pods, families, houses, universities, and the like (Peterson, 1992; Sergiovanni, 1994).

An Inclusive Continuum of Services:
From Place to Process

As we seek to mix students heterogeneously, we also attend in the United States to the federal legal requirement that schools provide a **continuum of placement options** to meet the needs of children with disabilities. These options must include instruction in regular classes, special classes, special schools, home instruction, instruction in hospitals and institutions, and provision for supplementary services in the general education classroom (IDEA, 2004). Figure 5.5 provides an illustration of this continuum of placement options as first popularized by Deno (1970).

The model assumes that the more intensive a service, the more segregated the placement. Frequently, the need to maintain this continuum has been used as one argument against inclusive education. Taylor (1988) suggested alternatively that linking intensive services with segregation is not necessary. Services at very different levels of intensity may be delivered in general education classrooms. Virtually any support service can be effectively delivered in general education. In Figure 5.6 we've provided an illustrative example of an **inclusive continuum of services**. What changes is not the physical location where the student spends his or her time. Rather, the type, intensity, and duration of various supports and services change based on the needs of the student and teachers. Thus any particular place, including a general education class, could have intensive services. This model has important implications for both practice and policy.

FIGURE 5.5

Continuum of Services: Traditional Model

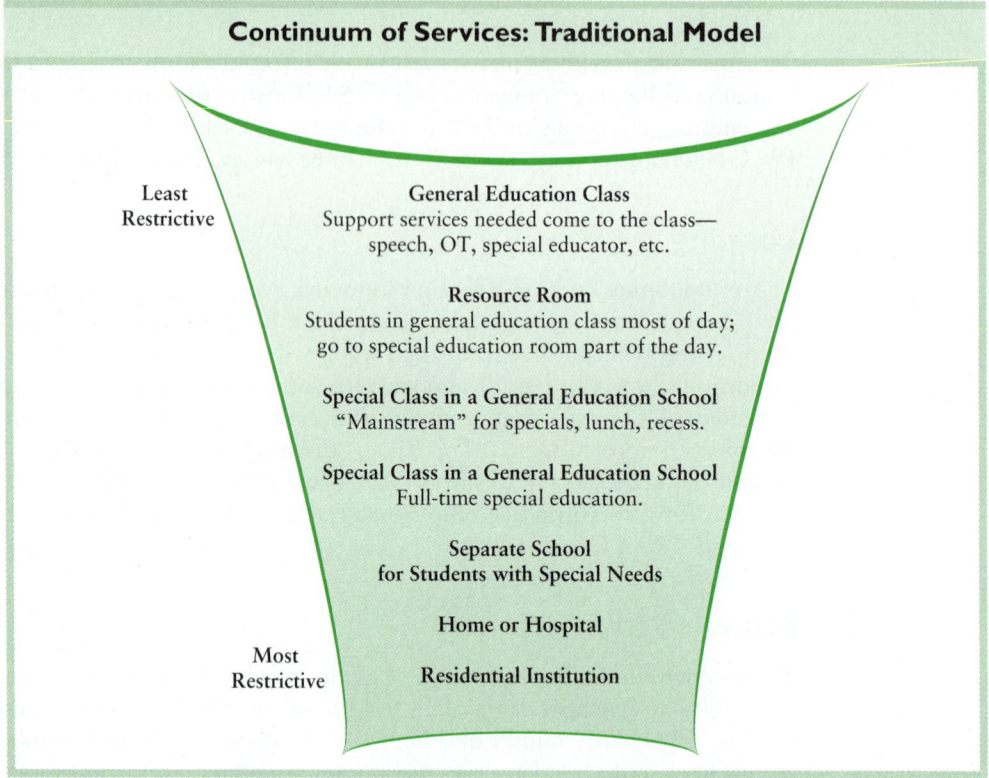

Least Restrictive

General Education Class
Support services needed come to the class—
speech, OT, special educator, etc.

Resource Room
Students in general education class most of day;
go to special education room part of the day.

Special Class in a General Education School
"Mainstream" for specials, lunch, recess.

Special Class in a General Education School
Full-time special education.

**Separate School
for Students with Special Needs**

Home or Hospital

Residential Institution

Most Restrictive

Source: Adapted from Deno (1970). This diagram represents one representation of a continuum of services, now known in federal law as a continuum of placement options, moving from most restrictive (bottom) to least restrictive and more normalized (top).

FIGURE 5.6

Continuum of Services: Inclusive Model

Greatest supports and services

All services listed below plus any additional consultative or direct services (e.g., therapist for child and family, psychiatrist).

In-class support coteacher works more than half to full time. Circles of support/friends.

Paraprofessional aide works part to full time.

Specialist assistance: Speech therapy, occupational therapy, rehabilitation teachers, orientation and mobility, etc.

In-class support coteacher provides periodic in-class assistance in adapting lessons and instructs special students or the whole class. Intentional assistance from classmates.

Collaborative consultation: Periodic consultation with teacher either in or out of class. Building relationships in the classroom.

Least supports and services

Collaborative team planning: General and special education, parents, other professionals.

External Partnerships for Professional Development and Facilitating Coteaching

SCHOOLS
to VISIT

Thompson Elementary School
1110 18th Avenue SW
Vero Beach, FL 32960

Thompson Elementary is located in a low-income area of town. When Martin O'Neal became principal of Thompson Elementary he relished the challenge of including children and improving learning for all.

The district adopted Quality Designs for Instruction (QDI) and Thompson Elementary was one of the first schools to sign up for the training, which was facilitated by staff from the Florida Inclusion Network. QDI helps schools examine staffing patterns and adjust roles of personnel to better meet the needs of students in general education classrooms.

Martin first worked to build teamwork. A special education teacher was assigned to each grade level and attended weekly meetings. Common planning time was established to allow special and general education teachers to meet consistently to plan curriculum and to identify accommodations.

The school created an Inclusion Task Force composed of the principal, general and special education teachers, paraprofessionals, parents, the district inclusion coordinator, and critical friends from the Florida Inclusion Network (FIN) and the University of Florida. The group met monthly to help the school move from being reactive to being proactive.

The first step was to establish a cotaught K–1 multiage classroom that proved to be a tremendous success, with significant academic and social gains made by both general and special education students. Thompson next planned a 2–3 coteaching model and began plans for a 4–5 multiage class.

Staff participated in professional development from several partners. Training in coteaching was provided by FUSE (Florida Uniting Students in Education). Staff obtained on-site modeling and training in curriculum and instructional strategies and assistive technologies and attended a summer conference, obtained support from the Assistive Technology Education Network (ATEN) and Dr. Diane Ryndak of the University of Florida trained paraprofessionals, with assistance of the district's inclusion specialist, regarding their roles in providing academic, behavioral, and physical supports.

Thompson Elementary continues to change and grow, utilizing support from both outside and inside and recognizing the importance of developing a team capable of including all children.

By Rick Reardon, Program Specialist, Indian River County Schools; edited by Michael Peterson.

Using Collaborative Teaming to Provide Support
Gathering the School Community

Effective inclusive schools build a culture of mutual help and support among all staff—teachers, secretaries, support staff, custodians. Helping children is the overriding aim, but all concerned understand that helping one another is a prerequisite for this to occur. Within such a culture, staff and volunteers work in collaborative teams. Let's explore teams we see in inclusive schools.

Collaborative Teacher Teams

Collaborative teams involve two or more teachers who work together at various levels of intensity, from periodic collaboration on a learning activity to teaching lessons collaboratively to a larger group of students. A special education teacher and/or other support person is an integral member of the team. Traditionally, teachers have been organized by grade levels in elementary schools and by departments (e.g., science and math, English and social studies) in secondary schools. As looping and multiage classrooms become more prevalent, however, it makes less sense to cluster teachers by grade levels. In elementary schools, teachers often think of themselves as "early elementary" and "upper elementary" and work in formal and informal teams. In other schools, classes at different grade levels are intentionally placed next to one another so that faculty can develop collaborative, multiage instruction, linking activities in their classes. Innovative secondary schools often use **interdisciplinary teams of teachers:** Social studies, literacy, math, science, and special education teachers work together rather than within separate subject departments (Fisher, Sax, & Pumpian, 1999; Walther-Thomas et al., 2000). Teacher teams often use themes to link the subjects and to bring their classes together in learning (Kovalik & Olsaen, 1997; Manning, Manning, & Long, 1994). In one school, for example, a team of teachers, including special education and **Title I support teachers,** used a yearlong theme of oceans and space as an organizer for many activities. They met across grade levels to plan instruction throughout the year (Peterson et al., 2002).

School Support Team

In effective inclusive schools, the **support staff**—special education teachers, Title I and bilingual teachers, counselors, social workers, psychologists, and others—work as a collaborative team to develop a comprehensive system of support. In Jamestown High School, for example, specialists meet together frequently to discuss children, the needs of teachers, and strategies for particular students. They develop coordinated schedules of support in classes, sometimes intentionally working together in a class, and at other times arranging to be in different classes, depending on teacher and student needs. Similarly, in Three Rivers Elementary, support staff meet formally early in the morning biweekly to discuss students and coordinate schedules (Noell & Witt, 1999; Snell & Janney, 2000; Walther-Thomas et al., 2000).

In less effective schools, in contrast, specialists tend to work in parallel, seeing only the children assigned to their own caseloads and scheduling separately from one another. For example, in one school the special education support teacher and the gifted education specialist both work with children in one fifth-grade class, but they do not coordinate their services or talk together about how to support the teacher in instructing students with such differing abilities (Noell & Witt, 1999; Snell & Janney, 2000; Walther-Thomas et al., 2000).

Inclusive schools organize **child study teams** through which teachers can bring concerns regarding a child to the attention of other staff. Such teams often meet either weekly or biweekly and are attended by the teacher who has referred the student, other teacher representatives, the principal, parents and family members, and support staff in the building—often a special education and Title I teacher (if applicable), counselor, social worker, or psychologist. These teams are called by many names: child study teams, prereferral intervention teams, student and teacher support teams, and more. Sometimes children attend these meetings as well. When the child is present, the team tends to focus more positively on communicating with both child and parent. The child is given responsibility for being part of decision making.

In some cases support teams are built around specific needs and respond to crises, behavioral challenges, or student academic problems. Increasingly, however, to use staff time and energy more efficiently, schools are creating one team that will deal with multiple issues, recognizing that problems are often linked (Fisher, Sax et al., 1999; Walther-Thomas et al., 2000).

A key purpose of effective team meetings is to provide assistance to a teacher or staff member who is concerned about an issue in his or her class. This is the process referred to as **collaborative consultation** (see Chapter 4), in which a teacher presents an issue and obtains assistance from others. One teacher, for example, was concerned about Randy, a child in her class who had diabetes. Randy's blood sugar level was not stabilized, and he frequently needed to stop work and ask the teacher to help him administer a simple blood sugar test. The teacher was particularly worried about the rest of the class and felt a need for backup from others. She obtained input from other teachers, two nurses who attended the meeting, and support staff—a psychologist, a special education teacher, and the principal. She went away from the meeting with commitments from support staff to help her monitor Randy's situation and deal with the class (Idol et al., 1994; Peterson et al., 2002).

Individual Student Teams

As we discussed in Chapter 4, teams are also built around students with special needs as part of an Individualized Education Plan (IEP), a Section 504 plan, or plan for dominant-language learning or supports for students who are gifted and talented. The more intense such needs, the more people may be involved to provide support and assistance. For example, Belita, a student with a mild learning disability whose first language is Spanish, has the special, bilingual, and general education teachers and the school psychologist on

her team. Jonathan, a student with a complex medical condition and severe mental retardation who uses a wheelchair and a computerized communication device, has a large team—special education teacher, speech therapist, occupational therapist, assistive technology consultant, general education teacher, and nurse. A support staff person will coordinate services to each student and provides some direct support (Bauwens & Hourcade, 1998; Ford et al., 1997; Giangreco, 1997; Noell & Witt, 1999).

Volunteer Support and Community Agency Collaboration

Finally, the larger community can provide wonderful sources of support for schools and teachers. In many schools parents not only volunteer for projects such as baking cookies but also operate parent resource centers, read stories to the class, or mentor individual students during or after school. Community agencies may also bring specialized resources to the school (Kretzmann & McKnight, 1993). Nationally, for example, Communities in Schools helps connect schools to community resources. At Merrill Elementary School a hospital sends interns into classes on a weekly basis to teach students science lessons related to the body. A violence prevention organization called Common Ground brings a special program into schools to provide emotional support via group meetings with students and to train students in conflict resolution (Peterson et al., 2002).

Schoolwide Student Support Services
Using Resources for Inclusive Teaching

Most schools employ support staff to provide services to children and families, and these staffers often provide direct and indirect support to teachers as well.

Counselors, Social Workers, and Psychologists

Counselors, social workers, and psychologists consult with teachers regarding student academic and emotional needs, suggest strategies, and provide helpful information. They can provide direct individual or group counseling, contact families, serve on a crisis team, and provide in-class support. For example, a psychologist might offer advice to teachers about self-esteem and conflict resolution. A psychologist–social worker team may facilitate circles of support (Bowen & Glenn, 1998; Carpenter et al., 1998; Quigney & Studer, 1999).

Media Specialists

Media specialists can be invaluable in locating written materials at various levels of difficulty, in providing assistance to individuals and groups of students engaged in research projects, and in training students in the use of computers and other media. Media specialists are increasingly becoming skilled in helping teachers design authentic, multilevel instruction and in working with students with special needs (Peterson et al., 2002).

Learning Support Centers

Learning support centers, or simply learning centers, are physical locations in schools where any student, not just those with special needs, may obtain assistance for academic, emotional, or physical needs. Centers are staffed by one or more teachers, and students may visit these centers for help or hang out during their lunch period. A laidback style often makes a learning center a preferred gathering place for students. For

JOURNEY into the CLASSROOM

Two Coteaching Relationships

Sarah and Melanie have been working together for 11 years. Melanie is an upper elementary teacher who has spent her career focusing on how to be a better inclusive teacher. She met Sarah in her first year of teaching, and over the years a strong relationship has developed. Now when they coteach, the relationship has a fluid sense to it. Once a week they sit down and plan lessons together. Sarah has a busy schedule with other classes. However, she works with Melanie in her room 1 hour a day. They plan their time in writing or science. Melanie comes to the meeting having thought out what she wants to do that week during the hour. Sarah and she then talk through what each person will do, who gathers the materials, and what adaptations need to be made for the several students on Sarah's caseload.

The plans change with the lessons. If they are writing, usually one teacher is walking around encouraging the writers with ideas, while the other is running one-on-one conferences. Sometimes one teacher will take a small group for a focused lesson on one topic. In science, often they are utilizing the lab and each teacher focuses on three tables as they work through doing and writing about an experiment. Once a month, they have a larger team meeting centered around one child in Melanie's room who is both visually impaired and has a cognitive disability. Like many people who have been together a long time, they can communicate ideas with few words being

said. They are flexible and supportive of what the other person needs, knowing that each one is focused on the benefit of the students.

In another coteaching model, Burnadette works with sixth graders in a middle school and plans with a team of four teachers. In each class period, she is right there helping explain content and lessons to children. Her role is one of support. In walking around talking to children, however, she clearly helps all children and not just her caseload. When the team meets to plan once a week, she organizes materials, study sheets, and other materials for her identified students. However, one of her ideas is now being used with the whole class. She was taking a PowerPoint® and making it into sheets with writing space for taking notes. It is working so well that she is now making that for all of the students. She has 1 hour a day in which the students come to her separately to work on classwork that they did not finish. She has a passion for her students and a solid, respectful relationship with her coteachers as well.

Reflection: For sure, coteaching is something of a professional marriage. Like marriages, good coteachers adhere to key principles and practices. However, these can be implemented using a wide range of individual teaching and personality styles. Most teachers who learn to coteach would never voluntarily go back. They feel more successful and they see the positive impact on their students.

some students, time in the learning support center may be scheduled as a daily class. However, students should *choose* to come.

Coteaching
Partnerships for Student Learning

Coteaching, by which we mean general education teachers working collaboratively with support staff to help students learn, is one key source of support. Coteaching involves making important changes as we decide to move beyond being a "lone ranger" and to work with others. In effective inclusive schools, teachers have choices regarding collaboration and professional supports. For example, Nancy is a seventh-grade teacher who teaches children with very different abilities together in creative ways. However, she neither asks for nor wants additional staff support in her classroom. She is able to manage just fine, enjoys teaching by herself, and successfully facilitates mutual support among her students. Jane, on the other hand, teaches sixth grade and thrives on teaming with support staff, collaboratively planning and implementing instruction, and using the strengths of others to complement her own abilities. For Jane, collaboration is the lifeblood of teaching. The point is that there is no one way to be an effective inclusive teacher. The key is to know ourselves, our working style, and our desire or need for additional support. If we do seek support, developing our collaborative skills will be critical.

The Purpose and Practice of Coteaching: Three Approaches

There are three key approaches by which support staff provide support to teachers, each based on different goals and strategies (Peterson et al., 2002). Understanding these approaches will help us decide how we want to work with support staff in our class.

Design and Implement Inclusive Multilevel Teaching. Most importantly, support staff will work with general education teachers to design and implement multilevel curriculum and instructional activities (see Chapters 11–13). The assumption is that instruction can be designed and implemented manageably for very diverse ability levels so that all students benefit.

Design and Implement Differentiated and Adapted Instruction for Individual Students. Support staff may work with children in the regular classroom, developing strategies for individual students who need differentiation and adaptations to instruction. An adaptation involves a strategy, specifically selected for an individual student, that varies from typical instruction and is designed to help the student succeed. In adapting curriculum, support staff typically work within the existing curriculum and instructional approach (Ford et al., 1997).

Support Needs of Teachers. All teachers have both strengths and needs, and support staff can help general education strengthen areas in which improvement is needed. In one situation, for example, the support teacher for students who are at risk was skilled in teaching science—so she led the science lesson two or three times a week while the general education teacher worked with students who were having difficulty. This provided both support and teacher development. In another case a teacher wanted to use a running record (a systematic analysis of errors in a reading sample) for each child but needed to learn better how to employ the strategy. The reading clinician spent 30 minutes twice a week demonstrating lessons in the class and mentoring the teacher (Peterson et al., 2002).

Methods of Organizing Coteaching

There are many types of staff with whom we may have the opportunity to teach collaboratively. As we work with specialists, we can use one of several methods of organizing our work together.

Team Teaching. Perhaps the most common method of collaborative teaching is team teaching between two or more general education teachers. In one elementary school two multiage classes (Grades 2–3) adjoin, and the teachers engage in collaborative instruction. At MacNeilson Elementary School two teachers decide to teach together in a larger room and combine their two classes for 1 year; other teachers work together on units organized by themes or collaborate in teaching particular subjects. At Dellian High School, interdisciplinary teams of science, social studies, language arts, and special education teachers

A general and special education teacher lead a discussion regarding the economy. The class is watching CNBC as President Obama is scheduled to talk to the country about plans to improve the economy. One student shares that her mother lost her job last week.

have adjoining rooms and work together on projects throughout the year. One high school class reads and writes with students in Grades 1 to 3 once each month, visiting the elementary school for 2 hours in the morning. Similarly, many upper elementary classes pair with students in Grade 1 for buddy reading and special projects. All these arrangements provide additional support and collaborative opportunities for both students and teachers (Fisher, Sax et al., 1999; Peterson et al., 2002; Walther-Thomas et al., 2000).

In-Class Collaborative Teaching by Support Teachers. Many teachers who specialize in a particular student population may work in a given school. These specialists, who previously taught students in separate rooms, now often work in the general education classroom, helping us teach. These teachers are typically associated with specially funded programs that include:

- Special education
- Title I (federal funds for schools with high concentrations of low-income students)
- Bilingual education
- Gifted and talented education

Special education and bilingual teachers will have specific students assigned to their caseload, for whom they are responsible. However, they are also allowed to work with the total class as long as the individual needs of the students are met (see Figure 5.7) (Dover, 1994). In one classroom, for example, Susan, the special education teacher, and Janet, the general education teacher, plan and teach collaborative lessons. They trade roles in leading the class, helping groups work on projects, and providing direct skills instruction to individuals or small groups as needed.

Szabo (2000) described a useful framework for related services specialists (see p. 166) that is also applicable to coteachers. Specialists may provide direct services in the general education classroom as well as indirect, consultative services to assist the teacher (see Figure 5.8). Professional organizations have endorsed these approaches as good standards of practice.

FIGURE 5.7

Roles of Support Teachers

1. Plan with the principal and teachers for new approaches to providing learning supports:
   - Organize in-service training.
   - Work with consultants.
   - Serve on inclusive education planning committee.

2. Plan for individual students:
   - Facilitate person-centered planning/IEPs.
   - Consult with individual families and attend parent meetings.
   - Advocate on behalf of individual students and families.

3. Assist in multilevel instruction and adaptations for students:
   - Take leadership in promoting collaborative teaching and cooperative learning.
   - Work with teachers to identify strategies for accommodating students.
   - Develop or acquire needed materials.
   - Help general education teachers coordinate with related services in the classroom.
   - Provide direct support and instruction with the general teacher.

4. Facilitate community connections and family involvement:
   - Facilitate involvement of students in school-sponsored extracurricular activities.
   - Contact Boy Scouts/Girl Scouts, community recreation.
   - Connect families to one another to provide support.

Source: Adapted from Tashie, Shapiro-Barnard, Donoghue-Dillon, Jorgenson, and Nisbet (1993).

Understanding these various roles is very critical in effective coteaching. If coteachers perceive their only role as direct instruction with students, this may actually limit their effectiveness. As coteachers are able to help general education teachers implement effective multilevel, differentiated instruction by designing lessons or obtaining useful instructional materials they are often needed less for direct instruction. When this occurs they use their time most effectively and expand their impact.

In-Class Collaborative Teaching by Related Services Specialists. Many other specialists provide what IDEA calls *related services:* "transportation and such developmental, corrective, and other supportive services as are required to assist a child with a disability to benefit from special education" (IDEA, 1999; Snell & Janney, 2000; Thomas, Correa, & Morsink, 1995).

- *Sign language interpreters* help students who are deaf understand what is happening in the class and communicate with others.
- *Speech therapists* help students with difficulties in producing sounds and communicating effectively.
- *Audiologists* evaluate hearing ability and make recommendations to maximize students' ability to hear and understand sounds.
- *Rehabilitation teachers* assist students who are blind or visually impaired in using accommodations, adaptive equipment, and materials for daily living and communication.
- *Orientation and mobility specialists* aid persons who are blind or visually impaired in using adaptive strategies to move around from place to place—canes, guide dogs, and so on.

■ *Occupational therapists* help students improve fine motor coordination and use of the upper extremities to accomplish functional tasks.
■ *Physical therapists* help people improve their gross motor abilities—walking, gait, and so on.
■ *School nurses* provide assistance related to health issues and coordinate in-school services with medical services outside the school.

In most of these specialties there is controversy over whether to provide the service in the context of a general education class or in a clinic. For example, speech therapists traditionally work with individual students on speech articulation and other communication strategies in a separate room. In inclusive education models, however, speech therapists come into the classroom and assist students in class communication activities. The therapist often works with a small group and sometimes with the whole class, helping promote language development of all the children while targeting the specific needs of a student with special needs. For example, a speech therapist may work with a student or small group of students on the articulation and production of specific sounds as the children sing a song or read text aloud. The same IEP goals and objectives can be practiced during literature circles or small group discussions. Peers serve as fluent role models and supporters for students with speech/language challenges, naturally reinforcing and expanding the assistance provided by the speech therapist.

Specialists very often benefit the total class. For example, students at Garland High School take sign language courses from sign language interpreters and earn foreign language credit. At Hamilton Elementary School, an interpreter facilitates communication between a child who is hard of hearing and her classmates. The interpreter and the child cotaught a weekly sign language class to all 75 students at that grade level. Classmates quickly discovered that learning a new language is challenging and fun. The classmates' parents were pleased that their children were learning sign language, and many children taught family members basic signs.

FIGURE 5.8

Related Services: Inclusive Models

DIRECT SERVICES

One-on-one therapy	*Small group therapy*
The therapist works with the student during a classroom activity to facilitate his or her participation. Therapy can also occur during activities in the gymnasium, on the playground, or at a community site.	The therapist works with the student with special needs and a group of classmates on an activity that promotes a therapeutic goal for the student with special needs; such as a craft project involving fine motor manipulation for all students that meets needs of the special student.

INDIRECT SERVICES

Consultation	*Monitoring*
The therapist recommends and instructs other professionals to carry out therapeutic programs, including instructional or environmental modification, activity enhancement, adaptation of materials, routine or scheduling alterations, or training.	The therapist maintains contact to monitor status, including scheduling checkups on a regular basis in the classroom.

Source: Adapted from Szabo (2000, p. 16).

Other professionals also assist the total class while meeting the needs of the student with special needs. While helping a student who is blind learn how to get around the school, an orientation and mobility specialist teaches the whole class how to function as a "sighted guide." Classmates explore interactions of body, space, and sensation as they learn how the student navigates the school without seeing. An assistive technology specialist identifies a communication device and simultaneously trains the student user and the rest of the class. Special services thus give the class new opportunities for learning, and the student with special needs has an opportunity to shine in front of his or her peers (Etscheidt & Bartlett, 1999; Friend & Bursuck, 1999; Giangreco, 1997).

In-Class Team Instruction. In some schools teams of support staff collaborate to support teachers. In some elementary schools, for example, teams in the lower grades assist classroom teachers in intensive literacy instruction. At Harper Elementary School a reading specialist supervises a team of one teacher and three paraprofessionals—individuals who are not certified as teachers but are hired to provide instructional assistance—who spend 45 minutes each day in the first- and second-grade classes working with the classroom teacher. They break the children into small groups for reading and writing instruction. At MacNeilson Elementary School the speech therapist and special education teacher team with the classroom teacher to do whole class and small group literacy instruction.

In-Class Support by Paraprofessionals. Paraprofessionals provide support in many schools. Their roles and relationship with teachers, however, must be carefully defined, and care must be taken to avoid some common problems. As teachers we take responsibility for all students, and we should expect the paraprofessional to work with all students as well as to attend to a student with special needs. A paraprofessional must be supervised by a teacher who is responsible for instruction and student support. We should plan with the paraprofessional at least once a week, defining his or her role in instruction. Paraprofessionals may (McVay, 1998):

1. Lead small group instruction.
2. Provide assistance for personal care and other physical needs.
3. Assist students in completing directions given by the teacher (*all* students, not just a student with special needs).
4. Facilitate interactions among students.
5. Adapt lessons under the teacher's guidance.
6. Implement other needed tasks.

At best, the teacher and paraprofessional share responsibility for all students within the class. The best paraprofessionals learn about the culture of the classroom; find ways to help under the guidance of the teacher; and figure ways to subtly encourage interactions, providing needed support but drawing back to encourage child-to-child engagement. Such paraprofessionals move throughout the classroom, helping all students so that a casual visitor would not see them as assisting primarily one student. The teacher and the paraprofessional constantly look for ways that children can support one another; they coach classmates in ways of being of assistance, consider peers as members of a student's team, and seek to facilitate independence on the part of children with special needs (Doyle, 1997; Friend & Bursuck, 1999; Marks, Schrader, & Levine, 1999; McVay, 1998).

Sometimes, however, problematic practices occur. Giangreco (1997) and Marks and colleagues (1999) found that many paraprofessionals spent much of their time close to a student with a disability. These paraprofessionals further perceived a major portion of their job as ensuring that the student was not a bother to the teacher and assumed the role of functioning as the expert on the student, oftentimes taking major responsibility for instructional decisions. In such situations the teacher had little responsibility for student instruction or for supervision of the paraprofessional. In some cases the paraprofessional and the student literally worked together in a separate place in the classroom, effectively creating their own isolated environment. Parents may request a paraprofessional to assist with inclusion, assuming that this will give their child support and ensure success—and often treating the paraprofessional as the person most knowledgeable about their child. Similarly, a teacher may welcome the paraprofessional, initially seeing the person as taking responsibility for the child off their shoulders. We will need to work proactively to use best practices and prevent such problems.

Consultation. A teacher consultant may visit a class, observe students, and consult with the classroom teacher regarding effective strategies. A consultant may also obtain materials, facilitate referrals to other services, and coordinate communication with parents. However, a teacher consultant does not often engage in actual instruction. In many situations consultation is provided in response to a short-term need to solve a problem (e.g., inability to complete class work, aggressive behavior) (Boudah, Schumacher, & Deschler, 1997; Idol et al., 1994). However, the long-term goal is to empower the classroom teacher to solve similar problems in the future (Friend & Cook, 1996; Noell & Witt, 1999).

Considerations for Success

How can we be effective in collaboration? Collaborative relationships are much like a marriage: They can be heaven, or they can be hell. As in marriages, however, we have considerable power to shift direction. A lot will depend on how we decide to work together. In some cases styles, ways of thinking, and methods of communication between teachers click so well that we fall into a terrific working relationship almost effortlessly. In other cases we are so different that we must work very hard to make the relationship productive. Figure 5.9 summarizes findings by Friend and Cook (1996) regarding characteristics of good collaboration and barriers that sometimes get in our way.

FIGURE 5.9

Collaboration: Success and Barriers

CHARACTERISTICS OF SUCCESSFUL COLLABORATION	BARRIERS TO COLLABORATION
■ Collaboration is based on voluntary relationships.	■ Time for planning is insufficient.
■ Collaboration involves a mutual goal.	■ Administrative support is lacking.
■ Each person is equally valued.	■ Scheduling problems exist.
■ Each has equal decision-making power.	■ Personal misunderstandings occur.
■ Responsibilities, accountability, and resources are shared.	■ Roles are unclear.
	■ Power struggles and hidden agendas exist.

Source: Friend and Cook (1996).

BUMpS IN THE ROAD

Getting Around Barriers to Coteaching

When the support for planning and teaching is working well it can be a very powerful feeling. There is that old saying that two heads are better than one and that is often the case. Conversely, however, there will be times in any teaching career where the collaborative working relationship you dreamed of is simply not there. What do we do then? Do we give up our dreams of an inclusive classroom that welcomes all children? While we always have a solid goal in mind understand that getting there is a process and, like the children we teach, we can only start with what we have. If you find yourself in a school with limited support set into the everyday classroom and the main teacher you find yourself working with, whether a general education teacher or a special education teacher, is very traditional in her approach and is not looking to gain new ideas, then you have some choices to make. Keep in mind that no matter how tough the situation, there are always things that can be done to make it better. Here are a few thoughts related to some common problems.

Problems in Creating an Inclusive Classroom	Ideas to Make the Situation Better
Children are pulled out for all services.	Talk to the special education teacher. Ask for support in including the child in a subject. Ask if he or she can come in twice a week to work with your class and observe how things are going.
Special education teacher is resistant to trying inclusive teaching for her children.	Create a written plan of how you will provide what the child needs. Talk to the parents and get them involved in the decision.
A general education teacher is nervous about having a student far below grade level in her class during reading.	Offer to sit down and plan with her for the success of that student. Offer to model a reader's workshop lesson for her and how that might work at that level.
Parents are unsure how you are going to meet the student's needs.	Write out your reasons for wanting the child included so that you can speak clearly. Then be willing to track the progress of the child and arrange a meeting after some time to discuss how it is going.

Keeping Children First. Sometimes adults get caught up in their own issues—hurts with roots in childhood or anxiety and fears of incompetence. If we can acknowledge these feelings while at the same time keeping our focus on children, we will be more likely to find common ground. This is actually more difficult than it seems, because adults must recognize when their behavior has to do more with their own needs than with the needs of children.

Power. Who is in control of what? At best, we come together with support staff and cede some control, developing a shared decision-making approach in which the opinions and perspectives of each person are respected. Differences in competence, philosophy, personal style, and needs can dramatically affect how this plays out. We must seek to develop effective collaborative relationships. However, we will not cede control when we feel that our partners will not or cannot use best practice approaches. At best, both parties identify and share what we see as our areas of strength and learn from and with one another.

What are the areas in which power is most important? At bottom line is the decision about what is to be done, when, where, with what materials, and using which instructional approach. The issue of whose discipline is perceived as more important may also be evident. For example, if our school has a reading clinician who is providing support to teachers in reading, do we defer and follow that person's direction, or do we engage with the clinician as equal partners in dialogue, expecting that we bring equal perspectives to the table? These are issues we may have to work through with both patience and strength.

Philosophy. Some teachers aim toward innovative teaching philosophies and approaches; others stand by traditional teaching methods such as worksheets, lectures, and fill-in-the-blank or multiple-choice tests. Many incorporate elements of both in their teaching. In collaborative relationships we may have to work through differences in philosophies. In some cases, we may give very specific directions to support staff regarding what we would have them do in our classroom, mentoring support staff and helping them learn innovative teaching techniques. In other cases, support staff will teach us new strategies and will have unique and important knowledge that strengthens our understanding of students with special needs. As we work together, both partners in a collaboration must be flexible and yet clear regarding our own approaches to teaching.

Balancing and Sharing Competence. All of us have areas of strength and need. Sometimes we are aware of these, sometimes not. The balance between collaborating partners can go either way. A support staff person may be the more skilled teacher. If this is the case, such an individual can be a mentor and professional development guide. In one school, for example, teachers were having difficulty teaching math at multiple levels using a new math program. The district hired a support teacher who worked half time in the building and taught a 30-minute demonstration lesson each week. The regular teachers thus learned new skills that they used throughout the week.

If we understand ourselves, we know how we can contribute in a partnership and we know where to ask for help. The concept of multiple intelligences (see Chapter 12) can help us think about our own strengths, needs, and styles, as well as about those of our students. As we talk with our partner in collaboration, it is helpful to recognize these different styles, strengths, and needs and to express a respect for the differences between us. If we can develop trust and ask for help in our weaker areas, we will build a bond as a foundation of our work together. We can both contribute to and draw from strengths of others in collaborative teaching.

A physical education teacher leads the class in exercises. One boy with autism is upset and a paraprofessional is helping him. She'll shortly try to connect him with another student as they do the exercises.

Beyond Disciplinary Territory. We will likely work with specialists from different disciplines—special educators, counselors, social workers, and more. Traditionally, different aspects of human beings have been claimed as the territory of different disciplines. In an interdisciplinary model, the team looks together at all the needs of the individual as a totality. In practical terms, all would look together at literacy, behavioral, social, and sensory–physical needs. This approach brings the wisdom of the total team into play and enhances the capacity of the team to engage in needed work.

Coteaching Strategies

What is it that support people actually *do* to help us? As we discussed earlier, this will vary greatly depending on our personal approach to including and supporting diverse students in our classroom, our philosophy, and our associated strategies. The framework on which this book is based would lead to the following roles for support people:

1. Designing curriculum, instruction, physical layout, and resources for students with diverse abilities
2. Team teaching
3. Building a community of learners
4. Developing needed adaptations
5. Addressing behavioral challenges, physical and sensory needs, communication, and assistive technology
6. Evaluating students

Depending on our needs and the resources available in the school, this support might involve direct work with students, indirect consultation and assistance, and intensive or mild assistance. As we develop our teaching style over the years, our skills at teaching multiple levels and building a community will grow, and we may find that we need less support.

Friend and Cook (1996) identified several methods of collaborative instruction. In the first, *one teach, one observe*, one teacher is responsible for instruction while the other observes a student, a small group, or the entire class to monitor learning and develop strategies to improve instruction. Teachers then later discuss observations and use them to drive teaching. In another approach, *one teach, one drift*, one teacher is responsible for instruction while the other teacher circulates to answer questions, bring students back to attention, or provide mini-lessons and assistance. A third setup, *station teaching*, occurs when students are placed at "stations" around the room engaging in different activities about a topic. Each teacher delivers instruction to one certain activity. Certain activities are done independently. Groups switch from one station to another at identified times. In *parallel teaching*, the class is split in two groups, and two teachers work simultaneously, each teacher with one group. In *alternate teaching*, one teacher manages the majority of the class while the other teacher pulls a small heterogeneous group aside to preview, review, assess, or provide enrichment. The purposes and membership of this small group change with each lesson and content area. Finally, when two teachers are *teaching together* they manage and instruct the class at the same time, flexibly interacting in the various instructional formats being used—small groups, partners, individual work, and centers.

Villa, Thousand, and Nevin (2004) describe four coteaching approaches in similar but different terms: (1) supportive; (2) parallel; (3) complementary; and (4) team teaching. With *supportive teaching*, one teacher leads the lesson while the other teacher does something that complements, supplements or enhances the lesson such as asking questions, monitoring students, restating importing information, asking for clarification, adding examples, and modeling for students. In *parallel teaching*, both teachers plan lessons together. Then each teacher instructs different groups of students at the same time. They may teach the same or different content. There are several examples of parallel teaching: split class, station teaching/learning centers, coteacher rotate, cooperative group monitoring, experiment or lab monitoring, learning style focus and supplementary instruction. With *complementary teaching*, both teachers share in the delivery of the lesson, but may use different methods. For example one teacher may lecture or read aloud while the other takes notes on chart paper. One teacher may also paraphrase the other teacher's statements on the overhead projector. In *team teaching*, both teachers equally share responsibilities for planning, teaching and assessing. It is common for team teachers to divide the curriculum according to each person's curriculum content mastery, preferences and training. More face-to-face time is required in this approach because more time is needed for planning.

The major differences boil down to answering the question, Is our collaborating partner "teaching with" us or "helping" us? In most of the effective inclusive classrooms we've observed, collaborating teachers use all of these strategies at one time or another. Sometimes it's helpful to have one person stand back and observe or help a few students. Sometimes we break students into small cooperative groups or "centers," and both of us rotate throughout the room. Sometimes we divide the class into two groups and actually teach the same content in these smaller groups. Truly collaborative coteachers switch in and out of these various roles frequently, often shifting with minimal conversation, as a glance or request will do. Other times, teachers very intentionally plan roles for the day or week and stick to these (Tashie, Shapiro-Barnard, Donoghue-Dillon, Jorgenson, & Nisbet, 1993; Wood, 1998).

In effective coteaching each teacher takes responsibility for all students in the room. Each teacher also has input into grading and contact with parents. The general education teacher takes responsibility for all students in the class; the special education teacher does not grade only students on his or her caseload. Teachers communicate to parents and students alike that there are two teachers in the room for all children. At best, students do not understand that one is a "special education" or "bilingual" teacher. They know only that they have two teachers in the room. This does not mean, however, that students do not know that their peers have some learning challenges. In a good inclusive classroom the needs of all the children in the class are explicitly talked about, as are the methods for supporting and growing these areas (Patriarcha, Freeman, Hendricks, & Swift, 1996; Snell & Janney, 2000; Tarrant, 1993; Vaughn, Schumm, & Arguelles, 1997; York, Kronberg, Medwetz, & Doyle, 1993).

As we seek to work together in the classroom with other educators, of course, there are many areas in which we may have various perspectives. Figure 5.10 illustrates and provides some examples of some issues that we will need to negotiate as we work together. How we work through these also depends on the style of the individuals involved. Those who have more flexible and laid-back personalities will largely work through these issues as they arise on a day-to-day basis. For others who feel the need to map out work in advance it may be important to have conversations ahead of time. You might find this list useful to provide a series of topics to discuss with your teaching partner(s).

To get a sense of how this works, let's hear Erin Herold, a fifth-grade teacher, describe how she and her special education coteacher work together in her classroom. Erin explains (Herold, 1998):

I have been coteaching for two years. It has been a successful experience. Here are a few things that we do to create a positive learning environment for all our students.

FIGURE 5.10

Issues for Coteaching Teaching

KEY QUESTIONS

To what degree have collaborating partners developed agreed-on strategies? Negotiated roles with one another? Share power and influence instead of struggling for control?

AREAS IN WHICH DIFFERENCES MAY ARISE	SOME EXAMPLES
Parent communication and partnership Formality of relationship with parents; understanding and acceptance of diverse family backgrounds, styles, and problems	One reaches out to parents, giving home phone numbers and connecting on the weekend. The other maintains distance. Teachers come from different cultural backgrounds and have cultural and religious differences.
Collaborative relationship Goals and expectations in the working relationship	One wants to be a friend, the other maintains professional distance. One expects to be in charge, the other wants sharing of control.
Student progress Expectations related to assessment tools and strategies to be used; degree of focus on the standardized test	One teacher believes all should be on grade level or retained. The other does not believe in grading but in individual development. One teacher believes that the standardized test should guide all they do in the class. The other believes assessment should be based on authentic student work.
Planning Time for planning; degree and detail of planning; planning ahead; designing for diversity; planning meetings, forms, and record-keeping	One teacher is very systematic, planning carefully and in detail sequences for each day. The other plans global approaches and obtains materials but anticipates students leading the learning in unanticipated directions. One keeps detailed charts and records of each student. The other asks students to do this in their portfolios.
Academic instruction Instructional strategies; assessment strategies; assignment of grades; adaptation and modification of lessons; sharing teaching roles; trying new approaches	One teacher believes children need structure and information needs to be transmitted. He lectures, gives tests, and expects students to be quiet. The other teacher uses cooperative learning and inquiry approaches, believes students should be active in creating their own learning.
Community building and behavioral challenges Classroom rules and routines; behavioral management and discipline; trying new approaches	One teacher believes in a strict enforcement of codes of conduct and strict discipline. The other teacher believes that order comes out of students building a community and that students must be given choices and options.
Classroom design, space, and materials Planning and organizing classroom space; designing the classroom for the different abilities and learning styles of students; making accommodations and adaptations; trying new approaches	Having personal space that she controls is very important to one teacher. Another teacher feels space belongs to the class and should be designed and used collaboratively. One teacher feels that structure in the class is important for children and so uses desks placed in rows. The other believes collaboration is critical and groups children around tables.

Planning: We meet every Thursday morning to go over the next week's schedule. I usually come up with the topic and the general assignments and projects, and she will give feedback. We decide who will teach which component during this planning time. . . . We spend a bit of time talking about which student may have trouble with the assignment and how we can modify it. All the modification plans are prepared beforehand, but we both know that we can adapt on the spot if needed. This seems like it takes a long time, but it doesn't! . . . Approximate time: 30 minutes.

Teaching: My coteacher leads the starter activity . . . . I then go over the daily agenda. Either one of us will lead the lesson. When one is teaching, the other is either standing in the back, monitoring behaviors, or else sitting with individual students. Occasionally, we will pull out individual kids to work with either of us one on one. Once a week, we try to do some type of bounce back and forth where she will talk, then me, then her, etc.

Review of students: Once every few weeks we discuss each individual student. We focus on their progress, strengths, weaknesses, behaviors, etc. My coteacher put together a guide of each student's goals for the year, and every few months we review these goals during our whole team meeting to see if and how we are helping them meet these goals.

Writing: We came up with a personal goal that we wanted one strong, solid piece of writing from each of the students on her caseload. We worked together with her students and walked them through answering an essay question from start to finish. We met with each student individually, either after school, before school, or during lunch. Once their piece was finished, we made copies as an example of their best writing. This was put in their IEP record as well.

These are just some of the things that we do that have been successful. The one thing I can say is that teachers involved in coteaching really have to make it their own. They have to develop their own style with which they are most comfortable.

In Figure 5.11 we've listed a few practical dos and don'ts for collaborative teaching. We've seen firsthand both very successful and very unsuccessful practices. The key for inclusive collaborative teaching is this: *All children should be a part of the class working at their own level.* When people enter our class, if they can easily find students with special needs doing different things in different places from the other children, we have a problem. Relatedly, if a visitor can observe our room and immediately know that a collaborating professional is there for specific students, we have a problem. In both instances we are sending powerful, deep messages to children that they don't belong to the class and that the collaborating professional is not a real teacher. In the process, we are laying the foundation for ongoing problems of acceptance and community in our classrooms (Peterson et al., 2002).

Caseloads of Support Staff

The term *caseload* refers to the number and type of students and classes that are assigned to a special education or bilingual teacher or a related services professional. Typical caseloads for special education teachers in inclusive schools are around 20 students, though this may vary. Speech therapists typically have much higher numbers often ranging from 40 to 60. The certification structure of special education teachers can sometimes create difficulties. In many states, special education teachers get certification in a specific disability—for example, learning disabilities, cognitive disabilities, autism, and so on. Other states have more flexible, cross-categorical certification, often along the lines of severity of disability or high incidence (e.g., learning disabilities, cognitive disabilities, and emotional impairment) and low incidence (typically students who are blind, hearing impaired, or have severe disabilities). Increasingly, inclusive special education teachers will obtain multiple certifications since they are dealing with students with a wide range of disabilities in inclusive classes.

In one approach, a special education teacher would provide service only to those students for which they have a certification. Thus, two or three special education teachers might be working in one general education class that had students with learning disabilities, cognitive disabilities, and emotional impairment. This practice, however, is problematic in that it can be very confusing for the general education teacher to deal

FIGURE 5.11

Principles and Practices for Inclusive Coteaching

DOS	DON'TS
Really, you can do this! We've seen many teachers collaborating in these ways.	*Really, these are practices we've seen in some actual schools! We hope you don't do them.*
Consider students with special needs as full members of your class.	Cluster all the students with disabilities in one place in the room—at the back, on one side of the room, in their own row.
Work with your coteacher as a real partner, negotiating and sharing all aspects of work in the class.	Have the coteacher act as a teacher helper, copying or filling out forms.
Collaborating staff share responsibility for all students in the class. Students know that there are "two [or more] teachers" in the room.	Have the coteacher, aide, or other specialist work only with students with disabilities or with other students who are on his or her "caseload" separately from the rest of the class in the back or in a corner of the room.
Make sure that students with special needs are part of all aspects of the class so that outsiders find it difficult or impossible to identify the "special kids."	Enclose an "included" student within a wall of file cabinets to keep behaviors in check.
Work together to design teaching at multiple levels that includes all students. Spend 90% of your collaborative time this way and 10% of your time doing accommodations and adaptations.	Use the coteacher or other professional primarily to develop adaptations to your lessons; ignore (or refrain from asking for) advice on how to teach differently for all students.

with so many special education teachers coming in and out of the class. Other schools assign special education teachers to classes and expect them to provide support to all students with disabilities obtaining consultation from other special education teachers as needed. This has tended to be a more successful practice and has the advantage of increasing skills and knowledge of staff over time.

If students are clustered, special education and other support teachers are typically assigned to only one general education classroom. We have already reviewed the problems with this approach. When heterogeneous student placement occurs, support teachers will work in several general education classrooms, typically three or four. They will negotiate with the teachers involved how to set up their schedule to maximize their effectiveness.

Scheduling and Coteaching

As collaborating partners start working together, we need time for planning. Effective inclusive schools have developed strategies that allow teachers time for collaborative planning (Agnew, Van Cleaf, Camblin, & Shaffer, 1994). Monroe Elementary School schedules "specials" (art, music, gym) at the same time so that teams of teachers can meet together. Hernandez Elementary School blocks specials for all lower elementary teachers in the morning and in the afternoon for upper elementary to allow for collaborative planning time. Still another school, Napoleon High School, closes early one day each week to allow a half day for teacher planning time and in-service development. Incorporating time for collaboration is critical for success.

Collaborating support teachers who work with several general education teachers develop their schedule to address both the needs of classroom teachers for support and the practical limitations of their own timetable. Support teachers are often assigned to teams of teachers. In elementary schools that use multiage teaching, one support teacher might be assigned to "lower el" (K–2) and another to "upper el" (Grades 3–5). In a middle or high school that is using interdisciplinary teams, a support teacher might work with one team of four teachers (Wiedmeyer & Leyman, 1991). In a traditional departmentalized high school, on the other hand, a support teacher might be assigned to each department—math, science, language arts, and so forth (Boudah et al., 1997).

Coteachers and other staff can help design our teaching for diverse students. We can talk together about our students, about the curriculum, about teaching and support strategies that use multiple intelligences, various learning styles, and multilevel teaching. For example, Marvin felt unprepared to teach science in his fourth-grade classroom. He and Mary, the support teacher, developed a plan in which Mary designed and taught the science lesson each day, as she had strong skills in this area. During this time Marvin assisted the support teacher and helped students with special needs. In another situation, a high school English teacher knew he would have several students in his fourth period who were well below "grade level." He and the special education teacher agreed that she would come to the class for this whole period throughout the first weeks of school. Later, as the semester developed and he gained confidence in his ability to work with these students, she shifted her schedule to another time slot. Figure 5.12 provides a picture from the point of view of the classroom teacher.

Professional Development and Growth

As we begin inclusive teaching, we will likely ask for as much help as we can get. That's a natural reaction. As we develop skills and confidence, however, we will often need less assistance, or at least different types of assistance. That's why support for professional growth and development is a critical piece of inclusive teaching. If all goes well, we will become master inclusive teachers who can then provide support to other new teachers coming on board, sharing our learning at conferences, on listservs, and in daily informal conversations with other teachers. What are key ways we can obtain support to grow and develop as teachers? We'll describe a few exemplary strategies and structures.

Professional Development Inquiry and Dialogue Groups. Many are increasingly critical of the typical one-shot staff development workshops in which a consultant comes in for an afternoon or a day, gives a talk, and then leaves. Little real growth occurs from such events. More effective are professional development strategies that enable teachers to study and reflect on their own practice.

All over the country, different structures are being developed by which small groups of teachers meet to learn together in their own schools. For example, in three elementary schools in Detroit, teachers and a faculty member from a local university meet together once a month, read a book regarding exemplary teaching practice, and discuss instructional strategies. In another school a professional development coordinator initiated similar teacher study groups. In still other schools teachers engage in collaborative teaching and demonstrate a new strategy directly in the classroom (Vargo, 1998).

Support Networks of Teachers—Gatherings and Online. In many communities teachers, parents, and university faculty have come together to provide mutual support and work together to improve schools and influence policy. Teachers are increasingly using listservs and chat rooms online to share successes, ask questions, and engage in dialogue about best practices. The Inclusion listserv out of the University of Alberta, with members

FIGURE 5.12

Sample Schedule for a Day of Collaborative Teaching in an Elementary Classroom

TIME	TEACHER	PROFESSIONAL SUPPORT	COMMUNITY PARTNERS IN THE CLASS
8:30	Class meeting. Check certain students' planners to ensure they are writing what is needed.		
8:50	Journal writing. Model writing in own notebook. Occasionally share.		
9:00	Writing workshop—start with whole class 10-minute lesson. Then, small group mini-lessons and one-on-one conferences on content ideas or editing, and assessments.	Special education teacher and speech therapist work with groups. All teachers collaborate in supporting all students.	Peer relations program teaches social skills once a week.
9:45	Reading workshop—due date conferences, and one-on-one reading conferences. Two days a week do guided reading groups. Three days a week do spelling groups.	Special education teacher goes with class to library once a week. Bilingual teacher does whole class lessons twice a week.	
10:45	Instructional read aloud, model comprehension strategies out loud.		Several parents or community volunteers per month read books.
11:05	Exploration learning—approve learning choice for the day, rove and push thinking skills with questions.	Special education teacher conferences with student earlier in the day about what they would like to work on during this choice time.	Residents from local hospital talk to class once a month.
11:30	Specials.		
12:10	Lunch/Recess.		
1:00	Math—one of two groups, same math skills at different levels through spiraling curriculum. Student experts.	Class divides in two with students with special needs in both groups. Both teachers work with individual students providing help as needed.	
2:00	Multiple intelligences themed centers—lead the logical-mathematical center. Integrate science, social studies, literacy, etc.	Teachers share ideas for multi-level teaching and resources for centers.	Volunteers help run interpersonal center once a week. Engineers work with students on building and racing toys cars once a week.

BACK
PACK

> **Power of 2 and Paraprofessionals**
>
> **Power of 2** A comprehensive site for coteaching in inclusive classrooms named after a good video by the same name. Lots of resources and ideas. www.powerof2.org/
>
> **Project Evolve** This site provides resources for training of paraprofessionals. www.uvm.edu/~cdci/paraprep/

all over the world, is a forum for daily intense discussion among parents, teachers, and university faculty regarding strategies for inclusive teaching of students with special needs (go to www.quasar.ualberta.ca/ddc/incl/intro.html). Many teachers have found both live gatherings and online communication to be valuable sources.

Critical Friends and Consultants from Outside the School. An external partner, often called a "critical friend," is important in facilitating positive change and growth in a school. Such an individual comes to know the school well, pulls in additional resources and people, and acts as a supportive critic. For example, Jorgensen (1998) describes working with Souhegan High School and providing assistance in planning and implementing an approach to inclusive schooling. Many faculty at universities have developed partnerships with schools, often supported by grants or contracts. Regional support centers also provide a range of services to schools—video and other media resources, consultants and in-service trainers on various topics, information regarding grants and collaborative opportunities, and professional development programs.

Support for the Road

We hope by now you are beginning to have a few concrete pictures regarding how support is provided in inclusive schools. We also suspect that you may be having a range of reactions. You may be feeling: "This is a fairy tale. No school does these things. Certainly, it won't happen in my school!" It is certainly true that the supports we've described don't yet exist fully in every school. However, in most areas some schools are working hard to put such systems in place. You may also be feeling: "Wow! This is wonderful. I had no idea schools were doing work like this to support teachers and students." If so, we confirm that yes, they are. Support is a foundation for inclusive teaching. When supports are effectively provided, the whole teaching enterprise is strengthened; teachers feel new energy and engagement (Pugach & Johnson, 1995; Rankin et al., 1994); and students increase their learning (Saint-Laurent et al., 1998). In subsequent chapters we will build on these ideas, strategies, tools, and information. You will meet teachers, other professionals, parents, and community groups all collaborating in supporting students in inclusive classes.

Traveling Notes

Learning to collaborate with other professionals in supporting children with real differences in our classroom is a new skill for many teachers. As the journey to becoming a real inclusive teacher continues, we can collaborate with other educators to help ensure that our students are successful. However, we need to use effective strategies and not re-create segregation and isolation within general education classes. Here are some notes of key practices we can follow.

1. Students should be heterogeneously placed in classes and heterogeneously grouped within a class.

2. Educators need to work together in teams to support learning. Every school needs a team of support staff who engage in collaborative consultation with teachers and coordinate support services. Teaching teams of grade-level teachers are important in providing mutual support and facilitating collaborative learning projects.

3. Children should be inclusively grouped, and strategies for building a community where children help one another are specifically taught. The children know what each person needs to work on and a climate of respect is evident. Some specific organizational strategies include multiage teaching, looping, the "school within a school" approach, peer tutoring and mentoring, circles of support, and cooperative learning.

4. Support teachers, paraprofessionals, and related services personnel should provide in-class support and coteaching with general education teachers.

5. Support should involve direct instruction and indirect supports aimed at helping the general education teacher design and implementation of multilevel, differentiated instruction.

6. While coteachers may initially provide help and assistance to the general education teacher, over time teachers should move toward collaborative coteaching where they both share responsibilities for planning and implementation of instruction.

7. Coteachers should be working with all students in the class and avoid pulling students with special needs to the side or back of the class.

8. Teachers should alternate roles within the classroom, using different types of coteaching methods. They work in different setups depending on the lesson: small group, whole group, centers.

9. Support staff have a schedule that allows them to work in several rooms and can adjust to best utilize their time and services.

10. Support teachers, specialists, and general education teachers should have a comfortable, flexible working relationship where they easily work through issues, bounce ideas off each other, and respect the other person.

11. Teachers should receive support as well as the students. This does not always mean teaching support in the classroom. It could be a group that gets together to talk over progress, a strong relationship with one of the support teachers, or a close relationship with some of the families.

Stepping Stones

Following are some activities that will help extend your understanding and actions you may take to improve supports for inclusive teaching in your school.

1. Find out how support services are delivered in your school. Where are the special education teachers, and what do they do? How are services delivered to dominant-language learners? Do you see evidence of racial separation of students? How is gifted and talented education structured? What about other specialists—speech therapists, psychologists, gifted educators, social workers?

2. Identify a student with special needs in your class who is presently being pulled out of your class to obtain assistance. Talk with a support person about how he or she might provide support in your room instead. Start very small if need be.

3. If you already have support staff in your room, how well is the collaboration working? What model of support is being used? How would you like to see this collaboration improved?

Set up a time to talk with support staff about collaborative teaching in your room and how improvements might be made.

4. Interview someone who has successfully dealt with a great challenge. This might be an adult with a disability who has a good job, someone who was once on welfare, or someone who suffered the death of a very close friend. Talk with the person about his or her experiences. What types of support did the person receive? From whom? What difference did the support make? What are the implications for support for inclusive teaching.

5. Visit two classrooms, one in which effective in-class supports are operating and the other in a school that has a reputation for not supporting teachers and where special education uses a pull-out model. Talk with the teachers and students. Ask the teachers about problems and challenges with students. What support do they receive, and what is the impact?

6

Partnering with Families and the Community

Building Relationships for Learning

CHAPTER GOAL

Grasp theoretical and practical aspects of partnering with families in the education of students with special needs.

CHAPTER OBJECTIVES

1. Become more sensitive to the challenges facing families and develop strategies for working effectively with families of children with special needs.
2. Utilize strategies for communication, collaborative problem solving, and support of families.
3. Understand system-, child-, and family-centered approaches to services.
4. Identify ways to connect with community resources that support families and promote learning.

Building Relationships for Learning

A few years ago, a teacher made the following comment at the conclusion of a class focusing on partnering with families: "Before I took this class, I thought that I would be teaching math, science, reading, and social studies. Now I know that I will be teaching children, and with children come families." If we are to be effective teachers of all children, understanding parents is critical.

We are visiting with a parent support group, part of a state-funded parent-to-parent network of families of children with special needs who meet periodically.

We arrive at the home of Ramla, the group's facilitator, and find 15 parents sitting in the living room, some in chairs, some on the floor. We're struck immediately by the diversity represented. Although most participants are women, they come from many different ethnic groups. Some, we are told, have very low incomes; others have moderate to high incomes.

After a welcome from Ramla, Frieda begins. "I am excited about how Melanie's high school drama teacher is reaching out to my daughter," she says with a big smile. Melanie has a severe learning disability and has had trouble with teachers who would not try to help her. "Mr. Kizewski really went out of his way to include Melanie in the school play. With his encouragement she is really blossoming!" she exclaims. "He met with Melanie to make suggestions about how she might practice and how we could help at home. She is having so much fun. It has brought out a side of her we have never seen. Amazingly, this new confidence is spilling over into some of her other courses."

Ramla, the group facilitator, draws a lesson. "We need to look for teachers who develop partnerships with parents," she said. "They need our support. However, others have stories that we need to hear tonight."

"Yes," said Dennis, one of the two fathers at the meeting. "We are very frustrated and would appreciate your support." Looking burdened and with a sigh, Dennis describes his efforts to get his son Matt, a 14-year-old with Down syndrome, into regular academic and industrial arts courses at high school. Dennis became convinced that Matt should be in a regular class after attending conferences and obtaining information from other parents about how much their children were learning.

"We just don't know what to do," Dennis says. "We met with the special education director, principal, and special education teacher. We visited some classes. The industrial arts teacher was encouraging, but he seemed nervous. The special education director told us that inclusion is inappropriate for Matt because Matt's abilities are too low. He says that Matt's special needs can be met only in a special education class. He doesn't even consider, it seems, how much Matt can learn by being with other children. The special education director will not even visit schools that are doing this successfully. We really do not want to take them to a hearing. We also do not want to have to sell our house and move to another district like some other families we know. What are we to do?"

Ramla asks for feedback from the group: "What ideas do you have?" They ask Dennis additional questions and share other stories of frustration. Throughout the next 2 hours, parents discuss concerns and experiences, some of them tearfully. As we leave, we are amazed at the degree of openness, emotional support, and practical advice and help these parents provide to one another. Some stories fill us with hope; others with despair. We ponder how these stories reflect both good and bad practices.

Toward Inclusive, Family-Centered Education
Building Genuine Partnerships

Research clearly demonstrates that if children are to learn and grow, teachers must reach beyond the classroom to partner with families and community members (Ballen & Moles, 1994; Barnett, 1997; Becher, 1984; Epstein, 1994). This is particularly true of children who have learning, social, and/or physical challenges (Bishop, Woll, & Arango, 1993; O'Shea, O'Shea, Algozzine, & Hammitte, 2001). In this part of our journey, we explore ways to connect with parents of students with special needs and harness the power of family partnerships.

The U.S. Department of Education (Ballen & Moles, 1994) has championed the strengthening of partnerships between schools and families by providing grant funds for demonstration programs, helping develop publications that promote effective parent–school partnerships, and encouraging research. Despite this national thrust on partnering with parents, however, parents of children with special needs often find their problems compounded by difficult interactions with teachers and school staff. Parents often sense that teachers do not care about their children. They often receive ongoing negative feedback that makes them feel unwelcome and unsupported. Even the most informed, educated, and committed parents often struggle to get help for their child. In virtually every school district, when parents of children with disabilities talk together, they share stories of pain and struggle like Dennis's story (Turnbull & Turnbull, 1997). Parents from low-income or minority backgrounds who have children with special needs are particularly likely to have difficulties (Comer, 1988; Fialka & Mikus, 1999; Moles, 1993; Villa & Thousand, 1996; Villa, Thousand, Stainback, & Stainback, 1992).

Some teachers and schools do not share this mindset, however. In many communities schools serve as potent centers of the community, reaching out to parents in partnership. These same schools are engaged in effective teaching practices and in active reform efforts.

Sights TO SEE

Engaging Parents in the Education of Their Child

Parent Involvement in Schools This YouTube video is useful in showing parents how they can be connected in the education of their children. www.youtube.com/watch?v=ZEkMidcy960

Family and Community Challenges

What is a family? In the 20th century we thought mostly about the nuclear family—mother and father with children. Grandparents, aunts, and uncles are the extended family. For most of history (and prehistory), however, "family" meant the full village—mother and father, extended family, neighbors, and friends. Everyone in a local community considered children "theirs" and saw themselves as having personal responsibilities to these children. The focus on the nuclear family is recent.

Today, in response to the need for stable relationships and support systems, people are finding new ways of forming social bonds. This trend is causing the definition of what constitutes a family to broaden and shift. If we understand the family of each child as a network of people who are intimately connected to and responsible for one another, we can then more naturally connect with the whole range of people in the life of a child—grandparents, family friends, and mentors (Dunst, 1987; Kagan & Weissbourd, 1994; O'Shea et al., 2001).

Local communities face many challenges, as do the families who live in them. Some of the problems are reported in the newspaper on a daily basis—teenage pregnancy, violence, crime, poverty, unemployment, divorce, illiteracy, disease, substance abuse, illness, and disability. People are isolated and often have few resources to draw upon. Neighbors may know little if anything about one another and may have infrequent interactions (Rankin & Quane, 2000).

As a result of these dynamics, when families encounter problems—such as the loss of a job, divorce, or serious illness—they often feel overwhelmed and alone. For example, perhaps a child with mental retardation is born. Families with children who have disabilities or other health issues may have few resources to call on for support. Human service agencies are often too understaffed and overburdened to provide the level of assistance needed to those encountering these difficulties (Kagan & Weissbourd, 1994; Turnbull & Turnbull, 1997).

Typically, too, such stressors do not occur in isolation. Poor families may occupy substandard housing, have trouble getting employment with a living wage, and live in environments that can contribute to children's learning problems or other disabilities. For example, lead poisoning, long known to damage the learning ability of children, is far more prevalent in housing in low-income neighborhoods (Schmidt, 1999). Many schools in low-income areas are in great disrepair, sometimes causing health and learning problems for children (Agron, 1998; Fraser, Clickner, Everett, & Viet, 1991; Grubb & Diamantes, 1998). Children also come to school with things as basic as daily survival on their mind. This gets in the way of learning. Another kind of difficulty faces the executive who lives in a "nice neighborhood": He or she may be under great pressure to maintain the family's standard of living and may therefore spend little time at home. Also, children in families under stress are more vulnerable to abuse or neglect (Barnett, 1997; Bishop et al., 1993; Coleman, 1994; Dunst, 1987). The family that speaks another language will be wary of interacting with adults at school, knowing the language barrier is great. The child is then moving back and forth between two cultures. As we deal with parents of children with disabilities and other special needs, we must bear all this in mind, trying to understand the world from their point of view.

The Importance of Family and Community for Child Development: An Ecological Framework

For many years the importance of total family and community interactions, the "life ecology" of children, was not well understood. Researchers studied learning in controlled clinical settings, focusing at most on mother–child interactions, rather than

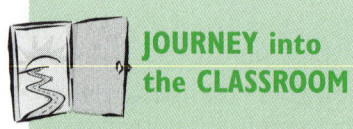

Practical Strategies for Building Positive Working Relationships with Parents:
Conversation with a Middle School Language Arts and Social Studies Teacher

Martin Hiller has a very positive reputation among parents and students alike in his middle school. He is known for his work with diverse students and for the respect he shows parents in his ethnically diverse community. We interviewed Martin about how he works for parents. He shared some practical, useful insights.

Michael: Martin, we hear that you have a very positive working relationship with many of your parents. Can you share with us what you do?

Martin: Well, thanks for asking. I believe that I must work hard to build a relationship with parents of my students. Parents entrust me with their most precious asset, their children. If I am going to be an effective teacher, I must make this a priority.

First priority is to understand the children that I teach. Often, they have many things going on in their lives. I need to understand why things are happening. For example, Melinda comes 30 minutes late almost every day. Initially, I was very irritated. She often missed the opening meeting where our team makes announcements and we get students started in the class. (I work with an interdisciplinary team of four teachers for the sixth grade. We start every day with a gathering of all 90 of our students.) However, when I talked with her I found that her mother works until 4 in the morning and Melinda lets her sleep the extra half hour because she knows how exhausted she is. There are similar issues with the kids involved in our sports team. They want to win the tournament this year and spend a lot of time into many evenings in practices. It's critical that I understand what is happening and then work out a solution with students and parents rather than just reacting.

Next, I also have a responsibility in helping make parents' lives easier. Sometimes all I can do is listen and show that I care. Many parents have never experienced this with a teacher and they really appreciate it. I pride myself on working to know about resources in the community that I can suggest to parents. I've connected parents with resources ranging from Big Brothers to a local store that sells appliances that have been repaired and sell at a low price. Knowing someone is behind them and cares about their family makes such a difference.

Often, parents begin to consider me like a part of the family! As they begin to trust me, I have often been invited to dances, birthday parties, or church functions. I vividly remember the first birthday party I attended. The student was handing out birthday invitations to some students in class. He walked up to me and with a big smile handed me his card. Now I had a choice: I could gently tell him I had something to do and get out of it. However, I chose to attend the party. It was the beginning of an important connection that made a huge difference as their son faced a major crisis later in the year.

Of course, to develop relationships I have to take the time to communicate with parents. There are so many ways to make communicating easy. At the first of the year I make a personal contact by phone or in person with each parent. You'll be thinking, of course, that with 90 students this takes a lot of time. For sure it does. My goal, however, is to talk to all parents no later than the first week of school. I start calling the week before school starts. I am not calling to discuss a problem but to simply introduce myself, see if they have any questions, get to know them a bit, and also ask them for ideas that may help their child learn. I make notes on a recording form I've developed for this (see Figure 6.1). I add to this throughout the year. By the time classes start, I know a lot already about my students.

The school curriculum night is not the time to do this, by the way. That night I build on a relationship that has already begun. Today, of course, e-mail is often a quick and effective way to discuss things with parents. I even have parents who will e-mail a response back to me and ask me to let the child read it. I also have students keep a planner in which parents can write notes and check daily. I send home a weekly newsletter that tells what is going on in the class and lists my email so parents can contact me.

FIGURE 6.1

Notes About Parents and Students

STUDENT NAME	PARENT NAME/ CONTACT INFO	INFO ABOUT THE PARENT (Interests, possible contributions to the class, background, etc.)	SUGGESTIONS FOR LEARNING (Interests, learning style, difficulties, etc.)
Reggie	Reginald/Natasha Williams	Mom is a nurse, father works for GM, willing to read to class	Loves sports, interest in reading a concern
Mya	Tanya Blake	Works long hours, concern about who can help her with school	Math a concern, basic facts, loves to sing, very social
Colin	Daren Troy	Mechanic, recent divorce	Very into working on own, social concerns, loves to read, science, and put things together
Maurice	Lachrise Tyler	Willing to help make props for school	Very active, loves to act, sing, and play football
Jenna	James/Belinda Byran	Father works with computers, mom interested in helping w/class books at home	Loves school, loves to help others, loves computers

A few children in my room will be on a weekly report that lists what they have completed and how their behavior has been. There are also a few students who are on a daily report. This is for those who are really struggling with either behavior or completing work. These reports can be very valuable if I have talked with the parent about this strategy and we have agreed to work together.

An open door to parents is also a huge relationship builder. If parents know they are welcome in my room, this changes how they feel when I contact them. Sometimes I invite them to participate in a lesson, to connect with their children at recess on their lunch hour once a week, read a book to the class, or share information about their job. With many working parents, they cannot come into school but they may be able to contribute outside of school time. The possibilities are endless. For example, I may ask parents to help collect art supplies, create flyers for an event, or anything else that comes to mind. Parents will feel invested in my classroom if they feel they are a part of it.

Michael: Martin, thanks for sharing these thoughts. However, I am struck by how much energy and thought you put into dealing with the parents, in addition to your students. Can teachers really be expected to do this?

Martin: Well, I know that many teachers complain that they do not have time to relate to parents. However, if I want students to succeed I *must* take the time. When I do this, I find that, over the long run, it actually *saves time* because when problems occur we have a relationship where we usually can get to a working solution quickly. If I haven't taken this time, I will be embedded in a crisis. It just helps my students be more successful and helps me enjoy my job more as a teacher!

Reflection: Many teachers feel that their greatest challenge is not the students but the parents of students! Yet, parents can also be our greatest allies and supporters. Martin gives us a lot to think about regarding how we can invest in positive relationships.

seeking to understand the complex influences of family and community. Urie Bronfenbrenner (1979) developed a widely utilized theory, an adaptation of which is graphically presented in Figure 6.2, that broke with this tradition and posited an ecological model of human development. This ecological framework posits that all aspects of the environment have an impact on child development and growth. A hierarchy of interacting influences is apparent. Those most critical are in inner circles—family, intimate relationships, close friends, and community mentors. For optimum growth and development, a child will be supported by this inner circle—which is, in turn, supported by key community institutions—such as church, synagogue, school, or the business community. When this framework breaks down, children have problems.

The implications of this ecological theory for teachers and schools are substantial. What are teachers and educators to do if a child does not have a caring social support system? Comer (1997) and others (Ballen & Moles, 1994; Hyde, Burchard, & Woodworth, 1996; Moles, 1993) suggest that the school must become a caring community where children are nurtured and where adults and other children become a support system for the child. Kretzman and McKnight (1993) suggest that the school develop partnerships with the community to link community resources to parents; providing support for parents, in turn, can make them better able to care for their children. We will find that our approach to parents of children with special challenges is key to building a truly caring learning community for all families and their children. Let us consider, then, the needs and challenges of such parents.

Principles and Practices for an Inclusive, Family-Centered School

Our goal is to make the family the center of learning where services are available and easily accessible. What do we mean by this? Understanding the differences among system-centered, child-centered, and family-centered approaches, as summarized in Figure 6.3, gives us a framework to answer this question.

System-centered services are organized for the convenience of the system—for the organization providing services and those in it rather than for the child or the family. This is both the most typical and the least desirable approach. Each of the three examples given in Figure 6.3 is driven by the needs and requirements of the system rather than by those of the family. In some cases, as with the example of the requirement for assessment, the original intent may have been to provide more effective services for children. However, such requirements often develop into inflexible bureaucratic procedures that no longer serve the child or family well.

Child-centered services focus on the needs of the child, usually without looking at the child in the context of the total family unit. In the examples in Figure 6.3, service providers give directives to a family to assist their child, but without dialogue or consideration of family circumstances. For example, if library books are sent home and the parents themselves are marginally literate, these books will not be read and the child may receive negative feedback about reading. If a communication device is sent home without the involvement of the family, family members may not know how to use it.

Family-centered services, on the other hand, focus on the total family unit. The child is considered in the context of the entire family. Families are given choices for meeting times and choices regarding services for their children that fit into their overall structures and needs. They are given support and assistance (e.g., child care provided by the school) so they can attend meetings. Families can meet with school people based on their convenience, so it is unnecessary to leave work to attend an important meeting. These strategies, of course, require that schools and other organizations rethink how they provide services. The fact is that in most systems the customers fit the system's needs,

FIGURE 6.2

Ecological Framework for Child Development

COMMUNITY (Microsystem)

Circle 1   Inner circle: family, close friends, spouse
Circle 2   Friends and acquaintances
Circle 3   Participation: acquaintances in local stores, community groups, or associations

PAID HELPERS (Mesosystem)

Circle 4   Paid helpers: doctors, teachers, dentists
Circle 5   Special human services: vocational rehabilitation, welfare caseworkers

ADMINISTRATION AND POLICY (Exosystem)

Policymakers and administrations: city council and school board, state legislature, U.S. Department of Education

SOCIETY AND CULTURE (Macrosystem)

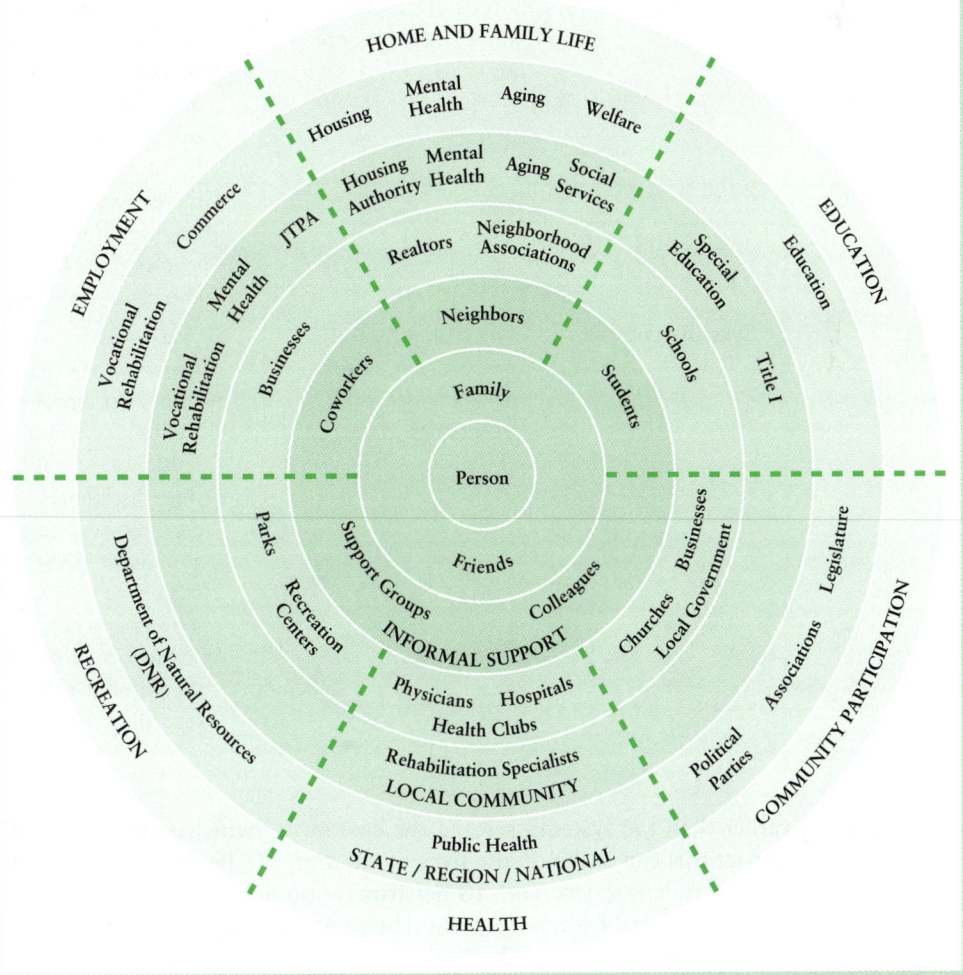

FIGURE 6.3

Family-, Child-, and System-Centered Services

TYPE OF SERVICE	DEFINITION	EXAMPLES
Family-centered	The priorities and choices of the family drive the delivery of services.	Child care is provided while a parent and child have a conference with the teacher. The school provides space for parent-to-parent support groups to meet at night or during the day. Meetings for IEPs are arranged based on the family schedule. A teacher and parent together develop a plan to have a child do grocery lists for the family to help the child improve in writing.
Child-centered	The strengths and needs of the child drive the delivery of services.	The school psychologist asks a family to spend time each night with a child doing schoolwork. The speech therapist orders an augmentative communication device that will be used both at home and school. Children with special needs are sent books home to read without involving the family in these choices or how they might be used.
System-centered	The strengths and needs of the system drive the delivery of services.	Office hours for a case manager, a mental health professional who helps coordinate services for children and families, are 9:00 a.m. to 4:00 p.m. M–F. An interdisciplinary assessment of psychological, cognitive, personality, and motor skills is required for a student to receive special education services and assistance. An educational plan is given to the parent to sign at a meeting regarding the child.

rather than the system's serving the customer—which in this case is the family. Yet the impact this can make on the lives of children can be enormous. One parent of a middle school student shared with us her frustration at not being able to get in touch with her child's teacher. "I work late, and when I get off she is never here. She has no method of weekly communication, like Friday folders or assignment books; she does not return my phone calls, and I am very worried about my daughter's reading. I can't just take off work to come talk to her." The system was failing this parent (Allen & Petr, 1995; Kagan & Weissbourd, 1994; Knoll, 1994).

In sum, system-, child-, and family-centered services represent very different perspectives on education and other human services. Family-centered services are the most effective, recognizing the needs of the entire family unit and the important influence of the family in the life of the child. Several principles provide guidance as we develop family-centered education practices. From these principles flow a series of practices that schools can use to effectively engage parents as they educate children.

Engage Families as Partners. Partnership between two or more parties implies equality of power. As representatives of the school system, we hold great power. For a partnership to work, then, we must make conscious efforts to equalize the power between schools and parents. This is difficult but very rewarding. As described earlier in this chapter, rather than making demands of parents, we must seek their suggestions and ideas, offer choices, and invite them to participate in their child's school (Allen & Petr, 1995; Dunst, 1987; Knoll, 1994). One teacher shared a beautiful example of how valuable parents' suggestions can be. She was very worried about a little boy labeled "trainable mentally retarded" in her fifth-grade classroom. In talking with the mother, the teacher commented that the boy was having great difficulty settling down and keeping his hands to himself. "I just couldn't understand what the problem was. He never used to be this difficult." The boy's mom explained that he had not been able to run and play for the last 6 weeks because of an air cast on his ankle. "It was hidden by his clothing, so I had forgotten it. Suddenly his behavior made sense."

Affirm and Build on Family Strengths and Gifts. All families have strengths. It is our job to see, understand, and draw on those strengths. This is sometimes very difficult, for we live in a culture that focuses on people's deficits. For example, a mother may be a drug addict, live in an apartment in great disrepair, and not have worked in 2 years. Some people, unable to see beyond her problems, might say she doesn't care about her children. However, as you confer with her you see how she talks about her son, see how hard she is trying to do better. This recognition becomes a way to connect with her, as we acknowledge her efforts and give someone with whom she can talk. Then we can find many strengths on which to build (Bishop et al., 1993; Dunst, 1987; Knoll, 1994).

Matt has been working very hard on his assignments. He had lots of difficulties early in the year but all his teachers and his mother feel very good about the efforts he's been putting forth. They want him to know they appreciate his work.

Honor Cultural Diversity. Truly honoring cultural diversity is much easier to say than to do. We must develop a sense of who we are, an understanding of our own culture and of how it has influenced our thinking and values. A mistake we often make is to fail to understand how our own cultural perceptions actually differ from those of others and to assume that our own judgments are unbiased or that they even transcend cultural mores.

We also must recognize that our school has its own culture and expectations—which are often different from the culture of the child. This "cultural mismatch" can be very problematic. Faltis (2000), for example, tells of a teacher who was concerned about a girl who did not engage in movement and choice activities and would never share in partner time. The teacher discovered, however, that in the girl's family culture, children were expected to talk little and to listen much when around adults. Once the teacher understood this, she and the parents were able to talk about ways that the student could share what she was thinking in the class. At first the student did this through writing in a journal, which she shared with a classmate. It often happens that as we understand the culture of a child's family, we can create conditions in our classroom that match better, thus increasing our capacity to know what the child's responses mean and providing a link between learning at home and the school. Families can and will often be our teachers in this regard if we let them (Bishop et al., 1993; Dunst, 1987; Faltis, 2000; Knoll, 1994).

Virtually all cultures have their own ways of viewing children with disabilities. In some cultures, great shame is brought on the family. In others, the family sees the child as a special person from God and seeks to build a nurturing (though often heavily protective) circle around the child. In the former case, we have to help the parents see the strengths of the child and model acceptance through our own behavior. In the latter, we can draw from the caring tradition of the family, yet suggest and model ways that the child can become more independent (Turnbull & Turnbull, 1997).

Treat Families with Respect and Dignity. Particularly when families are experiencing difficulty or when they challenge us, teachers can feel threatened and react in unhelpful ways. When a mother living in poverty is concerned for her child's safety in her neighborhood but is also frightened of the school, she may be angry and defensive with the teachers. When a parent is concerned about her child's treatment by teachers, she may act suspicious or hostile. All of this requires that we try and understand why. We look for the strengths of families and are firmly grounded in a commitment to listen to families and treat them with respect, seeking to put ourselves in their shoes. As we take the initiative to reach out and communicate, we will often encourage trust and may have opportunities to see assets as well as problems. When we do this, we will earn families' respect (Bishop et al., 1993; Turnbull & Turnbull, 1997).

Promote Family Choices. Providing choices is particularly important for families of children with disabilities or other special needs. Too often families have been given very restrictive choices and have been pressured by schools to accept the recommendations of educators with little or no consultation. This is particularly likely to occur when children are identified by the school as having academic or behavioral difficulties (O'Shea et al., 2001; Turnbull & Turnbull, 1997).

These principles ground us in our mission to develop effective family-centered services and lead us to partnership with families. You should note that these principles and practices relate to parents of all students, not only to those identified as having "special needs." However, family-centered education is particularly important for these families. With special students we particularly need inclusive family partnerships—so that their special needs and issues can be addressed not in separate meetings and structures but in the context of other parent partnership activities. Let's now consider specific practices through which we can partner with and support parents of children with special needs in our teaching.

Welcome Parents into the School as Partners. Schools that support families look for ways to welcome families as genuine partners in the life of the school. As teachers we are an important part of this process. Welcoming can be as simple as a friendly greeting in the hall when we encounter parents—or as complex as inviting elected

SCHOOLS to VISIT

Listening to Families and the Community

Puesta del Sol Elementary
450 Southern Boulevard SE
Rio Rancho, NM 87124

One school that listens to families is Puesta del Sol Elementary. The school serves a moderate-to-middle-income group of families representing a cross section of New Mexico's ethnic diversity and is one of the 11 collaborating schools involved with the Dual License Program of the University of New Mexico, a teacher education program in which student teachers are certified in both general and special education to support inclusive teaching. As a member of the Coalition of Essential Schools, Puesta consciously practices the philosophy of building an inclusive community.

The principal, Connie Chene, came to Puesta with both an appreciation for special education and an awareness of the need to do things differently. Her previous experience, as an assistant principal in a school that served students with severe disabilities by teaching them on separate sides of the campus, opened her eyes to the issues of segregation. When she began at Puesta del Sol, 100 students were schooled in the main building and in 32 outside portable buildings. All the special education programs were outside. Connie said the special education students and teachers "had been made second-class citizens just by the physical placement of the programs." Connie listened to her teachers, parents, and children.

Teachers helped provide the impetus for change. They wanted to team-teach, to talk to one another, and, most importantly, to make special education more a part of the school. "The reform efforts began here with special education knocking on the door and insisting that we open," Connie says; it was inclusion before Connie and her faculty had a name for it. The initial idea was to share resources, to be aware that everyone had something to offer someone else, and to know that there was a lot more they could do.

The voices of parents advocating for their individual children catalyzed more change. Of the children who were bused to schools outside the community, one boy with Down syndrome received maximum special education services. His mom wanted him to attend Puesta and learn to socialize with other children. Connie arranged to have him attend Puesta with the following conditions: The people involved (teacher, parent, administrator, and special education department) communicated almost daily, and a dual certified teacher worked with him in the general education classroom. The voices and caring behavior of the 25 general education children in the room demonstrated to this student how school works; they played with him and he taught them. The next year, a general and special educator team taught. Staff took a hammer to a separating wall in a double-wide portable classroom and broke down the barrier. This became the first inclusive classroom at the school, and many others have become a reality since that time.

By Liz Keefe and Pam Rossi, University of New Mexico.

representatives to serve on the local school board with authority to hire and fire the principal or on the school improvement committee. For all parents, coming into a school can be unsettling. This is particularly true of low-income parents and of parents who themselves did poorly in school (Ballen & Moles, 1994). They may remember feelings of rejection or hurt. However, even parents who have high status may feel that they are entering another world, a world they only partially understand. Reaching out to welcome people, making people comfortable, helping them feel ownership is important (Barnett, 1997; Coleman, 1994; Epstein, 1994).

Welcome and Care About Children with Special Needs. Although it may seem simplistic, a most important element in working with parents who have children with disabilities is to welcome their children into our classrooms and show that we care about them. The experience of many families of such children is that teachers and other professionals reject their children because they feel untrained, fearful, or disinterested (University of Alberta, 2000). When we simply welcome these children into our classes and communicate to families, we can make a difference to that child and family in many positive ways.

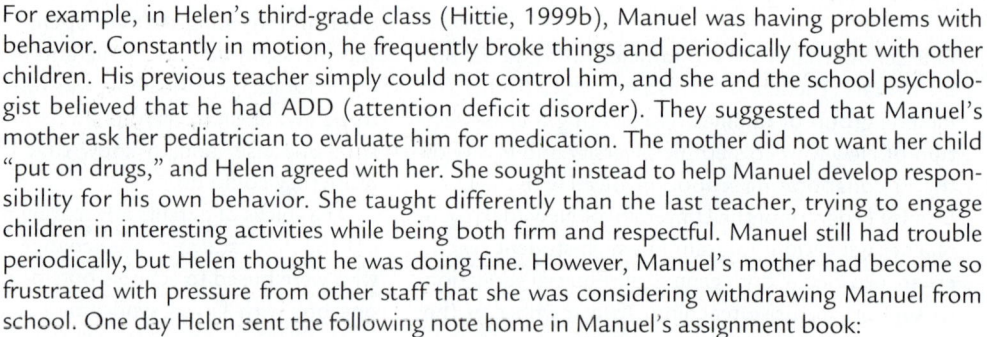

For example, in Helen's third-grade class (Hittie, 1999b), Manuel was having problems with behavior. Constantly in motion, he frequently broke things and periodically fought with other children. His previous teacher simply could not control him, and she and the school psychologist believed that he had ADD (attention deficit disorder). They suggested that Manuel's mother ask her pediatrician to evaluate him for medication. The mother did not want her child "put on drugs," and Helen agreed with her. She sought instead to help Manuel develop responsibility for his own behavior. She taught differently than the last teacher, trying to engage children in interesting activities while being both firm and respectful. Manuel still had trouble periodically, but Helen thought he was doing fine. However, Manuel's mother had become so frustrated with pressure from other staff that she was considering withdrawing Manuel from school. One day Helen sent the following note home in Manuel's assignment book:

> Mrs. Acosta, I am going to continue to do my best with Manuel. I have a new idea to try. I want him to pick one goal each day. What do you think? Give me some time with him before you give up on us.

Helen received the following response from this parent—a person described as "difficult" by others in the school:

> Thank you! So much. This is the only good thing that has been said to me. Yes, please, whatever you can do to help me. I will be glad to see ideas you have. Goals sound good. Let us go that way. Please write or call me at any time. [She then gave three phone numbers.] I'm really trying hard. I'm in tears almost every night for my son. Thank you again.

In this example, a simple act of communication on the part of this teacher made an enormous difference for this parent. Throughout the year Manuel's mother worked with Helen. Manuel, her son, continued to do better in this class than in any prior year. This story powerfully illustrates the impact that a simple welcome can have on a parent. It also illustrates the pressure that educators sometimes put on parents to obtain medication for their children—and suggests that a more effective approach may be working with the child and trying new strategies.

Communicate Effectively with Families. One of our most important jobs as teachers is communicating with families of the children with whom we work. We may have difficulty responding to parents who get angry, appear unreasonable, or want us to cure the problems their child is having. It is easy to feel scared and to get defensive, return the anger, or blame the parents. In fact, too often this is what parents experience from teachers. We need strategies that will enable us to communicate effectively. This is particularly important when we need to talk with parents regarding concerns we are having about their children. Next we discuss helpful strategies.

Explain how our teaching works and helps children learn. If we are using best practice teaching strategies (discussed in Chapters 6, 8, 11, and 14), it is highly probable that what goes on in our class looks very different from what the parents of our children experienced. We will need to be able to explain to parents what we are doing and why, helping parents understand the theory of learning that undergirds our approach. As we do this, parents will become our best supporters and will also be learning how to be better partners with us in helping their children learn (Oglan, 1997).

Be a resource and support for families. We must expand our role from being solely centered in the classroom to caring about the whole lives of the children we teach. Teachers are constantly aware of needs, and we often encounter opportunities to serve as resources, even within a limited amount of time. As teachers assist families in these broader ways, we gain credibility among parents and community members (Epstein, 1994).

The following story illustrates how one principal played a key role in the life of one family. It was Steven Davis's first day as a principal of an elementary school that served many low-income children. Steven was told to watch out for Jim, a young boy who had started a fire in the office last year, and he decided to make a home visit to talk with Jim's parents. As he drove down the dirt road to the dilapidated mobile home, he saw Jim's father step out looking as if no one had set foot on his property in years. Jim's father yelled, "What do you want?" Steven replied, "I'm the new principal. Just came by to chat a bit." Jim's father replied, "You wanna talk, come down to the barn." So Steven and the entire family walked down to the barn and sat on bales of hay among the pigs and talked. After an hour of conversation, Steven drove home. Jim continued to have some minor problems at school over the next few years, but nothing as drastic as setting a fire.

Almost 3 years later Steven answered the phone at his home one evening. Jim's father said somberly, "Mr. Davis, my wife just shot herself, and I'm not sure what to tell the children. If you could come and sit with us for a while, we sure would appreciate it." Steven drove back out to the mobile home to sit, talk, and support Jim and his family (Arnold, 1998).

Listen reflectively. We recently visited a high school on parent–teacher conference night and overheard several conversations between parents and teachers.

"We have been getting such negative notes about Andrew in school. Why can't you tell us something positive?" we heard a parent ask 10th-grade teacher Rosa Sanchez. "Mrs. Rodriguez, you know your son has not been turning in his homework and has been causing trouble in the lunchroom," said Rosa. "It has just got to stop. You must control your son." Mrs. Rodriguez became more angry. We wondered what else was going on in Andrew's life that was influencing his behavioral choices.

Shortly we came upon a similar conversation. Mr. Hall was speaking to the English teacher Randy Brookes. "You called last night expressing concern that my daughter Shirley has missed several classes and did not turn in an important paper. We did not know about this! Why have you not called before now?" Randy responded, "Mr. Hall, I am so glad you came in. Last night I was checking my records and realized I did not have her paper and called right away. You seem concerned about Shirley." Mr. Hall visibly seemed to relax and settled in the chair. They continued to talk.

Austin lives with his grandparents. Ginger, his teacher, shares about Austin's progress and some help he needs. She makes suggestions how Austin's grandparents can support his learning at home.

These two anecdotes illustrate, respectively, poor and good reflective listening. We must seek to listen carefully to parents (and children) as they talk with us. We must first attend to what they say, and second understand the feelings and deeper meanings underneath the spoken words. A simple but powerful communication technique involves several steps (Benjamin, 1981; Carkhuff, 2000):

1. Listen carefully to the person.
2. Check your accuracy by summarizing what the person says.
3. Probe for additional information or depth.

In the first example, Rosa Sanchez defended her own actions rather than really listening to the parent and probing what was happening. In the process she created an adversary rather than a partner. Randy Brookes, on the other hand, simply explained his actions and reflected back to Mr. Hall his observation that the father seemed concerned about Shirley. Mr. Hall continued talking about his daughter in the spirit of trust that Randy had begun to build through this simple response. Rosa might have responded similarly: "Mrs. Rodriguez, I appreciate your coming to talk to me. I know it must be hard hearing that Andrew is having trouble. I have been concerned about him, and I am sorry if you've only heard bad things. Let's talk together."

As we work with families of children with disabilities, we will have many occasions to listen reflectively. Parents are trying to help their children, cope with stress at home and work, and deal with unfriendly schools and services, and they may become frustrated. If we listen reflectively and let parents know that we hear them and care about their children, we can build trust and provide support to parents. Of course, we must be genuine as we do so, not just acting as if we care. Parents will quickly recognize artificiality and withdraw (O'Shea et al., 2001; Turnbull & Turnbull, 1997).

Communicate positively about children. Many children with disabilities have academic or social difficulties in the classroom—typically either doing poorly in their academic work or demonstrating problematic behaviors. As a result, unfortunately, families often receive repeated negative feedback from teachers that makes them feel defensive, creating conditions in which it is hard to engage in positive planning discussions. This does not mean that teachers should not address problems, but it does mean that we should do so in a way that recognizes the strengths and interests as well as the needs of the child. Here are some simple but effective guidelines for communicating positively with parents:

1. Frequently communicate positive strengths of the child—through notes home, comments to parents as they pick the child up in the afternoon, parent–teacher conferences, or telephone calls. Such actions build up an "emotional bank account" of positive rapport that makes dealing with problems much easier.
2. When a problem arises that needs to be communicated, do it as personally and as positively as possible. Ask for the family's input.
3. Develop a plan that involves a partnership between parent and teacher in which both have input. Establish a time and method for communicating progress.

Ask for input, ideas, and involvement of families. Families know more about their children than anyone and can provide us with some very valuable information if we ask and listen respectfully and carefully. As we develop teaching strategies for children, asking for the input and ideas of families regarding learning goals and strategies is invaluable. The caution, however, is to refrain from expecting parents to solve the problems about which we are concerned.

Engage in parent–teacher conferences and planning meetings. Key times for teachers and parents to talk together are the times virtually all schools set aside for parent–teacher conferences. Many schools are using innovative approaches to these conferences, involving students and parents in more active and positive roles. **Student-led conferences** are particularly powerful ways to help parents see what has been occurring in class and student learning. For children with special needs, teachers will often have special conferences with parents that involve an **interdisciplinary team,** a group of professionals who help support a student; these teams often include a teacher, a psychologist, a social worker, an occupational therapist, a speech therapist, and others. The intent of these meetings is to provide an opportunity to review progress and develop plans for students. These include Individualized Education Plans (IEPs) for students who have been identified as having disabilities and who qualify for special education services and 504 plans for students with disabilities who do not qualify for special education (see Chapter 4). At other times, meetings may be called with the parents and children that bring together teachers and support staff who are concerned about a particular student. Ultimately, the aim is the same as the typical parent–teacher conference. They provide an opportunity to develop needed supports and accommodations in greater depth with the input of multiple professionals. Ongoing, informal communication with parents, however, is critical to make these meetings effective. If teachers and parents are communicating on an ongoing basis, they will be working together to arrive at many of the goals and strategies that will be formalized with other professionals in a meeting.

Respond to the Special Needs of Families

As we work to partner with parents in an inclusive, family-centered approach to schooling, we will use the strategies we have just discussed in ways that respond to the unique needs and characteristics of students and families. Let's look at needs and approaches to various types of families.

BUMpS IN THE ROAD   *Parents of My Kids Don't Care! Parents of MY Kids Care Too Much!*

Perhaps the biggest bump in the road for effective, inclusive schools are negative attitudes of educators. There is no doubt that when things go wrong in schools, educators and parents often point fingers of blame toward one another. The more stress that occurs in the school environment, the more this happens. For example, anger and blame are often present in schools that serve poor families from minority groups, with parents (of any ethnic group or socioeconomic status) who have children with special needs who work hard to advocate for their children, and with parents of children considered gifted and talented who want teachers to challenge and support the growth of their children.

According to *Time* magazine (Gibbs, 2005), some educators reported some parents as:

- Helicopter parents—who hover over their children and get in the way of their developing self-reliance.
- Teacher's pests—who ask too much of the teacher and school.
- Monster parents—who are constantly looking for reasons to disagree with educators.
- Dry-cleaner parents—who drop off their rambunctious kids and want them all cleaned up and proper by the end of the day.

This same article reported that while 90% of teachers felt that parent involvement was important, only 25% were satisfied with their connections with parents. In fact, 31% identified parents as their major challenge as a teacher, whereas 73% said many parents treat schools and teachers as enemies.

As we look at this list we can see a pattern. Parents are criticized for either being involved too much or too little, particularly if the parents are poor or members of minority ethnic or cultural groups (Nakagawa, 2000). Parents, on the other side, report that educators sometimes retaliate against their efforts to respectfully advocate for their children by (1) delaying, (2) responding in ways to threaten or seek to cause fear, and (3) engaging in acts that try to punish parents.

What do we make of this? Certainly parents are human beings and they will make mistakes. However, these characterizations don't really help build the partnership or suggest respectful strategies. It seems to us that we have a responsibility to do the best we can to develop respectful relationships with parents. We must go the extra mile. If we experience some of these actions, we first (and continually) ask: "Why is this parent reacting this way? What legitimate need underlies this behavior?" If we can listen and seek to understand, we may gain the trust of parents. When we do so we may be in a position to help parents better support the learning and growth of their children.

Families with Ethnic, Cultural, and Language Differences

Parents of children who have a different cultural background have another layer of filters to sort through when communicating with teachers. They live in between two worlds. Keeping their heritage alive in their family is often important. They may speak another language, dress according to their cultural norms, and observe customs with which we are not familiar.

Families who come from different ethnic groups face substantial challenges in schools. We discussed some of these from the perspective of students in Chapter 1 and 2. As we discussed in Chapter 2, families of color are also more likely to be poor. In some cultural groups, teachers are seen to represent authority and they are seldom questioned. These parents may be particularly quiet and withdrawn in our presence. Other parents may have had bad experiences with previous teachers, feeling that their children were treated poorly or that teachers acted as if the parents were unintelligent. We will have to work very hard to build their trust and be careful not to personalize their anger and resentment.

Parents from minority ethnic groups report particular concern about the cultural environment of schools. Public Agenda (2006), for example, reports:

> If an adult had to work in an environment where disrespect, bad language, fighting and drug and alcohol abuse are practiced by a relative few, but tolerated or winked at by management, it might be considered a "hostile workplace." Yet, this is precisely the environment that many minority students face when they go to school. For too many youngsters, the data suggest, rowdy, unsettled schools are a significant hurdle to learning.

This reality is particularly true for minority parents who are poor.

Of course, this is not always true. We may be dealing with parents who have moved to areas where they hope the schools and neighborhood is better. In fact, communities all over the world are becoming more culturally and ethnically diverse. In such situations, for minority parents they often are moving into areas where members of their ethnic group are in the minority. Frequently these parents will have experienced a range of reactions in the local area from outright racist, rejecting responses to a sense of isolation. Many local communities are working hard to create acceptance and valuing of racial and ethnic diversity.

The point is, of course, we need to be sensitive to and seek to understand the past experiences of parents. This is critical to establishing trust and working relationships. Here are some key strategies we can do to build working relationships with parents from varied cultural and ethnic groups (Carasquillo, 1996; Comer, 1988; Education Alliance at Brown University, 2008; Gross, 2008; Moore, 1999; Pang, 2005; Townsend, 2000):

We will work hard to help parents and families feel comfortable in our classroom. Let them know they can come to our class at any time. Many teachers provide parents numerous methods of contacting them including e-mail addresses and cell phone numbers.

We can show interest in the culture and experiences of the family. We want to communicate that we see the parents and family as having important assets and contributions. Ask questions. As we come to understand, incorporate aspects of this culture into our classroom instruction and how our room is decorated. Ask family members to come in and share their personal story and information about their home country and/or culture. We must remember that this goes far beyond an ethnic food fair! Be attuned to issues of social justice, the political dynamics of their home country, and their experiences in schools and the community. When we show a listening ear and honor family experiences we'll often be surprised how we may be accepted into the family and culture itself.

We also seek to understand social customs and interaction styles. Schools have their own culture and expectations that often conflict with cultural norms of families. For example, students may be taught to be submissive to authority figures, including teachers. These students may not talk in class. We may consider, on the other hand, children from other cultures as loud, boisterous, and even aggressive. This stereotype is often applied to boys who have ethnic roots in Africa, for example. As we understand cultural patterns of social interaction, we'll be in a better place to communicate with parents and our students.

Attending events in the neighborhood of the family, particularly those tied to cultural events, can give us a presence in the local community and put us in a new role where parents can see us as real people, more than just an authority figure and professional. We can also visit local community centers and explore the neighborhoods in which our students live (we discuss this later in the chapter). Families will see that we actually care about their community, which can help deepen support and respect for us as teachers.

We can also work with others in the school to create forums and opportunities where families can express their feelings and where their input can be used to help improve the school and organize events where families have a meaningful part in connecting with their children's education. For example, some schools have had "science nights," "math nights," or "writing nights" where families and children engage in a collaborative learning activity. Such events can help families understand how their children are learning and help us strengthen relationships with them.

Families Who Are Poor

Parents who are poor struggle in ways that make it hard for them to reach out to teachers. Daily life is difficult in ways that are hard to comprehend. All parents have dreams and goals for their children. They love them and want what is best for them. However, for some daily reality is so harsh that those dreams and goals take a backseat to daily survival. Such parents may be thinking: "How can I expect to plan for my child's future if I do not know if I have any food to put on the table for dinner and I am scared for their safety every time they leave my doors?"

Many teachers are vocal in their complaints about the lack of involvement of parents in lower socioeconomic areas. They say that parents do not care and their interactions are often negative and judgmental. Yet, another group of teachers realize that, far from not caring, these parents are doing the best they know how for their children.

What can and should we do with parents who are very poor? Here are a few suggestions:

First and foremost, we must treat these parents with the same respect as we do any other parent. We can work to establish a relationship, understand their daily struggles and living situation, and make them feel welcome.

Often poor families may be difficult to contact. They may not have a phone, and notes carried from students may not reliably be delivered to parents. We need to consider various ways to make an initial contact. One strategy is a visit to the parents' home to introduce ourselves, establish rapport, and make a connection. We need to understand that parents may be ashamed, but if we treat them with respect and gentleness we may create an important trusting relationship. Oftentimes, of course, families who are poor live in areas that are considered "bad." However, when we choose to see positive qualities that are there in any neighborhood and show courage in arranging to safely visit a home, parents will understand and appreciate how we are reaching out to them.

Second, we need to be thoughtful about how some school expectations can cause great difficulty and stress for parents who are poor. These include school fees and supplies, homework, and access to books and reading material. Typical school requests for supplies or fees when going on a field trip may be a great source of stress and shame for parents who are poor. We should work with other teachers in the school and local agencies to obtain funds that we can use for students from poor homes. We might conduct fund-raisers during the year for this purpose or access any special funds available to the school such as Title I monies.

We need to understand also that students who are very poor have home conditions where doing homework is difficult if not impossible. Therefore, it is important that we create opportunities for students to work on homework at school. If a student is in an after-school program, ensure that the child does homework during that time. If in secondary school, help the student incorporate a time to do homework as part of his or her class schedule. Many secondary schools have "advisory" times daily when students can meet with advisors and work on school projects. Study periods may also be scheduled.

A very practical way to develop relationships with parents who are poor is to make it our business to know about helping resources in the community and seek to connect parents with such resources that may be helpful to them. If we know agencies, for example, that provide wrap-around services (see below) or help families who have children with special needs, we may be able to facilitate an important connection that will make a difference in the lives of the family and their children (our students).

Families of Children Who Are Gifted and Talented

Families who have children considered gifted and talented are often challenging to teachers in a very different way. While a common complaint from teachers is that parents are not adequately involved with their children, with these families traditional teachers feel that families are *too* involved! These parents are often successful and professional people who have high expectations for their children and their teachers.

Key in connecting with these families is understanding the perspective and hopes of parents and communicating to them how we plan to both challenge and support their children at high levels of learning. As inclusive teachers we may surprise parents of gifted and talented children. It is common for parents of gifted and talented children to express concerns regarding having lower ability students included in our classes. Frequently, parents have found teachers to "teach to the middle" and have not helped their children capitalize on their assets and gifts. A key in our developing a trusted relationship with these parents is to explain in clear terms how we work as inclusive, multilevel teachers, challenging and supporting each child at his or her own ability level. Many inclusive teachers report that such parents can actually become quite excited about the learning opportunities for their children, cognitively as well as socially. For truly inclusive classes, in fact, provide opportunities for very advanced learning of social skills and creative responsibility in a learning community.

We think of Dennis Mitchell, a parent of two children considered gifted. His daughter, Elana, was in Melanie Fitzgerald's third-grade class. That year Melanie had three children with cognitive impairments, two with learning disabilities, and two dominant-language learners. However, Dennis was amazed at what was happening in Melanie's class. While concerned at first, he began to see that Elana was being challenged. She did several in-depth creative projects during the school year. Yet, the students with cognitive disabilities were working on the same projects. Elana became good friends with one of these children, Maira. At the end of the year Dennis approached Melanie and told her this important story:

> You know, I have been so pleased with Elana's learning this year. She has progressed academically but she has also learned so much more. She has learned about helping other children who learn at a slower rate than she does. She's actually learned a lot about learning in the process. She and Maira have become good friends and her being a part of Maira's circle of friends was very important to her. She read a lot of information about Down syndrome and inclusion and wants to help Maira be part of her community. I have another daughter 3 years older than Elana. She went to a separate school for gifted children in Grades 3 to 5. While she was academically challenged socially she has suffered. Thanks for a good year!

Inclusive teachers have found that parents of children considered gifted and talented have always responded to the idea that all children will work at their own level of challenge, as long as the teachers actually made this happen. Like Dennis, if they understand what we are trying to do they can be our greatest allies with the school administration and with other families. When Melanie was involved with a local network of inclusive teachers who were organizing a conference, Dennis spoke about his experience in Melanie's inclusive classroom.

Families of Students Who Are Gay

What's perhaps most important with families of students who are gay is what we should *not do*. It's not our role to communicate to parents that their children are gay or lesbian. Given the attitudes prevalent, parents not infrequently may ask their children to leave home when they find out. We need to leave this issue to their children. We will, of course, be supportive of these families as we are with all families. If they have concerns, we can and should listen with empathy. It may happen that parents will want to share their concerns regarding homosexuality and their children with us. This may give us the opportunity to share resources and information that may help the parents rethink their position.

Families of Children with Special Needs

When we speak of families of children with special needs, we recognize that in one sense these families are like all other families. That is, all children are "special," presenting their own unique gifts and needs. On the other hand, some children place greater demands on the resources of the family, community, and school than others.

Responding to a Child with Special Needs. Being a parent is always challenging and exciting, and this is true of raising a child with special needs as well. Parents respond to a child with a disability in many ways, depending on their own personality, resources, and support. Some will be overwhelmed and angry; some will be thoughtful and reflective, gleaning insights into the challenge of human living. Some will be active advocates; others will cope by withdrawing. However parents may respond, they have much to share with us, and we can do much to support them.

Children with disabilities come into families in many different ways. Some have observable disabilities from birth. Some have a special need that may not be identified until the child enters school or later. Some families adopt children with special needs. For other families, a disability may occur as a result of a tragic accident.

Guilt. Families often struggle with guilt and issues of self-esteem. When a disability results from an accident, particularly from an accident that involved negligence, this can be particularly difficult. For example, one young father and his son were out fishing and the boat capsized. The boy survived but suffered severe brain damage. When genetic factors cause the disability, both parents may feel responsible for the struggles their child experiences (Fialka, 1997; O'Shea et al., 2001; Perske & Perske, 1981).

If the child has a severe disability, the family may take responsibility for home-based medical care requiring that they learn the use of medical equipment and obtain assistance from family, friends, and medical personnel. Daily routines of bathing, feeding, and play take more time and energy. Coupled with therapies and doctors' appointments, these substantial new responsibilities tax families' time, energy, emotions, and finances (Featherstone, 1980; Knoll, 1994).

Cycle of Grief. Families of children with disabilities often experience a cycle of grief that is not unlike dealing with death. All parents hope to have children who are bright, able, and talented. Most of us have to deal with the fact that our children have limitations. For parents of children with disabilities, however, this realization is often intensified. For example, the parents of a boy with severe mental retardation, whose language development by the first grade is very limited, know that he will not be a doctor, lawyer, or teacher. They also know that he will need significant support and assistance all his life. Such a family must allow the original desired image of their child to literally die so that they can accept their child as he is and rejoice in his strengths and capacities (Fialka, 1997; Turnbull & Turnbull, 1997).

Some family researchers, however, question the degree to which the experience of grieving is either typical or necessary. "It is misleading to describe parental reactions without also considering how professionals share the diagnosis," say Turnbull and Turnbull (1997, p. 137). O'Halloran (1995) takes a different approach. She describes a "celebration process" in which the emotions prompted by a diagnosis can be connected with deep reflections regarding hope for the future; the positive contributions of people with disabilities; and the capturing of negative emotions as a catalyst for energy, persistence, and learning.

The Tragedy of Abuse. Parents of children with disabilities develop strategies to cope with the stress of raising their children. Given the lack of support for parents, we sometimes see patterns emerge that limit or even directly harm children. Approximately 25% of the caseloads of welfare agencies dealing with abused children, for example, involve children with disabilities (Finkelhor & Hashima, 2001; Sobsey & Doe, 1991). Some parents believe that their children cannot learn, do not expect anything of them, and reinforce negative behaviors. As such children grow older, they sometimes are violent when their wants are not met immediately; parents may then withdraw, intimidated (Ammerman, Van Hassett, & Hersen, 1988; Finkelhor & Hashima, 2001; Sobsey & Doe, 1991).

Informal Support for Families. Parents of children with disabilities find themselves coping with other problems. Babysitters are often very difficult to find. In some cases, having a child with a disability is seen as a great shame to the family. Some families have experienced increased social isolation as neighbors and friends are uncomfortable being around a child with a disability. People may even make hurtful comments, clearly indicating that the child with disabilities is not accepted. In such situations the weakened bonds of community and neighbor relationships represent a dwindling support network just when families face increased responsibilities (Fialka, 1997; Knoll, 1994; O'Shea et al., 2001; Perske & Perske, 1981).

However, families and their allies also are developing alternative social supports to help them cope. The type of parent support meeting we described at the beginning of this chapter is one powerful example. Networks of family support groups and parent-to-parent connections are growing throughout the country (Bishop et al., 1993; O'Shea et al., 2001). Circles of support that bring people together around children with special needs also provide enormous assistance to families (Falvey et al., 1998; O'Brien & O'Brien, 1996). Parent-based advocacy organizations help parents connect with others who face similar challenges (Turnbull & Turnbull, 1997).

Professional Services and Supports. Professionals in medical, educational, and other social service agencies can make an enormous difference in the lives of families, and an expanding network of support programs now exists (Knoll, 1994). A growing number of physicians have training related to the disabilities of children (Society for Developmental and Behavioral Pediatrics, 2001). Mental health programs help families locate resources and provide **respite care,** a service that allows the family to leave their child with trained caregivers and have some time to themselves. Although these programs are generally inadequately funded, they do provide needed support to families (Knoll, 1994; Shelton, Jeppson, & Johnson, 1992).

Yet professionals often display attitudes, ignorance, and disrespect that greatly increase the stress on the families of children with disabilities (Turnbull & Turnbull, 1997). To be sure, these families encounter many professionals whom they deeply respect and appreciate; still, virtually all such families have dealt with a significant number of professionals who have caused serious problems.

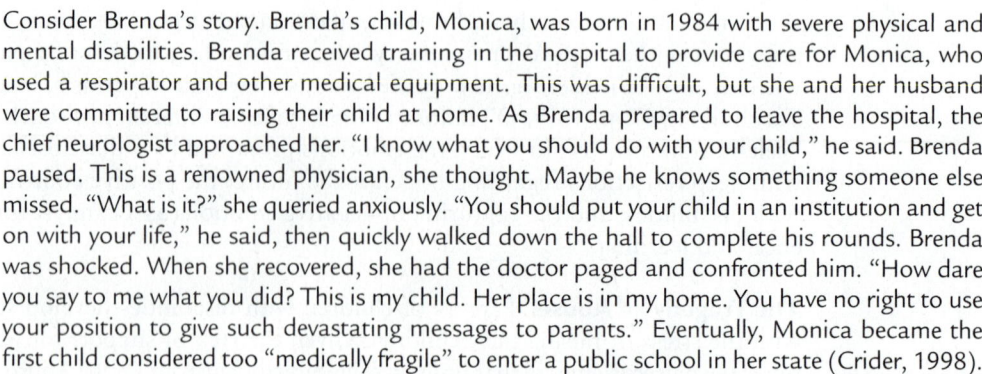

Consider Brenda's story. Brenda's child, Monica, was born in 1984 with severe physical and mental disabilities. Brenda received training in the hospital to provide care for Monica, who used a respirator and other medical equipment. This was difficult, but she and her husband were committed to raising their child at home. As Brenda prepared to leave the hospital, the chief neurologist approached her. "I know what you should do with your child," he said. Brenda paused. This is a renowned physician, she thought. Maybe he knows something someone else missed. "What is it?" she queried anxiously. "You should put your child in an institution and get on with your life," he said, then quickly walked down the hall to complete his rounds. Brenda was shocked. When she recovered, she had the doctor paged and confronted him. "How dare you say to me what you did? This is my child. Her place is in my home. You have no right to use your position to give such devastating messages to parents." Eventually, Monica became the first child considered too "medically fragile" to enter a public school in her state (Crider, 1998).

Many families continue to receive such messages from many kinds of professionals, despite gradual changes and the move away from the practice of institutionalizing young children. After experiences like Brenda's, a parent may naturally come to be cautious and defensive. As teachers, we must bear this in mind. When we communicate with the families of children with disabilities, we must seek to understand the experiences of the family.

Rethinking Life and the Road to Inclusion. In the midst of all these challenges, many parents of children with special needs rethink their view of life. They learn to look at strengths differently. They also ask difficult questions about where their child belongs in their community—and in school. Many professionals and extended family members suggest that their children belong in special places with other children who are "like them," hoping they will be protected from rejection, safe from harm, and able to find friendship with other children with disabilities. Parents of children in segregated schools often develop close and mutually supportive bonds with one another. In many locations, in fact, segregated schools were initially developed by parents' groups and have been virtually the only option available.

A growing number of parents, however, are beginning to question segregated special education. They often come across the idea of inclusive education by happenstance—in a talk with another parent or at a local conference. In school districts where inclusive education has become part of the natural order, parents are given much support in understanding inclusive education as well as other placement options on the continuum. Schools that have not embraced inclusive education, however, typically provide little information and often resist efforts by parents to have their children in general education full time. Some parents report that embracing inclusion means giving up their connection with and support from other parents of children with disabilities, who are fearful of having their child leave a segregated class or school. Yet the opportunity for their child to grow, learn, and become a real member of the community helps these parents continue to push for inclusion and to seek allies and support from others (Fialka & Mikus, 1999; Hampel, 2000; Turnbull & Turnbull, 1997).

Advocacy and Parents. The difficulty of caring for their children while meeting—too often—with frustrating responses from professionals has often thrust parents into a new role as advocates for their children. Over time parents have had enormous impact on policy. Parent advocacy, however, is in the midst of a substantive paradigm shift. Parent advocacy is torn between advocacy for inclusion and support in the mainstream and provision of special services.

The initial efforts of parent advocates were to develop special, segregated programs for their children in education, mental health, and rehabilitation—special education schools, separate classes, sheltered workshops, group homes. Many parents became convinced that the only way their children could be safe and that the families could have a life of their own was through segregated programs.

Melissa, Dayo's 5th grade teacher, explains to his mother this Dayo seems to have a gift of being able to express himself in writing, telling compelling stories about his experiences. She shares the story the Dayo wrote and illustrated about one of his classmates who has a significant disability who has become a good friend.

However, a growing number of parents are seeing a new vision of community life for their children that begins with being part of the regular school (Fialka & Mikus, 1999; Hampel, 2000; Ryndak et al., 1995; Turnbull & Turnbull, 1997), and new advocacy efforts have emerged that have taken several tracks. Most centrally, parents work very hard to advocate for their own child—interacting with teachers, principals, even school board members. A growing number of court cases have resulted from such individual advocacy efforts. However, parents also network with one another for support, often seeking to build collaborative efforts to have impact on the policies of a local school, district, or state. Nationally, TASH, which developed as a coalition of parents and university faculty, has been a major force for inclusive education since the early 1980s. Many other organizations have joined in this effort, and many state networks of parents working toward inclusive education have been established.

The Gift Teachers Have for Parents

All this means is that when parents come to our class, they often bring a long history of struggles, learning, isolation, and dreams for a better day. What they want most of all is a teacher they can trust who will welcome their child into the class, seeking to teach their child effectively and willingly. We have a special opportunity and responsibility to parents of children with disabilities and other differences. Rather than merely tolerating such parents and their children, we can reach out, helping parents understand that our class, our school is theirs also. We can help break the cycle of isolation, rejection, and hurt. We can come together with our principal and other teachers to say that our school is for *all children,* communicating this message in multiple ways:

- We can help develop brochures about the school that highlight our commitment to children of difference learning together, specifically stating that children of different colors, cultures, economic resources, and abilities are welcome. We might give an example of a child with autism who has succeeded in our school, along with children from different ethnic groups.

Parent and Family Involvement

National Coalition for Parent Involvement in Education This organization seeks to advocate for the involvement of parents and families in their children's education, and to foster relationships between home, school, and community to enhance the education of all our nation's young people. www.ncpie.org/

PEAK Parent Center The center provides resources to equip families of children with disabilities to advocate successfully for their children to help them live rich, active lives as full members of their schools and communities. www.peakparent.org/

- We can distribute this information to offices of physicians, agencies, and parent advisory councils for special education in our district and county.
- We can incorporate students with disabilities and their parents into literally every aspect of school life.
- We can help parents of any culture obtain information and make connections in the language they can access.

Our potential for having dramatic impact on children, parents, and the total culture of our school is very high as we welcome parents into the life of our school. Let's discuss principles and practices by which we can be supportive of families of our students.

Leia shared a story after a recent meeting with school staff that shows the potential of our impact as educators. Her son, Sean, is a second grader who has epilepsy and autism, who is being included in general education classes.

> We have been pushing for inclusion since we moved to this district last year. They have been doing a good job this year. During the meeting many wonderful positive things were said! You could tell that Sean had really found a place in the hearts of his team. The second-grade teacher said her dream for Sean was that he be in her class without a para-educator. Wow! On the one hand this is exciting. On the other hand it is scary. Sean has behavioral issues, and when he is done with something he is ready to leave. The teacher is a miracle. She and Sean have connected. She has a sister with autism and is able to see Sean in a different light. With her on Sean's side this year, full inclusion is a real possibility. (Holly, 2000)

Linking Parents, School, and Community
Resources for Learning and Family Support

A most critical element in working with parents is linking home, school, and community learning. Let's survey some examples of ways to link home and classroom learning (Ballen & Moles, 1994; Epstein & Salinas, 1998). Figure 6.4 provides a survey that we may send home to parents to obtain their input regarding how they might like to participate in our classroom.

Linking Home and Classroom Learning

We can use several strategies to link learning in the home and classroom. Let's look at a few of these.

Home Learning Activities. Teachers can collaborate with parents to identify tasks that are part of the family routine and that children can perform as learning activities at home. This allows parents to help children develop skills using authentic tasks that fit

FIGURE 6.4

Parent Preferences for Home–School Involvement

We would like to know your preferences regarding ways to become involved. Please check your preferences and we'll try to do our best to involve you in the ways that are most helpful to you and your child.

A. Meetings. When meetings are necessary, what arrangements are most convenient for you?

The best days for me are:

The best times for me are:

Anything else that we should think about when arranging meetings?

B. Other Ways to Communicate. What other ways should we use to communicate?
_____ Daily notebook or assignment log
_____ Brief phone calls. The best time to call is _____
_____ Drop-in before or after school
_____ Occasional notes
_____ Parent group meetings
_____ Other

C. Information. What information is critical to share?
_____ Upcoming themes/units/books
_____ When performance is slipping
_____ Homework assignments
_____ Changes in medication
_____ Behavioral issues
_____ Health-related concerns
_____ Friendship possibilities
_____ After-school activities
_____ Unusual events/rough days
_____ Exceptionally good days

D. Involvement. I could see myself becoming involved in the following ways:
_____ Coming in to problem solve around situations that arise related to my child
_____ Sharing adapted materials that we sometimes use at home
_____ Sharing information and resources that will help you understand my child and his/her educational needs
_____ Participating in a schoolwide planning committee/task force
_____ Coming in and demonstrating techniques that have been successful with my child
_____ Sharing videotapes from home
_____ Providing encouragement—compliments, cookies, comforting words
_____ Being in contact with another parent whose child may attend this school
_____ Using my network to bring in speakers
_____ Volunteering in class—reading; helping out; sharing a unique talent such as _____
_____ Talking with the school administration, school board, or others when an important issue arises
_____ Attending team meetings occasionally
_____ Preparing materials
_____ Other

E. Other. What else might you want to share about how you might be involved in your child's learning?
_____

Source: Information from Ford, Fitzgerald, Glodoski, and Waterbury (1997).

into the daily functioning needs of the family. For example, as families engage in various activities together (from going grocery shopping to taking family trips), a child can collect artifacts, take pictures, and write or tape-record a description of the activity that becomes part of a family-focused educational portfolio.

Meaningful, Engaging Homework. Homework can become a powerful tool for linking home and school learning. Typical homework often involves completion of worksheets of math problems, spelling words, or additional reading. In contrast, authentic homework that links to family and community life can provide an opportunity for

DESPERATE PARENTS RESORT TO
ESTABLISHING THEIR OWN
"FREQUENT INCLUDER PROGRAM."

children and parents to engage in an enjoyable, educational project together at the child's own level of ability. For example, one teacher asked students to do a project that lasted several weeks and focused on heroes in their lives. One student interviewed an aunt who was a singer and produced a poster. Another student met with a friend of the family who was a photographer, and together they took pictures and made a display. Students presented their projects in class. Several had their heroes come to the class with them. Other examples of such meaningful homework might include:

- Writing out the grocery list and shopping with a family member to obtain items. While shopping, the child can be responsible for adding up the prices of the items and helping decide how much money should be available for weekly grocery shopping.
- Helping prepare dinner, including reading recipes, measuring, and cooking.
- Researching historical community events and developing a presentation.

Reading Together. Families can be asked to read to and with their children. We must be careful, however, to ascertain the ability of the parent. If a parent cannot read well, this activity may be embarrassing and the parent may unintentionally discourage the child. Teachers can suggest and make available simple books that can be read aloud to children, or can provide books on tape for loan to a family. If the children are living in a home where books are unavailable, then providing some resources to read is critical. Create a system in which classroom books can be checked out, as long as they are returned responsibly.

Connecting with Community Resources

If we are to be effective teachers, we must also help families access resources and supports in the community. This becomes much easier if our school is committed to community partnerships. As we develop outreach relationships between the school and the wider community, we identify a wide range of possible resources for teachers, children, and families. By understanding the interests, needs, and skills of our families and their children and knowing about resources in the community, we can help link families to community. Schools and teachers who are effective use three key approaches:

1. Bring resources—people, organizations, materials—*into the school* to support learning and provide support for children and families.
2. *Connect learning* to the local community.
3. Engage children and the school community in activities that strengthen the neighborhood and community.

Let's see how this works in a process developed by Kretzmann and McKnight (1993).

Map Resources in the School. First, we can identify school resources that might be used in partnership with others in the community. What resources does our school possess? How might we make these available in new ways to families and the community? The most valuable resource of all is people—teachers; students in classes, who have enormous gifts to bring to the community; and families of students. Schools also have many other resources: space to be used for people to meet, office equipment, and so on. It can be helpful to compose a written list of all potential resources.

Map Community Resources Surrounding the School. Learning to view the assets, rather than deficits, of neighborhoods, families, and children is the key to what Kretzmann and McKnight (1993) call **assets-based community development (ABCD)**. Too often, particularly in low-income communities, only the deficits and problems are reported. Figure 6.5 contrasts assets- and deficits-based neighborhood maps or descriptions. However, any community is rich in positive resources. For a community to become stronger, people must identify and build on strengths rather than trying to repair deficits. A critical starting point is simply to identify what is good about a community. Notice that this way of thinking closely parallels suggestions earlier in this chapter that we build on the strengths of families, an approach that applies directly to students with special needs as well.

Each community is composed of five key building blocks (Kretzmann & McKnight, 1993):

1. Individuals (children, youth, elderly people, people with disabilities).
2. Associations (formal clubs, church choirs, the local garden club).
3. Spaces (parks, downtown area, lakes, etc.)
4. Institutions (schools, hospitals, welfare offices, mental health services).
5. Businesses (stores, law offices, etc.).

Associations, according to Kretzmann and McKnight (1993), are the most powerful resources. Whereas schools often gravitate toward the large organizations in their communities—government officials, businesses, hospitals, and the like—smaller-scale associations bring people together voluntarily based on their interests. This is their power and contribution, because they can connect people who have interests and gifts to contribute with other people with similar interests. A local garden club might involve a class of students in planting flowers on the school grounds and invite specific students who are interested in plants to be part of the monthly meetings. A local block club might work with a class to investigate the block—interviewing residents, doing presentations on the history of the block, helping clean up a vacant lot, or researching why the city had not cleaned it. As students learn to see the rich resources available in their community,

FIGURE 6.5

Assets and Deficits-Based Neighborhood Maps

ASSETS MAP	DEFICITS MAP
Gifts of Individuals	Crime
Artists	Graffiti
Elderly people	Mental disability
Labeled people	Child abuse
Youth	
	Broken families
Citizen's Associations	Slum housing
Churches	Welfare recipients
Block clubs	
Cultural groups	Gangs
Interest groups	Unemployment
	Truancy
Institutions	Illiteracy
Schools	Lead poisoning
Libraries	Dropouts
Parks	
Hospitals	
Community colleges	
Businesses	
Locally owned	
Corporate	

Note: Assets and deficits describe two very different views of the same phenomenon, whether neighborhood, family, school, or a child. One gives a way to build on strengths, whereas the other tries, most often unsuccessfully, to "fix" deficits.

they come into contact with positive role models and acquire ideas about productive ways to grow and learn.

As teachers we can identify concrete ways for adults in the community to help children and their families. As we gather information, we will begin to build relationships with various community people. We can, for example:

1. Conduct interviews of local residents regarding their skills, interests, and so on. Have students conduct these interviews in pairs and develop reports of what the people said.
2. Draw maps and take photographs or draw pictures of the local community.
3. Divide the class into teams to explore each of the building blocks of a community—individuals, associations, businesses, and institutions. Have each team collect information about the resources and assets of its "building blocks."
4. Invite 5 to 10 community leaders to the school and hold a focus group with teachers and students serving as the interviewers. Record this on tape and video.
5. Send a survey to community associations asking them what they do, what they think needs to be done to make the community better, and what one thing they could do that is not a part of their normal activities. Students could draft, compile, and interpret this survey with assistance from local community people.

We can use our findings in many ways: compile them into a book, make a bulletin board with changing components, or publish sections in the newsletter. This project itself could be published by a local community association after being illustrated with art, photography, and written work by students.

Develop School–Community Partnerships. As schools gather information about what they have to offer and the resources in the community, teachers can develop specific partnerships with community people. The possibilities are infinite. The key is to start small, have fun, and build trust. It starts when people get together and explore how to link the interests, needs, and gifts of people or organizations with one another (Kretzmann & McKnight, 1993).

- A teacher invites a local artist to school to share her work. They discuss ways in which the class and this artist might be involved with each other. One student who wants to be an artist is invited to see the studio of the artist.
- A local family support group is created to help parents deal with the problems and challenges of being a parent.
- The members of the school support team (psychologist, special education teachers, Title I teachers) meet with three local block clubs to discuss how they might work together to build circles of support in neighborhoods for families.
- The school sponsors a meeting of local block clubs to talk about how they can work together.
- When the city recreation department holds a community planning meeting for a local park, the school takes a group to provide ideas.

Develop Connections for Families and Children in the Community

Once we have identified resources in the community, we are in a position to connect children and families with these resources. First, we identify the gifts, interests, and needs of the child or family. As we get to know children, we will also get to know their families. We can have special nights when children and families come together and share their gifts and interests with one another.

We then match the interests or gifts of the family and child to community resources. We can have an evening workshop for families, teach them how to identify community resources, and encourage them to assist one another in locating such resources. Individually, we can look for resources throughout the year and work to make connections with families.

Get Help from Community Guides in the Area. In every neighborhood and community there are wonderful people known by many in the community. McKnight (1995) called these individuals **community guides**: trusted community members who know the neighborhood inside and out and who can be invaluable sources of information and connections for the school, children, and families. McKnight (1995) identified their key traits. Community guides are first and foremost people who see gifts in their community and the gifts in people. They see possibilities more than problems. Such people are also very connected to and involved in their community. They know many people and are, in turn, trusted and respected. This gives them access to a great number of people and resources in the community. Not surprisingly, they see their community as a caring, welcoming place and are willing and able to help connect people who need support and welcome. If we can locate these individuals, we can tap into a valuable resource for our school, our children, and their families. For example, they can help build a mentoring program, establish circles of support in a local community center, or run potluck dinners where families gather for fun and recreation in the school.

Community Agency Resources for Families

Numerous human service agencies have been established to provide assistance for families. Some specifically target families of children with special needs. We should be aware of agencies that may be helpful. Figure 6.6 provides a listing of comprehensive family support services available through one or more agencies.

Parent Training and Support Programs. Most states have programs that organize parent-to-parent help. A growing number of programs in the country also provide parent support groups. Such programs often have a staff of parents of children with disabilities who facilitate and coordinate a statewide network of support groups for

FIGURE 6.6

Components of a Comprehensive Family Support System

RESPITE AND CHILD CARE

SPECIAL NEEDS
Transportation
Special diet
Special clothing
Utilities
Health insurance
Home repairs
Rent assistance

INFORMATION AND RESOURCES
Information and referral
Advocacy
Futures and financial planning
Training

EMOTIONAL SUPPORT
Family counseling
Family support groups
Sibling support groups
Individual counseling

IN-HOME ASSISTANCE
Homemaker
Attendant care
Home health care
Chores

ENVIRONMENTAL ADAPTATIONS
Adaptive equipment
Home modification
Vehicle modification

RECREATION
Accessible recreation services
Day and summer camp

DEVELOPMENTAL SERVICES
Behavior management
Speech therapy
Occupational therapy
Medical/dental care
Physical therapy
Nursing

CASE MANAGEMENT AND SERVICE COORDINATION

FINANCIAL ASSISTANCE
Direct cash subsidy
Allowances
Vouchers
Line of credit

Source: Information from Knoll (1994).

parents of children with disabilities and special health care needs (Briggs, 1996; Briggs, Koroloff, Richards, & Friesen, 1993).

The U.S. Department of Education funds a national network of *parent training centers* that provide information to parents regarding their rights under special education law. Sometimes these centers also provide parent advocates who will attend IEP meetings with a family, sponsor a variety of informational seminars, or conduct other types of family support programs (Office of Special Education Programs, 2000a).

Early Intervention and Family Support. Public Law 99-457 provided funds for early intervention assistance to babies and young children through age 3 who show clear signs of disability or who are at risk for developmental delay. States have developed interagency coordination plans to provide services based on the family-centered principles. That is, services must be developed in the context of the needs of the total family and documented in an Individualized Family Services Plan (IFSP) (see Chapter 4). In each area of the country, one agency will be designated as the coordinating agency from which services and assistance can be requested. Teachers working in early childhood programs may contact the local agency for more information (Bishop et al., 1993; O'Shea et al., 2001).

Protection and Advocacy. Each state also operates a program funded by the federal Developmental Disabilities Act whose intent is to protect the rights of children and adults with developmental disabilities or mental illness. Typically housed in the state's department of mental health or mental retardation, protection and advocacy agencies provide training and can be called on for legal assistance when violations of state or federal laws occur (National Association of Protection and Advocacy Systems, 2000).

Family Financial Assistance. Some programs provide financial assistance to families who need help coping with the high medical and care needs of children with severe disabilities. In an increasing number of states, a family support subsidy provides a flat fee for parents of certain children with more severe disabilities whose income does not exceed a certain level. A Medicaid-funded program, usually called a Medicaid Waiver plan, also provides funds for the health care and related needs of children with severe disabilities. Both of these funding sources are most often coordinated by a local mental health agency (Bishop et al., 1993; O'Shea et al., 2001).

Community Mental Health Services. Numerous therapists provide family therapy, in which counseling is provided for the family unit. Family therapists view the family as a system and see family members' emotional difficulties as a function of the family dynamic and relationships rather than as the problem of individual members. Supportive family therapists can give important assistance to families. In addition, community mental health agencies can provide additional practical services—respite care, to give families a chance to get away from the care of children with high needs; information and referral; adaptive equipment; assistance with therapies; summer camps; and parent training on many issues (Knoll, 1994).

Neighborhood Family Resource Centers. In many communities centers have been established to provide a range of family services under one roof. The most effective of these function as community centers, combining activities for children with supportive services for families. Parents obtain counseling while their children receive tutoring and are involved in arts and recreational activities. Oftentimes, parent-to-parent support groups will meet in such centers (Kretzmann & McKnight, 1993).

Wraparound Services. Public family services fall under the jurisdiction of multiple federal, state, and local agencies. Nonprofit organizations receive government funds to operate services and often compete for clients in local areas. Private family services typically are funded by payments from individuals with higher levels of income or insurance. This multiplicity of organizations has made the provision of coordinated services difficult. Numerous efforts have been made over the years to promote interagency coordination. One of the most recent and most promising attempts is the model of wraparound services. In this model multiple agencies commit to work as a team around a specific family—to "wrap their services around" the family. In addition, this model is based on family-centered principles and provides flexible access to funds and resources based on the practical needs of the family. Such programs will also work to partner with informal resources in the community. Wraparound services are governed by a family–professional board that attempts to develop an effective partnership between public agency resources and the resources of the local community (Hyde et al., 1996; Melaville, Blank, & Asayesh, 1993; Yoe, Santarcangelo, Atkins, & Burchard, 1996).

Full-Service Schools. Schools are at the center of every family's life until the family's children are about 18. Yet schools have often been isolated from the larger community and from other service organizations that assist families. Many schools throughout the country have made a commitment to function as a community center for families, to house multiple services that can provide assistance to families—in other words, to be **full-service schools.** Such schools, in partnership with other human service agencies, include many services on-site (Dryfoos, 1994).

 ## Welcome Home

In this chapter we have described family-centered teaching and schooling. Rather than seeing the community and the family as helping schools, we need to do the opposite. We must see ourselves and our school as both supporting and learning from families, as building a "village" in which people care for one another. These are vastly different practices and entail a huge paradigm shift. As educators we can implement new ideas for involving parents and families in the educational process. We can serve not only as partners in the children's education but also as friends and members of the community. So we have begun our journey into inclusive schools by thinking about the community and parents—the two driving forces for the existence of schools in the first place.

Traveling Notes

Parents and teachers may find themselves at odds about how to teach children—and particularly children with special needs. Conversations in teachers' lounges often revolve around this problem. In a school that is working on creating powerful relationships with parents we would expect to see these things:

1. As teachers we empathize with parents and their situations. We work with parents to think of ways to help with whatever frustrations are an issue. *We will listen to and value them.*
2. We have multiple ways of sharing information with parents, from daily logs, notes in planners, home visits, e-mails, to an open-door policy for parents to stop in.

3. We are genuinely happy to see parents when they arrive, even if it is at a time that is not the best in the schedule. We are willing to talk about their concerns and let them know they can ask to come in for a more detailed talk if it is needed.

4. We make an effort to contact or visit every parent at the beginning of the school year to see if they have any questions or concerns that they want to talk about. This sets the tone for a relationship before any issues have had time to develop. Then, parents will later be more responsive to our requests.

5. We put families at the center rather than focusing primarily on the needs of the school (a system-centered approach) or the child alone (a child-centered approach).

6. We welcome all children into their classrooms. This is evident in the literature that is available about the school, in the books children are asked to read, and the work that lines our walls. We display multiple strategies for working with children that reflect best practices and are willing to spend the extra time and explain to parents the how and why of our approach to instruction.

7. We have a working knowledge of community resources that strengthen students' learning and provide helpful resources for both parents and children. We help link parents agencies that provide assistance to families.

Stepping Stones

Following are some activities that will help extend your understanding and actions you may take toward partnering with families.

1. Use the information and strategies in this chapter to develop a checklist of best practices regarding interactions with families and parents. Do a self-assessment.

2. Use the information in activity 1 to develop a plan to improve your relationships with families. Review this with another teacher or your principal to get their input.

3. Interview parents of a child with special needs in the family's home. Ask the parents to tell his or her story of the child and of past interactions with teachers.

4. Locate a teacher who has a reputation for partnering effectively with parents. Interview this teacher and ask about his or her philosophy and practices with parents. Join the teacher at a planning meeting where she is doing some collaborative problem solving with a parent. Implement some similar strategies at the next meeting with a parent from your own class.

5. Attend a support group meeting for parents of children with special needs. What do the parents discuss? What stories or issues do they bring up that have to do with interactions with teachers and other professionals? Ask their advice on how to effectively become an inclusive teacher.

6. Identify a local school that has a reputation for exemplary practices in partnering with parents. Interview the principal and observe some school activities. What do faculty and staff do?

7. Conduct a neighborhood map, involving children and parents together in the process. Use the information to help make a connection between a community resource and the needs of one family.

8. Obtain information about agencies that service the area in which your school is located. Pull out those that may be particularly helpful to families in your area.

7 Design an Inclusive School and Classroom

Using Space and Physical Resources to Support All Students

CHAPTER GOAL
Understand how to design and use space and physical resources to support all students in learning together.

CHAPTER OBJECTIVES

1. Understand universal design and the principles of healthy learning environments.
2. Recognize schoolwide methods of using and designing space.
3. Explore and identify classroom approaches to using space, technology, and resources to respond to students' learning styles and abilities.
4. Examine strategies for community-based learning experiences.

The first of the year is always hard and exciting all at once. We come into our classroom and look around at the bare walls and the boxes and boxes of materials. "How will the year go?" we wonder. We imagine the room filled with students. How do we arrange the physical environment of our classroom to promote effective teaching of diverse students? That's what this chapter is about. Let's first visit two schools that are working hard to develop positive learning environments.

A High School for Learning

We are impressed by the attractiveness of Santa Fe High School. Walking through the entrance, we see bright banners proclaiming WE ARE A LEARNING COMMUNITY in the commons area, a large open area at the building entrance next to the principal's office. Part of this commons area is the cafeteria, which has movable tables that can be folded away as needed for community and extracurricular events. As we visit classrooms, we discover that many rooms are connected to encourage interdisciplinary teaching. Students are working at tables in groups; others are working at computers using software that converts text to spoken language. Another student, who does not read or write well, is working with a partner on a story, dictating it into a computer that converts speech to text. Teachers are organized in interdisciplinary teams—each team including science, social studies, language arts, art, and special education. Students are also divided: into "colleges" of some 200 students each, with whom the same team of teachers will work for all 3 years. There are no special education rooms in the school. A learning resource center is staffed by a teacher and a counselor and is available for any students at any time during the day. This is a fun room where students can study, get special help, take adapted tests, or just hang out.

This school seems like home. We are struck by how warm Edwardo Elementary School feels. The office feels open and comfortable; secretaries welcome all who come in with a genuine smile, and the principal chats with children, teachers, and parents. We are particularly interested in the book projects displayed throughout the entrance hall, with students' artistic renderings or other representations of parts of books they have read. Classrooms, too, are filled with student work—not only on the walls but also hanging from ceilings. We also see all sorts of children—one in a wheelchair, another with a sign language interpreter. The student in the wheelchair has a communication device that speaks for her. Her friends are learning to use this device. Again, there are no special education classes in this school; special education teachers and paraprofessionals spend most of their time teaming with general education teachers in the classroom. We want to come visit again.

Designing Classrooms

Classroom Architect A great site where you can design a layout for your classroom. classroom.4teachers.org/

Emint National Center From the University of Missouri, this site has many resources for classroom design. www.emints.org/ethemes/resources/S00001368.shtml

Boundless Playgrounds We thought you might enjoy seeing more about this work! www.boundlessplaygrounds.org/

Environments have a big impact on our lives, and we put a lot of time and energy into arranging them. Yet so much of our teaching environment often feels given, unchangeable—a large, older high school building, a dreary classroom, inaccessible steps. Even so, we can always shape our environment as well as be shaped by it. Our goal is to structure the learning environment, to the degree possible, to support best practices in teaching and learning. What will make an environment most conducive to teaching diverse learners well together? What will enable us to use best practices in teaching and learning? What specific tools can we use to create effective inclusive learning environments? We will address these questions in this chapter.

The Learning Environment
A Tool for Learning and Growth

What is our learning environment? As teachers, we may automatically answer, "Our classroom, of course!" We suggest that our learning environment is much more. At minimum, our "extended classroom" encompasses (1) the school building and grounds, (2) the classroom, and (3) the community surrounding the school. If we think of our learning environment in this way, we will find numerous ways to use these many places and spaces to structure learning. This chapter will discuss each of these learning environments in order. First, however, let's think in a more general way about what is needed for students of diverse abilities to learn together. Two interactive frameworks are helpful: (1) universal design and (2) guidelines for healthy environments. Let's discuss each of these.

Universal Design

Architects and other design professionals are using a new concept to inform the shaping and organization of space and resources—*universal design*. Like the concept of designing teaching for diversity, on which this book is based, universal design involves a conceptual revolution. In the past, environments and products have most often been designed to fit the physical characteristics of average human beings. In contrast, universal designers seek to develop "products and environments to be usable by all people, to the greatest extent possible, without the need for adaptation or specialized design" (Steinfeld, 1994). Here are a few examples:

- Ramps and automatic doors are helpful not only to people in wheelchairs but also to many other people who must struggle with stairs or heavy doors—shoppers with packages, parents pushing strollers, older people with canes.

FIGURE 7.1

The Principles of Universal Design

PRINCIPLE 1: EQUITABLE USE

The design is useful and marketable to people with diverse abilities.

1a. Provide the same means of use for all users: identical whenever possible, equivalent when not.

1b. Avoid segregating or stigmatizing any users.

1c. Provisions for privacy, security, and safety should be equally available to all users.

1d. Make the design appealing to all users.

PRINCIPLE 2: FLEXIBILITY IN USE

The design accommodates a wide range of individual preferences and abilities.

2a. Provide choice in methods of use.

2b. Accommodate right- or left-handed use.

2c. Facilitate the user's accuracy and precision.

2d. Provide adaptability to the user's pace.

PRINCIPLE 3: SIMPLE AND INTUITIVE USE

Use of the design is easy to understand, regardless of the user's experience, knowledge, language skills, or current concentration level.

3a. Eliminate unnecessary complexity.

3b. Make use consistent with user expectations and intuition.

3c. Accommodate a wide range of literacy and language skills.

3d. Arrange information consistent with importance.

3e. Provide effective prompting and feedback during and after task completion.

PRINCIPLE 4: PERCEPTIBLE INFORMATION

The design communicates necessary information effectively to the user, regardless of ambient conditions or the user's sensory abilities.

4a. Use different modes (pictorial, verbal, tactile) to provide redundant presentation of essential information.

4b. Provide adequate contrast between essential information and its surroundings.

4c. Maximize "legibility" of essential information.

4d. Differentiate elements in ways that can be described (i.e., make it easy to give instructions or directions).

4e. Provide compatibility with a variety of techniques or devices used by people with sensory limitations.

PRINCIPLE 5: TOLERANCE FOR ERROR

The design minimizes hazards and the adverse consequences of accidental or unintended actions.

5a. Arrange elements to minimize hazards and errors: Most used elements should be most accessible; hazardous elements should be eliminated, isolated, or shielded.

5b. Provide warnings of hazards and errors.

5c. Provide fail-safe features.

5d. Discourage unconscious action in tasks that require vigilance.

PRINCIPLE 6: LOW PHYSICAL EFFORT

The design can be used efficiently and comfortably and with a minimum of fatigue.

6a. Allow user to maintain neutral body position.

6b. Use reasonable operating forces.

6c. Minimize repetitive actions.

6d. Minimize sustained physical effort.

PRINCIPLE 7: SIZE AND SPACE FOR APPROACH AND USE

Appropriate size and space is provided for approach, reach, manipulation, and use, regardless of user's body size, posture, or mobility.

7a. Provide a clear line of sight to important elements for any seated or standing user.

7b. Make reach to all components comfortable for any seated or standing user.

7c. Accommodate variations in hand and grip size.

7d. Provide adequate space for the use of assistive devices or personal assistance.

Source: Information from Connell et al. (1997).

- Talking software, originally developed for people with visual impairments, is being marketed for all people. In some technical devices the talking computer interfaces have increased productivity by some 25%.
- Recorded books, long used by blind people, are now commercially marketed for travelers; people who enjoy listening to books read aloud; and people with limited reading challenges, such as individuals with learning disabilities.

The Center for Universal Design (Connell et al., 1997) developed seven principles for designing environments and products to take into account the full diversity of human abilities (Figure 7.1). These principles constitute a powerful set of statements that can help us evaluate our present teaching practices and the way that the learning environment either contributes to or detracts from inclusive teaching.

Universal design is being applied to some degree in the architectural design of schools, particularly with the explosion of technology. We can involve our students in answering the basic question: "How do we arrange our physical environment in ways that meet our needs and promote learning among students of different abilities, races, and cultures?"

Figure 7.2 provides some ideas for using the principles of universal design to shape environments so that they are accessible and encouraging to all students, limiting the need for individual accommodations. Notice that the chart uses the three environments of school, classroom, and community in interaction with the three key areas around which we have structured this book—(1) academic learning, (2) social–emotional needs, and (3) physical–sensory abilities. This chart offers ideas to get you started as you plan your class at the beginning of the year.

Healthy Learning Environments

Architects say that "form follows function." In other words, if our environment is to be effective, it should be structured based on the functions that we want it to perform (Greenman, 1988; Meek, 1995). If we see our classroom as a place of control, the environment will be structured to control. If we see our classroom as a place of joy, fun, choice, and learning, the room will come bit by bit to look this way. If we seek to design inclusive learning environments, we also ensure that our environment promotes health and well-being; stimulates optimum intellectual, emotional, and physical functioning; and aids us in implementing best practices for teaching and learning. Figure 7.3 lists some guidelines drawn from literature on universal design, healthy environments, and school design. Let's look briefly at each guideline.

Stimulate Positive Awareness of Ourselves and Our Students. At best our school and class are tools through which students can become more aware of who they are—places of student self-expression where young people can better understand themselves. On any given day, students see their own products. When we visited Mitchell Elementary School to observe student-led conferences, one fourth grader spent an hour showing her work—literally walking through the classroom, showing her portfolio, hands-on lessons located on tables, her work on the walls, and hanging from the ceiling. This student clearly felt ownership of this classroom and saw expressions of her inner self all over the room.

Enhance Our Connections with Nature, Culture, and People. Our learning environment helps us develop multiple connections—with varied peoples, with cultural

FIGURE 7.2

Toward Universal Design of Learning Environments

	SCHOOL	CLASSROOM	COMMUNITY
Academic	■ Student work all over the building ■ Total school staff who see themselves as supporting student learning ■ Effective library and media center that is accessible to students and offers materials at many different levels ■ Computers in the media center that have talking software, speech to text, scanners, etc.	■ Books and other resources for different ability levels ■ Talking computer software ■ Multiple tools to use to express learning—speech-to-text software, graphics, audiotapes ■ Sound amplification devices; FM receivers available as needed ■ Visual magnification devices available; large-print display and software for computers ■ Sign language offered as a foreign language class	■ Mentors who come into the school and read or do investigations with students ■ Community organizations that host student learning activities ■ Accessible playgrounds and museums
Social–emotional	■ Welcoming place—student and staff greeters ■ Parent and community volunteers ■ Supportive and caring culture ■ Cheerful building with work of students highlighted throughout	■ Places to work together, or alone in privacy ■ Peer buddies ■ Circles of support ■ Student participation in organizing and decorating of room ■ Classrooms filled with student work	■ Local places where businesspeople and community members welcome students ■ After-school mentors and circles ■ After-school programs involving community members and parents
Sensory–physical	■ Wheelchair access ■ Clear signs using both words and pictures ■ Displays of student work that encourage looking, touching	■ Talking software and input devices ■ Braille printout from computers ■ Places for movement in the class ■ Allowance for drink and food ■ Clear labels for materials in the class with picture cues ■ Spaces for wheelchair access	■ Accessible playground equipment ■ Accessible public buildings and businesses

expressions, with nature. Our school is filled with the art, music, and literature of varied cultures—particularly those in our local area. In an inclusive school, our students connect with classmates from various cultural and socioeconomic backgrounds as well as with youngsters with disabilities.

FIGURE 7.3

Guidelines for Healthy Learning Environments

1. Stimulate positive awareness of ourselves and our students.
2. Enhance our connections with nature, culture, and people.
3. Do us no physical harm.
4. Be beautiful and inviting.
5. Provide for meaningful, varying stimuli.
6. Encourage times of relaxation and privacy.
7. Balance constancy and flexibility.
8. Use resources flexibly for multiple purposes.

Do Us No Physical Harm. It might seem almost too obvious to state, but we don't want our environment to hurt us. Unfortunately, this requirement is sometimes not met. In many older schools, buildings still contain lead or asbestos that can have negative effects on the well-being of children. Similarly, the neighborhoods in which some children live are physically unhealthy. If we work in such situations, we will face many challenges and will need to work hard in our own classroom and to interact with local community people to deal with these issues. In any classroom, however, it is our responsibility to organize our space so it is as safe as possible.

Be Beautiful and Inviting. Carol Venolia (1988) stated that "the creation and experience of beauty is immediate, whole, and healing. It enlivens our senses, warms our hearts, relaxes us, and puts us at one with the entire surroundings" (p. 15). A beautiful environment can help stimulate students and help promote a sense of safety and security (Greenman, 1988; Mann, 1997; Meek, 1995).

Provide for Meaningful, Varying Stimuli. We allow for multiple ways for students to be grouped and move about the classroom and school and draw on multiple intelligences to ensure that students have many ways to obtain information, express themselves, and learn. We establish locations where students can talk, be alone, read quietly, make noise, sit, run, and jump. We have a working space for projects involving the integration of literacy, art, music, dance, and drama.

Encourage Times of Relaxation and Privacy. Teachers and students need space and time for periodic relaxation and privacy, allowing students to regroup, to let their minds settle. Although this guideline may seem very difficult to implement in a crowded school, we can find ways if we are creative. Students need places to be alone—to think, read, or even cry.

Balance Constancy and Flexibility. The brain-based need for "relaxed alertness" (see Chapter 11) means that there is ongoing interaction between involvement in challenging activities and the ability to move away. In physical terms, it also means that we periodically change the environment—displaying new student work, shifting tables for a special project—but also maintain stability and predictability. The brain needs both novelty and security for learning, and our skill in providing both opportunities for stimulation and stability will help establish conditions for the linkages of academic learning, emotional calm, and community building.

An Exemplary High School: The Met

SCHOOLS
to VISIT

The Metropolitan Regional Career and Technical Center, a high school in Providence, Rhode Island, was founded in 1996 with 50 students. The school has served students who have done poorly at other schools with dramatic improvements in learning. Ninety-eight percent of the students go on to college, most first-generation college students often from impoverished backgrounds. Since its beginning, the Met has expanded to a network of small schools with 120 students each.

The entire curriculum for each student is centered around students' personal interests and goals. However, high standards are maintained as students demonstrate proficiency in traditional school subjects by applying such skills in real community-based learning. A student may learn math skills by selling a house or physics by building a boat. Rather than following the order of a textbook for learning, students meet with staff mentors frequently, both individually and in small groups, to develop a personalized curriculum around each student's needs and interests. This mentorship system allows one adult to get to know each student well, making what is already a small school even smaller.

Students are involved in internships related to their interests with businesses and community organizations. Students get school credit but are not paid. Students are involved in a wide range of work based on their personal interests and goals. One student, for example, interned with a clothing designer. For her final project, she designed and created six outfits for a local spring fashion show with support from her mentor.

Students are also required to complete a Senior Thesis project to graduate that will demonstrate their learning and involve a significant production and contribution to the community. Following are some examples of student projects from the Class of 2002:

- *Met Baseball Team.* Organized the Met's first baseball team, including recruiting student players, gathering necessary health forms, fundraising to buy equipment, leading practices with a mentor, and communicating with other local high school teams to organize competitive games.
- *Catering Business.* Established an independent catering business and catered five events, including the Mentor Breakfast serving approximately 300 people.
- *Met Yearbook.* Coedited and produced the Met's yearbook, including planning, designing, organizing, and laying out the format; learning Adobe PhotoShop and Quark; facilitating meetings; spearheading the advertising sales; and selling the yearbooks to Met students (two students).
- *Foster Care System.* Served as a Big Sister to a foster care child, including doing an intensive research project on the number of children in foster care in Rhode Island, the effectiveness of the system, and what happens to children after they leave it. Concluded by reporting on the project to DCYF staff.
- *Men's Group.* Ran the schools' Men's Group for its third year, including organizing and facilitating the weekly meetings; doing research on young men's issues; and organizing field trips to help the group bond and share positive experiences.
- *Costa Rica.* Traveled to Costa Rica for 3 weeks to study Spanish and volunteer at an orphanage after fund-raising, organizing, and planning the trip with a committee. Concluded by presenting an extensive research paper on Costa Rica's geography, culture, and the importance of saving its rain forest.

Source: The Big Picture, 2008. As of 2008, the Big Picture Company was involved in replicating this personalized design in 34 schools in 12 states throughout the United States.

Use Resources Flexibly for Multiple Purposes. Space and physical resources are often categorized as fulfilling one function, for example copy room and hall. However, if we are designing healthy environments, we realize that any space can be effectively used in multiple ways. Because resources are limited, such flexible and creative use of space has the effect of expanding our capacity. For example, some teachers assign each desk to one student.

The School

Creating a Welcoming Place for All

Trends in school design reflect our evolving images of school. In the early 20th century, the idea that bigger is better—and more efficient—was dominant. That period was the time of the growth of large industries. It also was the time when many elementary schools were built to house more than 1,000 children and when high schools were designed to dominate local neighborhoods. In these buildings desks were arranged in precise rows, often bolted to the floor (Meek, 1995). Today, however, our understanding of the connection between social interactions and learning has greatly shifted our thinking about how to design space. Let's survey the elements of a welcoming school.

A Welcoming Place to Be

We want to promote a spirit of community and common ownership rather than seeing the school as belonging only to the power structure. This spirit is communicated in the smallest matters. We display a lot of student work prominently on walls and in display cases. Artwork, essays, photographs of a class play or of community projects, and other student work reflect the cultural and ethnic diversity of the area. Colors are attractive and bright rather than institutional green, even in classrooms of older children. We post signs of welcome and encouragement throughout the building, many made by students. Our school office has comfortable chairs and an open, inviting atmosphere (Greenman, 1988; Meek, 1995).

Four first graders read in this literature rich class. Note how the teacher has arranged the classroom to make it comfortable and inviting.

Commons

A commons area may be located in a central area of the building with park benches, water fountains, and other amenities to encourage conversation and interaction. A commons gives students a place to gather before and after school and at lunch, and serves as a gathering point for groups. Schools often intentionally locate their commons next to the school administration office to convey a sense of openness, and administrators often interact informally with students and parents (Greenman, 1988; Meek, 1995).

School Within a School

A smaller school size, optimally 100 to 200 students, can make a big difference in students' sense of community (Meek, 1995). Large high schools were designed to provide adequate numbers for many programs; increasingly, however, smaller schools are being built, or schools are being designed to allow the student body to be broken into smaller groups. Schools often seek to arrange space where these teachers work together in flexible ways—linking classrooms in older buildings by doors or cutaways, placing offices between classrooms where teachers can work together, or fitting rooms with movable walls that allow teachers to combine their classes or work separately.

Parent and Community Center

It is very helpful to have a designated space where parents and community members can work, study, or just be while in the school. This space can be a separate room, or it can be part of an area such as the media center (library) or support staff offices.

Media Center/Library

In many ways, the media center is the heart of the school. In many schools media specialists run programs to help students learn the basics of word processing, using the Internet, and accessing information. In a school that focuses on a love of reading, there will be times of open circulation that children are free to come and browse through books on their own, with a class, or with a parent. Media specialists can also be a fount of useful information on ways to integrate computer use into the classrooms; on teacher- and child-friendly Internet sites to explore; and on books to use for any purpose, from a read aloud on a certain subject to literature circles.

Space and Inclusive Classes

Schools can send powerful messages about who belongs and who does not. The "special education class" or "resource room" is often down at the end of the hall. Students cycle in and out of the speech therapist's office. Talk to almost any student who has been in these special places and they can tell you of the fear, dread, and embarrassment they feel.

 Jordan, a student who was placed in a special education room when he was in the fifth grade, was terribly ashamed and simply would not stay in the room. He wandered the halls to prevent his former classmates from seeing him in the special education room and making fun of him. He was eventually kicked out of several schools and sent to a special education center—where his fondest dream was to go to a "regular" high school.

In an inclusive school we do not have special classes for students with labels. Rather, students are heterogeneously mixed in general education classes. Figure 7.4 contrasts uses of space in inclusive and segregated schools, classrooms, and communities.

FIGURE 7.4

Segregated and Inclusive Uses of Space

INCLUSIVE	SEGREGATED
SCHOOL	
■ There are no special education, bilingual, or Title I classrooms. Specialists are housed as teams in offices. ■ Technology and "specials" are integrated into ongoing classroom instruction, and special and general education classroom teachers work together to integrate instruction.	■ The school has special classes for special education, bilingual, and Title I classes that are most often at the end of the hall. ■ Specialists' offices are separate from those of the rest of the school staff.
CLASSROOM	
■ Students work in groups at tables or clusters of desks; there is a hum of activity. ■ Groups of students include diverse ability levels, ethnic and cultural groups, genders. ■ Students' work covers the walls, hangs from the ceiling, is displayed outside the room. ■ Students are seen in many places—at desks and tables, sitting on the floor and on bean bags, out in the halls working in pairs. ■ Speech therapists, special education teachers, and other support staff come into the class and help with students. However, you can't tell who they are there to work with.	■ Desks are arranged in rows; some desks are at edge of room. ■ Students are grouped by ability levels as they engage in activities. ■ Students of color are most often in the lower-level ability groups. ■ Teacher-made bulletin boards abound with rules and lists of consequences for infractions. ■ Students sit at desks. The teacher attempts to ensure that they are quiet, in their seats, and working independently. ■ Some students leave periodically for special help, causing a good deal of coming and going. ■ Students with disabilities are not allowed to mix with other students, even at recess or lunch.
COMMUNITY	
■ Students frequently go on short or longer study trips into the community. ■ Local community organizations and individuals come into the school. ■ The school has an active community and parent center where local people organize their work in classrooms and student engagement in the community. ■ Students in the school are actively involved in studying local community issues.	■ Students stay in the school building all day, except when they go to the playground. There is little connection with the local community. ■ When students with disabilities finish school, they go to sheltered workshops and group homes.

When educators begin to learn about inclusive schooling, a frequent question is: "How much does it depend on money? Can only rich districts do this?" In schools that serve low-income people, particularly in cities, this question gets turned into one of space. "We already have 35 kids in a class," said the principal of a very segregated middle school. "If we put kids with disabilities in these classes, we would have classes much too large." However, when you begin to look at the data, these concerns do not hold true.

JOURNEY into the CLASSROOM

Places to Be Alone

It was February, more than halfway through the school year, when third-grade teacher Mia agreed to switch from her Title I support position to one of classroom teacher. This class of 27 students had been through multiple teachers and substitutes that year. When Mia entered the classroom to take stock of its current environment, she found a classroom that was not designed well for anyone to function. The rectangle-shaped desks were organized in a large square. The teacher's desk was front and center. There were long cabinets along each wall and they were piled with photocopies.

Clearly, this classroom had no spaces that provided places for the children to have some private space throughout the course of the day. Mia knew these were very active children and had caused teachers lots of trouble this year. These students obviously needed an environment that worked better for them.

She set out to arrange the classroom so that it would work for a classroom of challenging and diverse children. She cleared out all the stacks of papers, cleaned cupboards, and put up bright bulletin boards.

However, she was most concerned about how she might provide some spaces where students could be more private. With the help of two other teachers whose opinions and teaching style she trusted, she began to create a different environment. She grouped all the desks in clusters of five so that children could work in a small group and help one another. This opened up space at the front for a group area which she set off with a bookshelf and a rocking chair that she had purchased. She created working areas for different types of activities by turning the cabinets, which were not attached, at a right angle to the wall. As she moved tables into spaces created by these cabinets, she intentionally left some small spaces between cabinets and walls that were perfect for small children.

She also found a study carrel that had been used to separate one student from others. Instead she created a "safe place" to which any child could go to unwind. She assembled a bucket filled with all sorts of useful objects: a stuffed animal to hug, squeeze balls and worry stones to handle, colored paper and pens on which to write notes. She put up bright pictures on the walls. She also moved her desk off to the side of the room. She utilized one side of it so that students could work at it on the other. She knew that students would like sitting in the space underneath the table, so she turned it where this space would be out of eyesight of the other children. She also took a small table and put it in her line of sight in the hallway, where children could work. The area by the back door was set off with hanging plants and a large cushion to turn it into a private space.

So, with very little money and a lot of creativity she turned the classroom into a welcoming, fun place to be. When the children entered the classroom for the first time their faces showed stunned pleasure. One child even turned around and left thinking he had entered the wrong room.

Mia certainly had her work cut out for her with this class. However, very quickly she discovered that providing students with places and tools with which to unwind and comfort themselves paid off.

Reflection: Here we see a teacher who considered the needs of her students, to imagine herself in their shoes, so to speak. It led her to creating space that made a real difference. Very quickly students in the class, particularly those with the greatest challenges, discovered that this teacher really did care for them.

Let's look at Georgetown High School as an example. The school is located in a poor but very racially diverse area. Some 30% of the students are African American, 30% Latino, and the rest are an even mix of Whites from the Appalachian region and Asian Americans. In this school 40 teachers serve about 1,000 students. Of the teachers, 18 are "general education" teachers, each of whom has 35 students. The other 22 faculty members teach in segregated classrooms; they include 9 special education teachers, 9 bilingual teachers, and 4 teachers of students who are at risk, each of whom has 10 to 15 students.

All these teachers know that their students would rather be in general education classes. Now let's do a bit of math. If all teachers took all students, the teacher-to-student ratio would be 1:20, an amazing figure in this district. Although teachers would need new training to address student needs, this could work.

Let's consider another option. If 30 teachers were general education teachers and the other 10 were support teachers, the student teacher ratio would be 1:33—high, but still less than the present ratio. Each of the 10 support teachers could work with 3 general education teachers; in other words, each general education teacher would have the equivalent of a support specialist working with the class one third of the time. It becomes clear that many options, both in use of funds and classroom arrangements are available if we decide to look for them.

Effective Use of Limited Space

Having inclusive classes also helps schools use space most effectively. In the Georgetown example, shifting to inclusive education would free up space in a very crowded school. Belle Elementary School provides another example of possibilities. As in other schools in this district, the school library had virtually disappeared, a fact that was of great concern to teachers and the principal. The room that had been the school library was being used for a special education class. The special education teacher convinced her principal to let her students attend general education classes, thereby allowing her room to be used as a library and teacher workroom.

Space for Specialists

In an inclusive school, specialists seldom use offices for pull-out services. Because such specialists spend most of their time in the classroom, they often have designated work space there. Some classrooms may have two desks, one for the general education teacher and the other for a specialist or support teacher. In other classrooms specialists and the teacher might have one desk, since they are seldom in that area for any length of time. Often these professionals will be housed together in an office, freeing up some space where teachers can counsel individual students and parents or work with small groups of students in activities. Housing a small group of specialists together also has potential to increase day-by-day communication regarding issues, needs, and strategies being implemented with specific students.

Lunch and Recess

Given their relative lack of structure, lunchtime, recess, and extracurricular activities present both opportunities and potential problems. How schools structure and foster community, responsibility, and inclusion during these times is particularly important. Teachers are usually on their break, and there are easily 200 to 300 students in one area at a time. At lunch students must all be able to eat and get back to classes on time and in an orderly fashion. If a student is not accepted, it is at this time that he or she is most likely alone, rejected, even ridiculed. Similarly, if there are racial tensions, they are most likely to become evident during lunchtime. On the other hand, it is during this time that students have a chance to really talk, play, and engage one another as people, and relationships can flourish.

A typical reaction to lunchtime tumult is to ask students to sit quietly without talking at assigned tables. However, this is one of the few times in the day when students can chat with friends and interact without interrupting someone's learning. Students need this break. Instead of trying to control their actions, we should devise ways to teach them to make responsible choices during unstructured periods.

What might make students comfortable, keep their interest, and encourage positive interaction during lunch, recess, and in extracurricular activities? Effective elementary and secondary schools establish a selection of interesting activities students may engage in during their free time with the help of teachers, aides, and community volunteers. Students rotate between activities, changing who gets first choice every day. This idea works well at all ages. Some of the ideas schools have organized include:

- Computer time
- Outside organized games
- Art areas
- Board games
- Literacy rooms, where kids are led in group activities like poetry and singing
- Tutoring room
- Gym time with games and exercise classes

Torland City High School, for example, runs such a program with community volunteers. A student with autism at the school has made friends with some other students in the weight-lifting program. This has reduced his sense of isolation, which was a great concern for all.

In addition, many schools assign older students jobs during lunchtime. In some schools teachers choose to eat lunch with their students. Other teachers meet several times a week with different student groups, eat lunch, discuss ways to help one another, and do fun things together.

Using Materials for All Students

In inclusive schools, materials bought through different programs benefit all students. In other words, materials purchased with Title I, special education, or gifted and talented funds are not locked in closets when the special teacher isn't using them with a labeled population of children; instead, these materials are used throughout the school.

Getting Places

Some students with disabilities have special needs for transportation that are difficult to meet on conventional school buses. Consequently, special education programs often purchase small buses that can transport children who use wheelchairs or have other special transportation needs. However, the "handicapped bus," like a special education classroom on wheels, separates students with disabilities. What to do? First, many students with disabilities can be transported on a typical school bus. Increasingly, buses are being designed with lifts and space and locks designed for wheelchairs. Older buses can be retrofitted: Taking out some seats provides a place for the wheelchair. It is also possible, although this is a less desirable solution, to arrange routes so that some students without disabilities ride in the special bus with wheelchair access. Students who have needs other than wheelchairs can be paired with other students in their area and ride the regular bus, or an aide may ride the bus to provide assistance. In addition, many students come to school through car pools, and parents can work out arrangements with one another. Whatever the solution, a team of general and special educators working together can help put inclusive transportation into action.

Inclusive Playgrounds

One physical location that is important to all children is the school playground. Nationally and internationally, people are beginning to use the principles of universal design to develop inclusive playgrounds. As part of this movement, an organization called Boundless Playgrounds was created in 1997 as a grassroots movement inspired by Amy and Peter Barzach of West Hartford, Connecticut.

In the summer of 1994, [Amy and Peter] observed a beautiful little girl in a wheelchair watching bravely with quiet tears while other children enjoyed a playground that this child was not able to use. Five months later, the couple's nine-month-old son, Jonathan, died from spinal muscular atrophy. To work through their grief, a bereavement counselor encouraged them to do something in his memory. The couple recruited and mobilized an army of 1,200 volunteers to create a playground where children of *all* abilities could play together—including children like the little girl they had seen at the park. Research, creativity, hard work, and community support combined to form an extraordinary and universally accessible 25,000-square-foot playground, "Jonathan's Dream." Opened in 1996, it is the first Boundless Playgrounds children's park. (Boundless Playgrounds, 2001)

When an article appeared in *Time* magazine, Amy and Peter Barzach received hundreds of requests for assistance from around the world. In 1997 Boundless Playgrounds was formed, and by 2001 the organization was operating 24 projects in disadvantaged communities.

The National Center on Accessibility (2000) developed guidelines for parks based on the Americans with Disabilities Act that can be helpful to schools. An interesting project for students would be to investigate how to make play accessible for all children using these guidelines. To meet the guidelines, at least one of each type of *ground-level play* components on a playground, such as spring rockers, swings, and stand-alone climbers, must be accessible. Although not all *elevated play* structures will be accessible, access to ground-level play structures is used to offset this. For example, if a play area has 10 elevated play components, at least 5 must be accessible. In addition, at least 3 accessible ground-level components are required, each of a different type. At least half of elevated play areas must be accessible by ramp or by transfer via a special platform. *Soft contained play structures*—such as ball pools, slides, climbing nets, and crawl tubes—are enclosed and made of pliable materials such as plastic, netting, and fabric. These

Bookshelves in Mishael Hittie's fifth-grade class are arranged by subject and genre and provide students reading materials on many topics at a wide range of reading levels.

devices must provide access to the entry points of each structure and should be accessible via ramp, transfer system, or platform lift.

In addition, designers of play components should consider:

- Space for wheelchair maneuvering to and from the play component
- Wheelchair space
- Height and clearances of play tables
- Height of entry points or seats
- Provision of transfer supports (such as a grippable edge or some other means of support)
- Surfaces soft enough to limit injury from falls but also firm and stable enough for wheelchair maneuvering

Once we begin to understand and think about how space is or is not accessible to all children, we don't take it for granted that some children have to be excluded. We realize that we can work to change the environment.

The Classroom

Designing an Inclusive Learning Community

Our own classroom, of course, is the space most important to us. How do we design an inclusive classroom? How do we improve our teaching and learning environment over time? Here are several key guidelines to consider:

1. Establish a comfortable, homelike atmosphere: colorful carpets, beanbag chairs, group area.
2. Allow for different learning styles, providing tools and resources that give students alternative points of access to information.
3. Design multiple ways for students to obtain information and express their learning.
4. Ensure sensory and physical access.
5. Use space in the school and class to support inclusive teaching.

We seek to design our class so it includes all, provides emotional support, and allows us to teach effectively. We want people to walk in and know this is a place where real learning is happening for very diverse learners.

Classroom Design for Inclusive Teaching

Our use of space is one important way we move toward or away from best practices. Traditional teaching is organized hierarchically: Students are involved in individual, rather than collaborative, work and are focused on minute skill development rather than on authentic and meaningful tasks; classes are dominated by teacher lecture rather than by student-initiated work (Goodlad, 1984a; Haberman, 1998; Kohn, 1999). It is not surprising that in traditional classrooms the arrangement of physical space is designed to reinforce this approach. Traditional images die hard. Like lecturing at the board, moment-by-moment teacher domination of the learning process is still preeminent—and so are the traditional rows of desks.

If we seek to implement best practices for diverse students, however, we will use space and physical resources differently. If we are to build community in our class, we must organize space to encourage student interactions, cooperative work, and collaboration. If we are to teach authentically, our class will begin to look like a workshop.

Making a Home in Our Class

Students of all grade levels learn best in classrooms that are inviting, warm, and cozy rather than formal and stress inducing. The more we can create relaxed and secure class-rooms, the more students will take risks, and the more they will learn. To start, we assess our classroom. Where are the windows, outlets, doors, tables, cabinets, computers, the sink? What arrangement of areas will make the room work practically and make it stimulating? Many effective elementary teachers put quiet areas, like reading, writing, or lis-tening centers, on one side of the room and louder areas, like science, math, and art, on the other. We can use windows to create a science area that includes growing plants or birds at a feeder, and we might put the aquarium or art center by the sink. Plants and lamps add to the appeal of these areas and create a comfortable atmosphere. An area does not have to be large to be effective. A poetry area could simply be a bucket full of poetry books located near a poetry bulletin board that the children change weekly (Fisher, 1995; Zutes, personal communication, March 17, 2000).

In a middle or high school class, we can use similar strategies. We may have activity areas for centers that focus on different activities, group work, and small group discus-sions; a video center with tapes, videotapes, and CD-ROMs; a place for art and design work. Computers may be either in one part of the room or spread around. Plants and animals can be valuable in a secondary class as well. In all, we seek to provide a sense of home and comfort, areas and resources that work for different learning styles, and tools to facilitate different modalities of information access and expression.

Classroom Decor and Ownership

We talked to Mark about how he decorates his eighth-grade classroom. "When I began teach-ing," he said, "I made a conscious decision not to use commercial posters or materials on bulletin boards. I put up bright fadeless paper with colorful borders, and a few things such as a calendar and some titles as to what might go on the boards. When the students arrive, they see a brightly colored classroom that has only begun to evolve." He went on to explain that he involves students the first day in discussing how bulletin boards might be used, how they would fill them with student work throughout the year, and who would be in charge of rotating them.

Part of building a learning community is creating an environment both students and teach-ers enjoy. This is important for secondary as well as elementary students. The walls can be a collage of interesting materials to explore and from which to draw ideas. These will include student work, book covers, artwork, artifacts from places being studied, informa-tion on famous people, multiple posters, a calendar, maps, interactive bulletin boards to do in spare time, pictures, and anything else that will pique students' interest. We involve stu-dents in deciding what types of work and artifacts should be displayed. We might even take a hint from some restaurants, which cover the tables with white paper and give out crayons. Some items, such as detailed self-portraits, will decorate the room all year; how-ever to keep the brain alert, the environment has to change periodically as well. It even works best if we coordinate a change of materials with the start of a new unit. The associ-ation with new materials will help imprint the new learning in the children's minds.

The Teacher's Desk. In a traditional classroom the teacher's desk is the focus of the room, and a few students' desks are often placed "close to the teacher." In best practice teaching, however, we are constantly moving: assessing, reviewing, helping, and encour-aging students, engaging in experiments, creating projects based on research, and writ-ing. With this change in teaching style, the room also shifts its focus. The teacher's desk is off to one side or in a corner. In some classrooms teachers have a small area on a table

CHAMPIONS OF INCLUSION CHALLENGE
students with disabilities to work their best toward high standards.

There are still many teachers who do not act like students with disabilities can succeed. They do not expose these students to high levels of teaching and learning. They do not promote students' independence, and they do not hold students to high standards.

Champions of inclusion are:

- The classmates who cheer for Ernesto (who has a mobility impairment) to run his fastest and make it to first base.
- The speech therapist who labors with Stephanie, encouraging her to make a clearer "th" sound.
- The language arts teacher who pushes Robert (who has learning disabilities) to read more challenging books with his adaptive equipment.
- The parent who, despite the recommendations of a pediatrician, advocates that her son (who has developmental delays) starts school in the inclusive early childhood program.
- The assistant principal who meets with Sean (who has emotional disorders) after returning from a suspension for fighting and points out to

him ways he can more appropriately deal with his anger.
- The kindergarten teacher who won't let Cherelle (who has multiple disabilities) play with the blocks until she finishes drawing her circle.
- The parent volunteer who calls the mother of Frankie (who has Down syndrome) and both reviews the school's home reading contract policy and offers suggestions for fulfilling it.
- The special education meeting facilitator who shares ideas as to why and how Tommy (who has mild cognitive delays) can now start riding the regular school bus.
- The math teacher who convinces Connor (who has autism) and his mother that he should participate in the AP math class in high school.
- And James (who has learning disabilities and attention deficits) who works extra hours in school and at home to prepare an excellent science project.

By Bill Henderson, Principal, O'Hearn Elementary School, Boston, MA.

or counter—or carry their main supplies in a large bucket and have no desk at all. One teacher laughingly said, "My desk is basically a place to stack materials I need that day and for students' work. By the end of the day, it usually resembles a small tornado!" In another room the students used the desk more than the teacher, as she allowed them to sit at it and work (Fisher, 1995; Zutes, personal communication, March 30, 2000).

Student Seating. We learn a lot about a teacher by observing his or her class. If students are expected to stay in their individual seats and not interact with others, we can be sure that the teacher spends a lot of time and effort trying to control students. Students do not want to stay by themselves for 6 hours a day, so they will inevitably push their limits. In such a situation, students who have different learning styles or need the help of peers will become problems. Control-oriented teachers respond by removing such students, often alienating others through fear.

In an effective inclusive class, in contrast, students sit in groups in which we encourage social interaction. Yet we also structure places where students can be alone, and for this purpose we find that using tables instead of individual desks is most helpful. However, many districts are unable to spend the money to replace their individual desks. In these schools we can push desks together to form clusters where students can work together as teams.

Creating ways to let students move throughout the day allows students who are stimulated through kinesthetic movement to learn more effectively. However, for some students this will not be enough; flexibility in seating is also important. We can allow kids choices about whom to sit with. One 10th-grade computer lab teacher says, "You may sit anywhere, as long as you are working!" What is important is not that students are sitting in their seats but that they are learning and having fun. We find that given choices, students will end up in many varied seating arrangements. Having places where kids can sit in chairs is only one option. Other approaches:

1. Provide pillows and carpet squares to sit and work on.
2. Demarcate standing stations at cabinets, podiums, or counters for when students need to work but are tired of sitting.
3. Furnish old easy chairs or rockers to be comfortable on.
4. Plan areas that are under, behind, or beside things where students can feel private.
5. Allow students to sit on tables and cabinets.
6. Let students work in the hallway at an extra desk or table or on the floor.
7. Clearly state that students can sit at anyone's seat as long as they respect the person's possessions.

Encouraging daily interactions by teaming students makes sense on several levels. Young people need to feel that they belong to a team and that their ideas are valuable. Seating students in groups also helps us foster community by providing ongoing, natural opportunities for interaction and sharing.

We are careful, however, not to cluster students by ability. Rather, we intentionally structure heterogeneous groups based on multiple variables—racial backgrounds, abilities of various sorts, personalities, genders. Erasing ability lines does not mean putting students together at tables in any haphazard way.

1. What personalities will complement each other?
2. What students are unable to interact well together?
3. What are the academic strengths and weaknesses of each student?
4. Do certain students need friends they have connected with nearby?
5. Are certain areas better equipped for certain students—for example, for students who daydream, need to move a lot, need to be alone, or need to be social?

Finally, we also organize space so that there is room between tables or clusters of desks. Open space is essential for students who use wheelchairs or who have difficulty walking, such as students with cerebral palsy. Providing open space further allows students to work easily in different places—on the floor, at other students' desks, under desks, or in the group area. In areas where this is difficult due to limited space, create an open pathway from one area to another.

Group Area. Every classroom needs an area where the class can meet to conduct whole class activities. Whether the teacher is reading or explaining an experiment, the group is working on a math problem, or a class meeting is being run, gathering students together increases the feeling of community that is vital to helping students grow. The area should be defined so that it is recognized as a separate place. There may be a rug, individual carpet squares to sit on, or a chair. Whether there is a carpet or a rocking chair by the open space, this area becomes the focal point of the room (Fisher, 1995).

Individual Space. In an environment in which we expect students to interact peacefully together for a long period of time, we specifically design ways for students to find private time and work individually. We can do this in many different ways. For example, in rooms where there are movable cabinets or bookshelves, we can often turn these to extend out from the wall, automatically creating dividers that children can sit around and behind. We can place tables or pillows in the hall. Separate desks can be designated for students who choose to sit by themselves. While we may be concerned that we cannot see all our students, we can learn to listen well. One sixth-grade teacher said to her class,

ISLAND IN THE MAINSTREAM
MRS. JONES AND MRS. COOPER ARE
STILL TRYING TO FIGURE OUT WHY FRED
DOESN'T FEEL LIKE PART OF THE CLASS.

"I can tell that some people have gotten off task, because the noise no longer sounds like working noise but playing noise. I would ask some of you to make different choices." She then proceeded to walk around and talk to several students (Fisher, 1995).

Learning Centers. In a well-structured environment, we plan ahead for students who finish early. Some of these students fulfill their need for social interaction by helping others with their work. Others will want different choices. Having *learning centers* with which students are familiar encourages them to engage in meaningful activities without taking our time away from students who still need help. Learning centers can be used for all ages of students. They should be easily recognizable, and the students should be taught how to use them ahead of time. Directions should be left by the area, and supplies should be easily accessible. In any given center directions for different levels of learning can be left, allowing for children to choose the level of assignment that is best suited to them. For example, a math center in a fifth-grade classroom could be left with directions for three different games, one practicing basic facts, one practicing adding fractions, and one practicing division. Some children also have independent studies that they contract to work on when they have completed other work. This arrangement gives students shared responsibility for continuing learning and maintaining order in the area, stimulates independence, and adds to the homey feeling of school. Some examples include (Fisher, 1995; Jensen, 1995):

1. Opportunities to create plays and develop songs, using music synthesizers on the computer, to illustrate the class topic
2. Microscope setup with slides provided
3. Class museum on current topic
4. Activities that involve maps: map hunts, map puzzles, maps to create own trip plans
5. Theme-related books
6. Listening center with books on tape (even for older students)
7. Math puzzlers: problem stumpers on current topic

8. Writing center where students can find a story starter, write poems, write letters to friends, make cards, or "publish" books
9. Spelling games: word hunts, games that use letters, crossword puzzles, magnetic letters to practice spelling
10. Math games that use cards, dice, and handmade gameboards to practice skills

Hallways as Learning Places.   In an inclusive school, space is used in creative ways for learning. In many schools, students work in hallways—alone, in pairs, or in small groups of three or four. When you ask students why they are there, it's never because they were misbehaving. Many like the novelty of working in the hallway; for others it is a quieter place to concentrate.

Many teachers devise creative spaces in or near the classroom for one-on-one or small group work. In these spaces teachers bring students together for multiple purposes, to receive assistance from a volunteer, or to work together on a collaborative project such as writing and rehearsing a play. One elementary school teacher took a large cardboard box that had housed a new refrigerator and, together with the students, cut and decorated it so that it looked like a castle. She placed it right outside the entrance to her room. Students use it as a reading corner or a place for two peers to talk or work on a project together. Other teachers obtain similar results by using a small tent, either in the classroom or just outside the classroom.

Movement, Food, and Drink.   We can also give students opportunities for movement— over and above walking down the hall with a pass to the bathroom. In one fifth-grade class, as the students finished work, they joined a "parade around the classroom" in which students quietly walked, making gestures as in a parade. Another teacher put on loud music chosen by the students to which they danced individually or in a simple line dance as a 5-minute transition activity. Other teachers have 5-minute aerobic exercises or activities that involve sharing information, such as searching for clock partners throughout the class for a few minutes.

Some students also need food and drink to function at their best. If we think about ourselves, how often are we munching on a snack or drinking coffee or water as we work? The simple act of drinking water has shown to keep the brain more alert and ready to learn. Provision for eating and drinking can look different ways in different classrooms. Many high schools have drink and snack machines in the commons area; one of the best ways to gather people together is to provide food, so this draws students together as a community. Similarly, teachers can allow snacks or water bottles in the classroom. We can establish simple structures for keeping the mess picked up and avoiding accidents. Engaging students in this process increases their independence and responsibility.

Multiple Strategies to Support Access to Information and Expression of Learning

In an inclusive classroom we also need materials, tools, and media to help all students obtain information, develop products that demonstrate learning, and deal with their limitations—whether these limitations are in reading ability or in ability to walk or hear or see. The more resources we have for all students, the easier inclusive teaching becomes. What are strategies we can use?

Multiple Intelligences and Learning Styles.   Over time we work to collect a wide range of learning materials at differing levels of ability for different student interests, topics of study, and sensory input modalities. These will include (1) books; (2) alternative print access resources (scanners that can be used with talking software, books on tape, braille,

Fourth-grade students outline their research projects on early American settlers on the carpet in the reading and group area of the classroom. Students are working individually but also can share with and help one another as they need. A sense of community pervades this classroom as students work together.

sign language books on video); (3) computers; (4) media—video, CD-ROMs, tape recorders; (5) contacts for experiences in the community; and (6) materials for hands-on activities—simulations and authentic experiences. We can use our knowledge of multiple intelligences as a framework to help us think about providing avenues for both input of information and expression of learning (Jensen, 1995).

Disability as a Tool for Designing Our Class for All Learners. In an inclusive school, we want learning environments to include all students without necessitating special adaptations. That's the goal. A simple way to start is to analyze our school and classroom from the perspective of individuals with different types of limitations. We could even go farther and ask different people with disabilities to come to our class and help us think through how we use space, materials, computers, and other learning resources. We can also involve students in thinking from this perspective. It's a terrific way to help them learn about disability in a framework that is positive and proactive rather than focused on deficits. Maybe we could borrow a child-sized wheelchair and have a student use it for a couple of days and make recommendations. We could do the same for hearing: All of us could wear earplugs and then identify ways to make the class better. Same for vision: Perhaps several students could wear blindfolds, and we could teach other students how to be sighted guides and help them go from place to place. We could all think together about how to make the class better for these students.

Also, when we know that a student with a particular limitation will be in our room, we can think about the design of our room with this specific student in mind. We can contact the family and arrange for the student to walk through and become familiar with the environment before school begins.

Students with ADHD often need more access to private areas where they can concentrate than do some other students. A student who is easily distracted can have problems in areas that would not bother another person. The buzzing of the overhead,

FIGURE 7.5

Disability Analysis for Learning

DISABILITY	ISSUE	STRATEGIES	BENEFIT TO OTHER STUDENTS
ADHD	Trouble sitting still; need for movement and places to be alone periodically	Movement around the class within certain guidelines as part of the daily routine Places in the class for privacy and being alone	Many other students also may need to move and be alone at different times.
Mental retardation	Limited reading ability Trouble understanding complex directions	Print materials with a wide range of ability levels and pictures Scanner and talking software Picture cues for tasks—teacher or student designed Peer buddies Cooperative groups	Students with limited reading ability benefit, as does any student who likes to hear a story. Other students can see different ways of communicating; strategies give them ways of synthesizing the key elements of a task.
Blindness	Inability to see print (reading books, directions) Inability to see videos	Books on tape Peer buddy for reading Adult volunteers Books on disk or CD with talking software Peer buddies to explain pictures Descriptions of key elements of pictures by teacher	Students with limited reading ability benefit, as does any student who likes to hear a story. Peer buddies focus on video content. Teacher's descriptions help students focus on key elements in video.
Deafness	Inability to hear teacher instructions Inability to hear videos	Interpreter Sign language instruction for classmates and teacher Closed-captioned films	Students learn another language; those with needs to move can do this as they talk. Comprehension increases for all. Students can talk while watching the video!
Epilepsy	Seizures	Carpeted areas; move furniture to prevent harm	Students learn sensitivity and are taught about preventing injuries.
Need to use wheelchair	Need for space to get around and access to materials	Books and resources at lower level Tables and spaces organized to allow for wheelchair access	All students have easy access. There is space for movement, creating a greater sense of openness in the room.

people talking in the hall, or the chatter of birds can all distract certain youngsters but have no effect on others. Having areas to which students can retreat (and feel that it is perfectly acceptable) can break up the distractions of a large room. Finding out who works best in what situation is important, as long as it is understood that every student is part of the community and that where he or she works best is somewhere in this room (Zutes, personal communication, March 30, 2000).

In Figure 7.5 we've sketched some examples of how you might start this kind of "disability analysis" and chart out what you find. Take the simple matter of talking software.

Initially many teachers acquire this for students with visual impairments and students who have difficulty reading—but discover that when their most able readers use the software on occasion, interest and comprehension rise dramatically for those students as well.

Books and Print Resources. Whether we teach high school math or physics, fifth grade, or kindergarten, we need a multitude of books available at a wide range of levels. In specific subject classes, the books may revolve around one topic, but we will want a choice of genres, from fiction and nonfiction to poetry; from chapter books to references. Materials about any subject can be found in almost any genre (Fisher, 1995).

Some publishers provide identified reading levels of their publications. We should use such information, however, to guide students rather than restricting them to identified levels. We particularly should not have students self-identifying their level in a particular system. This can easily promote, on the one hand, a sense of elitism and, on the other hand, discouragement if students feel they are not advancing to higher levels.

To teach students to care for books, we must have and model a system. We need our books organized so students can easily find and replace materials. Some teachers organize books by author's last name, title, subject, or genre. Some group them in rectangular plastic bins, with the cover facing out; other teachers place books on bookshelves with the spines facing out. Or we can remove the doors from a conventional storage cabinet to make it accessible to students as special shelving for books about the current subject being studied. Or books on a current topic can be placed on a designated bookshelf or laid on a table to capture the interest of students as they walk by. Returning books to their proper place, taking care with books when we read them, and organizing books all requires constant review and modeling, even with older students. Putting certain students in charge of the classroom library gives them ownership of the process.

Computers and Technology. As computers and related learning technology have increasingly become part of school life, the question of space to house them has become an issue. Many schools initially set aside a special room as the "computer lab" and cycled

AFTER RULING OUT A MEDICAL REASON,
BOBBY SUE'S PARENTS COME TO THE
CONCLUSION THAT THERE'S JUST A LOT
MORE TO BE AWAKE FOR IN REGULAR CLASS.

whole classrooms of students through it. More recently there has been a move to incorporate computers as part of the school media center and classrooms. The uses of computers in the classroom, too, have gone through phases. In some early applications, software was used essentially as computerized worksheets that could track student responses.

We now understand, however, that technology can help us embrace the principles of universal design, expanding our capacity to teach students with vastly differing abilities well together. Computers, rather than being taught as a separate subject, can function as ongoing tools, much like a blackboard, in the classroom. Rather than using computers only to fill out electronic worksheets, students are learning to use word-processing programs, spreadsheets, databases, graphics software, and other electronic tools to obtain information in a variety of formats and to produce learning products. Computers can enable students to generate text, graphics, animation, video, and sound, and even to control robots.

For example, suppose we want students to obtain information about the Civil War. Traditionally they would read information in the textbook, which might have a few illustrations and photographs. With a computer, however, students could:

1. Have the text read aloud via a speech synthesizer while they follow along in the book or simply listen.
2. Access a multimedia encyclopedia in which text could be read aloud and illustrated by graphics, pictorial illustrations, and even video clips demonstrating concepts or enactments of events of the era.
3. Access information at varying degrees of difficulty or complexity.
4. Use speech-to-text software to dictate a report rather than writing.
5. Create a presentation combining words and pictures to display knowledge.
6. Use bulletin boards, chatrooms, and online journals.
7. Create multimedia lessons and interesting projects for other students.
8. Develop electronic portfolios to demonstrate learning.

Many teachers increasingly communicate with parents via e-mail. Teachers may set up electronic bulletin boards for working groups of students and for open communication with parents. Student work may be demonstrated on a Web site or bulletin board, providing another way to facilitate interaction between school, home, and even the community. Teachers can access videos on many subjects and interesting lesson plans (through sites like www.UnitedStreaming.com).

Hearing and Learning. In active classrooms noise can be a problem. Teachers may be tempted to talk loudly or may spend a lot of time trying to get students quiet so they can be heard. In one research study, however, Barnett (1982) found that the hum of engaged learning in a busy classroom actually helps students to screen noises and concentrate.

One important tool used in many schools is voice amplification. A microphone can be used to raise the loudness of the teacher's voice just a few decibels. This can allow the voice of the teacher—or of a student who might use the device—to be slightly above the classroom noise so that a normal tone of voice can be easily heard. Amplification makes it unnecessary for teachers to raise their voices in pitch and thus makes the whole environment more pleasant.

Learning Styles and the Learning Environment

By recognizing diverse learning styles, we can create the conditions that are most conducive for learning. An understanding of learning styles helps us build on students' strengths and design instruction to respond to their needs. In addition, we can teach

Too often in schools, teachers and other educators focus more on controlling behavior of students rather than teaching them how to be responsible, how to learn, how to care for others. You see this in the way whole schools and classrooms are organized—as places of control and restriction. Such schools and classrooms are most often the least inclusive. They don't meet the needs of children and children respond in kind, creating an ongoing battle between students and teaching staff.

What are the physical structures that are designed to control rather than teach? Here's some of what you will see:

- *Arranging desks in rows.* The purpose for this organization is to focus on the teacher as the one "in charge" and to keep the children quiet and discourage interaction, to keep students at their seats. Typically in such classes students are not allowed to talk to one another and must raise their hand to move anywhere else in the room. Not surprisingly the teacher puts a great deal of energy into enforcing these rules so that there are constant commands to "be quiet and work" or "get back in your seat and do your work."

- *Isolating students who are seen as problematic.* Again, rather than teaching students how to act and be responsible, in these classrooms teachers isolate students. This is done in several ways: A student's desk may be placed on an outside row and turned so that it faces away from the other students. The teacher's intent is to reduce opportunities for what are perceived as problematic interactions with other students. We've also seen classes in which teachers literally built barriers around a student. In one class, for example, a student with autism who had challenging behaviors had a desk surrounded by a bookcase and two four-drawer file cabinets. Once again, the intent was to control behavior that was seen as problematic.

- *Creating places for "bad students."* Often teachers in these types of classes will create places that they put students who are bad. Often, of course, this means sending them out of the classroom and to the principal's office.

The problem is that these teachers really believe that such restrictive, punishing approaches are all that is possible, that creating a welcoming environment will not work for "their children." They think their students are too difficult, too disrespectful, and too challenging to function in a setting with choices and cooperative and active learning. They do not realize that organizing restrictive environments to try to control student behavior actually exacerbates the situation. Human beings are social creatures; we cannot learn in silence. When students are isolated or removed from the classroom, this may control their behavior in the short term but it does not teach them different ways of being. Students in such classes go into a fight or flight mode and cannot learn effectively. Their minds literally shut down and they become angry and resentful and always find ways of expressing this.

The teachers themselves are so focused on others' behavior that they have forgotten that the only behavior they can control is their own. The teachers are not modeling and teaching behaviors they want their students to learn.

It's also not surprising that these are not very inclusive teachers. Frequently, they have the most suspensions, the most students sent to the principal's office, and the most students referred to special education (in the hopes that they will leave their classroom).

What to do? First, we must consider if, in fact, we are such a teacher or have tendencies in this direction. Are we trying to control students' behavior or teach them to be responsible people? If so, are we willing to question our assumptions and beliefs and work in a different direction? That's the key, of course.

Second, if we are teaching with teachers who are in this controlling mode, there is no doubt that their actions impact on our classroom and the culture of the entire school. At best, we can try to get to know these teachers, hear their concerns, and tell them strategies that we use and the results we get with students. We might even agree to take a student from that classroom with whom the teacher is having lots of trouble. When we are successful in working with the student (as will be the case if we're using the approach articulated in this book) we may gain credibility with this teacher and be able to help him or her learn different strategies.

students to *understand their own learning styles.* When we do so we give them another tool for understanding themselves and becoming partners in designing instruction that meets their needs.

Learning styles have to do with how people are most comfortable learning and most receptive to learning. Learning styles can involve many specific variables, and many different approaches have been developed. Many are familiar with Grinder's (1991) description of visual, auditory, and kinesthetic learners. Jacobson (2002) has focused on the more sequential, analytic "left brain" versus the more global, intuitive "right brain."

Rita and Ken Dunn (1987; Dunn, 1996) have developed a useful comprehensive framework that incorporates detailed considerations of context (Figure 7.6). We can use the framework to structure our classroom to give students opportunities to respond to their own learning styles.

FIGURE 7.6

Contextual Elements of Learning Style

STIMULI	ELEMENTS			
Environmental	Sound: Amount of sound. Music and talking for some; silence for others.	Light: Bright versus dim light.	Temperature: Warm versus cool.	Design: Formal versus informal. Sitting in chairs or lying on the floor with pillows.
Emotional	Motivation: High versus low motivation. What tasks or situations create?	Persistence: Ongoing attention to task versus need for frequent breaks.	Responsibility: Conforming versus needing choices and creativity.	Structure: Need for structured guidelines or only for general direction.
Sociological	Responses to being with people while learning. Desire to work alone, with colleagues in a group or team, or with one other person in a pair. Preferences for working with an authority such as a teacher. Or preference for varied work relationships.			
Physical	Perceptual: Preferred sensory input. Auditory: listening and verbal. Visual: print, art, shapes. Tactile/kinesthetic: touch and movement.	Intake: Eating, drinking, chewing to help concentration.	Time: Energy and alertness levels at times of day, as in "morning person," "night person." When do peaks occur?	Mobility: Staying still versus needing to move.
Psychological	Analytic–global: Sequential, step-by-step versus global, intuitive. Left brain versus right brain.	Locus of control: External needs for approval versus internal goal setting.		Reflective–impulsive: Thinking deeply but not volunteering answers versus reacting immediately.

Sources: Information from Dunn and Dunn (1987) and Dunn (1996). For more information, see **www.learningstyles.net/.**

Environmental stimuli. We can enable students to vary sound, light, temperature, and the formality of the learning situation in our class. For example, we provide headphones so that some students can listen to music while engaging in learning. Earmuffs are available to let some students shut out noise; other students work best in learning groups in which talk is encouraged. Similarly, various types of lighting are available in the classroom and in other areas, such as study carrels with dimmer illumination. To vary the temperature we allow students to wear less or more clothing and have portable heaters or fans available. Finally, parts of our classroom are informal—a couch, pillows on the floor, and so on—whereas in other parts we have formal chairs at tables.

Emotional stimuli. We can design our teaching for varied emotional styles. Seeing lower levels of motivation as a strength is particularly difficult for us. However, if we accept this trait in students and seek ways to connect with those students' interests and needs, they will feel accepted and ultimately will perform more effectively. Similarly, we can provide opportunities for some students to work intensively on some projects while allowing others to take frequent breaks, perhaps shifting from topic to topic. To do this we structure our classroom time so that there are ongoing blocks of time for individual and small group work on assignments. For some students we provide highly structured assignments; we give others more global directions and provide support as they need it.

Sociological stimuli. As we design our classes for diversity, we will want to provide students with a range of opportunities for working alone or with other people. In the learning process some students desire and actually need to work individually. Others will seek opportunities to work with a buddy, with an adult (this could be a teacher, a volunteer, or someone at home or in the community), with a group of students who work as a team, or even with students from another class. Allowing time for both types of activities is important.

Physical stimuli. A diverse classroom will also attend to opportunities for visual, auditory, or kinesthetic learning experiences. Students should be allowed to snack or drink while working on projects. Teachers report that when they begin to allow such intake in their classrooms, they set a few basic rules. Initially almost all the students will bring food or drink. After the novelty wears off, however, they settle into their personal style patterns, and only the few who really need this continue. Some teachers actually have small refrigerators in their classrooms where students can keep food and drink they bring to school. We can also help students understand their own best learning times and how to structure their class time and projects based on this knowledge. Finally, we devise ways to allow students to move about the room. Here again, teachers report that they set some basic ground rules. Within these simple guidelines students can move from place to place, stand while reading, or walk around the room thinking about a project.

Psychological stimuli. Psychological aspects of learning styles require teachers to recognize and appreciate the variations in the way students' minds function and to respond to them accordingly. With students who are analytical, we draw on their strengths to help them sequentially develop work tasks. Yet we may also pair them with globally oriented students who teach them to look at whole concepts, to be less rigid, and to see relationships. We can similarly recognize each student's individual locus of control and build on the natural strengths inherent in this trait, helping students expand their repertoire. Students who have external locus of control will be very sensitive, for example, to the opinions and perceptions of other people and may help those with internal locus of control to hear what people are saying. By the same token, those who tend to act impulsively may demonstrate responsiveness and a sense of action, encouraging more reflective students to speak out. These latter students can, on the other hand, help impulsive students to think through issues more carefully.

How do we identify the learning styles of students? We find that the best and most efficient way is simply to watch our students carefully—a process we call "kid watching." We made a similar recommendation when we discussed multiple intelligences earlier. Kid watching simply means that we pay close attention to what happens with our students. We keep logs or journals and make notes about different students, particularly those about whom we are most concerned; we also keep an ongoing portfolio of illustrative student work. As we teach and watch our students, we will constantly be asking questions about how they learn and about the arenas in which they are most accomplished. Notes help us remember and organize that information. When students puzzle us, we will review our notes, study their work samples, and reflect on our teaching strategies, interactions, and relationships with them. By paying attention in this way, we can learn a lot; we can better understand our students and constantly improve our teaching practice.

The Local Community
Local Resources for Learning

The local neighborhood and community is potentially an important learning environment as well. Although some schools divorce themselves from their neighborhood, others see their surroundings as a key learning resource—whether the area is filled with broken glass and a landfill or the school sits next to the city library and art museum.

If we look carefully at the instructional strategies described in Chapters 11 through 13, we will see what Kovalik and Olsaen (1997) call a hierarchy of preferred learning. In brief, rich immersion in complex experience is critical for learning, and the most powerful learning strategies immerse students in hands-on experiences and real-world events. This means that the local community can be the most valuable teaching resource that we have.

However, schools traditionally don't connect well with neighborhoods. The reality remains that schools are often physically separated from local community resources. Although it might seem natural and obvious, for example, to cluster schools and other community resources—local businesses, libraries, art museums, social service organizations—we seldom see this. Consequently, we always have logistical difficulties in connecting with local communities. The most traditional procedure is the infrequent field trip, an event in which a busload of students is driven somewhere and then returned to the school. Yet this kind of experience is very limited. Given our constraints, how might we routinely see the local community as a learning environment? In Chapter 6 we explored some ideas taken largely from the work of Kretzmann and McKnight (1993). Here are a few others.

Almost all schools are located in areas with local resources. Residences, businesses, community institutions, even open fields can offer a wealth of learning opportunities. We have to think and look. We might start with questions about the area that students could explore. For example, if our school is in a neighborhood of houses, we might ask:

1. Who lives here? Where do they come from? Why do people live here?
2. What are the relationships among people in the local area? What types of problems exist? What do people think ought to be done about them?

We might gather information from the Internet, ask community members to talk to our class, conduct door-to-door interviews, walk through the neighborhood. We will likely find that as we follow leads and connect with area people, we will find opportunities to link literally everything in our curriculum to local resources.

In a movement called *place-based education*, a growing number of educational writers and reformers, including the leaders of the Annenberg Rural Challenge initiative, are calling for schools to center their study in the local community. Given the interdependence of communities throughout the world, this is not a return to a parochial view of the world. Rather, it is a way of connecting the larger influences, ideas, and needs in the world to the experience of students and their families.

As teachers we may have particular concerns about this approach if our school is located in a low-income neighborhood that many consider dangerous. Yet this is where our students live. This is their neighborhood. The fact that few teachers live in the area in such schools makes a place-based approach the more needed and powerful. We may begin to see new resources to strengthen learning in ways that we have not imagined; and we will likely gain important understanding and appreciation of the lives of our students, their parents, and the area.

One school we know well, for example, is located in a low-income area in a large city. Across from the entrance of the school are a series of houses, one of which burned to the ground and seriously damaged some of the other houses. The school has been broken into several times, and computers have been stolen. Behind the school is an empty lot; across the lot are a pipe-threading shop and large outside storage areas for metal structures. The school has no playground. About two blocks from this school are two major streets and two large churches, both very old.

What might this area offer for study? We could start with the questions we asked previously. Who lives here and why? Likely there are some very interesting people across the street who would appreciate the opportunity to share their experiences and ideas. What about the vacant lot? How big is it? Who owns it, and why is it vacant? What plants, insects, and animals live in this lot? The businesses across the lot—what do they make and for whom? What connections do their products have with other countries? Who works there, and where do they live?

Graves, Graves, Schauber, and Beasley (1999) and Russell (1998) have developed guides to help teachers devise lessons based on neighborhood studies and use of the school grounds and local areas for learning investigations; we recommend such guides to expand these ideas.

Students can be involved in important, real neighborhood projects that connect with others who are trying to improve the community. Lewis (1998a, 1998b) developed useful teacher guides for student involvement in social action and service projects, and Graves and Graves (1997) have described an interdisciplinary process by which students can engage in community planning. Other guides from the Center for the Understanding of the Built Environment (CUBE), too, can be very helpful to teachers. The potential for engaging inquiries that would involve literacy, math, science, social studies, art, and physical exercise is substantial. Such inquiries engage students in real experience, offering opportunities for children at multiple levels of ability to work together in pairs, small groups, and even large groups.

Sights TO SEE

Including Nick

Nick YouTube video regarding Nick, an elementary child with Down syndrome, being included in general education classes. www.youtube.com/watch?v=ji3R30PT1PQ

Toward Inclusive Learning Places

In this chapter we've thought about applying the principles of universal design to our schools, classrooms, and communities to support the learning of all students. This is both a complex and an exciting challenge. We know that what we've outlined here only gets us started. Yet we can build over time. Together with Chapters 11 through 13, this chapter begins to give us a picture of how we might design academic instruction for all learners, build community that supports students emotionally, and design the physical learning environment to include all students learning together and to support best practices in teaching and learning. Over time, as we expand and hone our thinking, gather materials, and seek to use these ideas, we'll have some of the most exciting, creative, fun classrooms around—classrooms in which many students naturally thrive.

Traveling Notes

Teachers and students spend a lot of time in classrooms. It's important that we create as comfortable and usable a space as possible. Here are a few notes from this chapter of key ideas you can take with you.

1. Universal design is a concept and practice that helps us design environments and tools to take into account the full range of human variability. This concept is parallel to our designing for diversity strategy and can help us think about our school and classroom.

2. Schools and classes need to be based on guidelines for healthy environments: They should stimulate, enhance connections, do no harm, be beautiful and inviting, provide varied stimuli, encourage relaxation and privacy, balance constancy and flexibility, and use resources flexibly for multiple purposes. We want to see schools and classrooms in which people feel comfortable where the environment is welcoming and space is used well.

3. Schools can work to use the ideas of universal design in schoolwide design through a range of strategies. Among the most important concepts are the following: a sense of welcome; a commons area; small schools and schools within a school; parent and community center; use of all space inclusively, no segregated classrooms; inclusive transportation to school—no special buses. As we look at schools and classrooms, provision of space that all children, even those with wheelchairs and other physical limitations, can access, both inside and outside is critical.

4. In our own classroom we can use space and resources to respond to our students' differing learning abilities, intelligences, and physical capabilities. Some strategies include multiple places to work and be—teacher's desk, space in the hall, floors, comfortable chairs, tables; varied books and print resources at differing ability levels; classrooms with spaces where students can be alone and also work in pairs and small groups.

5. Use technology to access information including use of text-to-speech and speech-to-text software; space that is organized to provide access and movement for all; and use of the local neighborhood and community as extensions of the classroom. Learning expeditions can start right on the school grounds.

6. Resources are used for all children. Whether books on different levels, science experiment kits, or talking software, materials are housed in a place that can be accessed by all.

Stepping Stones

Following are some activities that will help extend your understanding and actions you may take to improve design of your school and classroom for inclusive teaching.

1. Think about a place you love to be, where you are comfortable and feel that you could be your best in learning new things. Identify this place, describe the setting, and explain what about it makes it a good learning place for you. What are implications for your classroom and teaching? How might these implications relate to students with special needs?

2. Conduct an assessment to determine how well your school is designed to promote community, engage children in learning, and be inclusive. This would be a great thematic study for children in your class. What does the school do well? What might be improved? How?

3. Teach your students about the idea of universal design. Engage the students in a unit in which they think about and design different types of environments that are responsive to the needs and characteristics of all people (a great science project!).

4. Visit a traditional classroom that is organized with desks in rows and uses a textbook and worksheet-driven curriculum. With the teacher's help, identify one student in that class who is having difficulty. During a class, watch what goes on. What are the needs of this student based on what you see and know from the teacher? How is the use of space, teaching resources, and learning tools helping or hindering his or her learning? What might be done to improve learning for this student?

5. Visit a school that is designing curriculum to address multiple intelligences. How does this approach influence the way that the school and its teachers organize space? What tools and materials do faculty have in their rooms that recognize multiple intelligences?

6. Using Figure 7.4 and conduct a disability analysis of your classroom or that of another teacher. Involve your students. Have students themselves identify practical ways that your classroom could be structured to accommodate each disability. Have them also talk about how such accommodations might help (or hurt) other students. What do you and they learn?

7. Visit a traditional classroom that is organized with desks in rows and uses a textbook- and worksheet-driven curriculum. With the teacher's help, identify one student in the class who is having difficulty. During a class, watch what goes on. What are the needs of this student, based on what you see and know from the teacher? How are the uses of space, teaching resources, and learning tools helping or hindering the student's learning? What might be done to improve learning for this student? What might be the impact on other students if these changes were made?

8

Make Environmental Accommodations and Use Assistive Technology

Tools That Extend Human Capacity and Promote Learning

CHAPTER GOAL

Develop an awareness of technology that can be used to extend the capabilities of students with special needs, and understand the contributions technology can make to student learning.

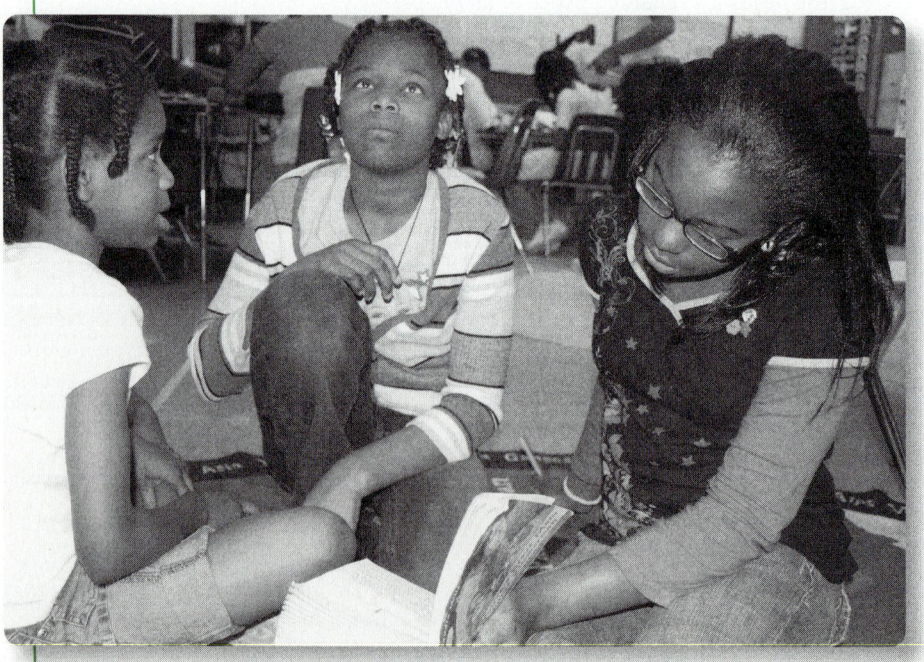

CHAPTER OBJECTIVES

1. Learn about assistive technology and resources for more information.
2. Understand ways that the school learning environment may be designed and modified to facilitate access and participation.
3. Explore and recognize low-, mid-, and high-tech tools that help students with special needs accomplish many functional tasks—from reading and understanding language to driving a vehicle.
4. Examine how assistive technology may be used in the classroom to the benefit of all students.

Including Cedric, a Student with a Severe Disability, with Help from Assistive Technology

Cedric is a fifth-grade student at Glenwood Elementary School. We really don't know what goes on in his mind or how much he understands. From one perspective, Cedric has several difficulties. His peripheral vision is poor. He has a cognitive disability, has no verbal language, and has difficulty walking, sometimes getting tired in the afternoon and using his wheelchair. He is, however, very social, and he communicates his likes and dislikes in many ways. He's an interesting guy.

We visit Cedric's class to see how technology is being used to assist him. On his desk he has a simple communication device—a rectangular plastic device about 4 by 12 inches that has two large buttons. The green button has the word yes printed on it; the red one, no. Cedric can use this device to respond to questions. When he presses a button, an electronic voice says the word aloud.

As we enter the room, Cedric is using a computer program that matches sounds to pictures with the help of a paraprofessional. After a few minutes, Pat Squires, the teacher, calls the kids to the rug area at the front of the room. She says, "Tell me something good." Cedric's peer buddy encourages Cedric to raise his hand. When Pat calls on Cedric he presses a button on a device that announces, "I went to the new library." "You did?" says Pat. "The new one downtown?" Cedric signs "Yes" with his hand. Later, when all go to centers, Cedric uses a tape recorder with headphones to listen to directions for the activity or a story being read.

"I was nervous at the first of the year," recalls Pat. "I have never had a student with disabilities as severe as Cedric's. Yet he has done fine. He likes my class. His buddies are learning a lot about helping other people. We all are learning how technology can be used to help Cedric communicate." Although Pat was also anxious about these new technological gadgets, she has become more comfortable with experience. "For Cedric," she says, "learning how to use these tools is an important part of his learning." She compared this use of assistive technology to other students' proficiency with computers.

Shannon is a senior at Longview High School and is planning to be a lawyer. She is also blind. As we talk, she says, "The school has really been great! A specialist came to the high school when we moved here, and together we thought about what help I would need." An orientation and mobility specialist familiarized Shannon with the layout of the school. She traverses the campus quite easily with the help of her cane. She describes how she uses assistive technology:

- Student buddies read books aloud and help her in other ways.
- Shannon accesses books on tape, using an MP3 player.
- She can read books on CD by using talking software.
- She writes her papers on a word processor, and her words are read back to her via a software program called DragonSpeak.
- She also has dictation software, but she likes to use the keyboard now that she has learned to type.

"It's interesting," Terrance, her guidance counselor, says, "how other kids responded to the technology designed to help Shannon. Several are now using the text-to-speech software, and teachers say it is helping them."

We follow Shannon to her American history class, which is studying the civil rights movement. The teacher has broken the students into groups representing different parts of the community in Little Rock, Arkansas, in 1954. Shannon has used a scanning program at the school to put the text from the book on a disk, which she has read at home using speech synthesis software. The groups are developing presentations to be moderated in a "town meeting." Shannon takes notes on a laptop.

Cedric and Shannon represent important examples of how technology can support inclusive teaching. Technology is an important tool for adapting the environment and providing support.

How do we utilize assistive technology in our class? On the one hand, we can accept and encourage use of adaptive tools and learn how to help students master assistive technology. On the other hand, students with disabilities and the technology they bring provide important learning opportunities for all our students. Assistive technology can give all of us a fresh perspective regarding how technology can interact with human beings—an interdisciplinary lesson in science, social studies, psychology, and literacy, which we receive just by interacting with a student with special needs and technology. Throughout the year we could involve students in exploring questions like the following: How is technology being used to help people with their limitations? What is being developed now? What might we like to see? The many positive outcomes can include:

- Increased self-motivation
- Increased independence
- Greater participation
- More accountability
- Expanded learning and life experiences

Sights TO SEE

Including Stacey and Shawn with Assistive Technology

Stacey As a sixth grader, Stacey has a significant hearing loss. Technology tools helped her in learning and functioning. From the *I Can Soar* video of the National Center for Technology Innovation. www.nationaltechcenter.org/index.php/2007/03/ 04/stacey/

Sean A junior in high school, Sean is blind. Technology makes a real difference in his schooling and life. From the *I Can Soar* video of the National Center for Technology Innovation. www.nationaltechcenter.org/index.php/2007/03/05/sean/

- New opportunities for interactions and communication
- Changed visions of a child's potential on the part of adults, peers, and the child (Sheets & Wirkus, 1997)

An Introduction to Assistive Technology
Technology Expands the Capabilities of All

First, here are some comments about language. The phrases *assistive technology, adaptive technology*, and *enabling technology* are used interchangeably (Cook & Hussey, 1995). Each term refers to technology that helps a person with special needs learn or perform a task he or she could not otherwise do. The term **rehabilitation engineering** refers similarly to the skills of an engineer to develop technological adaptations to assist in people's rehabilitation or to enhance ability to function at work, at home, in school, or in the community. When we speak of the modification of physical places, we talk about environmental "accessibility," "modifications," or "accommodations." The Technology-Related Assistance Act of 1988 (PL 100-407) and IDEA define assistive technology as including "any item, piece of equipment, or product system . . . that is used to increase, maintain, or improve functional capabilities of individuals with disabilities" (IDEA, 2004, section 602)—capabilities such as "speaking, writing, listening, seeing, eating, drinking, moving around one's home or community, using the telephone or computer, opening and closing doors, turning lights on and off" (King, 1999, p. 13).

Is assistive technology only for individuals with "special needs"? Truthfully, all of us use technology to compensate for our limitations or expand our capacities. No human being, for example, can run at 40 miles an hour, even though some animals do. Compared to those other species, we have a physical disability. By the same token, compared to cats, we have a visual disability: Our capacity to see in the dark is much more limited.

Because human beings have limitations, technology has been a powerful force in human history. As human beings developed tools for plowing and cultivating land, for example, they could survive in one location rather than constantly moving to hunt for prey. The rapid development of technology in the 19th century produced what we now call the Industrial Revolution. Most people in the United States rely on an adaptive technology device called an automobile, communication devices called telephones, and adaptive writing devices called computers. These are all tools to compensate for human inadequacies.

Once we begin to think about technology in this way, tools used to aid people who have specific types of limitations don't look so different. Given that all of us use technology to help us accomplish valued tasks, adaptations originally designed to compensate for limitations in people with disabilities are often useful to others as well. The rise of the field of universal design recognizes this fact.

Categories of Assistive Technology

We can view assistive technology through many lenses. Categories help us organize information and ways of thinking about how we use technology in our classroom.

First, many find it helpful to distinguish between low and high technology. **Low-tech** solutions are often simple manual adaptations that require little cost or sophistication—though they often reflect great creativity (Cook & Hussey, 1995). Examples include:

- A rubber pad on a desk to help materials adhere more easily, for students with limitations in their control of their arm and hand movements (such as children with cerebral palsy)

FIGURE 8.1

Examples of Assistive Technology

LOW-TECH	MID-TECH	HIGH-TECH
Post-it notes, erasable highlighter, colored paper, colored overlays, picture schedule, special grips, highlighter tapes, graphic organizer, sentence strips, communication board, large print	Calculator, AlphaSmart, talking dictionary, IntelliKeys, switches, digital voice recorder, tape recorder, word scanners, talking watch or clock, braille, powered toy	Desktop, notebook and handheld computers, typing software, Write Out Loud, Read and Write Gold, head or eye-gaze control of a computer, scanner, math software, electronic books, voice output device, amplification system, hearing aids

- Large pencils or foam blankets for pens to make these implements easier to grasp
- Communication boards that have pictures or simple words to which a student can point to communicate

Mid-tech involves the use of more common technological tools as indicated in Figure 8.1 that teachers and students use often. These may include tape recorders, cell phones, microphones, computers, and scanners.

High-tech devices, on the other hand, involve more sophisticated engineering (Beukelman & Mirenda, 1992; Brett & Provenzo, 1995). Obvious examples include:

- Computers, including scanners and systems that run talking software
- Electronic alternative communication devices with which students use eye gaze or head bands to focus on words or pictures, causing the device to say words aloud in digital speech
- Electric wheelchairs that are guided by a joystick or by "puff-and-sip" commands activated by the person's mouth

This distinction between high, mid, and low technology is useful in that it helps us think broadly about the term *technology*—meaning the use of any tool or device that can help a person perform a task or learn.

Software and *hardware* are two other useful categories. When we are talking about computers, *software* refers to the programs that perform the work—word processors, spreadsheets, databases, statistical analysis programs. *Hardware,* on the other hand, is the actual physical structure of the computer—monitor, disk drives, central processing unit (CPU), and so forth. In assistive technology, the actual devices are hardware. However, the information and skills people need to possess in order to use the devices, or the manuals in which information is contained, are the software. The ways in which people can be of assistance, as in reading aloud for people who are blind, also can be thought of as software (Brett & Provenzo, 1995).

We can further categorize assistive technology based on what it helps a person *do*. Assistive technology fills various functional needs of individuals. For each of these functional activities, many different types of devices can be used. Most would be considered mid-tech tools. Organizing assistive technology based on functional needs is helpful; for example:

1. Numerous devices help people with *communication;* these range from simple devices that record one to three spoken messages to complex communication aids.

2. Other devices such as wheelchairs, adapted automobiles, or leader guide dogs aid people in *mobility,* or getting from one place to another.
3. Some devices may assist primarily in *written communication*—scanners and talking software, books on tape, dictation software.
4. Other technology may help with *hearing or interpretation of sounds*—hearing aids, software that converts recordings to text, sign language interpreters (Cook & Hussey, 1995; King, 1999).

At other times we develop categories of *types* of assistive devices. Examples include wheelchair, computer, interface between technology and the person (e.g., computer keyboard, touch screen, on–off switch, control panel), automobile, optical magnifying lenses, and augmentative and alternative communication device (AAC). In some cases there is an obvious correspondence between type of device and function; for example, a wheelchair is used for mobility. In other cases, however, a device will be used for multiple purposes. A computer, for example, can be used to access print, to communicate, to control other devices at home or in the school classroom. Similarly, an on–off switch can be used to activate any number of messages, other devices, lights, and so on (Cook & Hussey, 1995; King, 1999).

Adaptive Technology Information and Services

With the growing importance of adaptive technology, numerous efforts are under way to make these available. The cost of developing and producing devices presents a serious hurdle, particularly when the target group is small. Consequently, assistive technology is both funded by governmental programs and marketed for profit by companies that specialize in assistive technologies. As universal design principles become more widely used, separate assistive technology devices for persons with special needs may be needed less and less and costs will go down dramatically (Orkwis & McLane, 1998; Steinfeld, 1994).

Every state in the United States has resources for assistive technology. In some states these form a comprehensive network and work effectively. In others, resources are more scarce and uncoordinated. Most states have established at least one resource center for assistive technology and are members of the **Alliance for Technology Access.** The federal government provides funds to assist states in developing coordinated assistive technology systems. In some cases centers associate with rehabilitation hospitals that work with injured adults or with hospitals for children with special health care needs. In other cases centers operate as freestanding organizations. In such centers specialists assess individuals and help select wheelchairs, seating devices, and other low- and high-tech solutions to the daily life needs of the individual (Flippo, Inge, & Barcus, 1995; Kelker & Holt, 2000).

Assistive, or adaptive, technology is required under IDEA for students with disabilities and can be written into a student's IEP (Kelker & Holt, 2000). Given this requirement, most state variations on intermediate school districts provide support for assistive technology for students with special needs. Large school districts may have their own staff and center established for this purpose.

In addition, national organizations provide ongoing research and development and information—publications, reviews of hardware and software, and other relevant resources. The *Center for Applied Special Technology (CAST)* has developed a model of universal curriculum design and has produced tools designed to move in this direction. **Closing the Gap** provides both an online and a hard-copy catalog of hardware and software. A network of "rehabilitation engineering centers" conduct research and development on various types of adaptive technology for both children and adults with disabilities. These organizations often develop new solutions to problems that may then be marketed through private companies.

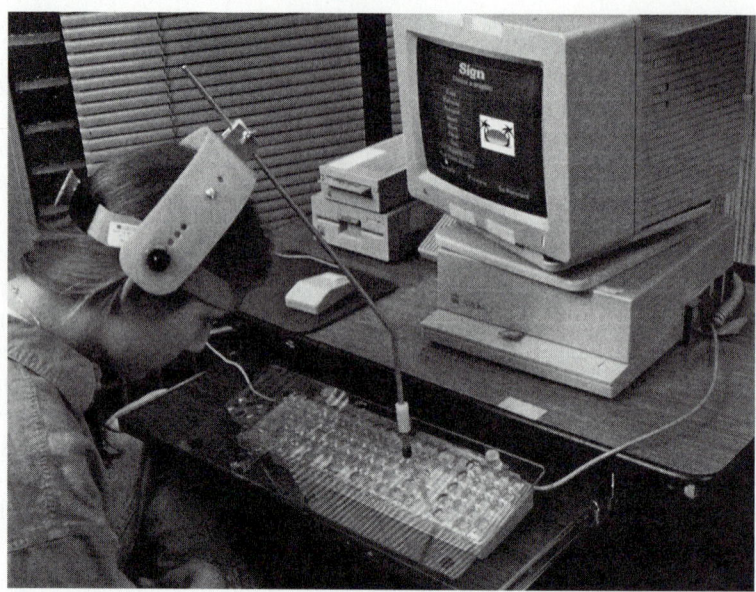

This student has limited ability to use his hands. This special device allows him to use his head motions to type on the computer.

Many companies produce and sell assistive technology for profit. As with any product, it can be difficult to judge which product is the best or whether a given device really meets a need.

In addition, assistive technology is gradually developing as a professional field in its own right. Assistive technology crosses many traditional fields but is not dominant in any—engineering, occupational therapy, physical therapy, speech therapy, special education. Some university programs, however, now offer courses or even degree programs in assistive technology. Although training and expertise is not as widely available as needed, many people are working in this field, and the number is constantly growing (Cook & Hussey, 1995; King, 1999).

Professionals from different fields tend to specialize in specific types of assistive technology, though this is not a hard-and-fast practice. For example, speech therapists tend to be most knowledgeable about augmentative and alternative communication (AAC) devices. Engineers often work with adaptive use of computers, mobility, and workstation design. Occupational therapists use many low-tech devices to aid individuals in activities such as reaching and using a pen—all functions of the upper extremities, the area of focus for occupational therapists (Cook & Hussey, 1995; King, 1999). For teachers, of course, learning to use technology is part of ongoing professional development. Technology is changing rapidly, and new tools are constantly being developed.

Selecting Assistive Technology

With any technological device, we seek to match the person with the most helpful tool. We can do this informally or more systematically. Two models in everyday life serve for comparison—shopping for a car and buying glasses. In the first model, we don't tend to go to experts for a "car–person assessment." Rather, we take it upon ourselves to review car ads, test-drive cars, and study consumer data about different cars. This is true despite the fact that automobile purchases are very expensive. Many people also adhere to this model in obtaining assistive technology. One way to identify helpful tools for our class is to follow a similar strategy. Assistive technology centers often allow people to "test-drive" various technological tools. Similarly, vendors of assistive technology help people select materials of interest and try them out (Kelker & Holt, 2000).

However, another approach is more like when we buy a pair of glasses. In this case, we go to a specialist who measures our eyesight and prescribes glasses with the precise lenses that we need to best see. Similar services are increasingly available in both for-profit companies and government-funded agencies in which an assistive technology specialist obtains detailed information about the functioning capacity of the person through interviews, observations, or performance testing. The specialist also obtains information about desired uses of technology and may visit the locations in which technology will be used—the home, a classroom, a job site—and conduct a detailed "environmental analysis" of these environments. Specialists then use this information to recommend different technological tools (Cook & Hussey, 1995).

IEPs for students such as Cedric and Shannon cover assistive technology and specify that the students receive assistance from one or more assistive technology specialists. As teachers we may receive assistance from our intermediate school district (or our state's equivalent structure). However, we can decide to use a local or state assistive technology center that is not directly connected with our school system (Flippo et al., 1995; Kelker & Holt, 2000; Ryndak & Alper, 1996).

Selecting technology that works for a person is complex. Some assistive technology research indicates that almost one third of devices obtained—at the cost of much time and money—are not used. This occurs for many reasons. Sometimes the devices don't work well or break down. Other times, however, a device is hard to learn to use or may be an embarrassment to the individual. Technology specialists refer to these latter issues as "human factors" (King, 1999).

As in Cedric's and Shannon's cases, our role as teacher is critical, even when (or maybe especially when) we are new to the technology our students are using. A law for technology use has been developed that can be stated rather simply: Motivation is the key to using technology. Said more fully, when time and physical, cognitive, and linguistic effort required for use of a technology exceed the motivation to learn, the technology will be discarded. The implications are clear. If, even unintentionally, we make a student uncomfortable in using an assistive tool, then we contribute to a failure in learning and growth that the technology could have helped mitigate. However, if we welcome and support the student (thus reducing effort), then we help make the student's chances of success much, much higher (King, 1999).

Modifications to the School and Classroom Environment

Creating Access

When designing or retrofitting a school for all learners, we seek to develop an environment that both allows and invites all students to be active participants. We do this with care, for it is certainly possible to make extensive modifications for a specific student in ways that isolate the child from other classmates, even in the same room. Following are key areas for consideration (Sheets & Wirkus, 1997).

Building Access

School buildings and classrooms should provide access for students with different types of limitations. The school must provide ramps with smooth access to the building; doors should be easy to open or be motor assisted so that they open with a gentle push. When the school is an older building, this will necessarily require retrofitting—creating ramps, installing elevators to higher floors. Grab rails throughout the building support students with poor balance or general weakness.

Similarly, *bathrooms* should provide access for students with poor balance or limited strength. For young children, "training" commode chairs may be needed. A light switch extension allows a student in a wheelchair to turn lights on and off; a motion sensor automatically turns water on and off (Sheets & Wirkus, 1997).

We should also consider access of students with physical disabilities to the *playground* or other recreational facilities. In one school, for example, a student was physically challenged and could not hold onto the swing chains. Another student could not use the slide because he couldn't get himself in a safe position. The school purchased an adapted swing and placed rails at the top of the slide that allowed children to stabilize themselves. They also attractively paved the sidewalk through the play area to allow easier access by a student in a wheelchair (Sheets & Wirkus, 1997).

Classroom Modifications

Classrooms also may need modifications. We ensure adequate *floor space* for a student in a wheelchair by organizing students in clusters of tables rather than individual desks, creating pathways in and through the classroom, and organizing spaces for centers. This allows physical access for students with mobility limitations; it also breaks up the space into smaller units, providing a sense of security and focus for distractible students, and establishes a known pathway for students who are visually impaired. We arrange *shelves* so students who cannot stand can access materials on lower levels. Again, grab rails serve as balance supports for students with many kinds of weaknesses.

A *couch* can support a student unable to sit independently on a regular chair because of neurological, muscular, or sensory motor impairments. A couch also encourages cooperative play, because two or three children often sit on it at a time. *Chairs with arms* such as captain's chairs or substitute chairs such as cube chairs or beanbags also offer more support for students with poor posture control, weak sensory orientation, or a very short attention span. Nonslip surfaces for tables and chairs also can provide greater stability (Sheets & Wirkus, 1997).

For students who have difficulties reaching and grasping, *desks* can be difficult. Students may have trouble leaning over to see materials on their desk and may constantly knock off pencils, paper, or other materials. A variety of simple items can help solve this problem. For example (Ryndak & Alper, 1996; Sheets & Wirkus, 1997):

- Paper or object stabilizers include double-sided tape, Post-it tape, clamps, or magnets (if the desk is metal). Also, rubberized pads mounted on a desk help materials move less easily.
- Various-sized drawing utensils include large and regular crayons, markers, and sponge brushes.
- Modified grippers attach to the hand and clamp to a pen; pens with enlarged bodies or covers can be easier to hold.
- Adapted scissors include loop-handled scissors and large-handled scissors or regular scissors.
- A portable slant tabletop made to fit an entire table can allow eight children to work at one time. This allows students to see work more easily, reduce fatigue, and help students with poor visual skills get closer to the work.
- Desks and tables can be made adjustable.
- One adapted desk is designed so the top functions like a lazy Susan and students can rotate it to access different objects (Cook & Hussey, 1995).

Assistive Technology in the Classroom

Let's visit three classes to see examples of how assistive technology is being used in real classes.

Manuel, a second grader in Sonya Chases's class, uses an augmentative and alternative communication (AAC) device to aid in play during recess. Manuel is a very pleasant boy, but he has some significant disabilities. Manuel contracted a serious illness when he was 2 weeks old and now is considered quadriplegic (he can move his arms a bit but can't use his hands or fingers to grasp well, and he can't walk) and nonverbal (though he can say yes and no). Manuel needs assistance with self-help skills, which an aide (sometimes with help from another student) provides. He uses a power wheelchair and a Light Talker, an augmentative communication device in which a light beam scans visual icons; when selected, the icons "talk" with synthesized speech.

We arrive for a visit as the class is heading out to the playground for recess. "Manuel has asked Eugene to be his buddy today at recess," Sonya says; "several of the boys have really become friends with Manuel." We watch Eugene wrap his arm around Manuel as he walks beside the buzzing, slightly meandering wheelchair. Manuel and Eugene join a group of children, and we hear Manuel's Light Talker say for him, "I like you Eugene." Eugene beams. Then, "Let's play ball." We're a bit surprised to see the children include Manuel in their softball game. One of his classmates hits for him, and he "runs" in his power wheelchair. He makes it to first base!

In an elementary school Latisha, a minimally verbal student, was having difficulty participating in story time. The teachers could not tell if she was understanding or if she was even involved in the story. When they asked Latisha questions, she would point vaguely and make sounds they could not understand. Another student, Aaron, who had physical disabilities was in a specially designed seat and also was not always involved. To deal with this problem, they used a range of strategies. They put beanbag and cube chairs on the reading carpet where the children sat on the floor in a semicircle around the teacher. These allowed extra support for both Latisha and Aaron. A grab rail mounted near the teacher allowed Aaron

to pull himself up to participate, using felt or Velcro boards. They also used a range of augmentative communication and interactive story extensions that included gestures, animated facial expressions, sign language, communication boards, puppets, and Velcro boards. An easily programmable, augmentative communication device allowed both children to comment on the story or to ask or answer questions. They found that verbal students, too, often used the augmentative communication devices as well as talking. In addition, many shy children or those lacking confidence participated more often, using a voice output device that eventually gave them enough confidence to begin speaking more often (Sheets & Wirkus, 1997).

In a middle school, Jena, a student with a severe disability, was able to make meaningful contributions by using some simple communication aids—the Speakeasy, BIGmack, and Step-by-Step75 (all produced by AbleNet, www.ablenetinc.com/). These programmable devices allowed students to do the following (and more) (Wise, 1999):

- Greet classmates
- Introduce self/classmates/coworkers
- Respond to attendance call
- Give directions for activity/assignment/work task
- Give an individual/group report, with classmates recording student's portion
- Share joke, riddle, or quote of the day
- Share weekend activities, with classmates transcribing in journal
- Answer comprehension question
- Make announcements over public address system
- Join in choral reading activity or recite lines of a skit
- Request assistance in holding/using materials
- Share the day's events with family, with message(s) recorded by peer

In Nan Sheldon's senior English class, students are working on a project for the yearbook, editing stories and incorporating these with photographs that

(*continued*)

the graphic arts class will use to design the layout and cover. Nan has a series of computers in her class. Jasmine, a student who is deaf, is at one of these. She has had to work hard to learn to write well and is now working with a partner. "We have our computers networked," Nan says as we watch. "Jasmine and the other kids have figured out that the best way for them to work together is to use the computers to send e-mail back and forth. This way Jasmine can read what is said and doesn't need the help of an interpreter." Nan explains that Jasmine sometimes does use a sign language interpreter and that over the year several of the students have gotten pretty good at basic conversation with her. "Also," she says, "some of the kids take notes for her. It's worked out well."

In her ninth-grade algebra class, Jan Larson has several students who have learning disabilities and one student, Brian, who has a cognitive disability. Jan has broken students into groups and given them projects that involve the use of a range of mathematics skills, including algebraic equations and geometry. Brian is working with a group that is designing the size and structure of a radio tower in a valley. (Jan tells us that she has been collaborating on some of these projects with the art and social studies teachers.) The students are building a scale model of the valley and the tower.

We're interested to see how Brian is involved with the group. He pulls out a measuring tape and measures the height of the tower and the mountain. The tape speaks the measurement in synthesized speech! Jan explains that she tries to have Brian work with students on projects like this at his own ability level. "However, the other students are helping him understand the most basic algebraic equations and what they might be used for," Jan says. When we ask about other uses of technology, she says that Brian especially likes the interactive math and graphics software she has in the class. "The software has been particularly helpful for Sue," she adds, "who has a learning disability. The software engages the students in using mathematics concepts in applied situations rather than having them simply calculate equations they don't understand."

Reflection: Technology makes a huge difference in all of our lives. Assistive technology has the potential to create greatly expanded opportunities for students with disabilities. Rather than being afraid of technology that is new to us, however, such tools can be used valuably by many of our students. Having this technology in our classroom is like having our own science lab to explore the interaction of technology and human capability. Kids love it!

Functional Applications of Assistive Technology
Using Technology to Live and Learn

In addition to focusing on general environmental adaptations, technology has many specific functional applications. Let's consider the key areas in which assistive technology can aid both children and adults.

Aids to Assist in Understanding and Remembering

A variety of aids are created to help students understand or remember. We already use helpful low-tech tools. For example, on our classroom walls we often have a list of the daily schedule, assignments and due dates, word walls, or lists of technical terms. Similar individualized tools can be created for students (Weisgerber, Dahl, & Appleby, 1980):

- A daily pictorial schedule that shows a clock with a time, a picture of an activity, and the words that represent this activity can be made for one student, several, or posted for the whole class.
- Tape-recorded instructions for an activity can indicate steps to be carried out.
- Checklists (with pictures if needed) enumerate steps for a particular activity.

Manipulating and Controlling the Environment

We rely on technology in our home—we use lights, oven, air conditioner, radio, TV, DVD player. The same goes for the classroom, where we depend on lights, timers, computers, DVD player, transparency projector. Children and adults with significant disabilities, however, have difficulty using typical controls—difficulty reaching, turning, moving around the room. A wide variety of low- and high-tech tools for manipulating and controlling the environment can provide assistance (Cook & Hussey, 1995; King, 1999).

Low-Tech Aids for Manipulation. Low-tech aids are designed as *general purpose* tools for numerous functions or activities. In contrast, *special purpose* devices are specifically designed for one particular function. In addition, some are designed to *augment* a person's ability to perform a task in a standard way; others use *alternative* means of accomplishing a task. Let's look at ways that devices can help.

Mouthsticks and head pointers are two general purpose aids frequently used for direct manipulation of objects by people who cannot use their hands and fingers well. They are used to turn the pages of books; to write (with a ballpoint pen attached to the end); to pick up objects (by means of a pincher attachment opened and closed by tongue action); and to grip objects (with a suction cup attached). They can also help people dial a telephone, type, and turn lights on and off.

Reachers help a person reach and grasp objects and are useful for a person who cannot stand (or for any of us when an object is on a high shelf). A handle grip is on one end of a pole that has grasping jaws, often covered with rubber or another nonslip material. With this mechanism a person can pick up and move many objects—cans, packages, books, paper, tapes, CDs, and so forth.

Special purpose aids most often involve specialized handles on tools designed for specific purposes. These might include, for example, a brush with an extended handle, a pen or pencil with an enlarged grip, a key holder with a large grip, a spoon with a bent handle for scooping or with a swivel handle. Electronic aids include page turners and feeders; feeders help people with limited use of arms or hands to eat more independently (Cook & Hussey, 1995).

Switches and Environmental Control Units. A wide range of adapted switches can control numerous devices. Switches fall into the following categories: (1) direct selection, (2) scanning, and (3) coded access.

Direct selection occurs when the individual directly selects the item—by hand and finger movement, by use of a mouthstick, or even via an electronic pointer mounted on the person's head. Such switches may be flip switches (like a typical light switch), buttons, or turn knobs.

Scanning involves an electronic device in which choices are provided and a cursor or light moves from one to the other. The switch is activated by the person when the correct choice is indicated.

Finally, *coded access* typically involves the use of Morse code to send signals to units to activate switches. For any switch, selection may include a simple on–off function (called "latching"); variability (as with varied intensity of lighting); or "momentary" function, meaning that the switch is on as long as it is being pressed and off when released. This brief introduction to switches illustrates the potential complexity of what most of us take for granted (Cook & Hussey, 1995).

An interesting application of switches is the development of *environmental control units*. A single environmental control unit, which looks like a small box with multiple switches or controls, can control multiple functions—light switches, oven, tape recorder,

DVD player. Although these are used mostly in homes, such a unit could be used in a school to give a student with limited mobility the opportunity to control some operations within the classroom (Cook & Hussey, 1995).

How might an environmental control unit work in a classroom? One high school used three units with infrared remote capability that controlled multiple appliances and office machinery. Using these devices, several students with severe disabilities were able to engage actively in classes by turning on the following types of equipment:

- Overhead projector
- Tape player or stereo—to dance, exercise, or hang out
- Book light
- Tape recorder with test questions/answers and books on tape
- Kitchen appliance for class cooking activity
- Office machines such as paper shredder, stapler, or letter opener for a cooperative work task

This helped the students be a real part of the class. Other students were interested in the control units, which helped prompt positive social interaction (Wise, 1999).

Seating and Positioning

For any of us to work for a length of time, we must have comfortable seating and posture. For students with disabilities affecting body structure, balance, and/or muscle strength, this is sometimes difficult in typical seating. We should pay attention to students' positions on the floor, at a desk or table, or in their wheelchair, as well as to their posture during other daily activities—in the bathroom, at the pool, on the playground, or on the school bus (King, 1999).

Physical therapists can help us select and design adaptive seating for students with severe disabilities and can provide consultation regarding ways to support a student in our class. Working with a team, often in a special clinic, physical therapists conduct a careful assessment of the physical capacities and needs of the person, try various approaches to seating, and help a family obtain needed devices.

In addition to comfort, two major areas of focus are important when we consider seating and positioning: (1) postural control and deformity management and (2) pressure control (Cook & Hussey, 1995). Let's discuss these briefly and explore implications for the classroom.

Posture Control. Some individuals have muscle weakness and uncoordinated movements that make it difficult for them to sit upright in a wheelchair or other seating. If not dealt with, these difficulties can, over time, cause general health problems and skeletal deformities that worsen the disability. Students with cerebral palsy most often have this difficulty, as do those with muscular dystrophy and multiple sclerosis. Treadwell and Roxborough (1991) described three levels of postural control ability for which different types of assistance are needed:

- Hands-free sitter: The person can sit without using hands for support. Seating is designed to provide mobility and a stable, comfortable base of support.
- Hands-dependent sitter: Hands are used to maintain support. Seating helps provide pelvic or trunk support to free the person's hands for activities.
- Propped sitter: The person lacks any ability to support himself or herself. Seating provides total body support.

Here are a few examples of types of seating support:

- A seat raised on the outer side to prevent the person from sliding forward
- A seat belt, lap belt, or bar to assist the student in maintaining position and to offer pelvis stabilization
- Foot supports so that feet don't hang too low
- Adjustable supports on the sides of a wheelchair to help a person with severe scoliosis maintain a more erect posture
- Head supports on a wheelchair to help stabilize the neck
- Seat with custom contours specially designed to fit the body structure of the student

What is both tricky and important about developing and using supported seating is that it is vital, on the one hand, to help students maintain good posture to prevent worsening of their disability, and, on the other hand, to provide flexibility so that they can engage in activities—reaching, writing, drawing, reading.

We work with the parents, the physical therapist, and the student in thinking about the physical structure of the class and the various ways the student can participate—sitting at the desk, sitting on beanbag cushions on the floor, moving the wheelchair throughout

BUMpS IN THE ROAD   *Lack of Access*

While assistive technology offers many possibilities of expanding the opportunities for all students, including those with special needs, many problems occur that limit its use. Many educators simply are not familiar with assistive technology. Even if they have some general knowledge, they may be afraid of being overwhelmed.

Unfortunately, assistive technology is not yet part of the everyday life and structure of schools. Although almost all schools use computer-based technology and have staff at their school who work with and maintain this technology, few of these educators are familiar with assistive technology. It is still seen as a province for "those" children rather than a resource that should be part of school services. For example, one survey found that 87% of parents of students with disabilities said they had access to some form of technology in schools, but less than 12% indicated that their children had access to assistive technology (Dalton, 2002). Similarly, in a national survey of individuals with disabilities, 40% indicated that they had received "some" or "a lot" of information about assistive technology, while 60% received only "a little" or none (Carlson, Ehrlich, Berland, & Bailey, 2001). Assistive technology centers often report that their resources are underutilized.

So while use of technology in learning is rapidly expanding through the use of computers and the vast amount of information available on the Internet, many students with special needs cannot use these tools without access to assistive technology (Dalton, 2002; Kelker & Holt, 2000). The result is that learning of all students is diminished.

What to do?

Key is to try to get assistive technology integrated and incorporated into the overall technology plan for the school. Talk with the school principal. Share some tools like an Alpha Smart and dictation and text-to-speech software and talk about how these could be valuable to all students. Suggest that the principal, several teachers, and parents take a tour of the assistive technology center that serves your school district.

Second, make it a priority to reach out to the needs of your students. Do an analysis of your students' needs and contact the assistive technology center for your school. Find out how the tools it offers work and try to obtain resources for use in your class. Let your principal and other teachers know you are doing this. Maybe they will also become interested, especially if you begin to have success with your students.

the room. Start by thinking about a typical classroom day and the many movements of students as they engage in active learning; then enlist the advice and assistance of the physical therapist. Other students also can learn how to help the person navigate the classroom and sit properly.

Pressure Control. Students with spinal cord injuries have the greatest difficulties related to pressure. Because they have limited feeling, they may develop sores from pressure at particular points (technically, *decubitus ulcers*), which can be dangerous. Two key strategies are used to assist with this problem. First, good posture is maintained as discussed previously. Second, various types of cushions are used. Finally, individuals engage in pressure relief activities—namely, a routine of shifting the weight of the body in different directions or of sitting in a way that relieves pressure, lying down, lying back in a wheelchair, and so on. With some children with significant disabilities, we may periodically help them shift their weight to aid in both pressure and posture control. A physical therapist will help us understand when and how to do this.

Augmentative and Alternative Communication (AAC)

Many students with more severe disabilities have difficulties talking. In some cases, as with cerebral palsy, individuals have deficits in muscular control; they are able to speak but do so slowly and may be difficult to understand. For students who speak at some level, tools may *augment* or improve their communication abilities. For students who are not able to talk to any meaningful extent, we use *alternative* communication strategies. The **augmentative and alternative communication** (**AAC**) approaches we use sometimes rely on tools and technology ("aided" communication) and sometimes on use of the body or expression ("unaided" communication) (Beukelman & Mirenda, 1992; Chedd, 1995).

Physical Movement and Gestures. Some approaches are not technological but build on typical alternative communication tools. We all use our bodies to communicate in a variety of ways—through facial expressions, gestures, nodding our head, pointing, or touching (Cook & Hussey, 1995). We all use such methods as ways to augment what we say in words. Many students with severe disabilities who cannot talk otherwise

LABORATORY RETRIEVER

communicate much in these ways. *Sign language* is valuable not only for individuals with significant hearing losses but also for students who are unable to talk.

Facilitated Communication. **Facilitated communication** is a process in which a facilitator works with an individual, often at a computer, helping stabilize the person's hands as he or she types messages and information on a computer. Developed by Australian educator Rosemary Crossley, facilitated communication has been heralded by some as a way of giving voice to many individuals with severe disabilities, particularly those with cerebral palsy and autism, who have not communicated effectively before (Crossley, 1994). Biklen (1990, 1992) brought the technique to the United States, where it has spread rapidly throughout the country. The approach has been controversial, however, with many doubting that the communications are the product of the person rather than the facilitator (American Speech and Hearing Association, 1994; Jacobson & Mulick, 1992; Levine & Wharton, 1995; Shane, 1994). Research to date has demonstrated cause for cautious optimism that this strategy may be able to open up a new life for some individuals (Biklen, 1990, 1992). On the one hand, individuals on both sides of the controversy acknowledge that facilitators can and do influence what is said. On the other hand, studies have demonstrated that this technique has been effective in allowing people previously thought to have minimal intellectual abilities to communicate deep and complex ideas, feelings, and thoughts. The Web sites of the Facilitated Communication Institute (2001) at Syracuse University and of Rosemary Crossley's Australian center (2001), DEAL, offer further information, including links to critics.

Communication Boards ("No Tech"). Technological aids vary dramatically in their degrees of technological sophistication. At the lowest-tech level are locally or commercially produced **communication boards** of various sorts. The simplest type of

Robert laughs as he uses this augmentative communications device to tell a joke about one of his classmates to this speech therapist. She provides support to Robert helping him learn to use the AAC device to communicate effectively.

communication board might consist of pictures with words that express a meaning placed on a piece of cardboard. The student would point to the desired message—"Go to the bathroom," "I am hungry," "Yes," "No."

Simple Electronic Communication Aids ("Low Tech"). Other communication aids use technology to a limited degree. For example, Versascan is a simple aid that uses a few picture icons arranged in a circular pattern on a square board. A light shines behind each picture in turn. When the light arrives at the desired picture, the individual hits a simple switch and the message is spoken aloud in synthesized speech. A frequently used, simple communication device is the BIGmack, shaped like a large hamburger made of plastic. On this device one message may be recorded at a time and is then activated when the individual presses the top of the apparatus (Cook & Hussey, 1995; Sheets & Wirkus, 1997).

Sophisticated Electronic Communication Devices ("High Tech"). Voice output communication aids (VOCA) are portable speech output mechanisms, many of which are very sophisticated. VOCA appliances can be thought of as computerized electronic communication boards. Typically the size and shape of a laptop computer, they are often mounted on wheelchairs. Most are divided into rows and columns of squares on which icons for messages are located. In some cases the VOCA instrument is multilevel, which means that more than one message may be stored under each key. Some produce synthesized speech output—the "robot" sound. Many use digital speech, which sounds like a human voice, either male or female. A range of message selection systems are available: In *scanning* a light or cursor moves from selection to selection and the user activates messages using a switch; in *direct selection* the person may use touch, a mouse, a joystick, or a head-mounted pointing device. Some mechanisms support *eye gaze* as a way of selecting choices as well (Cook & Hussey, 1995).

Dynavox (made by Sentient Systems), for example, uses an icon display and is accessed via touch, single- or dual-switch scanning, joystick, or mouse. The Pathfinder (Prentke Romich) provides high-quality speech synthesis with different age and gender options. It also can be used as an alternate keyboard to most computers and operates a variety of environmental controls. The Touch Talker (Prentke Romich) has 128 touch-sensitive keys that can be custom programmed and use additional overlays. The instrument can be hooked to a printer and used as an input device to a computer. A much less expensive, commonly used system is the Wolf (AdamLab). The least sophisticated version of the Wolf looks like a child's portable tape recorder and has four programmable squares for icons and words. It can be turned on via touch or adapted for scanning (Beukelman & Mirenda, 1992; Closing the Gap, 2000; Sensory Access Foundation, 2000).

Adapted Computer Access

Computers are important tools for accessing information and producing work; according to Sheets and Wirkus (1997), various adapted computer formats can help to level the playing field for people with disabilities. Typically, to use a computer effectively, a person must be able to see a monitor screen, read what is on the screen, and type to input information. However, many students, including those with disabilities, have difficulty with one or more of these processes. Assistive technology identifies ways to help with these limitations. One example is to modify the placement of the monitor. Beyond monitor placement and access, three additional considerations are important:

- Computer interface—the way the individual provides input to the computer

- Computer output—how the person receives useful output from the computer
- Computer software—programs that are based on best practices and encourage learning at students' own ability levels

Computer Interface. Numerous tools are useful to modify and adapt input into the computer.

Alternatives to typing. Some students need alternative methods of providing input to the computer beyond the standard keyboard. The first type of adaptation uses a standard keyboard but alternative methods of typing, rather than hands. For example, a mouthstick or head stick allows head motions to press keys. A similar device attached to the hand with a splint allows hand, rather than finger, movements to press keys.

Adaptations to the standard keyboard. For some people with disabilities, the standard keyboard causes various problems for which there are software solutions. For example, a student with cerebral palsy might have difficulty pressing a letter in such a way that it does not repeat itself over and over. Both Windows and Macintosh have available software that delays the amount of time required before a letter is repeated (Alliance for Technology Access, 1996; Cook & Hussey, 1995).

Alternative keyboards. Special keyboards are useful for some individuals with limited ability to move fingers. These alternatives include (1) TouchWindow, a program that puts a keyboard on the screen that can be activated through touch; (2) Big Keys, a large-lettered, bright-colored keyboard on which the keys are arranged in alphabetical order; and (3) IntelliKeys, which allows for a single-switch adaptation and uses simpler, graphic-based commands to help students more easily navigate the use of software programs (Sheets & Wirkus, 1997).

Communication devices as alternative inputs. Some of the communication devices discussed earlier can provide input into the computer, thus requiring the person to learn commands for only one device. However, the device must be physically connected to the computer. In addition, there are sometimes technical problems; communication between some devices and the computer can require manual programming, thus complicating this option (Alliance for Technology Access, 1996; Cook & Hussey, 1995). Examples include:

- *Scanning and switch-controlled keyboard:* When an individual cannot use any type of keyboard because of physical limitations, then scanning or Morse code is used. Scanners provide on-screen choices to the individual, either a line at a time or with rows and columns that cover half of the screen (Cook & Hussey, 1995). The individual can employ control switches select items scanned on the screen, using a "sequentially stepping selection cursor" (King, 1999, p. 18).
- *Morse code:* Software is available that allows "sequenced pulses from special switches to operate the computer" (King, 1999, p. 18) in Morse code. Use of Morse code allows more flexibility; however, it also requires the individual to memorize complicated sequences. Additionally, some required commands, such as "space," are not easily conveyed via Morse code (Cook & Hussey, 1995).

Speech-to-text software. Dictation software allows individuals to speak to the computer to control functions and engage the different commands of different software programs (Cook & Hussey, 1995). Students who are not able to write may speak into the computer and the computer will write in an e-mail, word processor, or other software program. Thus, students with significant physical limitations, like those with cerebral palsy, as well as students with significant cognitive limitations may be able to create written documents as well as control typical programs—graphics, presentation, e-mail, spreadsheet, and database. Both Windows and Macintosh operating systems come with speech-to-text and text-to-speech software built in. Dragon NaturallySpeaking (www.nuance .com/naturallyspeaking/) is used with Windows computers and MacSpeech's Dictate (www.macspeech.com/) and ViaVoice (www.nuance.com/viavoice/) are similar programs for use on Macintosh computers. Although speech-to-text and text-to-speech software are particularly important for students with special needs, these programs can be used with all of our students. In fact, many people are using such programs at home and in the workplace to reduce physical stress of typing on a computer and to increase productivity.

Computer Output. We are familiar with typical computer output—words and images on a screen and/or printed materials. However, a variety of other outputs are available.

Text-to-speech software. For both Windows and Macintosh operating systems, software is available that converts text to speech on personal computers. Some text-to-speech programs are specifically designed to assist in promoting literacy development with elementary-age students. According to the Sensory Access Foundation (2000), both a voice synthesis card and screen review software are required. Newer computers come with voice synthesis built into the operating systems for both Windows machines and Macintosh (VoiceOver); older computers may require a separate voice synthesis card. In addition, external voice synthesizers may be used. ReadPlease (www.readplease .com/), Natural Readers (www.naturalreaders.com/), IBM's Natural Voices, and TextAloud are all programs for Windows computers. Programs for Macintosh include TextSpeech Pro (www.digitalfuturesoft.com/) and GhostReader.

Two types of speech output are used with computers and other devices based on the use of microchips: digitized and synthesized speech. *Digitized speech* has been recorded onto some medium such as a magnetic tape, hard drive, or a read-only-memory (ROM) chip and produces a natural human sound. *Synthesized speech,* in contrast, uses complex rules to produce sounds based on spelling and syntax and produces a definitely "electronic" sound (Sensory Access Foundation, 2000).

Screen-reading programs work with the synthesizer to convert information on the screen into spoken words. By means of a screen reader, a blind user can read anything on the screen, from a single character to the entire screen display; and the screen review software can even notify the user that something has "popped up" on the monitor. With a single keystroke the user can command the synthesizer to speak out a word, a sentence, a paragraph, or an entire document. The only such program available for the Macintosh is Berkeley Systems's outSPOKEN, which works with the speech synthesizer built into the operating system. Numerous such programs are available for both DOS and Windows-based computers. Additionally, work is under way, though in its infancy, to convert graphics on the screen (graphical user interface, or GUI) to spoken words (Cook & Hussey, 1995; Sensory Access Foundation, 2000).

Magnified screen images. For persons with partial sight, enlargement of text on the computer screen can make an important difference. Magnification can be done by means of magnification software or through use of a closed-circuit television (CCTV). Software can be installed that magnifies images on the screen and changes colors and contrast so that materials read more easily. One such program built into the operating system for the

Macintosh is Closeview, which magnifies text and graphics 2 to 16 times. Similar programs are available for Windows-based computers. This software can also change the color of the text and background. For example, if users are light sensitive but need contrast, they can have the text displayed in bright yellow on a soft gray or powder blue. Many students find this beneficial, particularly students with visual processing disabilities. In addition, optical screen magnifiers placed over monitors or CCTV systems not only magnify printed materials but also enlarge information on a computer screen (Alliance for Technology Access, 1996; Cook & Hussey, 1995; Sensory Access Foundation, 2000).

Tactile output. Also available for computers are appliances that produce tactile output in two formats—letter shapes and braille. The **Optacon** is a device that creates a "tactile facsimile" of print, using pins that vibrate in the shape of each letter. Braille output can be accessed either as an electronic display or as hard-copy printed braille. An electronic braille display converts text on the screen to pins that raise and lower so they can be felt. The person can use the device to control access to the computer without switching back and forth. Such units, however, are very costly. Also available are braille printers, which, like any printer, vary in speed and quality. Two frequently used printers sell for as low as $500, although higher quality braille printers can cost thousands of dollars (Alliance for Technology Access, 1996; Cook & Hussey, 1995; Sensory Access Foundation, 2000).

Computer Software: Scaffolding Learning with Technology. Computers and software provide powerful tools for many of our students. What is *not* particularly useful, however, is to use computer programs as automated worksheets. Unfortunately, much educational software, particularly in packages sold to school districts, encourages just this type of use. However, software can provide multiple ways of presenting information to students and multiple ways to allow them to express information, including:

- Text- and graphics-based reference books such as encyclopedias on CDs.
- Interactive programs based on best teaching practices.
- Speech synthesis software and programs that allow books to be read and accompanied by pictures and graphics.
- Games that incorporate skills in literacy, mathematics, science, social studies, and other disciplines (e.g., space exploration programs that require calculations of fuel use, resource use of different colonies, etc.).
- Instructional software that teaches students how to use computer-based production programs—word processors, graphics, and so on. Many instructional programs are designed with graphics and sound to appeal to children.
- Word prediction software that predicts the words a student is trying to type. Students can then select the word they want. This is particularly helpful for students with learning disabilities and those who find it difficult to type, such as students with cerebral palsy.

That's just a start. Computers also offer students wonderful opportunities to produce evidence of learning that draws on different intelligences. Many programs have been developed to appeal to children of different ages with different levels of skill and sophistication. Among them are:

- Word processors
- Presentation software (PowerPoint; KidPics, a children's version of such a program)
- Graphics software—for drawing, painting, and so forth
- Spreadsheets

Teaching Students Successfully in General Education

SCHOOLS to VISIT

Fulton Elementary School
Lancaster, PA 17603

Fulton Elementary School is home to 472 students in kindergarten through Grade 5. Ninety percent of the children come from families with incomes at or below the poverty level; 42% are Latino, 33% African American, 24% White, and 1% Asian American.

Over the last 8 years Fulton Elementary has made great changes. At that time 25% of its students were in special education, most in segregated classes. Now 4% of students receive special education services and all are included in general education classes. "It's a culture," says principal Drue Miles. "Nobody talks special education or thinks in out-of-my-classroom strategies. We simply use a variety of strategies to make learning available to everyone."

The district and school have traditionally used a three-step process to serve students. Tier 1 is a teacher's requesting individual consultation regarding a student. Tier 2 is the formation of a small team for consultation. Tier 3 is a coordinating council that considers referral to special education. Drue, however, suspended tier 3 meetings and expected all students to be served by teachers with consultation and assistance.

Once the vehicle for passing a student to special education ("I'm not able to teach this student") was eliminated, the practice of taking what was considered the lower portion of students and recommending special education came to a halt.

Drue believed that educators in the school had the required talents to keep all children in the classroom. He created a resource bank based on assets-based community development of staff skills, talents, and interests. Today, each time a faculty member approaches Drue about a student, the principal searches the resource bank for the person with the solution. For example, it has been common that a first grader with phonemic awareness deficits would be referred to special education. The Fulton Elementary speech therapist now goes into the classroom to help all students with phonemic awareness.

Drue explains his motivation for inclusion: "I was a special education teacher, and I dealt with the reality of teachers' not wanting children in their classrooms. I wanted to purify special education. Now teachers can do real inclusion, and special education teachers can be a real part of the school community."

By Thomas J. Neuville, Millersville University, Millersville, Pennsylvania.

- Databases
- Music writing programs
- Web site development software

Such programs allow students to develop products. When used with adaptive input technology, these programs allow students with a wide range of academic abilities to write, draw, develop songs, assemble slide presentations, or create pictures. These productions can be used as a basis for other activities in the classroom; for example, a group might act out a story written by a student, use computer-generated graphics to design props for a play, organize a class sing-along based on songs written on the computer by a student (or group of students), maintain a database of books in the class library, or create a class book that incorporates students' graphics and research on a current topic of study (Alliance for Technology Access, 1996; Center for Applied Special Technology, 2008).

Aids for Students with Partial Sight or Total Blindness

Students with visual impairments range greatly in their visual acuity, field of vision, and other characteristics. Individuals with partial sight benefit from a variety of magnification tools that can help them make the most of the vision they have. Individuals who have no useful sight also can access information with the help of a growing range of strategies and tools.

Magnification Devices. Perhaps the most common form of assistive technology, used by a large part of the population, are devices that help us see better. Many people wear glasses or contacts. As people get older, almost everyone uses some sort of "corrective eyewear" or combinations thereof—contacts with reading glasses, prescription sunglasses, sports glasses, and so on. For people with more extreme visual impairments, other optical devices are available. These include various types of optical or electronic magnifiers of all sorts and sizes—from handheld to desk magnifiers. **Closed-circuit television (CCTV)** can function as an electronic magnifier: A camera focuses on a document or is connected electronically to a computer and sends the image to a television screen that enlarges the image. Different versions are available, including a handheld camera using an NTS interface that connects to a typical television, other portable cameras that use a table on which documents are placed and are connected to a computer monitor, and stand-alone units (Sensory Access Foundation, 2000).

Recorded Materials. For individuals who have no useful vision, a great variety of devices and tools are available. Although these require training to use, technology increasingly provides blind individuals with access to information. Many books are available through commercial companies that provide books on tape, through the Library of Congress, or through local services that often provide access to newspapers and other materials. Materials available through libraries can also be accessed without charge for students who have learning disabilities or other problems accessing written materials (Sensory Access Foundation, 2000).

Braillers. *Braillers* operate like small typewriters. Mechanical braillers are as noisy as a manual typewriter; however, more recent versions operate like small laptop computers. The more recent versions, such as the BrailleNote and BrailleLite, allow students to edit work, hear it read back to them, and feel the letters they have typed in a set of pins, as the curser moves. Also, they can be hooked up to a laptop computer, so that when the student is typing the teacher can see what is being written on the screen. Additionally, a person may use these braille devices to record information and then have the computer convert this, if desired, to braille with either hard copy or electronic print (Cook & Hussey, 1995; Sensory Access Foundation, 2000).

Reading Systems. Technological devices give persons who are blind more independence in accessing information. Reading systems allow individuals who are blind or visually impaired to access printed material. They consist of a scanner, a computer to which the scanner is connected, and software to turn the scanned image into text that can be read aloud through speech synthesis and/or displayed in electronic braille format. Stand-alone systems consolidate the computer, software, and scanner into a single unit in which one keystroke engages the scanning and text conversion process. Software-based systems require more computer skills but have the capability of editing and printing information. Among reading systems are Arkenstone's Open Book and Open Book Unbound, Telesensory Corporation's Oscar, and Xerox Corporation's Reading Edge (Cook & Hussey, 1995; Sensory Access Foundation, 2000).

This student has a visual disability. She uses software to enlarge the words so that she can read them.

Adapted Tools and Measuring Devices. A wide range of adapted tools and measuring devices are available. Although designed largely for persons who are blind or visually impaired, they can be useful to our other students as well. They include rulers with raised markings, talking clocks, watches with raised markings, braille labels, light probes (used to determine if lights are turned on), and liquid level indicators that sound a tone when electrodes placed in a container reach a certain level, as in measuring ingredients for cooking (Weisgerber et al., 1980).

Assisted Hearing and Alternatives

Assistive devices to aid people in hearing are among the oldest and most used assistive technologies available. They are used by so many people that we no longer consider them unusual or think of them primarily in connection with people with limitations. For individuals who have partial ability to hear, assistive devices include:

- Hearing aids—electronic aids that are mounted behind the ear, in the ear, or in the ear canal
- Amplified telephones with volume controls
- Headphones that allow students to listen to tapes with increased volume
- Classroom amplification systems in which teachers use microphones and speakers mildly amplify the sound
- **FM units**, in which the speaker uses a microphone and amplified sound is accessed through a receiver carried by the individual with a hearing impairment

For individuals without functional hearing, we need alternative tools. We have discussed sign language. Technological tools are important as well.

Telephone Access. The telephone provides an important challenge. People who are deaf can communicate either with other deaf people or with hearing persons using a **telecommunications device for the deaf (TDD)**, a keypad device that acts as a modem. If another deaf person has such a device, when the telephone connects, the two TDD users can type messages and send them back and forth to each other. If a deaf person is calling a hearing individual, the telephone company provides a "relay operator," an individual who reads the message from a TDD and then translates this into speech for the hearing person. (Interestingly, AT&T employs blind people in these jobs; the relay operators receive incoming messages in electronic braille.)

Another option for telephone communication involves use of a computer and speech synthesis software with a touch-tone phone. The computer is connected directly to the telephone. As the person who is hearing impaired types messages, the computer converts the text to spoken language. The TDD used by the person who is deaf can function automatically as a bidirectional TDD, allowing the hearing person on the other end to use the keys of the telephone as a simple text input device. This technology has allowed widened opportunities, as it requires neither the use of special equipment by the hearing person nor dependence on a relay operator.

A final option, not yet in wide use, is video transmission—which would allow two deaf people to speak to each other using sign language. Given the enormous memory requirements for such transmission, this technology is not yet used over telephone lines. It can be used, however, with local area networks (LAN); video transmissions can link two persons who are deaf or even link a hearing individual, a person who is deaf, and an interpreter together (Cook & Hussey, 1995).

Speech Interpretation Aids. Two types of aids are sometimes used to help people who are deaf interpret oral communications. Lip-reading aids depend on specialized types of glasses. Upton glasses employ a microphone that helps people interpret difficult sounds by means of color codes for different sound categories. This allows people to increase their speech-reading ability (Cook & Hussey, 1995).

Alerting Devices. Many sounds are important in daily life—doorbells, ringing telephones, car horns, smoke alarms, a child's cry. For people with hearing loss, devices are available that detect these sounds and cause either a vibration that can be felt or a flashing light or both. Microphones may be placed in key areas—near the front door, near the telephone—to detect sounds and either turn on a flashing light or a wrist-worn vibrator. For smoke alarms a special frequency can be set to provide a unique signal. Alarm clocks or timers can be tactile (under a pillow, on a wrist, or in a pocket) or can activate a light (Cook & Hussey, 1995).

Aids for Persons Who Are Both Deaf and Blind. People who are both deaf and blind use tactile input to obtain information and communicate. The oldest method is called the Tadoma Method. Both people involved must know sign language (or have an interpreter). The person feels hand signs and finger spelling with his or her hands. An automated version of the Tadoma Method has also been developed, in which the speaker talks into a microphone and a device converts the sound to vibrating pins, as in the Optacon. An interesting piece of equipment currently under development connects a mechanical hand to a computer, which can receive input from a TDD or a speech-to-text speech synthesizer. The hand moves in finger spelling and sign as a real person's hand would (Cook & Hussey, 1995).

Mobility

By mobility, we mean our ability to move around in our immediate environment as well as our capacity to move safely and efficiently from one location to another. Some people with disabilities have many problems of mobility: It may be difficult or impossible for them to turn over in bed; climb stairs; walk; or access automobiles, planes, or buses. Numerous devices are available to help solve these problems.

Mobility for Persons Who Are Blind. A range of strategies are used to help persons who are visually impaired or blind move around from place to place. The most used approaches are low-tech:

- Professionals who provide training and assistance to support blind people in mobility are called *orientation and mobility (O&M) specialists.*
- *Sighted guides* are persons who can see who help people with visual impairments move safely from one place to the other. The person who is blind typically will grasp the arm of the guide. The sighted guide will alert the person for steps, pausing briefly just before descending or ascending, or for objects or barriers. Sighted guides do *not* take the hand of the person who is blind and pull; this takes away a sense of dignity.
- *Canes* allow blind individuals to independently traverse an area with which they have some familiarity, and *guide dogs* assist individuals in safely moving around and walking.

Electronic travel aids have been developed to overcome limitations of the cane. Each uses some device to sense objects and/or drop-offs and provides feedback to the user in the form of sounds—high- or low-frequency tones or clicks—or vibrations. For example, a *laser cane* extends the range of the standard cane and can detect drop-offs. Three narrow laser beams are emitted, which detect objects and provide different feedback depending on location—a high-pitched tone if the object is upward, a low-pitched tone for a drop-off, and a vibration for an object directly in front of the person (Cook & Hussey, 1995; Sensory Access Foundation, 2000).

Wheelchairs. For someone for whom walking is difficult or impossible, a wheelchair provides a way to move from place to place. The history of the wheelchair itself tells us a lot about changing views of disability. The oldest wheelchairs looked much like large wooden rocking chairs on wheels; they were designed so that it was impossible for an individual to propel themselves.

A wheelchair has several typical parts—a seat, armrests, footrest, and brake. Typically, a sling seat allows the wheelchair to be collapsed for placement in a car or closet (Cook & Hussey, 1995). A person propels a *manual wheelchair* by turning the outer rim of the wheel. In recent years a new breed of wheelchairs has been developed to accommodate individuals involved in sport. *Ultralight* wheelchairs often sport bright colors, do not have armrests, and are made of aluminum alloys, titanium, or similar lightweight materials rather than the steel of the conventional chair. These wheelchairs are often used in wheelchair basketball and in all sorts of sports involving persons with disabilities.

Some children or adults may not have adequate strength or agility to propel themselves adequately in a manual chair. Increasingly, *powered wheelchairs* have become available. The decision to use such a chair must be made carefully, however; as with driving a car, using a powered wheelchair requires training and skill. These wheelchairs have a power unit and may incorporate any of a range of control devices. The most typical control is a *four-way joystick* that controls both speed and direction of movement. Joysticks can be mounted in different locations to be used with the hand, chin, foot, or head. A *puff-and-sip* control is used by an individual who has limited movement of body parts other than the head. Two switches are activated. When both are puffed, the wheelchair moves forward; when both are sipped, it moves backward; and when only one switch is activated, the wheelchair turns. Different settings of speed and rates of braking

BACK PACK

Assistive Technology Goldmines

Closing the Gap This site provides comprehensive online resources related to assistive technology. A free trial period is available and yearly subscription is inexpensive. www.closingthegap.com/index.lasso

National Center for Technology Innovation NCTI seeks to foster innovation in use of technology to support individuals with disabilities. www.nationaltechcenter.org/

can be selected for indoor and outdoor use. Oftentimes people who use powered chairs also use other devices that are carried on the wheelchair—a respirator or an augmentative communication device, for example (Cook & Hussey, 1995).

Vehicle Accommodations. Automobiles, vans, and other vehicles can now be modified so that persons with very severe disabilities can drive safely. These accommodations open up opportunities for many individuals with physical disabilities and can be funded through state vocational rehabilitation agencies or insurance companies. The first issue is simple *access* to the vehicle. Transfers to and from a car can be assisted with use of sliding boards, bars to grab, and straps. If a person is not able to transfer independently to a car, a *van with a powered lift* can be used to move the wheelchair from the ground to the floor level of the van. Similar types of lifts are available for school and city buses. Once in the van, a *wheelchair tie-down* should be used to stabilize and ensure the safety of the person. Additionally, an "occupant restraint system"—a seat belt or similar device—will hold the individual in the wheelchair in case of an accident.

The primary driving controls of a vehicle govern steering, acceleration, and braking. *Acceleration and braking controls* can manually augment conventional controls so that they require less pressure; or, in the case of a missing limb, controls can be moved from one location to another. A lever arrangement can be placed next to the steering wheel; the person pushes to brake and pulls to accelerate. Variations include push–twist and crank options. *Steering,* too, may be accomplished through a range of adaptive aids (Cook & Hussey, 1995).

Embracing Assistive Technology

You have to agree: That's a lot of technology. If you are a technology enthusiast and this was new to you, you likely loved it and want to know more. There's much to learn about technology, and it's an exciting part of the journey. If you're not into computers and other technology, however, this discussion may have seemed a bit overwhelming. When the first personal computers came out, many adults were scared to death of them. Kids took to them naturally. Now, many of us can't imagine managing our jobs or our personal lives without a computer.

Assistive technology professionals talk about the **transparency of technology,** and the more transparent the better. Technology becomes transparent when it is so much a part of our lives that we literally don't think about it. We don't think of driving a car, calling someone on the telephone, typing a report on a word processor, or cleaning our eyeglasses as unusual.

What makes some of the technology described in this chapter different is that it is new and sometimes not so easy to use. In some instances there are many bugs to work out. Also, most of us have had little experience with some of the people who need to use such technology. Yet if we had grown up with these people as children, had known them as adults, and had become familiar with their new augmentative communication device when we were learning how to use our computer, neither they nor the technology would seem strange. They would be part of our landscape—"transparent," so to speak. That, of course, is what inclusive schooling is all about. One of the goals of inclusive schooling is to make the people and the aids and supports they use part of all of our lives.

What will likely help us truly embrace both assistive technology and the inclusion of students with severe disabilities in our classes, however, will be the moment when we discover the benefit for all our students as we become comfortable with these students and this special technology. By way of analogy, consider one of the key things we know about literacy—namely, the fact that we can always read a passage more easily when we have *background information*. As we develop experience with even one student, our fund of background information skyrockets, and we can build on that fund over time. Perhaps, the clearest signal of our own growth and learning will be the change that will occur when we don't think of this technology as "special" at all. When we teach we will simply incorporate a growing range of technology into the ways we share information with students and into the opportunities we give students to demonstrate their own learning—following the guidelines for universal design of the curriculum that we discussed in Chapter 7.

Traveling Notes

Technology makes a difference in all of our lives. From one perspective, we are all disabled, and technology helps us do things we could never accomplish otherwise. What is your own reaction to technology? Do you love figuring out all the new software and video and audio devices? Or do they scare you? How will your responses affect your use of assistive technology needed by students with disabilities? Following are a few notes to remember.

1. Assistive technology uses high-, mid-, and low-tech tools to help extend the capacities of students. We'll find that while these tools are particularly important for students with special needs, they will be valuable for all our students.
2. Special education funds can be used to purchase needed assistive technology. Every state has centers for assistive technology where people can explore and try out different types of devices. Specialists can help us understand how to incorporate particular tools into our teaching process.
3. Students who use assistive technology can provide interesting opportunities for learning about the interface of human beings and technology for all our students.
4. Modifications are often needed to school grounds, buildings, and classrooms to ensure accessibility to students with physical or sensory disabilities.
5. Many different types of tools and devices can help students accomplish tasks and extend their abilities. These range from talking computers to devices that convert print to braille and modifications that allow students to use hand controls to drive vehicles. Many of these devices may be used with all of our students, including those with special needs to great benefit.

Stepping Stones

Following are some activities that will help extend your understanding and actions you may take to use assistive technology in your school.

1. What technology and tools do you have in your school and classroom to help students compensate for disabilities or to provide additional help? Do an assessment of your classroom and school and identify three or four additional needs that should be addressed. Use the information in this chapter as a guide.

2. Visit a local center for assistive technology and experiment with different tools described in this chapter. Identify several you would like to see in your school and explain how they might benefit all students.

3. Talk with your principal and school technology coordinator about assistive technology. Suggest that a plan be developed to incorporate assistive technology into the technology plan for the school. Perhaps start with attempts to obtain tools you saw in your visit to the assistive technology center.

4. Obtain and install talking software and software that allows students to dictate stories. Watch what happens with student learning over several weeks. What do you see?

5. Contact vendors of assistive technology equipment or a local assistive technology center and arrange a hands-on demonstration fair for children, teachers, and parents. Make it a fun event!

6. Visit a classroom in which technology is being used to assist students. What do you see happening? Does technology help each student be part of the curriculum and the class? How do the teacher and other students react? How "transparent" is the technology in the class?

7. Interview an individual with a severe physical or sensory disability who uses technology—a wheelchair, talking software, and/or other devices. Talk with the person about his or her life story and the role that assistive technology is playing. What difference has technology made? What are the problems in its use?

9

Build a Community for Learning

Promoting Mutual Care, Support, and Celebration

CHAPTER GOAL

Visualize and understand how to create an inclusive community of learners in the school and classroom.

CHAPTER OBJECTIVES

1. Consider the relationships between meeting social and emotional needs and academic learning.
2. Learn strategies for strengthening community in the school as a whole.
3. Explore and utilize methods of building inclusive community in the classroom.
4. Understand how to explicitly and openly recognize and value differences among students in the classroom.

The Impact of Care and Community in Teaching

We're all sitting in the living room talking—a group of teachers who get together periodically. It's been a long day. Tonight we talk about our own experiences as students. What was good? What was bad? What influenced us? "I had one teacher who was absolutely cruel," says Linda. "He belittled students, called us stupid. Controlling the class was the most important thing to him, and he sent many to the office. I had fun causing trouble without getting caught!" She smiles, and everyone laughs, setting off a round of similar stories.

"But what was good?" Silence surrounds us as we are lost in thought. "I remember Miss Annie, my sixth-grade teacher," Rich says. "In many ways she was an old-style teacher. We diagrammed sentences, and more than once I got in trouble in her class. But one thing you knew about Miss Annie—she cared deeply for every one of us." After a pause Rich continues. "We had what we would today call a learning community. She taught us by example about caring and helped us create that with one another. Many of us continue to go by Miss Annie's house," he said, "even though she's been retired many years." One by one, all of us recall stories about teachers who made a deep difference in our lives—by being who they were as much as by the academic skills they taught us.

Our evening discussion highlights the importance of emotions, care, and a sense of community in our classrooms. We first remember people for whom we cared and who cared about us in school. Parents ask first, "How does this teacher treat my child?" and "Does this teacher really care about my child?" Our students do the same.

Let's visit classrooms and think about this.

Kyoko Tanaka's sixth-grade social studies classes are always interesting. Kyoko has a dynamic personality and engages students in lessons of discovery. We particularly want to observe how she includes Duane, a student with a severe disability who uses an electric wheelchair, has limited control of his arms and legs, and doesn't speak. As the students read from their social studies book and engage in discussion, a cluster of two boys and one girl stand or sit around Duane. One holds the book for him and points to the passage; he is a member of the class. Every now and then Kyoko directs the conversation to Duane. His eyes glisten and he smiles. Later Kyoko directs the students to get into groups of two or three and read with one another, talking and answering questions. Two children wheel Duane to a table in the corner of the class under which his wheelchair can fit, and the three of them work together.

We then talk with Jennifer, a third-grade teacher, as we watch her learners in their reading workshop. "I am teaching third grade this year after having 'looped' last year from fourth grade," she explains. "So I have a new group of kids. One of these is Kevin, a student who has been labeled 'as having a moderate cognitive disability.' He's a nice kid but he functions far below most students in my class. However, it's important to me that Kevin is welcomed and can work at his own level. I build community in my class, and the students help one another. Community has provided a basis for Kevin's learning and growth this year." As we walk around the class, Jennifer talks about the multiple ways she builds community in the classroom and how these interact with academic instruction. She uses cooperative learning groups, students helping one another as "experts," classroom meetings, and heterogeneous grouping of students with students who can help and learn from one another. "You should have seen Kevin showing his parents what he has been learning in his student-led conference," Jennifer says. "For Kevin, writing just a short sentence now is a lot, but he likes to write and read. It was terrific to watch him with his parents, who were a bit amazed."

We would hope that all teachers and all schools would seek to build community in classrooms and schools—to create safe havens for children, who are under increasing stress across the socioeconomic spectrum. Unfortunately, this is not the case. We've been in schools where we have seen teachers scream at children, where such teacher behavior has become an expected part of the school culture. We've seen some schools struggle mightily to develop a sense of community and care in their buildings, trying particularly to help children whose lives are traumatic; and we've seen other schools where tension, pressure, and anger are the rule of the day, where children with high emotional needs are criticized bitterly by school staff. We have choices to make: Do we seek to build community for all children, or do we react with power and punishment when children don't do what is expected, building a culture of competition and isolation? That's the core issue that this chapter addresses.

You may remember that in Chapter 2 we posed the question: "What is the purpose of school?" That question is very fundamental to this chapter. If the purpose of school is to create competitive winners, then teaching children to care for one another and take responsibility for the community makes no sense. If, on the other hand, we hope that children will be effective citizens contributing toward making the community a better place and caring for family, friends, and others, then helping children learn to care for one another, helping them learn how to build a caring community is very central.

We will find that creating a learning community where all students feel safe and accepted supports higher levels of academic and cognitive learning. We will also find that building community creates a positive environment and helps prevent conflict and behavior problems. Figure 9.1 illustrates the relationship between meeting social and emotional needs and the level of behavior problems and challenges in a school and classroom. Typically, some 80% of issues regarding social–emotional needs will be met if adults explicitly work toward building an inclusive community of learners, seeking to address social and emotional needs of children. However, there are always problems that occur. Another 15% of students may be involved in conflicts, hurt feelings, and other social and behavioral challenges. These students require a range of effective interventions and supports. A final 5% of students have very serious social and emotional problems for which intensive, interdisciplinary, individualized plans of service and support are needed (Noddings, 2007; Peterson, 2005). Note also, however, what happens when we do not seek to build community. The less this happens, the more social, emotional, and behavioral problems occur. We have been in schools where, instead of 10% to 15% of students having challenging behaviors, the bar moved down so that as many as 50% to 60% of students did.

Creating an effective learning community, therefore, is critical. In this chapter we explore strategies for building an inclusive community of learners. In Chapter 10 we'll

FIGURE 9.1

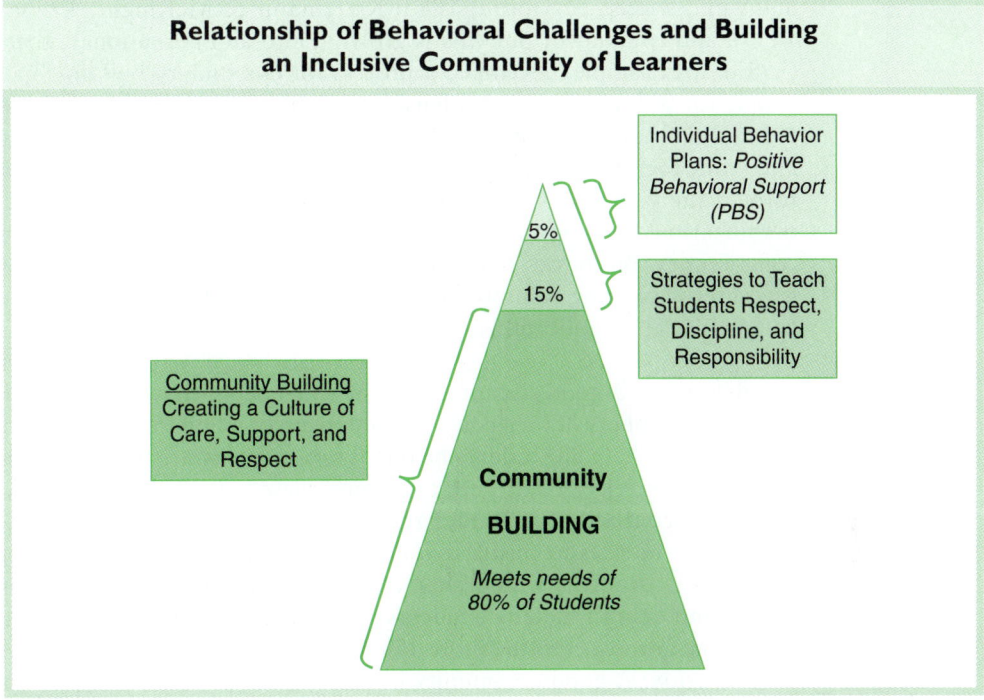

discuss proactive strategies for students who provide mild to serious behavior challenges. Let's start by considering what we mean by the word "community."

What Is Community?

Individual Growth Thriving with Care and Support

Students come to us with many strengths and abilities. They may also come to us with pain and hurt in their lives. Our challenge is to create in our classrooms a culture that helps students build on their strengths and heals their hurts so that learning can occur. Rather than focusing on the deficits of students, we attempt to build a caring community of learners in which they have emotional support and a safe place to deal with their concerns and needs (Noddings, 2007; Sapon-Shevin, 1999, 2007; Sergiovanni, 1994, 2004).

What is **community**? Community occurs when diverse people develop relationships and work together so that each person is supported by the group in growing, learning, and coping with challenges; when the group works together to accomplish common goals in an atmosphere of mutual respect and care; and when a flexible balance of emotional support and productivity occurs (Shaffer & Anundsen, 1993). The qualities required of members of real communities are commitment to one another, trust, honesty, compassion, and respect.

Solving problems through community building is as old as humanity. Over the last century or so, however, many social trends have contributed to increased isolation of individuals from one another and the weakening of community (McKnight, 1995), with attendant consequences of increased loneliness, drug abuse, child abuse, crime, and other social pathologies. In recent decades a growing host of writers and social activists have been calling for efforts to build and strengthen community (Bellah, Madsen, Sullivan, Swidler, & Tipton, 1985; Kretzmann & McKnight, 1993; Schwartz, 1992, 1997), and community building is growing into an international movement. Scott Peck (1987), for example, developed a process for community building, gathering groups of people for 3-day sessions of intense social interactions. In low-income neighborhoods, foundations have sponsored initiatives to help residents identify strengths and resources and work together to strengthen their community. Representatives from different cities formed the National Community Building Network (1995) to link individuals and organizations seeking to support comprehensive community building in low-income communities. Businesses talk about community building in the workplace, and educators discuss creating communities of learners. Let's look at key components of a good community and implications for teaching.

Belonging: A good community exists when people have a sense of belonging and feel valued as members of the group. The opposite of community is isolation and aloneness. As we seek to help all students belong, we become aware of the ways in which students are sometimes rejected and seek to counter these patterns. We explicitly deal with differences and conflicts that hinder relationships, connections, and acceptance and use numerous strategies to ensure that all members are part of the class. We are particularly observant of students whose characteristics may make them more susceptible to both feeling and being isolated—students with disabilities, students from minority cultural and ethnic groups, even the more able students.

Inclusion: A good community is *inclusive* when membership is open and we make intentional efforts to accommodate and value diversity. Segregated communities have historically been the norm, with people clustering together according to ethnic and cultural backgrounds or socioeconomic status. Gradually, however, new models of building inclusive communities are coming into being, and we have the opportunity to pave the way in our classrooms (Beaumont, 1999; E. Cohen, 1994; Sapon-Shevin, 1999, 2007).

Support and care: In a community members receive the support, assistance, mentoring, and caring that they need if they are to cope with the problems of their lives. Those with "special needs" are not separated from the community and put into "special places." In the classroom we help students learn about one another's needs and help one another. For example, Nathan, a student with autism, has difficulty coping with the noise level as the high school drama class readies for the presentation of their play; he screams loudly. A classmate simply helps him refocus. No one is distracted—they know their friend Nathan, and they go on (Sapon-Shevin, 2007).

Contributions and responsibility of all members: All members have both the opportunity and the responsibility to contribute to the good of the whole. In inclusive classes, all students, whatever their ability, contribute. No one is considered helpless. By providing support good communities enable each person to operate as an individual while caring about others in the group and about the dynamics and health of the community as a whole. Consequently, individualism and community are not contradictory but are complementary (Kohn, 1996, 1999; Peck, 1987; Sapon-Shevin, 1999). A student who is beginning to learn English may love bugs and poems and share with the class a poem she has written about a bug. A middle school student with diabetes may be encouraged and assisted in monitoring his blood sugar and shares with fellow students his excitement about a new monitoring device he has received from his doctor.

Democratic problem solving: In any group of people, conflicts regarding priorities or personal relationships are inevitable. In a community we engage members in dialogue to make decisions and deal with conflict. Many teachers, for example, begin their day with a morning meeting in which the class helps decide what will be accomplished during the

FIGURE 9.2

Seeing Community in a Classroom	
WHEN A CLASSROOM FUNCTIONS AS A COMMUNITY, WE SEE . . .	**WHEN A CLASSROOM IS *NOT* A COMMUNITY, WE SEE . . .**
■ Students constantly work with and help one another. ■ Students of vastly different ability levels, cultures, ethnic groups work together. You hear them talking about their differences and what each person needs or likes. ■ When conflicts occur, students have strategies to work through them (peer mediation, etc.). ■ Circles of friends operate with some students who want and need them. ■ Teachers and students frequently interact in classroom meetings to set rules and deal with problems.	■ Some students are ridiculed; others are isolated; cliques abound. ■ Students with learning differences are sent to special programs. ■ Students act out—either through direct aggressive verbal or physical acts or in passive–aggressive ways. ■ Teachers yell at students, frustrated that students will not "behave." ■ A lot of time and energy is put into controlling students. ■ Conflicts erupt in fights and arguments.

day and in what order. When conflicts occur among students, a classroom meeting is held in which students help develop solutions. We communicate directly and respectfully. Each person "speaks their own truth" when they are "moved to speak," in Peck's words (1987). Each person has the responsibility of listening and understanding as well as the right to articulate their own perspective.

Reaching out: Finally, a community *reaches out to and connects with* the larger world, making partnerships with other communities and groups (Gardner, 1989). In a school we seek to connect with parents, the community, other classes within our school, students in other schools. Parents are invited into class; students visit a local nursing home, developing relationships with the older people there; a high school English class comes to a third-grade elementary class once a week to read with them and work on joint projects.

When we walk into a school or class, we frequently sense almost immediately whether the culture fosters community or promotes exclusion and competition. Figure 9.2 describes what we might see in each type of culture; the tone and the impact on children of each type are unmistakable. When community is in place in a class, we are struck by the ongoing discussions and the way in which power is shared among students and the teacher. It's a class that feels like a place we would like to be.

Emotions, Relationships, and Learning

Community makes sense at one level. Yet in our society many powerful trends work to destroy community. People feel increasingly unsafe and limit relationships with others. Work demands reduce time available for community interactions, and financial pressures make the balance of home, family, and community life difficult. With increased mobility people frequently move away from family and friends and are constantly challenged to develop new relationships. Despite ongoing assaults, however, community survives as a basic human need. Community contributes powerfully to solving numerous human problems. Real community can (Shaffer, Anundsen, & Peck, 2005):

- Improve people's health. When people are in relationships and receive emotional support, they have reduced incidence of stress-related illnesses; cancer patients live longer, and birth problems are reduced.
- Help prevent addictions and assist people in recovering from addictions.
- Help people weather terrible crises in their lives.
- Promote learning and growth by providing a "safe place to grow."

Teachers make critical contributions to building a better society not only by teaching students academic skills in their classes, but also by giving students a chance to experience community. In this sense a very quiet revolution is occurring in which schools provide models for embracing, rather than destroying, diversity. Thus, inclusive teaching and community building are allied. Given the challenges to community, it's important that community be solidly grounded in our schools. Numerous educational researchers and writers provide a theoretical and practical foundation for community building in schools.

Community and Five Needs of Human Beings

William Glasser (1992) developed a model of schooling that he calls the **quality school,** which is being used in more than 1,000 schools. The quality school is a school in which the "bosses" of the school—teachers—interact with students in a noncoercive way. According to Glasser (1992), "lead management is the basic reform we need" in schools (p. 31). "Lead management" means talking with students and helping them think through better choices rather than dictating, directing, or controlling. According to Glasser, there are **five needs of human beings,** and as teachers, we provide students with opportunities to meet their five basic needs:

1. *Survival:* We help students survive, physically and emotionally, by creating safe places.
2. *Love and belonging:* Many of our students come to us having been rejected in one way or another in their lives. However, when we facilitate the connection of learners with one another, provide opportunities for collaboration, and ensure that each student is treated with respect, we provide the foundation out of which a sense of love and belonging may emerge.
3. *Power:* Helping students experience power is probably the most challenging. We are told in many ways that a key job of the teacher is to keep students under control. Yet creating community means giving students power along with responsibility. When we engage students in dialogue about the class—about how it will operate and how they will be evaluated—and when we listen to and act on what they say, we are sharing power with students. When we give students real opportunities to make decisions in small groups as they work on a project, we are giving power.
4. *Fun:* In a quality school, instruction is engaging and related to students' lives and, consequently, fun rather than boring.
5. *Freedom:* In such a school students have many opportunities for choices and can move around the classroom and school as they do their work, thus experiencing freedom.

Jeremy watches as Lochan reads a story about the history of their state.
Jeremy and Lochan have become friends this year.

Community and Maslow's Hierarchy of Needs

Maslow (1970) also identified five needs of individuals that occur in a hierarchy, beginning with lower-order and moving to higher-order needs:

1. Physiological needs: food, shelter, sexual gratification
2. Safety/security: physical and emotional survival and safety
3. Belonging/love/affiliation: being part of a community and experiencing caring
   relationships
4. Self-esteem: a positive sense of self, often attained through personal achievement
5. Self-actualization: the realization of the inner self's full potential in the world

According to Maslow (1970), we can't effectively move toward meeting higher-
order needs such as self-actualization until lower-order needs are met. First, the basic
physiological needs must be met; if they are not, it is very difficult to move to the following levels. This is why it's so hard for students who are homeless or hungry to function
well at school. Given the necessities for survival, people seek to ensure their *safety and
security*—both physical and emotional. Once safety is in place, needs for *belonging,
love,* and *connection,* or affiliation, with others become paramount. Our experience of
community, according to Maslow, is a prerequisite for achieving *self-esteem* and personal achievement. As people develop self-esteem, they often are restless to pursue their
unique gifts and talents, seeking to express the essence of who they are, a final need that
Maslow called *self-actualization.*

Kunc (1992) argued that schools often ensure that students with disabilities do *not*
have their needs met by expecting students to achieve self-esteem (and academic mastery) as a *prerequisite* to being able to join the school community. For example, students
who have been abused often have behavioral difficulties. We expect these students to
"behave" before we allow them to be part of the community. We expect students who

have significant learning problems to meet "seventh-grade standards" *before* they are allowed to be part of the general education classroom. Maslow's theory and decades of accompanying research demonstrate that this is exactly the wrong order. If students are to achieve and build a sense of self-esteem, these attainments must be built on the foundation of support and care in the community, not the other way around. We include students who have been abused to help them learn social skills. We include students with learning challenges with others in an engaging classroom environment so they can learn more effectively.

BUMpS IN THE ROAD   *Social Isolation Leads to Segregation*

As we are seeking to include students with differences, we simply must attend to their social relationships within our classes. However, sometimes this doesn't happen. Two stories illustrate this:

Cheryl, a third grader with Down syndrome Cheryl is considered by everyone to be just a cute girl. Her mother dresses her nicely and she is very well behaved. She likes being around other students and they seem to like her. Despite this, Cheryl has no friends. A paraprofessional has been assigned to Cheryl. Every day she brings in a tub of activities that the special education teacher organized that contains materials for lessons for Cheryl. She and Cheryl work together while the rest of the students in the class work on other activities. Even when they go to lunch the paraprofessional takes Cheryl and they sit alone at the end of the table.

We talked with the teacher, paraprofessional, and principal one day about this. "She needs her own activities because she can't do what the other children are doing," explained the principal who was clearly irritated that we had questioned this arrangement. "Her academics are more important than socializing. That's not the purpose of school." We were more than amazed because this same principal had talked with us in glowing terms about their hard work to make their school fully inclusive.

Some months later we were in the school and went to Cheryl's third-grade classroom. We did not see Cheryl there. "Oh, the mother decided to take her out of this school and put her in Streetlawn School," the teacher explained. (This is a segregated school only for students with cognitive disabilities.) When we

asked why she said, "The mother said she didn't have any friends and was lonely." When we asked what the teacher and others had tried to do to deal with this she said, "Well, we can't make other children be her friend." Clearly no one in this school took responsibility for how the structure they had created in the classroom had literally put a wall around Cheryl, cutting her off from natural interactions with other students.

Nathan, a middle school student with cerebral palsy and a cognitive disability A similar situation occurred with Nathan. Nathan had been fully included in general education classes beginning in the fifth grade. He was a sixth grader when we met him. Once again, Nathan was assigned a paraprofessional who went to all his classes with him. While all the other students worked at tables that seated five students each, Nathan was given an individual desk that faced away from the rest of the class. "He is very disruptive and can really act out sometimes. He touches the other students. So we have to keep him apart from them," explained the general and special education teachers. We recommended several strategies that they could use to help Nathan learn good social interactions skills, particularly suggesting that a circle of friends might be helpful.

"Would you like us to help you set up a circle?" we asked one day. When they expressed a willingness we explained how circles worked. We then asked Nathan if he would like to have a circle of classmates who would be with him and help him. He said yes. He also knew whom he would like to ask. We decided to get it started at lunchtime. After he had eaten, Nathan walked around and talked to several students. After a few minutes, 10 kids were gathered at a table at the back of the room. We went over with the teachers. After welcoming the students, we explained what a circle was. "Are all of you willing to meet periodically and work to help Nathan in your class?" we asked. They all said yes. One girl, Natalie, added, "We like Nathan but we don't get to talk with him much because he sits all by himself. He looks lonely." We brainstormed about what could happen to help Nathan participate with the other students and begin sitting at a table. This began an amazing discussion where the kids came up with all sorts of great ideas.

So we left that day leaving the teachers with some simple guidelines for keeping the circle going. We were hopeful.

A month later we were back in the school. As with Cheryl, however, we found that Nathan was not there. "He's left this school," explained Jeremy, the special education teacher. "His mother came in very angry one day saying that Nathan is depressed every day. She said she had talked many times to the principal and other staff about not separating Nathan in the classroom and she can't take it anymore. I don't think the mother understands just how severe her son's disability is." "What happened to the circle of support?" we asked Jeremy. "Oh that," he said. "That was too much work and there was no way those students were going to help Nathan. Those were some of the worst kids in this class." We were amazed at the lost opportunity. Nathan also is going to the Streetlawn School.

Relationships with other people matter. As human beings, this is a basic need. If we're to be successful teachers to students we must pay attention to this need and take action when we see students marginalized. In this case, of course, educators, well meaning though they were, actually structured situations that isolated students and then took no responsibility for the impact of their actions. In Nathan's case some students showed they were willing and interested in including him. For sure, calling something "inclusion" does not make it so.

Connections Between Academic Learning, the Emotions, and Community

In schools we often act as if we must choose between helping students with "academics" *or* with social–emotional needs. However, scientists are learning that the two are inextricably linked. In 1995 Daniel Goleman described the breakthrough research of Joseph LeDoux showing that emotional and academic learning are linked in the hard wiring of the brain, and emotional responses set the stage for academic and cognitive growth. According to Goleman (1995) **emotional intelligence,** or the ability to handle emotions well—interpersonal relationships, anger, feelings of sadness, and sense of self-worth—accounts for at least 50% of success in life. However, schools too often put little emphasis on emotional growth and development. This mismatch calls for a rethinking of the role of emotional learning in schools.

Building Resilience

Many researchers have become interested in **resilience,** the ability of some people to survive and become emotionally healthy when they are abused and mistreated or experience devastating circumstances, whereas others do not. We may have many children in our classes with whom we may feel helpless in light of their life circumstances. However, research has identified several characteristics of those who are able to weather traumatic circumstances to become healthy adults and has identified strategies that promote resiliency. These strategies give us hope. The strategies are twofold: (1) *Reduce* factors that increase the risk of harm, and (2) *increase* protective factors such as positive relationships, particularly with caring adults (see Figure 9.3) (Elias et al., 1997; Geller & Hunt, 1995; Noddings, 2007; Rutter, 1977).

FIGURE 9.3

Characteristics of Resilient Children and Protective Factors

CHARACTERISTICS OF RESILIENT CHILDREN	PROTECTIVE FACTORS THAT BUILD RESILIENT CHILDREN
Social competence ■ Good communication skills ■ Sense of humor ■ Caring attitude ■ Ability to see different sides ■ Adaptability ■ Positive relations with others	Warm and close adult relationships Positive relationships with other children High expectations for success Variety of opportunities (music, art, etc.)
Problem-solving skills ■ Ability to think abstractly and flexibly ■ Abililty to try different solutions	Youth participation and involvement Ablility to contribute meaningfully
Autonomy ■ Self-control, self-discipline ■ Clear sense of separate identity ■ Independence ■ Self-esteem ■ Exertion of control over environment	Acceptance and fulfillment of responsibilities Ablility to make decisions that affect them A safe and predictable environment
Sense of future and purpose ■ Goal orientation ■ Persistence ■ Achievement and education orientation ■ Hope for bright future ■ Sense of faith ■ Healthy expectations	Clear norms regarding tobacco, alcohol, and other drugs

Source: Adapted from Geller and Hunt (1995).

Behavior Management, Care, and Community: Beyond Punishments and Rewards

Perhaps no arena causes more concern for teachers than student behavior problems. Alfie Kohn (1996) tells of his frustration when he visited the classes of teachers who had reputations for dealing effectively with discipline. In Kohn's visits misbehavior seldom happened, so he did not get the opportunity to see how the teachers handled it. After a while, he says, "it dawned on me that this pattern couldn't be explained just by my timing. These classrooms were characterized by a chronic absence of problems." After concluding that these teachers were not simply "getting the good kids," he looked more carefully. He discovered that these teachers did *not* concentrate on being good disciplinarians; nor did their teaching stress worksheets and students' working alone at desks. Rather, what he saw were engaged classes working on interesting projects and classrooms in which community and care were actively and intentionally promoted.

Kohn (1996a) reviewed so-called **behavior management** programs and concluded that most are antithetical to good teaching. Relying on coercion through various forms of rewards and punishments, such programs reinforce an *external locus of control,* in which motivation is influenced primarily by others, rather than the more desired *internal locus of control,* in which drive and effort come from the internal interests and initiative of the person. Teachers often become frustrated at students' lack of inner motivation, their "not doing anything unless they are told," when that is what typical behavior management programs actually promote.

Kohn (1992, 1993, 1996a, 1999) and others (Goleman, 1995; Noddings, 2007; Sapon-Shevin, 1999, 2007) recommend that we assist students in taking control of their own learning; work to build community, respect, and responsibility in our classrooms; and move beyond competition to building cooperative learning and interactions (Johnson & Johnson, 1989a; 1994). When we do this, our behavior problems decrease.

Students with Differing Abilities in a Community of Learners

In a traditional competitive class, the self-esteem of students who don't do as well as others is always on the line as the class sorts itself into groups of nerds, jocks, and dummies. In an inclusive school, a student with rudimentary verbal language skills works in classes with a budding novelist, a gifted artist creates alongside others whose artistic abilities are very limited, a talented athlete teams up with an individual who has cerebral palsy and gets around in a wheelchair. Our goal, however, is for students to see differences yet learn to appreciate and value one another, working against the social sorting that breaks community. Rather than pretending that everyone is the same, students in effective inclusive schools recognize these differences and make a place for all, as the school and classroom community goes about its individual and corporate work. For students with obvious ability differences, a caring community provides a context in which they can build on their strengths, learning at their own level and developing self-esteem in the process (Grigal, 1998; Haring, Breen, Pitts-Conway, Lee, & Gaylord-Ross, 1998; Hughes et al., 1999; Johnson & Johnson, 1989a).

MYSTERIES OF FRIENDSHIP.

Building Community to Support Student Learning

West Orient Middle School
29805 S.E. Orient Drive
Gresham, OR 97080-8816

West Orient Middle School, with 430 students in Grades 5 through 8, has a long history of being a school that builds community. Several years ago, as the school construction committee worked on plans to remodel the old building set amidst farmland and tree nurseries, they invited students to join the planning committee. The students' first thought was: if the library was to be at a lower level, how would their friend Shawn get there? They were used to bumping his wheelchair across the rough playground and around the old school, but it was time to consider everyone's needs. Their question was not disability focused but friend focused. These students were key in reminding the adults that with the library at a lower level, there would need to be an elevator.

Today West Orient is a school that includes both students and parents in the development of school goals and in decision making. With concern about school safety on the minds of all parents, West Orient was a leader in making it a priority that all students feel safe and respected. This explicit goal is being accomplished through a focus on building relationships between teachers and students and student to student.

At West Orient, community means that every student, even those with significant disabilities, is a valued integral member of the school. It's not unusual to see the principal or the vice principal sitting in the cafeteria with a group of students, helping a student with significant disabilities eat lunch. This isn't seen as a job and relegated to an assistant or a teacher, but is a time for administrators to connect with students and enjoy the lunchroom commotion.

The students themselves know what community is about—not because it's a rule or they are supposed to be nice, but because they live it each day and watch their teachers value every child. Students see one another's value beyond what adults often see. When students look at Nick or Sarah or another friend who has a disability and see the enthusiasm that these friends bring to the class or recall that they are allowed to protest when they are upset or that they keep the most private of secrets, they see the depth of their friends. The students say things like "I hate it when Nick is sick, because he's the one who pipes up when things are getting boring. Sarah reminds the teacher to call on all of us—even when we're the quiet ones." Students are also quick to remind adults that teenagers need both time alone and time with their friends—not always with adults.

At West Orient it's the students who often lead the way in demonstrating that when we reach out to one another and build relationships, we build communities that are strong and supportive. It doesn't matter whether you have a disability, or are a fifth grader among eighth graders, or can't talk or read or write, or are the most athletic or musical; what matters is that you belong to the community at West Orient because you came through the door.

By Patti McVay, Outreach Center for Inclusive Education, Multnomah Education Service District, Portland, OR.

Building a Culture of Community in the School
Adults Collaborating and Caring

Nancy Creech (personal communication, June 21, 2000), a multiage teacher, says, "The key is that I teach *children*." Not English, not the sixth grade, not math, but children. We have choices. On the one hand, we can work to build community and support prosocial behavior. On the other hand, we can seek first and foremost to control children and punish them when we can't.

As we work to create community in our school and class, we can expect this process to occur in stages. Community doesn't just happen. It is created through hard work and perseverance. Peck (1987) described a series of stages through which a group of people go as they build community:

1. The process starts with **pseudocommunity,** a state in which people act as if they are community and are "nice" but do not connect.
2. Next, when people begin to speak the truth to communicate authentically, *chaos* ensues. Conflict occurs, and some people try to convince others that their position is correct. It is at this stage that people often give up. For example, staff may be angry at one another; students may get upset and withdraw sullenly.
3. If the group continues without falling apart, they next settle into *emptiness:* a time of waiting, listening, confusion. We literally do not know what to do, but we are there listening.
4. Eventually, people begin to communicate and listen to one another, reach out, and build an actual *community*—a state that is both felt and objectively real. This often starts with some genuine sharing on the part of one or two people. Gradually, their risk taking gives others courage, and others share too.
5. *Maintaining* community, of course, is an ongoing process as well. Oftentimes a group will recycle through earlier stages.

How does all this look with children and staff in a school? Sandy is a first-grade teacher and Michael a ninth-grade English teacher. Both seek to build community in their classes, and both describe some experiences that are similar each year. Both begin their year helping students get to know one another. They set up times to discuss how the classroom community is operating—each day for Sandy, once a week for Michael. Every year, they see Peck's cycle operate. At first, everyone is very friendly, chattering away. "I think they are actually hiding how nervous they are," explains Michael; Sandy nods her head in agreement. Then the conflicts begin. Each teacher facilitates discussions, but they allow students to air their feelings. "They really get angry!" says Sandy. She often has to resist jumping in too quickly. Watching such conflicts, the group will settle into silence. Then a student will say, "You hurt my feelings." Another might say, "My mom got her feelings hurt last night." Suddenly the real sharing begins, the basis of community.

If we understand these stages, we can more clearly appreciate the difficulties and the richness of the project as we work toward community in our teaching. We will know that "niceness" and "pleasantness" are not real community. We'll also know that conflict and chaos are inevitable as we and our students actually open up to one another and build authentic relationships. We'll know that community is born out of a struggle to listen, share, and communicate honestly and authentically with respect—and that this struggle is an ongoing process that is never complete.

The Foundations of School Community

Let's now explore specific strategies for building community. First, three basic foundation stones are important both schoolwide and within our classrooms (see Figure 9.4).

Democratic and Collaborative Decision Making. The first building block is democratic and collaborative decision making. For example: In a traditional school, the principal makes major decisions and tells teachers what to do; teachers in turn tell students. In an effective inclusive school, the principal allows teachers and other staff to work together to

FIGURE 9.4

Building Blocks of Community in the School

SCHOOLWIDE COMMUNITY

Child- and family-centered schooling   Collaborative learning groups
Culture of Respect   Schoolwide themes
Celebrations and assemblies   School celebrations for all

CLASSROOM COMMUNITY

Routines and structures
Class decorations and
   arrangements
What do we want to learn?
Democratic exercise of power
Classroom rules
Who are we? Getting to know our
   classroom community
Daily routines
Class meetings
Communicating respectfully
Making choices
Sharing

Student roles
Classroom leadership
Help others as experts
Buddies and peer mentors
Cross-age buddies and tutors
Circles of friends
Peer mediators

Dealing with difference
Ability differences up front
Children's literature
Thematic units

FOUNDATIONS OF THE SCHOOL COMMUNITY

DEMOCRATIC DECISION MAKING

SUPPORT TO TEACHERS AND STUDENTS

PARENT AND COMMUNITY CONNECTIONS

consider issues related to the whole school. At best, all school staff participate, including the secretary, the janitor, the teachers, the speech therapist, the lunch aides. Thus, teachers in the classrooms also utilize collaborative decision making on a regular basis, teaching children to make responsible decisions.

Democracy, of course, means that we can use our own influence, in collaboration with others, to make decisions and set directions—that is, to exercise power. In democracy we decide that our voice will be heard even, or perhaps especially, when those above us do not want to hear it. In standing for what we believe, we can model empowerment for students. We can create new energy and engage the support of others who are emboldened by our courage. This prevents the energy-draining disempowerment when we feel helpless (Apple, 1995; Banks, 1990; Skrtic, 1994).

Support for Teachers and Students. The second schoolwide foundation stone is the development of support for teachers, students, and others. In Chapter 5 we explored many support strategies and structures. As we collaborate, we form relationships and develop trust that mirrors the support and caring we give students in classrooms. It is very difficult to build community with our students if we do not have a supportive community among school staff. For example, as Fran, the art teacher, Cathy, the social studies teacher, and Randall, a special education teacher, work together to develop a multicultural unit on freedom, linking the experience of the Underground Railroad and the fight for freedom in South Africa, they develop a personal bond and enjoy one another. The students sense this, and it transforms the whole experience; and through the students' final assembly performance, the effects of the teachers' mutual support have an impact on the whole school.

Parent and Community Connections. The third foundation stone is involvement and connection with parents and the larger community. In Chapter 6 we explored ways to build these relationships and connections. Here we point out that these connections are a critical part of building community in the school as we bring many people into the lives of our students.

Key Schoolwide Practices That Promote Community

We can walk into any school and within a very few minutes get a feel for its culture. We may be treated rudely or ignored by a secretary, hear teachers yelling at students, see the principal acting tense. Or we may see friendly people who ask if they can help us in an open way. Students and parents feel the climate of a school as well, and respond.

Creating a Child- and Family-Centered Vision. First and foremost, we create a common vision of our school that is centered on children and families. If we see the school as driven by the goal of achieving higher test scores, we act differently than if our purpose is to create a supportive community where all grow and learn together. If we have a courageous and creative principal who supports child- and family-centered learning, we are fortunate. If we do not, we still can work toward this end and seek partners among other like-minded teachers and parents (Kohn, 1999; Schwartz & Pollishuke, 1990).

Building a Culture of Respect. A clear indicator of school culture is the way teachers talk to and about children and parents, particularly those with whom they are having difficulty. I walk into Sharon Watson's class and I see her talking with her first graders in highly respectful tones. "Class, let me introduce you to our visitor," she says. She asks students questions, gets their opinions, listens to them. She is concerned about one child with whom she has not yet been able to develop a good relationship.

Where respect flourishes, staff and students interact openly and spontaneously. Laughter and smiles are frequent. In other schools, however, tension fills the air; people talk hesitantly, with restraint, with forced smiles and with laughter that does not feel genuine. It is essential that we work to respect others, communicate in caring ways, and model honesty and directness.

Collaborative Learning Circles. How do we constantly renew ourselves, learn new teaching strategies, and build community with our coworkers? Increasingly, teachers gather, often supported by university faculty or staff development specialists, to share, talk, and explore innovative teaching. For example, at Barnard Elementary School, teachers meet every month after school as part of a "literacy circle." Teachers have taken the leadership in this group—deciding on scheduling, letting people know of meetings, setting the agenda. Learning circles are powerful, engaging, fun ways for teachers to grow that parallel best practices in our classrooms.

BACK PACK

Social and Emotional Support

Responsive Classrooms This site has many resources related to building community and addressing social and emotional needs of children. Very practical resources and materials. www.responsiveclassroom.org/

Tribes Tribes is a process of building community, respect, and responsibility in a community of learners in a school. This site provides an introduction and resources related to this approach. www.tribes.com/

Center for Social and Emotional Learning The center works to "promote positive and sustained school climate . . . that nurtures social, emotional, ethical, and intellectual skills and dispositions to enhance student performance, prevent drop outs, reduce physical violence, bullying, and develop healthy and positively engaged adults" by integrating "social and emotional learning with academic instruction." csee.net/climate/

Schoolwide or Multiclass Themes for Learning. Several teachers, or the whole school, adopt a common theme to organize learning. A high school, for example, might focus on "working for justice" to link subjects throughout the building. Or teachers in first, third, and fifth grades might decide to involve their students in the theme of animals in captivity. They link subjects around this theme and develop collaborative activities across grade levels (Manning et al., 1994; Zemelman, Daniels, & Hyde, 2005).

School Celebrations for All. We can promote community through schoolwide celebrations and assemblies, where we set a tone and demonstrate what we value. With the increased emphasis on raising standardized test scores, for example, many schools have assemblies honoring students who passed the test. Such awards ceremonies divide students who passed from those who did not.

In an inclusive school, celebrations recognize multiple talents and the gifts of all. We have awards for the most improved or the funniest; for hard workers; for caring and compassion; for creativity. Our assemblies are fun, involving students, parents, community members, and teachers. We sing songs; share stories; and break into small groups to act out a simple story involving teachers, students, and parents together. We look for ways to strengthen and celebrate our bonds with one another (Developmental Studies Center, 1994; Noddings, 2007).

Building a Community of Learners in Our Class
Valuing Our Differences and Helping One Another

When we use best teaching practices, we find multiple opportunities to build community. At the same time, as we have seen, community building supports academic learning. Let's now turn our attention to yearlong strategies and structures that help create community in our classroom.

Routines and Structures for Building Community: Getting Started and Building Throughout the Year

Community starts and ends with daily classroom routines, building through small, ever-present interactions and procedures. At the beginning of the year, we remember that first impressions, for adults as well as children, can endure; we seek from the beginning to set a tone and build a culture of mutual support. "What about the subjects—biology or spelling or math?" we are often asked. "Shouldn't we get into those right away?" Effective inclusive teachers take time for community-building activities. Teachers who intentionally work to build a community consistently believe this time to be well spent, establishing a foundation on which they build throughout the year (Denton & Kriete, 2000; Gibbs, 1998).

What Do We Want to Learn? We involve our students early on in talking about what they want to learn. Linda, an 11th-grade English teacher, for example, has students brainstorm ideas about the course, recording the suggestions on sheets of paper so all can see. The class then groups these ideas into workable themes. Linda has discovered that students often choose many ideas that she herself had and that are in the school curriculum. However, by helping shape the class, students gain the feeling that it belongs to them and they are not just visiting (Manning et al., 1994).

Promoting Student Ownership Through Democratic Exercise of Power. Students need to understand that the classroom belongs to everyone, not just the teacher. This understanding must be fostered through careful thought and consideration. Students need opportunities to help create the rules that will govern their lives in the classroom. This does not mean sitting down in one setting and creating a list of rules. Creating classroom rules should start with asking students this question: "How do you want your year to be in this class? What would make it a great year?" We lead students in discussing everyone's ideas and how these hopes can become real. We then get students to work in small groups to categorize and group the ideas and then develop a few rules that cover all the ideas contributed. We ensure that the voice of all students are heard and that some students do not dominate the conversation. This process is essential. We must be willing to give up the feeling of total control and to replace it with a feeling of pride in teaching students how to control themselves. Once the group agrees to the rules, we sign them, post them, and refer to them often. We might say, "Lorinzo, that breaks the agreement you made to abide by rule number four." This system puts the responsibility for actions on the students and reminds students of agreements made together (Manning et al., 1994; Peterson, 1992; Sapon-Shevin, 1999, 2007).

"You Can't Say You Can't Play": Classroom Rules That Promote Community. Any group of people can develop rules of conduct that encourage care and support or that create conflict, exclusion, and isolation. Students often reject one another, create cliques, or are cruel, reflecting the society around them. However, we will challenge students to promote rather than destroy community. When we see students creating divisive rules or acting out assumptions and prejudice, we ask them to think through these issues. Vivian Paley (1992) tells of her experience with a new rule she suggested to her kindergartners: "You can't say you can't play." She describes how her children sought to make this rule real and the dialogues that occurred as they presented their experience to older students. The rule helped children become more aware of ways in which they rejected one another and helped some isolated students join the classroom community.

Who Are We? Getting to Know Our Classroom Community. Early on we help students know each other, discovering commonalities and differences. During the first 2 weeks of the school year we intentionally engage in fun community activities, playing games that encourage interactions. This helps begin to build the culture of playing together. We ask students to bring pictures from home, make art projects together, organize classroom materials, read fun books, and share ideas. This begins to build the

CHAMPIONS OF INCLUSION

CREATIVELY adapt and UTILIZE appropriate strategies and materials to help students with disabilities learn and succeed.

There are still some who do not adequately adapt teaching and learning to provide sufficient opportunities for students who have disabilities to perform at their highest levels. Sometimes they may not be aware of the possibilities for differentiating instruction. Usually they do not spend enough time to seek out more information about possible adaptations, nor do they successfully solicit necessary supports to implement them. Champions of inclusion are:

- The classmates who figure out ways for Frankie (who has autism) to participate in the group's skit depicting a scene from the American Revolutionary War.
- The special education teacher who writes a simplified version of *Romeo and Juliet* for Juan (who has cognitive delays) so that he can grasp the key points of the play being discussed in the Grade 11 literature class.
- The behavior consultant who crafts a positive behavior plan for Rakeem (who has emotional disorders) so that he can stay on task more and become more successful.
- The speech therapist who organizes a set of picture symbols and voice recordings for Betsaida (who is nonverbal) so that she can communicate her needs more effectively.
- The Grade 5 teacher who learns how to use a computer with screen-reading software so that

Timothy (who has significant decoding problems) can follow some of the popular books read by his classmates.
- The basketball coach who designates and arranges tasks for Carmen (who has Down syndrome) so that she can serve as the assistant manager for the team on which many of her friends play.
- The occupational therapist who coordinates a school store where students with a variety of fine motor and social needs can practice useful tasks.
- The biology teacher who makes a chart for ways that Joshua (who has mild cognitive delays) can take responsibility for some of the activities in the lab.
- The teacher aide who identifies unobtrusive signals to keep Wong (who has ADHD) more on task.
- The art teacher who keeps a box of varying grips with her so that students with fine motor difficulties can better manipulate drawing and painting implements.
- And William (who has Asbergers) who shows his class a more efficient way to solve a math problem.

By Bill Henderson, Principal, O'Hearn Elementary School, Boston, MA.

idea that the classroom belongs to everyone and everyone is important, while also giving the teacher some baseline data from which to begin instruction.

Daily Routines. We either make or break community in daily routines. In elementary schools, going to the bathroom is one of the most important. For example: We enter Lowe Elementary School and see a class lined up. The teacher admonishes the children to stay quiet while trying to rush them to the bathroom. The noise of laughter and scuffling is heard through the bathroom door. In about 20 minutes, the teacher gets the class back to work. In another class Bob explains that children go as they need, waving a bathroom pass to ask permission without interrupting; he nods yes and checks the clock to make sure they are not gone too long. The children sign in and out, providing data for a conversation on responsibility should that become necessary. This process teaches children responsibility while not wasting learning time.

In this middle school, five teachers work as a team with 80 students. Each morning they start the day with a morning meeting for 30 minutes where students can share information, bring up concerns, and make plans for their learning community. Here the teacher leads a discussion regarding a problem that three girls have just presented—that some people are very boisterous and dangerous in the halls just before school.

We must help students take on responsibilities and provide supportive structures to enable them to do so. Each basic daily routine can be fun while teaching dependability. Let's take a look at some ways to build responsibility throughout the day of a fourth-grade classroom:

8:20 A.M.	Children enter the room and get materials out of their backpack and cubby for the day. They move a magnet with their name on it to hot or cold lunch. One student signs the lunch slip and will later hand out the cards to students with hot lunch. He asks Sara, a blind student, if she is having hot lunch, and signs her up. He then leaves, after waving at the teacher, and returns quickly for morning meeting.
8:30 A.M.	The children meet on the carpet for morning meeting. They bring daily planners that the school provides, in which they write down what homework is due and upcoming events. Children have homework buddies that check to see if each person has turned in his or her homework and written down the appropriate items.
8:50 A.M.	Children line up for specials. One child is the line leader, stopping at certain points that she has learned so the teacher can wait. There is no conversation from the students or teacher.
9:30 A.M.	During writing time, the children are working at their tables with partners, while the teacher meets with a small group. One child uses the sign language signal for bathroom to ask for permission. The teacher nods her head without interrupting the conversation with the group.
10:15 A.M.	When writing time is over, the teacher signals that by turning on a lively CD. The children dance to the theme as they transition to the

10:45 A.M.   carpet area for math. They bring math journals, dry erase boards, and markers to work on the teacher-directed math portion.

10:45 A.M.   The teacher begins singing songs from the class musical they are preparing for as the children move to play a math game to strengthen skills. When the children get too loud, the teacher moves to a designated spot in the room. As she moves to that spot, children begin to quiet automatically. She moves a rainstick around to get their attention and then waits. They quiet down and listen.

11:15 A.M.   The children get ready to leave for lunch. The teacher asks trivia questions related to their study as they move quickly around the room doing designated jobs. They stay quiet to hear the questions and move quickly to be allowed to leave for lunch.

Class Meetings. Classroom meetings are important tools for engaging students in decision making regarding needs and problems. Many effective teachers meet frequently, whether about teasing, staying on task, turning in homework, or celebrating an accomplishment. Meetings vary in length; some may be only 10 minutes, whereas others are longer. Both students and the teacher choose topics for classroom meetings by anonymously writing issue topics and putting them in a box, allowing those not comfortable with sharing aloud to have their needs addressed.

Classroom meetings are run by the children, not by the teacher—a difficult shift for some teachers. Students take turns in the roles of note taker and moderator. The class establishes basic rules that allow students to speak one at a time, often using a designated object (a "talking stick," for example) to pass to the person who has the floor to speak. Students are not required to speak and may pass if they want. Most importantly, when the class makes a decision, action occurs (Gibbs, 1998; Noddings, 2007; Sapon-Shevin, 1999).

Sharing: Celebration, Joys, Challenges, Grief, and Pain. If our class is a community, it must be first and foremost a place of sharing—sharing of hopes, dreams, joys, fears, challenges, and sometimes hurt, grief, and pain. As teachers we model by taking risks, sharing our own lives with students. This will encourage students similarly to share with one another. In an elementary classroom students write daily in journals about events in their lives and share them in "morning news," which we can record on chart paper and edit. This information could go into our weekly class newsletter. We can use a similar time in a high school class. The more trust we create, the more students will share during this time (Gibbs, 1998; Peterson, 1992; Sapon-Shevin, 1999). Teachers read journals when they are placed in a certain basket, responding quickly with highlighters and sticky notes, thus increasing the relationship between student and teacher.

Along with daily sharing, we also need routines for special times. Celebrating special events creates a feeling of community. We are alert for events in our students' lives—achievements, family events (weddings, graduations, etc.). We make sure that every birthday is celebrated, whether the parents do or not. We look for opportunities to tell students that we appreciate their work, help in class, or caring acts.

Sometimes, when a student is having a hard time, the total class helps the student. Perhaps a student's father has died and she is crying. We might ask if she would like to share what happened and tell the class about her father. Students could offer sympathy and practical ways to help. One year in Tanya's second-grade class a child had all of their Christmas gifts stolen and the family had no money for more. The children secretly called his mother and asked what he would like best. They then pitched in and bought him some Christmas gifts.

Communicating Respectfully. "When you are done writing, please match eyes with me so I'll know we can go on. Renae ready?" said Shawna. This is an example of a respectful strategy for interacting with students to move from topic to topic. Through respectful communication we promote acceptance in the class and do not embarrass students or put them on the spot. For example, anytime students don't want to talk, they just say "pass." They will be more likely to respond later. If they pass all the time, we talk with them individually. We invite students to participate but do not demand participation. As we make transitions, we say: "Would you bring your writing/conversation to a close, please?" Waiting respectfully, we say "Thank you" to those who do stop (Schiller, 1998). However, we do *not* compare students to one another: "I really like the way Renae stopped when I asked her to." Students recognize this as a manipulative ploy rather than true appreciation.

We communicate respect (or lack of it) as we respond to our most difficult students. In a fourth-grade class, Jennifer was arguing insistently with the teacher. Although the teacher tried to stay calm, she finally began yelling at Jennifer. Another student muttered, "Great! Now she'll be mad at all of us." When the teacher treats all students with respect, despite their behavior, they are more comfortable taking risks and sharing. When they feel intimidated or worried, however, the community bond is broken.

Making Choices. Children need both help from adults in the form of structure and freedom to make choices. We can establish many ways to give students reasonable choices. Often we can present options to the entire group and allow students to make selections through discussion. *Daily choices* students make include:

1. *Order of work:* We let students choose the order of work activities within the routine they have created. For example, math and theme studies are in the morning, but should they learn the new math lesson or go over homework first? The language arts block is in the afternoon. Should they do reading or writing workshop first?
2. *Day-to-day goals:* Students identify daily goals related to academics or behaviors. Teachers suggest, but do not demand, goals, chosen reflectively, that need improvement. This is done as a class at the beginning of the day, and the daily goal is posted in the room and is referenced often. The goal is revisited prior to choosing the goal for the following day.
3. *What to read/write:* During reading or writing workshop, students select books to read and stories to write. The teachers pick the genre, but students select the content.

Periodic choices include:

1. *What to learn:* At the beginning of the year or of each unit, we find out what students would like to learn and incorporate their ideas.
2. *Seating arrangement:* Although students have assigned seats for collaborative group work, a student rarely needs to sit in an assigned seat at other times. Students may sit in a preferred location as long as they are working. Teachers help students understand that the total room belongs to them all, no matter whose things are at a given seat. This provides many student options and facilitates more effective use of available space.
3. *Choice time:* Our curriculum is most often determined by our school district. Therefore, students do not often have the ability to choose topics of interest to them. However, we can provide time—whether at a certain time every day, an hour once a week, or the first 20 minutes of the class every Friday—for students to direct their own learning. This is important in developing lifelong learners. We can let them select their own topics or offer suggestions such as researching favorite basketball players online, conducting physics experiments on their own, creating a rich textural plan on paper and then building it with blocks, or reading books that are too easy but are fun and relaxing.

Games and Learning Activities That Build Community. Whether in the first 5 minutes of a class or during recess time, we can take time to play games that encourage community. Most games can be used, with adaptations, at all ages. Community-building games involve everyone in the class and are cooperative, as opposed to competitive: Students learn that for them to win, others do not have to lose. Rather, they learn that for one to win, all must cooperate and win together. Community games also teach conflict resolution and demonstrate commonalities and understanding of one another. Figure 9.5 summarizes some fun community-building games based on the work of Mara Sapon-Shevin (1999), many of which can be played in 10 or 15 minutes.

FIGURE 9.5

Games That Promote Community Building

GAME AND DESCRIPTION

1. *Cooperative musical chairs:* Children try to make sure that every person is on a chair, whether there are two people on a chair or six. This involves helping instead of pushing the slower and weaker ones out.

2. *Children write facts and fictions about themselves,* and class has to decide which is which. Or students write clues about themselves and class guesses who they are.

3. *Stand up/sit down* in categories or move to different walls. This shows students how they are alike and different.

4. *"Make a group":* Call out something, like a kind of breakfast food, and students who fit that category make groups of three or more. Change categories constantly so students are moving around a lot.

5. *Mimic others' actions:* For example, pretend to toss different objects while the other person catches them, or pass faces or sounds around a circle.

6. *Riddle concentration:* Each student has a card with either question or answer. Play like child's game Memory to find matches. Students can get help from classmates sitting on either side. Put matches in middle and cheer when all win.

7. *Get in groups by birthday month:* Each group makes rhyming chant about its month, then presents it.

8. *Hug tag:* Put in groups of two or three. One or more children are given a red flag or sock, which they try to give to other children. Children are "safe" if they are in a group that is hugging one another. When the teacher says "switch" the groups disband

and regroup while the "huggit" tries to give the flag away.

9. *Tug of peace:* Stand in circle with rope, hold out with two hands; all pull together, leaning back, to pull everyone up at same time; cheer; try to sit down without falling.

10. *Hula hoop pass:* In circle children hold hands and try to pass hula hoop from one person to next without letting go of the others' hands. Do with one then two together.

11. *Cooperative stories:* Retell aloud a story about a certain subject or chain of events. Each person adds line to story so it makes sense.

12. *Nonverbal lineups* on different topics. Students line up in order based on chosen topic. They must communicate without talking.

13. *Cooperative word sentences:* Put words on cards. One student has verbs, another adjectives, another with nouns, and so on. In groups of four to six, make different kinds of sentences—longest, funniest, and so on. Must use word from each person's set, and each person must be able to say the word to get credit, thus the peer tutoring aspect.

14. *Cooperative 20,000 pyramid:* In groups students generate clues to get people to guess items in a certain category—for example, among citrus fruits, to guess orange, lemon, and so on. Make sure clues are not misleading. Then play. Students need to use lots of skills to generate good clues. Can change skill level by selection of categories or by timing the game. Each team discusses as they hear each clue and decides whether to answer or ask for another clue.

Source: Adapted from Sapon-Shevin (1999).

Multilevel Cooperative Learning. Working together helps students accomplish tasks they could not do alone. Students can work together on any subject, whether reading a chapter book together or teaming up as editing partners or math homework partners. We create projects that require that students work together, but at different jobs requiring types and levels of expertise. For a science experiment, for example, differing students have the following job roles: obtain materials, set up the experiment, read directions, record results, share with the class, and draw a picture of what happened. Every student has a job at his or her own level on which others depend. Students learn that each person has different strengths to contribute (E. Cohen, 1994; Johnson & Johnson, 1989a, 1994).

Cross-Grade-Level Interactions. Interactions across grade levels also strengthen community. Older students might pair with younger partners to read once a week. Classes might do research or art projects together, take field trips, write a story together, or share completed work (Nesbitt, 1991; Sapon-Shevin, 1999).

Clock Partners. From kindergarten through high school, a good way to pair students for activities is the *clock partners* technique. Each student has a large clock drawn on a sheet of paper with a line at each hour. Students sign each other's clocks at the same time. For instance, Jeremy and Amy both decide to be two o'clock partners together. Students go around the room until they have a partner for each hour. They cannot have the same partner twice. Also, if someone asks, the student cannot say no. For an activity, we ask students to get their clocks and join up with, for example, their ten o'clock partner. This simple strategy removes the aggravations often associated with pairing students—no more hurt feelings or efforts to separate students who always work together.

Sharing Work. Sharing completed work gives students a sense of pride in their own accomplishments and appreciation for others, building self-esteem and community simultaneously. When a writing project is completed, we share together as a class, have a book signing to which adults are invited, or read stories to other classes. At the end of a unit, we can have a celebration for which children prepare activities and set up projects, skits, and written work showing their learning; we invite other classes or parents to attend. This raises the level of expectation, knowing there will be a real audience to prepare for and adds others into our community (Schiller, 1998).

Student Roles in the Learning Community

We develop opportunities and structures within which students can help and support one another. In addition, we explicitly teach students *how* to do this.

Student Classroom Leadership. When students exercise leadership, they increase their understanding, sense of responsibility, and self-esteem. In the class community every student has a job and takes responsibility for it without constant reminders. We recently observed a classroom in which all 25 students had meaningful and needed jobs—watering the plants, straightening books, passing out materials, helping on computers.

As students make choices, leadership roles often evolve naturally. We rely on some students to serve as peer mediators, to be members of circles of support, to give comfort, or to lead and facilitate discussions. Students may help design the way we approach the curriculum or give input as to how to help students who are having difficulty learning.

Sights TO SEE

Emotional and Academic Learning Together

Emotional Intelligence An Overview Many innovative school programs integrate social and emotional learning with more traditional academic areas, providing students with skills they'll need throughout their adult lives. This 7-minute video shows students putting on a student newscast and show daily. www.edutopia.org/emotional-intelligence-overview

Educating Hearts A Districtwide Commitment to Teaching How to Care A 10-minute video on how an Anchorage, Alaska, school system's investment in social and emotional learning is paying off both socially and academically. www.edutopia.org/anchorage-social-emotional-learning-video

Helping Others as Experts. Students need experience teaching others. To teach someone about something, a child must have a deeper understanding of that subject. By having children explain their thought processes to others, we teach a much needed skill and demonstrate that everyone can be an expert. Our class becomes transformed into a place where there are many people to ask for help, not merely one teacher who cannot be everywhere at once (Fuchs, Fuchs, Kazdan, & Allen, 1999). We also help students understand the difference between helping and doing the work for a peer.

Students often enjoy leading lessons they have seen taught several times. Maybe the physics class always starts out with an example problem that is discussed. We rotate students who choose the homework problem and lead the discussion. This strategy gives students a learning opportunity that is both powerful and fun; it also provides an excellent window into their thinking.

We can ask students to help others after finishing their work. Alternatively, we may ask one student to teach a few other students a new skill that the whole class needs to learn and then send others to this expert group for help. This is an excellent way for students who normally finish last to have experience being a leader.

Students can be experts on any subject—spelling, adding, dividing, proving theorems, capital letters, the Internet, quotation marks, making a cursive *m*, even quantum physics. The key is to teach the students to share knowledge—and to accept information from others (Au, Mason, & Scheu, 1995; Girard & Willing, 1996).

We are also careful to ensure that all students have the opportunity to share expertise as well as be helped by others. We will be particularly attentive to abilities that a student with a severe disability has to share with others and facilitate their being able to do so. When a student is learning our language, we look for ways she can share about her language and culture.

Buddies, Tutors, and Peer Mentors. Sometimes we formalize ways for learners to help one another. We might, for example, pair students on an ongoing basis as **study buddies.** (For older students, we'd call it something else, obviously—class partners.) Or we could shift such pairings more frequently; across subject pairing certain students in reading and others in math, or changing pairings from week to week (Girard & Willing, 1996; Sapon-Shevin, 1999).

More and more schools are utilizing **cross-age buddies and tutors:** older students who serve as tutors, reading buddies, and mentors for younger children. It is not unusual to walk into an elementary school and see a high school student reading with an 8-year-old or helping a fifth grader with his or her math assignment (Nesbitt, 1991). Students with special challenges themselves can also very effectively serve as tutors, mentors, and helpers for other students. For example, a sixth-grade student struggling to read sixth-grade material can fluently read a story to a first-grade student.

Some schools operate formal peer tutoring programs in which students receive training, provide tutoring, and receive credit. In one high school, students considered at risk because of academic and behavioral problems mentored students with mental retardation. The students with mental retardation developed friends and were able to negotiate the school environment. The self-esteem and academic performance of the students who were at risk increased dramatically as they were successful in a highly responsible role (Fitzgerald, Henning, & Feltz, 1997; Murray-Seegert, 1989).

Circles of Support. A circle of support (sometimes called circle of friends) is a powerful way to help when students need more intentional, intensive support. The idea is simple: We ask peers, friends, and family of a student to come together to provide support. Although circles were born to help students with disabilities, they are powerful tools for anyone. A student coming into our class having just immigrated to the United States may not speak our language well. A student with autism may have difficulty relating to others. A student with an abusive father may be doing poorly in school.

Can you spot the teacher lying on the floor leading the class in reading and discussing a book together? Lusala sits next to Sachit, the student in a wheelchair, so he will not feel excluded since getting on the floor is difficult for him.

To get started we ask students if they would like to have a circle of support. An adult acts as a facilitator for the group. A social worker or psychologist meets with students during the day after school or on the weekend to facilitate a circle meeting. Some teachers have met with circles on their lunch hour or during their planning period (Peterson et al., 2002). In other situations, teachers have taught students about circles and students conducted circles during the school day. Most school circles meet at the school building. Circles, however, may choose to meet at home or in a community setting.

Students themselves decide whom to invite to their circle. A student, with our help, can issue an open invitation to all students within a class. In other situations, when a student is new to our room and does not know anyone, we ask for class volunteers.

Once the group is selected and a meeting time and place established, the group meets. Most circles have found it helpful to use some form of person-centered planning, like the MAPS process described in Chapter 4, to focus. In a MAPS, the "focus person" and the group explore the dreams and fears of the student and develop an action plan, including assistance from circle members. One teacher used a very simple version of this process, asking a student what help he wanted. The circle then identified ways they could help (Peterson et al., 2002).

Circles have been very powerful. In Chapter 1 we described Judith Snow's experience with the first formalized circle of support. In schools circles have helped students with challenges by helping with many issues—homework, problems with relationships, the blues. In Kitchener, Ontario, we visited with the circle of friends of May, an eighth grader with Down syndrome. This group of young people had greatly helped May be part of their class. They decried the "life skills class," where, they said, May "was not learning anything." What was particularly interesting, however, was the critical thinking and problem solving going on among these students (Falvey et al., 1998; O'Brien & O'Brien, 1992).

When we spoke with Jennifer, early in this chapter, about Kevin, she also spoke of a circle of support. She talked with Kevin and his mother, asked him to suggest five children he wanted to be involved, and then she asked the children one-on-one. Even though these third graders gave up one recess a week and knew it was a working commitment, not one of them said no. "It says something about the community we have built," said Jennifer. "Children can meet very high expectations." The children began by deciding who would help Kevin with reading and other needs he expressed. We were struck by the fact that the children wanted to help Kevin with subjects in which they needed improvement also.

We can get more information through Inclusion Press (see www.inclusion.com). The developers of MAPS and circle of support concepts strongly urge that we invite friends and family to our own circle and MAPS session before facilitating a circle for someone else. You'll be surprised how valuable and fun this is (Falvey et al., 1998; O'Brien & O'Brien, 1992).

Celebrating Differences

We help students learn to understand and value one another. Simultaneously, we work to (1) understand common needs of all as human beings across our differences; and (2) explore ways in which human beings are different and ways in which these differences contribute to the total community. We seek to build an inclusive community in

JOURNEY into the CLASSROOM

A Circle of Friends Makes a Difference

The story of Brandon and his circle of support demonstrates the power of friendship and how children can help one another given the resources and opportunity. Brandon entered Trina's third-grade class with cognitive disabilities. He read and wrote at a prekindergarten level. He was sweet, emotionally young, and very likeable. Through the strong community that Trina built in her class, Brandon quickly found a group of friends that loved being with him. Two of these friends had also been in his first- and second-grade class where Brandon had been fully included.

At the end of the second grade, the school psychologist had recommended that Brandon go to a separate special education class in another school. This surprised the teachers and principal; they decided to visit the special education class. Trina went along as well. All were shocked at how much more Brandon was able to do than other students in the class and how limited the curriculum was. It was obvious that Brandon would regress in this situation. "Our Brandon simply can't go there," said Terry, a second-grade teacher. Marshall, the principal, and Trina heartily agreed.

Trina said, "I want Brandon to be in my class." They made plans for her to be supported by the special education teacher and the school's part-time occupational therapist. However, Brandon needed help and support from his peers as well.

One day Trina asked Brandon if he would like to have a circle of friends help him. As she explained, he liked the idea. She asked him for permission to invite friends to join them including the two friends he had been with for 2 years.

The first meeting was held at lunchtime and was fascinating. After discussing dreams and fears with Brandon, they began to come up with a plan. They decided that each of the five students in the circle would help him in a different subject. One student chose math because that was his favorite subject, and math with Brandon sounded like fun.

One little girl said she wanted to be in charge of helping with spelling. Trina was a bit taken back, as this student was not very strong herself at spelling. "Why would you like to do that, Lisa?" Trina asked. Lisa answered, "If I help Brandon with spelling, that will help me spell better also because it will give me more practice." "Out of the mouths of babes," thought Trina as she smiled.

After writing their plan they chose something fun to do together. This continued every week for the next 2 years (the teacher looped with her class). The weekly meeting always included plans to improve subjects, celebrations of what Brandon had done well that week, and discussion of how the other children were doing.

Over time the focus shifted from solely being on Brandon to how the whole group was doing in their lives. They always did something fun together, and as time went on they began to hang out together outside of school. When these children went on to fifth grade, Trina made sure they were in the same class and asked the teacher to provide them time to run their meetings each week. By the time they all reached middle school the group was functioning on its own, without an adult running it or even always being present. They were no longer doing something an adult had asked them to do, and they were not "helping" another student. They had become part of each other's lives. They had become a "kids' club" and were helping one another. Due to Trina taking the time and effort to help create and support this group, lifelong friendships were created and Brandon was provided support that helped him be successful. That is what good circles are all about.

Reflection: A major need in our society is the nurturing of people helping one another in communities. Circles of support provide students with special needs important supports in schools. As important, however, they give all students a concrete learning experience, leadership education you might say, in understanding how people can help one another. This is a life-changing experience with long-term positive impact.

which students notice, value, and celebrate differences that include race, culture, language, gender, sexual orientation, (dis)ability, age, and more. These differences provide a rich tapestry for learning and exploration that can cross subject areas. We help our students experience and understand different perspectives, the influences of life experiences, and the contribution that each person can make to the whole, enhancing learning and community building simultaneously.

Intentionally Promoting Inclusion and Relationships. Daily we work to support students in developing positive, caring relationships. If Jorge seems isolated, we look for opportunities to pair him with supportive classmates. If Anthony has a difficult time handling his emotions, we may ask some students if they could help Anthony out or group him with socially skilled, emotionally stable peers. If students seem afraid of Mary, a girl with severe cerebral palsy who must struggle to speak and is sometimes loud in the process, we ponder ways we can help classmates understand and support her. For it is certain that if some students do not have friendships and supportive relationships, these students are feeling isolated, fearful, sometimes angry, and our classroom community is weakened.

Fisher (2001) developed a helpful framework for understanding the social place of any child within the class (see Figure 9.6). If a child is at risk for being marginalized,

FIGURE 9.6

Frames of Relationship

FRAME	SAMPLE WORDS	SAMPLE ACTIONS
Ghost/guest	"Nothing to do with us!"	Being invisible, ignored, excluded
Inclusion kid/ different friend	"He is weird." "She is cute." "It's not nice to tease special students!"	Differential treatment by everyone Affection Politeness
Kid who needs help	"Can I push him to science?" "It's my turn to help her."	Helping
Just another kid	"It's no big deal." "Like everyone else."	Typical reciprocal interactions
One of my friends	"He's just my friend." "He's got my back."	Hanging Affection Invitations to parties Having fun together
Best friends forever	"Part of my life." "Best friend." "Trust with anything."	Hanging Having fun together

Source: Adapted from Fisher (2001).

this framework helps us consider our options. In ways, it is a more detailed break-down of the journey from benevolence to community that we described in Chapter 1. As we think about children, how do they interact? Is there one child who has no "regular friends" or "friends forever" but has many "helpers"? Is one child actually ignored by almost everyone (a "ghost/guest")? What might we do to change that? One teacher brought a situation like this to the attention of students, who subsequently invited the child to their house on the weekend. Do all children get to be helped? Perhaps Lisa, who is labeled gifted, is always helping other students but not receiving help herself. Might we suggest that a student with cerebral palsy help Lisa in an area in which he is strong?

Ability Differences Up Front. It is important to help students understand and accept that we all have different abilities and that these differences do not make us better or worse. Teaching students about multiple intelligences is one constructive way to do this. Personal knowledge of multiple intelligences helps students who function lower in some areas look at their strengths in other areas. We also help students understand that different students will be working at different levels.

As we do this, we are providing enormous learning that will benefit students in later life. Students learn to value and look for one another's abilities. They learn how to work effectively with people having very different abilities.

The example we set as we interact with students with obvious ability differences is most important. If we are frustrated with and belittle a student for lack of understanding, if we ignore or isolate such a student, we will promote these responses in other students as well. In contrast, we model respect and teach students practical strategies for supporting one another (Sapon-Shevin, 1999; Tomlinson, 2004).

Children's Literature. Literature is a powerful tool for engaging students in under-standing differences and experiencing the human condition from different perspec-tives. Many children's books deal explicitly with issues that confront children. We've listed just a few excellent resources in Figure 9.7. We can read and discuss such books aloud; or students may read and discuss them in literacy circles, write their own stories and compare their experiences with characters in the story, and/or act out parts, playing different roles and reflecting on the life of the person portrayed (Sapon-Shevin, 1999).

Thematic Units. We can study human differences as a **thematic unit.** We might even use the categories of difference listed previously. For example, one thematic unit could be: How do people differ in intellectual abilities? This question could lead into an exploration using multiple intelligences as a framework and include a study of IQ tests. Or we could explore the history of people who are deaf or differing ethnic groups. One teacher did an extended study project, for example, titled "Coming to America." Students read books, researched ways groups came to America, interviewed family members, and wrote the stories of their families, which were then read in class by par-ents. Another group of students investigated civil rights of persons with disabilities. They interviewed local people, invited presenters, and enacted a drama of the takeover of the president's office at Berkeley in California in 1972 (Manning et al., 1994; Zemelman et al., 2005).

FIGURE 9.7

Children's Literature Examples

Don't Feel Sorry for Paul. Wolf, 1974. Lippincott. I	Paul was born with incompletely formed hands and feet but is first and foremost a child—riding his bike, going to school, at a birthday party.
Rachel. Fanshawe, 1977. Bradbury. P	Picture book for young children that illustrates how Rachel navigates her life in a wheelchair—swimming, being part of a Brownie troop, going on vacations.
I Have a Sister—My Sister Is Deaf. Peterson, 1977. Harper. P	A sensitive book in which a girl tells about her sister and how she handles being deaf.
My Friend Jacob. Clifton, 1980. Dutton. P	Fiction; two high school students, one of whom has abilities far below typical for his age, are friends.
The Balancing Girl. Rabe, 1981. Dutton. P	Story of two students—one, in a wheelchair, can line up dominoes and then make them all fall down together; the other feels the need to knock down the dominoes. They work through this conflict.
Jamaica Tag-Along. Havill, 1989. Houghton Mifflin. P	An African American girl is rejected by her brother and does the same to a younger child. After she realizes that she's doing the same thing, they build a sand castle together, and finally her brother joins her as well.
Living in Two Worlds. Rosenberg, 1986. Lee & Shepard. I	Photo essay about biracial children that describes segregation and prejudice in housing, culture, and religion and conveys the pain of being teased.
Come Sit by Me. Merrifield, 1990. Women's Press. P	A young boy in a day care center has AIDS, and some children won't play with him—but Karen does.
The Big Orange Splot. Pinkwater, 1977. Scholastic. P	Mr Plumbean lives on a "neat street." He decides to paint his house to illustrate his dreams. At first the neighbors are upset, but by the end the street has all sorts of new designs!
Fly Away Home. Bunting, 1991. Clarion. P	A homeless boy scrounges for food and shelter at the airport where he lives with his father. He is given hope when a bird escapes from the terminal.
White Socks Only. Coleman, 1996. Albert Whitman. I	A young African American girl takes off her shoes and steps to the "Whites Only" water fountain in her white socks. A controversy ensues, ending with the removal of the sign on the fountain forever.
The Number on My Grandfather's Arm. Adler, 1987. UAHC Press. P	A little girl's grandfather tells her the story of the concentration camp in Hitler's Germany after she notices a number on his arm.
Sweet Clara and the Freedom Quilt. Hopkinson, 1993. Knopf. P	Twelve-year-old Clara, a seamstress slave, escapes on the Underground Railroad, leaving behind a quilt that shows the directions to the North for others.

P = Primary; I = Intermediate; A = Advanced
Source: Adapted from Sapon-Shevin (1999).

In the End
The Growing Circles of Community

At first building a community of third graders, eighth graders, or high school seniors may seem a bit far-fetched. After all, most of us have experienced schools where feelings were not considered important. Many of us probably long for deeper community—yet many of us have been hurt so often by interactions with others that the idea of a caring community seems questionable.

We would do well to look at ourselves and explore how our own needs for belonging, love, power, freedom, and fun are being met. What is our experience of community? What do we understand? Have we had positive experiences that lead us to understand community, or will we need to feel our way carefully from scratch?

The fact is that the hunger for an unmet need for community is strong for many people, underlining the potentially powerful impact of community in our class. This fact also makes the challenge greater as we learn. Yet it seems reasonable to hope that we can be community-building leaders in our schools. Teachers all over the world are building a literature of practices that far extend the beginnings we've sketched in this chapter. The community-building movement in neighborhoods, churches, businesses, and whole municipalities is similarly growing, and there is much from which to learn. We have to be wise in the process, of course. What Peck (1987) calls pseudo-community—everyone smiling and being nice—is not real. Community building is a journey that's full of both excitement and many false paths, but we'll find that it's key to teaching.

We may also find that the community we build with students contributes to a richness in our own lives that we wouldn't have thought possible. When we are greeted enthusiastically by students in the grocery store, when a college student we had in the fourth grade drops by to introduce us to his fiancee, when the student body throws us a farewell party as we move to another school, we'll reflect on community and the circling impacts of genuine care and support.

For students to learn, they must feel safe and emotionally secure. Otherwise they become tense and it is very difficult for them to take in new information. For this reason building a caring community in which students feel that they are welcome and that they belong is critical for learning. Caring classroom communities go far to help *prevent* many social and behavioral challenges and promote *problem solving* among the community when difficulties do occur. Creating a caring community throughout the school, through a warm atmosphere, friendly staff, and connections to the community is vital for encouraging learning and growth.

We intentionally build community in our class on a daily basis. Responding to the social and emotional needs are part of what we teach.

Traveling Notes

For students to learn, they must feel safe and emotionally secure. Otherwise they become tense and it is very difficult for them to take in new information. For this reason, building a caring community in which students feel that they are welcome and that they belong is critical for learning. Here are a few key ideas from this chapter that you can take with you.

1. Caring classroom communities go far to help *prevent* many social and behavioral challenges and provide a setting in which *problem solving* among the community can occur when difficulties do occur.
2. Creating a caring community throughout the school, through a warm atmosphere, friendly staff, and connections to the community is vital for encouraging learning and growth.
3. We intentionally build an inclusive, caring community moment by moment each day in our class. Responding to the social and emotional needs of our students is simply part of what we teach.
4. We have many strategies to build community—such as involving students in decorating the room, providing jobs that make students responsible for much of the functioning of the class, holding class meetings, promoting peer learning, and establishing circles of support.
5. When we foster emotionally safe classrooms, we find that more learning and higher-order thinking occurs because children are emotionally secure and are willing to take risks, regardless of the hurtful things going on in their lives.
6. We attend to helping students who are potentially marginalized be connected in class, creating interactive opportunities, facilitating problem solving, and developing structures through which students can develop friendships as well as support one another.
7. We explicitly help children learn about and appreciate differences among themselves, teaching them strategies to tap into classmates' strengths and to help one another.

Stepping Stones

Following are some learning activities that may extend your understanding of ideas and actions you may take toward building community in your school and classroom.

1. Make a checklist of the community-building practices we have described in this book. Check community-building practices you do and do not see being used. What is the impact on the behaviors and learning of students? How could you strengthen the community in your own classroom? Locate a teacher who uses circles of friends. Observe a meeting and interview the students involved. How do they feel about this responsibility? How has it enriched their own lives? How has it changed the lives of the students they are helping?

2. Interview a parent of a child who has been having "behavioral problems" in school. What has been occurring in the classroom? How is community built in the classroom and how has the teacher responded to the problems? What conclusions might you draw?

3. Find out what children are included in your local school district. Where do the children go who do not attend regular classrooms? Visit one of these rooms. Interview the students to find out how they feel about their school setting. What does this say about community?

4. Identify teachers in your school who are using different community-building strategies. Approach these teachers and talk with them about what they do. Ask to visit their class; write down notes of what you see, take pictures of what they do, and organize these into a booklet that you can pass out to all staff.

5. Locate a school that uses peer buddies and mentors. Observe and interview students involved in this process. What do they think? How does the system help them learn? How do they feel about the process?

6. Have a party and ask each teacher to talk about one positive happening with a child who is having difficulty in the class. Celebrate these achievements!

10 | Meet Needs of Students with Challenging Behaviors

Positive Strategies for Difficult Situations

CHAPTER GOAL

Develop knowledge and skills to build an understanding of how challenging behavior communicates needs of students; learn about proactive strategies for responding to social and behavioral problems.

CHAPTER OBJECTIVES

1. Evaluate and understand research on the effects of traditional practices utilizing rewards and punishments.
2. Visualize types of challenging behaviors and needs these behaviors may communicate.
3. Understand how imposing control rather than meeting needs strengthens problematic behaviors.
4. Explore and utilize proactive strategies for meeting student needs.
5. Understand legal requirements and procedures for developing Behavioral Intervention Plans.

These Kids Are Driving Me Crazy and I Don't Know What to Do!

"These kids are driving me crazy! I don't know what to do!" How do we respond to social and behavioral challenges? We've seen that the first strategy is to *prevent* problems by designing engaging instruction and by building a classroom community. Yet, despite our best efforts, we will experience problems with some students.

One of the other teachers was aghast, however. "There is no way this will work!" (Peterson, 1998). This reaction reflects the debate regarding behavioral challenges in schools. Do we try to control students through rewards and punishments? Do we label them as disturbed and get them out of our classes and into special education? Or do we work to build relationships, care, and respect? Do we seek to understand and respond to student needs? How can we meet our own needs also?

Quincy: A Student out of Control

We are talking with a young teacher who has developed a reputation for success with challenging students. William teaches Grades 4 and 5 and has been "looping" in a school serving a racially diverse, low-income area. We were immediately impressed by the student work that literally covers the walls, ceilings, and windows of William's classroom.

"I want to tell you about Quincy," William says.

"I can't do anything with him. He hits other students all the time." Quincy has quite a reputation, and several teachers think he should be in a class for students with emotional disorders. "I met Quincy my first year, when I took over his fourth-grade classroom," William continues. "I was the third teacher that year, and the class was in chaos." "What did you do?" we ask, thinking of stories about new teachers thrown into challenging classes.

"First, I made the classroom fun and inviting. Some friends helped me transform the room from drab to colorful. I wanted students to know this was going to be better and fun. However, Quincy hated everything, fought, and sometimes lashed out in a violent rage. He frequently turned over desks and jumped from tables. The only way I could get him to cooperate was to give him a choice of spending his time in class or in the office."

"He's afraid and angry at home, treated with disrespect at school." We expect William to tell us he tried to get Quincy in the special education class. Instead he says, "I really wanted Quincy

to be successful." His eyes flicker in anger. "I was incensed when I saw how the previous teacher had treated Quincy. She placed masking tape on the floor around his desk, creating an invisible jail. If I had been Quincy, I would have rebelled too!"

"Confused by what was making him act this way, I soon learned that Quincy was living in a small apartment with his mother and grandmother. His mother's boyfriend regularly beat her and did not like Quincy. The grandmother was threatening to kick Quincy and his mother out. I began to understand. Quincy was angry and scared. He did not feel safe or know if he would have a place to live!"

"The other teachers wanted to get rid of Quincy. Not my student!" William tells us that almost daily, teachers asked when Quincy would be sent to the center for children with emotional disturbance. Their answer was to get rid of him. Yet William persevered and began to experiment.

"I built on his interests and gave him choices." Quincy kept playing in the coat closet, swinging from the doors. "Rather than restrict him, I made him the coat closet monitor. This worked. He now had a reason to be there and was proud of his job. I also gave Quincy choices involving hands-on activities and work partners. I moved students who liked to help others to his table, and I got another student to read with him every day. During computer time I let him catch up on his work. He surprised me by working hard during this time."

"Quincy's behavior began to change. He knew I cared." William smiles again. "Quincy gradually improved. I remember the first day without having a real confrontation. I hugged him and congratulated him like he had just won the lottery! He began to listen to me when I asked him to sit down instead of fighting. One day he told me that a child was bothering him. I was so excited that he was thinking rather than just reacting. Another day, Quincy saw Karee's daily progress report, which listed things like 'Did you do all your work?' 'Did you follow the teacher's directions?' and 'Did you help the teacher?' He asked me if he could have a daily progress report. He was evaluating his own behavior. He also began to do nice things for me, such as putting away materials."

William responded to Quincy as a person, not by using M&M's or praise as manipulative tools. He gave feedback about personal growth and strengths. Quincy began to see him as a friend and ally, not as a controlling authority. William explains, "I think two things were responsible for Quincy's gradual change. First, my class was fun and he did not want to miss it. He had choices, and he could move around. No worksheets or invisible jail in my class. Second, he realized I cared about him and he responded.

"He began to do his academic work, and to learn. A few simple adaptations went a long way." As Quincy's behaviors began to improve, so did his academic work. "I became convinced that Quincy was afraid he could not do work and was refusing in order to save face. So I worked to make him feel comfortable and successful. He would read aloud with me or with a partner, not in front of the whole class. In spelling I allowed him to pick 5 words instead of 10. Although I expected less written work, my expectations continued to grow as he did more and more. On one report card he had As, Bs, and one C. When he saw his grades, he was shocked. 'Those are As . . . and Bs!' he exclaimed. I will never forget the proud look on his face."

"I invited Quincy home. We had fun and strengthened our relationship." William also reached out to Quincy beyond the school day. "This was the turning point. A couple of other teachers took selected students with high needs to their houses and encouraged me to do the same, despite negative teachers who warned me of lawsuits. The first time we had pizza. Quincy ran around the back yard wearing out my dog. It was terrific to see him playing and laughing. Over the next year I periodically had him for dinner, games, or swimming."

The most improved award for Quincy: "By the end of the year, Quincy was a different kid. He still had periodic problems. However, when a conflict arose, he would stop and think. At the honors assembly I was proud to give Quincy the Most Improved award. He wants to get on the academic honor roll next time."

FIGURE 10.1

Teachers on Dealing with Problem Behaviors

SOME COMMON PROBLEMS IN CLASSROOMS

The student:
- Is off task.
- Talks during instruction.
- Won't sit still.
- Attracts others' attention and gets them off task.
- Is unprepared for class.
- Makes excuses to leave class.
- Hits other students or the teacher.
- Insults other students.
- Acts belligerent.
- Withdraws and does not want to participate.

WHAT WORKS?

- Give students attention.
- Encourage cooperative learning and play groups.
- Teach in fun and engaging ways.
- Study culture or "difference" of the week in the room to promote understanding and acceptance of differences.
- Have students help make rules and structure learning activities in the classroom.
- Have students help other students—use peer mediation, peer buddies, circles of friends.
- Institute sharing time to talk about events in life.
- Show concern and care.
- Stop until the student gets under control.
- Emphasize group work. Ask "Do you need to . . . ?" Give options.

WHAT DOES NOT WORK!

- Boring, unengaging teaching
- Extra assignments
- Yelling
- Lack of respect—lashing out rudely, nagging, pleading, begging
- Intimidation—misuse of power
- Punishment
- Detention

In this vignette, we should recognize what William did not do. Yes, he ensured that Quincy did not hurt other students by keeping careful watch, helping Quincy think about his behavior, and getting other students to help Quincy. However, William did not spend most of his time focusing on Quincy's problems; nor did he refer him for special education or suggest medication. William knew his job was to meet Quincy's needs and to help him learn how to interact in positive ways, not to forcibly control his behavior. Quincy's story illustrates what is possible and highlights themes we will see throughout this chapter (Peterson & Hittie, 2000). (See Figure 10.1).

Sights TO SEE

Solving Social Problems

Resolving Conflict: O'Farrell Middle School At this school in San Diego, California, school leaders place equal emphasis on the social, intellectual, psychological, and physical needs of their students. www.edutopia.org/resolving-conflict-ofarrell-middle-school

Smart Hearts: Social and Emotional Learning Overview This 13-minute video provides an introduction to social and emotional learning and how this helps schools deal with serious challenging behaviors including bullying. www.edutopia.org/social-emotional-learning-overview-video

Creating a Positive, Student-Centered Approach

Educators are increasingly concerned about behavioral challenges and violence in schools. To deal with these problems, three general approaches are used:

1. Punishment
2. Rewards (technically, "reinforcers")
3. Meeting student needs and promoting growth and relationships

Many discipline programs promote use of power by adults, in the form of combinations of approaches 1 and 2, to control the behavior of children. Rather than helping children make choices based on their own internal values, interests, and motivation, an **internal locus of control,** most seek to control students' behavior through external rewards, incentives, or punishments, an **external locus of control.** Yet research clearly shows that both punishment and rewards often create more problems than they fix. Let's look briefly at these two very widely used strategies.

Rewards and Punishment to Control Behavior:
Typical Strategies That Deepen Problems

First, let's distinguish between the popular conception of rewards and punishment and the technical definitions used in behavioral psychology. In the popular parlance, **rewards** are perceived positive consequences or incentives bestowed by a person or persons with power in order to promote desired behavior. Such rewards may be social (a smile, praise, congratulations); sensory (a touch, a kiss, a pat on the back); fiscal (money, a gift certificate); or physical (food, books, a car).

A **reinforcer,** on the other hand, is an action associated with a behavior that *increases* the occurrence of the behavior. The point is that a reward is in the eye of the giver. A reinforcer, however, is defined by its impact on behavior. Reinforcers are of two types: (1) Positive reinforcement involves *providing* a stimulus to promote a behavior; (2) negative reinforcement involves *removing* something, typically something undesirable, when the desired behavior occurs. For example, if a student is promised time on the computer, for good behavior, that is positive reinforcement. When a student is isolated in the classroom, allowed only to return to the group when his behavior improves, that is negative reinforcement. Either way, to be called a reinforcer, an action must result in the increase of a behavior. In any case, we generally use the more popular term *reward* when describing efforts by those in authority to provide reinforcing consequences to obtain behavioral responses they desire (Charles, 1999; Janney & Snell, 2000b; Reavis & Andrews, 1999).

Similarly, **punishment** is popularly understood as an undesired consequence one person uses to *decrease* the behavior of another—taking away recess privileges, grounding a child, drawing frowny faces on a chart, requiring extra work. In the technical behavioral definition, however, a *punisher* is an aversive stimulus resulting in the reduction of a behavior. The other behavioral strategy for reducing behaviors is *extinction,* the withholding of stimuli that reinforce a behavior (Charles, 1999; Janney & Snell, 2000b; Kohn, 1993, 1996a; Reavis & Andrews, 1999).

How effective is punishment? Here is what research indicates:

- We can eliminate behaviors through punishment in the short run. However, this outcome occurs only if the punishment is sufficiently strong—and lasts only while punishment remains in effect (Beach Center on Families and Disability, 1994; Koegel, Koegel, & Dunlap, 1996; Martin & Pear, 1996).
- Punishment does not address underlying needs and new behavioral challenges often emerge (Carr et al., 1994; Hitzing, 1994; Janney & Snell, 2000b).
- A focus only on behavior prevents us from really understanding the person. We often distance ourselves from the "problem" student and depersonalize our reactions, thus setting the stage for additional future problems (Hitzing, 1994; Marin, Gilpin, Goodman, & Moses, 1996).
- Punishment reduces or eliminates guilt, ensuring that any change in behavior is caused by external force rather than internalized decisions (Cragg, 1992; Gilligan, 1996). As a result, "the more harshly we punish . . . the more violent they become; the punishment increases their feelings of shame and simultaneously decreases their capacities for feelings of love . . . and of guilt" (Gilligan, 1996, p. 110).

Many suggest that combined with consequences (punishments), we should provide rewards to reinforce positive behaviors. Most behavior management programs use this strategy (Kohn, 1992). At first glance this might seem rational and humane. However, Kohn (1993, 1999) conducted a comprehensive review of research and found that rewards:

- Punish—because (1) they are a form of control and (2) not everyone gets a reward. Someone is always left out.
- Rupture relationships—a person in power metes out rewards, and competition for rewards breaks a sense of community.
- Ignore the reasons for behaviors.
- Discourage risk taking—people do "exactly what is necessary to get [a reward] and no more" (Kohn, 1998, p. 63).
- Undermine intrinsic interest and motivation.
- Encourage mediocrity. Students who focus on rewards (grades, scholarships, praise) rather than on intrinsic interests are less likely to do well over time.
- Must be desired strongly enough to make an impact.
- Are effective only in the short run, as long as they "keep coming."

The impacts of traditional rewards on interest and motivation, and their consequent effects on learning and achievement, are particularly serious. In a comprehensive review, Lepper and Henderlong (2000) found that the motivation of students declines as they grow older, that the use of external rewards reduces interest in a task, and that performance declines as a result. Aware of this, many teachers say that they work hard *not* to reward students but help them become intrinsically motivated by pursuing their own interests.

How Could We Not Try?

Clearly the most important part of dealing effectively with students who have behavior challenges is for educators to make a commitment to helping them learn positive behaviors, to keep them in their classroom, and to care for them. This is hard work. Wesley's story illustrates how educators in real schools can commit to a child with challenging behavior and make a real difference in their lives.

One day Bobbie, the principal, talked with us about Wesley. "Wesley just has so many problems," she said. "Wesley would periodically hit, scream, and curse defiantly. One day he told his teacher he would kill her as he was put in a time-out room. We made a videotape of his acting out one day and showed it to his doctor. He told us that either you are crazy or a saint for keeping this kid. I don't know what we are but our staff has felt that they can see sometimes a wonderful child trying to come out. How can we not try to help him and keep him here? If we don't, if we let him go to a segregated special education program we know that we are likely, right now, committing him to a life in prison."

In other schools in which we've spent time, the entire staff would have turned against this child, seeking numerous ways to get him to leave the school. Not here. At Armstrong Elementary, the entire school staff, from principal to teachers to the school custodian, were pulling for this little guy.

While the staff members felt they didn't know what they were doing, they worked to develop a plan to help Wesley. At first, the key focus was just to get him to school and prevent outbreaks. Wesley was so anxious and tense. He said one day, "I don't want to be with kids!" Staff members were confused and concerned, but they listened. Cheryl, a paraprofessional, was assigned to be with Wesley. At first she spent much of the day in one-on-one activities in a small room, coming out for recess and lunch. She is a warm, easygoing, quiet person who is quite good with Wesley. He liked her. The staff continued to develop a behavior plan that would be effective. She took him part of the day to the kindergarten class where he sat at the end of a table and could be by himself. However, when we talked to Wesley one day,

he looked around the room and said, "All these people are my friends." Clearly, Wesley knew that people cared about him.

One day Michael (one of your textbook's authors) saw Wesley when he was in school. They had developed a good relationship and Wesley came over and hugged him with a big smile. But then Wesley got a wild look in his eyes and he began hitting Michael as hard as he could. Michael just held him close and he eventually quit. Why did this occur? No one understood, but we suspect that Wesley had learned that if you get too close to someone you risk getting hurt; he was protecting himself ahead of time.

On another day an event occurred that made matters much worse. Wesley was taken home by a driver, although he was supposed to have been taken to a relative's house on this particular day. Instead, the driver left him at home where no adults were present. Wesley tried to cook himself some lunch and ended up burning his house down. His sense of anxiety and fear seemed to pervade his being. He looked wild-eyed and he mumbled almost incoherently.

Soon after, a psychiatrist recommended termination of parental rights saying that the mother simply could not handle being a parent. Sharon, the kindergarten teacher, and Bobbie, the principal, were very concerned about what would happen with Wesley if he were taken away from his parents. "If they cannot find a family in this town, he'll likely go to another county and immediately be put in a segregated program," Sharon said with tears streaming down her cheeks. "I am afraid we are going to lose him."

This did not occur, however. They continued to work with Wesley, finding ways to help him express his feelings in drawings and songs. The paraprofessional continued to work one on one with him, but they gradually increased his time in the kindergarten room, connecting him with other students. The staff helped the other students understand how afraid Wesley felt and coached them in ways to interact with him. A few times he became angry and aggressive, but staff members were quick to pull him aside and help him express his feelings in other ways. Within a couple of months, Wesley was in the kindergarten class most of the day. When he first came to school, he would go to a therapy room first to ground himself and then go to class with the other children. The staff were delighted and hopeful. A family worker had been assigned to work with the family to help the mother cope better and learn parenting skills. It was having a good impact. By midyear Wesley was in the class full-time. Wesley's time with the paraprofessional was reduced, and the special education teacher and social worker spent an hour each day in the class helping the teacher facilitate social interactions and monitor Wesley's responses.

It's a work in progress and the outcome is hardly certain. Yet, this school and its staff demonstrated well that starting with a commitment fueled by caring and creativity can make a huge difference in a student's life.

Reflection: The most critical and important element in working with students with emotional and behavioral challenges is this: We must be *committed* to caring about and teaching them. If we are not, it doesn't matter what strategies and techniques we use. Students will sense we don't truly care about them and react. This story illustrates the power we have in our hands when we commit to students with challenging behavior and who have many needs.

Meeting Student Needs:
Promoting Growth and Relationships

Another approach is available: *positive behavioral support*. In this approach we seek to understand what behaviors communicate about needs and to help students meet their needs in a socially acceptable way. If a student curses in class, we want to know why that student is doing so. We'll be thinking about the student's needs and welfare as much as we are about prohibiting negative behavior. As other students understand that we care, we'll also be surprised how this helps to strengthen our classroom community. In effect, we are modeling how we'd like to see students help and support one another.

This does not mean that we condone disrespectful or problematic behavior. Quite the opposite. For example, if Lawrence enters our class cursing and calling us names, we pull him aside and ask him what is happening; we make it clear that his behavior is not acceptable but that we know something is bothering him. (In effective classes students know the class routines and will continue to work together, allowing the teacher time to talk with the student.) In doing so, we are helping Lawrence think about his behavior and showing we care about him, not just keeping him in line. Further, we gain the respect of students by being strong enough to attend to them as individuals rather than merely using our authority to demand compliance.

One way of contrasting the traditional and positive behavioral support approaches is pictured in Figure 10.2 (Albin, Horner, & O'Neill, 1994; Evans & Meyer, 1985; Faber, Mazlish, Nyberg, & Templeton, 1995; Hitzing, 1994; Kohn, 1996a). As the figure indicates, traditional behavior management focuses on controlling a student's behavior from the perspective of others in the environment, particularly adults. Positive behavioral support, however, seeks to respond to the needs of the student and to help the student learn respectful and proactive ways of having needs met. In the first approach, other people decide when the problem is resolved; in the second, the problem is not resolved until the student sees his or her needs being met.

FIGURE 10.2

Traditional Behavior Management Versus Positive Behavioral Support

	TRADITIONAL BEHAVIOR MANAGEMENT	POSITIVE BEHAVIORAL SUPPORT
Problem	Behavior is causing us or others trouble, so we want to eliminate it.	Behavior, which is learned, is *communicating* something important.
Assessment	Specify the problem behavior and determine frequency, strength, duration.	Conduct "functional analysis" to determine *reasons for* the behavior.
Goal	Eliminate problem behavior.	Help student learn better ways of communicating needs.
Intervention	Reduce reinforcement of behavior ("extinguish" by ignoring) or punish when target behavior occurs.	Develop a sense of safety and trust between teacher and student. Make the class fun and interesting so there is a "payoff" for positive participation. Provide support from another person; reduce frustration in the setting. Teach alternative ways to communicate. Teach how to tolerate school conditions.
Success	The behavior is eliminated and people in power view the situation as better.	The person's problem is solved from *his or her point of view.*

Source: Adapted from Hitzing (1994).

Creating a Student-Centered School

Throughout the world, schools are increasingly developing schoolwide approaches to challenging behaviors. Some schools rely heavily on efforts to control students, using what Kunc (1998) calls the "habits of exclusion"—**time-out, detention,** hall monitors directing the physical movement of students. In other schools control is maintained through rewards. Students are expected to learn the rules and create plays about them; teachers give daily tokens that can be turned in at the school store. Yet the focus is still more on controlling behaviors than on promoting real human growth.

What do schools look like that use a **student-centered** approach, one focused on student needs? Numerous schools are moving in this direction. Westside Elementary School provides one example. The school operates with only five rules: (1) Try, (2) be safe, (3) be kind, (4) work hard, and (5) be respectful. These are positive rules indicating what is *desired* rather than what is prohibited. Throughout the school, there is no punishment. When there is a conflict, staff assume that behavior signals an unmet need. For example, instead of missing recess or lunch, the class clown might be given 5 minutes a day to do a stand-up comedy routine. A bully "might become a tutor to the younger children he earlier terrorized. The clown needed attention and the bully needed to be admired by younger children" (Berg, 1989, p. 10B).

The school principal reports that such proactive strategies resolve more than 90% of discipline problems. When additional measures are needed, a child is expected to develop a plan, essentially a contract, in which the problem is defined and the student indicates what steps he or she will take to resolve it. The school seeks to help students learn new ways of responding. Building on William Glasser's **reality therapy**, staff lead students through a series of questions designed to help them think: "What did you want to happen? What did you accomplish? What are the pros and cons of your behavior? What do you want to do now? What do you need to do to get what you want?" (Glasser, 2000). Teachers use **cooperative learning** in the classroom, and the school holds periodic open meetings where children can "speak their minds without fear of reprisal from staff or peers" (Berg, 1989, p. 10B).

In another school, staff were concerned about their many behavior problems. The new principal said, "We won't look at students as being a problem but as *having* a problem." With this view in mind, he removed the school's "behavior room" and approached Helen—the warmest, most caring teacher—and asked her to work as a **mediator** with students and teachers. Whenever problems occurred, the student and teacher went to Helen's room and she helped them work out solutions. This became an opportunity for *learning* rather than punishment. After a while Helen said in a staff meeting, "I am glad you send students to me. However, at this point, if you have a conflict with a student, call me down and I will cover your class while you work out the problem yourself." She gradually began to spend most of her time providing such support for teachers (Kunc, 1998).

Comprehensive programs using a student-centered philosophy, at their best, incorporate the following components (Garbarino et al., 1992; Kay, 1999; Lantieri & Patti, 1996; McLane, Burnette, & Orkwis, 1997):

- Building community in the school
- Peer mediation and conflict resolution

Emily's teacher talks with her about some difficulties she's had with some other students in the class. "Why do you think they acted that way?" she just asked. "What are they feeling and needing do you think?" She tries to help students see each others' perspectives.

- Teaching students how to support one another through peer buddies and circles of support
- Professional support—individual and group counseling, support groups
- Mentors through such programs as Big Brothers and Big Sisters
- A building support team (see Chapter 5)
- Interagency support and intervention for families

School Patterns in Dealing with Behavioral Challenges

Schools vary dramatically in terms of how they use various responses to student behavioral challenges. However, consistent patterns are apparent in schools. Figure 10.3 illustrates some common patterns. In some schools and classrooms, there seems to be no

FIGURE 10.3

School Patterns in Dealing with Behavioral Challenges	
RESPONSE TO CHALLENGING BEHAVIOR	**DESCRIPTION**
Chaos: reactive responses	Teachers feel out of control; nothing works; no support systems in place; frustration. This often results in random lashing out at children and punitive responses. The pattern is often connected to punishment and expulsion.
Punishment and expulsion	Rules developed by the school or teacher with little to no student or parent input; administered inflexibly. When rules are broken or challenged, the prime mode of response is punishment, including taking away privileges, sending student home, and expulsion. Students are frequently referred for special education services to remove them from the class. Staff seldom work proactively with one another and a culture of blame is pervasive; often targeted at parents.
Staff control	This approach is often used in schools seeking to be inclusive but not clear on how to deal with challenging behaviors. Most often a paraprofessional is systematically assigned to a student with behavioral challenges. This pattern is particularly seen with students with autism.
Rules and rewards	Schools and teachers using this pattern focus on developing rules that are clear and provide rewards for compliance. This pattern often works hand in hand with punishment and expulsion and staff control. However, as the primary focus it provides a more positive culture. But the focus remains on control of student behaviors and the definition of appropriate behaviors by adults. In this approach, a focus on building community and responding to inner needs of children is typically secondary.
Community and positive behavioral support	In this pattern, individual teachers and the entire school culture explicitly and systematically attend to building a sense of care and community in the school. When problems occur, positive behavioral support is used and educators seek alternative ways of helping children have their needs met, developing behavior plans that provide support to students and modeling and teaching of problem solving and alternate behaviors. In such schools, we also see much effort to build community among adults. The work of Glasser and strategies such as Peace Clubs are tools toward these ends.

thought through response. Chaos and reactive responses rule the day. Of course, in such classes punishment is often front and center but it is so ineffective even in the short term that teachers literally don't know what to do. Punishment, suspension, and expulsion form the center of other patterns. In such schools and classrooms, it feels as if there is a literal war going on between teachers and students. The fact is that in such situations students almost always win: There are simply more of them. In some situations, staff are assigned to be with a given student every moment of the day. The theory is that they can control the behavior of the student on a moment-to-moment basis. Of course, such a strategy does nothing to help the student learn new behaviors so a constant guard is needed. Other schools decide to proactively teach all students in the school to follow rules. While this approach is more positive, typically students have had little to no input into the rules, little emphasis is placed on community building, and the focus is still control of student behavior. It's a move toward more positive practices but still has a ways to go. Finally, there are schools where building community is a key, front-and-center agenda. In such schools, when problematic behavior occurs teachers look first at the needs of the student and develop strategies to use all in the learning community to help the student learn new, more positive ways to have his or her needs met.

Teacher Roles and Perspectives

We watch our students as they arrive in the morning. George, whose parents were divorced a month ago, looks better today. Nicole is laughing, but she's abused at home and children's teasing sometimes sets her off in a violent fit. Keith is withdrawn. Classified as "mentally retarded," he's been working really hard lately, learning to read a book he enjoys. There's Patricia. Thank goodness for children whose home lives are together. She's a leader and has been particularly helpful with Keith and Nicole.

What are some of the strategies that successful teachers use to deal with challenging students? To help George cope with his parents' divorce, we seat him with very nurturing students at his table, and a special friend talks with him about anything he needs to talk about for the first 10 minutes of class. The teacher has organized **informal peer supports**, connecting George with other students who make sure he has someone to play with at recess. Because he loves to draw, he is helping the art teacher make the backdrop for the school musical. This keeps him busy, which always helps when people are hurting.

Nicole needs a lot of support. She has a circle of friends that meet once a week who help her with her homework and are teaching her to be a good friend by example. They are patient with her. When she gets really upset, they sing with her.

Keith is growing by leaps and bounds, thanks to his mother and his special group. They read with him in the mornings, sit with him in the group area to help keep him focused, remind the teacher to write down instructions for him, and play with him at recess. He does not read or write at the same level, but the whole class works on individualized materials, so he does not stand out. The students are aware of his limits and congratulate him when he tries hard and learns something new.

As we look at the many needs of our students, we also come face to face with ourselves. There is no other arena in which students' responses will raise more personal issues—issues about our own lives, relationships, and abilities to handle emotions. As we seek to understand students, we must do the same for ourselves. Why do we respond the way we do? What do our responses mean, and how can we grow? How were we raised? What was and is our relationship with our parents? Were we abused? How did teachers and others in authority treat us? How do we feel about ourselves? Were we provided models of joy, hope, and support? Do we know how to have fun while working hard? We are challenged to understand ourselves but not to lay blame. The fact is, if we can't and don't do this with ourselves, neither will we be able to do it with our students. The good news is that our seeking to work positively with students can simultaneously help both us and our students.

A Few Practical Tools

The key, of course, is to use strategies to help prevent problems in the first place. If we use the numerous strategies in Chapter 9 to help build community in our class we'll prevent many difficulties. When we do have difficulties, however, putting a few practical strategies into place can help deal with these in a respectful way that helps meet student needs.

1. *Daily e-mails to parents on progress:* With parents who use e-mail, we can send quick notes regarding any issues that arise once we have established a relationship with the parents.
2. *Weekly progress report:* Use a simple rating scale with behaviors on which the student is working. We check off how well they did for that day. We let the student choose categories with our assistance and then type a copy to use.
3. *Hourly progress report:* Have a conversation with the student about what he or she wants out of school and how we can accomplish that. Each hour mark with a plus or zero whether the student completes assignments and manages behavior. Do this together with the student so that he or she recognizes the behavior.
4. *Mini conversations:* Twice a day pull the student aside to verbally ask how he or she thinks it is going. Set one or two goals to focus on. This is not a time for us to fuss over the student, but to listen and help direct his or her thinking.
5. *A safe place that the student can work:* This is not a place to which we would send students as a punishment. We ask students ahead of time what place they might go to help them calm down if a problem arises. They can then choose to go to this place or we can suggest it if problems are occurring.
6. *Needs focus:* We can spend time *thinking and planning* to focus on why the student is doing what he or she is doing, not how to stop the behavior. What need(s) does the student have that is (are) not being met? This is best done on a regular basis.
7. *Circle of support:* Construct a group that is a *circle of support* for that student.

BACK PACK

Positive Approaches to Behavior Challenges

Reclaiming Youth Network Reclaiming Youth is an organization dedicated to transforming education and human services by creating respectful ways of dealing with youth. This work is based on the Circle of Courage that addresses the universal needs of belonging, mastery, independence, and generosity. Great approach and resources here. www.reclaiming.com/

Positive Behavioral Support This federally funded research and training center has many practical resources related to positive behavioral support. rrtcpbs.fmhi.usf.edu/

Center for Effective Collaboration and Practice The center seeks to "foster the development and the adjustment of children with or at risk of developing serious emotional disturbance." The site offers many practical resources regarding effective practices for students with varied social and emotional challenges. cecp.air.org/

Key Strategies

The Foundation

We'll talk in greater depth about strategies later in this chapter. However, these are so important we wanted to discuss them early on. Here are questions we often ask ourselves as teachers: Is it *ever* OK to use rewards? Is there *any way* to get students to be responsible? *Are there* consequences for harmful behavior? Well, *yes*, *yes*, and *yes*. Four key strategies we want to highlight in response to these questions include (1) expressing appreciation, (2) celebrating achievements through student selected rewards, (3) learning social skills, and (4) using restorative justice. Let's discuss these amazing tools.

Expressing Appreciation

All of us value when people we respect say that they appreciate something we did or when they tell us they appreciate something about us—how kind we are, how well we sing, the artwork we create. The fact is that when this happens we feel rewarded. The difference, however, is that *people do not express appreciation for the purpose of controlling our behavior*. In fact, we use another word when people do that—manipulation which, of course, is seen as a punishment rather than a reward. If we are constantly looking for positive attributes of students and sharing with them what we appreciate, the fact is that this is likely to be reinforcing in the technical sense and help strengthen positive and proactive behaviors.

Celebrating Achievements

The idea of celebrating achievements is similar to showing appreciation. In fact, you could think of it as one way of showing appreciation to an individual student or a group of students. Key is the relationship between student and teacher. If a student sets daily goals, then she may choose her own reward or celebration for achieving her goals. There is an extreme difference between this and a reward that is selected by the teacher even if the teacher has tried to take the student's likes and dislikes into account. Allowing students to select their own rewards gives them a sense of control, power, and self-determination. We want to encourage these. It is that daily conversation that will account for the student learning to think about how to make changes and actually internalizing the goals. The reward then becomes a sideline. It is a celebration of what has already occurred, then the motivation for learning. The motivation is in the realization that someone cares about them and is willing to take the time each day to work with them on their goals and dreams.

Some teachers use celebrations for the entire class. There are two very different approaches. If the teacher says, "Class, if we have good behavior this morning and get all our work done you will get an extra recess," he is using the recess to try and motivate his students. Without teaching them self-motivation this will not succeed in the long run. A second teacher says at the end of the day, "Class, you have worked very hard today and I am proud of the progress you have made on your research project. What can we do to celebrate your success?" They talk. Several ideas are thrown out and the class picks an extra recess.

Sometimes students select rewards a teacher would never consider that involve additional work and learning. In a seventh-grade language arts class a student chose to type extra stories on the computer and create pictures as his reward for achieving his goals on his daily report. A fifth-grade student who was a good artist but struggled in academics chose to work on decorations for parties coming up for both classmates and teachers. His work was very detailed and received lots of acclaim. This improved his self-esteem and he became highly motivated to work hard on his classwork.

The key to using rewards effectively is that they create and strengthen the teacher's relationship with the students, and the improved sense of self that results. If the reward only helps the students learn to do what adults tell them to do, then nothing has changed inside the students' minds. We all need recognition for a job well done. When we work together to give children recognition in ways that improve their sense of self and the entire community, then we can say rewards help rather than hurt.

Learning Social Skills in Community

Students often come to school not knowing how to make friends, talk about problems, or interact pleasantly with people they don't like. **Social skills instruction** is an unwritten school curriculum that every teacher at every grade level must address daily. We use many strategies for helping students learn social skills. However, the most effective and manageable strategy is to incorporate these skills into the daily fabric of our teaching. Many useful curricula for teaching social skills have been developed and we use these to garner ideas on ways to incorporate the teachings (Amish, Gesten, Smith, & Clark, 1988; Elias et al., 1997; Kusche & Greenberg, 1994; L'Abate & Milan, 1989; McGinnis & Goldstein, 1984; Walker, Colvin, and Ramsey, 1995).

Rehearsal approaches are particularly powerful, giving students opportunities to practice how they could react. For this purpose Gray (1994) developed **social stories,** which depict situations of concern to children. Each social story describes a social inter-action in the first person, telling where the situation occurs, who is involved, what is happening, and why. Stories also describe the feelings of the individual. Students apply these stories to daily interactions as part of a learning process; the approach has been found effective with students with autism and with others who have difficulty learning social skills (Kuttler, Myles, & Carlson, 1998; Swaggart et al., 1995). Some educators have added music and other multimedia strategies when using social stories (Brownell, 2000). This helps children remember the skills they learn, as the brain can create associations to sounds or visuals.

Some teachers or support staff use social skills curricula in classes or groups on deal-ing with emotions, feelings, coping with loss, dealing with anger, and so on. However, we can also use these guides to infuse social skills instruction into our classroom in the form of "social mini-lessons." For example, when discussing negotiations between two countries regarding trade agreements, we help the class focus on negotiation as a skill; we provide some short information about listening and coming to win–win agreements, then have students practice in groups. Then, when a real conflict arises, we use this con-frontation to help the students learn to solve problems, drawing on resource materials.

Using Restorative Justice: Healing Hurt

A final key approach is to use restorative justice. Said simply, "If you break something, it is your responsibility to fix it. If you hurt someone, it is your responsibility to do what you can to heal the hurt." Rather than hurting students when they hurt others, we engage them in responsible behaviors to make it better. It's a powerful way of thinking and doing.

Beginning in classrooms and ending in courtrooms, the traditional notion of "justice" says we find who is at fault and punish him or her. Someone breaks a rule and there are consequences imposed by those in authority. Yet, punishment does not change undesirable behavior and weakens the community because those injured and the person who caused

Survival does not necessarily have to be objectively threatened. The threat to survival is what is *experienced* by the student and may be physical or emotional.

Love and Belonging. We have a powerful need to be loved, to belong with a group of people, to feel needed, wanted, and appreciated. For many students, however, this need is not met. In both high- and low-income families, students often do not receive adequate attention through personal time spent with parents, eating family dinners and discussing the day or reading books together. Some parents are so busy providing food and clothing that there is no time or energy left over. Other parents are involved with work or social commitments or keep their children too involved in activities to spend personal time with them. Many students have no close adult relationships and have limited experience of nurturing relationships.

When students do not feel a sense of love and belonging, they often react in many problematic ways—acting the class clown, breaking rules, making loud jokes or obscene gestures, constantly putting themselves at center stage (Albert, 1996; Gilligan, 1996; Paley, 1990). Other students join gangs involved in dangerous and illegal activities (Garbarino et al., 1992). Yet others withdraw. Underlying these actions are desperate needs for connection and care and feelings of unworthiness and low self-esteem.

Power. All people need some control over time, space, activities, or situations and chances to feel skilled or competent. For many reasons, however, students often feel overwhelmed, alone, restrained, and powerless. Parents may not give their children opportunities for choices. Schools make matters worse with structured and rigid classes. Students with special needs often have been in small, highly controlled special education classes. Some students come from homes in which they have been abused and where alcohol and drug abuse make their lives unstable, where they feel they cannot control even small parts of their lives. Students who are poor may feel that they are powerless in a nation of wealth.

When students feel a lack of power and competence, they may react in many negative ways. Some seek *revenge* for real or imagined hurts. Gilligan (1996) found that abused murderers committed their crimes seeking to achieve a sense of *justice,* "an eye for an eye." Others seek *avoidance of failure.* Believing that they can't be successful, they compensate by withdrawing and appearing inadequate, hoping that people will not remind them of their unworthiness. A teacher told this illustrative story:

One day I had the kids make a French calendar. They were to write the name of the month and days of the week. Vernon kept saying, "This is stupid Mrs. Kwoslo, this is stupid, stupid. . . ." Then he looked up at me and said, "This is hard, Mrs. Kwoslo." (B. Quinlan, personal communication, March 16, 2000)

Most disconcerting are occasions when students refuse to respond to our requests, most often called **noncompliance.** Kunc (1998) says we should think of this *no* as the tip of an iceberg. What might *no* mean? There are numerous possibilities: "Ask me later"; "I am afraid of failure"; "Not with you!"; "I am embarrassed."

Fun. We all need activities that are enjoyable and invigorating, simply fun. When students are bored, they will do almost anything to change that. Students daydream and escape in other ways—playing games, making faces, throwing spitballs. They may also become frustrated, get into conflicts, or tell us in many other ways, "I don't want to be here." The following story is illustrative.

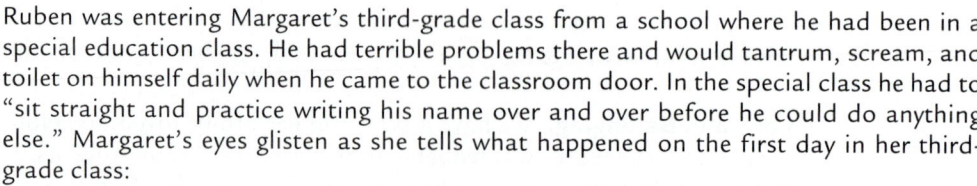

Ruben was entering Margaret's third-grade class from a school where he had been in a special education class. He had terrible problems there and would tantrum, scream, and toilet on himself daily when he came to the classroom door. In the special class he had to "sit straight and practice writing his name over and over before he could do anything else." Margaret's eyes glisten as she tells what happened on the first day in her third-grade class:

> On his way into class he started to become upset at the doorway, but I caught him casting a mildly interested eye at the fish tank. Before I was introduced to him or his parents, I handed him the fish food and asked him to feed the fish. End of a big problem with a long history. He walked right in happily. This great kid and the fish are flourishing. (M. Alkari, personal communication, September 12, 2000)

This child, with limited verbal communication abilities, had been saying by his behavior, "I hate this class. It is boring, repressive. I don't want to go." He fought with all his might. Several years of "behavior programs" based on behavior modification had done nothing; but the simple, attentive response of this teacher made a difference. Of course, Margaret built on this initial response, building an accepting, engaging community for Ruben.

Freedom. Freedom means both a lack of restraint and the ability to choose, to make decisions. If any single human need is the most widely ignored in schools, it is probably this one. In talking with groups of teachers about this topic, we frequently ask about the ways they got into trouble in school. Everyone laughs. "Why is this funny?" I ask. The reason it is funny is that one of the main causes of the trouble was always that the teacher was rigid and controlling; the problem behaviors defied an authoritarian regime in which rules were more important than people. We see over and over that teachers who provide students choices and freedom to move around and talk while they work have fewer problems in their classes. Of course such teachers spend a lot of time helping students learn how to handle their freedom, but they know how important it is.

Vicious Cycles

What happens when a student's needs are not met? According to Hitzing (1994) a vicious cycle often develops, in which negative behaviors and distrust spiral downward. Figure 10.4 demonstrates how this works. For example, suppose a student feels emotion based on an unmet need and reacts with unacceptable behavior. When he acts out or withdraws, he gets more of his needs met, though in a negative way. If the student wants greater control, he gets it; if attention, he gets this. In other words, rather than understanding needs and looking for positive ways to meet these, we often respond in ways that exacerbate the original problem. We may restrict the student, become angry, hold the student out of interesting activities. Consequently, problematic behaviors continue with increased intensity.

Students with social and emotional challenges often are struggling in very difficult situations. On the one hand, students *need* someone to care for and listen to them; they need attention, help in learning how to get what they need in positive ways, and someone to reach out to them. However, what they frequently *get* is punishment, anger, rejection, and segregation—responses that ensure that they feel more anger, hurt, and loneliness (see Figure 10.5). They also are often placed in an "alternative school" or in special education classes for students with emotional disturbance (Kauffman, 2008) with other students having similar difficulties—in a setting where positive role models are not available and where students learn poor behaviors from one another.

FIGURE 10.4

Vicious Cycle in Behavioral Challenges

Source: From "Support and Positive Teaching Strategies," by W. Hitzing, 1994. In S. Stainback & W. Stainback (Eds.), *Inclusion: A guide for educators.* Baltimore: Paul H. Brookes Publishing Co., Inc. Adapted by permission.

FIGURE 10.5

Needs of Students and Typical Responses

WHAT STUDENTS NEED	WHAT THEY OFTEN GET
Care and love	Rejection
Sense of belonging	Segregation (special education class, alternative school)
Support	
Attention	Anger
Respect	Punishment
Help with learning positive ways to get needs and desires met	Humiliation
Encouragement	

Proactive Responses to Social and Behavioral Challenges:
From Punishment and Control to Choice and Care

There is good news, however. Surprising as it may seem, when we respond proactively to students based on the principles we outline in this chapter, students often will move toward prosocial, responsible behavior. It's the difference between being kept in a jail by hated taskmasters and joining a family that has fun together. Responding proactively is not easy, of course, though on occasion we'll be surprised as a serious problem seems simply to vanish. Perhaps hardest for us will be learning how to shift from teacher-centered to student-centered teaching. Let's look at some key strategies that promote positive interactions and prevent vicious cycles.

Meeting Student Needs

When we see puzzling and troubling student behavior we ask, "What need is not being met for this child?" Every action communicates a message. When we work to meet student needs we do so in two ways: (1) preventive and (2) responsive (Janney & Snell, 2000b). For each need we constantly seek to provide opportunities that *prevent* problems from occurring. We work to create a class that is fun, safe, and emotionally secure. In other words, if we want students to act respectfully, our class must be a place they enjoy, where they feel physically and emotionally safe, where they know we care about them. Anything short of this and we become one of the factors creating behavioral problems (Albert, 1996; Hitzing, 1994; Kohn, 1996b, 1999).

We also see a student always as a *person*. As students cause us trouble, we can too easily focus only on their problem behavior. We get angry or upset and often distance ourselves, depersonalize our actions. By doing this we may actually exacerbate problems. Treating our students with respect as people is a simple but powerful approach. We talk with respect, no matter what students have done (Glasser, 1992, 2000; Kameenui & Darch, 1995; Lovett, 1996; Maag, 1997; Paley 1990). When teachers lose control of their words, they have forgotten that the only person whose behavior they can control is their own and they have jeopardized the community in the classroom. We are always modeling what we want students to do in challenging situations.

We also seek to *respond* effectively, understanding that challenging behaviors demonstrate unmet needs. We help students find ways to meet their needs in positive ways. To explore proactive strategies, let's again use Glasser's (1992, 2000) model of human needs.

Survival. Many children come to school with their basic needs insufficiently met. We cannot change their home environments, but we need to be aware of their intense feelings. To help, we can keep some basic food supplies from the cafeteria in the room for students who are hungry, allow water bottles, and find people with whom students can talk. We can also be aware of how children respond emotionally, sometimes feeling a sense of panic and fear. Some children with autism, for example, respond with panic to loud noises. For such students we can reduce noises and provide extra support through social stories and other strategies.

Love. Many children do not feel loved and accepted. One way to combat this is to create times and places where socializing is part of classroom activities. When students need approval, we ask them to take a message to a group, send them to talk to another student who is upset, or simply get very excited over an assignment they have done well and ask them to share it with another student. Of course, preventing students from being segregated into special classes is a key strategy in helping reduce isolation and create a sense of belonging. In addition, teaching that utilizes cooperative learning and peer buddies provides opportunities for the growth of relationships (Amado, 1993; Hughes et al., 1999). When students cause problems, we figure ways to meet the situation positively. A seventh-grade teacher told about Erma, a student who frequently left her desk to go talk to friends when she was supposed to be completing her work. The teacher decided to incorporate more social time, not less, into Erma's daily schedule.

Power. Students who have been denied power can be the most challenging. When students act out, our instinct is often to want to *reduce* their efforts to achieve power. Therefore, when we intentionally develop strategies to give these students *more* power, it can feel very risky. Yet we can find ways to do so that will make a difference (Kunc, 1998; Smull & Harrison, 1992; Walker & Walker, 1991). Examples:

■ A student stands up in the middle of class and tells us this lesson is crap. We ask to meet with him at the end of the class. We ask him if he would work with us to redesign how we teach the lesson. Surprised, he agrees.

■ Jay is always bullying younger students. We tell him that we can't let that happen. We ask him what he would like to do to make amends. We give him some choices—tutoring children after school (under supervision), taking a child on a field trip with a group, volunteering to help at a local circus.

■ Create classroom jobs for each student so each one has control over a specific area or type of classroom situation. These jobs stay constant all year so the student truly owns the job and has both the control and the responsibility of it.

■ Have each student be an "expert" in something he or she can share with others. The teacher then intentionally sends students to the expert for help.

■ Involve students in making decisions—choosing topics on which to focus, solving problems in the classroom, selecting order of activities for the day. The teacher then puts into action the choices that were made by the students.

Fun. Making our class fun is an ongoing process. We use students' interests to get them into learning. If a student is interested in cars, for example, we can take a physics concept and revolve it around cars; in language arts we can provide reading materials and research information for a project on types of transportation. We can use many other strategies too:

■ Incorporating multiple intelligences—music, dance, art, drama—on a daily basis into the learning

■ Playing games, particularly cooperative games, that connect to learning material in a fun way

■ Laughing a lot, telling funny jokes, using humor

■ Sharing aspects of our lives, at the start of the day and particularly in reading any material when we are modeling making connections to the work

When students react in ways that tell us they are not having fun, rather than punishing and making our class even more grim, we look for ways to respond. If Jalessa interrupts the class by making funny faces, we give her the job of telling a joke to the class once a week. Or suppose students at the back of our high school algebra class, who have been having trouble with the class work, are constantly laughing together. We ask them to lead the class in a discussion regarding how to make algebra fun. They surprise us by making a play out of a homework assignment.

Freedom. If we have a class in which there is little chance of choice and freedom, students will create their own choices. How can we provide freedom for students in our class when we are supposed to be "in charge" as the teacher? Here are some examples:

■ Provide choice time, a time when students may choose from any of several different activity options related to the study topic.

■ Allow students to sit where they want.

■ Have water or snacks that can be taken when needed.

■ Have students choose books to read and write stories on subjects they select.

Starting Inclusion with Students Labeled Emotionally Disturbed

Emily Dickinson School
725 West End Avenue
New York, NY 10025

The Emily Dickinson School (P.S. 75) on the Upper West Side of Manhattan has more than 700 students in kindergarten through fifth grade. The school's population reflects the full diversity of the United States, including students of many races, ethnicities, home languages, and with a large range of achievement (with no special gifted and talented program). Since 1997, led by a new principal—Bob O'Brien—the school has become a leader in quality and inclusive education.

Initially, the staff of P.S. 75 decided to focus their inclusive efforts on students from a nearby special education school who were labeled severely emotionally disturbed. P.S. 75 has subsequently supported students with diverse labels, including autism, multiple disabilities, and severe cognitive disabilities.

Working closely with Philip Santise, the principal of the self-contained special education school, Bob asked teachers to volunteer for the inclusion program—which was initially supported by the New York Statewide Systems Change Project. That first year, two third-grade teachers successfully included one student in each classroom. In 2002, approximately 100 children with IEPs who required special education teacher support were fully included in 15 different general education classrooms at every grade level, including 7 students in dual-language classrooms (Spanish/English).

The principal and the teachers were relieved to find that as more and more students with disabilities were fully included, schoolwide test scores increased, particularly for children who were considered "at risk" and had lower test scores. Support by special education teachers helped make this difference. There are currently six special education teachers who spend their days in two or three classrooms each, supporting not only the 100 children with IEPs but the general education students as well. These teachers provide support services including team teaching, small group instruction, curriculum adaptations and modifications, and some pull-out services for groups of children.

The teachers at P.S. 75 have benefited from the expertise of the special education teachers and administrators, particularly in regard to positive behavioral support plans and ways to work with children in emotional crisis. The administrators from the two schools blended resources to provide joint professional development resources and ongoing in-class supports.

By Celia Oyler, Associate Professor, Teachers College, Columbia University, NY. Edited by Michael Peterson.

Providing Information for Learning: Moving Beyond Constant Power Struggles

To communicate respectfully with students, we need the strength to communicate clearly to them our expectations along with the warmth through which we show we care. Too often we vacillate between being overly warm and being too strong. The more information we can give students—feedback, strategies, ways to think, and more—the less we have to use power to control their behavior (Figure 10.6) (Kunc, 1998). Let's look at specific strategies for giving students information in respectful ways.

Communicating to Promote Learning. Figure 10.7 summarizes contrasting approaches of control versus respect (Faber et al., 1995; Kunc, 1998). The feature illustrates some helpful strategies—and some practices to avoid or minimize. Let's explore

FIGURE 10.6

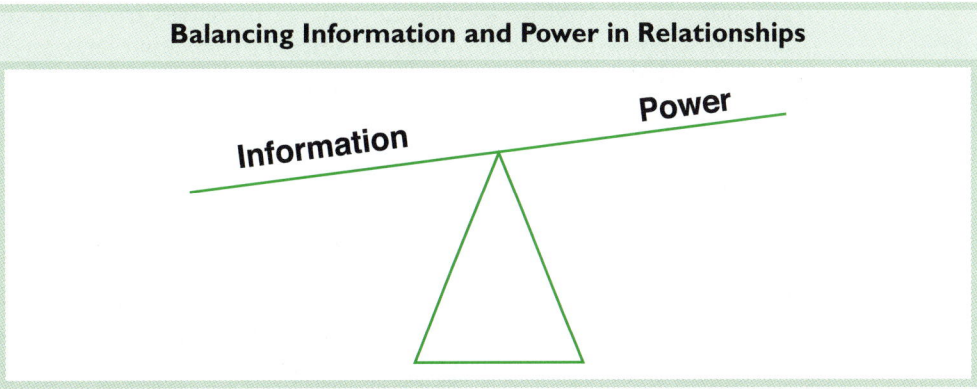

Balancing Information and Power in Relationships

Source: Kunc (1998).

these strategies and practices a bit. A student is running down the hall screaming. Rather than *assuming* we know what is going on ("That Brad is screwing around again, just showing off"), we can express *curiosity:* "Wow, what is going on? What's up?" This response prompts us to attend to the student in a different way.

In the same situation, one teacher might yell, "Don't run in the hall! You know the rules!"—an obvious demand that calls on authority. Another teacher seeing the same student might say, "Walk, please," a request. One response *demands* obedience, whereas the other respectfully *requests* compliance. A demand gives a student no choice; a request conveys the power to choose.

As we work through conflicts, we explore multiple ways to solve problems. Rather than assuming we know *the* way, we can work out solutions. Relatedly, as we interact with students we can help them *understand the rationale* for our requests as opposed to using our *authority* and the implied force behind it.

We also seek to use clear **I-statements.** Rather than saying, "You must not leave campus to go to lunch," we say, "I want you to be safe. This rule was made to help keep you safe. I hope you will follow it because I care about you." The difference is tremendous. Once again, we become a person and they are given choices.

FIGURE 10.7

Communication Based on Respect or Control: Philosophies at War in Practice

RESPECT	CONTROL
Curiosity	Assumption of intent
Request	Demand
Third alternative	One right way
Rationale/explanation	Authority
Clear I-statements	"You should" statements
Sharing/disclosure	Professional distance
Listening/support	Domination/coercion
Negotiation	Rewards/punishments

Source: Adapted from Kunc (1998).

Often we hear that we should maintain a professional distance from our students and not get involved personally. Distancing ourselves from our students and their families supposedly enhances our authority. In fact, however, our real impact comes from the relationships with our students and the care they feel from us. Therefore, we *share about our life,* our feelings, our thoughts. We help students see us processing what to do, share our own insecurities. We may fear that this will promote a sense of weakness, but the opposite actually occurs. As William reached out to Quincy earlier in this chapter, so we can connect with our students on a personal level. We can move to being a person rather than only an authority figure.

We also *listen* to students. Stephen Covey (1989) stated that a characteristic of effective people is that they seek "first to understand, and then to be understood." Further, we use good facilitation skills to *reflect back to them* what we hear them saying and the underlying thoughts or feelings that are coming through. "Morice, you seem tense. I know you've been under a lot of stress lately." "Jean, you're telling me that you're exhausted because you were sick all night. That must make you feel a lot of pressure right now." This approach contrasts dramatically with discipline by domination and coercion: "Morice, get in your seat right now." "Jean, I don't care what happened last night, you know your responsibilities."

We *negotiate* with students to help them meet their needs. We try constantly to understand students; we are neither a pushover nor a dictator but set expectations, communicate these, and work out arrangements so the needs of all can be met.

We help students understand themselves, too, and help them *set their own goals and evaluate their behavior.* Reality therapy, as mentioned earlier, is one useful approach for this purpose. In reality therapy a teacher approaches a student and poses a series of questions that go something like this: "You are doing this. What do you think the result of this action will be? Is this what you want? If not, what do you want? What do you need to do to get what you want?"

A Time for Power and Control

On occasion, we will need to use our power to control a situation that is out of hand (Kunc, 1998). In order to understand when to respond this way, however, we can think through our *"nonnegotiables"*—conduct that is simply intolerable. What is nonnegotiable and why? Too often we create difficulties when we define reasonably minor items as nonnegotiables. Do we seek greater control and compliance than is useful or necessary? In some situations, what is considered nonnegotiable may actually not be that important—rules about raising one's hand to talk, being quiet, and staying seated unless permission is asked. Other situations, however, are dangerous; for example, a student may be hitting other students, kicking, or throwing chairs. When students do cross the line, we may have to use our power and control. When we need to assert direct authority, it will be easier if we have a history of positive relationships. It is also important to exert control in a respectful manner:

1. Use a caring tone of voice and gestures.
2. Provide a reason why something is nonnegotiable.
3. Be respectful. "I know this is important to you, but . . ." (Kunc, 1998).

Engaging the Classroom Community in Problem Solving

In typical classrooms, when behavioral problems occur, the teacher takes charge of the situation and metes out rewards and punishments. In a more effective class, however, the classroom community is involved. As teachers, we do have responsibility for our class.

To fulfill this responsibility effectively, however, we support students in their efforts both to master the curriculum and to grapple with social and behavioral issues. For this support to work, our classroom community must have mechanisms and forums by which conflicts and problems are solved.

Class Meetings. Class meetings are an effective way to solve daily problems. These can be scheduled or created on the spur of the moment. In these meetings the teacher is a participant, not a leader, in a problem-solving discussion. Students discuss, create, and implement solutions (Developmental Studies Center, 1994; Elias et al., 1997; Glasser, 1992). Let's observe such a meeting.

Stephanie is a high school English teacher. As we enter her class, she is in the corner of the room in an intense conversation with two boys. The two students clearly were in a conflict with each other and the teacher earlier in the class. The tension among the three of them is strong.

As we sit down, Stephanie is describing her feelings to Mark and Nathan regarding their rude actions. She explains why their behavior was not helpful. She clearly is upset, but she speaks calmly, with no judgment in her inflections. After talking awhile, Stephanie and the boys join the rest of the class, who gather at the front of the room. She asks Mark and Nathan to explain their reactions. Classmates then share how they felt. They are encouraged to use I-statements, such as "I felt mad when you said that to me" but are not permitted to interrupt, yell, or accuse. Following their discussion, the class creates a plan for what to do the next time. The boys reluctantly suggest they read a funny skit tomorrow and decide to write in a special journal that Stephanie will keep available when they have something vital to tell her.

Later in the day, in contrast to this, the teacher down the hall has the same two students. When they act out, she first tries sarcasm, then yells at them. Finally they are sent to the office, where they receive 2 days' suspension. Unfortunately, there is no plan in place for the next time, and they certainly do not feel that this teacher cares about them.

Circles of Friends. As we discussed in Chapter 9, circles of friends can be a powerful tool both to prevent problems and to deal with challenges. Any student who needs support can have such a group, and many children benefit by participating in one.

Peer and Conflict Mediation. Many schools are establishing school- and districtwide "peacemaker programs" to train volunteer students in **conflict resolution** and **peer mediation** (Fisher & Ury, 1991; Fletcher, 1986; Johnson & Johnson, 1995; Lane & McWhitter, 1992; Porro, 1996). However, we can do this in our own class as well (Paley, 1992). Conflict resolution programs give opportunities for certain children to volunteer to be "peacemakers" or peer mediators. It is important that volunteers represent a mix of the class—that they come from different ability levels, genders, and ethnic groups, for example. Students receive training in helping other students. Here's how it works in the peacemaker program. If two or more children are having a problem, they approach a child designated as a peacemaker, who asks each student: "Do you want to solve a problem?" Each child then gets a turn to tell his or her story. When one speaks, the other listens. When each understands the other, the peacemaker facilitates a discussion regarding solutions. In several schools teachers report that peacemaking has become an integral part of teaching and problem solving at their school. Children begin using language like "I feel" and "I need" and begin listening to others' points of view. One urban school reported that parents were even learning such skills from their children (Baer, 1994; Fine, 1994).

Peer Supports. Students can help one another in many ways. We create structures to encourage this, such as "peer buddy" programs, in which students work together on certain assigned topics or help a newcomer become accustomed to the school. When a

At William Grace Elementary students with severe disabilities are included as part of the learning community. Students love helping Kasandra be a full part of their class. Here they are on the playground.

community has been built, however, students also will naturally help each other in unpredictable ways. They will read together, help with classwork, talk to a hurting student, or calm down an angry friend. When we expect learners to help and teach them how, they do so in ways that are invaluable in encouraging those with behavior struggles. No matter what the problem—whether it is about the loss of a boyfriend, a bad grade, or calling names, and whether the children are very young or in high school— students can help each other through problems. Indeed, students often accept the help of a peer when they will not talk openly to an adult (Farmer, Pearl, & Van Acker, 1996; Hughes et al., 1999; Rosenberg, McKeon, & Dinero, 1999).

Giving Students and Ourselves a Break

Sometimes teachers and students simply need a break from one another. Typically, teachers send students to the office as a punishment. We suggest that this and similar tactics be used less as punishments than as ways of giving us and students a break. Explain this idea to the student and suggest that we both might use the time to think and then get together to talk. We also make arrangements with colleagues to allow the student to come to their classroom, or ask the school social worker or psychologist to assist us when things get to be too much.

Better yet, we can create places for breaks for students to get away on their own initiative, a "safe place." These could be locations in or near our classroom—under our desk, in the reading corner, in the hall. Some high schools have established open student support rooms where students can come at any time for help or to study, talk, or just hang out. Similarly, one elementary school established a quiet, pleasant location next to the principal's office where students could come when they needed to get away. Often a safe place has supplemental items to help the children calm down. These vary by age of the students but include squishy balls to manipulate, a small blanket or stuffed animal to cuddle up with, paper and colored pens to write a note to a trusted friend, or a CD with relaxing music and headphones. All these strategies are helpful in giving a student a place to be alone to process emotions.

Taking a break allows us to break the cycle of conflict and to regather our thoughts and emotions. This approach is also a sharp contrast to forced "time-outs" for students, which require that students sit out their lunchtime or recess in the school office, and to in-school suspension, in which students are required to go to a special room supervised by a counselor or teacher.

Utilizing Professional and Community Supports

A range of professional supports are available for working with social and behavioral difficulties. Here are a few of the most widely available types of services; many additional variations have been developed based on unique resources in local communities (Garbarino et al., 1992; McLane et al., 1997):

1. **Support groups** for students with special problems and needs—divorcing parents, death in the family, drug abuse, pregnancy, and so on
2. Consultation support concerning student needs, provided to teachers by a psychologist, social worker, or counselor
3. Individual counseling
4. Group counseling; most effective when students participate voluntarily rather than being referred for "behavior problems"

Although these professional services can be helpful, they are not sufficient to help students solve serious behavioral problems. Counseling and support groups help students begin to understand themselves—to identify, label, and think about their feelings. However, students need daily practice and learning through modeling and gentle instruction. Our class is a key place where this occurs.

Engaging Parents in Partnership

Engaging parents is critical. We want to reach out to parents as partners. We walk a fine line here, however, for a parent may be an important contributor to the social or behavioral problem a child is having. We have to reach out, communicate, and listen carefully. On the other hand, we have to be careful not to make unwarranted assumptions (Garbarino et al., 1992; Koegel, Koegel, Kellegrew, & Mullen, 1996). Several strategies are particularly useful when we are dealing with families in relation to behavioral concerns:

- Be aware of the history of the family, of the challenges the family faces, and of how these have affected the child. Ask the parents about their lives.
- Tell parents the problems that are showing up in school and ask whether they see similar things at home. Ask their opinion as to what to do.
- Although families of children with behavioral problems often have many problems themselves, look at the strengths of the family. Focus and build on these.
- Communicate with the family about positive attributes of the child and about the child's growth and successes as well as about his or her problems.
- With some students, consider sending home frequent "behavior reports."
- Also be aware, however, of the dynamics in the family. In some situations in which children are being abused, negative reports from the school can set off additional abuse.

FIGURE 10.8

Selected Proactive Approaches to Social and Behavioral Challenges	
NAME OF APPROACH	**KEY RESOURCE**
Conscious discipline	Becky Bailey (2001). *Conscious Discipline*. Love Guidance Press.
Circle of courage	Larry Brendtro (2003). *Reclaiming Youth at Risk*. Solution Tree Press.
Collaborative problem solving	Ross Greene (2008). *Lost at School: Why Our Kids with Behavioral Challenges Are Falling through the Cracks and How We Can Help Them*. Scribner.
Limit setting	Robert J. MacKenzie (2003). *Setting Limits in the Classroom: How to Move Beyond the Dance of Discipline*. Three Rivers Press.
Cooperative discipline	Linda Albert (1996). *Cooperative Discipline*. AGS.

A Few Useful Resources

A plethora of books are available that deal with challenging behaviors of students. These vary greatly in philosophy and approach. In Figure 10.8 we provide some selected resources that use the strategies and ways of thinking suggested in this chapter and that provide much more extensive information.

Individualized Differentiation for Behavior:
The Behavioral Intervention Plan

Educators who utilize the positive approaches outlined in this chapter (and in recommended references) will be fulfilling both the spirit and the letter of the law. Sometimes, however, students' behavioral problems are so puzzling and challenging that we need to develop a formal **Behavioral Intervention Plan (BIP)** for a student. This may be part of a student's IEP, Section 504 plan, or part of a plan desired by the school staff or parents. Although the student's problem may be complex, the BIP steps are simple (see Albin et al., 1994; Hitzing, 1994; Janney & Snell, 2000b; Koegel, Koegel, & Dunlap, 1996).

Step 1: Identify Social and Behavioral Problem(s). We first identify the behaviors about which we are concerned, explaining in clear terms exactly what a student does. Rather than saying, "Justine is angry all the time," we describe what exactly Justine does, how she shows her anger. "Many times when boys in the class talk with Justine, she will grimace at them and tell them loudly to go away. She argues with friends during lunch and sits at the back of the class and sulks." This paints a clearer picture. To raise our level of awareness further, we keep a running record in which we describe students' academic, social, and behavioral actions. This illuminates the interconnections between instruction and the behaviors.

Step 2: Develop a Student-Centered Theory. Recently we talked with a teacher who was having a lot of trouble with a student. She was desperate to figure out a strategy that would "control this student's behavior." However, when we asked, "*Why* is this student acting this way?" she did not know. The question had not been asked by anyone. When we go through a systematic process of looking at a student's behavior to determine its strength and the underlying causes or situations that trigger the problem, we are doing a version of a **functional assessment** (O'Neill, Horner, Albin, Storey, & Sprague, 1996). Rather than responding only to the behavior itself (most often merely symptomatic of the real issue), we seek to understand what is going on and to develop a theory that will give us a sound basis for devising strategies to help the student. Rather than asking, "How can I control this kid?" we then ask questions like the following (Albin et al., 1994; Evans & Meyer, 1985; Hitzing, 1994; Janney & Snell, 2000b):

- What is the quality of life for the student?
- Why is this behavior occurring? What is the person trying to communicate through this behavior? What legitimate human need is being signaled?
- To what people, places, choices, and activities is the student connected?
- What is going on at home or in the community that affects the student?
- From what resources does the student draw emotional strength and support?
- How well does the student communicate? Through what modalities most effectively?
- Why does this behavior concern me? Is it really important, or is the problem more about my need for control?
- How can I help the student not feel the need to react this way?

With these questions in mind we gather information. We talk with students, have them write about their homes and lives as part of classroom literacy activities, observe them in the school, talk with parents and others who know the students, and make home visits. The key here is to focus on understanding the student but not to be rigid about how we gather information. We seek to understand the *student's story* as it is now and as it has unfolded in the past.

Often we will need to think carefully about what was going on before and around the time that a behavioral incident occurred—what behaviorists call "antecedent information." This information signals a specific need or feeling the person is trying to communicate. Useful questions include (Janney & Snell, 2000b):

- *Who* is present? How many people? Is someone coming or going?
- *What* is going on when the behavior occurs? Is there a pattern? What is happening when the behavior *never* occurs? In what type of task is the student involved—reading, math, gym? Is the task too hard or too easy? Is the student waiting a turn?
- *When* does the behavior occur? Is there a pattern? Before lunch? Just before the end of the day?
- *Where* does the behavior occur? On the playground? In class, in the office, at home, at the movies, at the grocery store? In a large open space or a closed space?

As we look at the *behavior itself,* we count and record the time of day, duration, and strength of the behavior. Recording forms exist for this purpose, and we use them to graph behaviors. Behavioral interventionists often use such charts to track the impact of strategies on behaviors. Such information focuses our thoughts more clearly on the problem.

We also want to pay attention to the *consequences* of the behavior. What occurred after the behavior? Did the person obtain desired outcomes? We also look for clues in the student's total life, bringing together what we know about the student's story, life, behaviors, and expressions of thoughts and feelings as we listen for *patterns* (Evans & Meyer, 1985; Hitzing, 1994; Janney & Snell, 2000b).

As we proceed, we develop a theory about what is happening. This theory will guide our subsequent efforts to develop strategies to meet the students' needs. Out of this process we articulate a coherent, if tentative, view regarding (1) why the behaviors are occurring, the (2) underlying needs of the student, and (3) strategies to help the student meet his or her needs in a more positive way.

We involve the student in all parts of this process. It should come as no surprise to the student that we are targeting certain behaviors. We want to know what students think of their own behavior and whether they think it needs to change. We engage families and students in gathering information, in helping us all to understand what is going on. Most important, we communicate with students about their needs and desires and explore better ways to meet these. What is important in the whole process is that we seek to be a partner with students and families rather than sitting back as the "professional authority."

Step 3: Develop and Implement a Plan. When students exhibit serious behavioral problems, we develop a written plan that can be part of the IEP or Section 504 plan (see chapter 4) for a student or a tool that is used informally in class. Whether we develop a formal written plan or an informal working strategy, we need the same information (Albin et al., 1994; Hitzing, 1994).

- Behaviors of concern
- Planned responses to behaviors or strategies to prevent and respond to behavioral problems
- Roles of teachers, support staff, parents, and others
- Method of evaluating the success of the plan
- A mechanism for reviewing the outcome and making necessary revisions.

Many different formats are used for documentation. Especially important are forms for recording strategies that include space for (1) prevention, (2) teaching new social and behavioral skills, and (3) responding to crisis situations (Janney & Snell, 2000b).

Step 4: Evaluate Outcomes Together. A key difference between control strategies and student-centered approaches lies in the question, "How do we know when an approach that aims to deal with a behavioral problem actually works?" Under a control philosophy, authority figures identify the problem. A strategy is deemed successful when the problem behavior disappears or when desired behaviors occur: The student quits fighting, or he reads when he is told.

However, a student-centered approach turns this around. Although the perspective of others in the setting will be important, we are *most* interested in the viewpoint of the student. For if behaviors are related to a range of individual needs, it will not be possible to eliminate or create behaviors without addressing the key needs of the person. In this view, the problem is solved when the needs of the person are met according to the *student's* viewpoint (Hitzing, 1994; Lovett, 1996).

Nonviolent Crisis Intervention

The strategies we've outlined will be sufficient to deal with most social and behavioral problems. Sometimes, however, crises erupt after building over a long period of time. At these moments, we need strategies for nonviolent crisis intervention.

Fisher and Ury (1991) describe three types of negotiating styles used in crisis situations: (1) soft, (2) hard, and (3) principled. **Soft negotiators** tend to focus on the relationship and may even fear conflict more than the problem itself. Such individuals often try to ignore issues rather than deal with them. **Hard negotiators**, on the other hand, seek to win no matter what the costs. **Principled negotiators** avoid both of these extremes. Separating the person from the problem, they seek a situation where all have their needs met and are treated with respect.

In some cases problems may escalate into a crisis in which a student loses control and may become dangerous. Figure 10.9 illustrates five typical stages of crisis and a range of both helpful and counterproductive responses. At any point in time during a crisis, the problem may escalate to a higher or lower level of threat depending on how those involved respond.

Often the development of a crisis begins with an individual who is experiencing unusual *anxiety*. This anxiety may show itself in several forms—noncompliance, disruption, extreme withdrawal. If we can listen, be supportive, be curious, and expect positive results, students are likely to settle down. However, if we act in authoritarian ways—directing students to act, setting limits, or labeling them or their behaviors—we often push them to the next level.

At the next level, some action may spark a response. Often this **trigger** will be trivial—a dirty look, a nasty comment, one person's stepping on another's shoes; but such triggers often set off feelings of rejection, unworthiness, and consequent shame (Gilligan, 1996). In this stage we see student challenges escalate—questioning, refusals to comply, emotional outbursts of anger or crying. Nonhelpful but too typical responses involve demands for compliance, threats, and punishment. The person does not feel heard, and the anxiety he or she felt in the first place goes up.

Depending on the person and the situation, the highest levels of *crisis* can take many forms, ranging from intimidation and threats to serious violence to property or people. Those using a paradigm of control will simply match the force of the person with force of their own—moving in, showing anger, and threatening either in words or in actions to retaliate and punish.

Lantieri and Patti (1996) outlined options in this stage: (1) avoid; (2) diffuse; or (3) confront, either (a) violently or (b) nonviolently. Soft negotiators tend to avoid the conflict, although this is often problematic. Hard negotiators tend to move toward the use of violence to "take down" students. However, those involved in **nonviolent crisis intervention** use other strategies, as shown in Figure 10.9. These negotiators suggest that we take steps to cool off, share our view of what is occurring while agreeing to work out a solution, and brainstorm solutions. In the most desperate of situations, such actions often help calm the person and allow us to find alternatives that prevent violence and actually promote learning and growth.

What might this kind of intervention look like? Consider this scenario.

Darius came in looking very glum this morning. Carmen, his teacher, knew he'd been having a tough time lately. Before she knew it, however, things escalated. Darius was at the back of the room, screaming and holding a knife on Mitchell. Terrified, Carmen nevertheless stopped, breathed deeply, and said, "Darius, you're really making us afraid. We know you've had a hard time lately and we all want to help you. We can do that. Would you please give me the knife." She stopped and waited, watching him and making eye contact. It seemed an eternity. However, he slumped just a bit, handed the knife to her, and sat down at the back of the class with his arms over his head.

The subsequent phases following the crisis provide an opportunity to help students think about their reactions. This is not a time for blame but a time for listening, sharing,

FIGURE 10.9

Proactive Crisis Management

STAGES OF CRISIS DEVELOPMENT	COUNTERPRODUCTIVE RESPONSES	HELPFUL RESPONSES
Anxiety demonstrated by . . . Noncompliance Disruption Unusual actions	*Issue Directive:* "Do this!" *Set limits:* "You can't do that." *Establish consequences:* "If you do this, I will . . ." *Label the student:* "You're . . . a problem, an angry child . . ."	*Listen and reflect:* "Mary, you seem upset today." *Express curiosity:* "What's going on?" *Be supportive:* "I'm here if you want to talk." *Partner:* "Let's work together on this." *Express healthy expectations:* "It will be OK."
Trigger: Action sets crisis in motion . . . Questioning—"Why do we have to?" Refusal Emotional outburst *Crisis:* A serious crisis develops. We see . . . Intimidation Threat Violence	*Demand compliance:* "Sit down!" *Apply consequences:* "You will get an F for this course." *Make threat/intimidate:* "Stop or I will call your mother." *Show anger:* "Back off!" With loud voice and flushed face. *Move in:* Move toward screaming student to stop him. *Retaliate/expel:* "Go to the office now!" *Punish:* "You lose your privileges for the week!"	*Cool off:* Take some deep breaths, acknowledge feelings. *Agree to work it out:* Show willingness to solve problem and let person know you are ready to discuss issues. *Give personal point of view:* Give your point of view using I-statements. *Solve the problem:* Brainstorm win–win solutions.
Recovery: Student settles down and feels . . . Embarrassment Guilt Shame *Resolution* Calm	*Blame:* "You always act this way." *Use instruction to retaliate:* "I've told you, walk out when you feel upset. What is wrong with you?" *Remind of crisis:* "You were out of control earlier, you know." *Avoid:* Teacher won't look at student. *Expect recurrence:* "He's going to go off again if they don't get him out of my class."	*Listen:* "You look like you are sad." *Support:* "How can I help?" *Normalize crisis:* "All of us have times when we lose it." *Make personal disclosure:* "I did this when I was your age." *Collaborate:* "How can we work together to help you?" *Analyze:* "What happened? What would have helped you?" *Problem-solve:* "What would be better next time you have these feelings? How can we help you deal with the issues facing you?"

Sources: Adapted from Kunc (1998) and Lantier and Patti (1996).

and reflecting. It is a time for all involved to help students think through their needs and explore ways to get those needs met. Helping students find ways to make amends in interaction with the classroom community can be particularly effective and powerful.

IDEA and Behavioral Challenges
What the Special Education Law Says

The Individuals with Disabilities Education Improvement Act of 2004 maintained the procedures related to behavioral challenges of students with disabilities that became part of the law for the first time in 1997. Concerns with student discipline continued to spark substantial debate in Congress during the reauthorization process. The IDEA provisions include the following:

1. *Suspension and expulsion.* Schools frequently suspend and expel students who cause behavioral problems. However, as an assistant principal said, "We send students home for 3 days. They come back to school and cause more problems. We suspend them again. We are not doing anything." Schools using **suspension and expulsion** seldom have a strategy for helping students learn new ways of behaving. In response to this reality, the law stipulates that students with disabilities can be expelled or suspended for problem behaviors only if the behaviors are shown *not to be directly related to the disability* of the student. However, a student may be removed from the school for up to 10 days, even over the parents' objection, if such procedures are consistent with the treatment of students without disabilities. A student who brings a weapon to school or uses or sells illegal drugs may be removed from the school for up to 45 school days. During this time school personnel work with the student and parents to develop a Behavioral Intervention Plan (Janney & Snell, 2000b; Koegel, Koegel & Dunlap, 1996).

2. *Manifestation determination review.* A team must meet to determine if problematic behaviors are directly related to a student's disability. The team conducts a review of student information within no more than 10 days after a student is suspended or removed from the classroom for behavioral problems. If there is a direct relationship between the student's disability and his or her behavior, the school must develop a Behavioral Intervention Plan (BIP).

3. *Behavioral Intervention Plan (BIP).* A plan to address behavioral concerns must be developed by a team as part of the IEP when the "behavior impedes his or her learning or that of others, and must consider, when appropriate, strategies, including positive behavioral interventions, and supports" (IDEA, 2004). At best, a BIP will be developed when behavioral challenges are evident, rather than after a crisis has occurred. A BIP can be developed for any student with a disability, not only for those classified as emotionally disturbed.

4. *Functional assessment.* A *functional assessment* is required whenever a school removes a child from his or her current educational placement. The intent of such an assessment will be to assist the school in developing a BIP for the student.

Moving On to Respect

Dealing with social and emotional challenges is an important part of our journey. Students belong in caring classroom communities in which peers help them work out their problems. They deserve to be treated with respect and to have help in achieving their own goals and meeting their needs. They deserve teachers who are in control of

FIGURE 10.10

Characteristics of Classrooms Practicing Positive, Relationship-Based Behavioral Support

1. Adults demonstrate commitment to working with all students who are presenting behavioral difficulties—to keep them within the general education class and demonstrate to students that they are cared for.

2. Students are rewarded primarily through natural reinforcers such as genuine recognition and appreciation, valued activities, accomplishments; formal reward and punishment systems are avoided.

3. Children are supported in providing assistance to one another in dealing with feelings and behaviors through a variety of structures, including classroom meetings, training and implementation of conflict resolution, peer buddies, and circles of support.

4. Teachers incorporate instruction and learning regarding how to deal with conflict, feelings, and behaviors of concern as an integral part of the curriculum.

5. Educators treat students with respect and talk with them in ways that encourage them to communicate their feelings and concerns.

6. Teachers and other educators engage students in dialogue and negotiate goals and strategies concerning behaviors and responses to feelings on which they need to work.

7. When students have challenging behaviors, adults carefully consider what legitimate needs the students are trying to meet through the behaviors.

8. When students are so wounded and hurt emotionally that they need concrete rewards to aid them, adults negotiate such rewards with students based on their own interests, choices, and needs.

9. When students have serious emotional and behavioral challenges, teachers work with a school-based, interdisciplinary team to conduct an intensive assessment to determine the roots of the behaviors and develop an intervention plan.

10. A crisis team designed to provide support to defuse dangerous behavioral challenges supports teachers and other educators.

their own emotions and feelings and can react calmly and respectfully in a situation. They deserve teachers who have thought out a plan of action and are concerned with each student's success, a place where actions are intentional instead of random and reactionary. With this attitude and some solid strategies, we will find ourselves reaching more difficult students than we ever thought possible. Few experiences compare to the feeling of creating bonds with challenging students where they feel safe enough to change their defensive behaviors. It is the reason we continue to work toward a community that includes all children. Figure 10.10 provides a summary of our discussion in this chapter that helps us do this.

Traveling Notes

We are most successful with students when we reach out to develop a caring relationship, even in the midst of challenges; when we move away from power struggles; and when we seek to provide information, helping students learn how to manage their own behavior rather than using our power and authority. Here are a few notes regarding positive practices from this chapter.

1. Teachers who have clearly thought about what they think about teaching children social skills. The things they do in their class are not random or reactionary, but are well thought out and have a purpose.

2. Rewards are used appropriately. The children set goals for themselves and rewards that interest them, rather than being assigned random stickers or trips to a class store.
3. Teachers use goals to help children think about behaviors and how they can improve.
4. When behavior problems occur, teachers ask questions about why the problem is occurring and seek to find the answer in the student's life.
5. Teachers always speak in respectful tones, never yelling or threatening, no matter what the provocation. They model respect and care they want to see from students.
6. Teachers use class meetings to engage the students in problem solving, relinquishing traditional control to further the strengths of the community.
7. Teachers use Glasser's five needs (survival, love and belonging, power, fun, and freedom) to analyze behavior and develop strategies designed to help them meet their needs in positive ways.

Stepping Stones

Following are some activities that will help extend your understanding and actions you may take toward positive behavioral support in your classroom and school.

1. With one or two other teachers, identify the two or three children in your school who are having the worst behavior problems. Bring together a group to brainstorm ideas to help these students and provide teacher support. For each student:
   - Identify the behavior.
   - Seek to understand *why* the behavior is occurring. What *need* is being communicated?
   - Develop some ideas that focus on helping the student meet his or her needs in a more positive way while ensuring that other students and the teacher have their needs met as well.
   - Think together about how this student's situation relates to community—or to a lack of community—in the school.
   - Meet together periodically to assess what is happening, and use this assessment process as an opportunity to learn.
2. Keep a journal regarding how you deal with students in your class who have challenging behaviors. What do you do? Are you punitive, angry, and controlling, or are you seeking to meet the students' needs? Are you treating the students with respect or using power exclusively? If change is needed, what two strategies might you employ to try to shift what is happening?

3. Review the strategies outlined in this chapter and develop a plan regarding how you could make these part of your teaching practice this year. How will you get support for doing this? Share your ideas and plan with another teacher. Find a teacher who is having problems with a child or children in his or her class. (This should not be hard.) Visit the class. First, identify the behavior. Second, think about *why* the behavior is occurring. What *need* is being communicated? How is the current teacher meeting her students' needs? What needs are not being met? Develop some ideas that focus on helping the students meet needs while ensuring that other students and the teacher have their needs met as well.

4. Locate a teacher who has a reputation for dealing effectively with students with challenging behaviors. Talk with the teacher and explore this teacher's ideas about dealing with challenging behaviors.

11 Inclusive Academic Instruction, Part I

Planning Inclusive Lessons and Units

CHAPTER GOAL

Understand the need for improving instruction for all learners and a process for planning multilevel instruction that will support students of varied abilities learning together in inclusive classrooms.

CHAPTER OBJECTIVES

1. Explore best practices in learning and teaching and critique ineffective traditional instructional practices.
2. Understand the steps involved in developing inclusive unit and lesson plans.
3. Learn how to develop authentic topics of study that link several subjects.
4. Be able to state why multilevel instruction is important.
5. Know how to articulate overall learning goals and expectations of various levels of student learning.
6. Learn how to use a range of assessment tools and strategies to support inclusive academic instruction.
7. Understand strategies for enhancing student performance on standardized tests.

In this chapter we will begin a discussion of strategies for inclusive academic instruction. Can this really be done? Can students who are highly gifted really learn well together with students who have significant cognitive disabilities or other learning challenges? It's a great question. The answer, of course, is yes! If we use strategies aimed at helping every student begin from where they are and move to the next level, we'll find, in fact, that teaching is more rewarding, that learning increases, that the students are really enjoying our class, and that we are too!

One day we visited a 5th grade class that was a fully inclusive class. Donald, a student with a severe disability, was a member of this class. He clearly had many friends who helped him in many ways in the class. We talked with Joshua, his best buddy, who explained how Donald used alternative communication devices. He had a few words to say as to how the tool should be improved to help Donald. We thought how much this student was learning to think like an engineer. Later we watched the class working on a project related to maps of their state, and watched Sylvia and Donald working together (see the photo on p. 348). We also had a conversation with the entire class about diversity and about their experience of having Donald in their class. Donald, of course, was part of this discussion, which he clearly enjoyed. We were amazed at these kids. In many ways they said, "We have learned so much by having Donald in our class." That very day, in fact, they had been reading a story about the Holocaust and talking about how people of difference lived together. These students were clearly experiencing this lesson as they learned with Donald.

So let's explore inclusive academic instruction together. Let's start with an example of a lesson designed in a way that allowed students of very different abilities to learn together at their own level.

Sydney's Moose Project

Sydney is now in the ninth grade at Southfield High School. "I really like my school," she explains. "I like math. I like my teachers. I like my friends." Her grandmother, Delores, with whom she now lives says she is doing very well, particularly in algebra. "I work with her on her lessons," Delores says, "but she really does understand the concepts and is able to do the problems. I am proud of her." "Math is my favorite subject," Sydney comments. "My second favorite subject is biology." Sydney is a very active student. She plays clarinet in the band and is active in soccer and baseball. "She is a sports fanatic," says her grandmother with a smile. Sydney is taking all general education classes, though she can go to a media center in the library for help from special education teachers if she needs it. However, she doesn't do this much. "She had some great teachers this year," comments Delores. The algebra teacher even volunteered to meet with her after school.

We first met Sydney when she was in the fifth grade at Kenbrook Elementary School. That year, after many years of tentative steps toward inclusive teaching, the school staff had decided to close their separate classrooms for students with cognitive disabilities and to teach these students in general education classrooms. Sydney was one of those students. She has a cognitive disability, having been born with Down syndrome. Sydney did well that year, which provided a base for her to do well in coming years as well, being exposed to a much more demanding, and interesting, curriculum than she had been receiving in separate special education classes. One project of which she was particularly proud was what she

JOURNEY into the CLASSROOM

Plant and Animal Adaptations
Unit Plan

What you will learn

- The parts or structure of the plant or animal
- Where it lives (habitat)
- Adaptations it has made to survive
- Its survival needs (Where is it on the food chain—predator/prey, consumer/producer, herbivore, carnivore, omnivore?)
- Interesting or unusual facts about your plant or animal

What you will do

Your research

1. Choose a plant or animal that you want to learn about. Find books and Internet sites that will help you in your research. You must use at least two different sources of information.
2. On *index cards* write what you are learning about your plant or animal. This should be written in your own words. Include the title of the Web site, book, or other materials where you found the information.

Your product

1. You will create a *story about your plant or animal*. You may use one of the following two story

starters to get going. The more you know about your plant or animal, the more interesting and detailed your stories will be.

Story starters

- A day in the life: Describe a typical day in your life as if you are your plant or animal. (For example: What kind of place do you live in? How do you spend your day? How do you get along with other animals near you? How do you communicate with other animals?)
- What it would be like: Describe creatively what it would be like to have some of your plant or animal's characteristics. For example: How does it feel to be able to change your skin color and patterns? What does it feel like to have a body temperature that's exactly the same as the air temperature around you? What is it like to have two eyes that can each see different things?

2. In addition, you will *choose a way to present your learning* to the class. Possible ideas are creating a riddle book, a PowerPoint slide show, poetry, a habitat, a skit, or a song.

called her "moose project." In fact, Sydney came to a university class to read her poem and her moose report as a good example of multilevel instruction.

Sydney's moose project illustrates nicely some key elements of good authentic, multi-level instruction. In the Journey into the Classroom feature you see a copy of the lesson plan that her teachers developed. (Two fifth-grade teachers collaborated on many lessons this year. They taught across the hall.) Students had to select a plant or animal and find out specific information. Note how this assignment is open-ended. While criteria were identified, students could successfully complete the project at very different levels of sophistication. The teachers in this class expected the students to work at their **personal best level**. Similarly, you'll note that Sydney got the highest rating on the rubric and earned an A on the project. Does this mean that Sydney was necessarily functioning "at grade level"? No, but she worked hard, learned, made progress, and met all the expectations of the assignment. (You can see a bit of her work in the Journey into the Classroom box.) Other students considered gifted in this class were expected to gather information and develop much more sophisticated products. Sydney wrote one of her teachers, Rod Moeller, a letter of appreciation at the end of school. The teacher particularly thought this statement was important: "I was doing my important work." In other words, Sydney felt successful, valued, and engaged in learning that matters. You can't ask for much more than that in a student!

JOURNEY into the CLASSROOM

Plant and Animal Adaptations
Rubric

Name: Sydney Jones   **Grade: A**

Benchmark Ratings	1	2	3	4
	This doesn't sound like my project.			This sounds like my project
My Research I used my time wisely in class. I stayed focused and on task. I organized my learning and took care of my products, supplies, and materials. I met my deadline for completing my project. I turned in my research notecards and used the facts I learned to write my story and make my presentation. I used at least two different sources.				X X
My Products My narrative story was well written and revised for the Six Traits. I answered all the questions I was asked about my plant or animal. My project was a quality product that clearly demonstrated what I learned.				X X X
My Presentation I spoke clearly and loud enough to be heard. I had rehearsed and was well prepared. My presentation was well organized, well written, and a quality product.				X X

 **JOURNEY into the CLASSROOM** A Day in the Life of a Moose

Excerpt of report by: Sydney Jones (2004)

I am the largest member of the deer family. I can be found in the northern forest in North America, Europe, and Russia. I spend most of my day eating. My favorite foods are weeds, grasses, roots, willow, birch, and aspen twigs.

I will drink water in the lake and walk around. I like to see other animals around me. When walking through wet areas, I spread my toes apart and it makes it possible to move with ease. Some call me a clumsy looking animal, but despite my large size, I'm very fast. I can vanish without making a sound.

> Moose poem
>
> A moose is a mammal,
> It likes to eat plants and twigs
> a moose can be fast and agile,
> Even though they are very big
> If you want to see a moose
> go to the water early in the day,
> If you stay very quiet
> a moose might came your way.

Sydney in the fifth grade.

Sydney as a ninth grader.

 # Disabled Curriculum and Instruction

"Official" and "Classic" Theories of Learning

Early in the 20th century, the "factory" model of schooling—in which students sit in straight rows, listen to lectures, fill out worksheets, read from texts under the watchful eye of the teacher, and are tested by filling in blanks, responding to multiple-choice items, or answering true/false questions—was questioned and challenged, most notably by John Dewey (1938, 1943). He argued that rote study promoted shallow thinking and a dislike for learning; experience in meaningful, real situations, he claimed, was the key to learning.

These critiques continue. For example, Frank Smith (1998) contrasted what he called official and classic theories of learning. The "official" view says that learning is hard work, limited, dependent on rewards and punishment, based on effort, individualistic, easily forgotten, and ensured by testing and memorization. However, Smith points out that students are learning all the time, even though this

> is a frightening thought for many teachers . . . and the students can't help it. They even learn things they might be better off not learning. The problem in school is not that many students aren't learning but what they are learning. . . . If they leave thinking that "school things"—such as reading, writing, mathematics, or history—are boring, difficult, and irrelevant to their lives and that they are "dummies," . . . they learn to be nonreaders or . . . non-spellers or that they can't do mathematics. (F. Smith, 1998, p. 10)

Yet, according to the classic view of learning, learning is continual, effortless, independent of rewards and punishment, and social. Very simply, says Smith (1998) "you learn from the company you keep . . . you become like them . . . . This is learning that is permanent. We rarely forget the interests, attitudes, beliefs, and skills that we acquire simply by interacting with significant people in our lives" (p. 9).

None of the individual elements of traditional teaching is ineffective in itself. Worksheets, lectures, and textbooks can all have an effective place in a best practice class. The problem, however, is that such strategies often form the bulk of instruction. As a group, worksheets, lectures, and textbooks fit together into a paradigm—an integrated overall approach that, according to Kohn (1999) and Haberman (1998), has the following problems:

- The emphasis on memorization engenders little understanding, leading to shallow understanding and lack of motivation.
- Mastery of certain skills—mathematical algorithms, spelling, writing conventions—is seen as separate from the use of such skills and teachers seldom engage students in using skills for real-world purposes.
- Teaching materials are largely textbooks written at one particular level so students for whom the material is too difficult and students for whom it is too simple are both frustrated.
- Instruction occurs largely through strategies that put students in passive roles—lecture, DVDs, and periodic field trips, all. Many students simply disengage.
- Schoolwork is seen as an individual rather than a social effort. Students sit at desks in straight rows and get in trouble if they talk. Consequently, school fails to help students learn critical social skills simultaneously ignoring a powerful source of learning.
- As students get frustrated and bored, they find ways to make the class more interesting. Some act out, play jokes or get in fights. Others simply withdraw. As a result, teachers spend much time maintaining classroom control.
- Evaluation largely occurs through tests that emphasize short-term memorization—multiple-choice, fill-in-the-blank, or true/false exams. Such exams don't require students to demonstrate meaningful understanding or application of skills.

Despite these and other ongoing critiques, traditional schooling practices continue in large part, according to Tyack and Cuban (1995), because this is the mental image people have of what "school is." Public Agenda (1997) conducted a national survey of high school students exploring two questions: (1) What could teachers do to help you in your learning? (2) Do your teachers do these things? The answers were revealing and troubling. Students wanted teachers to know their subject, use engaging learning approaches, and present information in an interesting way. Yet only a small percentage of students reported that their teachers did so. (See Figure 11.1.)

These results correspond with those of another major study of U.S. schools in which researchers found, for example, "a repetitive reinforcement of basic skills . . . throughout the twelve grades—a heavy emphasis on mechanics, textbooks, workbooks, and

FIGURE 11.1

What Helps Students Learn and What Teachers Do: Feedback from Students

STATEMENT	% WHO SAY WOULD BE HELPFUL	% WHO SAY TEACHERS DO
Try to make lessons fun and interesting.	78	24
Are enthusiastic about the subjects they teach.	71	29
Know a lot about the subjects they teach.	71	46
Treat their students with respect.	69	41
Give students a lot of individual help.	69	31
Use hands-on projects and class discussions.	67	22
Explain lessons carefully.	66	33
Challenge students to do better.	66	33
Care about students.	64	30
Know how to handle disruptive students.	46	29

Source: Adapted from a study conducted by Public Agenda, *Getting by: What American Teenagers Really Think About Their Schools.* Summary published in *Education Week,* April 1997, pp. 20–21.

quizzes emphasizing short answers and the recall of specific information" (Goodlad, 1984a, p. 207). More recently, Haberman (1998) and Hale and Franklin (2001) report that such ineffective instructional approaches continue to be the norm, particularly in schools that serve low-income, urban children of color.

The Debate About Good Instruction

While there are many, many variations on teaching strategies, three basic forms stand out: (1) lecture–test instruction (often lecture–worksheet–test instruction); (2) direct instruction; and (3) workshop learning.

The most traditional approach to instruction is **lecture–test instruction.** We all know what this looks like. As in the history class at Garland Heights High School mentioned previously, teachers assign reading in a textbook and then lecture on that same material. Often teachers will include worksheets for practice and homework. Such worksheets typically focus on basic skills: fill-in-the-blank questions, matching words to one another, matching pictures to words, and so on. Students take notes and sometimes view videos. Teachers then give tests—most often multiple choice or true and false.

The second approach is **direct instruction.** This approach focuses on instruction in skills, most often used in reading and math. Students are taught skills by completing worksheets and drills on skills out of the context in which such skills are used. For example, if a teacher wants young children to learn phonemic skills, the most basic sounds in our language, the teacher may lead a lesson reading from a script in which she says words with the long "a" sound and then the students repeat the words.

Interestingly, both lecture–test and direct instruction have a symbiotic relationship. Lecture–test instruction often results in students who have difficulty functioning in these narrowly designed classes. Students are seen as lacking prerequisite skills. For students with special needs, this almost always results in direct instruction of skills—phonemic awareness, phonics, math skills, and so forth in a separate resource or special education classroom.

Workshop learning actively involves students in gathering information, studying critical questions, and working to create products that demonstrate learning. Skills and facts are learned in context of authentic activities. The focus of workshop learning is understanding, meaning, and critical thinking related to important issues.

For sure there are many variations on lecture-test, direct instruction, and workshop learning strategies that go by many names. Teachers also combine aspects of lecture-test and workshop learning to create a hybrid. Many strategies can be used to make lectures and direct instruction more interesting and involve some student interaction. This moves toward workshop learning. However, the basic structure is still the same. Additionally, all workshop classes involve sharing information with the total class to begin with and conducting mini-lessons for direct instruction on skills. Some teachers may even lecture and have students take notes but spend most of their time in workshop learning. Despite these potential overlaps and variations, it's helpful to understand clearly these very different approaches to instruction and their impact on successful inclusive teaching.

Interestingly, despite its prevalence, there is no advocacy supporting lecture–test learning. No research suggests that lecture–test learning is effective. Quite the opposite. The primary debate has been between advocates of meaning-focused workshop learning and direct instruction. The story of this debate is filled with curious political complexities. One issue is what research actually shows. The other issue relates to how research results have been communicated. Let's look at both of these related to debates regarding learning how to read.

To talk about what research shows, we need an agreement on what research is valuable. You might think that the answer is: "All research is valuable if it is conducted based on scientific standards." However, in the recent political environment you would be wrong. There are two major camps of research: *quantitative* and *qualitative*. **Quantitative** studies measure outcomes of various treatments that can be reduced to numbers—for example, counting the number of syllables spoken correctly, scores on a test, and so on. Experimental studies, where a "control group" that does not receive the treatment or learning strategy of interest is compared to an "experimental group," is considered the standard among quantitative researchers. **Qualitative** studies, on the other hand, engage a researcher in observing students in the process of learning. They may gather information including student written work, observe students in reading and writing, and interview students about what they are learning and their perceptions of the classroom, for example. Qualitative studies aim to understand dynamics of learning and look at processes and results that are too complex to be reduced to simple numbers.

In recent years, much has been made of "scientific research," a phrase embedded in the United States in the No Child Left Behind law. In that law, research is largely not considered valuable unless it is quantitative and uses experimental control groups. You might think, "So?" The bottom line is that this throws out thousands of valuable studies and tends to classify research that supports direct instruction as the only good research. However, true experimental research is difficult for many reasons. One is that the variables are always compounded. To compare, for example, a phonics direct instruction program with meaning-based reading instruction is difficult because children in the phonics program typically also get opportunities to read focusing on meaning, and meaning-based reading approaches also incorporate phonics skills instruction. Further, true experimental research is difficult because it would require withholding what is thought to be better instruction from some students.

The result is that many experimental studies involve students in experimental procedures that don't much matter and also don't really say much about students' use of skills in authentic situations. For example, much research that claims that direct instruction is superior for helping students develop reading skills involves students in reading "nonsense words"—for instance, collections of letters that are given as isolated lists and that are not part of real words. When students who engage in direct instruction are shown to be able to better "read" these nonsense words than students who are in meaning-based instruction, researchers draw the conclusion that direct instruction helps students read better. The presumption is that if students can "call" nonsense words, then they can read better. However, reading nonsense words is actually not reading at all. Reading involves taking meaning from text and using it for an authentic purpose. Such studies don't evaluate how well students understand or how much students read based on their own interest nor how well, for example, students are able to spell when doing their own writing. The results that more balanced researchers find are very different.

However, these problems have not kept such researchers from announcing publicly and with much fanfare that direct instruction is more effective. While there are many details in reading, writing, math, science, and more, the story is the same in all these fields. Let's look further, as an example, at what happened in recent years in the United States related to how children learn to read.

In 2000, a panel of experts was gathered by the U.S. Department of Education as the National Reading Panel with a goal of ending the "reading wars" between direct instruction and whole language advocates by conducting a comprehensive assessment of reading research. Unfortunately, that's not exactly what happened. Since the education officials of the administration at that time were advocates of direct instruction, they took action to ensure that direct instruction was identified as the best instructional method. They did this several ways: (1) The panel included a large predominance of advocates for direct instruction who were largely researchers; only one person who had ever taught reading was on the panel. (2) Out of some 100,000 research studies on reading they carefully considered only 428 and used only 38 as a basis for their conclusions (Smith, 2003). (3) The majority of these studies were based on teaching children sounds in clinical experimental situations. Most did not involve children in actually reading for meaning. (4) The report summary actually contradicted reviews of research published in its comprehensive report that suggested that meaning-focused workshop learning was more effective than direct instruction. The summary report stated, incorrectly according to its own reviews, that "scientific investigation" showed direct instruction to be superior in teaching children to read.

Based on this report and the requirement that direct instruction be used when federal funds are provided for reading initiatives, programs for teaching phonemic awareness and phonics as separate programs, disconnected from actually reading, have proliferated. Some programs actually mandate that children not be allowed to read real materials until they have learned the designated phonemic awareness skills.

As we shall see, numerous researchers have been working hard to provide a more balanced view of research and to promote educational practices based on a more engaging, effective approach to learning. Learning of skills, of course, is important but in these approaches skill development is incorporated into authentic, engaging learning tasks and reinforced in numerous ways in a rich learning environment.

We may well find ourselves in a school where the administration has believed the publications of direct instruction advocates and government agencies that promote direct instruction practices. What to do? First, we need to be clear about our own position and be able to explain it to others. We need to incorporate skill development into authentic learning and be able to explain to parents, other educators, and students themselves how this works. Our experience has been that we will get lots of support, over time, when:

1. Our students love being in our class, including students who have never felt successful in school. Parents will notice this and express appreciation and let our principal know as well.
2. Our class does better on the state standardized test than students in other classrooms (a frequent experience).

Guidelines for Effective Instruction for Diverse Learners

If traditional practices in schools based on lecture–test and direct instruction are not effective, how *should* we teach? It is here that we begin to see effective instruction for all children and inclusive teaching come together. In this section we'll look at recommendations from a wide range of professional sources. We'll note that these all are variations on what we've called workshop learning. As we discuss these sources, note the overlap and congruence of ideas and strategies.

What to Look for in a Classroom

Alfie Kohn (1998) described an effective inclusive classroom as well as pointing out practices that should cause us concern (Figure 11.2). Kohn paints a picture of what we will expect to see in an effective classroom and a classroom that is ineffective for many students. It's helpful to get a picture of each in our minds as we talk more about effective learning.

Brain-Based Learning

In recent years many scientists have conducted research on how the brain actually learns, **brain-based learning** (Caine & Caine, 1994, 1997; Goleman, 1995; Jensen, 1995, 1998). The implications of these findings on education are enormous and exciting. Quina (1995) synthesized these findings as follows.

First, the brain simultaneously makes connections between multiple ideas and engages in many activities and thought processes at once. Given this, the step-by-step lecture and worksheet design of most U.S. schools inhibits meaningful learning. Brain-based teaching, in contrast, facilitates deeper learning by building connections between multiple stimuli; for example, storytelling and drama to enhance learning, body sculpture to teach syntax, and metaphorical stories read to music.

Second, the brain processes parts and wholes at the same time. The "left brain," which breaks content into parts, and the "right brain," which sees wholes, interact constantly. This is how the brain builds patterns and connections for learning. Thus, when teachers focus only on parts—skills, phonics, multiplication tables—they limit learning. Students need *more* learning time when facts and skills are taught in isolation rather than in context.

Third, the search for meaning is automatic and basic. The brain needs the familiar and novel simultaneously. Therefore, we should build into every lesson (1) security (the familiar) and (2) novelty (the search for new connections and possibilities).

FIGURE 11.2

What to Look for in a Classroom

	GOOD SIGNS	POSSIBLE REASONS FOR CONCERN
Furniture	■ Chairs around tables to facilitate inter-action ■ Comfortable areas for learning	■ Desks in rows or chairs all facing forward
Walls	■ Covered with student projects ■ Evidence of student collaboration ■ Signs, exhibits, or lists created by students rather than teachers ■ Information about and mementos of those who spend time together in the classroom	■ Bare ■ Decorated with commercial posters ■ Lists of consequences for misbehavior ■ List of rules created by an adult ■ Stick or star chart or other evidence that students are rewarded or ranked ■ Student assignments displayed but they are *(a)* suspiciously flawless, *(b)* only "the best" students' work, or *(c)* virtually all alike
Sounds	■ Frequent hum of activities and ideas being exchanged	■ Frequent periods of silence ■ Teacher's voice the loudest or most often heard
Location of Teacher	■ Typically working with students so that it takes a moment to find	■ Typically front and center
Teacher's Voice	■ Respectful, genuine, warm	■ Controlling and imperious ■ Condescending and saccharine sweet
Students' Reaction to Visitor	■ Welcoming and eager to explain or demonstrate what they are doing or to use the visitor as a resource	■ Either unresponsive or hoping to be distracted from what they are doing
Class Discussion	■ Students address one another directly ■ Emphasis on thoughtful exploration of complicated issues ■ Students ask questions at least as often as the teacher	■ All exchanges involve (or directed by) teacher; students wait to be called on ■ Emphasis on facts and right answers ■ Students race to be first to answer teacher's "Who can tell me?" queries
Tasks	■ Different activities take place at the same time	■ All students usually do the same thing
Around the School	■ Inviting atmosphere ■ Students' projects fill hallways ■ Bathrooms in good condition ■ Faculty lounge warm and comfortable ■ Office staff welcoming toward visitors and students ■ Students helping in lunchroom, library, and with other school functions	■ Stark, institutional feel ■ Awards, trophies, and prizes displayed, suggesting emphasis on triumph rather than community

Source: Kohn, 1998. Used with permission.

Fourth, emotion and cognition are linked in the hard wiring of the brain. They cannot be separated. Teachers must deal with both together. The brain will "downshift" under threat; when students feel threatened thinking and learning literally stop. We must build a sense of community, safety, and support if learning is to occur.

Caine and Caine (1991, 1994, 1995) worked with staff of the Dry Creek Elementary School to develop approaches built on the findings of brain researchers. They articulated three simple but powerful principles:

1.   Ensure *a state of relaxed alertness* in a challenging but nonthreatening environment. "Relaxed alertness" is a condition in which children feel comfortable, safe, and at ease but also engaged, interested, involved, and curious. This combination creates the psychological state that is conducive to learning. On the other hand, when children do not feel safe, the control shifts to the brain stem. This part of the brain controls the basic needs to survive, and when children are upset the brain reverts to the "fight or flight" syndrome and they literally cannot focus on learning.

2.   *Orchestrate immersion in complex experience.* The brain thrives on complexity, seeking naturally to create its own sense of order out of multiple inputs. When structure is imposed rather than emerging as students grapple with complex materials, again learning is reduced. To maximize learning, we *maximize experience*, looking simultaneously at the big picture and small parts. We do not break down learning into small segments and present these in a sequence. Teachers guide, shape, and orchestrate experiences so that needs for order, safety, and novelty are met.

3.   Continuously *engage in active processing of experiences* to consolidate emerging mental models. To help the brain create its own structure, reflection, talk, and dialogue about experience is critical. Classroom discussions, journal writing, e-mail groups with students in other schools, small group discussions—all help learners process, understand, and remember what they've learned.

Two students play a game called "seal hop" in Mishael Hittie's fourth-grade class. They have been studying frozen worlds as a year-long theme and this game is played by Eskimo children in Alaska. This game provides an opportunity to move while deepening their academic understanding.

Best Practices: Emerging Standards for Teaching and Learning

In recent years, national professional organizations have worked to develop standards for the content and process of learning in various fields of education. A common consensus regarding **best practices for teaching and learning** emerged from an analysis of this work that is consistent with brain-based learning, Smith's classic approach, Kohn's picture of an effective classroom, and inclusive teaching. Classrooms, this consensus holds, can be engaging, caring places where learners of different races, cultures, abilities, and learning styles draw from one another. In addition, these national reports mirror research findings in regard to many specific groups—students with learning disabilities, students who are gifted, students with mental retardation, and others (Cline, 1999; Faltis, 2000; Freeman & Alkin, 2000; Vaughn, Gersten, & Chard, 2000).

The reports call for less emphasis on traditional lecture–text–test–grading and more emphasis on learning that is active, cooperative, authentic, and inclusive. In such classes students work on real issues that integrate several subjects at once. Classes are abuzz with activity, work, and learning noise as students take responsibility for projects from start to finish—developing ideas, finding information, developing products and methods of presentation. Evaluation is based on actual evidence of learning—presentations, writing, plays—rather than on traditional tests (Zemelman et al., 2005). (See Figure 11.3.)

Classes that use best practices create space for students of differing abilities, learning styles, and strengths to flourish. Authentic learning activities let students of different abilities work together on the same project. In one classroom example, students studied the construction of space stations. A student with severe mental retardation carried materials and learned some key words. When time came to build the mock space station, he helped color key parts and copied letters for signs. What better way to meet his IEP goals of following sequences, learning his letters, and increasing dexterity?

Culturally Responsive Pedagogy

Important work has also occurred in recent years to develop schooling practices that are responsive to culturally diverse students. Such instruction is based upon seven key principles and associated practices (Education Alliance at Brown University, 2008; Richards, Brown, & Forde, 2006):

1. *Positive perspectives on parents and families*: Teachers aim to partner with parents inviting participation in the education of the child while being aware of and responsive to cultural differences in families.
2. *Communication of high expectations:* All students should be given the message that they can attain high standards of learning.
3. *Learning within the context of culture:* Teachers should learn about the cultures of their students and work to bridge the frequent gap between school and home cultures, adapting lessons to reflect ways of communicating and learning that are familiar to students.
4. *Student-centered instruction:* Learning should be cooperative, collaborative, and community-focused where students are encouraged to direct their own learning and work with other students on projects that are relevant to them.
5. *Culturally mediated instruction:* Teachers should aim to use different ways of knowing, understanding, and describing information that draw from different cultural perspectives.
6. *Reshaping the curriculum:* The curriculum should be meaningful, student-centered, and interdisciplinary connecting with topics and interests related to the background and culture of students.

FIGURE 11.3

Common Recommendations of National Curriculum Reports

LESS OF . . .	MORE OF . . .
■ Whole class, teacher-directed instruction (e.g., lecturing)	■ Experiential, inductive, hands-on learning
■ Student passivity: sitting, listening, receiving, and absorbing information	■ Active learning in the classroom, with all the noise and movement of students doing, talking, and collaborating
■ Presentational, one-way transmission of information from teacher to student	■ Diverse roles for teachers, including coaching, demonstrating, and modeling
■ Prizing and rewarding of silence in the classroom	■ Emphasis on higher-order thinking: understanding of a field's key concepts and principles
■ Classroom time devoted to fill-in-the-blank worksheets, dittos, workbooks, and other "seatwork"	■ Deep study of a smaller number of topics, so that students internalize the field's way of inquiry
■ Student time spent reading textbooks and basal readers	■ Reading of real texts: whole books, primary sources, and nonfiction materials
■ Attempts by teachers to thinly "cover" large amounts of material in every subject area	■ Transfer to students of responsibility for their work: goal setting, record keeping, monitoring, sharing, exhibiting, and evaluating
■ Rote memorization of facts and details	■ Choice for students (e.g., choice of their own books, writing topics, team partners, and research projects)
■ Emphasis on competition and grades	■ Enacting and modeling of the principles of democracy in the school
■ Tracking or leveling students into ability groups	■ Attention to affective (emotional) needs and the varying cognitive styles of individual students
■ Use of pull-out special programs	■ Cooperative, collaborative activity; the classroom as an interdependent community
■ Use of and reliance on standardized tests	■ Heterogeneously grouped classrooms where individual needs are met through individualized activities, not through segregation of bodies

Source: Zemelman, Daniels, and Hyde, 2005.

7. *Teacher as facilitator:* Teachers should function primarily as guides, consultants, facilitators, and advocates for students, helping them connect their lives and cultures with learning that occurs in school.

Universal Design for Learning

As students with special needs have increasingly been in general education classrooms, researchers have been building on the ideas of **universal design** of physical spaces (see chapters 6 and 7) to work to create methods of learning that fit the ways that students are different. While much of this work has centered around the use of computers as learning tools, these educators have moved to develop a powerful framework and set of guidelines that ensure positive learning for all. Figure 11.4 illustrates the key principles along with practical instructional examples. According to this framework, to help student learning we must (1) use multiple ways to present information; (2) provide multiple pathways for students' action and expression; and (3) provide multiple ways to engage students including collaborative, interactive structures. We highly recommend two online resources filled with practical resources that support effective inclusive

FIGURE 11.4

Universal Design for Learning

1. USE MULTIPLE WAYS TO PRESENT INFORMATION	2. PROVIDE MULTIPLE PATHWAYS FOR STUDENTS' ACTION AND EXPRESSION	3. PROVIDE MULTIPLE WAYS TO ENGAGE STUDENTS
Provide a range of examples and counterexamples. Example: persuasive writing vs. factual article in a newspaper	*Provide flexible models of skilled performance.* Examples: Math demonstration drawing lines or using manipulatives	*Offer choices of content and tools.* Examples: choices of *literature, books* to study; choices of doing a written report, acting out a drama, or videotaping a presentation
Highlight critical features. Examples: teacher tone of voice; marker underline or highlight; pointing to words or phrases	*Provide opportunities to practice with supports.* Examples: teacher prompt a multistepped task; provide a rubric/checkbox to edit writing	*Provide adjustable levels of challenge.* Examples: range of materials at different reading difficulties; response formats with prompts vs. open-ended formats
Represent information in multiple media and formats. Examples: text version of book; books on tape	*Provide ongoing, relevant feedback.* Examples: questions and answers in classroom; quiz or test	*Offer a choice of rewards.* Example: provide a menu of reinforcements
Provide supports for limited background knowledge, and establish a context for learning. Examples: classroom resources; peer tutoring	*Provide flexible opportunities for demonstrating skill.* Examples: written, oral, or visual presentation; explanations; word process	*Offer a choice of learning context.* Examples: option to work in study carrel vs. open classroom; student use of headphones
	Provide novel problems to solve. Example: unique problems outside the initial instructional set to promote generalization and transfer	

Source: Adapted from CAST (2008). Universal design for learning guidelines version 1.0. Wakefield, MA: Author. © 2008 by CAST. Used with permission. All rights reserved.

teaching: Universal Design for Learning Web site hosted by the Center for Applied Special Technology (http://www.cast.org/policy/ncac/index.html) and the Access Center, a site devoted to enhancing access to the general education curriculum by students with disabilities (http://www.k8accesscenter.org/index.php).

Differentiated Instruction

Differentiation is an instructional approach in which teachers seek to understand student learning profiles, including their readiness or ability level, and use strategies of instruction that will meet them where they are, providing assistance to move to their next level of skill and knowledge (Hall, Strangman, & Meyer, 2003). Teachers can differentiate content, process, and/or product for students (Tomlinson, 2004b).

Differentiation of *content* refers to a change in the material being learned by the student. For example, if the classroom objective is for all students to write persuasive paragraphs, some of the students are learning to use a topic sentence and supporting details, while others are learning to use outside sources to defend their viewpoint. Differentiation of *process* refers to the way in which the student accesses material. One student explores a learning center while another student collects information from the Web. Differentiation of *product* refers to the way in which the student shows what he or she has learned. For example, to demonstrate understanding of the plot of a story, one student creates a skit, whereas another student writes a book report.

When teachers differentiate, they do so in response to students' readiness, interest, and/or learning profile. Readiness refers to the skill level and background knowledge of the child. Teachers use diagnostic assessments to determine students' readiness. Interest refers to topics that the students want to explore or that will motivate them. Teachers can ask students about their outside interests and even include students in the unit-planning process. Finally, the students' learning profiles include learning style (for example, is the student a visual, auditory, tactile, or kinesthetic learner), grouping preferences (for example, does the student work best individually, with a partner, or in a large group), and environmental preferences (for example, does the student need lots of space or a quiet area to work). When a teacher differentiates, all of these factors can be taken into account individually or in combination (Access Center, 2008).

Differentiated instruction has its roots in efforts to create opportunities for quality learning for students who are gifted in regular classrooms. The tools of differentiated instruction and the approach are very valuable, however, for all students. Differentiated instruction accommodates children at multiple levels in one classroom. We have preferred the term "multilevel" to emphasize the fact that our students function at many differing ability levels without having to create a separate lesson plan for each level. The idea of multilevel teaching takes the idea of working at different levels one step further. Instead of planning different activities or instruction for each level, multilevel teachers plan lessons in which students can automatically function at different levels.

Authentic Multilevel Instruction

In 2002, 10 general and special education teachers who had been identified as exemplary multilevel teachers met 1 day per month for a year to discuss **authentic multilevel instruction.** They identified principles that guide and describe practices in their classrooms that are highly effective for students with differing ability levels. These correlate very well with the studies and guidelines already discussed. We have found the ideas and strategies developed by this group of teachers to be useful as a guide. According to this panel of exemplary teachers, effective instruction will have the following characteristics:

Authentic. **Authentic learning** is foremost and central. Rather than involve students in "school work," authentic learning teaches through tasks that occur for a real purpose. For example, rather than writing practice letters to no one in particular, authentic writing involves students in such tasks as writing a company regarding how it may improve its product, thinking about and substantiating suggestions; or writing a letter to parents on Mother's and Father's Day.

Higher Order Thinking. In authentic, multilevel teaching, teachers involve all students in higher order thinking, in complex learning and projects at the higher end of Bloom's taxonomy.

Inclusive. Teachers include all students with special needs in general education classes, ensuring use of heterogeneous grouping and pairing in the classroom. Ability grouping is used minimally and under careful conditions. When ability groups are used, they are based on specific skill needs in common with other students—mini-skill lessons—and are short term.

BACK PACK

Universal Design and Multiple Intelligences

Center for Applied Special Technology The center develops innovative resources and strategies for educators based on the principles of universal design for learning. This site has a wealth of materials. www.cast.org/index.html

Project Zero This project is designed to "understand and enhance learning, thinking, and creativity in the arts" based on the ideas of multiple intelligences. www.pz .harvard.edu/index.cfm

Multilevel. Students are engaged in learning activities that allow them to function at their level of ability, yet are challenged at their zone of proximal development to continue growing and learning. "Just right" work for all students is expected and supported. Students are taught to understand the concept of multilevel instruction, helping to challenge and support one another.

Multimodal. Multimodel methods of obtaining information, engaging in learning, and demonstrating learning are used flexibly and naturally, including multiple intelligences and learning styles.

Scaffolding. Students are given support and assistance to move from their present level of functioning to the next level. Students are explicitly and systematically taught to help, support, and challenge one another as part of building community in their classroom. Specialists assist students and the general education teacher in the design of multilevel lessons and providing needed specific skill instruction, support, and assistance.

Guided Student Leadership and Direction. Children are given voice in the classroom and explicitly taught to help, support, and challenge one another. Students are taught how to judge just-right work and provided choices, instruction, and support in learning how to take responsibility for choices.

Evaluation Based on Learning and Growth. Student evaluation is based largely on (1) learning and growth, and (2) effort rather than standard levels of expected functioning (e.g., "grade level"). Assessment is performance based and authentic and skills are assessed in the context of authentic tasks.

When we compare these different efforts to create more effective teaching practices, the similarities of approaches are remarkable. We now turn to exploring in detail strategies, tools, and resources to make these ideas real as we teach our students.

Steps for Planning Authentic Multilevel Instruction Units and Lessons

To start at the beginning of how we create this ideal in our own classroom, we need to look at the basics of how we plan for units, lessons, and the students we have in our individual classrooms. All teachers have some method of planning for what they teach. However, if we seek to design our lessons in ways that are both authentic and multilevel, we need to include some additional considerations. Figure 11.5 lists the key steps. Here we'll introduce these steps and then look at each step in detail in this chapter and in Chapter 12.

Step 1. Select an authentic interdisciplinary theme.   Select a theme that will be of interest to students that can link various subjects. While all our instruction will not necessarily be linked around authentic themes, the more this is the case, the more successful we will be in promoting higher levels of learning.

FIGURE 11.5

Steps in Unit and Lesson Planning for Multilevel Differentiated Instruction

1. Select an authentic interdisciplinary theme.
2. Develop multilevel learning goals.
3. Design product, assessment, and evaluation.
4. Engage students in authentic multilevel learning activities.
5. Differentiate lessons for individual students.

Step 2. Develop multilevel learning goals.   Define an overall learning goal for the unit or lesson that is linked to one or more strands in the district curriculum. Once we know the overall learning goal, we think about the range of functioning of our students and articulate optimum expectations for our highest-, lowest-, and average-level learners.

Step 3. Design product, assessment, and evaluation.   Next we design student assessment. What product(s) will they develop? How will they demonstrate learning and how will we assign grades?

Step 4. Engage students in authentic multilevel learning activities using workshop-based learning.   We then design learning activities in which students obtain and use information at their own ability level while working collaboratively with other students. We use multilevel learning materials that allow students to access information at their level of ability in multiple modalities with multiple forms of representation.

Step 5. Differentiate lessons for individual students.   Finally, we consider special needs of students and individually differentiate lessons for some to ensure their participation and learning. We connect lessons to individual plans such as IEPs and plan how to use support from specialists such as bilingual paraprofessionals, special education teachers, and speech therapists. (See Chapter 5.)

Figure 11.6 provides a form to detail these steps. Of course, most of the time we do not complete such forms (though they are required in some schools). *Learning to think* naturally through our unit and lesson planning *using this process is the goal.* Let's explore each step in greater detail.

Step 1. Select an Authentic Interdisciplinary Theme

Themes provide a powerful way to organize teaching around key topics or issues that are important or of interest to students. Themes improve instruction in many ways. First, interesting topics engage students and increase their motivation. Second, when teachers link several subjects, we more effectively cover many topics simultaneously. Third, themes allow students to see connections among the various subjects and to apply them practically, enhancing understanding. Finally, thematic instruction creates opportunities for students of different ability levels to work together.

When thematic instruction is authentic instruction, it engages students in tasks connected to real life—to family, community, or larger society; to real-life problems they are likely to encounter outside the classroom. It can be incorporated into many instructional approaches but most often operates as a type of workshop-based learning. Newmann and Wehlage (1993) stated that authentic learning:

- Promotes higher order thinking
- Seeks depth of knowledge (fewer topics are engaged in greater depth)

FIGURE 11.6

Romeo and Juliet Today: Ninth-Grade English Multilevel Lesson

LEARNING GOALS

In groups, students will re-create a scene from Shakespeare's *Romeo and Juliet* into a modern interpretation, brainstorming ideas and writing a summary justifying how and why they made their re-creation as they did.

LEVELS

1. Understand how Shakespeare relates to the modern world by creating an original, updated interpretation of a scene.
2. Understand how a play is developed and written.
3. Identify ideas that will be beneficial to include in the play.

LEARNING ACTIVITIES

1. Choose which scene on which to concentrate.
2. Brainstorm ideas to use in the scene re-creation.
3. Write scripts with some stage direction.
4. Practice the scene, make revisions as a group if necessary.
5. Type the final draft and write the justification summary.
6. Present the finished product.

INCLUDING STUDENTS

- Students with natural leadership skills will automatically become essential figures.
- Students with limited communication skills can have a nonspeaking role in the play; answer yes or no questions in group during decision making.
- Students who are gifted may flourish making the justification summary or creating props/set.
- Students who are more creative but have poor reading/writing skills will be able to play a large part in the creation of props/set or stage direction.

MATERIALS

Romeo and Juliet (original version); variations—comic book, other takeoffs from Internet sites such as YouTube.

ASSESSMENT OF LEARNING

In order to accurately assess students, each group will give me a description of the roles of each member. At the end of the project, each student will fill out a peer evaluation for the group members. I will then use these items, the knowledge of each student's capabilities, and the final project to determine what type of grade should be given. If any discrepancies arise, I will have a private discussion with group members to determine the actual amount of effort given. Also, since most of the work will be done in class, I will be able to observe groups and see which members are putting in effort. For students who have disabilities that severely hinder their participation in the activity, I will ensure that they are given some responsibilities with additional assistance from a partner, and that they are able to focus on IEP or personal goals that are set for them; they will then be graded accordingly.

Source: Adapted from James (2005).

- Engages students in connecting to the world beyond the classroom
- Encourages student construction of knowledge

What *is* real? What is authentic? Two key aspects of authentic instruction are most important: (1) the topic of focus and (2) the method of engaging students. Topics are authentic when they connect directly to the lives of students and the local community in which they live. This does not mean that we ignore state, national, or global issues, but it does mean that we use the lives of students as the starting place. Sometimes such topics simply involve students in studying real places, events, or people in the community. Frequently topics center on concerns or issues for individuals or the community. A few examples might be useful:

- A student interviews individuals he considers "heroes" and learns about their lives, developing written materials, a poster, a video, or another depiction.
- Students study a forest at the edge of the school grounds, inventorying the types of animal life they see, writing stories as if they lived in the forest.
- In order to learn to write letters, the class writes a letter to the newspaper regarding an issue. When their letter is published in the paper, they get 600 responses!
- A student's grandparents visit from a country that is in the midst of war. The class studies the country and class members write letters welcoming the grandparents to the United States.
- A local industry has just closed, and many people have been laid off. At the same time a new shopping mall is opening and a high-tech industry is being built in a nearby town. A high school class studies why this is happening.

Following the choice of topics, there is the question of teaching strategies. At best, authentic learning engages students in activities that are meaningful, that are intended to make an impact on the environment or the social life of the community. Students don't do "practice" letters; they write real letters to real people about real issues for real purposes. Students read books for enjoyment, not materials programmed according to certain letter sound combinations. Students gather information regarding real issues.

Authentic learning, then, is not about *preparing* for life. Rather, authentic learning is about *living* life. Through such living experiences students learn at a deep level (Dewey, 1943). We will find that many different levels of ability can be naturally incorporated.

Create Interdisciplinary Themes

How do we identify authentic themes? Here are a few suggestions. First, obtain these materials:

- District curriculum (not the textbooks, but the concepts to teach)
- School calendar of card-marking dates
- Regular calendar
- An organized format to record the ideas (computer, monthly planner)
- Textbook of any subject with a mandated order

Then consider the following questions. How long do I want my themes to be: 4 weeks, 10 weeks? Would I prefer to organize themes around science or social studies? (These two subjects are the most natural source of authentic lessons as both deal with occurrences and objects in the real world.)

Start by looking at the curriculum guidelines for either social studies or science. Roughly plot a schedule for covering topics. Now look at the curriculum guidelines for other subjects and look for themes to link these together. Sometimes we can make obvious links as in the following examples: connecting pro/con writing with the civil rights movement; linking legends with the early history; putting a unit on motion with the industrialization period. In other cases, we conceptualize an underlying theme that is used to link many topics such as conflict between human beings; love; fear; beauty. Some concepts make sense at a certain time of year. Plants are better in the fall or spring; civics, around an election or at the beginning of the year when our class is creating its structure. The key is to use a topic that is clear but also very broad and open-ended. Such topics help structure multilevel lessons.

Once we have a topic, name it and then provide a short description. Here are a couple of additional examples:

- *Ancient Worlds: How land was formed and original people lived.* This unit includes rocks and rain from science, Native American history, fossils, and how glaciers formed in our state.
- *Exploration and New Beginnings: How they came and why they stayed.* This unit includes explorers and early settlers, how day/night and seasons are formed, energy in various forms, and the reading comprehension strategy of sensory images.

One useful tool in this process is a **curriculum web**. Figure 11.7 illustrates a web organized around a schoolwide theme—"Going to the Extremes," a study of how human beings fare and adapt in outer space and the depths of the ocean (Hittie, 1999a).

Themes are used at all grade levels effectively. Elementary teachers use this process to link subjects in their own class. Many middle and high schools are developing interdisciplinary teams who link language arts, social studies, science, math, and the arts in longer time blocks around authentic themes.

Once we have the themes for the whole year, we introduce them to students. We start with finding out what connections they see across the subject areas. In daily conversation and activities, we are constantly bringing the focus back to the connections we want the students to build in their mind. We frequently ask: "How does this connect to something else that we have learned?" For example, using the science topic of day/night and the seasons, we ask students how seasons and the passage of night would have affected the explorers—when they traveled, the time of year to travel, jobs early settlers had.

 An eighth-grade teacher team obtained input from their students around the following topics: racism, poverty, and how and why wars happen. This suggested a theme of conflict in communities around which they could link literacy, social studies, and math. Some students gathered information about conflicts in their community. They looked at information on the Internet and in magazines and books, and interviewed people. Students worked in small heterogeneous groups to gather information and present it to the class. Each group developed a plan that included individual responsibilities and ways to support one another. Literacy was involved as students read, wrote notes, and developed their presentation. Students used math to count, graph, and analyze information; and gathered information about the economy, socioeconomic status, and use of land in communities to see how economics related to these conflicts. The total class shared their results in an evening program for parents and the local community.

Students with special needs were able to participate fully in these groups. Each group identified key roles that each student played and support each student needed. For example, Keith, a student with a cognitive disability who read on the second-grade level, was very involved in interviews with a partner. He likes to draw and helped make presentation materials for the group. He participated in all group discussions about the information and brought his uncle to class who had been very involved in civil rights.

Involve Students in Selecting Topics for Learning

We can also involve students in selecting themes, asking them to brainstorm ideas that are interesting to them or to pick from several that we have developed. We can involve students in selecting themes on which the total class may work. If we use

FIGURE 11.7

Curriculum Web "Going to the Extremes"

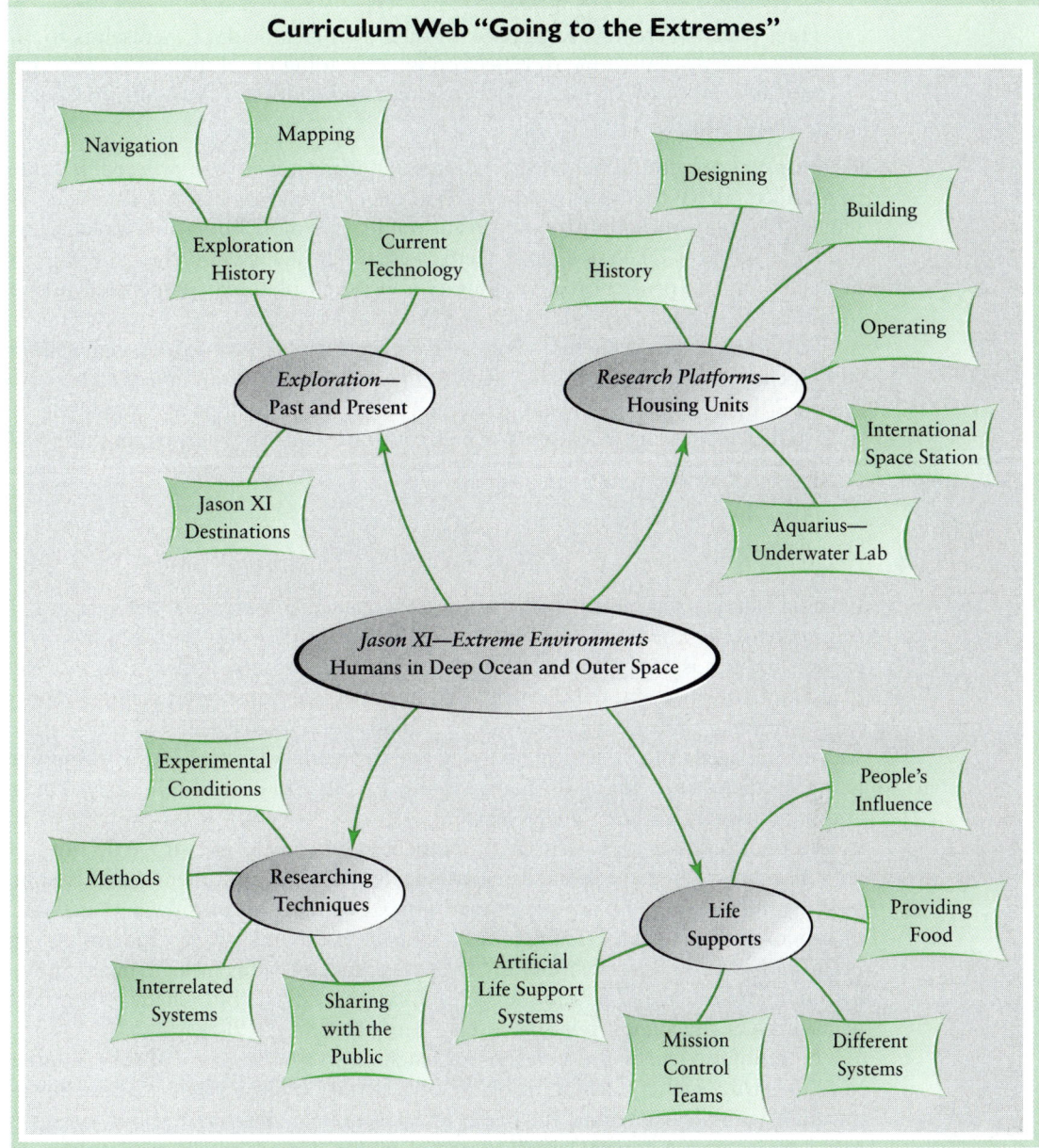

inquiry or problem-based learning in which students are involved in both individual and group learning projects, we will particularly want to engage them in selecting a topic of interest.

We do this by helping students reflect on their own lives and their interests, developing questions to ask. We can help students *formulate questions* in which they are interested. Students use a writing notebook in which they write down ideas about what matters to them, about things they want to know. Strategies to get students started include:

■ Break students into pairs, have them interview each other, and publish the interviews as part of a class newspaper.

- Ask students to interview their families and write "family stories" to share with the class.
- Have students create a scrapbook of their lives to introduce themselves to others.
- Give students daily time to reflect on what is going on in their lives, what questions they have about learning or their future, and create lists of things that puzzle them or worry them.

Teachers provide students with guidance in *planning* how to proceed. If students are to produce poetry or a short story, for example, we have them use a list, web, or sketch sequence to plan and organize important points. We model how this looks, sharing our thoughts out loud. Then, we assist them in creating their own. If they are to be involved in a collaborative project on a community issue, their plan may involve various methods of gathering and displaying information.

Students engage in these activities at multiple ability levels. In a high school social studies class, for example, a student with mental retardation interviewed his father and recorded the interview on tape. He listened carefully to the tape and used "picture writing" to develop a story. A classmate later transcribed the story into conventional text.

Why Multilevel Differentiated Instruction Is Important

Engaging students at multiple levels simultaneously is a critical part of best practices for several reasons. First, for students, the challenge of working with classmates of truly diverse abilities is an important "complex experience" all by itself. At an inclusive middle school, we once met with several eighth graders who had been a circle of friends for May, a student with Down syndrome. As these young people shared their experiences, we were amazed at their critical thinking and problem-solving skills. Working with May had provided them with an authentic course of study in critical thinking, management, and social issues, leading to deep learning.

Second, because students vary dramatically in their abilities, if we do not teach in a way that supports students at their own levels, we exclude students who cannot "keep up." School becomes a place of competition, of winning and losing, rather than a place of support and refuge. Learning is literally shifted downward, as students revert to the brain stem portion of their brain and the emotional reactions of fear, anger, and hostility became more prevalent. So multilevel teaching is a critical component of helping all students learn at the highest possible levels (Caine & Caine, 1995).

In multilevel teaching we design our teaching so that students of very different abilities can learn together, each at his or her own level of ability. When we base our teaching on brain-based learning and thematic, interdisciplinary instruction, our classes provide many *opportunities* for students to learn at multiple levels together. However, we must intentionally take advantage of these opportunities.

Vygotsky (1978) described an important concept for multilevel teaching, the **zone of proximal development (ZPD)**—the range of tasks just beyond a student's present level of ability that the student cannot yet perform independently but can perform with the help and guidance of others. We seek to take students where they are, provide support and assistance for tasks they cannot accomplish on their own, and challenge them to go to the next level. Thus, multilevel teaching does not mean that some have it "easy" and others must work "harder." Multilevel teaching means that all children are challenged to do their very best, no matter what their abilities.

Now contrast this scenario with what is more typical. Traditional schooling has all children learning the same material at the same level and at the same pace. In a traditional class we often hear people saying things like "He just can't do eighth-grade work. I think he should be referred to special education." In that same class we also usually observe some students who never study at all and yet always get A's. The first student daily experiences the message "I cannot learn" and probably comes to believe it. The other student thinks, "I am so smart I don't have to work." Neither message is healthy.

We should be clear that multilevel teaching counters traditional thinking. Typically, the goal is that every student will be on grade level. Grade level, on the one hand, outlines typical developmental expectations of children. However, said a different way, grade level is simply a point in a developmental continuum at which 50% of students will be above and 50% below. For many years now, we have asked teachers this question: "What is the range of grade level functioning of students in your room?" The very minimum response has been 3 grade levels. However, when teachers are honest they say 6 to 10 grade levels, *not counting* students with identified disabilities. If this is the case, focusing on instruction to the middle ensures that some students will be far beyond that level of instruction and others will be below. Both sets of students will be frustrated. This is what we call **mono-level instruction**, an approach directly contradictory to the best practice frameworks we discussed earlier in this chapter.

For multilevel instruction to work, students must be expected to engage in what teachers *call just-right work* or *personal excellence*. We teach students that all people are different but that, in our class, all are expected to work at their personal level of challenge and that all are to be supported and respected. Throughout the year, we help students understand how they are different and we teach them ways to help others learn. We teach students about multiple intelligences as part of this process and how they can better use their strengths to bridge the gap to the areas that are more challenging. Therefore, the next step in teaching using multilevel instruction is to develop multilevel learning goals.

Problems to Avoid in Designing Multilevel Differentiated Instruction

We need to avoid several traps as we work toward multilevel teaching. Let's first talk about situations we've seen in which students have been locked rigidly into specific ability levels. Any level planning is simply a template that changes as students grow and we better understand their abilities. It is also vital that we teach students to choose for themselves developmentally appropriate work that stretches their thinking. When we provide different levels of an activity, we do not preselect and assign students to an ability level. They will make mistakes that we will need to discuss, but that is all part of the learning process.

Some teachers do, in fact, lock in students and limit their abilities by creating elaborate leveling and management systems for different subject areas. One teacher codes books by colored stickers and assigns students their color to read. Another teacher uses blocks with different activities on the various faces and assigns each child a particular face (Kronberg, 1999). One teacher gives her students three choices of activities but designates these as A, B, and C activities for each particular child. These designations represent the highest grade that child could get in each activity, even if the work was at the child's level (Nunley, 1998). In all of these approaches students have no knowledge of how to choose appropriate work when the teacher is unavailable; nor do they have strategies for completing work that is more difficult by relying on those around them.

Schum, Vaughn, and Leavell (1994) suggest a pyramid for planning at three levels (1) what *all* students should learn, (2) what *most* but not all students will learn, and (3) what *some* students will learn (the highest level and the top of the pyramid). This approach helps us differentiate learning for students with higher abilities. However, this strategy

Students are using the microscope to conduct an investigation and record their observations. They will later participate in a classroom discussion. Working in a group provides each student both support and the ability to work at their own level of ability.

may be problematic for teaching that includes students with severe disabilities, depending on how we define "what all students should learn." If, for example, teachers routinely identify learning targets that are beyond the capabilities of a student with severe disabilities, what is to be done? At worst, this could easily result in the conclusion that the general education classroom is inappropriate for this student. At best, the process simply provides no guidance. You will notice that in our multilevel lesson planning approach (see Figure 11.10), we too identify three levels. However, instead of specifying the lowest level as what all students will learn, we suggest simply that this is the lowest level of ability for which we are targeting the lesson, a level that can be adjusted as we need.

As we design instruction, we also must not develop automatic and stereotypical approaches based on disability categories. There is no formula. Each student is unique, and our planning of multilevel instructional adaptations will be unique for each student. Similarly, we must also not be stuck in the mindset that we cannot teach this particular type of child because we do not have the training to deal with that. Multilevel teaching is as much a mindset as it is a set of tools for teaching. Once we have the mindset that we can teach all students, then regardless of the disability we will find a way to make it work.

Step 2. Develop Multilevel Learning Goals

Developing multilevel learning goals involves three key steps: (1) identify the overall goal of learning in a unit or lesson; (2) state anticipated demonstration of learning at different levels by students with highest, average, and lowest abilities in our classroom; and (3) consider needs for alternative learning goals for some of our students.

One of the difficulties that teachers often experience with students of both high and low ability is that we don't really understand what to expect. If, for example, a teacher expects that a student with a cognitive disability will function on grade level, she will be very frustrated and feel she is a failure when this does not happen. The clearer we can be about the type of performance that would demonstrate real learning for students of varied abilities, the better we will recognize their learning when we see it.

Develop Overall Learning Goals for the Unit or Lesson

Developing overall learning goals is very important. If we are using authentic themes to link several subjects, we'll want a learning goal statement that helps clarify the focus of the lesson. We'll also want to phrase learning goals in a way that supports higher order thinking and multilevel instruction. In our work with exemplary inclusive teachers, we've been struck with how they articulate learning goals and how they describe these to students. Consistently, these teachers state open-ended learning goals that require higher levels of thinking, whereas teachers who are not skilled at multi-level teaching identify learning goals largely as memorization of facts, a low level of learning.

Let's look at two contrasting examples of learning goals:

1. Students will memorize definitions of the parts of a plant.
2. Students will understand and demonstrate how plants grow and reproduce.

While these may seem similar, in fact, they represent very different ways of framing the learning goal. The first learning goal is traditional. Classrooms are replete with similar examples: memorizing state capitals or body parts. This is similar to the focus on "getting the right answers" in math calculations. What's the problem with these as learning goals? There are several. First, for all students, and particularly those with higher abilities, such goals simply are not interesting or challenging. The prevalence of such learning goals in classrooms helps explain the frustration of parents of children who are gifted who want lessons that engage higher levels of thinking. Curiously, at the same time, such goals make it much more difficult for lessons to be multilevel where each student can learn at his or her own level of ability. If the goal is to memorize parts of the plant, if a student cannot do this, the only thing to do is to create a parallel goal—for example, naming a plant. Although this is an important strategy on occasion, having learning goals that naturally allow students to move to their level of challenge makes instruction both easier and more effective.

Look at the second example. This is an open-ended goal in which students can learn in many different ways and at many different levels. For example, a student with a cognitive disability, who reads at the first-grade level, could use learning materials with many pictures and text that is read aloud on a computer to achieve the goal of learning about plant reproduction. This student's understanding may be basic but still meet the learning goal. At the same time, a student who is highly able can pursue this question at a very sophisticated level. Such a student could examine the process of plant growth in great technical detail, seeking to understand the impact of various environmental factors on plant health and growth. Indeed, many scientists have organized their entire careers around such a learning goal.

District curriculum guidelines typically state learning goals for different grade levels. These broad learning goals are often conducive to multilevel learning goals. Some typical examples follow. All of these goals are open-ended, allowing us to facilitate multilevel learning.

- Reading: Students will comprehend technical information in nonfiction.
- Spelling: Students will improve their spelling of words in their writing.
- Math: Students will improve their computation skills.
- Science: Students will utilize the scientific process to conduct research and experiments.
- Social Studies: Students will understand how the New World was founded.

As we explore the district or state curriculum guidelines, they become the basis for our lessons. We can easily demonstrate how our instruction is directly linked to the curriculum whenever this is needed, as ideas are pulled directly from these sources. This reinforces the validity of using best practice teaching. Use of district curriculum guidelines can also be very useful as we develop individualized plans for students with special needs. Law requires that all students with disabilities have *access to the general education curriculum*. If we use curriculum guidelines to target individualized learning goals for students, we better link such individual plans to ongoing instruction in our classroom.

Courses should be organized around *big ideas* and key knowledge. Three key questions can articulate these big ideas as course organizers: (1) Why are students learning information? What is the fundamental purpose for understanding and skill development? (2) What do people in various fields *do*? (3) How might we involve students in learning based upon activities of professionals in various fields—physicists, mathematicians, statisticians, historians, writers, and so on. Thinking this way will lead us to important questions that will be open-ended and allow multilevel instruction to occur. They also lead to learning activities that are engaging and practical, connected to real occupations and fields of study (Wiggins & McTighe, 1998).

Bloom's taxonomy of educational outcomes also crafts goals for higher order thinking and multilevel instruction (Bloom, 1956; Fowler, 1996). Figure 11.8 describes Bloom's taxonomy. Note that the closed goals we listed previously are part of the lowest level on Bloom's taxonomy—knowledge of facts. As we move up, outcomes involve students in higher orders of thinking and tend to make learning more engaging. It is simply more interesting to use information for a purpose, analyze data, synthesize various viewpoints, or evaluate the effectiveness of a program than to memorize and passively understand. These higher levels of outcomes naturally move towards authentic learning related to the real world.

Is it important that students know facts? Of course. However, the magic is that the higher levels naturally incorporate lower levels of learning. For example, if you are going to evaluate you must use facts and analyze and synthesize information. If you are going to apply information, you must understand and know it. As we involve students in interesting, complex tasks we find that they will remember more effectively rather than just memorizing facts for the test and then forgetting them.

At all levels, from knowledge to evaluation, there are degrees of sophistication or levels of ability that can be demonstrated. For example, if a class is involved in gathering water specimens in the creek next to the school, analyzing the water (analysis), and drawing conclusions about the effectiveness of a water filtration process that is supposed to help make the water more clean (evaluation), could a student with a cognitive disability be involved in this process? Absolutely. Let's say the student has no functional language except a reliable "Yes" and "No" made through sign language. How would this student be involved? One strategy: Other students in the class get his input by asking him yes and no questions while presenting simplified information to him. The wonder of this strategy is that these students are gaining much as they must put information and questions in very clear terms. They are also learning how to communicate highly technical information in typical language. In other words, the learning of all is being

FIGURE 11.8

Bloom's Taxonomy of Educational Outcomes

COMPETENCY	SKILLS DEMONSTRATED
Evaluation	**Presenting and defending opinions by making judgments about information, the validity of ideas, or the quality of work based on a set of criteria** *Question cues:* Assess, decide, rank, grade, test, measure, recommend, convince, select, judge, explain, discriminate, support, conclude, compare, summarize
Synthesis	**Compiling information together in a different way by combining elements in a new pattern or proposing alternative solutions** *Question cues:* Combine, integrate, modify, rearrange, substitute, plan, create, design, invent, ask "what if?", compose, formulate, prepare, generalize, rewrite
Analysis	**Examining and breaking information into parts by identifying motives or causes; making inferences and finding evidence to support generalizations** *Question cues:* Analyze, separate, order, explain, connect, classify, arrange, divide, compare, select, explain, infer
Application	**Solving problems by applying acquired knowledge, facts, techniques, and rules in a different way** *Questions cues:* Apply, demonstrate, calculate, complete, illustrate, show, solve, examine, modify, relate, change, classify, experiment, discover
Comprehension	**Demonstrating understanding of facts and ideas by organizing, comparing, translating, interpreting, giving descriptions, and stating main ideas** *Question cues:* Summarize, describe, interpret, contrast, predict, associate, distinguish, estimate, differentiate, discuss, extend
Knowledge	**Recalling facts, terms, basic concepts, and answers** *Question cues:* List, define, tell, describe, identify, show, label, collect, examine, tabulate, quote, name; ask who, when, where, etc.

Sources: Adapted from Bloom (1956); Counseling Services Learning Skills Program (2001); and Fowler (1996).

strengthened. This is a far cry from what typically happens with students with cognitive disabilities. Such students typically have a more simplified curriculum where they are taught to memorize the most basic of facts using very structured, closed learning materials for their entire school career.

CHAMPIONS OF INCLUSION COLLABORATE
with others to maximize students' development.

There are still some teachers who do not prioritize the time to meet with others to explore ways of improving teaching and learning for students with disabilities. They may not be receptive to new ideas. They may not want to commit the extra time. They may not feel comfortable interacting with others. Whatever the reasons, they are probably not exposing students with disabilities to as wide a range of possibilities as they could be.

Champions of inclusion are:

- The classmates who meet with Sammy (who has lost some mobility from an accident in his friend's car) to discuss ways of supporting him.
- The team of Grade 7 teachers who strategize with the behavior specialist ideas for connecting better with Marilyn (who has emotional disorders).
- The special education teacher who designs adapted activities for an astronomy unit with the Grade 4 teacher who includes students with various disabilities.
- The early childhood teacher who discusses with her part-time teacher aid better ways of engaging with Keisha (who is nonverbal) in play activities.

- The history teacher who agrees to share some of the techniques he uses with students who have cognitive delays with colleagues at an upcoming inservice.
- The computer specialist who devotes extra time demonstrating how to use screen-reading software on computers throughout the building.
- The special education administrator who listens to teachers' concerns, spends time becoming familiar with the issues by visiting classrooms, and then sets up follow-up meetings to deal with them.
- The parent leaders who, after meeting with staff leaders to prioritize needs, then coordinate activities to raise funds for more assistive technology.
- And Carlos (who is a blind high school student), who volunteers to tutor a struggling Grade 2 reader in an after-school program using appropriate-level print braille books.

By Bill Henderson, Principal, O'Hearn Elementary School, Boston, MA.

Describe Expected Performance Levels for Learning Goals

Once we develop effective overall learning goals, we describe expected levels of learning by students of differing ability levels. At first, making a few written notes will help us clarify our thinking. As with all aspects of this planning process, the more experience we have the more intuitive this will become. We want to consider students who function at the lowest levels, those who fall into the average range, and those with the highest abilities. We've labeled these in order levels 1, 2, and 3.

A level 1 learning goal would involve the simplest demonstrations of learning we would expect. Theoretically, there is no bottom level. However, we will target students at the lowest functioning levels in our class. A level 2 goal focuses on skills achievable by most students in the class. A level 3 activity will reflect what we'd expect of our students with the highest ability. We must be careful, however, to not create learning activities that separate students based on our expectations. We are then recreating segregation. Figure 11.9 illustrates an overall learning goal and multilevel expectations of a unit associated with the Jason Project.

Design Needed Alternative Learning Goals and Expectations

We may also need alternative learning goals for some students with more significant learning challenges. If we have effective multilevel learning goals, almost all students will be able to achieve this goal at some level. However, if we have a student for whom

FIGURE 11.9

Multiple Levels of Teaching Goals:
Example from "Going to the Extremes"—Jason Project

Unit Theme: *Human beings living in extreme conditions—in outer space and deep in the ocean*

Overall Learning Goal: Understand the conditions under which plants can grow.

Learning Activity: Small groups conduct a hydroponic experiment (growing plants without soil as scientists are doing in space), record multiple data, and compare results of data from two different sources.

Level 1	Level 2	Level 3
Help set up materials, working in a team. Do basic recording of the responses of the plant.	Learn how to work as a team. Plant seeds, record growth, and write simple conclusions.	Learn to lead a team. Plant seeds, record growth, and do projections of growth.

Sources: From Hittie (1999a).

this is not realistic, we may continue to have him or her be involved in the learning activity and general topic for different purposes. If we differentiate and adapt the learning goals, activity and materials, we will keep these as close as possible to what the rest of the class is using. In Chapter 4, we learned how to use a curriculum matrix to connect IEP goals (and similar goals for other students with special needs) to our classroom lessons. We can use the curriculum matrix to consider alternative or additional learning goals. For example, take the student involved in studying plants. In addition to learning about plants, however, the goal being addressed from his IEP is to identify colors and to interact well with other students. This can easily be incorporated into the lessons we have already created. Truth is, we will almost always have such additional alternative goals in our minds for all our students, even if we don't state them as a learning goal of the lesson.

In considering alternative goals, we also consider changing the amount or difficulty of work (Deschenes, Ebeling, & Sprague, 1994). Examples include:

- Allow calculator use in math.
- Have a student draw quick sequential sketches to record journal responses to a story read by the teacher or books on tape.
- Change the standard by which we evaluate the product a student produces (e.g., give credit for a simpler product).
- If the class is reading a Shakespearean play, have one student read a simpler version.
- Simplify directions by limiting words or number of steps.
- Adjust the number of pages of writing or reading, number of spelling words, length of a speech or presentation, or the number or length of homework assignments

We can also provide students opportunities to take additional time with the material. Three general strategies are useful (Deschenes et al., 1994).

- *Additional guided practice:* We gather students for mini-skills lessons; peer buddies provide in-class or out-of-class review and tutoring; we arrange occasions such as science nights when families engage in fun learning together.
- *Changes in the pace of instruction and performance:* We slow or increase the rate at which students are asked to obtain information and perform tasks. For some students, we provide additional time (often for fewer responses or performance tasks). For other students, we require more rapid performance on certain tasks.
- *Extra time:* We allow extra time within or outside of class for students to complete their work. If we give other students 1 hour to finish a project, we might give a particular child 2 hours. Of course, this also means that we may have to exempt the child from other work that some students complete.

Help Students Understand Fairness

How do we handle the situation when one student may get an A for work that is clearly not as sophisticated as the work that earns a C for another student? How do we respond when some students turn in very sophisticated and complex projects and another student turns in only a simple drawing? What about when one student reads three complex chapter books and another three simple picture books? How do we explain this to students and parents? Some people will say that this is not fair.

We'd like to respond by telling a story. We go to the playground and watch the children playing baseball. To our surprise we see a boy in a wheelchair at the batter's box. The boy hits the ball over first base and begins wheeling as fast as he can go. He manages to get to first base before the ball is thrown, yet the umpire shouts "Out!" The crowd yells in anger. The umpire explains, "He is supposed to run to first base. He used a wheelchair. That is not fair."

This is obviously not a true story, but we think it illustrates the point: Using his wheelchair was not unfair at all. In fact, it was quite the opposite. The wheelchair helped this child perform more equally. We can state a simple guiding principle about fairness: *Fairness is not about providing the same thing but about providing what each student needs.* We can think of other obvious examples. When people who are blind use braille, tape recorders, or readers, they are engaging in a task in a way that helps equalize their opportunity; the same is true with sign language interpreters, or when students who speak Spanish have texts in Spanish to read in class.

In an inclusive class we help students understand and appreciate how they are each different. As we have differing options and standards based on individual capacities and needs, students understand that we provide what each student needs rather than expecting them all to be the same. We will be surprised how much students understand and appreciate this approach. In fact, if we provide the same curriculum and expectations to all people despite their different intelligences, learning styles, and ability levels, this *is* unfair (Tomlinson, 2004b; Zemelman et al., 2005).

Step 3. Design Product, Assessment, and Evaluation

After we are clear about the goals of learning, we want to design ways of assessing and evaluating students. Assessment has two interactive purposes: (1) determining *what* students have learned, and (2) determining *how* students best learn. Assessment information guides teachers in developing, delivering, and differentiating curriculum and

BUMpS IN THE ROAD

Segregated Functional Skills Training Rather than Education

Some educators believe that academic instruction for students with moderate to severe disabilities (like Sydney) doesn't make sense. They argue that their program should focus on **functional skills**: personal hygiene and care; household chores such as making beds; learning to do simple food preparation; using a bus for transportation; and basic work skills often involving sorting, stacking, and moving objects. Such instruction typically occurs in segregated classes. Schools develop sheltered workshops where students engage in simple work tasks for little or no pay or use "community-based instruction" in which small groups go into the community where, for example, they purchase food at a McDonald's or a grocery store. Separate vocational training schools provide prevocational and vocational training.

These educators do not believe that learning academic skills is of value to these students. They believe that students need to learn such skills to be more independent in the community. However, the evidence simply doesn't show that such programs meet their goals. In part, this occurs because few people learn such functional skills until and unless there is an authentic need for them. Further, most of us learn such skills in the context in which they will be used—at home, in the community—with people who know how to use them.

Of great concern, of course, is that such programs segregate these students. Further, when we assume that students cannot benefit from academic learning, we automatically shut them out of rich learning experiences that broaden their world. Research is demonstrating that students with significant disabilities can benefit tremendously from participation in the general education curriculum where they obtain an education based on critical skills such as reading, writing, and being part of a community (see Chapter 2).

For sure, all people need to learn functional skills. However, this can be done in a way that does not segregate students and is based on skills they actually need as they engage in activities at home, in the community, and on the job. Children typically learn, for example, how to shop for groceries when they need to buy food to eat, most often going with parents or friends, sharing notes about how to get the best buys. Many people naturally develop these skills as they go to events in the community: movies, restaurants, shopping at the mall. Most children learn cooking, home chores, and more from their parents or, later, with roommates. Many inclusive opportunities do exist in schools for development of functional skills— school stores, homemaking courses, after-school programs, and activities in typical classroom instruction. In addition, most high schools operate vocational education and work-study programs in which students get credit for working part-time in community jobs obtaining job-related instruction from teachers. All of these are options that help students with special needs engage in functional activities the way the rest of us do without segregating them and restricting them from learning opportunities.

---

instruction. Evaluation involves making a judgment regarding the quality of student work. In most schools evaluation translates into assigning grades. While assessment and evaluation are related, they are very different functions.

Assessment should directly relate to the learning goals we establish for lessons and units. Some districts have developed report cards that are based on curriculum guidelines that list skills and content knowledge. Some provide developmental statements and allow a rating of quality of performance and knowledge. We can use district curriculum guidelines to help us develop learning goal statements and then develop tools to assess student performance of these skills. Rather than an overall semester grade that provides little information, such competency-based assessment helps us communicate clearly to parents and administrators the growth and learning of students.

Note, however, that we want to avoid rating students on skills as at, below, or above grade level. This implies comparison to other students and says little about the actual level of competency of the student or learning and progress they have made. For students who have cognitive and learning disabilities, this practice also ensures that they will always have low grades no matter how much they learn or how hard they work.

Of course if this process of assessment is to be effective, much depends upon the quality of the curriculum guidelines of the district. At best, such guidelines will focus on various skills (reading, writing, mathematics, scientific inquiry) and content knowledge (science, social studies, etc.). However, while the mission statements of most school districts indicate that they hope to develop the whole child, including responsibility, positive mental health, social skills, and citizenship, the fact is that districts seldom have ways of assessing and reporting such learning on the part of students. Some report cards do have places for items related to such issues but typically focus on student behavior. But, if we consider such areas important we can develop our own list and include this in the assessment process of our lessons and the way we report learning to parents.

We will use assessment to carefully determine how students are progressing and ways we may need to change instruction and support to help them. The math standards of the National Council of Teachers of Mathematics (NCTM), for example, state that one of the most important tools is to listen to students talk as they learn (1987, 1991). When teaching at multiple levels, we must assess students continually to know if they are being challenged at their level of success (Armstrong, 1994). If we do not know that all students are being challenged, then we do not know if they are all learning. When students are making a choice that is too easy or too hard, we discuss it with them. Does it stretch their abilities? Are they finishing too quickly? If they decide a new choice is in order, then we commend them for thinking it through. Given the proper support, students often make good choices.

We also work with specialists, such as speech therapists and special education teachers, to collaboratively conduct both assessment and assignment of grades in the class. Specialists should not take total responsibility for assessing and evaluating students with special needs. This must be a team effort. If students have IEPs or other individualized plans we will need to track and assess their achievement of the goals and objectives listed on these plans. We will track achievement of these on a special form, rating scale, or task analysis list. We may report numbers of responses, compute the percentage of a goal/objective completed, produce a qualitative narrative evaluation or rating, or simply complete a checklist that indicates satisfactory performance of various skills.

Products That Reflect Learning

Effective assessment is based on students developing authentic products that demonstrate their learning—reading real books at their own levels, producing a range of materials (drawing, building a model, writing a song or reflective poem) that demonstrate deep understanding of content, writing real stories, or participating in a student-developed play about a historical event. Rather than having students learn first and then show us what they learned, they learn while demonstrating. For example, if students are learning to write short stories, they don't read about writing and then write. They learn by writing, receiving critiques, rewriting, and editing (Daniels & Bizar, 1998). This approach to assessment helps schoolwork make sense to students with learning difficulties and deepens learning. Authentic assessment allows students to demonstrate learning at their own level (Neill et al., 1995; Tomlinson, 2004b; Wolf, 1989).

ANSWERING QUESTIONS
WITH QUESTIONS

Portfolios

Portfolios are collections of students' work that demonstrate growth and learning. Students choose examples of their best work in each subject, as well as work that shows improvement. They also complete an information sheet that describes what they learned and what they could have done better. In one high school class, for example, students included an early piece of work, a later piece of work, a description of their learning, and a reflective essay. Two copies of each portfolio were made, and one was sent home with a cover letter and photos of the student and the class (Kent, 1997; Wolf, 1989). Portfolios are typically used in student-led conferences. Once again, this form of assessment and sharing is based on personal excellence and just right work for each student.

Anecdotal Records

Anecdotal records are narrative records of what we see and hear as we observe students. The teacher carries a clipboard and jots notes regarding several students each day. By the end of the week she has made notes regarding all students in her class. We can also use Post-it notes placing them in a notebook with a section for each child. Observations help us gather valuable information (Calkins, 1994). Figure 11.10 illustrates one fifth-grade teacher's notes regarding her students' reading. The teacher took these notes when reading individually with students during reading workshop. The reading levels of books range from Grade 1 to Grade 7. Although some students are reading at a lower level, they still receive good grades because they are working hard and are making progress in reading and comprehending well at their level.

Rubrics

When teachers create **rubrics** for projects or assignments, they are beginning the teaching with the end in mind. They know exactly what they want the students to learn and show, and the students are able to frame their learning as well. A rubric or checklist of

FIGURE 11.10

Teacher Observation Notes on Students' Reading Performance

GRADE NOTES

C   Roger: *Shiloh* p. 27. Cases—got second time. Sounded out families. Sack = snack. Wheat = what. Reads kind of rough. Missing basic words like A and there that I know he knows. Bottles = boatels. Deposit = disposal. Totally missed aluminum.

A   Cathey: *A Wrinkle in Time* p. 79. Great flow. Not sure Cheshire—used magic E rule with prompt to figure out. Want = what.

A   Bryant: *Spiders*. It's = it is. Smooth flow—halted over few words not sure. Is = can. Halted over purring and fourth.

B   Joey: *Chang's Paper Pony* p. 48. Pete = pat. Galloped = growled. Dust = treasure. Spread = sprout. We worked on getting meaning from sentence.

A   Aaron: *Soccer Stars* p. 90. Reads nice flow. Corrected that to though. Needs more expression. While = we'll. Corrects most words but pauses to think.

specific skills or behaviors can be used as we conference with students, observe student work in progress, or evaluate a final project. For example, a teacher creates a checklist of key reading and verbal expression skills. He checks a skill with a date when he sees that skill mastered. When a teacher assigns a project, he gives students a rubric so they are aware of expectations. This tool can be particularly valuable in engaging children in thinking about what makes a quality example of the work. We can then guide them to create their own rubrics. Figure 11.11 illustrates a rubric for a computation game project.

FIGURE 11.11

Rubric for Computation Game Project

Name: _____

Item	Possible	Points Earned
Gameboard with interesting path	20	
Easily seen squares to draw cards	5	
Cards with math problems	15	
Answer sheet included and readable	10	
Thoughtful/creative/colorful	10	
Directions include setup, playing, and winning	20	
Explain to group in class and play	10	
Self-evaluation of game	10	
Total	**100**	

Performance Assessment

In **performance assessment** we evaluate products or performances of students—a story, a play depicting an episode in history, a science experiment, research on a social issue. We can assess skills involved as well as quality of the product and effort. One teacher had students write and illustrate stories. To do this we need to analyze each product to determine skills and knowledge that is demonstrated. These can then be placed on a rubric.

A middle school teacher had students create artwork with captions in response to a novel they read. A high school football player brought in a shoe box and told a story with action figures. The teacher wrote everything down the student said and handed him the text, saying: "You are a writer" (Herman, Aschbacher, & Winters, 1992). This allowed the student to express what he learned, while giving him exciting feedback on his progress as a learner.

Classroom Tests

Classroom pencil-and-paper tests can be useful, although they should be used sparingly. If students are learning through projects in which they develop projects, we will find that classroom tests don't assess well what is being learned. Often teachers divide the curriculum so that different groups of students study different parts of the same topic and then are expected to share. In this jigsaw approach, if pencil-and-paper tests are used, different groups take different tests. Classroom test questions can also be open-ended and can encourage a variety of answers. One teacher we know allowed her sixth-grade students to use any resource in the classroom to find answers they did not know. This required them both to know information and to possess research skills for finding answers. Another teacher formed study groups for the children to review for the tests and study for retakes. This group met during class time to share what they were still struggling with and go over answers to questions. This teacher knows that in reality children need strategies for taking tests; however, we also need to develop supports for being successful in this arena.

If we are relying primarily on multiple-choice or true/false tests, we may need adaptations for some of our students. Some strategies include (Deschenes et al., 1994; J. Wood, 1998):

- Reducing the number of test items or simplifying concepts
- Allowing all students to retake tests
- Having a student respond to the test orally and tape-recording the exam or having it recorded by a writer
- Allowing the use of helping devices on exams—computers and calculators
- Allowing time extensions
- Providing alternative test formats—short-answer, multiple-choice, oral, or essay questions
- Splitting administration of an exam over more than one session

Student-Led Conferences

In **student-led conferences** students show and explain their work and learning to parents. With teacher guidance, students decide which pieces of their work they put in their portfolios. The examples chosen demonstrate individual growth and progress, show exemplary work overall, or represent the individual student's interests and talents.

During the conference, the teacher serves as a greeter and facilitator as he greets each family and hands each student his or her portfolio. Multiple student-led conferences are conducted simultaneously. The student leads, showing each piece of work in the portfolio.

Students also show their families around the classroom, demonstrate daily routines, introduce classmates, and show parents classroom resources. Math activities, experiments, or other key learning activities are set up in which parents can participate. Student-led conferences provide opportunities for students to be positively involved in bridging home–school communications (Kent, 1997; Wolf, 1989).

Grading and Report Cards

When teaching students with diverse abilities, grading and assessment can be confusing. Will grades be adjusted to accommodate for individual students' disabilities? Will these adjustments be indicated on report cards? Will all students be graded on the same activities? These questions fit into the broader issues concerning best practices for evaluation and grading. As teaching practices shift from lecture and worksheet to best practices, evaluation of students changes as well.

Although much research indicates that grading is counterproductive to learning (Kohn, 1999), most schools continue to use some version of the traditional A–E grading system. A typical problem in grading practices is that some students work very hard and

---

Making Teamwork Fun

SCHOOLS to VISIT

Theodore Roosevelt High School
540 Eureka
Wyandotte, MI 48192

Roosevelt High School is located in Wyandotte, Michigan, a southwestern suburb of Detroit, known as "Down River." Most of the 1,300 students come from blue-collar, working-class families. In 1987, Roosevelt High School began its journey toward inclusive education. It developed a process of team teaching between general and special education teachers to provide support to students with mild to moderate disabilities in general education. Beginning with a small number of teachers, the program has grown. Certain classes are identified as team-taught classes. The general and special education teachers have, over the years, worked out very positive relationships and enjoy their work together. The special education staff sees itself as a support for all students in the class. They've also been about team building in the school. The special education office, located in the school's center, serves as planning center for teachers but also is the host of parties and celebrations for all involved in the coteaching effort.

In recent years, the school has hosted a special class of students with severe and multiple disabilities that come from 16 school districts in their county. They have sought to integrate these students as much as possible into general education classes throughout the school. Their special education class is located in the center of the school. Many general education students volunteer in the class, receiving service-learning credit, and help students participate in general education classes.

Roosevelt has a strong program of vocational–technical education and a strong art program. Students with special needs have particularly found such programs helpful. The horticulture program helps students apply biology knowledge through a school-run greenhouse and florist shop.

Recently, in concert with an initiative by the superintendent of the school system, general and special education staff have begun to work together to expand hands-on, activity-based learning throughout the school curriculum. Special education staff are developing a catalog of many practical examples of ways to teach using active learning methods that better meet the needs of students with special needs and other students as well.

yet get low grades, while other students do little and get all A's. The more we emphasize grades (or any type of test performance, for that matter), the more students lose interest in learning, focusing primarily on how they did rather than on the substance of what they are learning (Christiansen & Vogel, 1998; Kohn, 1999). If we are nevertheless required to give grades, as is the case in most schools, then we must strive to grade in a way that encourages and rewards students when they put forth effort and demonstrate an interest in learning. Effective inclusive teachers we have seen use the following three criteria for giving student grades:

1. Effort
2. Growth and improvement
3. Goals reached

Such a scheme is more fair than the typical method of assigning grades based on absolute criteria or on the percentage correct on a test. It also allows us to make good use of best practice assessment strategies described previously.

Grading should also be aligned with instruction. For example, if students have been writing stories by choosing their own topics and conferencing with peers, we do not then grade them by supplying a topic that they have to complete on their own.

We ask students to set goals for themselves in our classes. A goal might be expressed as a number of books to be read; as a set of skills on which a student would like to improve; or as a product, such as a short story, play, or artistic depiction, that the student would like to develop. Once students set goals, we provide simple forms on which they record progress toward such goals. However, know that students need explicit instruction and modeling on how to plan for goals and strive to reach them. Many of our students, particularly those living in poverty, come to us without this background knowledge, so we need to be very specific in teaching them how to plan and think in terms of long-range goals.

One useful strategy involves students in evaluating themselves and making grade proposals and justifications. At the end of the card-marking period, teachers ask students to propose the grade they should receive and to provide evidence that justifies this request. The forms that they use to track progress would be cited as evidence. We can also ask students to write reflective journals regarding what they have learned over a particular period. These strategies help involve students in thinking about their progress, thus increasing the meaning of the grades they receive.

Laura Schiller, a sixth-grade teacher, explains how she uses this process: "I have a range of kids in my class," she says, and "some talented and gifted kids have gotten E's because they did not push themselves and take risks." If students typically receive A's, their parents may be concerned about failing grades. However, we have students keep self-evaluations so when parents inquire the teacher simply explains her grading process and asks students to show their parents the papers in their folder. Students functioning at lower levels may get good grades if they are pushing themselves and working hard (Schiller, 1998).

In some cases we need to differentiate or adapt grading for students with special needs. In some cases no modification of grading is required. This occurs when the learning objectives are the same for all students, even though some additional specialized objectives may be included. However, when needed, we modify our grading procedures with these strategies (Christiansen & Vogel, 1998; Janney & Snell, 2000a; Price, Mayfield, McFadden, & Marsh, 1998):

■ Grading based on the accomplishment of learning goals established on the IEP or our own agreement with a student

Students are developing their presentation materials for their project on Alaska. Pairs of students worked together to gather information about a state in the United States. They will present this information to the class. This multilevel lesson allows both Emily, who is gifted, and Alice, who has a cognitive disability, to contribute and learn.

- Grading based on (1) improvement and (2) effort—standards of grading that some teachers prefer for all their students
- Providing additional projects for students to bring up grades

This type of individualized grading should be consistent with what we use for all of our students. At best we will establish individual learning goals for each student that we negotiate with them—and if we do so, this is very similar to what we will do with evaluating learning objectives established in IEPs.

How grades are recorded on a report card for students with special needs varies. Some schools indicate on the report card that the grade reflects an "adjusted" grading system. Other educators argue that grades are subjective in all cases and simply cannot reflect a uniform measure of student achievement. These educators do not indicate adaptations or "adjustments" in the grading system.

Standardized Tests

Standardized tests play a powerful role. Student scores on these tests often drive community opinions of schools. The tests themselves also drive what we teach, as these tests are based on the state standards. Although standardized tests have always been used in schools, in recent years their use has expanded dramatically and most schools are under great pressure to produce high test scores.

Many policy makers see standardized tests as procedures by which schools can be held accountable for producing effective learning (Popham, 2001). Others see them as harming effective learning. These analysts argue that tests focus on memorization of facts rather than on deep understanding (Kohn, 1999; Ohanian, 1999) and lead teachers to feel pressured to produce high test scores, even if this means a shift away from best teaching practices. Many schools are spending an increasing amount of instructional time in explicit preparation for tests (Hilliard, 2000; Kaiser, 2000; Kohn, 1999, 2000). Test scores may even be used to determine promotion from one grade to another or graduate students from high school, a purpose for which such tests were not designed (Heubert & Hauser, 1999; Popham, 2001; Townsend, 2000). Test results themselves are related to the socioeconomic status of students' parents (Heubert & Hauser, 1999; Hilliard, 2000).

Educators have hoped that the increased focus on standards, combined with IDEA's requirement that students with disabilities have access to the general education curriculum would assist students with disabilities in being included and better educated in general education classes (Office of Special Education Programs, 2000a). Others, however, are concerned that increasing numbers of students will be referred to segregated special education classes when they are not able to "keep up" with the standardized curriculum; some hope to exempt students with learning differences from the tests (Heubert & Hauser, 1999) or seek not to count these students' test scores to increase schools' average scores (Heubert & Hauser, 1999; Peterson et al., 2002; Thurlow, 2000).

What are best practices in relation to standardized testing? First, we keep the tests in perspective. We use standards to focus on topics to teach but resist organizing our teaching around the test. We understand that the best hope both for learning *and* for higher test scores is to use best instructional practices.

Second, we prepare students for the test using best teaching practices. We teach tests as a special genre of literature, teaching students to break the test apart, think about what it is really asking, and understand the tricks inherent in the test. We involve them in brainstorming strategies. Students write their own questions and share their efforts. We teach students that skilled test takers are those who can move easily from the text to questions and back. Students spend time learning to write and think in the formal English that test writers use. They learn not to expect the test to be interesting. In other words, we teach them the unwritten rules of test taking that good test takers know (see Calkins, Montgomery, Santman, and Falk, 1998).

Third, IDEA requires students with disabilities have the same opportunity as other students to take state standardized tests. This requirement was intended to prevent schools from unilaterally exempting all special education students so that their scores would not depress the scores of the school. The Americans with Disabilities Act and Section 504 of the Rehabilitation Act of 1973 require accommodations in the testing. To access accommodations, however, a student must have either a 504 plan or an Individualized Education Plan (IEP). Accommodations may include:

- Reading the questions to the student
- Having someone write the responses the student dictates
- Providing visual aids to enlarge the examination
- Presenting the exam in alternative formats—braille, the native language of the student, and so on
- Administering the exam in a location that is quiet
- Allowing for breaks and an extended time period

In addition, for students with moderate to severe disabilities, for whom the regular state test is deemed inappropriate, each state is required to develop an *alternative assessment* (IDEA, 2004). Only a maximum of 2% of students receiving services in special education, however, can take this alternative assessment.

Fourth, we can provide information to parents and others regarding how tests work and explain to parents their rights regarding exemptions for their children. In some states, taking the standardized test is mandatory. In others, parents have the right to exempt their children. The decision as to whether a child with learning difficulties

Sights TO SEE

Learning Styles and Assistive Technology

Knowing How You Learn: Schools Attuned At San Francisco's Gateway High School, a diverse group of students learn how their brains work and how to accommodate their learning styles. Most important, they discover that there is no one "right" way to learn. www.edutopia.org/knowing-how-you-learn

The Sound of Learning: Albano Berberi Assistive technology helps a blind computer science student and devoted gamer pursue his passions. www.edutopia.org/assistive-technology-albano-berberi-video

should take standardized exams must be made with consideration of the impact on the student. Many parents exempt their children from these examinations. Many teachers, too, are concerned about the negative impact of failing these exams on students' self-concept. Others want their children included in these tests if other students are required to take them (Peterson et al., 2002).

Finally, we can connect with the growing national movement to challenge standardized tests. We can educate ourselves regarding the impact of standardized tests, develop our own opinion, and become part of the effort to influence policy makers to create the conditions most effective for learning. See Kohn (1999) and Ohanian (1999), and see the FairTest Web site (www.fairtest.org) for comprehensive critiques of standardized testing.

Toward Inclusive Academic Learning

There's no doubt that shifting from a goal of having all children on grade level to having them learn at their personal best level is a major shift in the way we think about schooling. However, with a bit of reflection, we can see that the notion of grade level is actually the stranger goal. Clearly, the idea is literally based on seeing schooling as a type of factory. We all know how factories work. For what they are intended to do, the structure of a factory is very useful. The steps to produce a product are broken down, standardized, and performed by different workers. The production line, of course, must stay on schedule. If one worker is too slow, the entire production line slows. That's the model on which keeping students on grade level is based. We have standardized ideas about the "product"—thus standardized tests—and we have to stay on time and target to end up with this goal.

Does such a standardized, regimented structure work for the education and development of human beings? Many thoughtful people whom we discussed early in this chapter think that it does not, for human beings simply are not and cannot be standardized. We vary in all sorts of ways. When we treat human beings in formation—for example, children—as standardized pegs in a production line, we ignore their strengths, needs, unique gifts, challenges. In fact, if we are successful in creating a standardized product, we precisely rob students of some of their humanity and potential contributions in the process. By being successful, we lose.

It's why inclusive teaching that affirms that we should celebrate differing levels and types of outcomes of learning is so critical for having good schools for all children. We move beyond standardization to creating a process of learning where students, on the one hand, learn together as a community but also, on the other hand, achieve their personal best, nurturing their own gifts and talents framed by personal life goals.

Traveling Notes

When we design authentic, multilevel instruction we are using practices that are highly supported by research and the positions of many educational organizations. We will be creating classrooms where all students experience success based on their personal capabilities while being part of an inclusive classroom community. Here are a few notes regarding positive practices from this chapter.

1. Despite best practice information to the contrary, lectures, worksheets, and textbooks continue to form the bulk of instruction in many classrooms. This leads to shallow learning.
2. The brain can process many things at one time. This allows teachers to combine ideas and teach complex processes and minute parts simultaneously.
3. Educators from many perspectives are calling for more hands-on, relevant, multimodal learning in classrooms to reach all types of students including brain-based learning, best practices of national educational organizations, culturally relevant pedagogy, and universal design for instruction.
4. Multilevel instruction reaches all students at their ability level supporting them in moving to the next level, while enabling them to work with children at all levels in the classroom.
5. Planning for multilevel instruction involves several steps: plan a theme, plan multilevel goals, develop learning activities, look at certain students and make alterations to learning activities, and plan assessment.
6. Creating products becomes learning in and of itself as students develop representations of information and knowledge.
7. Effective assessment allows students to demonstrate learning in multiple and interesting ways—journals, portfolios, products, student-led conferences—moving away from multiple-choice, fill-in-the-blank tests.
8. Students do better on standardized tests when multilevel instruction is used. Students with special needs can take these tests with appropriate accommodations.

Stepping Stones

Following are some activities that will help extend your understanding and actions you may take toward multilevel instruction in your school.

1. Ask a teacher who does multilevel teaching if you can sit in on a planning session with him or her. How does the teacher create thematic lessons and plan lessons that reach all levels of students?
2. Use the district curriculum and identify themes that could link multiple subjects throughout the year. Identify overall learning goals and describe varied levels of learning you might expect from students with differing abilities.
3. Discuss the ideas of multilevel learning goals and multilevel assessment with a group of teachers (at best a team with whom you

teach). Identify ways you might begin to incorporate these ideas and strategies into your teaching practice.
4. Observe in a classroom where the school puts great emphasis on being on grade level and utilizes one set of grade-level materials for all students. What problems do you see? What do you learn from this?
5. Develop a plan for using multimodal assessment tools in a unit of lessons in which students have options and choices.
6. Keep a journal about your feelings, thoughts, questions, and ideas. How do you feel about teaching using what we've called best practices? How do you feel about engaging learners at multiple ability levels? Why?

12 | Inclusive Academic Instruction, Part II

Multilevel and Differentiated Learning Activities

CHAPTER GOAL

Understand the need for improving instruction for all learners and a process for multilevel differentiated instruction planning.

CHAPTER OBJECTIVES

1. Understand strategies and tools for designing multilevel learning activities.
2. Know how to access and use multilevel learning materials that allow students to obtain information at their personal challenge level.
3. Utilize numerous strategies to support student learning including scaffolding and multiple intelligences.
4. Be able to design individualized differentiation for specific students.

Two Social Studies Classes: One for Sleeping, the Other for Learning

Let's visit two high schools to see how their efforts toward inclusive teaching are going. In a history class at Garland Heights High School, we watch 28 students laughing and jostling; yet 3 others are asleep. Belinda, the teacher, is reviewing a lesson about Vietnam for an exam. She has given a handout of facts she expects the students to know taken from the information required for the high school graduation test. She reads each question from the handout and has a student read the answer. "Any questions?" she asks after each one. Only about a third of the class is paying attention. "Frank! Turn around," she says as one student playfully smacks another on the leg. The special education teacher goes around to the 8 students with disabilities in the class. The students obviously like her. "These students are having a hard time," she comments. "Jamal has low reading abilities," she says about a student whose head is down on his desk. Finally, Belinda passes out a 50-item multiple-choice test. We hear groans and yawns and shuffling of feet as students start to work.

The next day, in a social studies class at Highlander High School, we find students all over the room in small groups. Ayo, the general education teacher, and Marla, the special education teacher, go from group to group answering questions, talking, challenging, and offering suggestions. Students occasionally laugh but are very intent on their work. They explain that the class is role-playing the passage of the Indian Removal Bill that led to the forced march of the Cherokee Indians from Georgia to territory in what later became Oklahoma. Each group represents a different constituency—the Cherokee Indians, the U.S. government under President Andrew Jackson, plantation owners and farmers, missionaries and northern reformers, and Black Seminoles. Each group is studying its own position, preparing a presentation for Congress, and trying to gain allies. The students are engaged, discussing very complex ideas (adapted from Bigelow, 1995).

After a while we locate students with disabilities in the class. Rihana, who has cerebral palsy and a mild cognitive disability, is with the Cherokee Indians group. She does not read well and uses a computer with key guards to type. Rihana is helping the group understand the rejection felt by the Cherokees based on her experiences with her disability. Juan, a bilingual student with learning disabilities, is part of the plantation owners group. He is a good artist and is making posters that document his group's perspective. Jonathan, a student with a severe cognitive disability, is part of the missionaries group. He has difficulty communicating more than a yes or no. As the group discusses strategies, they periodically turn to Jonathan and ask questions about what he thinks. Ayo explains, "It's interesting watching

BACK
PACK

Universal Design for Learning and Project-Based Learning

Access Center The center is a program funded by the U.S. Department of Education whose mission is to provide technical assistance that strengthens state and local capacity to help students with disabilities effectively learn in the general education curriculum. Its Web site is filled with useful resources related to universal design for learning, multilevel learning, and differentiated instruction. www.k8accesscenter.org/index.php

Edutopia This initiative of the George Lukas Foundation provides information and quality video regarding innovative teaching techniques including inquiry and problem-based learning. www.edutopia.org

Project-Based Learning Online This is a great resource that walks you through the process of designing project-based learning with many videos of classes in action. www.bie.org/index.php/site/PBL/pbl_online/

students with Jonathan. As they synthesize information to ask him yes and no questions, you can see that they are getting a clearer understanding of the material. Having Jonathan here is strengthening the learning of all the students in ways I didn't anticipate."

Step 4. Inclusive Instructional Strategies

If we are to be successful with students we need to use approaches to instruction that (1) engage students in learning they feel is meaningful and interesting; (2) provide students a feeling of success and efficacy; and (3) support students in growing and learning starting with where they are now and helping them move along to the next step. If all three of these criteria are not met students will simply not achieve and grow. Let's look at the three major approaches to instruction and explore how one, workshop learning, helps us fulfill these important criteria.

Introduction to Workshop Learning

In this chapter we provide strategies for workshop learning, and in Chapter 13 we'll see how workshop learning looks in school subjects. We'll start with an overview and then go into more depth.

As discussed in Chapter 11, we first *identify the topic and learning goals*. Sometimes, particularly if we are organizing workshop around a skill-based subject such as reading, writing, or math, we select the topics while allowing for some student input. However, in inquiry or problem-based learning, we help students select their own topic or question to pursue. We may also use authentic themes to link a variety of skill-based subjects as we explored in Chapter 11.

Workshop time begins with an introduction to the lesson or an activity to get the students interested. Once the learning process is under way, we will start each lesson with a short *mini-lesson* (usually 10–15 minutes) that provides key information, teaches skills, and engages students in discussion.

In all forms of workshop learning, students work individually, in pairs, and in small groups. This constant interplay of individual, paired, and small group work allows students to function as a learning community (see Chapter 9).

We then get students involved in the **learning process**. This involves the key way we will have students learning information, developing skills, and creating products that demonstrate their learning. In workshop learning the focus is on creating a product. All learning leads to and is organized around creating the final product—a poem, a story, a reflection, a report, an artistic rendition of an event, a play. The type of product depends on the field of study and the students' ability level. It's why we call this approach "workshop." Students are working, as in a home workshop, on an active project. For example, in one class students locate information on the Internet and create a PowerPoint presentation on Penguins as part of nonfiction reading. At the same time others write in their journals about facts they have found, or read books on their research subject and discuss their findings in groups. They are all reading nonfiction but in different ways.

As students are involved in the learning process they gather information and *draft* their product. Students *seek input and feedback to revise their drafts* in *peer conferences*. They meet with peers at an "editors' table" to review drafts and work with partners to revise their work.

During the class, teachers have several responsibilities. We move from student to student and group to group monitoring student work, answering questions, and providing needed assistance. We conduct *student conferences* to provide one-on-one assistance. We also conduct *mini-lessons* with small groups who need to work on similar skills. Now and then, of course, we stop and address the whole group to clarify an issue or do a brief mini-lesson related to a topic about which many students are having difficulty.

As student work is completed, we facilitate students *publishing* their products and *sharing and celebrating* their work by presenting to other students or to parents and community members via *student-led conferences* or learning fairs.

In workshop learning, all students are working on similar projects but can pursue their work at their own level of ability with support from the teacher, one another, and specialists, such as speech therapists, special education teachers, or gifted consultants. In studying erosion of the soil, for example, some students make simple drawings of rain washing away soil. Others engage in complex mathematical analysis and present charts of erosion under differing conditions. If students need intensive support, this is easily incorporated into the workshop process.

Workshop-based learning exists in several variations. We may have **workshops for typical school subjects** such as reading, writing, math, and science. In these, the focus of the workshop is on skills or content associated with that subject as well as content linked around an authentic theme.

Inquiry and problem-based learning are two related approaches for thematic learning in which students develop questions, seek answers to those questions, and develop products that demonstrate learning using the inquiry and authoring cycle shown in Figure 12.1. This approach is particularly useful in authentic, thematic units that link several subjects. Inquiry and problem-based learning could involve the total class in the same inquiry. Alternatively, small groups or individuals may select different inquiry topics. We can also have students select different inquiry topics around an overall theme. For example, students in Chapter 11 were involved in a class around the theme of "going to the extremes." Some groups explored people going deep underwater, whereas others had experiences in the Arctic and Antarctic, and yet others learned about outer space travel to the moon (Short, Harste, & Burke, 1996).

Expeditionary learning involves students in community activities organized around themes. An elementary school class, for example, focused on transportation and space exploration; activities included a demonstration of a hot-air balloon, a helicopter landing at the school, and a visit to an air show. In LaCrosse, Wisconsin, a school district

FIGURE 12.1

Inquiry and Authoring Cycle

START

Connect to life experiences

Develop questions for inquiry and plan approach

Plan new inquiries

Gather information, artifacts, engage in research, reflect

Build skills for inquiry

Draft product of inquiry—report, story, presentation, play

Share, publish, celebrate

Others help edit for publication

Explore meaning with others and gain new perspectives

Revise the content and self-edit for conventions

Source: Adapted from Short, Harste, and Burke (1996).

developed a School on the River program in which students learn how to canoe, fish, and sample the ecosystem of the Mississippi River (Pitsch, 1994).

In **microsociety** schools, teachers, and students operate a miniature civilization that includes a legislature, courts, banks, post office, newspaper, businesses, and an internal revenue service. In the morning students typically attend subject classes that are taught with a focus on real-world applications. For example, in the English class the emphasis may be on writing and publishing; in mathematics, on personal and social economics; in social studies, on government. In the afternoon students go to their "jobs" in student-run businesses, government agencies, and newspapers. A miniature marketplace, currency, and legal system are utilized. Students have jobs they can accomplish at their level of learning (Sommerfield, 1992).

Community-based learning involves students in learning in the community. Such experiences may be associated with specific classes. For example, in one high school, students obtained English credit working at the local newspaper, a nonprofit organization newsletter, and a local book publishing company. **Cooperative work study** is a form of community-based learning in which students go to classes a half day and then work in the community for a half day, obtaining school credit. Many schools require that

FIGURE 12.2

Learning Activities and Subjects Matrix

| | SUBJECTS | | | |
LEARNING ACTIVITIES	LANGUAGE ARTS	HISTORY	MATH	ART
Read the Bill of Rights as a group.	X	X		
Write and act out play regarding civil rights.				
Personal reflections: writing, tape, etc. Some students do individually, some in cooperative group based on choice.	X			X
Create song or drawing to illustrate one of the rights. Present to the class.		X		X
Observe and take notes in a location in the community. Present conclusions as a group or individually.	X		X	X
Interview a lawyer or civil rights leader about one of the rights. Develop written report, video, etc.	X			X
Conduct study regarding rights violations in a community—legal costs, economics, number of complaints lost and won.	X	X	X	
Write a short story, play, or poem regarding reflections on the importance of one of the rights.	X	X		X

students provide service in the community as part of their high school requirements. Such **service learning** experiences may include assisting in hospitals, museums, community agencies, schools, and other settings via internships and mentorships (Peterson, LeRoy, Field, & Wood, 1992; Richardson, 1994).

We will want to use a systematic process to link our learning activities related to a theme across disciplinary subjects that we teach. Figure 12.2 uses an adaptation of the multiple intelligences grid to link learning activities and multiple subjects.

Multilevel Learning Activities

Inclusive workshop learning activities facilitate students with substantial ability differences learning together. These can be broken into three broad categories:

1. *Multilevel learning activities* where learning goals, materials, and the nature of the learning activity allow students to naturally function at their just-right level.
2. *Tiered lessons* in which teachers design lessons with materials and assign activities at several levels of sophistication and complexity.

3. *Individualized differentiation and curriculum adaptations* that adapt or modify a lesson for an individual student.

Multilevel learning activities allow students naturally to operate at their own level of challenge without requiring the teacher to create lessons at different levels. Typically such learning activities are based on open-ended assignments that aim at higher levels of Bloom's taxonomy. Multilevel learning activities involve both individual and cooperative group tasks in which students explore important and complex questions. Students draw from strengths of others in the group and teachers pay attention to the structure and interactions of the group (Cohen, Lotan, Scarloss, & Arellano, 1999).

In Chapter 11 Sydney's moose project was a nice example of a multilevel lesson that involved aspects of both individual and small group work. If you'll remember, students were required to select a plant or animal about which they wanted to learn. They were to gather information and create a way to present what they had learned to the rest of the class. Students could do a good job on this project at very different levels of sophistication. You saw a bit of Sydney's work. These teachers also had several students who were considered gifted. One of these students, Marsha, produced a complex PowerPoint presentation. She got so interested in various species of birds that she also made a chart showing the locations around the world in which they lived and how the environment had spurred the birds to develop different adaptations. Sydney did a good job on her project and got an A. So did Marsha. Yet their learning products were at extremely different levels of complexity and sophistication. That's the wonder of good multilevel instruction. It allows all students to be challenged but does not require extra work of the teacher.

Multilevel learning activities can occur in various formats. Let's look at some of these.

Skill Learning via Authentic Applied Activities. Teaching skills such as reading, writing, and math are taught via inclusive, multilevel learning activities when students are involved in using the skills for a genuine purpose focusing on skills and using learning materials at their own level of ability.

For example, in **reading workshop**, students read just-right books and other written materials at their own challenge level. Some students may be reading complex chapter or nonfiction books on a theme the class is exploring. Other students may be reading picture books.

In **writing workshop**, students write for real audiences at their own level. Some students wrote poetry and fiction pieces working on using sophisticated metaphors. Other students told a simple story using pictures cut out from magazines and picture figures.

In **math workshop** students engage in applied activities using math. One class, for example, had groups of students develop and operate a business (either for real or in simulation). This allowed students to have varied roles and to use math skills in operating the business at their level of ability. As students in reading and writing workshop worked on skills and concepts at their own ability level, so students in math workshop worked on skills ranging from basic addition and subtraction to using complex statistics and algebra. We'll explore applications of inclusive, multilevel activities and workshop learning in typical subjects more in Chapter 13.

Open-Ended Individual Projects. Open-ended individual projects allow students to gather information and produce products at varied levels of sophistication. While projects may be individual projects, other students will also be involved. Other students review drafts. We have students share with one another their progress and learning in pairs or small groups. In "individual study" in a workshop class we will see students reading, obtaining information from the Internet, asking other students about something they don't understand, and having students review their drafts at the editors' table. In addition, student pairs and small groups can implement most open-ended individual projects.

Here are a few examples:

- Students gather information about different states or countries including their capital, economy, geography, and significant historical events.
- Students explore the concepts of love and hate as a theme linking several subjects over a semester. They are expected to find examples of various types of love and hate and how they have been expressed in people's lives.
- Students compare and contrast three approaches to the economy: capitalism, communism, and fascism.

Independent inquiry and problem-based learning. If part of our goal as teachers is to create lifelong learners, then we need to structure part of our class where we encourage students to explore topics in which they are interested. We can work with them to identify areas to explore and the type of product they will produce. We can help link **independent studies** to required curriculum guidelines. Students may then do their own work and research on a project, with the guidance and support of peers and specialists such as special education teachers or gifted consultants. Students will develop a product to share with classmates. For example, in a unit on ocean life, a student says he wants to learn more about whales. We help the student develop inquiry questions and guide him in collecting information. He may develop a presentation to the class using a poster or PowerPoint. When we use independent studies we want to ensure that students are engaged in just-right work at their own level of challenge to ensure high standards. We will help students develop a schedule for their project to help them stay on track and prevent procrastination. Having students use journals and logs to document their progress can be helpful.

Learning contracts. **Learning contracts** are similar. However, instead of supporting students in selecting their own topics, in learning contracts the teacher specifies the necessary skills or knowledge to be learned and expectations for the lesson. However, we allow the student to decide how she will complete the lesson. This allows us to have control over student learning while allowing students to make choices based on their own learning styles and preferences. We also are teaching students how to plan and work more independently. For example, a student completes a learning contract for a social studies project. We want students to explore an important event during the period in which the United States gained independence. She is interested in how Indians were treated during this time. She indicates that she will read information on this, create a poster explaining her findings, and write a report. We also ask the student to identify dates at which she will complete various aspects of the project. The contract is written out and signed by both teacher and student.

Learning centers. **Learning centers** are a way to manage interesting and complex learning experiences for individuals and small groups. We can create different activities on the same topic through which students rotate, or we can create centers with different topics. We can also use multiple intelligences to focus the learning of one topic in eight interesting ways. This allows students to use their strengths to learn specific content. Centers are motivating to students when they involve interesting work and an element of choice. Centers can also be used as enrichment where students study topics beyond the general curriculum.

We should have centers that allow students to engage at differing levels of ability with materials of different complexity. For example, a center on poetry might have a range of poems that students can read along with tape-recorded poems, and poems on a computer program accompanied by graphics. In addition, we can create some centers that are more complex and some that are simpler. We would expect students to select just-right centers for themselves.

Authentic homework. In workshop learning, **homework** is not used for rote practice of skills. When students are required to do homework that is filling out a worksheet or practicing math facts, it makes little difference in student learning. However, when the learning is real and connected to what they are doing in school it can greatly improve what students get out of the context. Homework should have real-life applications, receive immediate feedback, and involve the family in learning together.

For example, a sixth-grade social studies teacher was exploring heroes and explorers important in history. She assigned a multiweek homework project in which students were to interview a person about his or her hero and to share the information with someone else, not the person they interviewed, before they presented the project in class. I got a note back from the person with whom they shared. "One student," she explained,

> did a puppet show; another produced a video. One boy interviewed his older brother. His older brother's hero was Jackie Robinson so he found Jackie Robinson's baby picture and his brother's baby picture and made a poster. Another student made a poster on which were these words: "leader, teacher, better person, and friend." Each of the words represented a core theme from an interview with the student's mother. He had two pages of handwritten materials, an amazing amount of writing for this student! I was very proud of him.

Homework moves from being an onerous chore to be avoided to engaging work that deepens understanding of key concepts and provides an opportunity for the student and family to connect.

Open-Ended Group Projects. **Open-ended group projects** involve a group of students in study or development of a product (such as a play, poster, song, etc.) in which students can take varied roles, allowing differing levels of skill and ability. For example, one elementary class collaborated to investigate how their town looked and operated a century earlier. They then built a model of the town.

In group projects we ask questions that prompt students to think about where they might find information. We can design guides for conducting interviews and practice interviewing in class, give information on using particular resource tools, and bring materials and people into the class. We establish supports at the student's level. For example, a student who has difficulty reading and writing is planning to gather information through interviews and collect artifacts from local people. Perhaps the student and a buddy can work together, one of them asking questions and the other writing down the answers. We can help them work out mutual responsibilities.

Here are a few examples of possibilities:

- In a unit about the Civil War, students choose to work in groups on one of four topics: free labor and slave labor, key leaders in the North and South, the emergence of the Ku Klux Klan and lynchings, and impact on the economy.
- Students collect and analyze information regarding weather patterns in different parts of the world and develop and confirm hypotheses regarding causes of these patterns.

Process drama is a very powerful group learning strategy that uses theater to engage students and teachers in living through experiences that engage emotions, mind, and body. This strategy is both a way of presenting information and engaging students in a

Inclusive Creative Writing in Middle School

Laura Schiller (1998), a former middle school teacher, provides some pointers on conducting effective writing workshops that are applicable at all grade levels and provide excellent illustrations of scaffolding and multilevel instruction that also connect across learning styles and multiple intelligences.

In her class, she uses the following strategies to structure the year: (1) Start with poetry to develop an understanding of the craft of writing, (2) move to memoirs to develop depth, and (3) then use expository text supported by fiction. She seeks to get students involved immediately in the craft of writing, linking this to reading, and building on this throughout the year.

To help students get started, she uses **freewriting** to break down fears and inhibitions. "We ask them to turn off the internal censors and editors. Just see what comes out. Keep the pencils writing. Do this for no more than 7 minutes." Most often students respond saying, "Oh! We need more time. This gets students ASKING to write!" Often there are surprises in the creativity that emerges. Kids with disabilities often come up with new perspectives.

Poetry. Laura explains, "I ask kids, 'How many of you think you're poets?' Not many usually raise their hands. 'There is a very easy way. A **list poem**.' I show them a picture of a treasure chest. 'If you could put anything you wanted inside your treasure chest, what would you put?'" She then has students share what they wrote. Students are asked to make their list quickly. This helps students with special needs buy in. They can do a tiny piece. Students then revise and some read theirs out loud. The teacher point out concrete details, use of the senses, and the importance of threes—words that come in threes as a typical word rhythm in the craft of poetry. As they make revisions, we ask students to pare down language—eliminate unnecessary words. "The kids then handed in their poems," Laura explains. "We typed them up with their name next to their poem. We then made a video in which all read a line or two. This was shown at parents night in the school. Thus, we went from writing to performance."

Memoir. While poetry gets students thinking and feeling, the memoir deepens thinking. Laura asks her students to "Write what matters to you. Write what you know or can find out about." This moves us beyond typical action writing that has no depth. A couple of other strategies are useful in helping students get started. With **Heart MAP**, students draw a heart with pictures and words of what matters to them on it. They then use these ideas as the basis for writing about their lives. In **Neighborhood MAP**, students draw a map of (1) trips taken, (2) their bedroom, (3) and/or their neighborhood. The teacher can ask questions to help them think: "Where did you tell a lie? Where did the bully get you? Where did you like to play?"

If students get *stuck* Laura has them write "I am stuck" over and over *or* has them restate or rewrite what they started with in the first place. They must keep the pencil moving the whole time. While the students are writing the teacher models freewriting on a transparency. This is very helpful to students with special needs and breaks down inhibitions. Most writing in schools needs to be informal.

Reflection: Laura uses some great strategies that engage students in deep thinking. She challenges both students who are gifted and children with cognitive and learning disabilities while providing support to all. She often invites parents of children from various ethnic groups into the class to share stories from their lives as part of these learning projects and she is well respected in the community.

powerful learning activity. Using this process, teachers engage students in a play of historical events, taking different roles in the events, stopping periodically to reflect on what people may be feeling as the event unfolds. In these dramatic sessions teachers' problems with students virtually disappear. Many students who have trouble with writing and reading shine in dramatic learning (Rohd, 1998). Some students use these experiences as a springboard to develop their own play. Others write a story from the

This heterogeneous group of 5th graders is practicing making a play out of a book that they have read.

perspective of a character and read it to the class or draw pictures of the event (Douglas, 1997; Manley & O'Neill, 1997).

Teacher-Designed Leveled Lessons

In addition to multilevel lessons that naturally allow students to engage at multiple levels of ability, we can also design lessons where we create assignments with different directions and learning materials at different levels of ability. This requires additional work on our part, but is not as difficult as we might think at first. As we develop lessons, we can use them from year to year so that, over time, using leveled lessons becomes very manageable.

Tiered Assignments and Products. The key strategy—tiered assignments—involves keeping the overall learning goals and content of learning the same but creating assignments with different levels of complexity for each of the levels of learning goals we discussed in Chapter 11. We can adjust the level of complexity of learning materials, break information into smaller steps, adjust the number and complexity of expected student responses, the degree of abstractness versus concreteness, and the amount of support we may provide a student.

Tiered assignments may have three choices, each with a different level that can be assigned to a student. The best tiered lessons are all interesting activities, but while children in multilevel tasks would be doing similar work at different levels, tiered assignments are often very different in nature. The topic is the same, but what the children are doing can be very different. This is managed in several ways. Teachers create dice to roll with a different activity on each side. There are then different dice for different levels. A choice chart allows children to choose from different modalities to express their learning, and there would then be a different choice chart for each level. At this stage, great care must be taken so that we do not re-create ability grouping within the classroom, simply by grouping all the children who are similar in activity or level.

For example, as in Sydney's moose lesson in Chapter 11, students were expected to identify and study a plant or animal. Another teacher created a similar lesson where, rather than providing overall criteria, she specified expectations that students could meet at their own levels. For the most *basic* students, she expected them to identify by name the plant or animal and provide a picture in its habitat, the parts of which they could label. If they chose an animal, students were also expected to know the sound the animal made. Other students were expected to have this same information, but also to write a two-page report with pictures discussing how the plant or animal functioned in its environment. Other, more sophisticated students were expected to do all this, but also to gather statistical data on the population and movement over time of their plant or animal and create a graphic using Excel, a spreadsheet. The teacher created modified rubrics for each level of project all using similar criteria.

Curriculum Compacting. Curriculum compacting involves allowing students to move on to other curriculum topics if they already know what we are about to teach. To use curriculum compacting, we first assess the student to determine level of knowledge on the material to be studied and determine what skills or knowledge the student yet needs to master. If we decide that the student knows the materials, we develop alternate plans in enriched or accelerated study. For example, a third-grade class is learning to identify parts of fractions. Two students already know this. We give these students an assignment of learning how to add and subtract fractions. As with other students, we establish a way students can demonstrate and share what they have learned. We will want to have conversations with students engaged in curriculum compacting regarding what we want them to do and how this may be beneficial to them. Providing options related to the interests of students can be helpful.

Tiered Games for Practice and Review. An engaging way to learn information or practice skills is to participate in **tiered games**. Games have the same function as traditional worksheets but are much more engaging and motivating for students. To be effective, games should allow for students of differing abilities to play together. If the student who is higher functioning is always winning, then the other students will be frustrated and shut down. Learning will not occur. There are several ways to think about games to make them multilevel. One way is to have the children create a set of handmade gameboards. Then, the students can play on the same gameboard, but use the skills that they need to practice. They can practice different math skills or use different sets of fact cards. Often the students create their own cards on different topics; however, they are having fun and learning together at different levels. Many traditional children's outdoor games can be structured so that there is an element of learning involved as well. In this case, most children can be involved at some level in the outdoor play while learning the information. Another way to make the learning multilevel is to teach the children many games in the course of the class time. Then, when the children are partnered up they can decide what game they want to play that practices a skill they both want to work on. The key is to provide elements of choice and the ability for any student to win, no matter the learning level. Here are some examples.

One game involves *differentiated fact cards*. There is a stack of cards from which to draw in the center of the board with animals from varied habitats that students have been studying. Each student has a different section of cards spread out to look at for the match to that fact card. The cards are at different levels, but there is one in each level that connects to the same animal. The most basic has a picture of the animal and a picture of the habitat. The next level has a picture of the animal and facts about what it eats, where it lives, and what hunts it. The last level has very detailed facts. Students can learn at their own level, yet they interact on the same gameboard and they hear facts from all levels as the players read their matches out loud.

A second example would be a *bingo game that is played as review at the end of a unit*. As the unit progresses, a word wall is developed around the subject. To review, each student selects words that he or she has learned. This is where different levels are accommodated, as there are a range of words available. Then, instead of stating the word, the teacher reads a definition and the child matches the word. This is a fairly basic game that is intentionally leveled, and yet maintains that level of choice that children need.

A third example involves a basic game of *tag that is altered to learn the food web process*. One child is chosen as the predator. As the class forms a circle to discuss the game, the children list animals that are the prey of the chosen predator. Each child chooses one prey to be. They start at one end of the area, and the goal is to get to the other end without being tagged. The predator says he is hungry for some antelopes and all the children who chose antelopes run across the path. If they get tagged, they become another predator. When all children have had a chance to run, another predator is chosen. Between rounds, the teacher gathers them into a circle and talks about what happens

DESPITE HAVING A MASTER'S AND 18 YEARS OF EXPERIENCE, MRS. SNIPPETT TRIES TO CONVINCE MR. MOODY THAT THE STUDENT WITH DISABILITIES IN HER CLASS WOULD BE BETTER SERVED BY AN ASSISTANT WITH NO EXPERIENCE.

when there is plenty of prey: All the predators are healthy and multiply. Following rounds they discuss what happens when there is limited prey—the predators die out—or what happens when too much of a specific prey is eaten. The game is used to teach the concepts while involving children in active play together.

Multiple Intelligences: A Tool for Inclusive Workshop-Based Learning

Multiple intelligences is a useful tool in designing inclusive workshop lessons. Howard Gardner (1993) developed the idea of multiple intelligences in response to his dissatisfaction with typical intelligence tests. He posited that there are eight forms of human intelligence, or ways of being smart. Figure 12.3 provides a simple description of these intelligences and sample teaching techniques. As we focus on the ways students *think*, what they *love*, and what they *need*, we dramatically improve learning.

For example, students who have strong spatial intelligence think in images and pictures; love designing, drawing, visualizing, and doodling; and *need* art, movies, imagination games, mazes, illustrated books, and trips to art museums. Students with high levels of kinesthetic intelligence think through bodily sensations; love dancing, running, jumping, building, and touching; and *need* role-play, drama, movement, construction projects, sports, and hands-on learning. If students truly do *need* these types of activities, if they do not have them they will learn less, be less motivated, and often create problems (Armstrong, 1994).

If we take seriously the argument that students with various intelligences *need* particular experiences, then we must pay attention to this need. For example, allowing students to stand or lie on the floor while reading is a good start, but we could do more. Acting out parts of the text, having students represent concepts through art or illustrations, creating quick "body figures" that portray a key emotion or idea stretch the whole

FIGURE 12.3

Multiple Intelligences

INTELLIGENCES AND DESCRIPTIONS	THINKS . . . LOVES . . . NEEDS . . .	TEACHING MENU (A FEW IDEAS)
1. *Linguistic:* The capacity to use language to express ourselves and to understand other people. Examples: poet, writer, orator, lawyer, teacher.	Thinks in words. . . . Loves reading, writing, telling stories, playing word games. . . . Needs books, tapes, writing tools, paper, diaries, dialogue.	Use storytelling to explain. . . . Conduct a debate on. . . . Write a poem, legend, short play, or news article about. . . . Conduct an interview about. . . .
2. *Logical–mathematical:* Ability to use numbers effectively and to reason well logically. Examples: mathematician, accountant, computer programmer, scientist.	Thinks by reasoning. . . . Loves experimenting, questioning, figuring out logical puzzles. . . . Needs things to explore and think about, science materials, manipulatives.	Translate a . . . into a math formula. Design and conduct an experiment on. . . . Make up syllogisms to explain. . . . Describe patterns of symmetry in. . . .
3. *Spatial:* Competence to represent the spatial world internally in our mind and to use materials to impact the environment. Examples: hunter, scout, artist, architect, inventor.	Thinks in images and pictures. . . . Loves designing, drawing, visualizing, doodling. . . . Needs art, video, movies, imagination games, mazes, illustrated books, trips to art museums.	Chart, map, or graph. . . . Create a slide show, video, or photo album of. . . . Create a piece of art that illustrates. . . . Draw, paint, sketch or sculpt. . . .
4. *Bodily–kinesthetic:* Expertise in using our whole body to express ideas and feelings and ability to use our body to make or change things. Examples: actor, athlete, sculptor, mechanic, surgeon.	Thinks through bodily sensations. . . . Loves dancing, running, jumping, building, touching. . . . Needs role play, drama, movement, construction, activities, sports, hands-on learning.	Create a sequence of movements to explain. . . . Build or construct. . . . Plan and attend a field trip to. . . . Bring hands-on materials to demonstrate. . . .
5. *Musical:* Ability to think in music; to hear patterns, recognize them, remember them, manipulate them. Examples: singer, songwriter, composer, music critic.	Thinks via rhythms and melodies. . . . Loves singing, whistling, humming, tapping feet. . . . Needs sing-along time, music playing, musical instruments, music.	Give a presentation on . . . with musical accompaniment. Sing a rap or song that explains. . . . Explain how the music of a song is similar to. . . . Make an instrument and use it to demonstrate. . . .
6. *Interpersonal:* Ability to understand thoughts, feelings, motivations of other people and to interact well with them. Examples: politician, salesperson.	Thinks by talking with other people. . . . Loves leading, organizing, talking, mediating, partying. . . . Needs friends, group games, social events, mentors.	Conduct a meeting to address. . . . Participate in a service project to. . . . Teach someone about. . . . Practice giving and receiving feedback on. . . .

FIGURE 12.3

Continued		
INTELLIGENCES AND DESCRIPTIONS	**THINKS... LOVES... NEEDS...**	**TEACHING MENU (A FEW IDEAS)**
7. *Intrapersonal:* Understanding of ourself—of our feelings, and reactions to others—and ability to act on that understanding. Awareness of inner moods, capacities for self-discipline and deep reflection. Examples: philosopher, poet, counselor.	Thinks by reflecting deeply inside self. . . . Loves setting goals, meditating, dreaming, being quiet. . . . Needs secret places, time alone, self-paced projects, choices.	Describe qualities you have that will help you. . . . Develop a plan to. . . . Describe a personal value about. . . . Write a journal entry on. . . . Assess your own work in. . . .
8. *Naturalist:* High sensitivity and responsiveness to living beings (plants, animals), the natural world, and the environment. Examples: "street smart" student, hunter, farmer, botanist.	Thinks by interacting with nature and the environment. . . . Loves camping, moving around the community, organizing the environment. . . . Needs time in nature or the community, organizing events.	Create observation notebooks of. . . . Describe changes in the local community. . . . Care for pets, wildlife, gardens, or parks in. . . . Draw or photograph natural objects or the community.

Source: From *Multiple Intelligences in the Classroom,* 2nd Edition (pp. 4–5) by Thomas Armstrong. Alexandria, VA: ASCD. © 2000 by ASCD. Used with permission. Learn more about ASCD at www.ascd.org.

community's thinking and our comfort levels so that we have to learn along with our students (Armstrong, 1994).

There is often a mismatch between the multiple intelligences of students and typical instruction in schools. Teachers have estimated that 75% to 90% of the learning in schools relies heavily on linguistic and logical–mathematical intelligences. However, a minority of students excel in these intelligences. An estimated 60% of children in schools have high abilities in visual–spatial intelligence, in part because of the increasing prevalence of media. As children spend more time watching TV, playing video games, and surfing the Internet, this percentage continues to rise. Approximately 33% express their learning through music, while around 17% are strongly bodily–kinesthetic and another 17% are interpersonal (Gardner, 1993; Jensen, 1998).

Given this reality it is interesting to note that the number of children identified as having learning disabilities has grown rapidly. The areas in which these children have the most difficulty are language and mathematics, the two intelligences on which schools focus the most (Armstrong, 1994; Campbell & Campbell, 1999). We also know that these students often have high abilities in one or more of the other intelligences. For example, at age 14 Brad was identified as having a learning disability and was doing poorly in school. He felt stupid. Yet at home he designed and built shelves and cabinets and had a gift for repairing the lawn mower—talents that many of his linguistically oriented classmates did not share.

Multiple intelligences theory has several important implications (Armstrong, 1994):

1. *Each person possesses all eight intelligences.* We must not attempt to label students based on intelligences. Although some intelligences are more developed, most people

can develop all eight intelligences to a reasonable level. This means that we should structure opportunities for development of all intelligences.

2. *Although we describe the intelligences separately, they interact with one another.* For example, when we cook a meal, we read a recipe (drawing on linguistic intelligence), decide whether to double or halve the recipe (logical–mathematical), modify the recipe for the likes and dislikes of family members (interpersonal), and actually cook the food (bodily–kinesthetic—and perhaps interpersonal, if we are cooking with a partner or two).

3. *There is no one correct way to express any intelligence at a high level.* For example, a student who cannot read may be an amazing storyteller or speaker. Conversely, a person may be an avid reader and writer, yet fumble when asked to communicate orally.

Understanding multiple intelligences helps us recognize and build on students' strengths. We will often be amazed at positive attributes of students. For example, when we use drama and movement to teach concepts, we will note students who excel. When we ask students to express mathematical concepts through music or art, we will have other opportunities to identify student strengths. The student's strengths can then be used to bridge the gap to the weaker areas. Figure 12.3 illustrates how we can think about planning instruction using multiple intelligences.

We can use multiple intelligences to identify how a student *misbehaves* in class. Often such "behavioral problems" are expressions of the student's need to use a particular intelligence that is being stifled. For example, students who are highly spatial often doodle instead of taking notes. Students who are musically intelligent may hum constantly or daydream, listening to the music and rhythms in their minds. Students who are kinesthetically intelligent may move constantly, leave their seats, or tap the desk. (Often these children quickly get identified as having ADD, or attention deficit disorder, when they may in actuality be demonstrating an intelligence that is not very welcome in the classroom.) These behavioral clues can help us identify strengths while giving us strong signals that we need to allow these intelligences into our classroom.

Other good indicators of student intelligences are the ways they spend their free time. What do students choose? Do they read books, draw, talk with other students, move around the room from place to place, sit in the study carrel listening to music, or roam the Internet? We can keep a journal with observations and notes about our students to identify needs, particularly with those students who pose the greatest challenges.

A final useful strategy can be a simple checklist that helps us think about students' intelligences (Armstrong, 1994). A word of caution is needed here, however. Traditional intelligence tests, which measure linguistic and logical–mathematical intelligences, have been used to identify *deficits* of students. Multiple intelligences theory, in contrast, is used to identify *strengths* of students. We must be careful about labeling students in a new way—as the "art smart kids" or the "deep thinkers," for example. Intelligences are dynamic, and they can change.

Teaching students about multiple intelligences helps them better understand their own strengths and abilities. Ask specific questions: "How many people excel at speaking? How many love to write?" (linguistic). "How many of you love math? How many people enjoy science experiments?" (logical–mathematical). The more we incorporate the language of multiple intelligences into our daily speaking, the better students will get at understanding their strengths.

Multiple intelligences theory provides one lens to help teachers design instruction that will reach students with diverse abilities. The concept of multiple intelligences also is a natural fit with interdisciplinary instruction. That is, from one perspective the multiple intelligences correspond to many disciplines in the school—language arts, math, science, social studies. Knowing this, we can create different ways of approaching a topic.

Learning in any subject area can be strengthened when students draw upon multiple intelligences. Similarly, any particular intelligence can be strengthened through the others. Areas of strength can also be used to bridge the gap to areas that are struggling. This is particularly important when we have students who are struggling in a particular arena.

Let's look at an example. We are working in a high school as part of an interdisciplinary team involving social studies, language arts, and art to help students understand their own culture and learn how to interact respectfully with people of other cultures (interpersonal intelligence). We engage students in gathering information about and reading literature of cultures (linguistic intelligence), have multicultural events at which different customs and food are represented (bodily–kinesthetic, spatial, and musical intelligences), and dramatically act out a key event in the history of an ethnic group (bodily–kinesthetic intelligence). We recommend the following steps in using a grid to plan lessons based on multiple intelligences:

1. Identify your theme and the learning goals and objectives.
2. Brainstorm ideas that will actively engage students and that will help them demonstrate what they know and understand. Don't try yet to connect these ideas with the multiple intelligences. When you have several ideas for good learning activities, write these on the planning form in the Learning Activities column.
3. Use the matrix to indicate which of the multiple intelligences is strongly used in a particular activity. Then analyze the degree to which all the intelligences are utilized and make changes as needed.
4. Finalize your plans, adding more details for how each activity will be implemented in your class or with other teachers.
5. Use your awareness of multiple intelligences to devise alternative evaluation strategies for understanding what students have learned.

In the example in Figure 12.4, the teacher wanted to help students learn about the Bill of Rights. She created many good ideas for how to engage her students. As you can see, in this example the intelligences are often interactive, and both learning activities and demonstrations involve several intelligences at once.

Multiple intelligences is strength-based; as such, it removes pressure from an area of difficulty, identifies and builds on strengths, and uses the other intelligences to "surround" a weak area. Let's look at an example that is illustrated in Figure 12.5.

This student had a great deal of difficulty writing. He had to concentrate so much on controlling the pen or pencil that he was extremely slow. The teacher, in consultation with the student's parents, built on his strength—oral communication. She did not require him to write at all and had him read text only periodically for fun. Instead he listened to the text via text-to-speech software on the computer (while often following along in the book). The pressure to read and write, to struggle with areas in which he was having problems, was taken away. The student listened and participated in class assignments. Over time he gradually learned to use a computer for papers (a different form of writing production) and began reading to his infant sister. Ultimately, he began to read text that was closer to grade level; simultaneously, he was doing complex projects on the computer involving both mathematics and graphics (O. Smith, 1997). His area of strength bridged the gap to the area that was weaker.

When we talk with teachers about multiple intelligences, they often say, "But don't we want children to read?" Of course we do. However, it is counterproductive to pressure students to try harder on strategies that are not working. Recall our discussion on brain-based learning and the importance of "relaxed alertness." When we push students to perform in areas in which they feel like failures, they will not learn. In the example of the student with writing difficulties, the teacher and parents were able to work together

FIGURE 12.4

Multiple Intelligences Planning Matrix

Theme: *Human and Legal Rights*

Learning Goals and Objectives for Unit: *Understand the relationship between the Bill of Rights and the human rights it is designed to protect. Understand and describe specific examples of legal and advocacy strategies groups use to address human rights protected by the Bill of Rights.*

LEARNING ACTIVITIES	LING.	LOG.–MTH.	SPAT.	BOD.–KIN.	MUS.	INTER.	INTRA.	NAT.
Read the Bill of Rights as a group.	P					P		
Write and act out play regarding civil rights.	P		S	P		P		
Personal reflections: writing, tape, etc. Some students do individually, some in cooperative group based on choice.	P					S	P	
Create song or drawing to illustrate one of the rights. Present to the class.	S		P		P	S	S	
Conduct study regarding rights violations in a community—legal costs, economics, numbers of complaints lost and won.	S	P				S		S
Write a short story, play, or poem reflecting on the importance of one of the rights.	S		S	P	P		P	

P = primary intelligence associated with activity; S = secondary intelligence associated with activity.

to create a condition of relaxed alertness and to provide multiple avenues toward learning course content. The strategy worked.

Scaffolding Learning to Strengthen Understanding

When we have children of differing abilities learn together, we provide them support and assistance to reach the next level of learning—Vygotsky's (1978) zone of proximal development referred to earlier. The term **scaffolding** is often used to refer to this kind of support, in which teachers, other adults, or more competent students help students perform tasks that are within their zone of proximal development (Ormrod, 2000). Morocco and Zorfass (1996) describe effective scaffolds as (1) multilevel, (2) inclusive, (3) promoting higher level thinking, and (4) dynamic and evolving.

FIGURE 12.5

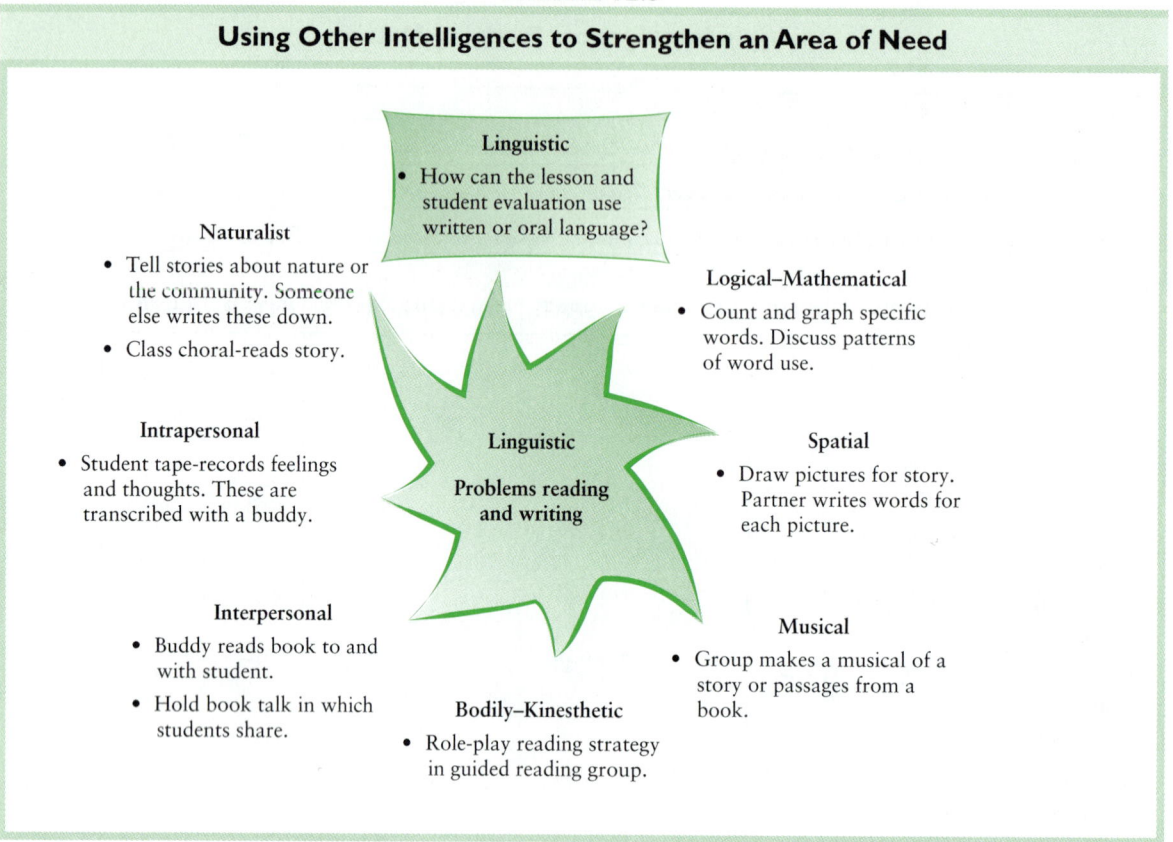

Using Other Intelligences to Strengthen an Area of Need

Linguistic
- How can the lesson and student evaluation use written or oral language?

Naturalist
- Tell stories about nature or the community. Someone else writes these down.
- Class choral-reads story.

Logical–Mathematical
- Count and graph specific words. Discuss patterns of word use.

Intrapersonal
- Student tape-records feelings and thoughts. These are transcribed with a buddy.

Linguistic

Problems reading and writing

Spatial
- Draw pictures for story. Partner writes words for each picture.

Interpersonal
- Buddy reads book to and with student.
- Hold book talk in which students share.

Musical
- Group makes a musical of a story or passages from a book.

Bodily–Kinesthetic
- Role-play reading strategy in guided reading group.

Construction crews use scaffolds to support a building while it is being constructed. Scaffolds in the classroom are similar. Teachers provide supports and assistance so that students can perform a task or activity *just beyond* their actual level of ability. Therefore, scaffolding engages students in work at a higher level while simultaneously supporting their learning and achievement. The teacher (or other helper) can provide the support before the activity to help activate student background knowledge, during the activity to build concept understanding, afterward to extend thinking, or a combination of all three (Graves & Graves 1994; Berk & Winsler, 1995). Scaffolding helps us avoid lowering our expectations—whether of students who are gifted or of students with special needs—to the point where children are not learning in our class, just occupying space (Graves & Graves, 1994).

What are some examples? Kathi Tarrant-Parks (1999a) conducted research investigating scaffolding strategies that promote inclusion in literacy instruction. Some additional examples include the following:

- A teacher or student reads a book to a student that the student likes but could not read independently.
- As a student reads, a more competent reading buddy reads along and helps with words the student doesn't know.
- One student records in the math journal for another student who has difficulty writing.
- A teacher arranges spaced blanks for words in a sentence for a child who has difficulty writing and separating words. The child then writes each word on its blank.

- A teacher provides a pictorial guide for a student to use in conducting a student-led conference. The teacher remains available to help the student, if needed, in conducting the conference.
- New vocabulary in a reading assignment is pretaught and then highlighted for the student, so it is easily identified.
- Students act out an emotional scene in a novel to understand concepts.
- The teacher or another student reads a student's work aloud so the student can hear which words are missing.

Morocco and Zorfass (1996) describe a project that illustrates how scaffolding and authentic learning build student strengths. In a middle school, an interdisciplinary team of teachers decided to engage in a "we-search" unit (Macrorie, 1988) organized around the theme of water ecology. The unit used an adaptation of the authoring cycle involving four phases: (1) identifying thematic questions for exploration, (2) developing a search plan, (3) gathering and integrating information, and (4) drafting, revising, and "publishing" a product.

First, teachers and students explored the topic. Teachers worked as an interdisciplinary team. Activities included viewing a video on water pollution, using a computer simulation on pollution and the environment, listening to an invited speaker from the local water commission, and reading Spanish and English comic books about waterborne diseases. In addition, the teachers took 100 students on a hike to the local river to collect and test water samples.

To ensure active involvement and learning for all, the teachers broke the students into cooperative learning groups, and each teacher (social studies, science, English, and special education) coached five to six groups, monitoring their progress. Scaffolds included worksheets to track progress as well as teacher discussions with each group regarding what they knew, what they wanted to know, and how they could obtain information. All teachers ensured that all students, including students with learning challenges, were an integral part of the project.

As the learning groups identified questions, they developed a plan to answer their questions. The teachers required each group to gather information in four ways: reading, watching, asking, and doing. They helped the groups develop a logistical plan and made sure that the groups established responsibilities and gave each group member support for doing his or her task.

As the groups began to gather information, the teachers recognized problems in students' interactions. Some were not taking responsibility, whereas others were dominating the groups. They decided that the special education support teacher, who was very skilled at dealing with emotional frustrations, would work with each group and "teach them how to discuss their frustrations constructively, using 'I' statements instead of fighting" (Morocco & Zorfass, 1996, p. 173). All the teachers helped students solve problems, using one another as resources. Teachers helped students identify interview questions for speakers and develop an interview guide for telephone interviews. Robert, a student with learning disabilities, was one student who conducted phone interviews. At one point, with help from the teacher, his group conducted a group interview with a speakerphone. This demonstration provided a model for Robert, who then rehearsed with support from the teacher and classmates. Though he was nervous and unsure at first, by the end of the rehearsal sessions his voice became confident. He learned much as he attempted to talk to people in government offices.

Finally, students used word processors to develop their reports. Again, teachers provided a detailed guide. Periodically a teacher would conduct a mini-lesson regarding a particular skill—grammatical structure, how to develop a lead, and so forth. Robert had great difficulty writing, so he talked about what he had discovered while another student wrote down his comments. Students invited more than 200 people to hear them as they shared their findings and made recommendations for how to solve some real ecological problems facing their community.

In this example, students were challenged at multiple levels and teachers used a range of constantly changing scaffolds. They modeled, conducted skill lessons, worked in small groups to further understanding, and arranged for a student to write for a peer who had difficulty. By participating in an engaging and meaningful problem-solving task, students who began at different levels arrived at a shared understanding. Robert could not have done this complex an activity on his own. With support from teachers and his peers, however, he was able to record his findings about water, conduct a phone interview, and learn about government bureaucracy. However, scaffolding should be thought of not as a teaching technique for struggling students but as a key strategy for all students. It extends students' zones of proximal development and gives them common experiences to talk about, write about, and share (Graves & Graves, 1994; Berk & Winsler, 1995).

A range of tools are useful in supporting scaffolding. A few include copy search, journaling, and organizers. **Copy search** is a useful multilevel tool to teach conventions in any subject. When students are having difficulty with any particular part of their work (e.g., how to start a paragraph or how to employ the scientific method), teachers have students look for models in resources. For example, if students are having trouble creating strong story leads, we would then ask them to work in groups to find examples of leads that grab their interest. "See what you notice. Share at your table." Such sharing helps structure language in the minds of students. The class then compiles a list of types of leads or of books with good examples to be referenced later. This approach allows all students to contribute (Schiller, 1998).

We can modify materials to help students understand. A few strategies include:

- *Highlighting* the important information in written materials. This can be done with a yellow highlighter by the teacher or aide or by peer helpers.
- *Summarizing* key points and information from texts and materials.
- Developing *study guides* for lessons.

Students play an active role in learning when they are constructing meaning based on what they already know. One way to help students construct meaning is to have them maintain written **journals** in which they record their thoughts, reactions, questions, and feelings about a subject. The writing is short, can be a combination of sketches or words, and is often used as a springboard for discussions. Journals can take many forms and are a useful tool to help students organize and retrieve thoughts and ideas. Students, for example, may write in a journal after a science lesson to record key facts or after a social studies lesson to review a concept discussed. They might use a math journal to describe how they understood a problem, or students might record their feelings about an event in their daily life and use this account later as an idea for a project. (Figure 12.6 illustrates some types of journals students may use.)

Another way to help students construct meaning and enhance understanding is to use **graphic organizers** which assist students in focusing on key elements of either fiction or expository text. By combining words, pictures, and color in story maps and webs, children remember important information in an easily accessible manner. These tools are particularly helpful for students with reading difficulties and can be applied across curriculum areas (Rhodes & Dudley-Marling, 1996; Strickland, 1995; Tomlinson, 2004b). Schools are increasingly using software such as Inspiration, which allow easy construction of such tools using computers (Genesis Technologies, 2001). Through consistent modeling of these tools by the teacher, children learn to organize their thoughts and

FIGURE 12.6

Types of Journaling

Freewriting	Students write as much as they can in a given time span on a given topic.
K-W-L	In three columns students write what they know, what they want to know, and later what they learned.
Dialogue journals	Written conversation about a topic goes back and forth between teacher and student or between student and student.
Learning logs	Continuous writing about what was learned that day, in an academic subject or a given topic. A student's learning log is a place to hold sketches, K-W-Ls, etc.
Book journal	Thoughts, predictions, likes/dislikes, or feelings about a story read.
Double entries	Journal pages divided into columns, where on one side problems can be worked out and on the other side the rationale is explained.
Writing notebook	Journal where ideas for a writing, snippets of thoughts, great descriptions of a single item or event, or lists of ideas are created for later use in the writing process.

Effective Adaptation of Curriculum

SCHOOLS to VISIT

Powell Valley Elementary School
4825 E. Powell Valley Road
Gresham, OR 97080-1951

Powell Valley Elementary School has 518 children in Grades K through 5. Curriculum adaptation is at the heart of the success of inclusive schooling at Powell Valley. When teachers look at upcoming activities and consider how they optimize every child's learning, they collaborate with other teachers, assistants, and the Supported Education Team. Collaboration and teaming meet the students' needs with the best of ideas while saving time.

Together the teachers have learned that adaptations begin with the work the whole class is doing. Some adapations are on the spot, such as a fold in the paper or the highlighting of some problems. Other ideas take a little more time and planning, but ideas always expand beyond one child, often being used to enhance the learning of many students. Teachers have discovered that when they begin designing adaptations by focusing on the work everyone in the class is

doing, they set up a natural opportunity for students to work together. If an "adaptation" is something totally different, peers can't help one another, because it isn't always clear what the work is about or how it ties to the current lesson. Consistently, teachers have discovered that when they look at another way to teach the general lesson to fit a certain child, they improve their own teaching and reach more children.

Curriculum adaptation is a product of teamwork and a belief in children. When teachers believe all children learn best when they are actively involved in their learning and when they use real-life situations for problem solving, every child has the opportunity to learn within his or her own learning style. When teachers practice the belief that all children can and want to learn, all children are welcomed and valued for what they as individuals bring to the classroom community. When teachers build a caring school community based on the belief that all children need to feel a strong sense of community and collaboration, all children are involved not only in their own learning but in the learning of others.

Source: By Patti McVay, Center for Inclusive Education, Multnomah Education Service District (MESD), Portland, OR. Edited by Michael Peterson.

learning. This is important as many children come to school without the skills to plan and organize. Some teachers use certain types of graphic organizers consistently with the same type of material to encourage connections within children's minds as they process information. Many teachers of writing teach in-depth web making prior to writing to organize thoughts and plots.

Step 5. Individualized Differentiation of Learning Activities

Sometimes our initial lesson design does not adequately meet the needs of an individual student. We may need to develop **individualized differentiation** of instruction for that student. We'll find, of course, that the more effective we are at using multilevel and tiered teaching strategies, the less we will need to develop individualized differentiation or curriculum adaptations for students. As we discussed in Chapter 4, anytime we need to do this, we will want to evaluate ways we could incorporate these into the overall design of our lesson. Individualized differentiation will most often be needed for student at the far ranges of ability—those much higher or much lower in ability than the average in our class.

Sometimes we find that teachers think that students must be advanced students working above their grade level to effectively engage in projects. We certainly could create expectations where this would be true. However, if we are using truly multilevel goals and learning activities that can be pursued at differing levels of sophistication, all students should be able to be successful. As we discussed in Chapter 4, we can provide additional supports to students and modify or adapt lessons to provide individualized differentiation around the needs of specific students. For example, for students with severe cognitive disabilities, we may need to simplify the information to its basic concepts.

We can use all the strategies discussed previously to help us think about individualized differentiation of learning activities for students. Such differentiation will need to focus on the specific needs of the student. Often, the focus will be on the *cognitive level of learning*. When this is the case, we will want to modify our lesson to allow the student to engage in learning at her level of ability. If the student is having *social or emotional challenges*, we may need to adapt the way students are working together, providing additional guidance and support and helping students problem solve. Students may also be having difficulties that deal with physical or sensory abilities. If a visual or hearing disability, for example, is getting in the way of learning in a lesson that relies heavily on either vision or hearing, we'll need to obtain resources to help or modify the lesson in some way.

As we seek to make adaptations and differentiation for individual students we have a range of general strategies from small to larger changes. Figure 12.7 illustrates these strategies. Let's discuss them.

FIGURE 12.7

Strategies for Differentiation of Cognitive Level of Learning

1. **No differentiation**—same goals, activities, teaching strategies and materials
2. **Adapted teaching strategies**—same goals, activities, and materials
3. **Adaptations to all parts of the lesson**—changes in learning goals, materials, teaching strategies, and activities
4. **Parallel activities**—different learning goals, learning activities, teaching strategies, and materials

At the simplest level (1) there is *no differentiation needed* at all. Goals, activities, teaching strategies, and materials are all the same. Again, this will occur most often if we intentionally are designing our learning activities using multilevel and tiered strategies. Let's use the example of Sydney and the lesson on learning about plants and animals in Chapter 11 to look at these strategies. Sydney needed slight differentiation in this lesson. Students considered gifted needed no differentiation in the lesson, though it was critical for all students to understand that they would work at their just-right level.

Second, we can *use different teaching strategies*, different ways that students may obtain information. This may involve using multiple intelligences, scaffolding of learning, learning styles (see Chapter 7), and other resources. In this step, learning goals, learning activities, and materials may stay the same or have minimal changes. In Sydney's lesson, she did need assistance in accessing information. Teachers helped her locate information on the Internet, used a screen reader to help her read material, and provided support to her in writing out her report and poem.

Third, we may *adapt all aspects of the lesson—learning goals, materials, learning activity, and teaching strategies*. A student with a severe cognitive disability, for example, may have participated in the lesson on learning about plants and animals. However, learning goals were made simpler for this student—to be able to say the name of the plant or animal and recognize a picture of its habitat. For such a student, a helper (peer, paraprofessional, or special education teacher) may have worked one on one with the student holding out pictures of different plants or animals and asking, "Which one do you want to study? This one or this one?" The student then chooses. The helper would sit next to the student and find information pointing out pictures and asking simple questions along the way. He or she may use a program such as Boardmaker to create simple pictures that represent key information. For example, three animals might be presented and a helper asks the question: "Which one is the penguin, Sherie?" Sherie points to her animal, the penguin, and so on. When designing adapted lessons of this sort we want, on the one hand, to create lessons at the students' level of ability but also keep the learning activity and materials as similar as possible to those used by other students. For

These boys are making a ramp on which they will race cars they have designed. They collect data on the impact of various car designs and the slope of the track on the outcome of the races.

a student who is gifted, it would be possible to modify the assignment so that the student would be expected to, for example, collect data by directly observing a plant or animal in the area and then gather information from government offices.

Finally, with students with significant differences in cognitive abilities we may have them *engaged in a different activity altogether with different learning goals and using different materials*. Again, it is helpful to keep the lesson as related to what the rest of the class is doing as possible. A student with a significant cognitive disability might be working on knowing colors while the rest of the class is working on the plant or animal project. In this case, a paraprofessional or peer might use colored pictures of different plants or animals and ask the student to name colors. For a student who is gifted, we might decide to instead have the student develop an individualized learning contract to engage in another study that would relate to a learning goal of the district curriculum. Perhaps in science the student is very interested in understanding energy alternatives that are being considered with the growing cost of oil. The student might engage in inquiry learning as already discussed. We make an agreement with him and he agrees to develop a learning product, present information to the class, and design a way that students in the class can engage in a knowledgeable discussion about the topic. He also agrees to allow Kendall, a student with a cognitive disability, to work with him on this project.

We can also use multiple intelligences to develop strategies for individualized differentiation in all subject areas. Figure 12.8 illustrates how this worked for one student.

Tools and Strategies for Inclusive Workshop Learning

So far in this chapter, we have discussed how workshop learning looks in summary and explored multiple intelligences and strategies and tools for designing inclusive learning activities in workshop learning classes. In this section, we want to discuss the tools of workshop learning that we introduced at the beginning of the chapter. These tools can facilitate students of very different abilities and characteristics learning together. They build on and contribute to the way we organize our classroom (Chapter 7), use assistive technology (Chapter 8), and build a sense of community (Chapters 9 and 10). These procedures provide the context in which we use the inclusive learning activities we just discussed. We'll see more clearly how workshop learning looks and feels and how we can support students in learning.

Whole Class Mini-Lessons and Discussions

When effective multilevel teachers present information, they work to ensure that all students have some level of understanding and comprehension. Teacher talk will be interspersed with times when we ask students to turn to one another and summarize what the teacher said, or give an example, or check the understanding of their partner and help them understand if they are not clear.

As we teach a mini-lesson at the beginning of a workshop session, we want to engage students in thinking about the lesson. We will be involving students of varied abilities in this process and want to ensure understanding of all while pushing all to higher levels of thinking. It's a bit of a balancing act. We prepare a list of questions about the topic the class will be studying and pose these questions to the class. We may need to

FIGURE 12.8

Using Multiple Intelligences for Individual Differentation

INTELLIGENCE	POTENTIAL PROBLEMS	SOME SOLUTIONS
Linguistic	Verbal and written language abilities either higher or lower than those of the majority of the class	Reading materials at multiple levels Buddies and partners who assist the student Study guides
Logical–Mathematical	Difficulty in thinking in logical sequences Difficulty in understanding mathematic concepts	Thinking organizers Task analysis Hands-on activities
Spatial	Visual disability Difficulty with spatial relationships (gets lost in the high school halls) Inability to draw or represent graphically	Using touch in place of sight—feeling objects, sculpting rather than drawing Orientation to the layout of the school by an orientation and mobility specialist Stick-figure drawing Supporting effort at own level
Bodily–Kinesthetic	Physical disabilities—uses wheelchair, weakened by physical condition Poor physical coordination Tactile-defensive	Modified rules of games to allow participation Unified Sports Play supporting role in sports—leading fan, etc
Musical	Tone deaf Difficulty with rhythms	Allow to participate at own level (if tone deaf, sing but moderate volume)
Interpersonal	High needs for attention Frequently angry and acting out Withdraws from other students	Listen, understand what student is feeling Connect with supportive students Circle of support
Intrapersonal	Fear of being alone Difficulty understanding own feelings	Develop opportunities for student to work with others in class projects Provide lessons to all students about how to identify emotions and healthy ways to respond
Naturalist	Difficulty synthesizing and seeing the how small pieces fit into the whole; gets lost in details	Work with others who can explain the relationship of the part to the "big ideas" of a lesson

vary the complexity of the questions or restate them depending on the ability level of the student. We'll encourage all students to ask and answer follow-up questions in the discussion. We also ask questions and give students a chance to write their ideas and then talk to a partner.

In an inclusive classroom, it is important for teachers to avoid calling on the same children all the time. We want all children to be thinking about the topic and yet we want to keep children in the relaxed state that will help them learn. This can be hard to do when students are waving their hand in the air, eager to answer. One way of making sure that all students have something to share, is to use partners. If the teacher posits a question, and then asks the students to discuss the question with their partner, when she calls on a student to answer the question he will have something to share, no matter what level the student functions at. It is also imperative to create a routine that does not allow hand waving and excited noises, as this will prevent students from learning. Some students' brains will literally shut down because they know someone else has the answer. So, creating a signal for raising hands is important.

Beyond the routines of dicussions, what do we discuss? **K-W-L** (What do we *k*now? What do we *w*ant to know? What did we *l*earn?) is an excellent thinking strategy. At the beginning of an idea, a K-W-L mini-lesson helps students plan their work by brainstorming what they know and what they want to know. Subsequently, the teacher models and assists them in organizing ways to research information, with different members of the group engaging in different research activities. As usually happens, when the biology teacher applied these strategies, the two students who had difficulty reading did much better. First, they participated as part of a group, engaging in tasks that required less sophisticated reading. Then one of the two students interviewed a parent who is a biologist to learn answers to some questions. The other student was the artist of the group. In addition, as the group reported back and discussed what they were finding, all the students learned through this oral communication more readily. One boy who was gifted decided that he would like to include complex pictorial descriptions in his projects and began to do so.

At other times when we are sharing information in a whole group setting, it is important to teach children using visuals. The brain needs something to connect the information we are sharing to. Given the rising number of children who are visual learners, teachers will increase the potential for retaining the information by outlining it in a graphic organizer. Some teachers have different graphic organizers for each type of information. Also, increasing the number of pictures and realistic examples that are shared with the information will help. The more teachers model using graphic organizers, the easier it is for students of all ability levels to begin to create their own.

Student Collaboration and Peer Support

We can use a range of strategies to organize students into learning groups in inclusive workshop-based instruction.

Flexible Grouping. Students work as part of many different groups depending on the task and/or content. Sometimes students are placed in groups based on readiness, other times based on interest and/or learning profile. Groups can either be assigned by the teacher or chosen by the students. Students can be assigned purposefully to a group or assigned randomly. As part of the workshop process, the knowledge we have about what students need is constantly changing. We are gaining new insights daily through conferencing, therefore the groups will change often—whether this is done every few weeks through a set assessment, or whether they change based on observational data.

The groups are short term and are constantly changing. We avoid having stable ability groups, knowing this changes the tone of our community and does not focus on what exactly the students need to know. This strategy allows students to work with a wide variety of peers and keeps them from being labeled as advanced or struggling. For example, in a reading class, we may assign groups based on readiness for phonics instruction, where each group focuses on a different phonics sound. The teacher would then allow students to choose their own groups for book reports, based on the book topic. To use flexible grouping and avoid stable ability grouping we need to use these guidelines:

- Ensure that all students have the opportunity to work with other students who are similar and dissimilar from themselves in terms of interest, readiness, and learning profile.
- Alternate purposeful assignment of groups with random assignment or student selection.
- Ensure that all students have been given the skills to work collaboratively.
- Provide clear guidelines for group functioning that are taught in advance of group work and consistently reinforced.

Classwide Peer Tutoring. **Classwide peer tutoring** is a teaching strategy that involves students in acting as both teacher and learner. The class is divided into two groups with the teacher aiming to ensure equal levels of ability. Students work in pairs. One student presents a stimulus such as a spelling word, a math problem, or direction for reading a passage aloud. The other student responds answering the question or following directions. The teacher student indicates whether or not the answer is right. Later, the two students switch roles. Learning tasks for each student are based on their abilities.

Classwide peer tutoring has the two groups compete for the highest scores. Students obtain points for correct answers—2 points for a correct answer with no help and 1 point for a correct answer with support. Totals for all pairs on each team are totaled and reported. Classwide peer tutoring incorporates seven features that are responsive to concepts of inclusive teaching and universal design for learning:

1. *Multimodal:* Students "hear," "see," "say," and "write" their responses, thus tapping into various learning modalities.
2. *Reciprocal practice:* Students are both teacher and tutee and get multiple opportunities for practice.
3. *Immediate correction of errors:* Students are immediately corrected and given the opportunity to practice three times.
4. *Gaming:* Students love to play games and this process incorporates that sense of enjoyment ensuring that all are successful, thus avoiding some of the problems associated with traditional competition.
5. *Built-in reinforcement:* Students naturally congratulate and support one another; all feel good when they cheer for their team.
6. *Success for every student:* Since learning tasks are developed to match each student, all are successful and challenged at their own level.
7. *Measured outcomes:* These are built into the process. Teachers use pre- and post-assessments. Points earned daily indicate learning outcomes along with written documents from tutoring sessions.

Classwide peer tutoring is particularly useful for engaging students in multilevel learning of information that is based in skills and content knowledge. It is less useful in open-ended exploration and inquiry tasks. However, teachers have experienced the approach as a fun way to engage students (Terry, 2005).

Partner Reading. In **partner reading** we pair students to read together. They sit side by side, reading the same book, taking turns reading and discussing the events of the story. Students of different ability levels can be paired together (Englert et al., 1995).

As a natural extension of partner reading, *literature circles* bring several children together to read and discuss a book. The students set up their own schedule and decide how they will share. Teachers often also assign simple jobs that rotate, such as finding a moving passage to get the conversation started. Literature circles take conversation to a new level, as students use their personal viewpoints as a springboard to analyze the text. Every child has a viewpoint to share (Daniels, 1994).

Work Groups. Small **work groups** can meet to work on a variety of projects, depending on the subject and topic. In math, a study group meets to work on division problems similar to those they have encountered in class or to go over the homework. In another class, a work group is involved in a complex science or social studies project.

Jigsaw. Organizing students into groups enables them to work together to find information and delve more deeply into a subject. The whole class may discuss a topic and divide it into smaller pieces. Different groups study different aspects of the material but are responsible for teaching their particular information to the rest of the class (Johnson & Johnson, 1989b).

Partner Clocks. Students need to be able to work in pairs in a manner that is easy to access and encourages students to work with those outside their normal group. This helps the community grow and ensures a heterogeneous mixing of students. One such idea is the **partner clock**. Create a sheet with a line by each hour on the clock. Students sign up for a partner for each hour. Then any hour can be assigned as the partner for that activity. This easily becomes part of the common routine.

Students as Experts. When we identify the skills of our students and encourage them to help one another, we greatly expand our learning resources. We take an environment that typically has one expert and too many children to reach and we teach children to rely on each other for support. Such student-to-student teaching occurs with teacher guidance and observation. For example, Lisa was writing a story but not using needed quotation marks. The teacher said to her, "Writers use quotation marks." She then asked Lisa to look for examples in books. "You've got it!" she said when Lisa shared what she had done. "Will you be willing to help others now?" Lisa said that she would. Later, when another student asked for help with quotation marks, the teacher said, "John, Lisa is good at quotation marks. Ask her for help." As John learned about quotation marks, the teacher asked him if he too would help other students. For the rest of the year, John and Lisa were the teachers for quotation marks.

Another teacher facilitated this process by developing a "yellow pages" that listed student skills. Students were asked to identify two or three skills in which they excelled and write an advertisement for themselves. These were compiled into a class yellow pages book. Students often consulted this book when they needed help on topics and as the class learned new skills, new advertisements were included. This project gave every child the opportunity to be the teacher, including students with special needs (Fisher, 1995; Kent, 1997; Schiller, 1998).

Experiments. Experiments should be ongoing in every classroom. For example, students may be studying light. Some students set up an experiment in which plants of the same type get exposure to differing amounts and types of light and record the plants' growth. Another student might have a different idea they want to try using plants. Teaching children to explore their own ideas using the scientific process allows for multilevel instruction. Experimenting is best done in groups of two to four, often with each student playing a different role—observer, recorder, setup person, reporter, and so on. These roles allow children to interact at multiple levels (American Association for the Advancement of Science, 1989).

Small Group Mini-Lessons

Sometimes students need explicit instruction on skills or content information. While we typically begin each day's lesson with a short mini-lesson with the whole class, we will often find it helpful to identify students who have similar needs and periodically group these students for short mini-lessons. Different lessons focus on different things for different groups.

In mini-lessons we are careful to truly be flexible in the way that we group students, ensuring that we do not create stable, ongoing ability groups. Most of the time we will have groups of students with varied skill levels even if they need to work on a similar skill. For example, one teacher had small groups of students working on reading with expression and fluency. In one of these fourth-grade groups were students who read at very different ability levels—one at the first-grade level and another at the seventh-grade level. However, each student read aloud to a partner and then to the whole group materials at his or her level of challenge, seeking to create meaning through engaging oral reading. When we do group students by ability level we are careful to mix students and not create ongoing ability groups of the same students.

To get started, we call a group together during workshop time when other students are busy with their projects. We may announce that we are going to conduct a mini-lesson on a skill and invite all students who want help to attend. Alternatively, we may ask certain students to join, mentioning that we noticed they have been struggling in this area and would find the mini-lesson helpful. When we can show how a skill will be helpful in work in which the student is engaged, students are usually interested and they learn the valuable skill of assessing their own work. Often there will be more students than anticipated at the meeting.

The mini-lesson can address anything from choosing books that are just right to fluency and expression in reading to borrowing in subtraction (Calkins, 1994; Fisher, 1995; Kohn, 1999; Schiller, 1998). Mini-lessons should be short (no more than 10 or 15 minutes), should focus on the same idea for several lessons, and should give the students something to try when they are done. Tools for mini-lessons include the following.

Strategy Lessons. In **strategy lessons** we use students' materials to focus on specific skills; for example, spelling sound combinations, editing skills, or other content area skills. The teacher calls groups to practice working on how to spell the long *o* sounds, as they are misspelling them in writing. This can be done through a scavenger hunt that looks for all the words that have the long *o* sound and sorts them by spellings. They can play a game to practice these sounds, such as listing many choices on the board together and then playing hot potato and saying a long *o* word each time. Then, they take it back to their own writing and edit the words. For editing skills, a small group can be called to work on indenting for paragraphs. They spend time looking in books and identifying what a paragraph is. Then they take turns reading their own work and having children put a thumb up when they think a new paragraph is needed. If students are needing additional work on adding fractions, they meet to use manipulatives to work on how this concept works. They take time to add them on paper and with manipulatives or they solve a real-world problem using pizza or candy bars to share.

Group Reflections and Dialogue. When students meet in groups, it is often to discuss an idea they are still struggling with or to reinforce something they are learning. For example, students who have a misconception about how day and night works can be called for small group lessons in which they read books together, use a globe and a flashlight to act out how it works, and watch a short video clip, all the while discussing what they see. When the class is hearing a instructional read aloud, the teacher calls one

mini-lesson of students who need more support in understanding the motivations of the main characters. They talk about what the character is doing and why. They act out the scenes that let them know that and create questions to share with the class to help them understand the ideas.

Learning Logs. Students keep "process journals" describing how they have approached an inquiry. Children are constantly writing what they are thinking about anything we are working on in class, whether it is science centers, a research project that involves early settlers, or the math topic of fractions. Then, mini-lessons are called together to discuss what the students are writing. This gives the teacher insights into what the children are retaining and thinking. It allows her to group students again for mini-lessons based on thoughts she wants to push, and gives the students another chance to hear the information in a different form.

At the end of the mini-lesson students write in their journals or logs making plans for what they will do next in the skills they need to learn. Of course, we don't expect one mini-lesson to provide all the learning students need. They use skills in ongoing lessons. We regroup students later to work on various aspects of the skills. Using mini-lessons, however, we can provide systematic, explicit instruction without stable, ability-based groups.

Student Conferences

When students are working, they are expected to confer with the teacher to share what they have learned and discuss what they'll do next to improve. Conferences are usually one-on-one and can focus on developing reading strategies, testing comprehension, sharing a new writing skill, editing a paper, or drafting a web to organize a writing or project. Student conferences give teachers a wonderful window into a child's learning, and the time for these vitally important conferences is one of the benefits of workshop-style learning. They are structured so that other children are working individually or in small groups while the teacher is conducting conferences (Calkins, 1994; Daniels & Bizar, 1998). Teachers keep anecdotal records that indicate what the child is working on so that at the next conference it can start with, "so how did the work on . . . go?" This provides consistency from conference to conference and keeps the teacher informed of each student's progress toward his or her goals.

Peer Conferences and Testing

As students are ready, they *draft* their product—a poem, a story, a reflection, a report, an artistic rendition of an event, a play. The type of product being produced depends on the field of study and the student's ability level.

Students share with others to gain new perspectives and explore the meaning of their work. Several strategies are useful:

- Sharing circles, in which students share work in progress and solicit comments, ideas, and reactions from others.
- Conferences, individual meetings with the teacher or another student to review work and obtain feedback.
- Student presentations to the entire class regarding their work; classmates ask questions, give feedback, and so on.

In *peer conferences,* students work with one another to exchange feedback on drafts. Schiller (1998) suggests that students comment using prompts such as the following: "This seems to be about . . .," "What if . . .," "I thought, . . .," "I wondered . . ." (p. 54). We ask students to keep records of their conferences in work folders. To get peer conferences started, we model the process for the class. Teachers can also select students to work with one another. For example, one teacher often linked students with higher and lower abilities to conference together. This raises the level of learning for both students, as one sees higher thinking modeled and the other learns at a deeper level by explaining material. Conference records provide an ongoing assessment record of the students' work.

Students will *revise* the product and subsequently obtain assistance for *final editing* for publication or presentation. This occurs in several ways: students meet at an editors' table to edit one another's work, or they work with partners to revise content.

Publishing

When students are learning in a workshop-style environment, they have to publish their work to show what they have learned. When we are teaching, there is a different set of expectations for finished work than for works in progress. Students can publish their work at many levels of sophistication. This can be adapted to multilevel teaching, as all children can work on a similar project and be expected to have brought it to different levels by the finished project. For example, children writing historical fiction create stories at a simplistic level with two or three facts inherent in the story, or they can create complex stories with many facts, including accurate clothes and descriptions from the time period. This can also be set up in a tiered environment, where teachers provide different publishing choices for the different levels. Regardless of the design, publishing for a purpose is an important part of authentic learning.

Sharing and Celebrations

Finally, students *share* their work. There are many ways of doing this in order to recognize and celebrate every student's achievement.

- Incorporate sharing of student products in student-led parent conferences.
- Compile products (poems, stories) around a theme and have a "book signing" at a local bookstore.
- Pair the students' writings with pictures of the students, compile them in a binder, and add to the binder blank sheets that say "We welcome your comments." The teacher may then send the book home, first to those parents the teacher knows will write something to encourage others to contribute.
- These student books are added to the classroom library and enjoyed by others during quiet reading time.

The *sharing chair* is a valuable tool for student sharing of work. Students come together as a group and the student sits in a special chair or other props specifically set aside for this purpose. Some teachers use a decorated chair while others use a podium. We make it a special occasion. Tables are set with tablecloths, and hot cocoa and donuts are served in a coffeehouse style. We may have students present to one another or to other classes, or send invitations to parents and family.

When students share learning, they may use media such as art, video, music, computer technology, projects, plays, or poetry. For example, students create a mural to depict what they have learned in a book, write a poem about the differences between

BUMpS IN THE ROAD

Dealing with a Required Prescriptive Curriculum

Over the years there have been many efforts to develop "teacher proofed" curriculum programs that literally prescribe what the teacher is to do and say, what students are to do, and the materials to be used. Such efforts appear to be based on a belief that teachers cannot be trusted to develop lessons that will adequately engage and teach all students. Using such curricula, teachers become technicians rather than professionals whose job is to follow directions, grade assignments, and report results.

Clearly if we are required to use such prescriptive curricula, creating multilevel lessons around the needs of a range of students, creating themes that connect to the lives of students, and organizing workshop learning is going to be more difficult. So what to do?

We need to be clear on our beliefs about teaching. The temptation will be to give up on our goal of becoming an effective inclusive teacher that connects with our students. We need to keep our vision while also doing what we must do to keep our job.

Effective teachers have used the prescribed curriculum in the context of inclusive workshop learning strategies. This is easiest when the curriculum includes elements of inclusive workshop learning that we have discussed in this chapter, as is the case with Open Court and Success for All in literacy instruction. If the curriculum involves total emphasis on direct instruction in skills, our job is more difficult. We operate our class as a workshop using the materials of the prescribed curriculum as part of our resources—like some teachers use textbooks, taking each element of required curriculum and finding ways to match these with workshop learning strategies we'd like to use.

We can also display student work and label how it relates to the components of the prescribed curriculum. We can keep records of student performance and report them in the categories used by the prescribed curriculum. When we do this, when our principal, parents, or others visit our class or want to see how our students are doing in the prescribed curriculum, we can show them. One teacher we knew did exactly this and was held up as a model teacher for implementing the prescribed curriculum, even though she used the curriculum in the context of inclusive workshop instruction.

Here's what one teacher who had done this reported on a listserv:

We have two specialists who visit our classrooms regularly (from the organization that sponsors the prescribed curriculum). They have given my principal glowing reports, and were very taken with our actually doing the investigation/inquiry part of the program. I showed them records that documented knowledge of parts of speech, genre, character analysis and some extras I have added—"hooks," words that describe character, other words for *said,* ideas to talk about in book clubs and our "Magic School Box," an idea coming from the students which houses summaries and personal reviews the students write about the classroom library books they read so others can check for books they might also like to read. I also showed them how I have integrated the current curriculum theme into most of what we do throughout the day. The theme . . . really lends itself to everything we do and how we do it and helps with learning how to work in an at least partially-based-on-inquiry classroom. (Sharon, 2003)

two countries, or create a multimedia presentation on the ocean. If students are learning about economics, have them make holiday cards, then market and sell them. One teacher of a grades 3–5 multiage class states, "In my class, I have seen students who could not memorize facts about the unit they were studying, but when given the freedom to create, they made creations that took my breath away and illustrated a depth of understanding that surprised me" (S. Huellmantel, personal communication, September 2001).

Multilevel Learning Materials

A key to effective multilevel teaching and workshop-based learning is availability of learning materials that allow students to learn about topics at their own ability level and also provide us many different ways to present information to students in multiple modalities with multiple forms of representation. This means that good multilevel teachers are on the constant lookout for good books and other resources at different ability levels. Most budgets include funds every year for purchasing such materials. These include:

- Written materials regarding topics on many ability levels. Some publishers provide identified reading levels of their publications. We should use such information, however, to guide students rather than restricting them to identified levels. We particularly should not have students self-identifying their level in a particular system. Rather, teach them how to choose material they can read no matter where it is found.
- Graphics materials—photographs, figures, and drawings.
- Tools by which written materials may be read aloud: text-to-speech software; students reading to one another; reading by a special education teacher or paraprofessional; books on tape.
- Software programs that combine words spoken with graphics, emphasizing key words.
- Quality Internet sites that combine text and graphics with key links to information, often in combination with text-to-speech software.
- Videos on topics.
- Interview of community members and parents recording on audio- or videotape as well as taking notes.
- *Picture booklets* showing step-by-step instructions. These could be developed by a support person or student. Making such booklets could even be part of a group activity and would help all the students better understand the procedure.
- PowerPoint presentations of key concepts in reading materials that incorporate graphics to illustrate key points.
- "Thinking worksheets": Effective inclusive teachers often use forms developed for various projects that ask students to record observations, journal notes, conclusions, questions, and more. These provide ways for students to record what are essentially working notes that the teacher can use to check for understanding.

When we use a range of learning materials that are based on combinations of varied learning styles (see Chapter 7), multiple intelligences (see later in this chapter), and ability levels using varied modalities and different ways of presenting information, we help students make connections and engage the material so that they will better understand and remember information and deepen skill development.

Let's also be clear about what learning materials are not multilevel and make inclusive teaching more difficult. These include:

- *Textbooks:* By definition, a textbook is at one level of ability. Students don't use other materials such as trade books that may be written at differing ability levels. Effective inclusive teachers use textbooks as one resource, often as a reference book.
- *Worksheets of basic skills:* Worksheets that are presented at only one ability level make it difficult for students with both higher and lower abilities. Effective inclusive teachers do not use these types of worksheets often but instead use "thinking worksheets" as discussed previously.

Students are sharing regarding books they have read. The teacher has provided them questions to ask each other to prompt discussion and dialogue. Georgio, a student with a learning disability, shares the key story line and a funny event that happened.

Including Students in Lecture–Worksheet–Test Instruction

Despite the usefulness of workshop learning, it is still possible, though more difficult, to successfully teach students of varied abilities successfully in lecture–worksheet–test classes. First, lecture–worksheet–test teachers should work to make their lectures more engaging and interesting and provide some opportunities for student engagement. Here are a few suggestions that will help you reach more students and facilitate learning:

- *Lecture and group discussion:* Introduce information and content and pose a question to the students. Involve them in a group discussion, going back and forth between lecturing and discussion. Call on a variety of students taking care to provide all students opportunities for sharing.
- *Think–pair–share:* Again, introduce information and content and ask a question. Ask each student to think for 60 seconds, share with a partner, and then for that pair to share with another pair or the whole class.
- *PowerPoint:* Using transparencies, or better yet, presentation software such as Microsoft PowerPoint or Apple's Keynote. At best, provide simple summaries of the content via the presentation slides. Use graphics, video, and music to introduce additional modalities.
- *Supports for note taking:* If you want students to take notes, provide them training and support in taking good notes. Print out your presentation slides and give them to students as a handout. For students who have difficulty taking notes, consider asking one student to share her notes with other students, perhaps using carbonized paper to easily make a copy of the notes.
- *Alternatives to lecture:* Consider some alternatives to lecture and testing on material. For example, you could have students work in small groups and develop summaries of reading materials. You could ask groups to present to the total class or

Multilevel Project-Based Learning

View these videos and think about specific strategies by which students of varied abilities could participate in and learn through these great learning activities.

Learning Landscape: Kids Monitor Terrain with Tech Students at this Minnesota elementary school use new technology to study the ancient ecology of a vast prairie wetland. www.edutopia.org/wetland-ecology-technology-video

A Night in the Global Village: Role-Playing Life in Poverty At Heifer International's re-creation of communities in developing countries, in Perryville, Arkansas, Colorado middle school students experience firsthand how to survive in substandard living conditions. www.edutopia.org/night-global-village

Smart Moves: The New PE Collaborative games, zip lining, and classroom aikido are part of a new physical education movement that makes kids smarter. www.edutopia.org/new-physical-education-movement-video

engage in a group discussion. This will ensure that students read the material. Use assistive technology to provide written materials on tape or text-to-speech software. For students with cognitive disabilities, you might ask other students in the group to do simple summaries of the material using pictures and graphics.

Second, you can use strategies that improve the validity of typical tests for students with a range of abilities. You can use these related to worksheets of content and skills. Here are a few suggestions:

- *Tests at differing ability levels:* You will want to create tests on the material at differing levels of ability so that students who are considered gifted, students who are middle range and students with cognitive or learning disabilities get material at different levels of complexity. You'll need to experiment with this over time. At first, it will require more work. However, you should be able to use each test you develop multiple times. One of the difficulties with this strategy, as with tiered assignments discussed previously, is that you have to decide which students get what test. You can get assistance from specialists such as special education teachers, bilingual consultants, and gifted consultants.
- *Number of items:* Some teachers ask students with lower abilities to do a smaller number of items and students with higher abilities to do more.
- *Review sheets:* Provide review sheets at each level that state exactly what is going to be tested. Give students time to study in study groups within the class period and take time for questions that have come up in their review prior to taking the test.

Making Schools Work for All Students:
The Beginning and End of the Journey

We talked recently with a group of teachers in a school that is seeking to become an inclusive school. A student with a very severe disability, Denise, is in the sixth grade with support by a paraprofessional. Several students with autism are also in general education classes full time. One day we watched as Denise's whole class was energetically engaged in discussing questions they would e-mail to a man who was making a movie in the northern part of the state. The students called out all sorts of good ideas; a student recorder wrote them down. I thought, "This is a terrific authentic writing project." Afterward the teacher explained to us that the man making the movie is Denise's father, to whom she is very close. Partly because he'll be out on the movie set for the next few months, Denise has been very down and depressed. The teacher came up with this authentic activity, connected to their ongoing class objectives, to help Denise feel better. "Denise," she said to this student, whose eyes sparkle and connect as the teacher talks but who has no verbal language, "we are going to ask your dad these questions and he's going to write us back!" Denise laughed.

We held a focus group discussion with teachers regarding their progress toward inclusive teaching and listened carefully as Denise's teacher talked. "What we have to realize," she said, "is that we don't ask ourselves, 'How do I include this one kid?' We ask ourselves, 'How do I help create a culture and way of teaching in my class that welcomes all, where all students can work to their own potential?' "

We agree with Denise's teacher. In this chapter we've reviewed some best practices in teaching. We've suggested that these practices offer us many strategies to help students learn at multiple levels. Our challenge and opportunity is to teach and to build a classroom culture in ways that really do support students in learning together. As we think about it, the sun shines a bit more brightly in our mind's eye. We see schools full of teaching and learning and laughter and interest, beyond the dark and dismal images of learning that lie behind us on this road we are traveling.

Traveling Notes

For many teachers, it's a bit of a wonder to realize that best strategies for instruction are the same as those that facilitate our including students with a wide range of differences and abilities in learning together. How might we make these the center of our teaching practice? Following are a few notes to remember.

1. Traditional teaching practices ensure failure among many students. Their emphasis on narrow skills and worksheets causes many students to get bored and lose interest in learning. In addition, "one-level" instruction is far below the level of many students, offering them no challenge; for others, it is too high level and frustrating.
2. Both research and the judgment of national professional organizations call for moving away from such traditional practices to more engaging, hands-on, collaborative ways of learning.
3. Three fundamental formats for teaching are apparent in classrooms: lecture–worksheet–test instruction, direct instruction, and workshop-based learning. Workshop learning involves students in active learning where they work individually, in pairs, and in small groups to access information and develop products that demonstrate their learning.
4. Multiple intelligences theory helps us design instruction based on eight ways in which students can be smart, thus building on student strengths.
5. Multilevel instruction allows students to learn and be challenged at their own level of ability while working with others at different levels: materials at differing levels, open-ended projects, and group work in which students take differing roles are some of many strategies.
6. Tiered instruction allows children to work on different assignments about the same topic at their level of instruction.

7. There are several ways to provide individual differentiation for students who need support beyond what they already get in multilevel instruction. These range from making minimal adaptations to creating parallel activities, a seldom used strategy.

8. Workshop learning involves a range of tools and strategies that include mini-lessons at the beginning of instruction and in small groups, multilevel and multi-modal learning activities, peer conferences to review drafts, teacher conferences with students, publishing, and sharing and celebrations of work.

9. Scaffolding helps us support students in moving to their next level of challenge in learning and strengthen their learning.

10. Inclusive teaching in lecture–worksheet–test classes is possible when teachers find ways to make lectures more engaging and connected, provide alternative ways that students can access information from the text, and make modifications to tests.

Stepping Stones

Following are some activities that will help extend your understanding and actions you may take to use best practices and the four building blocks in your teaching practice.

1. Outline a thematic unit based on the concepts of inclusive workshop learning, using format like that in Figure 11.6 in Chapter 11. Follow these steps:
   - Sketch your learning goals and levels of goals.
   - Identify learning products and assessment strategies.
   - Brainstorm some engaging learning activities based on open-ended individual and group projects.
   - Use the learning activities and subjects matrix and the multiple intelligences matrix to see how the activities match to both subjects and intelligences. Study the matches. Make modifications to ensure coverage of the multiple intelligences and linkages with subjects.
   - List the materials you will need.
   - Consider various students in your class— those with learning challenges, students who are gifted, and so on and make notes regarding how they will participate at their ability level based on their needs.

2. Develop a rubric based on the ideas in this chapter regarding inclusive workshop learning. Conduct an analysis of the strengths and needs in your own teaching. If possible, get another teacher to do this also or a teacher team (third-grade teachers, seventh-grade team). Discuss strategies for working on improving your teaching as an inclusive workshop teacher.

3. Consider your own "intelligences." What are your strongest areas of performance and learning? If you were to design a perfect school just for you, what would it look like? What would students do? How would teachers teach? What are the implications for your own teaching practice?

4. Teach students about multilevel learning and setting personal best goals and engaging in just-right work. Lead a discussion about what this means in the classroom. Get their ideas.

5. Teach students about multiple intelligences and learning styles. Have them determine their own intelligences and learning styles. Then have them talk with each other and get ideas for how they might learn the best.

13

Inclusive Academic Instruction, Part III

Applications in Subjects

CHAPTER GOAL

Understand how inclusive workshop learning plays out in the different subject areas.

CHAPTER OBJECTIVES

1. Learn how to implement inclusive literacy workshop learning in elementary and secondary school.

2. Understand trends and guidelines for professional practice in mathematics education that support inclusive multilevel learning.

3. Utilize inclusive workshop learning in science and social studies.

4. Understand how to include diverse students in art, music, and physical education.

Inclusive Literacy in Action: A Visit to the First Grade and a High School Language Arts Class

We walk into Joanne Butler's **first-grade class** and see students all over the room, some on the floor, some at their desks, a few in groups of two or three. She welcomes us and explains that this is "reading workshop" time. All the students are reading—most in picture books with a few words, but a couple in chapter books. Joanne helps her students select books in which they are interested. "Earlier this week," she says, "we all got down on the floor and picked out books. They helped each other. I asked them to get one book that was easy, one that was just right, and one that they liked but was challenging." Some students are reading silently alone. Others are reading in pairs. Students meet together to talk about their books. This helps all the students have experiences with different books and learn to ask questions. Joanne reads some of the harder books aloud to the class as a group.

Joanne points out a few students to us. One girl, Midha, recently immigrated from Iran to this country. She reads picture books with large words with other students in pairs. "The other children are really good with her. She is beginning to learn our language quickly," Joanne comments. One student, Chad, has autistic-like behaviors. He has taken an interest in reading books about dogs. "Rosalita is my highest reader in the class," Joanne explains. "She, too, is reading about dogs and she and Chad get together now and then. They've been good for each other. I have worked out an arrangement with Rosalita where she is linking extra-credit projects in science and even math with her interest in dogs. It's been fun."

Curious, we ask, "How are they learning their phonics?" She replies that she observes the students reading and writing and talks with them, figuring out what problems they are having. "I might cluster students for a mini-lesson, say on the different ways to say the letter g. As I figure out who is good at particular skills, I have students learn to come to one another for help so that I am actually ending up with 24 teachers in this room rather than just myself," Joanne laughs (Peterson et al., 2002).

We also visit Akio Kudo's **high school literature class** over several days. Students have been reading Alan Paton's *Cry, the Beloved Country*, a novel of South Africa, and have become intrigued with the history of Africa, colonialism, and apartheid in South Africa. They want to explore these issues more.

Akio recently decided to push his teaching a bit by allowing students to propose projects and chose this topic to try it out. He's also been growing as an inclusive teacher. He moved recently from a racially homogeneous school that also segregated students with special needs to Cortes High School, a racially mixed school that also has been working over the last 10 years to include students with special needs in general education classes. He was pleased to see that students with special needs worked well in all these projects and that his students with higher functioning skills were challenged as well, learning how to work with other students in leadership positions.

As a total class Akio helped students brainstorm ideas for projects. Once he approved these, students broke into groups based on their interests. One group wanted to compare racial relations in Africa and what has occurred in the United States and develop a multimedia presentation. Another group decided to develop a play of a key event in the historical struggle with apartheid. Yet another small group explored art in South Africa and how it related to social conditions in the country. Akio approved these projects and they got to work.

The class was abuzz. Students accessed information via google searches on the Internet where they found good information, maps, and hyperlinked videos to some key events. Books in the library were also useful. Two students had family members who had been to South Africa when apartheid was enforced and students interviewed them. Nakia, a great dancer, developed an interpretive dance related to protest music and her partners video-taped her performance. Students often shared across groups.

Akio was amazed and excited at how engaged the students were.

After 3 weeks of work, students presented their projects. The presentations and discussion took 2 days but were amazing, involving students' thinking and feeling at a deep level. All of the students with special needs were given an integral part in the presentations. Students thought this was so cool, they proposed to have a forum to involve other classes and community members in the same experience. (Adapted from International Reading Association & National Council of Teachers of English, 1996)

In Chapters 11 and 12, we provided a framework and process for designing inclusive units and lessons across all subjects. In this chapter we'll look in greater detail at how these strategies for inclusive workshop learning play out in select subjects. Our intent is to help connect the strategies of inclusive teaching with effective workshop learning practices in various subjects. Many other books and resources provide strategies that are consistent with those that we are presenting in this book, even if the authors do not specifically use the language of inclusive teaching and multilevel differentiated instruction. If we think about these connections, however, we discover that there are a great many possibilities for extending the ideas and strategies presented in this text. Let's start with literacy and language arts.

Literacy and Language Arts

Literacy is a foundational skill upon which much of our learning and human functioning is based. For all our students, helping them become literate, in the broadest sense of the term, is very important for life success. Language arts and literacy, like all other subjects,

BACK PACK

It's Just Good Teaching

It's Just Good Teaching The Northwestern Research Educational Laboratory (NWREL) provides a series on inclusive classrooms in math and science downloadable as pdf documents. www.nwrel.org/msec/resources/justgood.php

Annenberg Media This site provides teacher resources across ages and subjects. It has many useful materials including videos of exemplary lessons. www.learner.org

are both similar and different in elementary, middle, and high school. Children obviously grow larger, know more, have more experiences, and move toward adulthood over time. Yet, no matter the age of the students, we teach them that reading is an important part of their life. This is the focus of how we lead any workshop session.

Yet, in effective instruction there are many parallels between elementary and secondary school. For example, in elementary school we involve students in reading for meaning: considering plots in a story, what characters feel, and issues that develop. We continue this in secondary school, often at greater depth and complexity. However, given that we will have students at all grade levels who function at very different levels of ability, in all classes students will be exploring themes and issues at differing levels of sophistication. As we discussed in Chapter 11, this is the heart of multilevel learning goals.

Another important shift is that while traditional secondary teachers expect students to know the skills of reading and writing, the reality is that all students need to continue to expand and deepen their skills. There will be students in high school who read on a third-grade level, and they will need to work on basic skills. All students will need continued work on strategies of comprehension. In writing, some students will be working on basic spelling, phonics, and grammar skills. All students (throughout their lifetime) will be working on how to write with clarity and meaning. So secondary language arts classes will also incorporate reading, writing, spelling, and grammar instruction in language arts classes. Below we explore a range of strategies that can be used in both elementary and secondary classes.

What *Is* Literacy?

Given that literacy is so essential, it's important that we are clear on *exactly* what literacy is. **Literacy** is a process by which human beings utilize symbols and tools in communicating. Traditionally, this has meant reading and writing. However, if the focus is on communication of meaning, we should consider an expanded understanding based upon diverse communication systems human beings actually use. These include (Oglan, 2003):

- Reading by which individuals construct meaning from print using their prior knowledge
- Writing text in words
- Speaking and listening
- Viewing
- Representing, either physically, in drama, movement, or in pictures
- Signing, facial expression, and gestures of hands, legs, or other body parts
- Using technology to facilitate access to written and graphic materials and to communicate in writing and orally

What's the point? Simply this: If we are trying to get students to use symbols to convey or access meaning we have many choices. Using multiple options we can devise effective strategies for students who have difficulties.

Challenges in Literacy Education

Children who have been exposed to reading and books and given opportunities to express themselves come to school with a hunger to read and write. Yet, too often this hunger is quashed by practices that make reading and writing an oppressive process that seems to have little to do with the actual lives of students. How does this happen? Here are some of the prevalent practices:

- Using curricula where a teacher reads out commands and students chant the desired answer in unison. This could involve "reading" a nonsense word, a series of words that have the same sound, or matching the meaning of different words. Students in such instruction are taught that learning is following commands.
- Filling out worksheets in which students complete phrases or match words to pictures and definitions.
- All students taking turns reading the same level text, regardless of what level they currently read at.
- Students being allowed to read only texts designed around reinforcing various phonics concepts even though the stories are not interesting and of poor quality.

In other words, students are involved in all sorts of drill activities related to aspects of reading and writing but spend *little, if any time actually reading and writing.* Advocates of direct instruction state that these strategies are necessary so that students may obtain basic skills such as decoding and spelling. Some suggest that such strategies may be learned as students are engaged in actual reading and writing. However, most teachers who use these strategies extensively find that there is not time to do both. Of course, the more difficulty students have in acquiring these basic skills, the more they are emphasized. Students who have special needs may, in fact, spend their entire public school career working on basic skills and never actually using them to read and write for an authentic purpose.

What is clear is that, for students with special needs, by the time they reach the third or fourth grade, they have been told in many ways that they have difficulties in reading and writing. Lots of pressure has been put on them to work hard to improve their skills and they have spent more and more time in skills and drills. The result: These students begin to believe they cannot learn to read and write. More importantly, they quit trying. We participated recently in a study group of K–12 teachers in an urban school district that was trying to improve reading and writing of students with special needs. As part of this work they conducted an interview with several high school students regarding their previous involvement in literacy. Their high school teachers reported, "We can't get them to read anything! Not comics, not materials about stuff in which they are interested. Nothing!" When did this start? The third grade. The fact is that few people will continue to work hard at a task that everyone says we do poorly. This story is repeated over and over.

Does it have to be this way? Absolutely not. If we adhere to the standards of quality instruction and focus on involving students in reading and writing where meaning and purpose are the central focal point, all students can be productively involved in reading and writing. Will all be on grade level? No, human beings are too diverse for this to happen. However, all students can be literate at some level and enjoy and value the process, while making progress toward doing it more effectively. Effective learning in literacy involves two key components—reading and writing workshop. Let's look at how these work with diverse students.

Standards in Literacy Learning

The **standards for language arts** developed jointly by the International Reading Association and the National Council of Teachers of English (1996) indicate that students from elementary through high school should be engaged in active involvement in language, reading, and writing for authentic purposes, linking literacy to social studies, science, math, and other arenas of their lives as we saw in the two previous scenarios. According to these standards, effective literacy and language arts instruction should include the following characteristics:

- Students read a wide range of literature and genres to develop understanding and experience personal fulfillment.
- Students learn to use many strategies to understand written material drawing on their prior experiences, interactions, and knowledge of word identification strategies, sound–letter relationships, and writing structures.
- Students learn to vary their use of language to communicate verbally and in writing with different groups of people.
- Students develop abilities to use language conventions (e.g., spelling, punctuation, etc.) to critique and think about texts.
- Students engage in research on issues by developing questions, posing problems, and gathering information.
- Students use a range of resources to gather information.
- Students use language to achieve their own goals, to learn, to persuade, and to share information and ideas.

In other words, we want students, based on their own interests, needs, and abilities, to read, write, and communicate to accomplish important purposes in their own lives and become effective citizens in their communities.

Reading Workshop

Reading workshop involves several components that allow students of different levels to work together, and yet pushes all students to do their best. These include:

1. Reading assessment to identify skills and needs of students in decoding and comprehension
2. Instructional read aloud, a shared reading time that introduces new literature at higher levels and models comprehension strategies.
3. Mini-lessons and guided reading in small groups to work on reading strategies
4. Individual reading of just-right books
5. Student dialogue and sharing of books they have read
6. Assessment to demonstrate comprehension and understanding

We teach students how the process of reading workshop operates so they know what to expect each day. We start slowly at the beginning of the year, adding one workshop piece at a time until the result is a complex time with many things going on simultaneously and flexible time for teachers. Figure 13.1 illustrates the way we communicate the steps to students. Let's look at the literacy workshop process in more detail.

In reading workshop many things are going on simultaneously. Students select books to read at their own level of challenge. During this time they may read alone, in pairs, or in small groups. Students write in journals regarding their books. We conduct conferences with students to talk about their reading plan, discuss how to think about a book, assess comprehension, or share reading strategies. We gather students together for a mini-lesson based on a specific reading strategy or to meet with guided reading groups. This structure allows us the flexibility we need to meet all their needs.

Instructional Read Aloud. At all grade levels, including middle and high school, **read alouds** are a valuable part of literacy and language arts instruction. In a read aloud all students get a chance to simply listen and think about the meaning of the words. During the read aloud we model what is going on in our head. We stop to share connections we

FIGURE 13.1

Reading Workshop Cycle

- Choose a just-right book.
- Prove it is just right to the teacher and set a due date.
- Read the book, marking comprehension strategies with sticky notes.
- Summarize your understanding of the book by addressing these questions: What was the problem and solution? What did the characters feel and do? What connections do you see between the book and yourself, the world, and other books you have read?
- Have a student orally test you on the book.
- Take to the teacher for a conference.
- Choose another just-right book.

have, questions that we wonder, or to describe visual images that we see that go beyond what is written in the book. In other words, we model strategies of comprehension and facilitate discussion to prompt deeper understanding and thinking regarding the reading. Instructional read alouds help promote the notion that good reading is not just "getting through" the book but engaging with the writer in a deep way.

Reading Assessment and Just-Right Books. At the beginning of the year, we test each student on fluency and comprehension to get an understanding of his or her reading level. We can do this using a formal assessment tool or simply have a student read a passage to us. This enables us to help students learn to identify what their **just-right** level is.

In an effective multilevel classroom, we do not tell students their reading level nor do we publicly display on books a reading level and expect students to read only books in their tested level. This can promote a focus on reading level and inadvertently make some students feel inferior and others superior. Further, when we restrict students to certain reading materials coded at their level, we are not teaching them how to select books for themselves. Students should assume responsibility for choosing reading at their level.

We teach students to identify a just-right book by how many words they are unsure of on a page. Being unsure of two to four words shows the book is a just-right book. If they don't know or are unsure of five or more words, it is too difficult. If they know all the words or are unsure of just one, it is too easy. When students have difficulty finding books that have words they do not know, then a discussion of what content challenges and engages the mind without frustrating the child is relevant.

Individual Reading of Just-Right Books. We contract with students for how many books they will read. Depending on the nature of the books the number can vary dramatically from student to student. For example, if a seventh grader is reading at college level, she may read 3 complex novels in a marking period while another student, functioning at second-grade level, may read 30 books with lots of pictures. We give extra credit if students want to read more books than the minimum for which they have contracted. However, this new amount, in subsequent contracts, becomes the new just-right minimum. Again, we give options for extra credit and again increase the minimum requirements. We can do this at all levels of functioning, of course. It's a way to encourage students to read more without using a system that pushes reading by rewarding the students who read the most with prizes or points. This method of encouraging students to read lets students set their own pace and level of challenge.

We have students put sticky notes on pages as they make connections to their own experiences (to self), to other books they have read (to text), or to something in the broader world and environment (to world). They mark things they think will be important later in the book, questions that they have, and places where the words gave them a great visual image. The sticky notes have their own code to help identify the type of comprehension strategy they are marking. They then have detailed notes of their thinking to share with groups or the teacher or to review when they finish the book to deepen their thinking and understanding.

Book Clubs and Books the Whole Class Reads. While it is important for children to read just-right books individually, children also need the social aspect of reading with small groups or even the whole class to discuss what they are reading and deepen their understanding of various elements. Students meet on a daily or weekly basis, depending on the structure of the class, to discuss parts of the book, reactions to characters, and to answer thought-provoking questions. This particularly occurs in middle and high school. When students are reading books at one level, we'll need to provide scaffolds and support for students whose abilities are not at the level of the reading. As we've discussed in other chapters, we can use several strategies: (1) do read alouds by the teacher for part of the reading, engaging students in discussion of the meaning of the text; (2) do partner reading, where a partner reads aloud to a student; and (3) use oral reading technology such as books on tape or CD or text-to-speech software. Sometimes we can obtain software that will have text-to-speech capabilities that also incorporates graphics that help illustrate the meaning of the text. This can be helpful and enjoyable to all our students.

Strategy Mini-Lessons. These begin in small groups after students have been reading with us individually for several weeks so we have time to identify strategies on which students need to work. While students are reading individually, we can pull students together to learn about a particular skill. The lesson varies depending on what is being studied. Students are often given an assignment to work on throughout the week while they are reading and the students bring their books to share how they have been working on their strategy with the group. Some examples of strategies include:

- Choosing just-right books
- Reading with expression
- Reading fluently, using punctuation to mark breaths and pauses
- Figuring out a variety of sounds in unknown words
- Figuring out the meaning of a word or phrase in context of known words
- Identifying comprehension strategies being used with sticky notes
- Completing paperwork that shows what they know—students interview one another asking questions provided by the teacher and rating the response of the student.

There are many substrategies and skills that may develop. However, note that we do not mention the strategy of decoding words. All students, not just those who are lowest functioning, need work learning the sounds of letters and combinations of letters that we attribute to decoding. However, this is a very different skill than reading. All students, not just those who are highest functioning, also need to learn to think about what they read to improve their comprehension. Reading is about understanding meaning from text: having pictures form in their brain as they read, thinking of questions and answers, what will happen next and why, and issues in the plot of the story. Learning how to sound out words and spell them we call **word study**, more traditionally known as *spelling*. These are two very different ideas and no child should receive instruction in only one or the other. All students need both to learn and grow.

MRS. KING SPORTS HER
WORN SOFTBALL CAP AS A REMINDER
THAT INDIVIDUALIZING TO MEET
UNIQUE STUDENT NEEDS IS
OLD HAT TO GOOD TEACHERS.

Guided Reading. **Guided reading** is an approach to working with students on reading skills in small groups. We gather a small group of students who function at similar levels of ability, read a book together, and model and discuss specific reading strategies. In early elementary, we will use predictable books, choral reading, dramatic play of events in a reading section, and Big Books. We guide students in making predictions from pictures, have them read with partners, discuss the text, and write responses in journals regarding what they read. We use different levels of text involving students in rereading several times during the week. Although students are grouped by ability, in a workshop-based classroom this would be the only occasion where that might happen, and since it is only one small part of the literacy instruction it can be fun and motivating for students. If the students are not grouped by ability, then care will need to be taken to ensure that all have access to the literature.

Strategies for Comprehension. As students read, we ask them to use strategies that help them understand and remember what they learn. We emphasize that good readers are always thinking about what they read and we are going to share some of the ways they think about reading. All students, no matter what level they read at, should work on the comprehension strategies that good readers do. These key comprehension strategies include making connections, asking questions, visualizing, determining importance, inferring, and synthesizing (Harvey & Goudis, 2000). Let's discuss these key strategies briefly and how we teach students to use them.

1. *Making Connections*: This refers to readers' ability to think of other things while they are reading. For example, if reading about a character who told a funny story makes me think about last night when my husband told a funny story, then I made a connection. There are three kinds of connections: text to text, where I think about other books; text to self, where I think about things from my past and life; and text to world, where I think about things from the TV or area around me.

2. *Asking Questions*: This skill is when readers are always thinking about the questions of who, what, when, where, why, and how. For example, why did that character say

Two fourth-grade students read a book together in a reading corner in Mishael Hittie's class. Pairing students provides support from one student to another, making reading a fun activity and increasing student motivation. Allowing students to read where they want—on the floor, at desks, in the hall—strengthens learning.

something mean to his friend? Good readers also are always thinking of possible answers to the questions. Hopefully, the story will either validate their thoughts or change them at some point.

3. *Visualizing*: Good readers are always running a picture in their mind, much like a personal television screen. They add details that are not listed in the story, thus personalizing the story and making it their own.

4. *Determining Importance*: This refers to the ability to sense what is going to happen later in the story. Can readers begin to think like the author and figure out what is going to be important to the overall plot as the story unfolds?

5. *Inferring*: When students make inferences, they are making predictions about what they think will happen next in the story, based on some piece of information that is in the story. If I think the character will run away from the slave owner, I base this inference on the fact that the character has been very interested in what the word *freedom* means and how you get it.

6. *Synthesizing*: This is a complex skill that allows children to take a story and retell the most important points in a concise paragraph. When students synthesize, they are learning to make general statements that cover a host of small actions. This is done at the end of the book to share learning, at the end of the chapter, or after reading a magazine article.

For any of these strategies, students learn them by first hearing teachers model how they think about these things in their head, then they receive guided practice with teachers and small groups of students, finally they move to working on their own. We also encourage students to read at home, communicating these expectations to parents. This helps students make reading part of their life and not something they do just at school.

Sharing with Other Students. We structure opportunities where students can share with one another about their reading. This pushes their thinking beyond simple recall and can be done a number of ways that include:

- Students making a presentation to the class about their book, focusing on one particular section of the book.
- Making posters, media presentations, or sculptures depicting key themes in the reading
- Forming book clubs where small groups come together to share about what they are reading, particularly useful if we group students whose books have overlapping or connected themes

Assessment. We use multiple strategies to assess students understanding and comprehension of their reading if we are to get a clear picture. One useful strategy is to have students assess one another using a series of questions that we have generated. Figure 13.2 illustrates one set of questions from which students can select. These are generic questions

FIGURE 13.2

Book Assessment Questions

These questions make the oral testing situation simpler and easy to use with any level of reader simply because they are generic to any book. They also give the listener a window into what is happening inside the reader's mind, as well as a chance for the students to develop the skill of talking about what they are reading.

FICTION QUESTIONS

1. What was the main problem and how is it solved?
2. What words would you use to describe the main character and why?
3. What was the most exciting part of the story and why?
4. Did you like the ending? Why or why not?

NONFICTION QUESTIONS

1. Summarize 6 key things that you learned about this topic.
2. What was the most important thing you learned that you would share with others?
3. What was the strangest thing you learned?
4. What questions do you still have about this topic?

that can be applied to all fiction. The testing student can select one question from each section of possibilities. The questions simply rate the student on how well he or she responded. These questions make the oral testing situation simpler and easy to use with any level of reader simply because they are generic to any book. They also give the listener a window into what is happening inside the reader's mind, as well as a chance for the students to develop the skill of talking about what they are reading.

Other strategies for assessment include:

- Holding individual conferences with the teacher
- Writing about the book
- Sharing with other students in small or whole group
- Final report on each book. Students use notes taken while they were reading to describe how they are using comprehension strategies by providing an example illustrating how they used each strategy. They also describe their thoughts and perceptions of the book.

Teacher Conference. We will also conference with individual students, setting a specific number each day. We check on the reading progress of students, have them read to us to update our understanding of their skills, and identify the mini-lessons to which we will assign them to increase their skills.

Teacher Roles and Responsibilities. The structure of reading workshop allows us to use our time helping and working with students individually and in small groups in many ways. These will include:

1. Holding individual conferences with students about progress on due dates and paperwork that is due when a book is complete
2. Reading for 2 or 3 minutes with a student to help model comprehension strategies
3. Meeting with small groups to teach a mini-lesson or conduct a guided reading session
4. Congratulating students on their accomplishments, recognizing real achievements relative to the skill ability of each student

BUMpS IN THE ROAD | *Gifted Students and Inclusive Classes*

Some people continue to argue that for students with substantive ability differences, particularly students with learning and cognitive disabilities and students who are gifted, the general education classroom simply doesn't provide adequate challenge or support. Parents of students considered gifted, in particular, are known for insisting on separate classes and even schools for their students.

What is the answer?

One day we had a conversation with some teachers we respect regarding having students with mixed abilities, including students considered gifted, in their classes. We found the discussion enlightening. Here is what Frederick, a middle school science teacher; Ginger, a high school English teacher; and Lazar, an elementary 4th grade teacher told us:

Lazar started by saying, "Having students with a mix of abilities in class benefits all students academically and socially. However, when gifted students are pulled out for special classes or enrichment programs, they never become a part of the classroom community. Most often they feel either isolated or superior. Additionally, it seems that often teachers then assume that this meets the needs of gifted children, so that just following the teacher's scripted lesson plan in the curriculum materials is adequate. I've actually done this myself!"

Frederick continued, stating, "There are always kids who are frustrated by the lesson because it is too difficult while other kids are bored because they are far beyond the skills taught and practiced in the lesson. Often the highly able students simply quietly do what they are told, finishing very quickly and then doodling or wasting time until they go to their enrichment classes. Other times, these became discipline problems. When you teach this mono-level way, both lower and higher level kids are often rejected by the other students, which constantly causes problems."

All three teachers had also been fortunate enough to be in schools where there was an emphasis on multilevel differentiated instruction and any support services were brought into the general education classroom to enrich learning for all students. Ginger

said, "When I work to have lessons that connect to the interests and abilities of all my students the class just goes much better. It's certainly not easier, of course! However, as I have gotten the hang of how to do this it's really not a lot harder either. Kids are not bored or frustrated by classwork. Rather, they are excited."

Frederick added, "I have them work often with partners. Sometimes they pick those with whom they will work. Other times I pick. I have found it interesting that gifted students don't necessarily pick other gifted students with whom to work. Rather, they pick partners who have the same interests and they learn how to help each other. One student may be able to read more difficult books while the other student has more knowledge or experience or insight that the other student values. They can help each other see different perspectives on the material."

Lazar said, as the other teachers nodded in agreement, "The most important thing is that students get to explore their own interests at their own rate and level of learning based on their best learning modes. It's also important that they have a variety of options for demonstrating their learning through writing, art, drama, dance, etc. As a teacher I must have materials available to support and challenge all kids, and students must have free access to those materials. As we develop a strong sense of community in the classroom, we support students in taking the necessary risks in their learning process."

All agreed that students who are considered gifted and talented can be challenged and supported in an inclusive general education class. They can achieve and be challenged at their own level while also providing real support and helping to challenge other students in the class.

Ginger finally addressed a critical issue, that of communicating with parents of students who are gifted or talented. "Often parents are themselves highly engaged and motivated and they are very clear about wanting opportunities for their children. It's not unusual for some students to get very low grades on their first card marking. Their parents show up

(continued)

very quickly! But when I explain to them that my goal is that their child will make progress from where they are now and that I will expect them to do that, as I do with all the students in my class, I've never had a parent who didn't want the same thing. In fact, these parents become my supporters. One of my parents made a presentation at a local parent conference this last year. He compared the experience of his two daughters, both considered gifted. One child, Amanda, went to a special school for gifted children. The other child, Emily, was in my class with another gifted student and several students with significant disabilities. He said that both of his children were taught enriched learning lessons, but that Amanda suffered socially while Emily developed important social skills and truly enjoyed her class. That really made me feel good!"

Reflection: If we're clear about what we're about we really can support students at all levels in learning well together, including those with the highest abilities. An inclusive classroom becomes a place of enriched, enhanced learning for all. If we are clear about what we are doing and why, we can also explain this in ways that parents, other teachers, and administrators understand. When students all learn and love our class, even doing well on standardized tests, we'll get support for our work as an inclusive teacher.

Writing Workshop

Writing is also a very important piece of literacy that we stress should become part of the students' lives. Writing workshop is similar to reading workshop in that students are all working on different goals and writing materials at their own ability level. Throughout the year, students will be exposed to various genres in reading workshop, and they will learn how to write various genres in writing workshop. As writers and readers, we will explore everything from adventures and fairy tales to historical fiction, persuasive writing, nonfiction writing, and more. Between studying genres we intersperse short 2-week units on revision and structure. Most genre units take about a month to complete.

Writing workshop also involves several components that will occur simultaneously. These include:

- Assessing student writing abilities
- Developing ideas for writing in a writing notebook
- Giving mini-lessons on craft and editing ideas
- Doing individual writing work
- Students reviewing drafts and providing feedback
- Editing (for grammar, spelling, and other mechanics of writing)
- Sharing
- Publishing

In elementary school, writing workshop should occur at least three or four times a week for 45 to 60 minutes. Any less time spent will not be effective. Although writing in other subject areas is important, it does not count as writing workshop. The workshop structure is important for students to learn how to craft writing. In middle and high school, writing workshop more often occurs as part of a literature block in conjunction with reading. However, given the various levels of student ability, we must continue to grow their writing skills.

Assessing Student Writing. As in reading workshop, at the beginning of the year, semester, or writing unit we will want to assess student writing ability. We do this by having students write pieces that are meaningful to them—a journal entry about their daily life, a letter to a parent, or a story about a character in a book. We look for the following to determine writing strengths and needs:

- Can the student plan a story with a web and use it to follow a sequence?
- Does the student have interesting ideas?
- Does the student use a variety of words, or are the same words repeated over and over (i.e., *said*, *went*, etc.)?
- Does the student have a sense of structure, such as paragraphs and beginning, middle, and end?
- Can the student use punctuation and grammar correctly?
- Does the writing have a strong, clear voice?

Developing Ideas for Writing: The Student Writing Notebook. This is a place for students to collect ideas for writing. They can make lists of things they love or that irritate them. Ideas can include pictures—from favorite people, trips, or possessions to a beautiful sunset. The notebook can also include maps of favorite places, descriptions of exciting events, or something in nature that caught their eye. As students learn to look at the world through a writer's eye, the possibilities are endless. Teachers model by sharing writing entries of their own.

A key in student writing is authenticity. Students should be writing for a real audience for a real purpose, not just as an abstract school exercise. This naturally leads to ways that students can share their writing. Teachers can help students think about what they would like to say and then help them locate places their writing can be shared.

Creating Mini-Lessons. Typically we start with a whole group mini-lesson that focuses on one topic for several lessons (10–15 minutes). We write and model for the students, thinking aloud as we write so students understand our thinking process. We may refer to a word wall or use other tools. Students may help us edit a drafted piece of work. We may read from a text, pointing out specific writing crafts that we encourage students to try. We focus on different parts of the writing process, a variety of topics and forms ranging from shorter, simpler pieces to longer, more complex writing.

Mini-lessons can involve basic skills, but they will also involve helping students understand how to best convey meaning in their writing.

Doing Individual Writing. Students then write individually. Each child will be at a different stage: planning, drafting, revising, editing, and publishing. In writing workshop students most often make three to five drafts and conference with other students and the teacher. Students select their own topics, often linked to their reading, a science project, or a social studies lesson using relevant genres—poetry, short stories, historical fiction, expository writing. Students keep journals regarding their writing process—ideas to write about, their feelings about the process, or a record of their activities. They write at their own level. As the teacher helps them complete a detailed web that plans the story, the drafting process becomes much easier. The teacher helps them separate *drafting* from *editing* through such strategies as freewriting, in which students write whatever comes to mind with no concern about grammar or spelling. The mechanics come later when students give feedback and assist one another in editing. Teachers are involved in final editing for *publication* only (Calkins, 1994; Cunningham & Allington, 1999; Graves, 1983; Holdaway, 1979; Routman, 1996).

Reviewing Drafts and Editing. Once the writing is completed, the student works with other students to edit, correcting spelling and grammar errors and ensuring the piece communicates well. Students share ideas, get feedback, and meet on a regular basis so that they learn strategies for helping one another and develop trust. This kind of collaboration increases the number of helpers from one—the teacher—to many (Calkins, 1994).

Sharing Writing. We end each day with a sharing time. This is very important in allowing students to hear good ideas and learn to identify them as well.

Publishing. At the end of the writing process, it is important that we demonstrate that student work is valued and honored in the way that their work is published and presented. No matter their ability, students have worked hard in completing their writing. They have written several drafts, and revised writing to use various strategies we have taught them to convey meaning. We compile students' work into a laminated classroom book, which provides authentic purpose for their writing and is sent home for parents to read. We structure varied opportunities where students' work is read publicly. Reading students' work in front of a caring group honors their achievement and is a wonderful teachable moment in which "both advanced and struggling writers can be nudged forward in their literacy development" by their feelings of accomplishment (Cunninham, Hall, & Defee, 1998, p. 656). We can do this many ways. We invite parents to attend a reading celebration in which each piece is honored by choral reading. Finished work is shared with a younger partner class with which they have shared many learning opportunities. Even a student with severe multiple disabilities is easily included in this multilevel process by working with a partner, who asks yes/no questions to help her write her own contribution to the book.

Performing Teacher Roles and Responsibilities. As students work, teachers are doing several things. We move around the classroom checking on students' progress and offering suggestions. We keep informal notes on each step—planning, drafting, revising, and editing. In one classroom, for example, Bobby is working on capital letters and periods and can create stories a few sentences long with a lot of effort. Julie writes nicely edited stories but needs to tap her creative and descriptive skills. In Julie's case, we would check back later and ask how her new idea is going. We may also:

- Set goals with students for a new piece of writing.
- Meet with a small group for a mini-lesson on a related topic.
- Model a type of writing on the overhead.
- Identify students who have excellent examples of a strategy, topic, or skill being worked on to share with other students.

Teaching Skills: Spelling, Phonics, and Grammar

In effective workshop reading and writing classes, we integrate skill learning into authentic reading and writing activities. Let's discuss some strategies for doing this in an authentic way.

Phonics and Spelling. Many times in classrooms, teachers confuse teaching phonics skills with teaching reading. Teaching **phonics**, or how the letters combine to make different sound combinations, is an important part of literacy instruction. As students progress with their abilities, they learn what suffixes and prefixes mean and how to recognize words that have a Latin derivative to help them derive the meaning of the word. These are very important skills, and yet they are separate from teaching reading. Reading is the ability to *find meaning* in words and stories. Effective teachers have found that teaching phonics in the context of spelling instruction is a valuable strategy.

FIGURE 13.3

Individualized Spelling Lists from Weather Journals

Cathy: probably, travels, autumn, evaporation, equator, movement, video, crystal, glacier, until

Norman: today, cloudy, explode, December, icy, windy, muddy, heat, earth, weather

Kami: revolves, half, certain, autumn, probably, glacier

Jordan: rain, snow, cloud, wet, year, make, some, black, sack, pack

Sean: eight, partly, temperature, degrees, which, blizzard, changes, climate, report, video

Individualized spelling lists may be selected from student writing, as illustrated in Figure 13.3. We select words that are incorrect but close as we grade students' writing. We ask students to give each other spelling tests under our supervision. Such an approach allows students to be successful, pulling words from their own writing.

In another useful approach, we group students for mini-lessons every 4 to 6 weeks by the type of spelling words they are missing. For example, we give a spelling placement test and group students who need to learn long *a* spellings and another group that is studying the rules for adding *s* or *es* to create plural words. Most teachers run five or fewer groups at a time. All groups are based on a specific need and change often. The reading workshop time is then extended so that students also work on spelling assignments. We meet with one guided reading, book club, or fluency group and two spelling groups a day as part of reading workshop.

Strategies for spelling and phonics instruction include (Cunningham et al., 1998; Hittie, 2008):

- Practicing reading words that have the target skills.
- Creating crossword puzzles of words with the target sounds.
- Playing games to practice the spelling or the sound, and listening to books to identify the sound.
- Displaying high-frequency words organized alphabetically and having students practice saying the words, clapping, snapping, and writing.
- Playing *round up the rhymes*. Students read poems with rhymes, focusing on the rhyming parts of words.
- Playing *guess the covered word*. This activity helps students check meaning with letter–sound connections. The teacher writes several sentences, covering a word in each sentence. As students guess the word, the teacher uncovers the first letter, then the second. This allows students to carefully connect letter sounds to words but in the context of making meaning.
- Playing *scavenger hunt* or *word search*. Ask students to search for a word type, such as an adjective or a word that ends with *own*, and mark it with sticky notes in their reading book to show you at the next strategy small group.
- Playing *word sort*. Students manipulate small papers with many words and a few titles into groups. As they visually sort the words by sound and spelling, they help the brain see the patterns in the words.

One of the interesting things is that groups are not always divided by reading level. Spelling and reading on grade level are not always connected. A child who reads on grade level could be mistaking the short *e* and short *i* and spend several weeks in the short vowel group until he masters that. When he tests again, he might move up to easy prefixes and suffixes if he does not miss words until then. The students do not move through each list linearly. They also enjoy tracking their own progress as a measure of what they have learned.

Grammar. As children progress through writing with more clarity and meaning, they will need some specific instruction on **grammar**. Grammar means the rules by which sentences are put together. It refers to the tense of verbs and the placement of words. As with other skills in writing workshop style, this can be addressed in several ways. It is not taught through worksheets that have students diagramming sentences. However, during whole group lessons, a particular skill may be focused on. A small group mini-lesson may be called to address another skill. If one student continues to struggle, a one-on-one conference may be needed. As with all other skills, it is addressed in the context of the work that is being created.

Individualized Differentiation in Literacy and Language Arts

We need many strategies to help students pursue personal excellence, learning that helps students achieve at their own level of capability yet pushes them to high standards. We can draw from many tools discussed in previous chapters. Here are a few key ideas.

Multiple Intelligences. As we discussed in Chapter 11, multiple intelligences can be used to bridge the gap in reading instruction from the stronger areas to the weaker ones. For example, as we get to know our students, we learn that a child who is struggling in reading is gifted in music. During multiple intelligence centers, the child is given time to lead a center and share the talent. As the complexity of what she creates musically increases, so does her self-confidence. One day, a connection is made in the brain and the reading takes off (Campbell, 1994).

Multilevel Reading Materials in the Classroom. An effective inclusive teacher will have a host of reading materials at a wide range of levels—trade books, picture books, reference books, and so on. We help students learn to select reading materials that are easy, just right, and challenging. As discussed earlier, most of the time we want students reading just-right books. At other times, however, students may want to challenge themselves with more complex materials, particularly in a subject of high interest to them (Cunningham & Allington, 1999; Duffey-Hester, 1999; Routman, 1996).

Individualized Differentiation in Reading. Students who struggle may read with partners, as we teach both students how to read together. We choose several books at different levels that will appeal to the students and then ask students to examine them and choose a book in which they are interested that they think is at their just-right level. This allows the students to make the choice. If they want to read a book that is too hard they can develop a plan with another student for how that will work.

Allowing students choices in what they learn is vitally important for making the connections within the brain that will help students feel relaxed, interested, and able to remember what they learn. Yet, what do we do when students who are struggling in literacy have difficulty selecting books they are able to read but also want to read? Here are a few helpful suggestions (Fielding & Roller, 1992):

- Help students determine books at their level of ability.
- Encourage students to read books the teacher has read as a read aloud.

- Suggest that students read with a friend and reread books that they enjoy.
- Set up programs where students can read to younger students (thus reading easier materials, but in a way that does not stigmatize the student).
- Have many interesting and informational books with pictures available.

Also, it's helpful to understand that there are at least three ways to "read" a book, each of which can be a valuable tool:

- "Pretend read" familiar storybooks.
- "Picture read" by looking at a book with many pictures and talking about what you see based on the pictures.
- Listen to the book read via tape, CD, talking software, or another reader, either a peer or adult volunteer or educator.
- Read the words of the text.

Individualized Differentiation in Writing. The multilevel nature of writing workshop makes it a centerpiece of effective literacy instruction that support all students. Writing is often a key way for students to become skilled readers. Students who have difficulties with very simple reading texts may be able to read their own messages in their writing notebooks and folders. We have many specific strategies that we can use in inclusive reading and writing workshop to scaffold and support student learning. Figure 13.4 lists some of these.

Assistive Technology. Assistive technology can be used as a powerful tool in literacy learning. Text-to-speech software and books on tape or CD can help students be able to access written materials that they would have difficulty reading alone. Consider this question: When a student who is blind uses such tools, is this considered reading for that student? Most people would say yes—this is the modality that most blind people use to access text. If that is true, what about students with learning or cognitive disabilities?

FIGURE 13.4

Literacy Scaffolding

- Daily modeling writing procedures, verbalized thinking in math, and so on
- Demonstration of key words: *who, what, why, first, next, finally,* and so on
- Word banks/picture dictionaries that students continually add to
- Cognitive maps to organize reading and writing processes
- Reader response logs to share thoughts
- Choral and partner reading, writing, spelling practice
- Flexible grouping (large group, small group, pairs, individual)
- Developmental spelling
- Structures that encourage participation, inquiry, and student talk
- Motivating activities that create desire to learn about a topic

- Guided reading strategies groups
- Choral reading in which teacher sits slightly behind students so they hear words and inflections
- Readers' Theater to interpret readings
- Heterogeneous groups doing jigsaw reading and sharing with other groups.
- Preteaching of vocabulary, content, and questioning
- Marking points in reading where students refer to questions to encourage thinking
- Semantic maps or time lines to organize information
- Deep content materials at different levels (e.g., books, Internet access, books on tape, videos, DVDs, community resources)
- Student "apprenticeships" in effective strategies used in a discipline

Source: Adapted from A. Tarrant (1999).

Sights TO SEE

Inclusive Academics in Action

View these videos, thinking about strategies by which students with high and low abilities could participate in and learn through these great activities.

Inclusive Reading Workshop In Mishael Hittie's fifth-grade class, reading and writing workshop are based on an inclusive workshop learning approach. Here you'll see components of reading workshop. www.wholeschooling.net/WS/Video/ReadworkshopMH.html

Cooperative Arithmetic: How to Teach Math as a Social Activity A master teacher in Anchorage, Alaska, establishes a cooperative-learning environment in an upper-elementary classroom. Imagine how students with differing ability levels may engage in different roles in this learning activity. www.edutopia.org/math-social-activity-sel-video

First-Class Citizens: Civics Isn't Just a Class Hudson High School has become a laboratory of democracy, challenging widely held assumptions about how schools can and should operate. www.edutopia.org/first-class-citizens-video

Bill Henderson, principal of the fully inclusive O'Hearn Elementary School in Boston, suggests that these students should be given such literacy supports as much as individuals who are blind. The key is to have such students access written information and gain meaning and understanding, using written information for an authentic purpose.

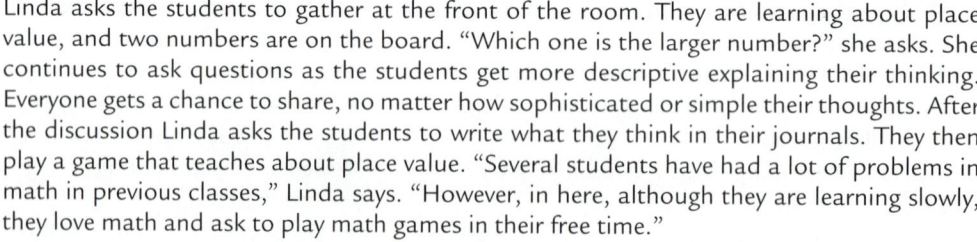

Mathematics

Students are often intimidated by math. Let's visit a classroom in which students are working on a worksheet of algebra problems.

We see examples on the board as the teacher walks around helping. Several students are finished and look very bored. Most are struggling. One student in the back of the room is simply staring at his paper, his head down, his eyes sad as he attempts to decipher the exercise. A buddy leans over and explains again, but he shakes his head, saying, "I can't do it." Later, the teacher too shakes his head: "Angus tries hard but he simply cannot do basic algebra." We leave feeling sad that both Angus and the teacher have given up on his math abilities.

What is it about math that intrigues some and makes others incredibly frustrated? What do we do about students like Angus? Fortunately, important changes are happening in the way we teach math. Let's visit another another class where we see very different results.

Linda asks the students to gather at the front of the room. They are learning about place value, and two numbers are on the board. "Which one is the larger number?" she asks. She continues to ask questions as the students get more descriptive explaining their thinking. Everyone gets a chance to share, no matter how sophisticated or simple their thoughts. After the discussion Linda asks the students to write what they think in their journals. They then play a game that teaches about place value. "Several students have had a lot of problems in math in previous classes," Linda says. "However, in here, although they are learning slowly, they love math and ask to play math games in their free time."

Challenges in Mathematics Education

For many people mathematics learning has become a fearful and distasteful process. In no other area of learning, besides early reading, is the emphasis on disconnected skill development and procedures for "getting the answer" emphasized more traditionally than in mathematics. It's fair to say that the vast majority of students in geometry and algebra have no clue how the many algorithms they are expected to learn in school relate to anything in the real world. Most forget what they knew within a short time from leaving class. Given this situation, it should not be surprising that students with special needs also often have difficulty in traditional math instruction.

Standards for Mathematics Instruction

The National Council of Teachers of Mathematics, or NCTM (1991, 2000), has established a reformed model of teaching mathematics to address many of these problems that takes important steps toward inclusive teaching. The standards call for less emphasis on worksheet computation and greater emphasis on mathematical reasoning and problem solving in actually using mathematics. Three key strategies are important:

1. Recognizing that "knowing mathematics is *doing* mathematics," that it is related to a purposeful activity.
2. Understanding that mathematics shifts from the traditional sequence of algebra–geometry–precalculus that was designed largely for engineering and the physical sciences to understanding mathematics in ways that can be applied to many disciplines.
3. Understanding that, the new curriculum recognizes the dramatic changes that technology has brought about in providing tools for solving mathematical problems. The new curriculum calls for use of calculators and computers as tools for computation, along with learning computation in the context of problem solving.

NCTM, on the one hand, recognizes that students vary dramatically in their mathematical abilities and interests but also suggests that all students must learn key content while allowing that the depth and sophistication of knowledge may vary substantially across students. The content standards for high school state that all students should be involved in 3 years of mathematical study in high school, with 4 years required for students who plan to go on to college. The core curriculum for all students in Grades 9 to 12 includes the following content: numbers and operations; measurement; geometry; data analysis and probability; and algebra (Access Center, 2006; National Council of Teachers of Mathematics, 1991).

NCTM emphasizes students engaging in discovery learning, using mathematical ideas, thus deepening understanding. Mathematics should work to build a community of learners where exploration, voice, and mutual support are seen as critical elements using the following strategies (National Council of Teachers of Mathematics, 1991, 2000):

- More time for students to explore and invent alternative strategies for computing mentally
- Increased focus on concrete experience, using objects rather than symbols
- Focus on mathematics as a way of thinking; emphasis on teachers listening to and understanding how students are thinking
- Discussion among students regarding approaches to solving mathematics problems
- Emphasis on taking students' thinking seriously—listening, coaching, reflecting, and challenging as students construct approaches to mathematical problems

The NCTM standards for teaching and learning help move mathematics learning in a new direction that involves students using and understanding mathematics at a deeper, applied level. This means moving from Bloom's lowest levels of understanding to higher levels of cognitive thinking. The move opens up opportunities for students with special needs to learn at a higher level and allows multilevel instruction to become a reality.

Inclusive Mathematics Instruction

Let's explore some valuable strategies for helping make mathematics accessible to all students, in response to the NCTM guidelines.

Use a Daily Lesson Format. Workshop learning in mathematics instruction involves a balance of whole group instruction, small groups, and individual work. Typically, we will meet with the entire class at the beginning of the lesson to connect with students personally, engage in a mini-lesson related to a particular skill, and allow students to report on the status of projects on which they are working. Then students may work on learning projects, either as a whole class, individually, in pairs, or in small groups. We pull small groups together for mini-lessons on needed topics and facilitate support for individual students in collaboration with a special education teacher or paraprofessional. We organize inclusive lessons using individual or small group multilevel learning projects that are linked to authentic themes and other subjects, tiered lessons, centers based on multiple intelligences or learning styles, and extension activities available for all students based on individual choices.

As we organize daily lessons for diverse students, we pay attention to two interactive areas: (1) developing inclusive learning structures in our classrooms such as multilevel projects or tiered assignments; and (2) using instructional strategies that enhance learning for all students, thus ensuring that students with special needs also are learning more effectively. Let's look at some key strategies for ensuring effective learning for all.

Emphasize Conceptual Understanding by Emphasizing "Big Ideas." While there is much to learn in mathematics, the major concepts are relatively few. Rather than "getting through the book," we identify the key big ideas and use these to focus instruction (Choike, 2000).

Make Connections Between the Real World and the Use of Mathematics. When students are presented with real-world situations and guided in using mathematics for functional, useful purposes, students both see the value of mathematics but also can be guided to understanding how mathematics actually works. They begin to think at some level as a mathematician rather than simply memorizing formulas that they don't understand.

For example, Zemelman and colleagues (2005, p. 107) describe a teacher who introduced algebraic equations with a lesson titled "Chocolate algebra." The teacher led students through a discussion regarding how many combinations of purchases of chocolate bars may be made when they had $10 to spend and Hershey bars cost $2 and Tootsie Rolls $1. They constructed a table of options and gradually came upon the need to create an equation. The class itself constructed this simple algebraic equation out of a real situation and need, and experienced both how such an equation might be used as well as the logic behind it.

We use multiple strategies to help students visualize mathematical operations. Students work together in pairs or small groups, thinking about math and creating, for example, their own methods for adding and subtracting. Curiously, Davis and Maher (1996) indicate that "the present evidence suggests that it is *easier* to invent one's own methods than it is to memorize methods conveyed by other people " (p. 71). Thus, students with learning challenges can excel as they are engaged in thinking with other students. Learning through hands-on activities is particularly helpful for students with special learning needs, as these activities make abstract concepts tangible (Romberg, 1995).

No doubt it is difficult to connect the skills sets in mathematics with applied situations. The fact is that in the real world, we use many types of mathematics skills simultaneously. Effective teachers work to create real-world connections for each skill set while also creating opportunities where students may use mathematics skills to engage in functional activities where multiple types and levels of skills might be used simultaneously. Here are a few examples:

- *Concept of 1 million.* One set of teachers involved a class of elementary students in conceptualizing "how big 1 million really is." They used real-world objects to actually construct a representation of 1 million. In the process they used math skills of counting, multiplication, representation, and even a bit of algebra.
- *Class store.* Students may be involved in running a simulation of a store or even in having an actual class store where many math skills can be practiced.
- *Interdisciplinary links.* Math, of course, is used in many disciplines, particularly relevant to science and social studies. Teachers can look for opportunities to use math skills in science experiments ranging from recording to making projections based on extrapolations of available data involving both statistics and algebra.
- *Home–community connections.* Have students investigate how math is used in their home life and in their community. Make connections with local scientists, community activists, and businesspeople to identify projects in which students may use mathematics.

Remember the curriculum matrix in Chapter 4? We used this tool to make connections between individualized student goals and the curriculum in our classroom. However, we can also use a variation on that matrix to connect mathematics skills to other subjects, home, and community. Making mathematics authentic, connected to the real lives of students, while also involving students in thinking through the meaning of mathematical solutions is the key to motivating students and to creating real understanding. It's also the key to having lessons that allow students to work on different levels and types of skills simultaneously.

Link Mathematical Learning to Student Interests and the Local Community. As we seek to involve students in concrete activities to explore and understand mathematical concepts, we will strengthen learning if we can connect to student interests. This will enhance their motivation and will help deepen their practical understanding of mathematics. For example, perhaps a student has become interested in sewing or another student wants to get new wallpaper for her bedroom. Both provide opportunities for using a range of mathematic skills. Per the previous discussion, we can involve students in helping identify places in their lives where mathematics can be used.

Move from Concrete to Representational to Abstract. Students can learn mathematics of all sorts most effectively when we move from concrete to representational to abstract, ensuring understanding along the way. The Access Center (2008) has outlined three steps to accomplish this:

- First, students use concrete materials to apply mathematical operations. These may include base 10 blocks, pattern blocks, or real-life artifacts.
- We next use semiconcrete representation of mathematic operations and concepts via graphics including circles, dots, stamps to imprint symbols, and other symbols.
- Finally, we move to the abstract using numbers and mathematical symbols only.

The Access Center (2008) suggests these strategies for moving students from concrete to representational:

- Have students work on the computer to use virtual manipulatives.
- Develop guided worksheets.
- Use cooperative groups and encourage students to talk their way through solving problems.

- Vary the type of manipulative that is used.
- Provide songs, rhymes, or rhythms to help remember the basic facts.
- Use flash cards for individual or group review of basic facts.
- Teach number facts in fact families. Chunk pieces of information and facts in sets of three.
- Provide multiple opportunities for practice and demonstration.
- Simplify the problem. (p. 21)

Strategies for moving students from representational to abstract (Access Center, 2008) include:

- Work with the student individually or in a small group to ensure that he or she understands the concept.
- Demonstrate how to solve problems with self-dialogue or think-aloud strategies.
- Fade the use of guided worksheets to prepare students for the abstract stage.
- Use cooperative groups and encourage students to talk their way through solving problems.
- Provide multiple opportunities for practice and demonstration. (p. 22)

Use Multiple Representations, Manipulatives, and Other Concrete Materials. Relatedly, we want to provide students multiple ways to understand a mathematical concepts by providing numerous representations of a concept.

Math **manipulatives** are helpful tools such as base 10s, pattern blocks, and geoboards to help students shift from knowing "how to do" a numerical operation (such as addition of three-digit numbers) to understanding "why it is done."

We can also use *multiple intelligences*. One example involves art and multiplication math facts. Even as late as April in a fifth-grade room, there are a group of students who do not know their math facts, but they are talented in art. So, they spend a significant amount of time making detailed artistic flash cards. Each picture is significantly different and the fact and answer are written right over the picture. This helps the students learn them, as they associate the picture with the fact. Thus, the art bridges the gap.

Mnemonic strategies may be useful in helping students remember difficult material. This is a strategy that can be applied in other subjects as well. A **mnemonic** is a tool to help people remember information by associating the desired information with something easily remembered—an abbreviation, a poem, a symbol, an image, or even a sound. The human mind more easily remembers spatial, personal, surprising, or funny information much more easily than abstract sequences and data. The Access Center (2008) has identified several forms of mnemonics: (1) keyword, (2) pegword, (3) letter, and (4) order. A *keyword* uses "a familiar word that sounds similar to the word or idea being taught" (p. 25). For example, in teaching students the 2 × family of multiplication tables, 2 × 2 might be associated with the word (and picture of) *skateboard*. *Pegwords* involve words that rhyme with numbers. For example, *fun* might be associated with the number 1. *Letter* uses acronyms, whereas *order* uses cute saying to help remember a sequence of operations. For example, the saying "**Many Dogs Are Smelly**" can be used to help remember that in a math problem like $(6 + 10) - (4 \times 6)$, multiplication (M) and division (D) are to be done before addition (A) and subtraction (S) (p. 34).

Graphic organizers can be valuable in mathematics as in other subjects. According to the Access Center (2008), three main types of graphic organizers can be used: (1) hierarchical diagrams in which the main idea is placed in the center connected to supporting information or details in surrounding boxes or circles; (2) compare and contrast charts such as a Venn diagram; and (3) sequence charts that illustrate how events or tasks are arranged in chronological order.

These 5th-graders share what they have learned about explorers in their state. They worked as a group to find information, organize it, and develop a presentation for the class. These students have a wide range of functioning abilities but all participated at their level.

Develop Authentic Multilevel and Tiered Lessons. As we use the previous strategies, we'll find that our lessons naturally often become *multilevel lessons* authentically connected to the real world. For example, if we have students operate a store or work together to create a model of an ecosystem and gather data regarding different aspects of that ecosystem, students can function in different roles using different mathematics skills. When we involve the whole class in exploring a concrete problem, students will have different levels of understanding. We can provide support via special educators or peer supporters to help students understand the key concepts.

We can also develop *tiered lessons*. We might give an assignment with different expectations and assignment directions for different groups of students. For example, in one fourth-grade class students were engaged in a lesson involving measurement. Some students learned how to use a ruler and a scale to measure objects within the closest inch and weigh objects to the closest pound rounding off. Other students did the same activity but were expected to measure objects with two decimal places. Two students who had good skills in basic measurement measured the diameter of objects and then calculated the perimeter. All students graphed their results and shared them in a classroom discussion.

Here's another example of a tiered lesson. In a middle school class, the teacher posed this consumer application problem involving basic algebra (National Council of Teachers of Mathematics, 1991, p. 132):

> Carlos deposits $100 in a savings account earning 6% interest compounded annually. Assuming a fixed interest rate, how much money will be in the account at the end of 10 years?

Several levels of learning may occur in this problem. At level 1, the lowest level, students multiply $100 by .06, obtain a new total, and conduct this same calculation 10 times.

At level 2, a student might express this calculation in an algebraic formula. At level 3 students could solve problems in which interest rates are calculated semiannually, quarterly, or monthly. In this scenario, students at level 1 would have opportunities to engage in similar problems to practice and understand the basic skill while students who functioned at a higher level could work on more advanced problems. Students who are more advanced may provide peer support to students at a lower level, deepening their understanding as they support other students.

We can *use mathematical materials for various purposes* to create tiered lessons. For example, we might use a worksheet for calculating division and multiplication problems for the class. We could create different versions of this worksheet at different levels of complexity. For a student still learning to identify basic numbers, we could ask the student to circle all the 2 and 5 numbers, for example. Or we could ask her to add instead of divide or multiple the same problems. This same strategy could be used with many materials.

We can also provide *extensions* for learners to extend their learning as they finish other work. In one teacher's class, two children finish the daily pages of the regular work. The teacher has created a chart with choices from which these students can pick. As they work, they look up from time to time and tune into the class discussion. Learners who are gifted have the ability to work on something else and listen to what the teacher is doing.

Create Understandable and Clear Math Problems. As we seek to involve students in using math, we'll want to present applied problems that involve use of various skills and concepts. Here are a few practical guidelines. First, we'll want to be sure that details of the problems don't actually distract. Choike (2000) provides one example in which a problem was posed regarding a CD player that was on sale for a down payment of $13.80 and a monthly payment of $22.69. He suggests that using numbers is distracting. Rather, simplify and use a similar problem with a down payment of $5 and a monthly payment of $10. Additionally, we want to make sure that the language of problems is clear and without ambiguity. Finally, consider the settings in which problems are placed. Use those that are familiar to students, expanding as needed into new contexts. Choike (2000) provided this example:

> As an illustration, consider the following setting. A turtle walks at five feet per minute, and a snail crawls at three feet per minute. The turtle and the snail start from an oak tree and head toward an elm tree that is located thirty feet from the oak tree. In this simple setting, students can investigate, through multiple representations, patterns in words, tables, symbols, and graphs. By having students link these representations with one another, they experience a rich lesson in many of the big ideas of algebra. When the class is familiar with this setting, use it again but with an additional twist: give the snail a nine-foot head start on the turtle. Students can then investigate how the various multiple representations have changed. (p. 4)

Listen Carefully to Students and Recognize Emerging Understandings. We need to listen carefully to students to see when they are developing understandings of a concept even though they may not express "the answer" in a traditional way. Choike (2000) gave this example. A teacher (whom he called Mr. Relentless) posed this problem:

> "Frank's car travels twenty-five miles in thirty minutes. What is the car's average speed?" The answer that Mr. Relentless expected to this question was fifty miles per hour. In class, he called on Kisha to give her answer to his question. Kisha responded, "The average speed of Frank's car is 5/6 mile per minute." Mr. Relentless brushed Kisha's answer aside as he asked whether anyone else in class could give the correct answer to this problem. (p. 557)

Clearly, Kisha understood key concepts even though her answer was hardly traditional. Listening carefully is important for all our students, but particularly for students with special needs who may have unusual (and often interesting) ways of framing understandings. The more we can capture emergent understandings, the more we can build on these to strengthen student learning.

Create a Sense of Safety, Community, and Belonging. Most critical in mathematics classes is to create an environment in which the voice of all is heard and respected and students have a sense of safety. In the experiences of many people, mathematics classes were places of fear and humiliation. If we can help students know that they are safe in exploring, in being wrong, in thinking together, then we will go far to helping students learn at a higher level.

Have Students Reflect on the Meaning and Use of Mathematics. We want to constantly involve students in thinking about and reflecting on their mathematical experiences. For example, students can keep **math journals** where they record work on different topics of interest to them. Writing about what they learn helps all students clarify the meaning and make stronger connections within the brain.

Science

Ms. Carrese was excited. A high school science teacher, she was returning from a conference at which she learned new approaches to teaching science. She decided to put these new ideas to work in a project she called "The Archeazoan Project." She set the stage for her students. "The town of Archeazo has no electricity," she explained. "The town board will hire several consulting firms representing solar, nuclear, chemical, hydro, and wind energy to develop proposals. The class will divide into groups forming consulting firms to advise citizens." She further explained that they were to prepare and present their proposals to include the following elements: "pros and cons, how your form of energy is converted to electricity, why yours is most beneficial, and hazards." "It was great. It was so much fun . . . and . . . I didn't have to stand there and say, 'This is solar energy.'" She talked about how helpful this project was to several students with disabilities. One student with ADHD seldom finished homework assignments. However, he became engaged with the hands-on Archeazoan activities and worked very hard. He was in charge of making the display that illustrated complex information in an interesting way. His parents were delighted that he was excited about learning. (Adapted from Champagne, Newell, & Goodnough, 1996, pp. 20–32)

Challenges in Science Education

Traditional instruction in science has centered on having students read textbooks, listen to lectures with an occasional video, and complete worksheets. At best, in such classes students have been involved in very narrowly prescribed laboratory experiments. Traditional science education has also focused on memorization of facts rather than using the scientific method and research procedures. This approach to science instruction often results in students losing interest. Further, students do not experience science as a dynamic, problem-solving learning process, nor do they engage in science using tools and processes that are used by practicing scientists. The result has been poor science learning.

Standards for Science Instruction

Beginning in the 1980s in the United States, major initiatives have sought to reform science learning, moving toward an inquiry-based model of workshop learning. In 1985, the American Association for the Advancement of Science (AAAS) began an initiative to reform K–12 science education in the United States titled Project 2061. The resulting document, *Science for All Americans* (American Association for the Advancement of Science, 1989), was followed in subsequent years by the *Benchmarks for Science Literacy* (American Association for the Advancement of Science, 1993) and the *Atlas of Science Literacy* (American Association for the Advancement of Science, 2001) which provided a curriculum framework. The National Research Council worked on a parallel project creating the *National Science Education Standards* (1996) followed in 2000 by the document *National Science Standards: A Guide for Teaching and Learning*. This document, along with the *Atlas of Science Literacy,* provide practical and extensive guidelines for effective workshop learning in science (Zemelman et al., 2005). Science for all suggests that *all students*, not just those who will go on for advanced studies in chemistry and physics, should know how science relates to their everyday lives.

Based on these recommendations, effective science instruction should include the following characteristics:

- Students must *do science* by conducting scientific inquiry, not just cover topics.
- Students should use a variety of scientific approaches and tools.
- Teachers must focus on helping students develop fundamental concepts and the big ideas of science, not just memorizing facts.
- Students learn via collaborative group work.
- Assessment must focus on students' understanding and engagement in scientific processes, not just the recall of facts.

Traditional science instruction in schools has been based on a variation of lecture–worksheet–test instruction: Students listen to lectures, read a textbook, and conduct prescribed experiments whose purpose is to verify facts of the lecture and reading. Students are assessed to determine their recall of basic facts. As with all lecture–test instruction, this approach results in poor learning of material, little understanding, and often a dislike of science altogether.

In inquiry learning, however, we involve students in actively generating their own questions, deciding how to conduct their own experiments or studies, actually engaging in studies, and analyzing and reporting processes and results. Students immerse themselves in doing science rather than "covering topics." Teachers help students articulate good scientific questions and obtain good data and evidence to answer these questions. Students use a range of scientific research tools and strategies to engage in inquiry becoming familiar with various approaches to scientific investigation. Teachers involve students in small group as part of inquiry learning and assess student learning via portfolios and performance tasks.

Let's compare traditional science instruction and inquiry learning. In one class, Julie decided to teach how mice learn to use mazes. She lectured about mice and operant conditioning, writing words on the board as students sat in rows listening. She then had students observe mice in a maze. They were told exactly what to look for. Unfortunately, the mice didn't cooperate and do what they were supposed to. One student said in dismay, "We didn't get the right answer!" (adapted from Walker, 2007). The teacher also became embarrassed and frustrated as students had all sorts of other questions to which she did not know the answers: "What sex are the mice? How can you tell?"

While this teacher thought that she was doing inquiry learning since part of the activity was hands-on, she actually was not. She generated the questions and designed the experiment but was not interested in the questions students had. This lesson demonstrates clearly how hands-on learning and inquiry are not the same thing.

Let's look at another lesson with another teacher, Sarah. She wanted to teach students about the sense of taste. She began by bringing all the students to the carpet area at the front of the room. She then began eating a banana. She asked, "Why does a banana taste like a banana? Why does it not taste like something else?" The class began to discuss this question.

> Sarah provided the students with an investigation question to start them off; "What effect does your sense of smell have on your sense of taste?" The students then had to develop a way of answering this problem themselves. Sarah prompted the class by asking them questions like, "What do you think will happen when you can't smell?" "Why?" "Have you ever actually tasted that?" "How could you do that?" The students were responsible for designing the experiment themselves, and at the end, they told Sarah what they had found. The students set up an experiment where one student was blindfolded and then fed different types of food. They had to guess what food it was. Next, the student had a peg put on their nose, and had to re-taste everything and guess again. The students found that it was more difficult to guess when you had a peg on your nose. (Walker, 2007, p. 36)

Sarah's lesson was closer to real inquiry. While she provided the initial stimulus question, she facilitated students asking their own follow-up questions and designing an experiment related to the question. These students took more control and thought about the issue in ways that Julie's students did not. In many classrooms, groups of students will be involved in creating different inquiry experiments, and the results of the original experiment will fuel the questions for the next experiment. Children learn that real science is a constantly rotating cycle of questioning and discovery.

Inclusive Inquiry Learning in Science

Inquiry learning in science is very conducive to authentic multilevel lessons. Students in small groups can take on roles involving varying degrees of ability and skill requirements. With scaffolding and support, all students, even those with the most severe disabilities, can participate in these lessons. Tiered lessons, particularly for individual projects, can also be useful.

Authentic Interdisciplinary Themes. Science provides a very natural arena to select themes around which we may link social studies, literacy, math, and the arts. We select themes involving social issues and the history, philosophy, and sociology of science that integrate science with other school subjects and the various science disciplines and build on student's curiosity. Two projects are rich sources of ideas for developing interdisciplinary themes related to science: (1) *Science, Technology, and Society (STS)* seeks to promote acceptance and celebration of diverse student contributions (Yager, 1990); and (2) the *Jason Project* links students through the Internet and teleconferencing to investigations of recognized scientists. We can use broad themes to anchor many specific inquiries in which students may engage.

A Daily Lesson Format. We can use a daily process to manage inquiry learning. Often we start the lesson with a mini-lesson related to a particular researching or experimenting skill or the content of a science concept. We can have students provide a brief review of the status of various projects. This allows students to have a sense of what others are doing. This is also a good time to brainstorm key challenges across projects to help us identify needed mini-lessons. Students are then given work time for their projects. They take notes, sketch experiment results, research topics, and graph data. Inquiry projects may be individual, small group, or even involve an entire class. The projects may be multilevel or tiered assignments and use helpful strategies such as centers based on multiple intelligences.

Let's look now at how the inquiry cycle looks in science learning.

Inquiry Lessons. Figure 12.1 in Chapter 12 provides a generic framework for inquiry learning that is the basis for workshop learning across subjects. This framework applies equally to science. However, science inquiry will add additional twists aiming to use tools and processes of actual scientists. Inquiry learning can be implemented as an individual assignment based on either multilevel or tiered assignments. It is most effective when we have small groups working together. In such a situation, students with varied abilities can take on varied roles that require different levels of ability.

As we begin an inquiry lesson with students, we first *introduce* the lesson or unit. If we have involved students in developing their own topics of inquiry, we can remind them of the steps they went through to identify them. We then aim to engage interest of the students by facilitating a discussion regarding what they know and think about a topic.

Next, we have students *generate questions and a hypothesis*. We engage students in pairs or small groups, exploring and creating questions that they have about the topic. We can involve students in categorizing and synthesizing their questions, helping them learn how to articulate effective questions. Students will then develop a hypothesis that can be tested using scientific data gathering and analysis procedures.

We then *facilitate student planning of an experiment* or other study to answer their questions and test their hypothesis. We help students directly connect their questions with the type of information that they will gather. In the process, we will be providing students with different models of scientific research: experimental studies with control groups; survey research; and qualitative observations. We will walk them through decisions regarding what types of information they need, the variables that are important, ways to gather information, and ways they can analyze the information. Students will also make decisions regarding practicalities of gathering and analyzing data.

This step, of course, can vary from very simple to highly complex. Many people spend their entire careers devoted to understanding various types of research procedures. Involving students in planning studies helps them act and think as scientists and researchers and deal with the complexities of design and the practicalities of gathering information.

The obvious next step is to *conduct the study to gather and analyze data and information*. We monitor students in following their plan, gathering information, making observations, setting up the experiment, and recording results. The study must be directly hands-on and directed by the students themselves. As students gather data, they will be involved in recording, summarizing, and analyzing the results to determine the answers to their questions.

Finally, students will *communicate and share results* of their study with others. This will involve creating posters, PowerPoint presentations, or other tools that can be used to share their original question or hypothesis, procedures that were used to gather and analyze data, and their results. We want to help students connect their inquiry to their everyday lives exploring practical implications for their results. For example, if students have explored level of pollution in a local stream and have found high levels, they can discuss why this matters and what needs to be done. Students may also be able to connect their own results with other situations. For example, they might be interested in comparing levels of pollution in other rivers and lakes.

Let's now look at examples of inclusive inquiry-based science learning in actual classrooms.

Layers of the Earth: Small Group Multilevel Project. In Melanie's Grades 3 to 5 multiage class students are working on an introductory project to explore the layering of the crust of the earth. Students had previously worked in pairs and made models of the earth with colored modeling clay, one color for the inner core, one for the outer core, and one for the mantle. The crust was blue and green, with blue representing water and green representing landmasses. She provided a plastic knife to each team and suggested that they simply slice the model in half. Once teams got their models sliced open—not an easy task—they all seemed to be amazed by the appearance of the cross section. The students were excited about their projects and shared them with visitors in the class.

Rather than simply viewing pictures of the earth's layers, this activity involved students in a concrete way. Kevin, the student with a cognitive disability, had worked with a partner. However, all the students were able to examine the layers of the earth, and complete the work together. Following the whole class lesson, students who wanted to pursue this project further were encouraged to do so during the thematic research project time that occurs three times a week.

Exploring Sound: Multiple Intelligence Centers. In Jasper's fifth-grade class, students are invited to rotate through several centers in small groups related to sound. The musical center has a variety of musical instruments, noisemaker toys, and eggs with items in them. The students make different sounds and discuss how they work. Two students who play in the orchestra are leading this center. In the bodily–kinesthetic center students list places in the school they think will be the best for creating echoes. They try them out and record what happens. In the artistic center, students create visual renderings of sound waves and vibrations. The linguistic center contains picture books on sound that students read and discuss. In the intrapersonal center students watch a video and write their thoughts in a journal. Students work together using soda (pop) bottles with different water levels to create a tune in the interpersonal center. At the logical–mathematics table, students create tables showing time sound takes to reach different distances. All of the students are learning about sound, accessing information based on different intelligences but also at their own level of challenge.

Making a Light: Small Group Multilevel Project. David, a fifth-grade teacher, likes to give students experiments to help them discover what works, what does not, and why. Students recorded data in a science log. The experiments are set up so that all students can succeed. As one example, the class was studying energy and electricity. The teacher gave the students a bag with a battery, light bulb, and wire. The first part of their task was to make the light bulb light up and draw a picture of what worked and what did not. The second part of the task was to end with a new question that will lead their personal experiment at the following work time. Some students asked for additional materials to create a way to light up two light bulbs from the same battery. One group asked for extra batteries to make the light bulb bright enough that the child with visual impairments in their group might be able to see it. The entire process was recorded on their experimentation log. Students worked together in heterogeneous ability groups. One student with a cognitive disability worked with a student who was highly gifted, who explained some key concepts. A paraprofessional helped one group pose yes and no questions to involve a student with severe disabilities. All children, regardless of ability, went through the process of doing a teacher-led experiment, to give them some background knowledge, and then through the inquiry process with their own experiment.

Understanding Density: A Tiered Lesson. Willis and Mann (2000) provided this example of a tiered science lesson in middle school:

> At Brownell Middle School . . . science teacher Marie DeLuca offers tiered assignments to help her 8th graders understand the concept of density. To start . . . DeLuca uses an introductory lab activity that allows the whole class to compare the differing weights of identical volumes of sand and oil. The object is to determine whether a ship could carry the same

amount of sand as it could oil, and how this manifests the property of density. From this starting point, DeLuca assigns students an Internet activity that explores the causes of the sinking of the Edmund Fitzgerald—but at different levels of synthesis and analysis, depending on student ability. Homework assignments ask higher-ability students to design cargo boats, grade-level students to float an egg, and below-level students to determine which is more dense: a can of Classic Coke or a can of Diet Coke. They must perform a water displacement experiment to come up with the correct answer. All students complete lab reports that DeLuca evaluates using a rubric. . . . Students can earn an A grade as long as they support their conclusions with evidence found in their own particular assignments. The tests DeLuca gives are also differentiated. . . . "It wouldn't be fair for everyone to do the same assignment and the same test," says DeLuca, "because everyone has different talents. The important thing is for everyone to have a certain degree of challenge." (p. 3)

Inclusion as a Catalyst to School Improvement for All

**SCHOOLS
to VISIT**

Patrick O'Hearn Elementary School
1669 Dorchester Avenue
Boston, MA

O'Hearn Elementary School is a *fully inclusive multiracial, high-achieving school* that serves an ethnically, linguistically, and racially diverse group of students in early childhood through Grade 5. Approximately 33% of the students have a disability, many of which are labeled significant. Based on the hard work of staff, O'Hearn is a high-performing school, student attendance approaches 95%, and there are few discipline referrals.

Inclusive teaching has served as a *catalyst for school improvement* that has benefited all students. Inclusion was initiated in 1989 as a result of parent advocacy. O'Hearn has sought to accomplish this mission "to help all students learn and succeed. Students involved in general education; students with mild, moderate, and severe disabilities; and students considered talented and gifted learn together and from each other."

Like other Boston schools, O'Hearn uses *workshop learning*. This approach supports multilevel differentiated learning and works well with all students. Sometimes *instructional adaptations*, however, are necessary. During literacy, for example, some students need books on cassette, assistive technology, or braille to access and respond to print. Other students need simplified versions of stories, simplified written responses, artistic

depictions, or gestures. Many of these adaptations have also proved beneficial to students without disabilities.

We see this interplay between multilevel teaching and adaptations in writing workshop. This provides a structured opportunity for students to express their thoughts in writing about a topic that they have selected or their teacher has suggested. After a brief mini-lesson with the whole class, students write. Some of the slant boards and special pens and markers that are necessary for students with fine motor skill difficulties have assisted other students. Some of the special software programs that show pictures or facilitate spelling for students with learning disabilities or cognitive delays have benefited others. Some of the strategies used by teachers to stimulate students with emotional disorders have sparked others. And some of the direct, even hand-over-hand techniques used by teachers with students with significant disabilities have definitely inspired others.

At the end of each writing workshop session a few students share their work. This provides an opportunity to highlight strengths and possible areas of improvement as well as to foster mutual respect and a sense of community.

We have also put great emphasis on *inclusive arts* at O'Hearn. Teachers have worked hard to learn how to include students with a wide range of abilities and characteristics. Arts have developed to be one of the strongest components of the school. Music, dance, the visual arts, and drama are used regularly throughout the curriculum. With support from other arts organizations in Boston, including Very Special Arts Massachusetts and the Community Music Center, students have staged many performances. These productions are connected to the curriculum and have elicited strong family involvement.

Collaboration between general education teachers and a range of specialists is an important component for creating success at O'Hearn Elementary. Collaborating with other adults in classrooms changes the dynamics of instruction. In some situations, one adult assumes responsibility for most of the class and another adult for just a few of the students. In other situations, adults share and switch responsibilities. They communicate regularly before, during, and after lessons. Good inclusion will not be successful unless there is also effective cooperation and continuous problem-solving among professionals. Speech therapists and occupational therapists also go into classrooms to facilitate oral communication and to assist with writing. The collaboration of these various professionals has expanded the variety of instructional supports used to help all students learn.

General education teachers, special education teachers, therapists, and arts teachers have all spent considerable *professional development* time on literacy. Together they study strategies for teaching reading and writing. Many of these strategies are also appropriate for and are used regularly with students with disabilities. For others, adaptations involving accommodations or modifications are necessary and appropriate strategies for these must also have been investigated.

Family and community involvement has also been a critical element in the success of O'Hearn. Since inclusion was initiated by parent advocacy, parents were invited to be part of a group to help set priorities and policies for the school. O'Hearn became one of a small number of schools in Boston to participate in school-based management directed by a council of school personnel and parents. The council decided to promote more reading at home as part of literacy learning, and parent volunteers have worked hard to promote participation in the home reading program.

An important source of improving instruction has involved teachers *reviewing students' work* together every other week. Initially teachers brought only samples of work that was either above or relatively close to the grade-level benchmarks. However, some teachers began sharing samples of assignments from students with significant disabilities. This loosened up the conversations and led to a decision to bring samples from students representing a range of performance levels and to examine just first drafts. Teachers became more comfortable talking frankly about students' needs and began to talk about instructional strategies that could help each student progress.

Finally, any school must have *resources and funds* to operate. Extra funds are provided in all school districts for students with disabilities. However, these funds are often used in separate special education programs and when students with disabilities are included in a general education school, funds do not follow them. At O'Hearn, we negotiated a different approach. We worked with the district administration to calculate the costs for students in segregated programs and then requested that these funds be transferred to O'Hearn. These funds have allowed us to determine personnel and other resource needs and use funds in a flexible way to support effective inclusive teaching.

School improvement is an ongoing process that requires the concerted energies of the entire school community. When effectively designed and implemented, inclusion can provide positive learning experiences for all students, including those with significant disabilities. At O'Hearn Elementary, inclusion has served as a dynamic catalyst for improvements that have benefited the whole school community.

By Bill Henderson, Principal, O'Hearn Elementary School, Boston, MA.

Social Studies

Dinah is a third-grade teacher. She is involving her class in a collaborative project in which they study the history of their town and make a model of the town in its early days. Today, she is having a conversation about what they need to get done. Students were given choices including which historical building they would research, how they would present information, and materials they would use. She asks kids where they are in making their buildings for the town model they are working on. They then start with working on their buildings—post office, Baptist church, cemetery, and so on—constructions of cardboard and wood. Later Dinah explains to the class that "tonight is curriculum night; we are going to write something to our parents or whoever is coming, and they will write back to you." Dinah asks, "What are some things you could say about school, your classroom? How do we end the letter?" They talk about different options. "You have about 20 minutes to work on your letter. Remember, the longer your letter is the more you will share." Dinah circulates through the room helping kids.

In this class two students have limited English-speaking abilities, two have cognitive disabilities, and two others have significant learning disabilities. All are distributed in heterogeneous working groups throughout the class. Dinah has connected their individual learning needs with this research and development project. (Peterson et al., 2002)

Challenges in Social Studies Education

Social studies involves a broad range of disciplines that seek to understand the human experience. These include psychology, sociology, history, and more. Given the importance of social studies and the need for students to be able to have a critical understanding of their social environment, this school discipline has the potential to be exciting and engaging, involving students in exploring the key issues of the day.

Unfortunately, traditional social studies doesn't approach this possibility. As in other subjects, traditional social studies particularly relies on students reading long, complicated, boring textbooks; listening to lectures; and taking multiple-choice tests based on facts—dates, names of inventions, key people, key events.

Standards for Social Studies Learning

The National Council for the Social Studies (NCSS) published curriculum standards for social studies in 1994 and instructional standards in 1997. The NCSS standards emphasized 10 broad thematic strands: culture; time and change; people, places, and environments; individuals, groups, and institutions; power and governance; production, distribution, and consumption; science, technology, and society; global connections; and civic ideals and practices. The standards also call for four skills: (1) acquiring and manipulating information, (2) creating arguments and stories related to policy, (3) constructing knowledge, and (4) participating in groups. Based on these standards, effective instruction in social studies should have the following characteristics:

- Students should investigate important topics in depth rather than having cursory "coverage."
- Students should be involved in inquiry involving open-ended questions based on their own interests and choices in individual and collaborative projects.
- Social studies learning should be linked to the community connections and participation.
- Students should use original source materials, not just textbooks.
- Students should engage in dialogue, engagement, and debates.
- Assessment should focus on key skills and attributes of citizenship, not the recall of facts.

The dialogue regarding the standards for social studies curriculum content, goals, and instruction has been substantive. Some advocate that social studies instruction should aim to preserve existing values and structures, and believe that advocating for social change should be avoided. Others feel that teachers help students critique social practices with the goal of encouraging social change and improvement of society (Hursh & Ross, 2000).

In many ways social studies is at the content center of the curriculum in schools because it touches on all aspects of our lives—work, home, community, politics, the economy. As such, involvement in learning social studies content can be a centerpiece for linking learning of all other subjects together: literacy, math, science, art, even physical education. If we are teaching in elementary school, we can literally link many if not all our subjects around important themes that are centered in social studies. If we teach in high school, we can partner with other teachers to again identify authentic themes from social studies that can be used to link subjects together.

In fact, some writers suggest that fundamental issues related to social studies form a spiraling curriculum that can be carried through the entire K–12 system. Postman (1996) suggests these five themes that can serve as the core focus for all learning in U.S. public schools: (1) spaceship earth—human beings as the stewards and caretakers of the planet; (2) the fallen angel—the struggle of good and evil in human existence, the interaction of knowledge and wisdom; (3) the American experiment—seeing this country as an experiment in whether true democracy can work; (4) the law of diversity—understanding difference in all of life, including society; and (5) the word weavers, the world makers—the impact of language and thought on human events.

Eisler (2000) has suggested that the most critical concern for human beings is the type of society that we create. She maintains that we have two fundamental options: (1) partnership and (2) dominator. How these two approaches to forming society play out over time, Eisler suggests, should be the organizing center for all studies in schools. These can be studied in a matrix where students explore how different subjects connect with different historical periods. Several cross themes link studies together: understanding partnership and dominator models in human events; partnership values and ethical/moral standards; partnership competencies (e.g., parenting, political, leadership); gender balance; diversity and multiculturalism; and the process of developing a society based on partnership.

Whether we adopt the suggestions of Postman or Eisler, it's easy to see how these powerful themes would engage students in deep and meaningful learning, linking many disparate facts together in genuine grappling with our condition as a people. Social studies moves from memorizing what seems to be meaningless trivia to exploring the key issues of humankind.

Inclusive Social Studies Learning

The standards for social studies clearly call for students to be actively engaged in studying, debating, and acting on topics and issues of importance in their social and political lives. When social studies learning uses this framework as the foundation for designing instruction and assessment, strategies for inclusive learning are naturally integrated into instruction. Social studies provides a natural opportunity to learn about issues and gain information but also to directly experience democracy, a sense of community, and inclusion. Experiences of students and families become key for making self-to-world connections, seeing the relationships of personal experiences to larger social and policy issues. Let's look at a few strategies and resources for using these ideas in the inquiry and workshop style of learning.

Studying and Acting on Issues. Social studies should involve students in understanding their communities and the larger political systems in which they operate. However, rather than just reading sterile descriptions in a textbook we involve students in exploring important issues. Inquiry learning here, as in science, can be directly applied. We can involve students in identifying important local issues, gathering information about different viewpoints, interviewing people, and visiting sites to gather information. In class we can involve students in presenting different perspectives, debating topics, and acting out important events and actions. We encourage children to develop their own questions and work together to discover the answers. This occurs most naturally in courses that deal with current topics. However, we can also bring history alive when we help students draw parallels between past and present events exploring questions like: "How are the events in Iraq and Vietnam similar and different?" "What issues that resulted in the Civil War in the United States are still active today? How?"

Sensitive social studies teachers are alert to the presence of issues and needs in our own classrooms. When the experience of students and their families provides a source for grappling with issues, we simultaneously connect with students' lives and provide an opportunity to address them. We can involve our students in discussing and identifying important issues in their community and in the school itself. We might raise issues like these: How do students from different racial groups get along in our school? In the local community? Is bullying present in our school and community? Why is this? Where do students with disabilities learn in our school district? Are they included or separated? Why? To identify issues, we can ask students to tell stories they know from their families and invite family and community members to the class to talk about issues. Such a process facilitates the voice of all being heard.

We will often have students work in small groups exploring a question, or have groups study related questions. For example, in a local community where major industries have shut down in the last 10 years, students may want to understand why this has happened and the impacts of the shutdowns on their community. The class could brainstorm issues and questions and develop working task forces to explore various aspects. When we do this, of course, students are engaging in processes often used in professional organizations. Not only are they learning content, they are understanding how collaborative task forces work. In such study groups, per our discussion in Chapter 9, we expect small groups to act as a community and identify roles for students with varying skills so they can make a contribution. This approach lends itself naturally to inclusive teaching (Bigelow, Christensen, Karp, Miner, & Peterson, 1994; Burke-Hengen & Gillespie, 1995; Isaac, 1992; Young, 1994).

Acting Out History. Process drama is a powerful group learning strategy that uses theater to both present information and engage students and teachers in living through experiences that engage emotions, mind, and body. Using this process, teachers engage students in a play of historical events, taking different roles in the event, stopping periodically to reflect on what people may be feeling as the event unfolds. In these dramatic sessions teachers' problems with students virtually disappear. Many students who have trouble with writing and reading shine in dramatic learning (Rohd, 1998). Again, the class lessons lead to time that is directed by the students and their own questions and wonderings. Some students use these experiences as a springboard to develop their own play. Others write a story from the perspective of a character and read it to the class or draw pictures of the event (Douglas, 1997; Manley & O'Neill, 1997). Here are a few examples of how this might work:

- A class acts out the roles of various people in the passage of the Indian Removal Bill involving the U.S. government, plantation owners, and the Cherokee Indians (see the beginning of Chapter 11 for more detail).
- A teacher involves high school students in acting out trials. The class is divided into three groups, each of which is given information on a trial involving different legal concepts. Each student takes two roles as a lawyer, witness, defendant, jury, or

JOURNEY into the CLASSROOM

Reflections on This Year's Journey Toward a Vision for Erin

In 2004, Erin was a senior in high school. Erin, who had Down syndrome, was always fully included in all general education classes and extracurricular activities and was never in a special education class. Her parents even kept her out of cotaught classrooms feeling that they replicated the look and feel of special education classes. During her senior year, Erin wrote, "I'm a cool senior at Westerville South High School. Go Wild Cats! I have my class ring, my letter jacket for Drama Club, and my senior pictures to give to my friends. I go to dances and parties and hang out with my friends at school." A few years earlier, as Erin began high school, Barb McKenzie, her mother, wrote these reflections regarding Erin's experience in general education classes (McKenzie, 2001).

Vision: To have a life in a community that values diversity and accentuates strengths and to contribute to that community. *What has happened?*

- Erin's excitement about sitting with friends at lunch and wanting to share that and other events that happen with friends in our talks each day after school.
- Being a "Dancing Tree" in the English class Mythology Play.
- "Her interest and enthusiasm has spilled over into the classroom and is a stimulus for other students who see Erin taking her classroom activities so seriously," her Ecology teacher wrote.
- "Thanks for your nice thoughts. It is I that is learning so much from Erin. I believe I am the lucky one to have her in my class. After 22 years of teaching, sometimes it takes a wonderful student like Erin to make us realize why we chose teaching as a profession in the first place," wrote Erin's English teacher.
- Interest that some ASAP (Active Students Advocating Peace) students seemed to take in brainstorming ideas for promoting an environment that encourages listening and understanding the diverse ways people communicate and valuing them, and looking at ways to be more intentional facilitators for students who need that assistance.

Vision: To have reciprocal relationships with friends; to communicate and advocate for herself. *What has happened?*

- The independent creation of her "commercial" for ecology—"Don't smoke! Yucky, Gross, Ugly! So there!"—became the creative idea for her science group and the basis for their group commercial.
- Erin's excitement about sitting with friends at lunch and on the bus.
- Working and conversing in lab groups.
- Reading "scary stories" around the pretend campfire in English.
- Asking more questions of other students in English and other places.
- Three great speeches on Erin's favorite topics in English.
- Choir! Choir! Singing in choir! Practicing for Choir! Erin's private singing lessons which she loves too.
- Ushering at plays—and then getting to watch them too.
- Learning about prejudice in the story *To Kill a Mockingbird* …

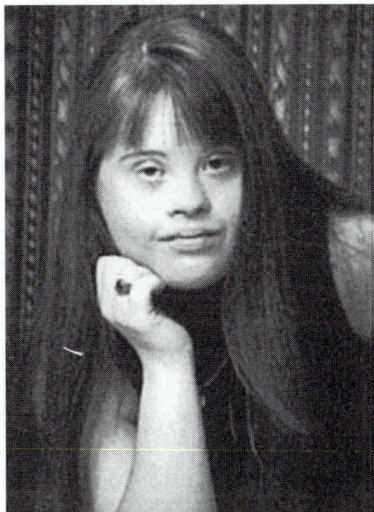

Erin McKenzie in her graduation photograph.

(continued)

Vision: To have the same opportunities as any other person to learn and participate in typical classroom, extracurricular, and community activities when they would typically happen. To graduate from high school in 2004 with her class and move on to post secondary options such as college and a career Erin is interested in. *What has happened?*

- Sitting in the Westerville South section at the Palace Theater for *The Scarlet Pimpernel*.
- Going to New York with the Heritage group, which included some South students, and seeing Erin's new favorite play/CD—*Phantom of the Opera*.
- When Erin turned on the bathroom fan/light and came running out to tell her dad and me about the air going out of our house, just like she had learned about in Ecology that day. Later, the humidity that Erin found in the bathroom because of the steam on the mirror.
- Learning the term "recycling" and connecting it to what we have always done with our newspapers, etc.
- Walking past the TV show that her dad was watching about the Aztecs and Tenochtitian

and saying, "Oh that's World History! The capital."
- Doing well with vocabulary games and on geography maps.
- Observing Erin easily maneuvering computer tools on a measuring program in math. Seeing her comfortably work with charts and other computer programs.
- Singing "Hail Holy Queen" from *Sister Act* for the Spring Concert.
- Following her daily schedule and getting to classes on time.

Tragically Erin died in 2004, shortly after graduating from high school. A "Welcoming Space" was created in the library at Otterbein College in honor of Erin. You can visit this at library.otterbein.edu/ErinMcKenzie/index.htm where you can also view Erin delivering a speech at a high school graduation week event. More reflections, narratives, and photographs that tell Erin's story of inclusion can be found in the book *Reflections of Erin—The Importance of Belonging, Relationships, and Learning With Each Other*, by Barbara McKenzie. Contact her at bmckenzie@columbus.rr.com.

judge. The group prepares and then conducts their trial in front of other students. This is followed by a class discussion of key concepts (Willis & Mann, 2000).

- Students act out the assassination of Martin Luther King and the responses of those pushing for both racial segregation and integration.
- Students explore segregation and discrimination against people with disabilities and role-play the time when individuals with disabilities took over the offices of Health, Education, and Welfare to protest for the development of regulations that would implement the first civil rights law for people with disabilities, Section 504 of the Rehabilitation Act of 1973.

In these examples, students have options to play many roles that call on different types and levels of skills. Students in groups work together so that all have valued parts, making these events natural for inclusive teaching.

Beyond the Textbook: Using Trade Books and Original Source Material for Learning. If we have students with wide ranges of abilities to read and write in our classes, total reliance on the text will create difficulties for many of these students. Many inclusive teachers do, in fact, use textbooks but only as a reference, not as the key source for the curriculum. We need to develop a classroom library of trade books on the topics we address that are at different reading levels, ranging from picture books to sophisticated analyses.

Moving beyond the textbook is important for other reasons as well. We need to be teaching students how to read original source material, synthesizing information and seeing different points of view. When students read trade books that provide different perspectives on, for example, the causes of the Civil War, we are helping students develop their ability to compare, contrast, and critically analyze information. When used together with materials at different reading levels, we lay the foundation for deeper thinking as well as inclusive teaching in our classes. Using original source material also easily and directly leads to having students study and take action on local issues and act out important events to deepen their understanding.

Calling on Technology. We can use technology to help our students access written materials as well as using text-to-speech software, for example, and speech-to-text software to help students who have difficulty getting ideas on paper. However, a growing number of valuable resources for social studies are available that can strengthen learning for all. The Internet provides a rich treasure-trove of sources that combine graphics (photos, videos, audio files) with typical text. Additionally, a growing number of interactive DVDs for various social studies issues are available.

The Arts and Physical Education

We decide to visit a middle school choir teacher, Abena Agyeman. She is working on a performance of *Jesus Christ Superstar* involving the entire choir along with a local youth rock group. We are interested because Abena has several students singing in the choir whose English is very limited and two students with moderate cognitive disabilities. We listen and watch as they practice. We note that one of the students with a cognitive disability sings a bit off key, and we wonder what Abena thinks about this. We ask her after practice. "Well," she says. "You'd be amazed at how much Sheryl has improved! But, yes, she is a bit off. We continue to work on that. But, you know, I recently had to ask myself the question. Am I a teacher or a conductor of a professional choir? The fact is, my students helped me make that decision. A few weeks ago we were at the state choir competition and, frankly, I had made a decision that Sheryl would sit out for the main competition. I thought she would hurt our chances. However, my students found out about this and they were angry. 'Ms. Agyeman, you know you teach us to respect and help one another. Sheryl is a member of our choir and she needs to participate.' So I allowed it. Interestingly, the judges found out about what had happened and they counted this act in our favor. So I've learned that I am a teacher first and foremost."

This time we visit an art class in Wadsworth Elementary School. Arnold Schoonover, the teacher, has a great sense of humor and is an excellent artist. However, we have heard that he has been very frustrated with some of the students. We follow a third-grade class down to his room with Jolinda, the teacher. "I'm not sure what is going on," she explains to us. "But every other day my students are sent back to my class early because of some behavior difficulty. Mr. Schoonover seems particularly concerned about Jared." As we come in Arnold is asking the students to be quiet. He is lecturing about the work of an artist who specialized in painting flowers. He is hoping that students might try to copy her techniques. As we look around we're surprised that there is no artwork up on the walls. We are further surprised as the lecture about the artist goes on for 20 minutes! Students are getting fidgety, Jared particularly. He stands up and twirls around as some of the other students start talking and giggling. Arnold tells them to be quiet and tries to continue his lecture. We notice, interestingly, that Jared is alternating between jumping up and looking around with plopping on the floor feverishly sketching a picture of a bear and a deer. The class gets noisy again. Arnold says, "OK. I've had enough. All of you go back to your room!" With lots of confusion and anger students get up and head back to Jolinda's classroom. As students leave we watch Arnold pick up Jared's drawing. "Jared!" he says. "This is a wonderful drawing." We look. So it is. Somehow Jared caught the real spirit of these animals. But Jared has already left.

These stories illustrate very different practices and philosophies about what arts education in schools should be about. Abena had become committed to being a true teacher of the arts, to involve students in performance to the best of their personal abilities, celebrating as a group. Arnold, on the other hand, seemed to forget that art is about expressing oneself. Rather, for him, art was again a list of facts and series of artistic techniques and skills. He had managed to make art much like a lecture–test class, in this case, a lecture–copy class. In the process, he missed some amazing artwork that a student did in spite of his lectures. All students were missing out in his class.

In this section, we discuss both the arts and physical education together. While very different in many ways, for inclusive teachers the arts (music, visual arts, drama, etc.) and physical education offer similar opportunities and challenges. In terms of multiple intelligence theory, these disciplines call on different intelligences than the linguistic and logical–mathematical intelligences that are the basis for most traditional instruction in public schools. Very naturally, the arts and physical education offer vast opportunities for students to engage in activities and development at very different levels of ability. Many students who struggle with reading, writing, and mathematics, for example, will often excel in sports or in some aspect of the arts.

Challenges in Arts and Physical Education

Despite the opportunities for inclusive teaching in the arts and physical education, we find surprising challenges.

In elementary school, the arts and physical education are thought of as "the specials." Typically art, music, and physical education teachers will see all students in the school in their programs. In elementary schools, some arts and physical education teachers feel that they are not considered equally important as other classroom teachers and that having students with special needs in their classes is just another example of being treated as second-class citizens. In fact, some schools integrate students with special needs only into the arts and physical education classes. In addition, the arts and some aspects of physical education have too often been seen as luxuries that are the first programs cut when school districts have budget difficulties. Some teachers show their anger in the way they treat students with special needs.

In secondary school, other challenges are present. In both middle and high school the arts and physical education, particularly sports, are tied up in competing with other schools to demonstrate their excellence—sport team competitions, art contests, and choir contests. Some teachers, as in Abena's story, may be tempted to not include students with special needs in these events. As did Abena, we have to make important decisions regarding whether our prime role is that of a teacher for all or whether we seek to win at all costs.

Other challenges come from the presence of special programs designed for students with disabilities to be involved in the arts and sports. Very Special Arts is an international organization designed to "create a society where all people with disabilities learn through, participate in and enjoy the arts" (Very Special Arts, 2008). This program sponsors events and activities aimed at promoting involvement of individuals with disabilities in the arts. However, sometimes these programs are essentially segregated programs just for children and adults with disabilities. Similarly, Special Olympics is a program "dedicated to empowering individuals with intellectual disabilities to become physically fit, productive and respected members of society through sports training and competition" (Special Olympics, 2008). This typically occurs through various levels of competitions involving children and adults with cognitive disabilities. Thus, the program often functions as a segregated program only for students with disabilities. Both programs offer separate activities based on the assumption that individuals with disabilities cannot participate in typical arts and sports programs in the community. However, as we shall see, both Very Special Arts and Special Olympics are also taking the lead in developing inclusive options for arts and physical education engagement rather than operating separate programs only for individuals with disabilities.

Standards for Arts and Physical Education

A consortium of arts organizations published the *National Standards for Art Education* in 1994 (Consortium of National Arts Education Associations, 1994). This document affirmed the value of the arts and outlined the need for students to be actively engaged in doing the arts. However, art was depicted often as a collection of facts to be memorized. Subsequent work reframed the arts in a more proactive direction and provided useful guidelines for arts educators. One document, *Gaining the Arts Advantage: Lessons from School Districts That Value Arts Education*, identified positive practices associated with schools in which the arts played a central role (Arts Education Partnership and the President's Committee on the Arts and the Humanities, 1998). The Arts Education Partnership (2002) published a document suggesting that the arts are central to learning the core academic subjects as well as subjects in their own right. Quality instruction in the arts should include the following characteristics (Zemelman et al., 2005):

- Students should *do* the arts, not just view or listen to them.
- The arts should be integrated into all subjects with all teachers engaging the arts.
- Students should have choices, be nurtured to find their strengths, create their own form of expression via the arts, and share their products and performances with others.
- Students should be involved in the world of the arts, experiencing various art genres, and connecting with arts events and artists.

Inclusive Arts and Physical Education

We will find, if we take these guidelines seriously, that the arts and physical education can naturally be inclusive. Here are a few ideas.

Involve Students in *Doing* Art and Physical Education. Inclusive arts classes are run as true workshops. The focus is on doing—creating visual artwork, performing with instruments, singing, engaging in physical education games. Skills lessons are taught as mini-lessons with the whole class for short periods and with small groups based on need. We can involve students in finding and discovering their inner voice and way to express themselves, whether we are an arts teacher or a general classroom teacher where art is integrated into the curriculum. When our primary goal is to help students learn how to express themselves via the arts, we find that all students, whatever their abilities, can participate valuably. We'll also be surprised at the talents that students with significant limitations sometimes show. Information about art techniques and tools, famous artists and musicians, knowledge of color or music—all become tools toward the end of self-expression rather than information in their own right.

Use Assistive Technology. For students with special needs, assistive technology can be helpful. This will range from low-tech tools, like paintbrushes with large handles, to higher tech tools, like drum machines that a student with only head movement might operate as part of participation in the band.

Include Cooperative Physical Education Games. Inclusive physical education teachers will work to create opportunities for learning that involve all students at their level of challenge. Cooperative games provide opportunities for students to help and challenge one another. One such example is field day. There are two ways of handling this traditional event. The traditional competitive way would have students competing against each other in a variety of sports and physical activities and earning first-place, second-place, and third-place ribbons. The noncompetitive way of running field day has 7 to 10 stations that students rotate through and play for fun. There are no ribbons given out, but the classes have a great time cheering for their classmates as they complete an obstacle course, play volleyball with a beach ball, run a race to fill a bucket with water, and play tug of war. The students have a great time doing physical exercises, without students feeling left out for not getting a ribbon.

Hold Inclusive Competitions. Inclusive arts and physical education teachers make the decision to include all students in arts or sports competitions. As all school districts move toward having students with special needs in these events, unfair advantages are balanced since all schools will have students with a mix of abilities. Competitions can also include points related to how well a team works together as well as the quality of the product. Judges may also take into account the learning demonstrated by students with special needs. As we move toward creating inclusive arts and physical education options many creative solutions can be developed.

When competitive games are used in physical education classes, teachers can assess the capabilities of students and develop teams with students that have balancing abilities. For example, a student with mild cerebral palsy might be on one team and a student with a moderate cognitive disability who is a slow runner on the other team.

For students with significant disabilities, physical education teachers may collaborate with physical therapists or adapted physical education teachers (teachers with specialized training in working with students with disabilities) who may provide support in integrating students with special needs into the class, helping them improve physical functioning. In addition, teachers can involve students in developing adaptations to games that allow students with significant disabilities to participate. In one elementary school, a student with a significant disability moved around slowly with a stand that held him upright. He could barely move his legs. However, the students came up with an adaptation in soccer where they periodically would stop and cheer for David to kick the ball (Reeves & Stein, 1999; Schilling & Coles, 1997; Villa & Thousand, 1996).

Unified Sports is a program that combines equal numbers of athletes with and without mental retardation and other disabilities, of similar age and ability, on teams that compete against other Unified Sports teams. Unified Sports was launched throughout the United States in 1989, with basketball, bowling, distance running and walking, soccer, softball, volleyball, and cycling; other sports are on the way (North Carolina Special Olympics, 2001). A manual for coaches is available, and most states now have coordinators who can give physical education teachers information on how to begin (Connecticut Interscholastic Athletic Conference, 2001).

Incorporate Arts and Physical Education in All Classes. All teachers should incorporate the arts and physical movement into their classes. Arts and physical education teachers can provide ideas and support to other teachers to accomplish this. An art teacher, for example, might coordinate a schoolwide visual arts program around a theme that connects art with interdisciplinary studies in other disciplines. Remember Sydney's moose project in Chapter 11? The school could have easily integrated art into that project with both classroom teachers and the art teacher collaborating in students using the arts as part of their project. This view encourages the production of art as a way of life for all, not merely for the specialized few. In best teaching practices, then, the arts become part of the total school and teachers of the arts become total school resource staff. In addition, therapists, such as art therapists and occupational therapists, can work collaboratively with arts teachers on projects that will enhance therapeutic goals for students (Johnson, 1997; Kovalik, 1994; Short et al., 1996; Young, 1994; Zemelman et al., 2005).

In a school that is seeking to use effective learning principles, physical movement, well-being, and skill can be integrated into and supportive of the total school curriculum rather than being an isolated subject. Physical education teachers can provide support and ideas for general education teachers. We might see elementary teachers incorporating dance and games into their thematic study about ancient Greece or a country in Africa. We might see math teachers using physical movements of the class as a way to demonstrate mathematical functions.

One school created a schoolwide mileage club. Each day, participating classes walked or ran around the school (4 times equaled a mile they discovered). The younger classes walked together, holding hands and discussing a question from the lesson as they walked. Some classes sang songs together. One class picked up trash as they went around. In a fifth-grade class students recorded the number of laps each day. The teacher used this as an opportunity to teach fractions, decimals, and percentages. For every 10 miles they completed, a paper foot was put on the wall with the child's name on it. As the year went on, the line went around the room and out the door. Students had an opportunity to engage in physical education in a very social way.

Toward Inclusive Workshop Learning

We recently went to dinner with four teachers who teach together as an interdisciplinary team in an urban high school. They included Edna, the math teacher; Devin, the science teacher; Kwame, the language arts and social studies teacher; and Aika, the special education teacher. Over the last 3 years they have been part of a school reform effort funded jointly by the Bill Gates Foundation and the Annenberg Foundation. Their school took on three initiatives which they joined together as part of a major school improvement initiative: (1) inclusive education in which they committed to including students with mild to moderate disabilities in general education classes; (2) implementation of authentic workshop-based learning; and (3) creation of smaller learning communities in the school through creation of several "communities" where teacher teams would follow students across Grades 9 through 12, working with them 4 years. We've heard good things about this effort and wanted to talk with these teachers.

After we ordered drinks and food, Kwame started the conversation by remembering how he felt 3 years ago when they began. "I was new in the job," he said. "I was absolutely overwhelmed! I thought they bit off way too much. Not one major change initiative but three! I told my wife that the school administration was crazy." As we look around the table we see lots of heads nodding in agreement along with smiles, like they are laughing a bit at themselves. "It's true for me too," said Aika. "Truth is, I was terrified. I had spent my 10-year career in special education in a self-contained special education classroom. I didn't know *anything* about the general education curriculum. I was also convinced that my students would be ridiculed and just lost."

"But it didn't turn out that way, we understand," Michael said. "No, it didn't," said Devin. "The fact is, looking back on it, we don't think that any one of these initiatives—smaller learning communities, inclusive education, and workshop learning—could have succeeded without being linked to the others." "Right!" said Edna. "As I began to figure out how to link math with real topics and issues in science, social studies, and language arts, I began to find so many ways to help all my students learn at their own level of ability. I had been absolutely lost thinking about what students with cognitive disabilities would do in an algebra class. But as we figured ways to have students involved in workshop learning on various topics, they learned what they needed to learn. And the practical, hands-on, inquiry learning we used help them understand so that many, in fact, have learned algebra skills. Looking back I am amazed."

"I feel the same way," said Devin. "Who would have thought that we could have students with such different abilities in our class and they actually enjoy helping one another and learning together? We've learned so much about how emotional and academic learning go hand in hand. I feel so fortunate to have been part of this school. The administration, as it has turned out, has been great. They've challenged us but also listened and have been very supportive."

"So is there anything else to do to improve your school?" Michael asked. The group erupts in laughter. "Oh yes," they say in unison. Kwame said "We are constantly learning. We are still working to help build community in our classroom and meet needs of kids with very serious problems. We're still aiming to have more of our lessons be real multilevel, rather than tiered lessons. Most important, there are still students with severe, multiple disabilities who should be attending our school. To tell you the truth, I am nervous and a bit scared if I can teach them. But I've learned that if I decide I want to it will likely be OK. So that's a next step," says.

We all agree that this team and school has traveled an amazing journey. It's the journey we all should be on. We wonder what the real impact would be if all schools and teachers took this journey. Maybe, just maybe all students really would find their special gifts, not only increasing academic and personal skills, but helping create better communities along the way. Maybe students would come out of school having grown to be real human beings who know, who have experienced how truly diverse people can live, learn, and work together. We agree that it's a goal worth pursuing with passion!

Traveling Notes

We've discussed strategies throughout this book regarding how to be inclusive teachers. In this chapter, we've focused on strategies that are specific to various subject areas. Here are a few notes from this chapter.

1. Literacy involves using many signing systems (written and oral words, pictures, gestures, etc.) to communicate meaning to another person.
2. Students gain skills in reading by reading at their own level with support to develop skills and strategies through mini-lessons and peer-to-peer support.
3. Students write to express their own perspectives. A key in helping students learn to write is to involve them in writing at their own level. Students can increase skills as they write through mini-lessons to the whole class and to small groups of students.
4. Direct instruction is not useful as the major or total curriculum for teaching literacy to any student. It focuses on skills, not the use of literacy to communicate meaning, and reduces student motivation.
5. Learning mathematics for all students must focus on understanding the meaning of concepts, not just following procedures to work problems.
6. Involving students in authentic learning of mathematics using concrete materials and resources helps strengthen student understanding.

7. Mathematics is not just for future engineers but is needed by all people. As teachers we need to commit to creating inclusive learning opportunities.

8. Science is about learning how to think and do as a scientist. It is not about memorizing a series of facts.

9. Involving students in inquiry and actual research, collecting and interpreting data, strengthens learning and understanding and provides a framework for effective multilevel differentiated lessons.

10. Social studies and science are two key subjects that can be used to organize authentic themes around which to link numerous subjects.

11. Social studies should focus on helping students understand how human beings function as social beings and the social structures by which this occurs. Social studies should involve students in learning about and understanding key, controversial social and political issues. It is not about memorizing facts and dates.

12. Involving students in active learning strategies such as acting out history or studying important local issues facilitates multilevel and tiered lessons to support inclusive teaching.

13. The arts and physical education are natural subjects for inclusive teaching as activities are organized to support students in performing at their own level of ability. They provide a place for students to show abilities in different types of intelligences.

14. The arts and physical education should be integrated into the curriculum throughout the school.

Stepping Stones

Following are some activities that will help extend your understanding and actions you may take in your journey toward becoming an inclusive teacher.

1. Use the information in this chapter and Chapters 11 and 12 and sketch out a semester-long series of lessons in your subject area based on workshop learning. Use multilevel and tiered instruction strategies for individual, small group, and whole class learning to create an inclusive approach to your lessons.

2. Obtain several lesson plans from other teachers or sources on the Internet. Use the information in Chapters 11 through 13 to critique these lesson plans. In what way are they conducive to inclusive teaching? What

problems do you see? How would you change these lesson plans so that they support inclusive teaching?

3. Do a google search titled "Inclusive Teaching My Subject" where "My Subject" is the subject you teach. Review at least three resources. Compare these to the ideas and strategies discussed in Chapters 11 through 13. Make notes that will add strategies or deepen your understanding.

4. Discuss the ideas of multilevel differentiated instruction for inclusive teaching with your principal and other trusted teacher colleagues. See if they would be interested in developing a working group to share effective strategies for inclusive teaching they are using in the classroom.

Looking Back and Going Forward!

Toward Creating Good Schools for ALL

Our journey together is ending now and it's time to part. We thought it might be good to help you look back at where we've been and then part with well wishes for your future as an inclusive teacher. We'll also propose a few reflective questions for you to consider as you look to the future. So let's look back together using the learning triangle from Chapter 2 to guide us (see Figure 14.1). As we consider where you have been and

FIGURE 14.1

Learning Pyramid in Effective Schools and Classrooms

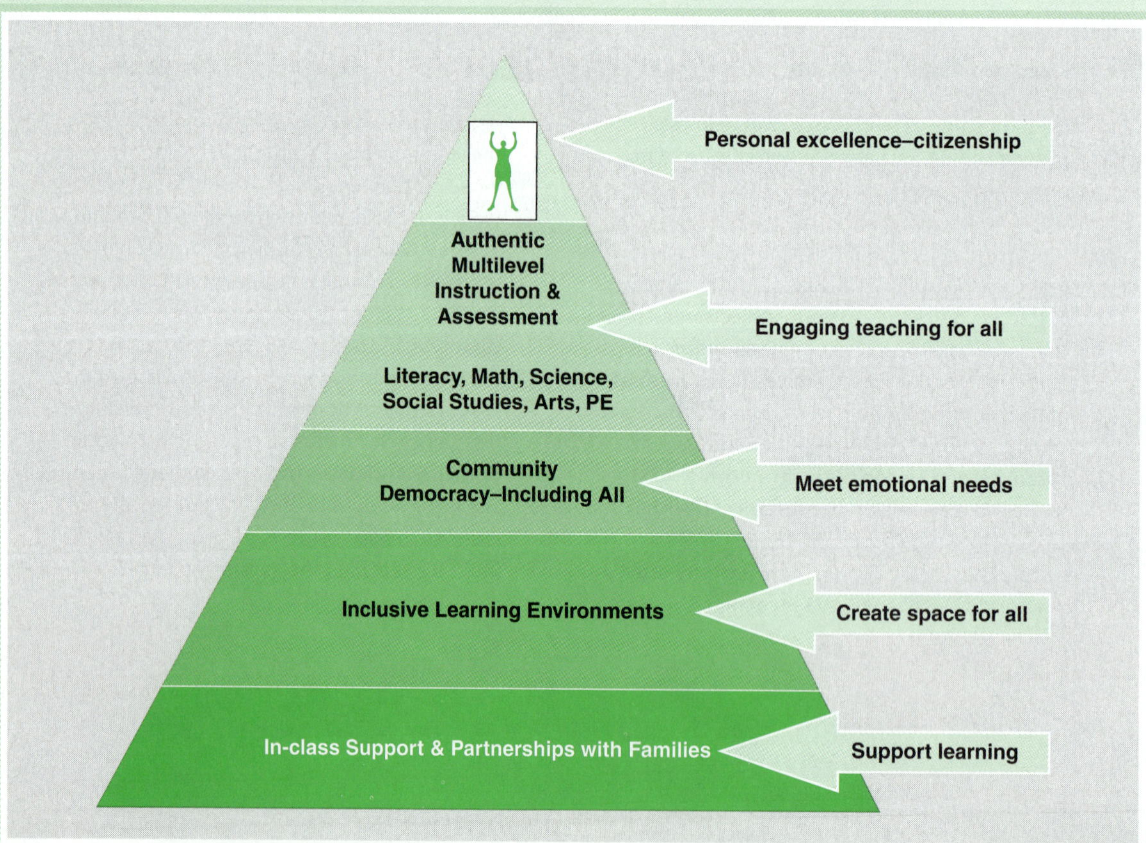

- Personal excellence–citizenship
- Authentic Multilevel Instruction & Assessment
- Engaging teaching for all
- Literacy, Math, Science, Social Studies, Arts, PE
- Community Democracy–Including All
- Meet emotional needs
- Inclusive Learning Environments
- Create space for all
- In-class Support & Partnerships with Families
- Support learning

where you are going in your journey, think about how this triangle builds on a foundation to produce personal best learning for each child.

First, the most fundamental question is this: *Do you* want *to be an inclusive teacher? If so, why? If not, why not? If you're still not sure, why is that?*

Second, if you think inclusive teaching is a good idea, then another question naturally follows: *What exactly are you* willing to do *to help quality inclusive teaching become a reality?* For good or for bad, it is likely, even if you are in a school that has been working toward inclusive teaching for a while, that you now know more than most educators you will meet about inclusive teaching. With knowledge comes responsibility. *What steps will you take? What's your intent and plan?* You might want to review ideas for teacher leadership presented in Chapter 1 as you think about this question.

You may remember that we spent several chapters exploring the reasons for inclusive teaching (Chapter 1), what research says (Chapter 2), and how an inclusive school looks (Chapter 2). Together, we looked at an image of schooling that works for all children, rather than considering some children as less worthy. Throughout the book, we've presented a central theme that we could summarize this way: *Good teaching and inclusive teaching are literally the same thing. When we use practices that help all children learn together, these are the same practices that promote the highest levels of learning and human development for all.* We began considering this thesis in Chapter 2, where we sketched out strategies for inclusive teaching. We pursued this further as we explored ways of thinking about differentiating for individual students in Chapter 4. Of course, the rest of the book expanded on this theme. *What do you think about this central thesis? Is good teaching inclusive teaching? Or is "inclusion" of special students a strange and unique undertaking that has little to do with teaching for "regular" students? Why do you think the way you do?*

Beginning in Chapters 5 and 6, we explored how parents and teachers and specialists can collaborate to provide mutual support and provide assistance to all learners. This calls for developing a true professional community in the school. *How might you use this information in a school to help create support for all students learning together?*

Beginning in Chapter 7, we delved into the key components of teaching—organizing the classroom, dealing with students' social and emotional needs, and designing academic instruction based on strategies that allow students with diverse abilities and characteristics to learn well together. In Chapters 7 and 8 we discussed how we can organize a classroom for active inclusive learning and use assistive technology to increase learning for all students. *How will you organize your classroom and use resources to promote inclusive teaching? What have you learned?*

In Chapters 9 and 10, we dealt with the social and emotional needs of students. A key thesis in those chapters is this: *We need to build a caring, mutually respectful community in our classrooms.* To the degree we do this, student learning will increase and our problems with student behaviors will decrease. We discussed what to do to support those students who have challenging behaviors in a respectful, caring manner. *What specific strategies will you use to build community in your classroom? How will you deal with conflicts and behavioral challenges to help students learn in a way that is positive and proactive? Do you believe, in fact, that we* should be *working to include students who have behavioral challenges? Why or why not? What will you do to put this belief into practice?*

Finally, in Chapters 11 through 13 we explored strategies for inclusive academic learning. We investigated ways to design lessons so they are naturally inclusive and ways

FIGURE 14.2

Sketching Inclusive Teaching in My Class

What are my strategies for _____?

Academic learning for all

Social–emotional–behavioral issues and building community

Learning environment

Collaboration with parents and specialists working in my classroom

to use tiered lessons and individualized differentiation. Finally, we glimpsed at some practicalities of how this looks in different subject areas. *What strategies will you use to develop multilevel and inclusive lessons? How will you gather resources to solve problems and to improve your skills in multilevel lesson design over time?*

You may also remember the teaching sketch pad in Chapter 2, where a teacher made a few notes about how he would teach his social studies class. This seems like a good time for you to make such a sketch in response to these questions we've just asked. Figure 14.2 provides you a blank form. Use your imagination and knowledge and literally, right now, create a summary image of how you will be an inclusive teacher.

Mishael Hittie and Michael Peterson

Well, that's it and that was a lot! You are to be congratulated if you've come to this resting point on the journey with a new vision of what teaching can be. Truth is, students and the world *need you*. We need people committed to creating success, respect, and care for all people. For out of that comes students who live full and successful lives and a better place for us all to live.

At this point, we want you to know we've been honored to journey with you. The journey has been hard and exciting and confusing all at the same time. At its end you may have more questions than when we began. We certainly do. But, ah yes! We've heard that happens when learning is at its best.

So the real journey is about to begin. We look forward to visiting you one day in your inclusive class, watching you engage kids of various races, cultures, and abilities, seeing you in a discussion with a group of teachers in your school as you ponder over the student problem of the day and rejoice in an amazing turn of learning and growth. We look forward to listening as you share at a conference with a team of students, parents, and teachers from your school the amazing wonders of growth, laughter, pain, sorrow, and learning in your inclusive classroom. We look forward to learning new lessons from you on those days. We'll smile and greet you knowing that, at the end, courage and comradeship are what really matters.

Until then,
We are Michael and Mishael

References

Access Center. (2006). *Strategies for accessing algebraic concepts K–8*. Washington, DC: American Institutes for Research.

Access Center. (2008). *Enhancing your instruction through differentiation: Differentiation strategies chart*. Washington, DC: Access Center, American Institutes for Research.

Achieve. (2004). *Case for action*. Retrieved September 10, 2006, from http://www.achieve.org/

Adam, B. (1978). *The survival of domination: Inferiorization and everyday life*. New York: Elsevier.

Affleck, J., Madge, S., Adams, A., & Lowenbraun, S. (1988). Integrated classroom versus resource model: Academic viability and effectiveness. *Exceptional Children, 54*, 339–348.

Agnew, J., Van Cleaf, D., Camblin, A., & Shaffer, M. (1994). Here's how: Successful scheduling for full inclusion. *Principal, 74*(2), 18–22.

Agron, J. (1998). The urban challenge: Meeting unique and diverse facility demands. *American School and University, 70*(11), 18–20.

Ainscow, M. (1999). *Understanding the development of inclusive schools*. London: Falmer Press.

Albert, L. (1996). *Cooperative discipline*. Circle Pines, MN: American Guidance Service.

Albin, R. W., Horner, R. H., & O'Neill, R. E. (1994). *Proactive behavioral support: Structuring and assessing environments*. Eugene, OR: Research and Training Center on Positive Behavioral Support.

Allen, R., & Petr, C. (1995). *Family-centered service delivery: A cross-disciplinary literature review and conceptualization*. Lawrence, KS: Beach Center on Families and Disability.

Alliance for Technology Access. (1996). *Computer resources for people with disabilities: A guide to exploring today's assistive technology*. Alameda, CA: Hunter House.

Allington, R. (1991). Children who find learning to read difficult: School responses to diversity. In E. Hiebert (Ed.), *Literacy for a diverse society: Perspective, practices, and policies*. New York: Teachers College Press.

Allington, R. (1993). The reading instruction provided readers of differing reading abilities. *The Elementary School Journal, 83*(5), 548–559.

Allington, R. (1994). What's so special about special programs for children who find learning to read difficult? *Journal of Reading Behavior, 26*(1), 95–115.

Altman, R., & Lewis, T. J. (1990). Social judgments of integrated and segregated students with mental retardation toward same-age peers. *Education and Training in Mental Retardation, 25*, 107–112.

Amado, A. (1993). *Friendships and community connections between people with and without developmental disabilities*. Baltimore: Brookes.

American Academy of Child and Adolescent Psychiatry. (2008). *Conduct disorder*. Retrieved January 31, 2008, from http://www.aacap.org/cs/root/facts_for_families/conduct_disorder

American Association for the Advancement of Science. (1989). *Science for all Americans: Project 2061*. Washington, DC: Author.

American Association for the Advancement of Science. (1993). *Benchmarks for science literacy*. Washington, DC: Author.

American Association for the Advancement of Science. (2001). *Atlas of science literacy*. Washington, DC: Author.

American Association of Intellectual and Developmental Disabilities. (2007). *Definition of mental retardation*. Retrieved November 29, 2007, from http://www.aamr.org/Policies/faq_mental_retardation.shtml

American Association of Physical Anthropologists. (1996). Statement on biological aspects of race. *American Journal of Physical Anthropology, 101*, 569–570.

American Cancer Society. (2000). *Cancer in children*. Retrieved July 1, 2002, from http://www.cancer.org/eprise/main/docroot/CRI/CR1_2x?sitearea=LRN&dt=7

American Psychiatric Association. (2000). *Diagnostic and statistical manual of mental disorders* (4th ed., text revision, pp. 92–93). Washington, DC: Author.

American Speech and Hearing Association. (1994). *Facilitated communication: Technical report*. Rockville, MD: Author.

Americans with Disabilities Act. (1990). 42 U.S.C.A. § 12101 *et seq.* (West 1993).

Ammerman, R., Van Hasselt, V., & Hersen, M. (1988). Abuse and neglect in handicapped children: A critical review. *Journal of Family Violence, 3*(2), 53–72.

Amish, P., Gesten, E., Smith, J., & Clark, H. (1988). Social problem-solving training for severely emotionally and behaviorally disturbed children. *Behavioral Disorders, 13*, 175–186.

Apple, M. (1995). *Democratic schools*. Alexandria, VA: Association for Supervision and Curriculum Development.

Armstrong, T. (1994). *Multiple intelligences in the classroom*. Alexandria, VA: Association for Supervision and Curriculum Development.

Armstrong, T. (1997). *The myth of the A.D.D child: 50 ways to improve your child's behavior and attention span without drugs, labels, or coercion*. New York: Plume Books.

Arnold, A. (1998, January). *Inclusion: Whole schooling*. Address presented at the University of Wisconsin–Stevens Point, Stevens Point, WI.

Arts Education Partnership. (2002). *Critical links: Learning in the arts and students' academic and social development*. Washington, DC: Author.

Arts Education Partnership and the President's Committee on the Arts and the Humanities. (1998). *Gaining the arts advantage: Lessons from school districts that value arts education*. Washington, DC: Author.

Au, K., Mason, J., & Scheu, J. (1995). *Literacy instruction for today*. New York: HarperCollins.

Baer, J. (1994). The web we weave: Creating the fabric of peacemaking. *Primary Voices: K–6, 2*(4), 12–14.

Baines, L., Baines, C., & Masterson, C. (1994). Mainstreaming: One school's reality. *Phi Delta Kappan, 76*(1), 39–40.

Baker, E. T. (1994). *Meta-analytic evidence for non-inclusive educational practices: Does educational research support current practice for special-needs students?* Unpublished doctoral dissertation, Temple University, Philadelphia.

Baker, E. T., Wang, M. C., & Walberg, H. J. (1994). The effects of inclusion on learning. *Educational Leadership, 52*(4), 33–35.

Baker, J., & Zigmond, N. (1995). The meaning and practice of inclusion for students with learning disabilities: Themes and implications from five case studies. *The Journal of Special Education, 29*(2), 163–180.

Balboni, M., Giulia, F., & Pedrabissi, L. (2000). Attitudes of Italian teachers and parents toward school inclusion of students with mental retardation: The role of experience. *Education and Training in Mental Retardation and Developmental Disabilities, 35*(2), 148–159.

Ballen, J., & Moles, O. (1994). *Strong families, strong schools.* Washington, DC: U.S. Department of Education.

Banerji, M., & Dailey, R. (1995). A study of the effects of an inclusion model on students with specific learning disabilities. *Journal of Learning Disabilities, 28,* 511–522.

Banks, J. (1990). Citizenship education for a pluralistic democratic society. *The Social Studies, 81,* 210–214.

Banks, J. (1994). *All of us together: The story of inclusion at the Kinzie School.* Washington, DC: Gallaudet University Press.

Banks, J. (1995). *Creating the multi-age classroom.* Edmonds, WA: CATS Publications.

Barnett, D. (1982). The effects of open-space versus traditional, self-contained classrooms on the auditory selective attending skills of elementary children. *Language, Speech, and Hearing Services in the Schools, 13,* 138–143.

Barnett, D. (1997). *Helping children learn: Comprehensive school-linked services.* Detroit: Wayne State University, Skillman Center for Children.

Bauer, A., & Myree-Brown, G. (2001). *Adolescents and inclusion: Transforming secondary schools.* Baltimore: Brookes.

Bauwens, J., & Hourcade, J. (1998). *Cooperative teaching: Rebuilding the schoolhouse for all students.* Austin, TX: Pro-Ed.

Beach Center on Families and Disability. (1994). *Positive behavioral support as a means to enhance successful inclusion of persons with challenging behavior.* Lawrence, KS: Author.

Beaumont, C. (1999). Dilemmas of peer assistance in a bilingual full inclusion classroom. *Elementary School Journal, 99*(3), 233–254.

Becher, R. (1984). *Parent involvement: A review of research and principles of successful practice.* Washington, DC: National Institute of Education.

Beegle, D. (2000). *Interrupting generational poverty: unpublished doctoral dissertation.* Portland, OR: Portland State University.

Beegle, D. (2003, October). Overcoming the silence of generational poverty. *Talking Points, 15*(1), 11–19.

Begali, V. (1992). *Head injury in children and adolescents: A resource and review for school and allied professionals.* Brandon, VT: Clinical Psychology.

Bell, T. (1994). Understanding students with traumatic brain injury: A guide for teachers and therapists. *School System: Special Interest Section Newsletter, 1*(2), 1–4.

Bellah, R., Madsen, R., Sullivan, W., Swidler, A., & Tipton, S. (1985). *Habits of the heart: Individualism and commitment in American life.* San Francisco: Harper & Row.

Bellamy, G. T., Rhodes, L., Mank, D., & Albin, J. (1988). *Supported employment: A community implementation guide.* Baltimore: Brookes.

Beloin, K. (1997). *Using read-alouds for students with intellectual disabilities in general education classrooms: Implications for educators.* Unpublished manuscript, Cardinal Stritch University, College of Education, Milwaukee, WI.

Beloin, K. (1998). Strategies for developing inclusive practices in small, rural schools. *Rural Special Education Quarterly, 17*(1), 12–20.

Bender, W. (1997). *Understanding ADHD: A practical guide for teachers and parents.* Upper Saddle River, NJ: Merrill/Pearson Education.

Benjamin, A. (1981). *A helping interview* (3rd ed.). Boston: Houghton Mifflin.

Berg, P. (1989, May 7). School runs with no punishment, just simple rules. *St. Paul Pioneer Press,* pp. 1b, 10b.

Berk, L., & Winsler, A. (1995). *Scaffolding children's learning: Vygotsky and early childhood education.* Washington, DC: National Association for the Education of Young Children.

Berrigan, C. (1994). *Schools in Italy: A national policy made actual.* Retrieved July 1, 2002, from Center on Human Policy, Syracuse University Web site: http://web.syr.edu/~thechp/italy.htm

Bertrand, J., Mars, A., Boyle, C., Bove, F., Yeargin-Allsopp, M., & Decoufle, P. (2001). Prevalence of autism in a United States population: The Brick Township, New Jersey, investigation. *Pediatrics, 108*(5), 1155–1161.

Beukelman, D., & Mirenda, P. (1992). *Augmentative and alternative communication: Management of severe communication disorders in children and adults.* Baltimore: Brookes.

Bigelow, B. (1995). Show, don't tell: Roleplays and social imagination. In M. Burke-Hengen & T. Gillespie (Eds.), *Building community: Social studies in the middle years.* Portsmouth, NH: Heinemann.

Bigelow, B., Christensen, L., Karp, S., Miner, B., & Peterson, B. (Eds.). (1994). *Rethinking our classrooms: Teaching for equity and justice.* Milwaukee, WI: Rethinking Schools.

Bigge, J. (1991). *Teaching individuals with physical and multiple disabilities* (3rd ed.). New York: Macmillan.

The Big Picture. (2008). *One student at a time.* Retrieved July 11, 2008, from http://www.bigpicture.org/

Biklen, D. (1985). *The complete school: Integrating special and general education.* New York: Teachers College Press.

Biklen, D. (1990). Communication unbound: Autism and praxis. *Harvard Educational Review, 60*(3), 291–314.

Biklen, D. (1992). Typing to talk: Facilitated communication. *American Journal of Speech-Language Pathology, 1*(2), 15–17.

Biklen, D., Corrigan, C., & Quick, D. (1989). Beyond obligation: Students' relation with each other in integrated classes. In D. Lipsky & A. Gartner (Eds.), *Beyond separate education: Quality education for all.* Baltimore: Brookes.

Bishop, K., Woll, J., & Arango, P. (1993). *Family/professional collaboration for children with special health needs and their families.* Burlington, VT: Department of Social Work.

Blanksby, D. (1999). Not quite eureka: Perceptions of a trial of cluster grouping as a model for addressing the diverse range of student abilities at a junior secondary school. *Educational Studies, 25*(1), 79–88.

Blatt, B. (1966). *Christmas in purgatory: A photographic essay on mental retardation.* Boston: Allyn & Bacon.

Bloom, B. S. (Ed.). (1956). *Taxonomy of educational objectives: The classification of educational goals: Handbook I. Cognitive domain.* New York/Toronto, Ontario, Canada: Longmans, Green.

Boger, C. (2005). *The socioeconomic composition of public schools: A crucial consideration for student assignment policy.* Chapel Hill, NC: University of North Carolina.

Boggiano, A. K., & Barrett, M. (1992). Gender differences in depression in children as a function of motivational orientation. *Sex Roles, 26*(1), 11–17.

Booth, T., & Ainscow, M. (1998). *From them to us: An international study of inclusion in education.* London: Creative Press and Design.

Borman, C. (2004). Accountability in a postdesegregation era: The continuing significance of racial segregation in Florida. *American Educational Research Journal, 41*(3), 605–620.

Boudah, D., Schumacher, J., & Deschler, D. (1997). Collaborative instruction: Is it an effective option for inclusion in secondary classrooms? *Learning Disabilities Quarterly, 20,* 293–316.

Boundless Playgrounds. (2001). *Welcome to Boundless Playgrounds.* Retrieved July 1, 2002, from http://www.boundlessplaygrounds.org/index.html

Bowen, M., & Glenn, E. (1998). Counseling interventions for students who have mild disabilities. *Professional School Counseling, 2*(1), 1–9.

Braddock, D., Hemp, R., Bachelder, L., & Fujiura, G. (1995). *The state of the states in developmental disabilities* (4th ed.). Washington, DC: American Association of Mental Retardation.

Brantlinger, E. (1995). *Sterilization of people with mental disabilities: Issues, perspectives, and cases.* Westport, CT: Auburn House.

Bredekamp, S., & Copple, C. (Eds.). (1997). *Developmentally appropriate practice in early childhood programs* (Rev. ed.). Washington, DC: National Association for the Education of Young Children.

Breeding, J. (1996). *The wildest colts make the best horses: What to do when your child is labeled a problem by the schools.* Austin, TX: Bright Books.

Breggin, G. (2000). *Ritalin class action suit filed.* Retrieved July 1, 2002, from http://www.breggin.com/classaction.html

Breggin, P. (2001). *Talking back to Ritalin: What doctors aren't telling you about stimulants for children.* Cambridge, MA: Perseus.

Breggin, P., & Ross-Breggin, G. (1994). *The war against children: How the drugs, programs, and theories of the psychiatric establishment are threatening America's children with a medical "cure" for violence.* New York: St. Martin's Press.

Brett, A., & Provenzo, E. (1995). *Adaptive technology for special human needs.* Albany: State University of New York Press.

Briggs, H. E. (1996). Creating independent voices: The emergence of statewide family networks. *Journal of Mental Health Administration, 23*(4), 447–457.

Briggs, H. E., Koroloff, N. M., Richards, K., & Friesen, B. J. (1993). *Family advocacy organizations: Advances in support and system reform.* Portland, OR: Portland State University, Research and Training Center on Family Support and Children's Mental Health.

Brinker, R. P., & Thorpe, M. E. (1984). Integration of severely handicapped students and the proportion of IEP objectives achieved. *Exceptional Children, 51*(2), 168–175.

Brolin, D. (1993). *Life-centered career education curriculum guide.* Reston, VA: Council for Exceptional Children.

Bronfenbrenner, U. (1979). *The ecology of human development: Experiments by nature and design.* Cambridge, MA: Harvard University Press.

Brooks, D., Clarke, V., Green, D., Kerby, K., & Riley, J. (2003). *Inclusive high school teaching guide. Unpublished report developed for SED 5600.* Detroit: Wayne State University.

Brownell, M. (2000). *The use of musically adapted social stories to modify behaviors in students with autism: Four case studies.* Lawrence: University of Kansas.

Bull, B. (2006). Is standards-based school reform consistent with schooling for personal liberty? *Studies in Philosophy and Education, 25*(1–2), 61–75.

Burke-Hengen, M., & Gillespie, T. (1995). *Building community: Social studies in the middle school years.* Portsmouth, NH: Heinemann.

Burnette, J. (1999). Critical behaviors and strategies for teaching culturally diverse students (*ERIC/OSEP Digest* E584). Retrieved from http://www.ericdigests.org/2000-3/critical.htm

Buysse, V., & Bailey, D. (1993). Behavioral and developmental outcomes in young children with disabilities in integrated and segregated settings: A review of comparative studies. *The Journal of Special Education, 26,* 434–461.

Caine, R. N., & Caine, G. (1991). *Making connections: Teaching and the human brain.* Alexandria, VA: Association for Supervision and Curriculum Development.

Caine, R. N., & Caine, G. (1995). Reinventing schools through brain-based learning. *Educational Leadership, 52*(2), 43–47.

Calkins, L. (1994). *The art of teaching writing.* Portsmouth, NH: Heinemann.

Calkins, L. M., Montgomery, R., Santman, D., & Falk, B. (1998). *A teacher's guide to standardized reading tests: Knowledge is power.* Portsmouth, NH: Heinemann.

Campbell, B. (1994). *The multiple intelligences handbook: Lesson plans and more.* Standwood, WA: Campbell and Associates.

Campbell, L., & Campbell, B. (1999). *Multiple intelligences and student achievement: Success stories from six schools.* Alexandria, VA: Association for Supervision and Curriculum Development.

Carkhuff, R. (2000). *The art of helping in the twenty-first century.* Amherst, MA: Human Resource Development Press.

Carlberg, C., & Kavale, K. (1980). The efficacy of special versus regular class placement for exceptional children: A meta-analysis. *The Journal of Special Education, 14,* 295–309.

Carpenter, S., King-Sears, M., & Keys, S. (1998). Counselors + educators + families as a transdisciplinary team = more effective inclusion for students with disabilities. *Professional School Counseling, 2*(1), 16–25.

Carr, E. G., Levin, L., McConnachie, G., Carlson, J., Kemp, D. C., & Smith, C. E. (1994). *Communication-based intervention for problem behavior: A user's guide for producing positive change.* Baltimore: Brookes.

Carlson, D., Ehrlich, N., Berland, J., & Bailey, N. (2001). *Assistive technology survey results: Continued benefits and needs reported by Americans with disabilities.* Rehabilitation Engineering and Assistive Technology Society of North America, Arlington, VA.

Ceifetz, C. (1997). *Inclusive education observation report.* Detroit: Wayne State University.

Center for Applied Special Technology. (2002). Retrieved July 1, 2002, from http://www.cast.org/

Center for Applied Special Technology. (2008). *Universal design for learning.* Wakefield, MA: Author.

Center for Effective Collaboration and Practice. (1994). *National agenda for achieving better results for children and youth with serious emotional disturbance.* Washington, DC: Office of Special Education and Rehabilitative Services, U.S. Department of Education.

Center for Effective Collaboration and Practice. (1999). *Think time strategy.* Retrieved July 1, 2002, from *Success Stories:* http://www.air-dc.org/cecp/resources/success/think_time.htm

Centers for Disease Control and Prevention. (1988). Perspectives in disease prevention and health promotion update: Universal precautions for prevention of transmission of human immunodeficiency virus, hepatitis B virus, and other bloodborne pathogens. *MMWR Weekly, 37*(24), 377–388.

Centers for Disease Control and Prevention. (2001). *HIV/AIDS surveillance report.* Retrieved from http://www.cdc.gov/hiv/stats/hasr1301/fig5.htm

Century Foundation. (2000). *Economic school integration.* New York: Author.

Cessna, K., & Skiba, R. (1996). Needs-based services: A responsible approach to inclusion. *Preventing School Failure, 40*(3), 117–123.

Champagne, A., Newell, S., & Goodnough, J. (1996). Trends in science education. In M. Pugach & C. Warger (Eds.), *Curriculum trends, special education, and reform: Refocusing the conversation.* New York: Teachers College Press.

Charles, M. (1999). *Building classroom discipline.* New York: Longman.

Chase, P., & Doan, J. (1994). *Full circle: A new look at multi-age education.* Portsmouth, NH: Heineman.

Chedd, N. (May, 1995). Getting started with augmentative communication. *Exceptional Children, 28*(5), 34–39.

Cheney, D., & Harvey, V. (1994). From segregation to inclusion: One district's program changes for students with emotional/behavioral disorders. *Education and Treatment of Children, 17*(3), 332–346.

Cheney, D., & Muscott, H. (1996). Preventing school failure for students with emotional and behavioral disabilities through responsible inclusion. *Preventing School Failure, 40*(2), 109–116.

Choike, J. (2000). Teaching strategies for algebra for all. *Mathematics Teacher, 93*(7).

Christiansen, J., & Vogel, J. (1998). A decision model for grading students with disabilities. *Teaching Exceptional Children, 31*(2), 30–35.

Clark, B. (1997). *Growing up gifted.* Upper Saddle River, NJ: Merrill/Pearson Education.

Cline, S. (1999). *Giftedness has many faces.* New York: Foundation for Concepts in Education.

Closing the Gap. (2000, February/March). *2000 Resource Directory: Hardware, Software, Producers, Organizations: A Guide to the Selection of the Latest Computer Related Products for Children and Adults with Special Needs, 18*(6).

Cogswell, A. (1984). *When the mind hears: A history of the deaf.* New York: Random House.

Cohen, E. (Ed.). (1994). *Designing groupwork: Strategies for the heterogeneous classroom.* New York: Teachers College Press.

Cohen, E. G., Lotan, R. A., Scarloss, B. A., Arellano, A. R. (1999). Complex instruction: Equity in cooperative learning classrooms. *Theory into Practice, 38*(2), 80–86.

Cohen, M. K. (1994, July). *Children on the boundary: The challenge posed by children with conduct disorders.* Alexandria, VA: Project FORUM, National Association of State Directors of Special Education.

Cohen, O. (1994, April 29). Inclusion should not include deaf students. *Education Week,* pp. 10–13.

Cohen, S. (1991). Adapting educational programs for students with traumatic brain injury. *Journal of Head Injury, 6*(1), 56–63.

Cole, D., & Meyer, L. H. (1991). Social integration and severe disabilities: A longitudinal analysis of child outcomes. *The Journal of Special Education, 19*(4), 483–492.

Coleman, J. S. (1994). Family involvement in education. In C. Fagnano & B. Werber (Eds.), *School, family, and community interaction: A view from the firing lines.* San Francisco: Westview Press.

Coles, C. (1987). *The learning mystique: A critical look at "learning disabilities."* New York: Pantheon Books.

Coles, G. (1998). *Reading lessons: The debate over literacy.* New York: Hill & Wang.

Comer, J. (1988, November). Educating poor minority children. *Scientific American,* pp. 42–48.

Comer, J. (1997). *Waiting for a miracle: Why schools can't solve our problems and how we can.* New York: Dutton.

Connecticut Interscholastic Athletic Conference. (2001). *Unified Sports coaches handbook.* Cheshire, CT: Author.

Connell, R., Jones, M., Mace, R., Mueller, J., Mullick, A., Ostroff, E., et al. (1997). *The principles of universal design.* Retrieved July 1, 2002 from Center for Universal Design Web site: http://www.design.ncsu.edu/cud/univ_design/principles/udprinciples.htm

Considine, J. (1995). *Restorative justice: Healing the effects of crime.* Lyttleton, New Zealand: Plowshares.

Consortium of National Arts Education Associations. (1994). *National standards for arts education: What every young American should know and be able to do.* Reston, VA: Author.

Cook, A., & Hussey, S. (1995). *Assistive technologies: Principles and practice.* New York: Mosby.

Cornelius, D. (1980). *Inside out.* Washington, DC: George Washington University, Regional Rehabilitation Institute.

Council for Exceptional Children. (1993). *CEC policy on inclusive schools and community settings.* Reston, VA: Author.

Counseling Services Learning Skills Program. (2001). *Bloom's taxonomy.* Victoria, British Columbia, Canada: University of Victoria.

Covey, S. (1989). *The seven habits of successful people: Restoring the character ethic.* New York: Simon & Schuster.

Cragg, W. (1992). *The practice of punishment: Toward a theory of restorative justice.* New York: Routledge.

Crider, B. (1998, April). *Families and professionals: A needed partnership for inclusion.* Presentation at the College of Education, Wayne State University, Detroit.

Criteria for determining the existence of a specific learning disability, 34 C.F.R. 300.541 (1997).

Crossley, R. (1994). *Facilitated communication training.* New York: Teachers College Press.

Cullinan, D., Epstein, M., & Sabornie, E. (1992). Selected characteristics of a national sample of seriously emotionally disturbed adolescents. *Behavioral Disorders, 17*(4), 273–280.

Cunningham, P., & Allington, R. (1999). *Classrooms that work: They can all read and write.* New York: Longman.

Dalton, E. (2002). Assistive technology in education. *Issues in Teaching and Learning, 1*(1), 14–21.

Daniels, H. (1994). *Literature circles: Voice and choice in the student-centered classroom.* York, ME: Stenhouse.

Daniels, H., & Bizar, M. (1998). *Methods that matter: Six structures for best practice classrooms.* York, ME: Stenhouse.

Danziger, S., & Haveman, R. (2001). *Understanding poverty.* New York: Russell Sage Foundation.

Davis, R., & Maher, C. (1996). A new view of the goals and means for school mathematics. In M. Pugach & C. Warger (Eds.), *Curriculum trends, special education, and reform: Refocusing the conversation.* New York: Teachers College Press.

DEAL Communications Center. (2001). Caulfield, Victoria, Australia. Retrieved July 1, 2002, from http://home.vicnet.net.au/~dealccinc/

de Jong, E. (2006). Integrated bilingual education: An alternative approach. *Bilingual Research, 30*(1), 23–44.

Delpit, L. (1995). *Other people's children: Cultural conflict in the classroom.* New York: New Press.

Deno, E. (1970). Special education as developmental capital. *Exceptional Children, 37,* 235.

Deno, S., Maruyama, G., Espin, C., & Cohen, C. (1990). Educating students with mild disabilities in general education classrooms: Minnesota alternatives. *Exceptional Children, 57*(2), 150–161.

Denton, P., & Kriete, R. (2000). *The first six weeks of school.* Greenfield, MA: Northeast Foundation for Children.

Deschenes, C., Ebeling, D., & Sprague, J. (1994). *Adapting curriculum and instruction in inclusive classrooms: A teacher's desk reference.* Bloomington: Indiana University, Institute for the Study of Developmental Disabilities.

Developmental Studies Center. (1994). *At home in our schools: A guide to school-wide activities that build community.* Oakland, CA: Author.

Dewey, J. (1938). *Experience and education.* New York: Collier.

Dewey, J. (1943). *The school and society.* Chicago: University of Chicago Press.

Diller, L. (1998). *Running on Ritalin: A physician reflects on children, society, and performance in a pill.* New York: Bantam.

Disability Rights Advocates. (1999). *Forgotten crimes: The Holocaust and people with disabilities.* Retrieved July 1, 2002, from http://www.dralegal.org/projects/disability/holocaust/

Douglas, R. (1997). Democracy and empowerment: The Nashville student sit-ins of the 1960's. In A. Manley & C. O'Neill (Eds.), *Dreamseekers: Creative approaches to the African-American heritage.* Portsmouth, NH: Heinemann.

Dover, W. (1994). *The inclusion facilitator.* Manhattan, KS: Master Teacher.

Doyle, M. (1997). *The paraprofessionals guide to the inclusive classroom: Working as a team.* Baltimore: Brookes.

Dryfoos, J. (1994). *Full-service schools: A revolution in health and social services for children, youth, and families.* San Francisco: Jossey-Bass.

Duffey-Hester, A. M. (1999). Teaching struggling readers in elementary school classrooms: A review of classroom reading programs and principles for instruction. *The Reading Teacher, 52*(5), 480–495.

Dunn, L. (1968). Special education for the mildly retarded: Is much of it justifiable? *Exceptional Children, 35*(1), 5–22.

Dunn, R. (1996). *How to implement and supervise a learning style program.* Alexandria, VA: Association for Supervision and Curriculum Development.

Dunst, C. (1987). *Enabling and empowering families: Conceptual and intervention issues.* Morgantown, NC: Western Carolina Center, Family Infant and Preschool Program.

Duttweiler, P. , & McEvoy, U. (2001). *Standards-based reform: What is missing?* Clemson, SC: Clemson University.

Eber, L., Nelson, C., & Miles, P. (1997). School-based wrap-around for students with emotional and behavioral challenges. *Exceptional Children, 63*(4), 539–555.

Edelsky, C. (Ed.). (1999). *Making justice our project: Teachers working toward critical whole language practice.* Urbana, IL: National Council of Teachers of English.

Education Alliance at Brown University. (2008). *Principles for culturally responsive teaching.* Teaching diverse learners: Equity and excellence for all. Retrieved from http://www.alliance.brown.edu/tdl/tl-strategies/crt-principles.shtml#perspectives

Elias, M., Zins, J., Weissberg, R., Frey, K., Greenberg, K., Haynes, N., et al. (1997). *Promoting social and emotional learning: Guidelines for educators.* Alexandria, VA: Association for Supervision and Curriculum Development.

Englert, C., Garmon, M., Mariage, T., Rozendal, M., Tarrant, K., & Urba, J. (1995). The early literacy project: Connecting across the curriculum. *Learning Disability Quarterly, 18*(3), 253–276.

Englert, C., Mariage, T., Garmon, M., & Tarrant, K. (1998). Accelerating reading progress in early literacy project classrooms: Three exploratory studies. *Remedial and Special Education, 19*(3), 142–159.

Epstein, J. (1994). Theory to practice: School and family partnerships lead to school improvement. In C. Fagnano & B. Werber (Eds.), *School, family, and community interaction: A view from the firing lines.* San Francisco: Westview Press.

Epstein, J., & Salinas, K. (1998). *TIPS: Teachers involve parents in schoolwork: Language arts and science/health: Interactive homework in the middle grades.* Baltimore: Johns Hopkins University, Center on Families, Communities, Schools and Children's Learning.

Etscheidt, S., & Bartlett, L. (1999). The IDEA amendments: A four-step approach for determining supplementary services. *Exceptional Children, 65*(2), 163–174.

Evans, I., & Meyer, L. (1985). *An educative approach to behavior problems: A practical decision model for interventions with severely handicapped learners.* Baltimore: Brookes.

Faber, A., Mazlish, E., Nyberg, L., & Templeton, R. (1995). *How to talk so kids can learn—at home and in school.* New York: Fireside.

Facilitated Communication Institute. (2001). Retrieved from Syracuse University Web site: http://soeweb.syr.edu/thefci/

Fairtest. (1995). *Principles and indicators for student assessment systems by the National Forum on Assessment.* Cambridge, MA: Author.

Faltis, C. (2000). *Joinfostering: Adapting teaching for the multilingual classroom.* Upper Saddle River, NJ: Merrill/Pearson Education.

Falvey, M., Forest, M., Pearpoint, J., & Rosenberg, R. (1998). *All my life's a circle: Using the tools—circles, MAPS, & PATH.* Toronto, Ontario, Canada: Inclusion Press.

Farmer, T., Pearl, R., & Van Acker, R. (1996). Expanding the social skills deficit framework: A developmental synthesis perspective, classroom social networks, and implications for the social growth of students with disabilities. *The Journal of Special Education, 30*(5) 232–256.

Federal Register: Assistance to state for education of children with disabilities and early intervention program for infants and toddlers with disabilities (1999, March 12). *Federal Register*, p. 12456.

Featherstone, H. (1980). *A difference in the family: Life with a disabled child.* Washington, DC: Association for the Care of Children's Health.

Feldman, J., & Gray, P. (1999, March). Some educational benefits of freely chosen age mixing among children and adolescents. *Phi Delta Kappan,* pp. 507–512.

Fialka, J. (1997). *It matters: Lessons from my son.* Huntington Woods, MI: Author.

Fialka, J., & Mikus, K. (1999). *Do you hear what I hear? Parents and professionals working together for children with special needs.* Ann Arbor, MI: Proctor Publications.

Field, S., Martin, J., Miller, R., Ward, M., & Wehmeyer, M. (1998). Self-determination for persons with disabilities: A position statement of the Division of Career Development and Transition. *Career Development for Exceptional Individuals, 21*(2), 113–128.

Fielding, L. , & Roller, D. (1992). Making difficult books accessible and easy books acceptable. *The Reading Teacher, 45,* 678–685.

Fine, E. (1994). Peacemaking as a tool for change. *Primary Voices: K–6, 2*(4), 2–11.

Finkelhor, D., & Hashima, P. (2001). The victimization of children and youth: A comprehensive overview. In S. White (Ed.), *Handbook of youth and justice.* New York: Plenum.

Fishbaugh, M. S., & Gum, P. (1994). *Inclusive education in Billings, MT: A prototype for rural schools.* (ERIC Document Reproduction Service No. ED369636)

Fisher, B. (1995). *Thinking and learning together: Curriculum and community in an elementary classroom.* Portsmouth, NH: Heinemann.

Fisher, D., Pumpian, I., & Sax, C. (1998). High school students' attitudes about and recommendations for their peers with significant disabilities. *Journal of the Association for Persons with Severe Handicaps, 23,* 272–280.

Fisher, D., Sax, C., & Grove, K. (2000). The resilience of changes promoting inclusiveness in an urban elementary school. *The Elementary School Journal, 100*(3), 213–227.

Fisher, D., Sax, C., & Pumpian, I. (1999). *Inclusive high schools: Learning from contemporary classrooms.* Baltimore: Brookes.

Fisher, D., Sax, C., Rodifer, K., & Pumpian, I. (1999). Teachers' perspectives of curriculum and climate changes: Benefits of inclusive education. *Journal for a Just and Caring Education, 5,* 256–268.

Fisher, M. (2001). Andre's story: Frames of friendship. In M. Grenot-Scheyer, M. Fisher, & D. Staub (Eds.), *At the end of the day: Lessons learned in inclusive education.* Baltimore: Brookes.

Fisher, R., & Ury, W. (1991). *Getting to yes: Negotiating agreements without giving in.* New York: Penguin.

Fitzgerald, M., Henning, G., & Feltz, S. (1997). *Youth mentoring youth: Case examples and perspectives of a student support program.* Milwaukee: University of Wisconsin–Milwaukee, Wisconsin Inclusion Project, and Waukesha West High School.

Fletcher, R. (1986). *Teaching peace.* New York: Harper & Row.

Flippo, K., Inge, K., & Barcus, J. (1995). *Assistive technology: A resource for school, work, and community.* Baltimore: Brookes.

Ford, A., Fitzgerald, M. A., Glodoski, J., & Waterbury, K. (1997). *Team planning to accommodate learners with disabilities.* Milwaukee: University of Wisconsin–Milwaukee, Wisconsin Inclusion Project.

Fowler, B. (1996). *Bloom's taxonomy and critical thinking: Critical thinking across the curriculum project.* Retrieved from Longview Community College Web site: http://www.kcmetro.cc.mo.us/longview/ctac/blooms.htm

Frankenberg, E., & Orfield, G. (Eds.). (2007). *Lessons in integration: Realizing the promise of racial diversity in American schools.* Charlottesville: University of Virginia Press.

Fraser, A., Clickner, R., Everett, N., & Viet, S. (1991). *Asbestos in schools: Evaluation of the Asbestos Hazard Emergency Response Act (AHERA): A summary report.* Washington, DC: U.S. Environmental Protection Agency.

Freeman, R. (2005). *Competing models for public education. Which model is best?* Retrieved September 10, 2006, from http://www.commondreams.org/views05/0226-25.htm

Freeman, S., & Alkin, M. (2000). Academic and social attainments of children with mental retardation in general education and special education settings. *Remedial and Special Education, 21*(1), 3–18.

Friend, M., & Bursuck, W. (1999). *Including students with special needs: A practical guide for classroom teachers.* Boston: Allyn & Bacon.

Friend, M., & Cook, L. (1996). *Interactions: Collaboration skills for school professionals.* White Plains, NY: Longman.

Fryxell, D., & Kennedy, C. H. (1995). Placement along the continuum of services and its impact on students' social relationships. *Journal of the Association for Persons with Severe Handicaps, 20*(4), 259–269.

Fuchs, D., & Fuchs, L. (1994). Inclusive schools movement and the radicalization of special education reform. *Exceptional Children, 60*(4), 294–309.

Fuchs, L., Fuchs, D., Kazdan, S., & Allen, S. (1999). Effects of peer-assisted learning strategies in reading with and without training in elaborated help giving. *The Elementary School Journal, 99*(3), 201–219.

Fullan, M. (1997). *Change forces: Probing the depths of educational reform.* New York: Falmer Press.

Garbarino, J., Dubrow, N., Kostelny, K., & Pardo, C. (1992). *Children in danger: Coping with the consequences of community violence.* San Francisco: Jossey-Bass.

Gardner, H. (1993). *Multiple intelligences: The theory in practice.* New York: Basic Books.

Gardner, J. (1989, Fall). Building community. *Kettering Review.*

Gaustad, J. (1998, December). Implementing looping (*ERIC Digest 123*). Portland: University of Oregon.

Geller, S., & Hunt, D. (1995, November). *Resilient children: Making healthy choices.* Presentation at the annual conference of The Association for Persons with Severe Handicaps (TASH), Chicago.

Genesis Technologies. (2001). *Inspiration 6.0.* Retrieved from http://www.academic-softwares.com/inspiration.asp

Gerard, G. (1997). Community-based restorative justice: A capacity-building tool for confronting crime. Retrieved July 1, 2002, from http://freenet.msp.mn.us/org/ssco/rj/rjpaper.htm

Gerring, J., & Carney, J. (1992). *Head trauma: Strategies for educational reintegration.* San Diego, CA: Singular Press.

Gething, L. (1992). *Person to person: A guide for professionals working with people with disabilities.* Baltimore: Brookes.

Giangreco, M. F. (1997). *Vermont interdependent services team approach: A guide to coordinating educational support services.* Baltimore: Brookes.

Giangreco, M. F., Dennis, R., Cloninger, C., Edelman, S., & Schattman, R. (1993). "I've counted Jon": Transformational experiences of teachers educating students with disabilities. *Exceptional Children, 54,* 415–425.

Gibb, G., & Dyches, T. (2000). *Guide to writing quality individualized education programs.* Boston: Allyn & Bacon.

Gibbs, J. (1998). *Guiding your school community to live a culture of care and learning: The process is called Tribes.* Sausalito, CA: Centersource Systems.

Gilligan, (1996). *Violence: Reflections on a national epidemic.* New York: Vintage.

Girard, S., & Willing, K. (1996). *Partnerships for classroom learning: From reading buddies to pen pals to the community and the world beyond.* Portsmouth, NH: Heinemann.

Glasser, W. (1992). *The quality school: Managing students without coercion.* New York: Harper.

Glasser, W. (2000). *Reality therapy in action.* New York: HarperCollins.

GLSEN. (2007). *Gay-straight alliances: Creating safer schools for LGBT students and their allies: GLSEN research brief.* Lakewood, CO: Gay, Lesbian, and Straight Education Network.

Goldstein, A. P. (1988). *The prepare curriculum: Teaching prosocial competencies.* Champaign, IL: Research Press.

Goleman, D. (1995). *Emotional intelligence.* New York: Bantam.

Goodlad, J. (1984a). *A place called school: Prospects for the future.* New York: McGraw-Hill.

Goodlad, J. (1984b). *What are schools for?* Bloomington, IN: Phi Delta Kappan.

Goodman, K. (1986). *What's whole in whole language?* Portsmouth, NH: Heinemann.

Gostin, L., & Beyer, H. (1993). *Americans with Disabilities Act: Rights and responsibilities of all Americans.* Baltimore: Brookes.

Grabb, E. (1997). *Theories of social inequality: Classical and contemporary perspectives.* New York: Harcourt Brace.

Grant, J. (1996). *The looping handbook: Teachers and students progressing together.* Peterborough, NH: Crystal Springs Books.

Graves, D. H. (1983). *Writing: Teachers and children at work.* Portsmouth, NH: Heinemann.

Graves, D. H., & Graves, G. (1997). *Box city: An interdisciplinary experience in community planning.* Prairie Village, KS: Center for Understanding of the Built Environment (CUBE).

Graves, D. H., Graves, G., Schauber, S., & Beasley, J. (1999). *Walk around the block.* Prairie Village, KS: Center for Understanding of the Built Environment (CUBE).

Graves, M., & Graves, B. (1994). *Scaffolding reading experiences: Designs for student success.* Norwood, MA: Christopher-Gordon.

Gray, C. (1994). *The social story kit.* Austin, TX: Future Horizons.

Greenman, J. (1988). *Caring space, learning places: Children's environments that work.* Redmond, WA: Exchange Press.

Gresham, F., & MacMillan, D. (1997). Autistic recovery? An analysis and critique of the empirical evidence on the early intervention project. *Behavioral Disorders, 22,* 185–201.

Gresham, F., MacMillan, D., & Bocian, K. (1996). Behavioral earthquakes: Low frequency, salient behavior events that differentiate students at-risk for behavioral disorders. *Behavioral Disorders, 21*(4), 277–292.

Grigal, M. (1998, July/August). The time–space continuum: Using natural supports in inclusive classrooms. *Teaching Exceptional Children,* pp. 44–51.

Grinder, M. (1991). *Righting the educational conveyer belt.* Portland, OR: Metamorphous Press.

Gross, B. (2008). *Diversity and complexity in the classroom: Considerations of race, ethnicity, and gender.* Retrieved

January 18, 2008, from http://honolulu.hawaii.edu/intranet/committees/FacDevCom/guidebk/teachtip/diverse.htm

Grubb, D., & Diamantes, T. (1998). Is your school sick? Five threats to healthy schools. *The Clearinghouse, 71,* 202–207.

Haberman, M. (1998). *The pedagogy of poverty versus good teaching.* Retrieved July 2, 2002, from http://equity.enc.org/equity/eqtyres/erg/111376/1376.htm

Hacker, A. (1993). *Two nations: Black and White, separate, hostile, unequal.* New York: Scribners.

Hale, J., & Franklin, V. (2001). *Learning while Black: Creating educational excellence for African-American children.* Baltimore: Johns Hopkins University Press.

Hall, L. J. (1994). A descriptive assessment of social relationships in integrated classrooms. *Journal of the Association for Persons with Severe Handicaps, 19*(4), 302–313.

Hampel, M. (2000, November 13). *Teachers partnering with parents of children with special needs: We need you!* Presentation at the College of Education, Wayne State University, Detroit.

Hardman, M., Drew, C., & Egan, M. (1996). *Human exceptionality: Society, school, and family.* Boston: Allyn & Bacon.

Haring, T., Breen, C., Pitts-Conway, V., Lee, M., & Gaylord-Ross, R. (1998). Adolescent peer tutoring and special friend experiences. *Journal of the Association for Persons with Severe Handicaps, 12*(4), 280–286.

Harris, D., & McArdle, N. (2004). *More than money: The spatial mismatch between where minorities can afford to live and where they actually reside.* Cambridge, MA: Harvard University, Civil Rights Project.

Hartmann, T. (1996). Are you a hunter or a farmer? In T. Hartmann & J. Bowman (Eds.), *Think fast! The ADD experience.* Grass Valley, CA: Underwood.

Harvey, S. , & Goudis, A. (2000). *Strategies that work: Teaching comprehension to enhance understanding.* York, ME: Stenhouse.

Heal, L., Haney, J., & Amado, A. (1988). *Integration of developmentally disabled individuals into the community.* Baltimore: Brookes.

Helmstetter, E., Peck, C. A., & Giangreco, M. F. (1994). Outcomes of interactions with peers with moderate or severe disabilities: A statewide survey of high school students. *Journal of the Association for Persons with Severe Handicaps, 19*(4), 263–276.

Henderson, W. (2000). *Inclusion: A catalyst for whole school reform.* Retrieved from http://www.coe.wayne.edu/CommunityBuilding/ARTInclCatalyst.html

Herman, J., Aschbacher, P., & Winters, L. (1992). *A practical guide to alternative assessment.* Alexandria, VA: Association for Supervision and Curriculum Development.

Herold, E. (1998). *Co-teaching in Erin Herold and Pam Gutierrez's class.* Unpublished manuscript provided for SED 705 Mainstreaming Handicapped Students at Wayne State University, Detroit.

Heubert, J., & Hauser, R. (1999). *High stakes: Testing for tracking, promotion, and graduation.* Washington, DC: National Academy Press.

Hickson, L., Blackman, L., & Reis, E. (1995). *Mental retardation: Foundations of educational programming.* Boston: Allyn & Bacon.

Hiibner, C., & Fracassi, K. (1999, June). *Three ways to differentiate curriculum.* Presentation at the Whole Schooling Summer Institute, Detroit.

Hill, B., & Lakin, C. (1984). *Classification of residential facilities for mentally retarded people.* Minneapolis: Center for Residential and Community Services, University of Minnesota, Department of Educational Psychology.

Hilliard, A. G. (2000). Excellence in education versus high-stakes standardized testing. *Journal of Teacher Education, 51*(4), 293–304.

Hindley, J. (1996). *In the company of children.* York, ME: Stenhouse.

Hinz, A. (1996). Inclusive education in Germany: The example of Hamburg. *The European Electronic Journal on Inclusive Education in Europe, 1.* Retrieved July 1, 2002, from http://www.uva.es/inclusion/texts/hinz01.htm

Hittie, M. (1999a). *Including a child with behavioral challenges.* Unpublished manuscript, Southfield Public Schools, Southfield, MI.

Hittie, M. (1999b). *Jason Project at Macarthur Elementary School.* Unpublished manuscript, Southfield Public Schools, Southfield, MI.

Hitzing, W. (1994). Support and positive teaching strategies. In S. Stainback & W. Stainback (Eds.), *Inclusion: A guide for educators.* Baltimore: Brookes.

Hodgkinson, H. (2006). *The whole child in a fractured world.* Alexandria, VA: Association for Supervision and Curriculum Develpment.

Holdaway, D. (1979). *The foundations of literacy.* New York: Scholastic.

Hollowood, T. A., Salisbury, C. L., Rainforth, B., & Palombaro, M. M. (1995). Use of instructional time in classrooms serving students with and without severe disabilities. *Exceptional Children, 61*(3), 242–253.

Holly, L. (2000, August 24). Message posted to http://www.quasar.ualberta.ca/ddc/inclusion/intro.html

Horowitz, S. M., Bility, K. M., Plichta, S. B., Leaf, P. J., & Haynes, N. (1998). Teachers assessments of behavioral disorders. *American Journal of Orthopsychiatry, 24*(3), 29–38.

Hoskins, B. (1996). *Developing inclusive schools: A guide.* Bloomington, IN: Forum on Education.

Hughes, C., & Agran, M. (1998). Self-determination: Signaling a systems change? *Journal of the Association for Persons with Severe Handicaps, 23*(1), 1–4.

Hughes, C., Guth, C., Hall, S., Presley, J., Dye, M., & Byers, C. (1999, May/June). "They are my best friends": Peer buddies promote inclusion in high school. *Teaching Exceptional Children,* pp. 32–37.

Hull, J. (2006). *Language diversity and southern schools: The growing challenge.* Atlanta, GA: Southern Legislative Conference.

Hundert, J., Mahoney, B., & Mundy, F. (1998). A descriptive analysis of developmental and social gains of children with severe disabilities in segregated and inclusive preschools in southern Ontario. *Early Childhood Research Quarterly—Special Issue: Inclusion in Early Childhood Settings, 13*(1), 49–65.

Hunt, P., Alwell, M., Farron-Davis, F., & Goetz, L. (1996). Creating socially supportive environments for fully included students who experience multiple disabilities. *Journal of the Association for Persons with Severe Handicaps, 21,* 53–71.

Hunt, P., & Farron-Davis, F. (1992). A preliminary investigation of IEP quality and content associated with placement in general education versus special education. *Journal of the Association for Persons with Severe Handicaps, 17,* 247–253.

Hunt, P., Farron-Davis, F., Beckstead, S., Curtis, D., & Goetz, L. (1994). Evaluating the effects of placement of students with severe disabilities in general education versus special education. *Journal of the Association for Persons with Severe Handicaps, 19*(3), 200–214.

Hunt, P., Goetz, L., & Anderson, J. (1986). The quality of IEP objectives associated with placement in integrated versus segregated school sites. *Journal of the Association for Persons with Severe Handicaps, 11*(2), 125–130.

Hunt, P., Staub, D., Alwell, M., & Goetz, L. (1994, Winter). Achievement by all students within the context of cooperative learning groups. *Journal of the Association for Persons with Severe Handicaps, 19*(4), 290–301.

Hurch, D., & Ross, W. (2000). *Democratic social education: Social studies for social change.* New York: Falmer Press.

Hyde, K., Burchard, J., & Woodworth, K. (1996). Wrapping services in an urban setting. *Journal of Child and Family Studies, 5*(1), 67–82.

Idol, L., Paolucci-Whitcomb, P., & Nevin, A. (1994). *Collaborative consultation* (2nd ed.). Rockville, MD: Aspen.

Individuals with Disabilities Education Act, Pub. L. No. 105-17, 20 U.S.C. 1400 (1997).

Individuals with Disabilities Education Act. (1999, March 12). Education of Children with Disabilities and Early Intervention Program, 34 C.F.R., 300 & 303, Vol. 64, No. 48.

Individuals with Disabilities Education Improvement Act, Pub. L. No. 108-446, 118 Stat. 2647 (2004).

International Reading Association & National Council of Teachers of English. (1996). *Standards for the English language arts.* Newark, DE: Authors.

Isaac, K. (1992). *Civics for democracy: A journey for teachers and students.* Washington, DC: Essential Books.

Jacob K. Javits Gifted and Talented Students Education Act, Title XIV, Pub. L. No. 103-398, U.S.C. (1994).

Jacobson, J., & Mulick, J. (1992). Speak for yourself, or . . . I can't quite put my finger on it! *Psychology in Mental Retardation and Developmental Disabilities, 17*(3), 5–7.

Jacobson, S. (2002). *Education about education with neuro-linguistic programming.* Lincoln, NE: iUniverse.

Janney, R., & Snell, M. (1997). How teachers include students with moderate and severe disabilities in elementary classes: The means and ends of inclusion. *Journal of the Association for Persons with Severe Handicaps, 22*(3), 159–169.

Janney, R., & Snell, M. (2000a). *Behavioral support: Teacher's guides to inclusive practices.* Baltimore: Brookes.

Janney, R., & Snell, M. (2000b). *Modifying schoolwork.* Baltimore: Brookes.

Jenkins, J., Jewell, M., Leicester, N., O'Connor, R. E., Jenkins, L., & Troutner, N. M. (1994). Accommodations for individual differences without classroom ability groups: An experiment in school restructuring. *Exceptional Children, 60*(4), 344–359.

Jensen, E. (1995). *Super teaching: Over 1,000 practical teaching strategies.* San Diego, CA: Brain Store.

Jensen, E. (1998). *Teaching with the brain in mind.* Alexandria, VA: Association for Supervision and Curriculum Development.

Johns, B. H., & Keenan, J. P. (1997). *Techniques for managing a safe school.* Denver, CO: Love.

Johnson, D. W., & Johnson, R. T. (1989a). *Cooperation and competition: Theory and research.* Edina, MN: Interaction.

Johnson, D. W., & Johnson, R. T. (1989b). *Leading the cooperative school.* Edina, MN: Interaction.

Johnson, D. W., & Johnson, R. T. (1994). *The new circles of learning: Cooperation in the classroom and school.* Alexandria, VA: Association for Supervision and Curriculum Development.

Johnson, D. W., & Johnson, R. T. (1995). *Reducing school violence through conflict resolution.* Alexandria, VA: Association for Supervision and Curriculum Development.

Johnson, L. (1996). Evolving transitions? *Teacher Education and Special Education, 19*(3).

Johnson, P. (1997). *Pictures and words together: Children illustrating and writing their own books.* Portsmouth, NH: Heinemann.

Jorgensen, C. (1998). *Restructuring high schools for all students: Taking inclusion to the next level.* Baltimore: Brookes.

Joseph, J. (1995). *Remaking America: How the benevolent traditions of many cultures are transforming our national life.* San Francisco: Jossey-Bass.

Jupp, K. (1994). *Living a full life.* London: Souvenir Press.

Kagan, S., & Weissbourd, B. (Eds.). (1994). *Putting families first: America's family support movement and the challenge of change.* San Francisco: Jossey-Bass.

Kahlenberg, R. (2007). *Rescuing* Brown v. Board of Education. New York: Century Foundation.

Kaiser, J. S. (2000). Are high-stakes tests taking control? *Schools in the Middles, 9*(7), 18–21.

Kameenui, E. J., & Darch, C. B. (1995). *Instructional classroom management: A proactive approach to behavior management.* White Plains, NY: Longman.

Kaskinen-Chapman, A. (1992). Saline area schools and inclusive community CONCEPTS (Collaborative Organization of Networks, Community Educators, Parents, the Workplace, and Students). In R. A. Villa, J. S. Thousand, W. Stainback, and S. Stainback (Eds.), *Restructuring for caring and effective education: An administrative guide to creating heterogeneous schools* (pp. 169–185). Baltimore: Brookes.

Katz, M. (1985). *In the shadow of the poorhouse: A social history of welfare in America.* New York: Basic Books.

Kauffman, J. (2008). *Characteristics of emotional and behavioral disorders of children and youth.* Upper Saddle River, NJ: Merrill/Pearson Education.

Kauffman, J., Lloyd, J., & Baker, J. (1995). Inclusion of all students with emotional or behavioral disorders? Let's think again. *Phi Delta Kappan, 76,* 542–546.

Kay, P. (1999). *Prevention strategies that work.* Burlington: University of Vermont.

Kelker, K., & Holt, R. (2000). *Family guide to assistive technology.* Cambridge, MA: Brookline.

Kennedy, C., Shulka, S., & Fryxell, D. (1997). Comparing the effects of educational placement on the social relationships of intermediate school students with severe disabilities. *Exceptional Children, 64*(1), 31–48.

Kennedy, D. (1995). Teaching the gifted in regular classrooms: Plain talk about creating a gifted-friendly classroom. *Roeper Review, 17*(4), 232–234.

Kent, R. (1997). *Room 109: The promise of a portfolio classroom.* Portsmouth, NH: Heinemann.

King, T. (1999). *Assistive technology: Essential human factors.* Boston: Allyn & Bacon.

Kirschenbaum, R., Armstrong, D., Ciner, D., & Landrum, M. (1999). Resource consultation model in gifted education to support talent development in today's inclusive schools. *Gifted Child Quarterly, 43*(1), 39–47.

Knoff, H. M., & Batsche, G. M. (1995). Project ACHIEVE: Analyzing a school reform process for at-risk and underachieving students. *School Psychology Review, 24,* 579–603.

Knoll, J. (1994, Summer). *Inclusive Communities: The Newsletter of the Developmental Disabilities Institute* (Wayne State University, Detroit), pp. 4–6.

Knowlton, E. (1998). Considerations in the design of personalized curricular supports for students with developmental disabilities. *Education and Training in Mental Retardation and Developmental Disabilities, 33*(2), 95–107.

Koegel, L. K., Koegel, R. L., & Dunlap, G. (1996). *Positive behavioral support: Including people with difficult behavior in the community.* Baltimore: Brookes.

Koegel, L. K., Koegel, R. L., Kellegrew, D., & Mullen, L. (1996). Parent education for prevention and reduction of severe problem behaviors. In L. K. Koegel, R. L. Koegel, & G. Dunlap (Eds.), *Positive behavioral support: Including people with difficult behavior in the community.* Baltimore: Brookes.

Koegel, R. L., & Koegel, L. K. (1995). *Teaching children with autism: Strategies for initiating positive interactions and improving learning opportunities.* Baltimore: Brookes.

Kohl, H. (1967). *36 children.* New York: New American Library.

Kohl, H. (1998). *The discipline of hope.* New York: Simon & Schuster.

Kohn, A. (1992). *No contest: The case against competition: Why we lose in our race to win.* New York: Houghton Mifflin.

Kohn, A. (1993). *Punished by rewards: The trouble with gold stars, incentive plans, A's, praise, and other bribes.* Boston: Houghton Mifflin.

Kohn, A. (1996a). *Beyond discipline: From compliance to community.* Alexandria, VA: Association for Supervision and Curriculum Development.

Kohn, A. (1996b). What to look for in a classroom. *Educational Leadership, 54*(1), 54–55.

Kohn, A. (1998). *What to look for in a classroom . . . and other essays.* San Francisco: Jossey-Bass.

Kohn, A. (1999). *The schools our children deserve: Moving beyond traditional classrooms and "tougher standards."* New York: Houghton Mifflin.

Kohn, A. (2000). *The case against standardized testing: Raising the scores, ruining our schools.* Portsmouth, NH: Heinemann.

Kortering, L. J., & Blackorby, J. (1992). High school dropouts and students identified with behavioral disorders. *Behavioral Disorders, 18*(1), 24–32.

Koski, W. (2001). Educational opportunity and accountability in an era of standards-based school reform. *Stanford Law & Policy Review, 12,* 301–322.

Kovalik, S. (1994). *Integrated thematic instruction.* Kent, WA: Books for Educators.

Kovalik, S., & Olsaen, K. (1997). *Integrated thematic instruction: The model.* Kent, WA: Books for Educators.

Kozol, J. (1991). *Savage inequalities: Children in America's schools.* New York: Crown.

Kretzmann, J. P., & McKnight, J. (1993). *Building communities from the inside out: A path toward finding and mobilizing a community's assets.* Chicago: Northwestern University, Center for Urban Affairs and Policy Research.

Kroll, J., & Bachrach, B. (1986). Child care and child abuse in early medieval Europe. *Journal of the American Academy of Child Psychiatry, 25*(4), 562–568.

Kronberg, R. (1999). *Coming to grips with the different learning levels in your classroom.* Torrance, CA: Staff Development Resources.

Kunc, N. (1992). The need to belong: Rediscovering Maslow's hierarchy of needs. In R. Villa, J. Thousand, W. Stainback, & S. Stainback (Eds.), *Restructuring for caring and effective education.* Baltimore: Brookes.

Kunc, N. (1998, July). *Learning to stand still.* Presentation at the Inclusion Summer Institute, Stevens Point, WI.

Kunc, N. (2000, June 27). *Do all kids belong in all classes? Equity or excellence in education.* Presentation at the International Education Summit, Detroit.

Kusche, C., & Greenberg, M. (1994). *PATHS curriculum.* Seattle, WA: Developmental Research and Programs.

Kuttler, S., Myles, B., & Carlson, J. (1998). The use of social stories to reduce precursors to tantrum behavior in students with autism. *Focus on Autism and Other Developmental Disorders, 13*(3), 176–182.

L'Abate, L., & Milan, M. (Eds.). (1989). *Handbook of social skills training and research.* New York: Wiley.

Lane, P., & McWhitter, J. (1992). A peer mediation model: Conflict resolution for elementary and middle school children. *Elementary School Guidance and Counseling, 27*(3) 10–15.

Lantieri, L., & Patti, J. (1996). *Waging peace in our schools.* Boston: Beacon Press.

Lee, C. (2004). *Racial segregation and educational outcomes in metropolitan Boston.* Cambridge, MA: Harvard University Civil Rights Project.

Lepper, M., & Henderlong, J. (2000). Turning "play" into "work" and "work" into "play": 25 years of research on intrinsic versus extrinsic motivation. In C. Sansone & J. Harackiewicz (Eds.), *Intrinsic and extrinsic motivation: The search for optimal motivation and performance.* New York: Academic Press.

LeRoy, B. (1990a). *The effect of classroom integration on teacher and student attitudes, behaviors, and performance in Saline area schools.* Detroit: Wayne State University, Developmental Disabilities Institute.

LeRoy, B. (1990b). *Inclusive education in Michigan: A preliminary status report.* Detroit: Wayne State University, Developmental Disabilities Institute.

LeRoy, B. (1995). *Michigan inclusive education initiative: Implementation report.* Detroit: Wayne State University, Developmental Disabilities Institute.

LeRoy, B., England, J., & Osbeck, T. (1994). *Facilitator guides to inclusive education.* Detroit: Wayne State University, Developmental Disabilities Institute.

Levine, K., & Wharton, R. (1995). Facilitated communication: What parents should know. *Exceptional Children, 28*(5), 40–53.

Lewis, B. (1998a). *The kid's guide to social action.* Prairie Village, KS: Center for Understanding of the Built Environment (CUBE).

Lewis, B. (1998b). *The kid's guide to service projects.* Prairie Village, KS: Center for Understanding of the Built Environment (CUBE).

Lewis, T. J., Chard, D., & Scott, T. M. (1994). Full inclusion and education of children and youth with emotional and behavioral disorders. *Behavioral Disorders, 19*(4), 277–293.

Lipskey, D. K., & Gartner, A. (1997). *Inclusion and school reform: Transforming America's classrooms.* Baltimore: Brookes.

Lofkuist, L., & Dawes, R. (1980). Vocational needs, work reinforcers and job satisfaction. In B. Bolton & D. Cook, (Eds.), *Rehabilitation client assessment.* Baltimore: University Park Press.

Logan, K., Bakeman, R., & Keefe, E. (1997). Effects of instructional variables on engaged behavior of students with disabilities in general education classrooms. *Exceptional Children, 63*(4), 481–498.

Lovaas, O. (1987). The autistic child: Language development through behavior modification. *Journal of Consulting and Clinical Psychology, 55*(1), 3–9.

Lovett, H. (1996). *Learning to listen: Positive approaches and people with difficult behavior.* Baltimore: Brookes.

Ludlow, B., Turnbull, A., & Luckasson, R. (1988). *Transitions to adult life for people with mental retardation: Principles and practices.* Baltimore: Brookes.

Ma, J. (2002). *What works for children: What we know and don't know about bilingual education.* Cambridge, MA: Harvard University Civil Rights Project.

Maag, J. (1997). Managing resistance: Looking beyond the child and into the mirror. In P. Zionts (Ed.), *Inclusion strategies problems.* Austin, TX: Pro-Ed.

MacGillivray, I. K. (2000). Educational equity for gay, lesbian, bisexual, transgendered and queer/questioning students: The demands of democracy and social justice for America's schools. *Education and Urban Society, 32*(3), 303–323.

MacGillivray, I. (2004). Implementing school non-discrimination policy that includes sexual orientation: A case study in school and community politics. *International Journal of Qualitative Studies in Education, 17*(3), 347–370.

Macrorie, K. (1988). *The I-search paper.* Portsmouth, NH: Boynton/Cook.

Manley, A., & O'Neill, C. (Eds.). (1997). *Dreamseekers: Creative approaches to the African-American heritage.* Portsmouth, NH: Heinemann.

Mann, L. (1997). Designing the learning environment. *Education Update, 39*(6), 1–5.

Manning, M., Manning, G., & Long, R. (1994). *Theme immersion: Inquiry-based curriculum in elementary and middle schools.* Portsmouth, NH: Heinemann.

Manset, G., & Semmel, M. (1997). Are inclusive programs for students with mild disabilities effective? A comparative review of model programs. *The Journal of Special Education, 31,* 155–180.

March, R., & Sprague, J. (1999). *Effective behavior support (EBS): A school-wide behavioral support program.* Portland: University of Oregon, Institute on Violence and Destructive Behavior.

Marin, M., Gilpin, M., Goodman, S., & Moses, M. (1996). *Positive behavioral support: An interagency project.* Lansing: Michigan Department of Community Health, Michigan State Training Team.

Marks, S., Schrader, C., & Levine, M. (1999). Para-educator experiences in inclusive settings: Helping, hovering, or holding their own? *Exceptional Children, 65*(3), 315–328.

Marston, D. (1996). A comparison of inclusion only, pull-out only, and combined services models for students with mild disabilities. *The Journal of Special Education, 30,* 121–132.

Martin, G., & Pear, J. (1996). *Behavior modification: What it is and how to do it* (5th ed.). Upper Saddle River, NJ: Merrill/Pearson Education.

Maslow, A. (1970). *Motivation and personality.* New York: Harper & Row.

Mayer, G. O. (1995). Preventing antisocial behavior in the schools. *Journal of Applied Behavior Analysis, 28*(4), 467–478.

McAdamis, S. (2001). Individual paths; teachers tailor their instruction to meet a variety of student needs. *Journal of Staff Development, 22*(2), 15–18.

McClellan, D. (1994). Research on multiage grouping: Implications for education. In P. Chase & J. Doan (Eds.), *Full circle: A new look at multiage education.* Portsmouth, NH: Heinemann.

McClellan, D., & Kinsey, S. (1999). Children's social behavior in relationship to participation in mixed-age or same-age classrooms. *Early Childhood Research and Practice, 1*(1), 22–30.

McCormick, L., Loeb, D., & Schiefelbusch, R. (1997). *Supporting children with communication difficulties in inclusive settings: School-based language intervention.* Boston: Allyn & Bacon.

McDonnell, J., Hardman, M., Hightower, J., & Kiefer-O'Donnell, R. (1991). Variables associated with in-school and after-school integration of secondary students with severe disabilities. *Education and Training in Mental Retardation, 26,* 243–257.

McDonnell, J., Hardman, M., Hightower, J., & Kiefer-O'Donnell, R. (1997). Academic engaged time of students with low-incidence disabilities in general education classes. *Mental Retardation, 35*(1), 18–26.

McGinnis, E., & Goldstein, A. (1984). *Skillstreaming the elementary school child.* Champaign, IL: Research Press.

McGonigel, M., Kaufmann, R., & Johnson, B. (Eds.). (1991). *Guidelines and recommended practices for the individualized family service plan* (2nd ed.). Bethesda, MD: Association for the Care of Children's Health.

McGregor, G., & Vogelsberg, T. (1998). *Inclusive schooling practices: Pedagogical and research foundations: A synthesis of the literature that informs best practices about inclusive schooling.* Baltimore: Brookes.

McIntosh, R., Vaughn, S., Schumm, J. S., Haager, D., & Lee, O. (1993). Observations of students with learning disabilities in general education classrooms. *Exceptional Children, 60,* 249–261.

McKnight, J. (1995). *The careless society: Community and its counterfeits.* New York: Basic Books.

McLane, K., Burnette, J., & Orkwis, R. (1997). School-wide behavioral management systems. *Research Connections, 1*(1), 1–8.

McLeskey, J., Waldron, N., & Pacchiano, D. (1993, April). *Inclusive elementary school programs: Teachers' perceptions of strengths and challenges.* Paper presented at the Council for Exceptional Children Annual Convention, San Antonio, TX.

McVay, P. (1998). Paraprofessionals in the classroom: What role do they play? *Disability Solutions, 3*(1), 3–14.

Meek, A. (Ed.). (1995). *Designing places for learning.* Alexandria, VA: Association for Supervision and Curriculum Development.

Melaville, A., Blank, M., & Asayesh, G. (1993). *Together we can.* Washington, DC: U.S. Department of Education.

Merrell, K., & Walker, H. (2004). Deconstructing a definition: Social maladjustment versus emotional disturbance and moving the EBD field forward. *Psychology in the Schools, 41*(3), 899–910.

Metz, M. H. (1994). Desegregation as necessity and challenge. *Journal of Negro Education, 63*(1), 64–76.

Meyer, L., Peck, C., & Brown, L. (1991). *Critical issues in the lives of people with severe disabilities.* Baltimore: Brookes.

Michigan Department of Education. (1999). *Individualized education program team manual.* Lansing, MI: Author.

Microsoft. (2008). *Encarta world English dictionary.* Retrieved January 24, 2008, from http://encarta.msn.com/

Miles, M. (1999). Historical background of educational and social responses to disabilities in Anglophone eastern and southern Africa: Introduction and bibliography. *Disabilities and Childhood in Eastern and Southern Africa.* Retrieved July 2, 2002, from http://www.socsci.kun.nl/ped/whp/histeduc/mmiles/aesabib.html

Miller, B. (1995). *Children at the center: Implementing the multiage classroom.* Eugene, OR: ERIC Clearinghouse on Educational Management. (ERIC Document Reproduction Service No. EA025954)

Miller-Lachmann, L., & Taylor, L. (1995). *Schools for all: Educating children in a diverse society.* New York: Delmar.

Moles, O. C. (1993). Collaboration between schools and disadvantaged parents: Obstacles and openings. In N. Chavkin (Ed.), *Families and schools in a pluralistic society.* Albany: State University of New York Press.

Monastra, V. (2004). *Parenting children with ADHD: 10 lessons that medicine cannot teach.* Washington, DC: American Psychological Association.

Montgomery, R. (2008). What is the difference between emotionally disordered and socially maladjusted? Retrieved from http://www.behavior-consultant.com/social.htm

Moody, S., Vaughn, S., & Hughes, M. (2000). Reading instruction in the resource room: Set up for failure. *Exceptional Children, 66*(3), 305–316.

Moore, A. (1999). *Teaching multi-cultured students: Culturalism and anti-culturalism in school classrooms.* New York: Falmer Press.

Morocco, C., & Zorfass, J. (1996). Unpacking scaffolding: Supporting students with disabilities in literacy development. In M. Pugach & C. Warger (Eds.), *Curriculum trends, special education, and reform: Refocusing the conversation.* New York: Teachers College Press.

Murphy, S., & Rogan, P. (1995). *Closing the shop: Conversion from sheltered to integrated work.* Baltimore: Brookes.

Murray-Seegert, C. (1989). Nasty girls, thugs, and humans like us. In M. Falvey, *Community-based curriculum: Instructional strategies for students with severe handicaps.* Baltimore: Brookes.

Nakagawa, K. (2000). Unthreading the ties that bind: Questioning the discourse of parent involvement. *Educational Policy, 14*(4), 895–904.

Naicker, S. M. (1999). *Curriculum 2005: A space for all: An introduction to inclusive education.* Cape Town, South Africa: Renaissance.

National Association of Protection and Advocacy Systems. (2000). *Protection and advocacy systems.* Retrieved from http://www.protectionandadvocacy.com/

National Association of School Boards of Education. (1994). *Winners all: A call for inclusive education.* Washington, DC: Author.

National Center for Educational Restructuring and Inclusion. (1995). *National study of inclusion.* New York: Author.

National Center on Accessibility. (2000, November 20). Americans with Disabilities Act (ADA) accessibility guidelines for buildings and facilities; play areas. 36 Fed. Reg., Part 1191.

National Commission on Excellence in Education. (1983). *A nation at risk.* Washington, DC: Author.

National Community Building Network. (1995). *Statement of principles.* Oakland, CA: Urban Strategies Council.

National Council of Teachers of English. (2005). *Supporting linguistically and culturally diverse learners in English education.* Paper presented at the Conference on English Education Leadership and Policy Summit, Atlanta, GA.

National Council of Teachers of Mathematics. (1987). *Curriculum and evaluation standards for school mathematics.* Reston, VA: Author.

National Council of Teachers of Mathematics. (1991). *Professional standards for teaching mathematics.* Reston, VA: Author.

National Council of Teachers of Mathematics. (2000). *Principles and standards for school mathematics.* Reston, VA: Author.

National Institute of Mental Health. (2001). *Attention deficit hyperactivity disorder (ADHD): Questions and answers.* Retrieved from http://www.nimh.nih.gov/publicat/adhdqa.cfm

National Law Center on Homelessness and Poverty. (2000). *Separate and unequal: A report on educational barriers for homeless children and youth.* Washington, DC: Author.

Neill, M., Bursh, P., Schaeffer, B., Thall, C., Yohe, M., & Zappardino, P. (1995). *Implementing performance assessments: A guide to classroom, school, and system reform.* Cambridge, MA: National Center for Fair and Open Testing.

Nelson, C. (1992). Searching for the meaning in the behavior of antisocial pupils, public school educators, and lawmakers. *School Psychology Review, 21*(1), 35–39.

Nelson, C. (1996). Rhythms of the racing brain. In T. Hartmann & J. Bowman (Eds.), *Think fast! The ADD experience.* Grass Valley, CA: Underwood.

Nelson, C. (1998, February). *Hyperactive hearts and minds: Toward a unified model of attention difficulty.* Paper presented at the meeting of Mind–Brain Sciences Colloquium, Palm Springs, FL.

Nesbitt, N. (1991, March). Cross-age tutoring in mathematics: Sixth graders helping students who are moderately handicapped. *Education and Training in Mental Retardation,* pp. 89–97.

Newmann, F., & Wehlage, G. (1993, April). Five standards of authentic instruction. *Educational Leadership,* pp. 8–12.

Noddings, N. (2007). *Critical lessons: What our schools should teach.* Cambridge, MA: Cambridge University Press.

Noell, G., & Witt, J. (1999). When does consultation lead to intervention implementation? *The Journal of Special Education, 33*(1), 29–35.

North, S., Fontanive, L., Hechlik, J., Lamp, S., Sheehy, J., & Nichols, A. (1995). *Integrating exceptional individuals with diverse needs: A resource guide.* Detroit: Wayne State University.

North Carolina Special Olympics. (2001). *Unified Sports.* Retrieved from http://www.sosc.org/unified.htm

Nunley, K. (1998). *The regular educator's guide to layered curriculum.* South Jordan, UT: Kathie Nunley.

Oakes, J. (1985). *Keeping track: How schools structure inequality.* New Haven, CT: Yale University Press.

O'Brien, J., & O'Brien, C. (1992). Members of each other: Perspectives on social support for people with severe disabilities. In J. Nisbet (Ed.), *Natural supports in schools, at work, and in the community for people with severe disabilities.* Baltimore: Brookes.

O'Brien, J., & O'Brien, C. (1996). *Members of each other: Building community in company with people with developmental disabilities.* Toronto, Ontario, Canada: Inclusion Press.

O'Brien, J., & O'Brien, C. (Eds.). (1998). *A little book about person centered planning.* Toronto, Ontario, Canada: Inclusion Press.

O'Brien, J., O'Brien, C., & Jacob, G. (1998). *Celebrating the ordinary: The emergence of options in community living as a thoughtful organization.* Toronto, Ontario, Canada: Inclusion Press.

Odom, S. L., Deklyen, M., & Jenkins, J. R. (1984). Integrating handicapped and nonhandicapped preschoolers: Developmental impact on nonhandicapped children. *Exceptional Children, 51*(1), 41–48.

Office of Special Education and Rehabilitative Services. (1991, September 16). *AD(H)D and special education services: Memorandum.* Washinton, DC: U.S. Department of Education.

Office of Special Education and Rehabilitative Services. (2000). *A guide to the Individualized Education Program.* Retrieved from http://www.ed.gov/offices/OSERS/OSEP/IEP_Guide/

Office of Special Education Programs. (1999). *Twenty-first annual report to Congress.* Washington, DC: Author.

Office of Special Education Programs. (2000a). *Parent training and information centers.* Retrieved from http://www.taalliance.org/PTIs.htm

Office of Special Education Programs. (2000b). *Twenty-second annual report to Congress.* Washington, DC: Author.

Office of Special Education Programs. (2001). *Twenty-third annual report to Congress.* Washington, DC: Author.

Oglan, G. (1997). *Parents, learning and whole language classrooms.* Urbana, IL: National Council of Teachers of English.

Oglan, Gerald. (2003). *Write, right, rite!* Boston: Allyn & Bacon.

Ogle, D., Pink, W., & Jones, B. F. (Eds.). (1990). *Restructuring to promote learning in America's schools.* Columbus, OH: Zaner-Bloser.

O'Halloran, J. (1995). The celebration process. In *Parent articles.* Phoenix, AZ: Psychological Corporation.

Ohanian, S. (1999). *One size fits few: The folly of educational standards.* Portsmouth, NH: Heinemann.

O'Neill, R. E., Horner, R. H., Albin, R. W., Storey, K., & Sprague, J. R. (1996). *Functional assessment and program development for problem behavior: A practical handbook* (2nd ed.). Pacific Grove, CA: Brooks/Cole.

Orelove, F., & Sobsey, D. (1987). *Educating children with multiple disabilities.* Baltimore: Brookes.

Orfield, G. (2001, April 3). *Housing segregation: Causes, effects, possible cures.* Cambridge, MA: Harvard University, Civil Rights Project.

Orfield, G. (Ed.). (2004). *Dropouts in America: Confronting the graduation crisis.* Cambridge, MA: Harvard Education Press.

Orfield, G., & Lee, C. (2005). *Why segregation matters: Poverty and educational inequality.* Cambridge, MA: Harvard University, Civil Rights Project.

Orfield, G., & Lee, C. (2007). *Historic reversals: Accelerating resegregation and the need for new integration strategies.* Los Angeles: University of California–Los Angeles, Civil Rights Project.

Orfield, G., Losen, Wald, J., & Swanson, C. (2004). *Losing our future: How minority youth are being left behind by the graduation rate crisis.* Cambridge, MA: Harvard University, Civil Rights Project.

Orkwis, R., & McLane, K. (1998). *A curriculum every student can use: Design principles for student access.* Reston, VA: Council for Exceptional Children.

Ormrod, J. (2000). *Educational psychology: Developing learners* (3rd ed.). Upper Saddle River, NJ: Merrill/Pearson Education.

O'Shea, D., O'Shea, L., Algozzine, R., & Hammitte, D. (2001). *Families and teachers of individuals with disabilities: Collaborative orientations and responsive practices.* Boston: Allyn & Bacon.

Osher, D., & Hanley, T. V. (1996). Implications of the national agenda to improve results for children and youth with serious emotional disturbance. In R. Illback & C. Nelson (Eds.), *Emerging school-based approaches for children with emotional and behavioral problems: Research and practice in service integration.* Binghamton, NY: Haworth.

Osher, D. M., & Osher, T. W. (1996). The national agenda for children and youth with serious emotional disturbance (SED). In C. Nelson, R. Rutherford, Jr., & B. Wolford (Eds.), *Comprehensive and collaborative systems that work for troubled youth: A national agenda.* Richmond: Eastern Kentucky University, National Juvenile Detention Association.

Paley, V. (1990). *The boy who would be helicopter: The uses of storytelling in the classroom.* Cambridge, MA: Harvard University Press.

Paley, V. (1992). *You can't say you can't play.* Cambridge, MA: Harvard University Press.

Palmer, P. (1998). *The courage to teach: Exploring the inner landscape of a teacher's life.* San Francisco: Jossey-Bass.

Pang, V. (2005). *Multicultural education: A caring-centered, reflective approach.* New York: McGraw-Hill.

Parent Education Project. (1998a). *How to build a better IEP.* West Allis, WI: Author.

Parent Education Project. (1998b). *Parent rights, roles, and responsibilities: A look at special education and its impact on your child.* West Allis, WI: Author.

Patriarcha, L., Freeman, G., Hendricks, J., & Swift, C. (1996). *Understanding, improving, and promoting effective co-teaching: Final report.* Lansing: Michigan Department of Education.

Peck, C. A., Carlson, P., & Helmstetter, E. (1992). Parent and teacher perceptions of outcomes for typically developing children enrolled in integrated early childhood programs: A statewide survey. *Journal of Early Intervention, 16*(1), 53–63.

Peck, S. (1987). *The different drum: Community making and peace.* New York: Simon & Schuster.

People for the American Way. (2008). *The truth about gay and lesbian issues in the public schools.* New York: Body Health Resources Corporation.

Perin, C. (1988). *Belonging in America: Reading between the lines.* Madison: University of Wisconsin Press.

Perske, R., & Perske, M. (1981). *Hope for families: New directions for parents of persons with retardation or other disabilities.* Nashville, TN: Abingdon.

Peterson, M. (1993). A study of support, instruction, and outcomes in inclusive education. Detroit: Wayne State University, Whole Schooling Consortium.

Peterson, M. (1998). *Teacher focus group.* Unpublished field notes, Wayne State University, Detroit.

Peterson, M. (1999). Unpublished field notes of observations of mainstreaming and inclusive education, Wayne State University, Detroit.

Peterson, M., & Hittie, M. (2000). *Whole Schooling Research Project field notes.* Wayne State University, Detroit.

Peterson, M., LeRoy, B., Field, S., & Wood, P. (1992). Community-referenced learning in inclusive schools. In S. Stainback & W. Stainback (Eds.), *Curriculum considerations in inclusive schooling.* Baltimore: Brookes.

Peterson, M. (2001a). *Improving learning through student assessment: Beyond the standardization of learning.* Detroit: Wayne State University, College of Education, Whole Schooling Consortium.

Peterson, M. (2001b). *Interaction of quality of teaching, support, and student learning: A study of relationships.* Detroit: Wayne State University, Whole Schooling Consortium.

Peterson, M., Tamor, L., Feen, H., & Silagy, M. (2002). *Lessons about connecting inclusive education to whole school improvement.* Retrieved October 24, 2006, from http://www.wholeschooling.net/WS/WSPress/WSRptMI/WSR%20AToc.html

Peterson, M. (2005). *Whole schooling: An inclusive framework for school renewal and professional inquiry.* Paper presented at the Inclusive and Supported Education Conference, Glasgow, Scotland.

Peterson, M., & Tamor, L. (2009). *Good teaching 4 all: Building an effective, inclusive community of learners.* Thousand Oaks, CA: Corwin Press.

Peterson, R. (1992). *Life in a crowded place: Making a learning community.* Portsmouth, NH: Heinemann.

Phillips, W. C., Alfred, K., Brulli, A. R., & Shank, K. S. (1990). The Regular Education Initiative: The will and skill of regular educators. *Teacher Education and Special Education, 13*(3–4), 182–186.

Pierangelo, R., & Giulani, G. (2007). *Classroom management techniques for students with ADHD: A step-by-step guide for educators.* Thousand Oaks, CA: Corwin Press.

Piers, M. (1978). *Infanticide.* New York: Norton.

Pitsch, M. (1994, October 12). Mississippi learning. *Education Week,* pp. 29–30.

Popham, J. (2001). *The truth about testing: An educator's call to action.* Alexandria, VA: Association for Supervision and Curriculum Development.

Porro, B. (1996). *Talk it out: Conflict resolution in the elementary classroom.* Alexandria, VA: Association for Supervision and Curriculum Development.

Postman, N. (1996). *The end of education: Redefining the value of school.* New York: Vintage Books.

Prager, D., & Telushkin, J. (1983). *Why the Jews? The reason for antisemitism.* New York: Simon & Schuster.

Price, B., Mayfield, P., McFadden, A., & Marsh, G. (1998). *Collaborative teaching: Special education for inclusive classrooms.* Retrieved July 2, 2002, from Parrot Publishing Web site: http://www.parrotpublishing.com/Inclusion_Chapter_1.htm

Procedures for evaluation and determination of eligibility, 34 C.F.R. 300.530–300.536 (1999).

Public Agenda. (1997, April). Getting by: What American teenagers really think about their schools. *Education Week,* pp. 20–21.

Public Agenda. (2006). *How Black and Hispanic families rate their schools.* New York: Author.

Pugach, M. C., & Johnson, L. (1995). Unlocking expertise among classroom teachers through structured dialogue: Extending research on peer collaboration. *Exceptional Children, 62*(2), 101–110.

Pugach, M. C., & Wesson, C. L. (1995). Teachers' and students' views of team teaching of general education and learning disabled students in two fifth-grade classes. *Elementary School Journal, 95,* 279–295.

Putnam, J. (1993). *Cooperative learning and strategies for inclusion.* Baltimore: Brookes.

Quigney, T., & Studer, J. (1999). Touching strands of the educational web: The professional school counselor's role in inclusion. *Professional School Counseling, 2*(1), 77–82.

Quina, J. (1995). *Principles of accelerated learning.* Unpublished manuscript, College of Education, Wayne State University, Detroit.

Rainforth, B. (1992). *The effects of full inclusion on regular education teachers.* San Francisco: California Research Institute.

Rankin, B., & Quane, J. (2000). Neighborhood poverty and the social isolation of inner city African American families. *Social Forces, 79*(1), 139–164.

Rankin, D., Hallick, A., Ban, S., Hartley, P., Bost, C., & Uggla, N. (1994). Who's dreaming? A general education perspective on inclusion. *Journal of the Association for Persons with Severe Disabilities, 19*(3), 235–237.

Reavis, K., & Andrews, D. (1999). *Behavioral and educational strategies for teachers—B.E.S.T.* Salt Lake City, UT: B.E.S.T. Project.

Reeves, L., & Stein, J. (1999). Developmentally appropriate pedagogy and inclusion: Don't put the cart before the horse. *Physical Educator, 56,* 2–7.

RESA, Wayne County. (2004). *Social maladjustment: A guide to differential diagnosis and educational options.* Wayne, MI: Wayne County Regional Educational Service Agency (RESA).

Rhodes, L., & Dudley-Marling, C. (1996). *Readers and writers with a difference: A holistic approach to teaching struggling readers and writers.* Portsmouth, NH: Heinemann.

Richards, H. , Brown, A., & Forde, T. (2006). *Addressing diversity in schools: Culturally responsive pedagogy.* Tempe: Arizona State University, National Center for Culturally Responsive Educational Systems.

Richardson, J. (1994, Novermber 9). Adventures in learning. *Education Week,* pp. 25–28.

Rief, S. (2005). *How to reach and teach children with ADD/ADHD: Practical techniques, strategies, and interventions* San Francisco: Jossey-Bass.

Riester, A. E. (1998). *A guide for developing IEPs for students with behavioral and emotional disorders.* San Antonio, TX: Psychological Corporation.

Roach, V., with Ascroft, J., & Kysilko, D. (1995). *Winning ways: Creating inclusive schools, classrooms, and communities.* Alexandria, VA: National Association of School Boards of Education.

Roberts, C., & Zubrick, S. (1992). Factors influencing the social status of children with mild academic disabilities in regular classrooms. *Exceptional Children, 49,* 192–202.

Rohd, M. (1998). *Theatre for community, conflict, and dialogue: The hope is vital training manual.* Portsmouth, NH: Heinemann.

Romberg, T. (1995). *Reform in school mathematics and authentic assessment.* New York: State University of New York Press.

Rosenberg, S., McKeon, L., & Dinero, T. (1999, October). Positive peer solutions: One answer for the rejected student. *Phi Delta Kappan,* pp. 114–118.

Roth, M., Bartlinski, A., & Courson, P. (1994). *Modifying essential curriculum for the typical classroom.* Baltimore: Maryland Neighborhood Inclusion Project.

Rothman, D. (1990). *The discovery of the asylum: Social order and disorder in the new republic.* Boston: Little, Brown.

Routman, R. (1996). *Literacy at the crossroads: Crucial talk about reading, writing, and other teaching dilemmas.* Portsmouth, NH: Heinemann.

Russell, H. (1998). *Ten-minute field trips: A teacher's guide to using the school grounds for environmental studies.* Arlington, VA: National Science Teachers Association.

Rutter, M. (1977). Protective factors in children's responses to stress and disadvantage. In M. W. Kent & J. E. Rolf (Eds.), *Primary prevention of psychopathology: Vol. 3. Social competence in children.* Hanover, NH: University Press of New England.

Ryan, A. (2004). Communicating about school performance. Retrieved September 9, 2006, from http://www.businessroundtable.org//taskForces/taskforce/index.aspx?qs=14A5BF159F8

Ryndak, D. L., & Alper, S. (1996). *Curriculum content for students with moderate and severe disabilities in inclusive settings.* Boston: Allyn & Bacon.

Ryndak, D. L., Downing, J. E., Jacqueline, L. R., & Morrison, A. P. (1995). Parents' perceptions after inclusion of their children with moderate or severe disabilities. *Journal of the Association for Persons with Severe Handicaps, 10*(2), 147–157.

Ryndak, D. L., Morrison, A., & Sommerstein, L. (1999). Literacy before and after inclusion in general education settings: A case study. *Journal of the Association for Persons with Severe Handicaps, 24*(1), 5–22.

Sacks, O. (1989). *Seeing voices: A journey into the world of the deaf.* Berkeley: University of California Press.

Saha, N., Enright, B., & Timberflake, M. (1996). *Schools as inclusive communities: Training seminar series.* Orono: University of Maine, Center for Community Inclusion.

Saint-Laurent, L., Glasson, J., Royer, E., Simard, C., & Pierard, B. (1998). Academic achievement effects of an in-class service model on students with and without disabilities. *Exceptional Children, 64*(2), 239–253.

Saint-Laurent, L., & Lessard, J. C. (1991). Comparison of three educational programs for students with moderate or severe disabilities. *Education and Training in Mental Retardation, 26*(4), 370–380.

Salend, S., & Duhaney, G. (1999). The impact of inclusion on students with and without disabilities and their educators. *Remedial and Special Education, 20*(2), 114–126.

Salisbury, C., Palombaro, M. M., & Hollowood, T. M. (1993). On the nature and change of an inclusive elementary school. *Journal of the Association for Persons with Severe Handicaps, 13*(1), 41–53.

Sapon-Shevin, M. (1994a). Celebrating diversity, creating community: Curriculum that honors and builds on differences. In S. Stainback & W. Stainback (Eds.), *Inclusion: A guide for educators.* Baltimore: Brookes.

Sapon-Shevin, M. (1994b). *Playing favorites: Gifted education and the disruption of community.* Albany: State University of New York Press.

Sapon-Shevin, M. (1999). *Because we can change the world: A practical guide to building cooperative, inclusive classroom communities.* Boston: Allyn & Bacon.

Sapon-Shevin, M. (2007). *Widening the circle: The power of inclusive classrooms.* Boston: Beacon Press.

Schaefer, N. (1997). *Yes! She knows she's here.* Toronto, Ontario, Canada: Inclusion Press.

Schiller, L. (1998). *Increasing the success of your sixth grade students: Writing and reading strategies that work: Resource handbook.* Bellevue, WA: Bureau of Education and Research.

Schilling, M., & Coles, R. (1997). From exclusion to inclusion: A historical glimpse at the past and reflection of the future. *Journal of Physical Education, Recreation and Dance, 68,* 22–24.

Schleien, S., Ray, T., & Green, F. (1997). *Community recreation and people with disabilities: Strategies for inclusion.* Baltimore: Brookes.

Schmidt, C. (1999). Poisoning young minds. *Environmental Health Perspectives, 107*(6), A302–A307.

Schum, J. S., Vaughn, S., & Leavell, A. (1994). Planning pyramid: A framework for planning for diverse student needs during content area instruction. *The Reading Teacher, 47*(8), 608–615.

Schwartz, D. (1992). *Crossing the river: Creating a conceptual revolution in community and disability.* Cambridge, MA: Brookline.

Schwartz, D. (1997). *Who cares: Rediscovering community.* Boulder, CO: Westview Press.

Schwartz, S., & Pollishuke, M. (1990). *Creating the child-centred classroom.* Toronto, Ontario, Canada: Irwin.

Scotch, R. (1984). *From good will to civil rights: Transforming federal disability policy.* Philadelphia: Temple University Press.

Scruggs, T. E., & Mastropieri, M. A. (1994). Successful mainstreaming in elementary science classes: A qualitative study of three reputational cases. *American Educational Research Journal, 31*(4), 785–811.

Seattle Public Schools. (2008). *Advanced learning: Eligibility process.* Seattle, WA: Seattle Public Schools.

Sensory Access Foundation. (2000). *Access technology.* Retrieved from http://www.sensoryaccess.com/

Sergiovanni, T. (1994). *Building community in our schools.* San Francisco: Jossey-Bass.

Sergiovanni, T. (2004). *Strengthening the heartbeat: Leading and learning together in schools.* San Francisco: Jossey-Bass.

Seyler, A., & Buswell, B. (2001). *Individual education plans: Involved effective parents.* Colorado Springs, CO: PEAK Parent Center.

Shaffer, C., & Anundsen, K. (1993). *Creating community anywhere: Finding support and connection in a fragmented world.* New York: Putnam.

Shane, H. (1994). *Facilitated communication: The clinical and social phenomenon.* Florence, KY: Thomson Learning.

Shapiro, J. (1993a). *No pity: People with disabilities forging a new civil rights movement.* New York: Times Books.

Shapiro, J. (1993b, December 13). Separate and unequal. *Newsweek,* pp. 46–60.

Sharpe, M. N., York, J. L., & Knight, J. (1994). Effects of inclusion on the academic performance of classmates without disabilities. *Remedial and Special Education, 15*(5), 281–287.

Sharon, T. (2003). Open court and workshop learning: E-mail posted on listserv October 30, 2003.

Sheets, L., & Wirkus, M. (1997, April/May). Everyone's classroom: An environment designed to invite and facilitate active participation. Retrieved July 2, 2002, from Closing the Gap Web site: http://www.closingthegap.com/cgi-bin/lib/libDsply.pl?a=1050+b=4&c=1

Shelton, T., Jeppson, E., & Johnson, B. (1992). *Family-centered care for children with special health care needs.* Bethesda, MD: Association for the Care of Children's Health.

Short, K. G., Harste, J., & Burke, C. (1996). *Creating classrooms for authors and inquirers.* Portsmouth, NH: Heinemann.

Silver, M. (2004). *Trends in school reform.* Seattle, WA:

Simpson, E. (1999, June 23). Passing life's tests: Hard work and persistence pay off in a regular diploma for a student with Down syndrome. *Virginian–Pilot,* p. E1.

Sinclair, E., & Alexson, J. (1992). Relationship of behavioral characteristics to educational needs. *Behavioral Disorders, 17*(4), 296–304.

Skiba, R., & Grizzle, K. (1992). Qualifications v. logic and data: Excluding conduct disorders from the SED definition. *School Psychology Review, 21*(1), 23–28.

Skrtic, T. (1994). *Democracy and special education.* New York: Bantam.

Smith, D. (1998). *Inclusion: Schools for all students.* Boston: Wadsworth.

Smith, F. (1998). *The book of learning and forgetting.* New York: Teachers College Press.

Smith, F. (2003). *Unspeakable acts, Unnatural practices: Flaws and fallacies in "scientific" reading research.* Portsmouth, NH: Heinemann.

Smith, O. (1997). *Case study of an elementary student with severe learning disabilities.* Unpublished study, Okemus, MI.

Smith, R. (2008). Diversity in public high schools: A look at the experiences of gay and lesbian students. Retrieved February 15, 2008, from http://www.mtholyoke.edu/~rlsmith/gayandlesbianadolescents.html

Smull, M., & Harrison, S. (1992). *Supporting people with severe reputations in the community.* Alexandria, VA: National Association of State Mental Retardation Program Directors.

Snell, M., & Janney, R. (2000). *Collaborative teaming.* Baltimore: Brookes.

Snow, J. (1998b). *What's really worth doing and how to do it: A book for people who love someone labeled disabled (possibly yourself).* Toronto, Ontario, Canada: Inclusion Press.

Sobsey, R., & Doe, K. (1991). Patterns of sexual abuse and assault. *Sexuality and Disability, 9*(3), 243–259.

Society for Developmental and Behavioral Pediatrics. (2001). *Education programs.* Retrieved from http://www.sdbp.org/education/index.cfm

Sommerfield, M. (1992). Micro-society schools tackle real-world woes. *Education Week, 12*(13), 1, 8.

Spear-Swerling, L., & Sternberg, R. (1998). *Off track: When poor readers become learning disabled.* Boulder, CO: Westview Press.

Special Olympics. (2008). *About Special Olympics.* Retrieved from http://www.specialolympics.org/

Stainback, W., Stainback, S., Moravec, J., & Jackson, H. J. (1992). Concerns about full inclusion: An ethnographic investigation. In R. Villa, J. Thousand, W. Stainback, & S. Stainback (Eds.), *Restructuring for caring and effective education: An administrative guide to creating heterogeneous schools.* Baltimore: Brookes.

Staub, D., Schwartz, E., Gallucci, C., & Peck, C. (1994). Four portraits of friendship at an inclusive school. *Journal of the Association for Persons with Severe Handicaps, 19*(4), 314–325.

Staub, D., Spaulding, M., Peck, C. A., Gallucci, C., & Schwartz, I. (1996). Using nondisabled peers to support the inclusion of students with disabilities at the junior high school level. *Journal of the Association for Persons with Severe Handicaps, 21*(4), 194–205.

Stein, D. (1999). *Ritalin is not the answer: A drug-free practical program for children diagnosed with ADD or ADHD.* San Francisco: Jossey-Bass.

Steinfeld, E. (1994). *The concept of universal design.* Retrieved from http://www.ap.buffalo.edu/~idea/publications/free_pubs/pubs_cud.html

Stepanek, J. (1999). *The inclusive classroom: Meeting the needs of gifted students: Differentiating mathematics and science instruction.* Portland, OR: Northwest Regional Educational Laboratory.

Sternberg, R., & Grigorenko, E. (1999). *Our labeled children: What every parent and teacher needs to know about learning disabilities.* Reading, MA: Perseus.

Stevahn, L., Johnson, D. W., Johnson, R. T., Laginski, A. M., & O'Coin, I. (1996). Effects on high school students of integrating conflict resolution and peer mediation training into an academic unit. *Mediation Quarterly, 14*(1), 21–36.

Stolov, W., & Clowers, M. (1981). *Handbook of severe disability: A text for rehabilitation counselors, other vocational practitioners, and allied health professionals.* Fed. Reg. 65,083 (December 29, 1977). Washington, DC: U.S. Government Printing Office.

Strickland, K. (1995). *Literacy not labels: Celebrating students' strengths through whole language.* Portsmouth, NH: Boynton/Cook.

Swaggart, B., Gagnon, E., Bock, S., Earles, T., Quinn, C., Myles, B., et al. (1995). Using social stories to teach social and behavioral skills to children with autism. *Focus on Autistic Behavior, 10*(1), 1–15.

Szabo, J. (2000). Maddie's story: Inclusion through physical and occupational therapy. *Journal of Teaching Exceptional Children, 33*(2), 12–18.

Tarrant, K. (1993). *Teachers' beliefs about literacy, the instructional needs of special education students, and inclusion.* Paper presented at the Annual Meeting of the American Education Research Association, Atlanta, GA.

Tarrant, K. (1999a, June 22–24). *Building communities of practice between general and special education: Teachers and students working together to enact an early literacy curriculum inclusive of all students.* Presentation at the Whole Schooling Summer Institute, Wayne State University, Detroit.

Tarrant, A. (1999). *Learning disabilities.* Unpublished paper, Western Michigan University, College of Education, Kalamazoo, MI.

Tarrant, K. (1999b). *The collaborative implementation of an early literacy curriculum in a full-inclusion primary grade classroom: Co-teachers and students working together to accomplish literacy goals.* Doctoral dissertation, Michigan State University, East Lansing, MI.

Tashie, C., Shapiro-Barnard, S., Donoghue-Dillon, A., Jorgenson, C., & Nisbet, J. (1993). *Changes in latitudes, changes in attitudes: The role of the inclusion facilitator.* Durham: University of New Hampshire, Institute on Disability.

Taylor, S. (1988). Caught in the continuum: A critical analysis of the principle of least restrictive environment. *Journal of the Association for Persons with Severe Handicaps, 18*(2), 75–83.

Taylor, S., & Searl, S. (1987). The disabled in America: History, policy, and trends. In P. Knoblock (Ed.), *Understanding exceptional children and youth* (pp. 5–64). New York: Little, Brown.

Terry, B. (2005). An introduction to classwide peer tutoring [Electronic version]. *Special Connections,* retrieved from http://www.specialconnections.ku.edu/cgi-bin/cgiwrap/specconn/main.php?cat=instruction&section=cwpt/main

Thomas, C., Correa, V., & Morsink, C. (1995). *Interactive teaming: Consultation and collaboration in special programs.* Upper Saddle River, NJ: Merrill/Pearson Education.

Thurlow, M. (2000). Including special needs students in standards-based assessments. In *Including special needs students in standards-based reform: A report on McREL's Diversity Roundtable III.* Aurora, CO: Mid-continent Research for Education and Learning.

Tomlinson, C. (2004a). *The differentiated classroom: Responding to the needs of all learners.* Alexandria, VA: Association for Supervision and Curriculum Development.

Tomlinson, C. (2004b). *How to differentiate instruction in mixed-ability classrooms.* Alexandria, VA: Association for Supervision and Curriculum Development.

Tomlinson, C., Kaplan, S., Renzulli, J., Purcell, J., Lwepien, J., & Burns, D. (2002). *The parallel curriculum: A design to develop high potential and challenge high-ability learners.* Thousand Oaks, CA: Corwin Press.

Townsend, B. (2000). Standards-based school reform and culturally diverse learners: Implications for effective leadership when the stakes are even higher. In *Including special needs students in standards-based reform: A Report on McREL's Diversity Roundtable III.* Aurora, CO: Mid-continent Research for Education and Learning.

Treadwell, S., & Roxborough, L. (1991). Cerebral palsy seating. In M. Letts (Ed.), *Principles of seating the disabled.* Boca Raton, FL: Council for Exceptional Children Press.

Turnbull, A., & Turnbull, R. (1997). *Families, professionals, and exceptionality: A special partnership.* Upper Saddle River, NJ: Merrill/Pearson Education.

Tyack, D., & Cuban, L. (1995). *Tinkering toward utopia: A century of public school reform.* Cambridge, MA: Harvard University Press.

United Cerebral Palsy Association. (1993). *Policy on full inclusion of individuals with disabilities.* Washington, DC: Author.

United Nations Educational, Scientific and Cultural Organization. (1994, June 3). *The Salamanca statement and framework for action on special needs education.* Document produced at the World Conference on Special Needs Education: Access and Quality, Salamanca, Spain.

University of Alberta. (2000). *Inclusion listserv archives.* Retrieved July 2, 2002, from http://www.ualberta.ca/htbin/lwgate/INCLUSION/

University of Oregon. (1999). *First Step to Success.* Retrieved from http://cecp.air.org/resources/success/firststep.asp

U.S. Congress. (1988). Technology-Related Assistance Act, Pub. L. No. 100-407, § 3.1.

U.S. Department of Education. (1995). *Model strategies in bilingual education.* Washington, DC: Author.

Vargo, S. (1998, January/February). Consulting: Teacher to teacher. *Teaching Exceptional Children,* pp. 54–55.

Varin, R. (1998). *Autism and its history in education: An outline of past and current effective educational options.* Retrieved July 2, 2002, from home.earthlink.net/~varin/infopub/infopub/in01002.htm

Vaughn, S., Bos, C., & Schumm, J. (1997). *Teaching mainstreamed, diverse, and at-risk students in the general education classroom.* Boston: Allyn & Bacon.

Vaughn, S., Gersten, R., & Chard, D. (2000). The underlying message in LD intervention research: Findings from research syntheses. *Exceptional Children, 67*(1), 99–115.

Vaughn, S., Moody, S., Schumm, J. (1998). Broken promises: Reading instruction in the resource room. *Exceptional Children, 64,* 211–225.

Vaughn, S., Schumm, J., & Arguelles, M. (1997). The ABCDE's of co-teaching. *Teaching Exceptional Children, 30*(2), 4–10.

Venolia, C. (1988). *Healing environments: Your guide to indoor well-being.* Berkeley, CA: Celestial Arts.

Very Special Arts. (2008). *About Very Special Arts.* Retrieved July 7, 2008, from http://www.vsarts.org/x16.xml

Villa, R., & Thousand, J. (1992). Restructuring public school systems: Strategies for organizational change and progress. In R. Villa, J. Thousand, W. Stainback, & S. Stainback (Eds.), *Restructuring for caring and effective education: An administrative guide to creating heterogeneous schools* (pp. 109–137). Baltimore: Brookes.

Villa, R. A., & Thousand, J. S. (1996). *Creating the inclusive school.* Alexandria, VA: Association for Supervision and Curriculum Development.

Villa, R. A., Thousand, J. S., Meyers, H., & Nevin, A. (1996). Teacher and administrator perceptions of heterogeneous education. *Exceptional Children, 63*(1), 29–45.

Villa, R. A., Thousand, J. S., & Nevin, A. *A guide to co-teaching: Practical tips for facilitating student learning.* Thousand Oaks, CA: Corwin Press.

Villa, R. A., Thousand, J. S., Stainback, W., & Stainback, S. (Eds.). (1992). *Restructuring for caring and effective education: An administrative guide to creating heterogeneous schools.* Baltimore: Brookes.

Vitello, S. J., & Mithaug, D. E. (1998). *Inclusive schooling: National and international perspectives.* Mahwah, NJ: Erlbaum.

Vygotsky, L. (1978). *Mind in society: The development of higher psychological processes.* Cambridge, MA: Harvard University Press.

Wagner, M. (1995). Outcomes for youths with serious emotional disturbance in secondary school and early adulthood. *The Future of Children: Critical Issues for Children and Youths, 5*(4), 90–112.

Wagner, M., Blackorby, J., Cameto, R., Hebbeler, K., & Newman, L. (1993). *The transition experiences of young people with disabilities.* Menlo Park, CA: SRI International.

Wagner, S. (1999). *Inclusive programming for elementary students with autism.* Arlington, TX: Future Horizons.

Waldron, N., & McLeskey, J. (1998). The effects of an inclusive school program on students with mild and severe learning disabilities. *Exceptional Children, 64*(2), 395–405.

Walker, H., Colvin, G., & Ramsey, E. (1995). *Antisocial behavior in school: Strategies and best practices.* Pacific Grove, CA: Brooks/Cole.

Walker, H., & Walker, J. (1991). *Coping with noncompliance in the classroom: A positive approach for teachers.* Austin, TX: Pro-Ed.

Walker, M. (2007). *Teaching inquiry-based science: A guide for middle and high school teachers.* Retrieved from http://www.worlddeer.org/markwalker/new1inquiry.Doc

Walther-Thomas, C., Korinek, L., McLaughlin, V., & Toler Williams, B. (2000). *Collaboration for inclusive education: Developing successful programs.* Boston: Allyn & Bacon.

Wang, M. C., & Baker, E. (1986). Mainstreaming programs: Design features and effects. *The Journal of Special Education, 19*(4), 503–521.

Wang, M. C., & Birch, J. W. (1984). Effective special education in regular classes. *Exceptional Children, 50,* 391–398.

Weaver, J. (1994). What I've learned as an ADHDer about the problems and needs of students with ADHD. In C. Weaver (Ed.), *Success at last: Helping students with AD(H)D achieve their potential.* Portsmouth, NH: Heinemann.

Weber, M. (Ed.). (1978). *Economy and society.* Berkeley: University of California Press.

Wehman, P. (1993). *The ADA mandate for social change.* Baltimore: Brookes.

Weiner-Zivolich, J. (1995). If not now, when? The case against waiting for sheltered workshop changeover. *Journal of the Association for Persons with Severe Handicaps, 20*(4), 311–312.

Weisgerber, R., Dahl, P., & Appleby, J. (1980). *Training the handicapped for productive employment.* Rockville, MD: Aspen.

Werts, M. G., Wolery, M., Snyder, E. D., & Caldwell, N. K. (1996). Teachers' perceptions of the supports critical to the success of inclusion programs. *Journal of the Association for Persons with Severe Handicaps, 21*(1), 9–21.

West, C. (1993). *Race matters.* Boston: Beacon Press.

Wheelock, A. (1992). *Crossing the tracks: How "untracking" can save America's schools.* New York: New Press.

Wiedmeyer, D., & Leyman, J. (1991). The house plan: Approach to collaborative teaching and consultation. *Teaching Exceptional Children, 23*(2), 6–10.

Wiggins, G., & McTighe, J. (1998). *Understanding by design.* Alexandria, VA: Association for Supervision and Curriculum Development

Wilcox, B., & Bellamy, T. (1987). *A comprehensive guide to the activities catalogue: An alternative curriculum for youth and adults with severe disabilities.* Baltimore: Brookes.

Wilkes, P. (2000). Using the Piirto Pyramid of talent development in the inclusionary classroom. *Gifted Child Today, 23*(6), 32–33, 51–52.

Will, M. (1986). *Educating students with learning problems: A shared responsibility.* Washington, DC: Office of Special Education and Rehabilitative Services, U.S. Department of Education.

Williams, W., Fox, T., Monley, M., McDermott, A., & Fox, W. (1989). *Individual program design series.* Burlington: University of Vermont.

Willis, S. (1995, February). Mainstreaming the gifted. *Education Update, 37*(3), 4–5.

Willis, S., & Mann, L. (2000). Differentiating instruction: Finding manageable ways to meet individual needs. *Curriculum Update.*

Winebrenner, S. (2001). *Teaching gifted kids in the regular classroom: Strategies and techniques every teacher can use.* Minneapolis, MN: Free Spirit.

Wise, M. (1999, February/March). Participating in high school and beyond: A six-pack for success. Retrieved July 2, 2002, from Closing the Gap Web site: http://www.closingthegap.com/cgi-bin/lib/libDsply.p1?a=1180&b=2&c=2

Wolf, D. (1989). Portfolio assessment: Sampling student work. *Educational Leadership, 46*(7), 35–39.

Wolfensberger, W. (1972). *Normalization: The principle of normalization in human services.* Toronto, Ontario, Canada: National Institute on Mental Retardation.

Wood, J. (1998). *Adapting instruction to accommodate students in inclusive settings.* Upper Saddle River, NJ: Merrill/Pearson Education.

Wood, M. (1998). Whose job is it anyway? Educational roles in inclusion. *Exceptional Children, 64*(2), 181–195.

Wood, T. (1997). *Creating safe schools for lesbian and gay students: A resource guide for school staff.* Youth Pride, Inc.

Wormeli, R. (2006). *Fair isn't always equal: Assessing and grading in the differentiated classroom.* Portland, ME: Stenhouse.

Yager, R. (1987). Assess all five domains of science. *The Science Teacher, 54*(7), 33–37.

Yager, R. (1990). Science, technology, and society (STS): Thinking over the years. *The Science Teacher, 57*(3), 52–55.

Yoe, J., Santarcangelo, S., Atkins, S., & Burchard, J. (1996, March). Wraparound care in Vermont: Program development, implementation, and evaluation of a statewide system of individualized services. *Journal of Child and Family Studies, 5*(1), 23–29.

York, J., Kronberg, R., Medwetz, L., & Doyle, M. (1993). *Creating inclusive school communities.* Minneapolis: University of Minnesota.

Young, K. (1994). *Constructing buildings, bridges, and minds: Building an integrated curriculum through social studies.* Portsmouth, NH: Heinemann.

Young, M. (1995). *Restorative community justice: A call to action.* Washington, DC: National Organization for Victim Assistance.

Zahn-Waxler, C. (1993). Warriors and worriers: Gender and psychopathology. *Development and Psychopathology, 5*(2), 79–89.

Zemelman, S., Daniels, H., & Hyde, A. (2005). *Best practice: New standards for teaching and learning in America's schools.* Portsmouth, NH: Heinemann.

Zigmond, N., & Baker, J. (1995). Concluding comments: Current and future practices in inclusive schooling. *The Journal of Special Education, 29*(2), 245–250.

Zigmun, N., Jenkins, J., & Fuchs, L. (1995). Special education and restructured schools: Findings from three multiyear studies. *Phi Delta Kappan, 76,* 531–540.

Zionts, P. (Ed.). (1997). *Inclusion strategies for students with learning and behavior problems: Perspectives, experiences, and best practices.* Austin, TX: Pro-Ed.

Author Index

Page numbers followed by "f" refer to figures.

Subject Index

Page numbers followed by "f" refer to figures.